TATE BRITAIN ▲ 206

HARRODS ▲ 2

NATIONAL GALLERY ▲ 286

BRITISH MUSEUM ▲ 300

SOUTH BANK CENTRE... ▲ 322

BUCKINGHAM PALACE
An icon of monarchy, surrounded by the royal parks.

HYDE PARK
This expanse of green, along with Kensington Gardens, is dear to the hearts of Londoners.

COVENT GARDEN
This lively area round the restored Royal Opera and the old market abounds in restaurants and fashionable shops.

ST JAMES'S ST, BOND ST, REGENT ST
The home of English chic. Savile Row tailors are among the best in the world.

NATIONAL GALLERY
It gives an authoritative history of art, from the early Italian painters to the Impressionists.

BRITISH MUSEUM
An overview of all civilizations; the treasures of Antiquity include the Rosetta Stone.

SOUTH BANK CENTRE AND TATE MODERN
The new center of London cultural life.

LONDON

EVERYMAN GUIDES

● Encyclopedia section

■ **NATURE** The natural heritage: species and habitats characteristic to the area covered by the guide, annotated and illustrated by naturalist authors and artists.
HISTORY The impact of international historical events on local history, from the arrival of the first inhabitants, with key dates appearing in a timeline above the text.
ART AND TRADITIONS Customs and traditions and their continuing role in contemporary life.
ARCHITECTURE The architectural heritage, focusing on style and topology, a look at rural and urban buildings, major civil, religious and military monuments.
AS SEEN BY PAINTERS A selection of paintings of the city or country by different artists and schools, arranged chronologically or thematically.
AS SEEN BY WRITERS An anthology of texts focusing on the city or country, taken from works of all periods and countries, arranged thematically.

▲ Itineraries

Each itinerary begins with a map of the area to be explored.
✪ **SPECIAL INTEREST** These sites are not to be missed. They are highlighted in gray boxes in the margins.
★ **EDITOR'S CHOICE** Sites singled out by the editors for special attention.
INSETS On richly illustrated double pages, these insets turn the spotlight on subjects deserving more in-depth treatment.

◆ Practical information

All the travel information you will need before you go and when you get there.
SIGHTSEEING A handy table of addresses and opening hours.
USEFUL ADDRESSES A selection of the best hotels and restaurants compiled by an expert.
APPENDICES Bibliography, list of illustrations and general index.
MAP SECTION Maps of all the areas covered by the guide, followed by an index; these maps are marked out with letters and figures making it easy for the reader to pinpoint a town, region or site.

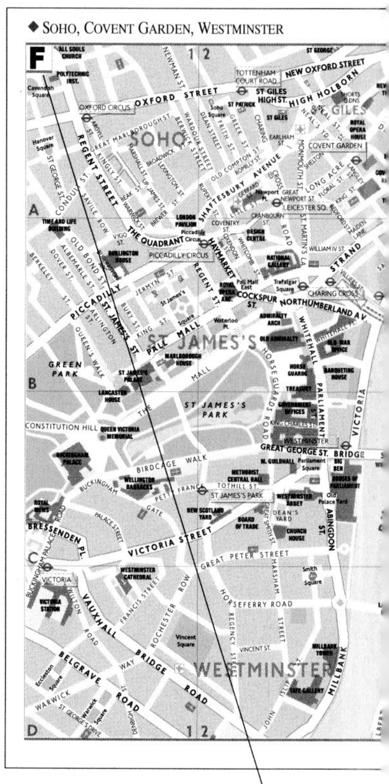

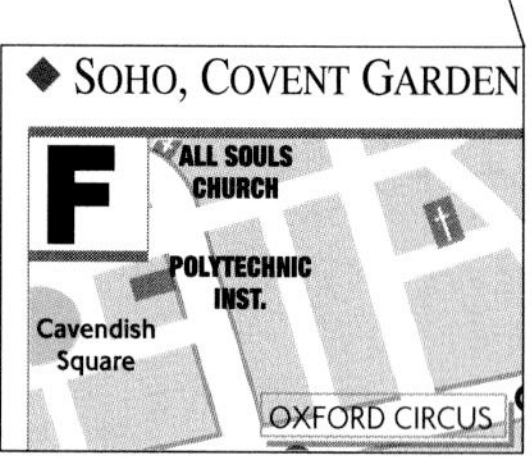

Each map in the map section is designated by a letter. In the itineraries, all the sites of interest are given a map reference (for example: **F** B2).

The itinerary map shows the main sites, the editor's choices and the places of special interest.

● ▲ ◆
The above symbols within the text provide cross-references to a place or a theme discussed elsewhere in the guide.

The mini-map pinpoints the itinerary within the wider area covered by the guide.

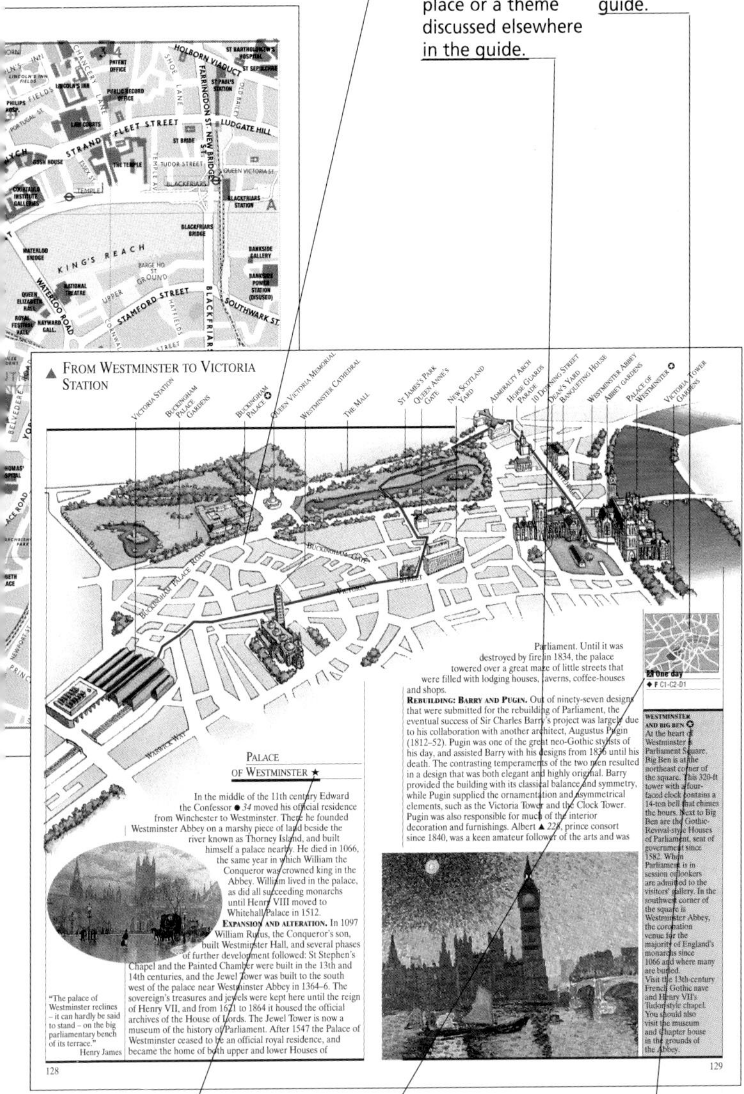

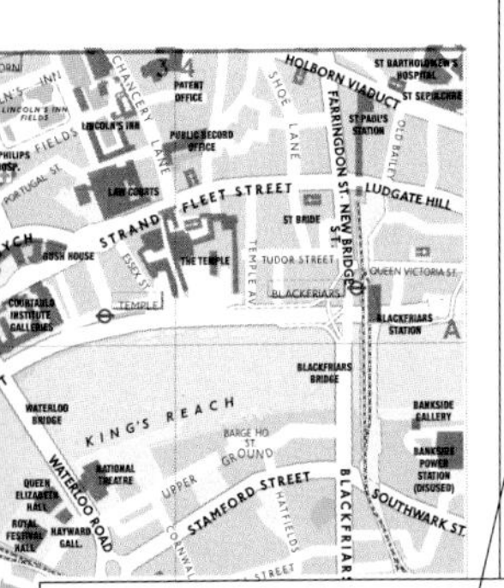

▲ FROM WESTMINSTER TO VICTORIA STATION

VICTORIA STATION · BUCKINGHAM PALACE GARDENS · BUCKINGHAM PALACE ✪ · QUEEN VICTORIA MEMORIAL · WESTMINSTER CATHEDRAL · THE MALL · ST JAMES'S PARK · QUEEN ANNE'S GATE · NEW SCOTLAND YARD · ADMIRALTY ARCH · HORSE GUARDS PARADE · 10 DOWNING STREET · DEAN'S YARD · BANQUETING HOUSE · WESTMINSTER ABBEY · ABBEY GARDENS · PALACE OF WESTMINSTER ✪ · VICTORIA TOWER GARDENS

PALACE OF WESTMINSTER ★

In the middle of the 11th century Edward the Confessor ● *34* moved his official residence from Winchester to Westminster. There he founded Westminster Abbey on a marshy piece of land beside the river known as Thorney Island, and built himself a palace nearby. He died in 1066, the same year in which William the Conqueror was crowned king in the Abbey. William lived in the palace, as did all succeeding monarchs until Henry VIII moved to Whitehall Palace in 1512.

EXPANSION AND ALTERATION. In 1097 William Rufus, the Conqueror's son, built Westminster Hall, and several phases of further development followed: St Stephen's Chapel and the Painted Chamber were built in the 13th and 14th centuries, and the Jewel Tower was built to the south west of the palace near Westminster Abbey in 1364–6. The sovereign's treasures and jewels were kept here until the reign of Henry VII, and from 1621 to 1864 it housed the official archives of the House of Lords. The Jewel Tower is now a museum of the history of Parliament. After 1547 the Palace of Westminster ceased to be an official royal residence, and became the home of both upper and lower Houses of Parliament. Until it was destroyed by fire in 1834, the palace towered over a great maze of little streets that were filled with lodging houses, taverns, coffee-houses and shops.

REBUILDING: BARRY AND PUGIN. Out of ninety-seven designs that were submitted for the rebuilding of Parliament, the eventual success of Sir Charles Barry's project was largely due to his collaboration with another architect, Augustus Pugin (1812–52). Pugin was one of the great neo-Gothic stylists of his day, and assisted Barry with his designs from 1836 until his death. The contrasting temperaments of the two men resulted in a design that was both elegant and highly original. Barry provided the building with its classical balance and symmetry, while Pugin supplied the ornamentation and asymmetrical elements, such as the Victoria Tower and the Clock Tower. Pugin was also responsible for much of the interior decoration and furnishings. Albert ▲ 228, prince consort since 1840, was a keen amateur follower of the arts and was

"The palace of Westminster reclines – it can hardly be said to stand – on the big parliamentary bench of its terrace."
Henry James

One day
◆ F C1-C2-D1

WESTMINSTER AND BIG BEN ✪
At the heart of Westminster is Parliament Square. Big Ben is at the northeast corner of the square. This 320-ft tower with a four-faced clock contains a 14-ton bell that chimes the hours. Next to Big Ben are the Gothic-Revival-style Houses of Parliament, seat of government since 1582. When Parliament is in session onlookers are admitted to the visitors' gallery. In the southwest corner of the square is Westminster Abbey, the coronation venue for the majority of England's monarchs since 1066 and where many are buried. Visit the 13th-century French Gothic nave and Henry VII's Tudor-style chapel. You should also visit the museum and Chapter house in the grounds of the Abbey.

128 | 129

At the beginning of each itinerary, the distance, the suggested means of travel and the time it will take to cover the area are indicated beneath the maps:
- By foot
- By car

★ The star symbol signifies sites singled out by the editors for special attention.

✪ This symbol indicates places of special interest.

● Encyclopedia section

▲ Itineraries in London

◆ Practical information

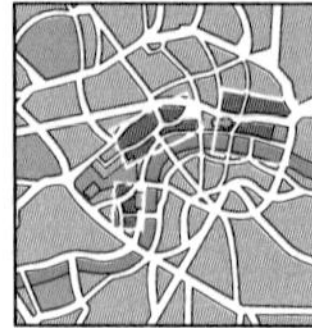

THE SIGHTS OF LONDON ▲ 127
The Houses of Parliament and Westminster Abbey, home of coronations and royal tombs, dominate the Thames, while, further up the river, the City and the Law Courts are a hive of activity.

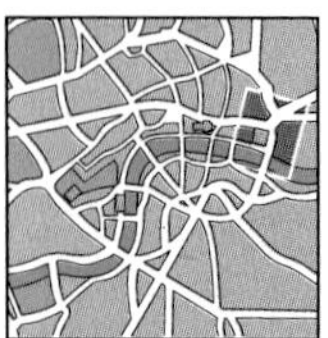

HISTORICAL JOURNEY ▲ 169
Between the neoclassical dome of St Paul and the artistic center of the Barbican, traces of the original London Wall still remain. Further away loom the legendary Tower of London and Tower Bridge.

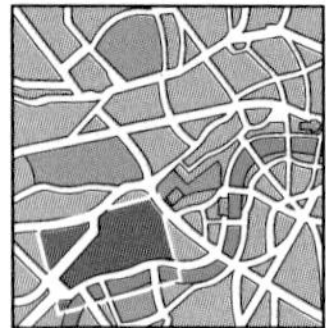

VILLAGES AND MUSEUMS ▲ 193
Just a step away from chic Chelsea, trendy since the 60's and 70's, the Tate Britain displays its treasures. The charms of Pimlico and Vauxhall Gardens rival those of Belgravia and Kensington, lined with beautiful houses and museums.

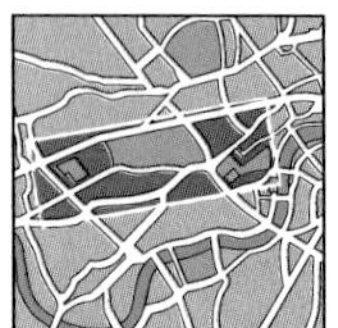

LONDON'S PARKS ▲ 237
Green Park, St James's Park, Hyde Park, Kensington Gardens… A walk through this green oasis can stretch as far as Marylebone or the picturesque Regent's Canal. As for the little gardens of Hampstead and Highgate, they seem to preserve a village atmosphere.

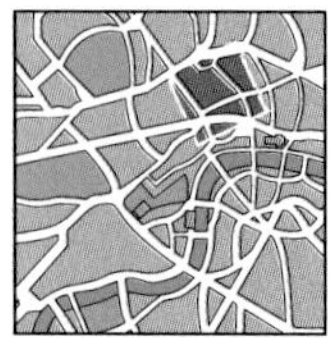

THE WEST END ▲ 265
Activity and entertainment are guaranteed in this part of London which includes Soho, Covent Garden, St James's, Trafalgar Square and Mayfair. In the midst of all this action, the British Museum in tranquil Bloomsbury invites contemplation.

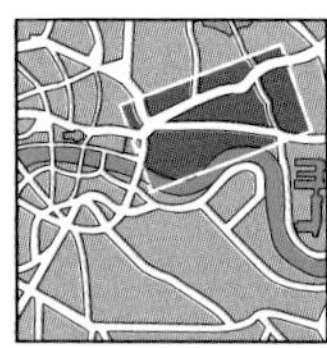

AROUND THE EAST END ▲ 309
The shadow of Jack the Ripper still hangs over some of the poorer areas, but Spitalfields and Whitechapel, relatively spared from concrete, now attract a lot of interest.

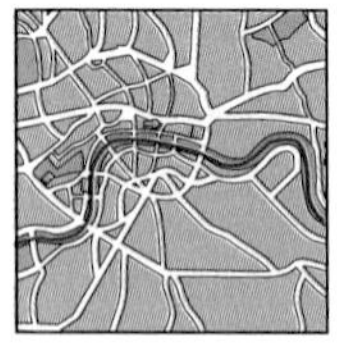

ALONG THE THAMES ▲ 317
The South Bank of the Thames between Waterloo and Tower Bridge is one of the new centers of creative activity, and, like the Docklands, now a fashionable area. The other riverside village is Chelsea, home of artists and intellectuals.

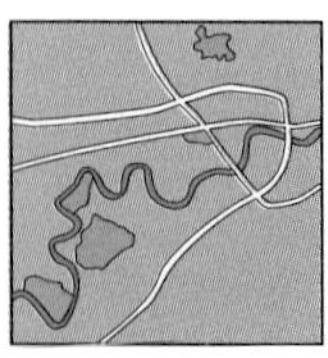

OUTSIDE THE CENTER ▲ 341
Charming excursions can be made along the Thames, past parks, castles and little villages: Putney, Richmond-upon-Thames, Hampton Court Palace, Windsor… not forgetting the famous village of Eton.

Numerous specialists and academics have contributed to this guide.

Encyclopedia section

NATURE
Tony Hare
HISTORY AND LANGUAGE
Catherine Cullen,
Michel Rapoport
LONDON LIFE
Catherine Cullen
ARCHITECTURE
Elain Harwood
LONDON AS SEEN BY PAINTERS
Suzanne Bosman

London itineraries

Catherine Cullen, Michel Rapoport,
assisted by Nathalie Bonnin,
Hélène Borraz and Agnès Robin

Practical information

Yvonne Worth, Michèle Delagneau,
Nicolas Christitch

Everyman Guides are published by Alfred A. Knopf, New York

Completely revised and updated edition published February 2004

Translated by
Clive Unger-Hamilton

Edited and typeset by
Book Creation Services, London

Printed and bound in Italy by
Editoriale Lloyd

Everyman Guides
Northburgh house
10 Northburgh Street
London EC1V 0AT
guides@everyman.uk.com

LONDON

EDITOR
Maylis de Kerangal assisted by: Patrick Jézéquel, Josyane Magniant (London life), Odile Simon (Nature)

LAYOUT
Isabelle Roller, Fabienne Cassayré, Laurent Gourdon (Practical information)

PICTURE RESEARCH
Suzanne Bosman

ILLUSTRATIONS
Nature: Jean Chevallier, Richard Coombes, François Crozat, François Desbordes, William Donohoe, Claire Felloni, Catherine Lachaux, Ruth Lindsey, Guy Michel, Pascal Robin, John Wilkinson
Nature plates: Frédéric Bony
Architecture: Peter Bull, Hugh Dixon, William Donohoe, Chris Forsey, Trevor Hill, Roger Hutchines, Claudine Legastellois, Michael Shoebridge, Edward Stuart, Antony Townsand
Maps: Vincent Bruno; Jean-Yves Duhoo, Françoise Genit, Stéphane Girel, Frédéric Liéval, Jean-Pierre Poncabare, Christine Adam and Jean-Claude Senée (colour work)
Computer graphics: Elizabeth Cohat

PHOTOGRAPHY
Eric Guillemot *assisted by* Patrick Léger *with* Leonardo Castellucci

We would like to thank: Siena Artworks (London), Peter Jackson, Anthony Kerstin, Emily Lane, Eileen Tweedy, Jonathon Green and Flora Fraser.

AND ALSO
Catherine Cullen, Michel Rapoport; David Gentleman for authorising us to reproduce several drawings from his book 'London' (Weidenfeld and Nicolson).
The text for some of the restaurants (p. 375) was written by Matthew Fort, and first appeared in the Everyman Guide to England & Wales.

Encyclopedia section

"Huge barges, each steered by a single man at the end of a pair of giant oars, lumbered and swirled downstream at all angles. Occasionally a tug snorted busily past, flashing its red and green signals and dragging an unwieldy tail of barges in its wake."

Arnold Bennett

Flat-bottomed Thames barges passing Greenwich, seen from the bridge of a boat coming up-river.

On August 6, 1939 100,000 people came to see the the liner *Mauritania* make its way cautiously into King George V Dock.

"A few customers came, chiefly for bathing-suits and hat-guards, and on Saturday night the cheapest straw hats and ties, and Mr Polly found himself more and more drawn towards the shop door and the social charm of the street." H.G. Wells

NATURE

The Thames Barrier was built to prevent the river from flooding. It is more than 550 yards wide at this point.

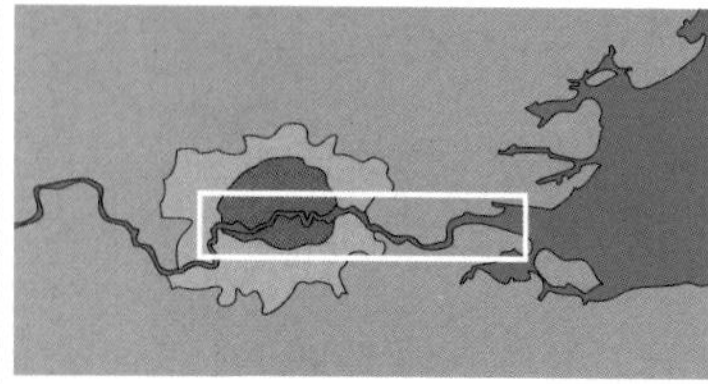

A wide freshwater river, the Thames is influenced by the sea up beyond London, where the water is still briny and tidal. Leaving behind the grassy meadows along its banks, the river flows past the docks and quaysides of the capital and broadens out in the grazing lands and saltmarshes toward the estuary. In the course of the forty miles in which the river meanders through Greater London, its flora and fauna are very varied. There are gulls, cormorants and eels. Even salmon are once again to be found living in the river.

Elephant hawkmoth

GREAT HAIRY WILLOWHERB

Upstream from London, the Thames ceases to be tidal.

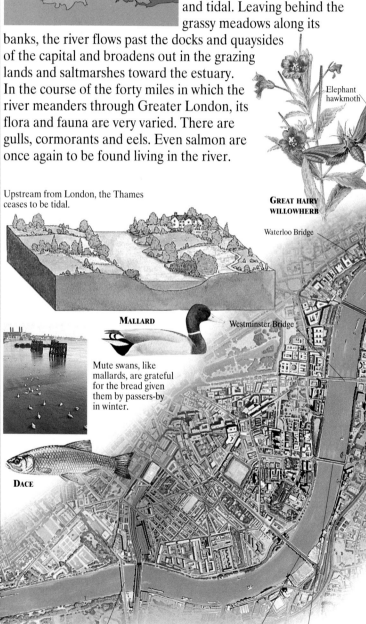

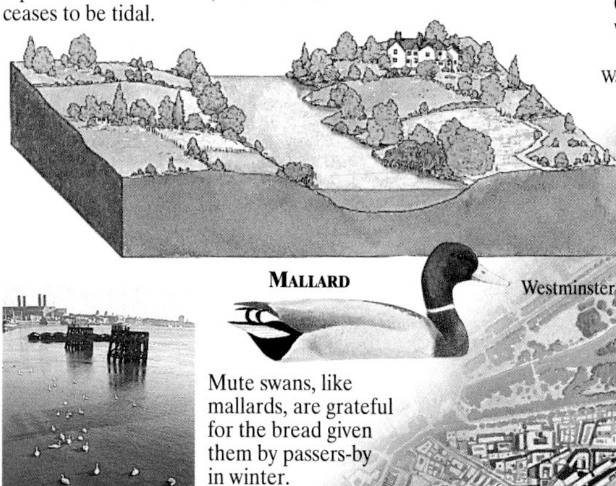

Waterloo Bridge

MALLARD

Westminster Bridge

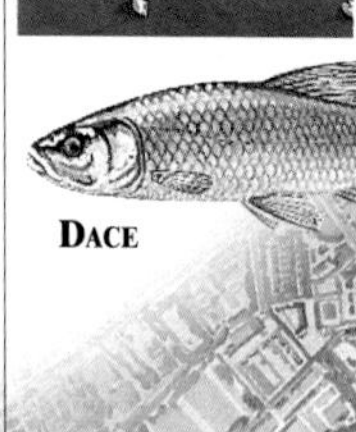

Mute swans, like mallards, are grateful for the bread given them by passers-by in winter.

DACE

Chelsea Bridge

Vauxhall Bridge

Lambeth Bridge

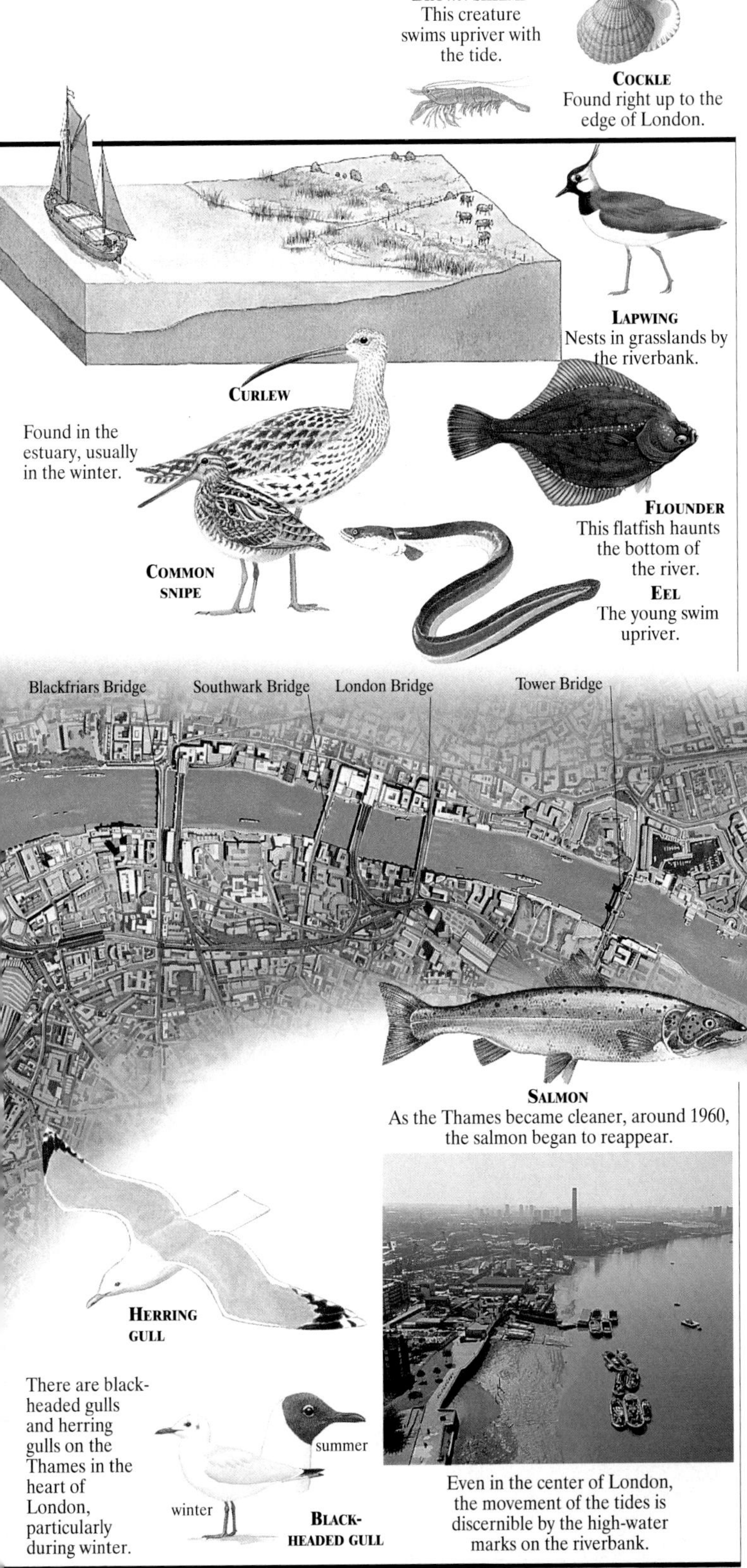

Brown shrimp
This creature swims upriver with the tide.
Cockle
Found right up to the edge of London.
Lapwing
Nests in grasslands by the riverbank.
Curlew
Found in the estuary, usually in the winter.
Flounder
This flatfish haunts the bottom of the river.
Common snipe
Eel
The young swim upriver.
Blackfriars Bridge
Southwark Bridge
London Bridge
Tower Bridge
Salmon
As the Thames became cleaner, around 1960, the salmon began to reappear.
Herring gull
There are black-headed gulls and herring gulls on the Thames in the heart of London, particularly during winter.
summer
winter
Black-headed gull

Even in the center of London, the movement of the tides is discernible by the high-water marks on the riverbank.

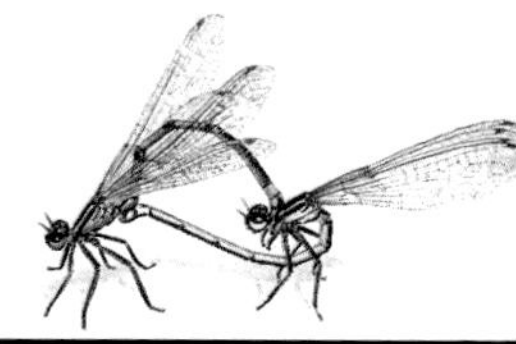

AZURE DAMSELFLIES
Commonly found flying near water, they make tasty prey for birds.

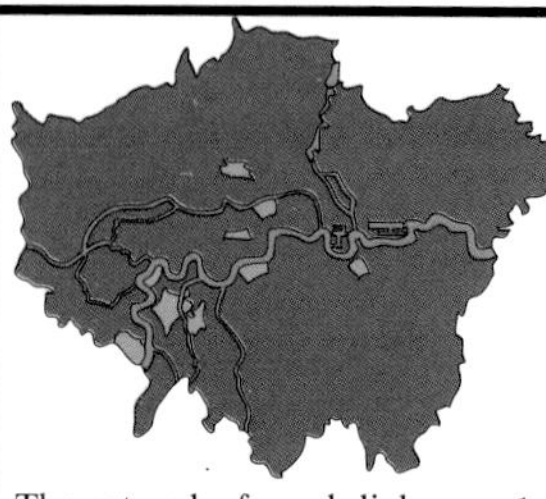

The network of canals links Birmingham and the north with the port of London.

These manmade waterways are strips of real countryside running through the heart of the city. An astonishing variety of wildlife has grown up in the water and on the banks of the canals. The water is relatively clean and the flora can be just as varied as that which flourishes along a riverbank. Canals are excellent lines of communication for wildlife as well as for man. They have been colonized by all kinds of animals. Pike, for example, are found in the larger ones. The towpaths make a delightful walk.

COOT
Small flocks of these birds are often seen on the canals in winter if the water is not frozen.

SWIFT

In the clean waters of London's canals, a variety of water plants will grow and spread vigorously.

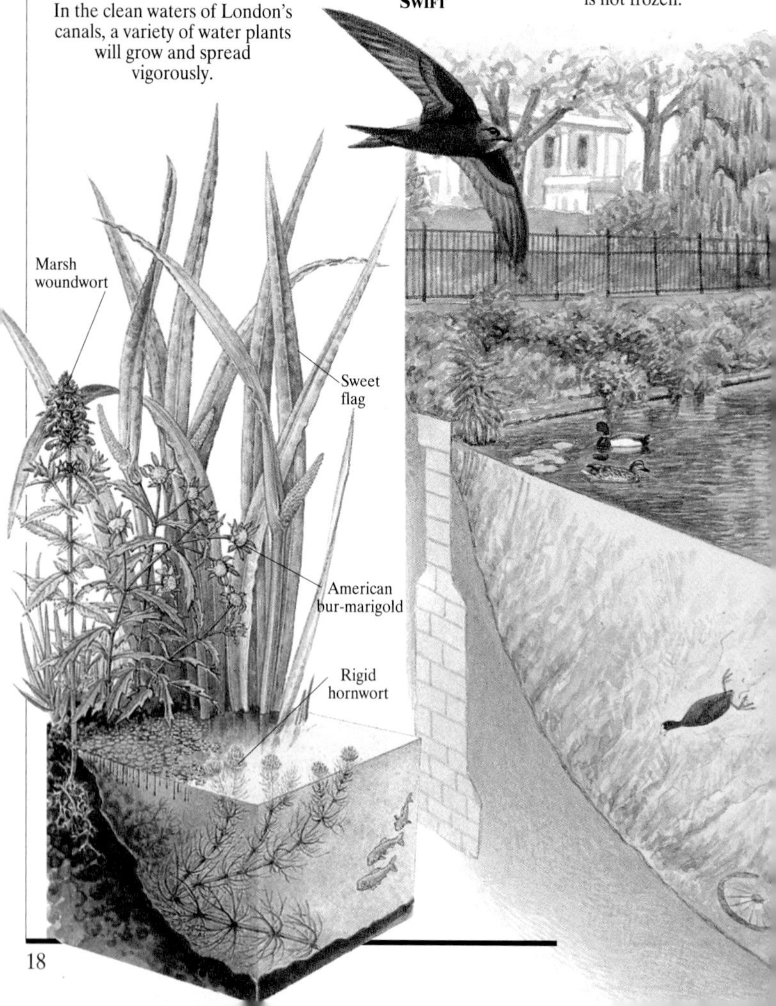

Marsh woundwort

Sweet flag

American bur-marigold

Rigid hornwort

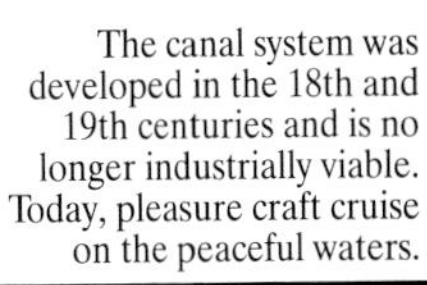

The canal system was developed in the 18th and 19th centuries and is no longer industrially viable. Today, pleasure craft cruise on the peaceful waters.

Mallard

The most common ducks in Britain, they can be seen nesting in the center of London.

Bleak

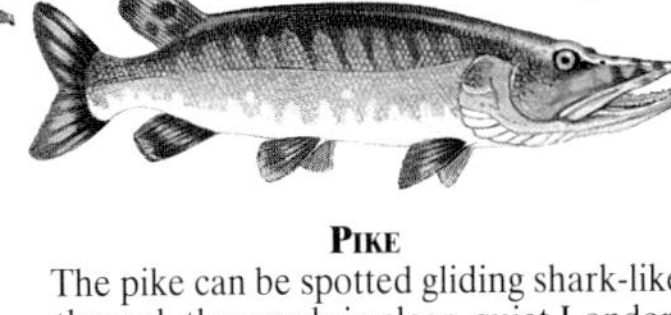

Pike

The pike can be spotted gliding shark-like through the weeds in clear, quiet London canals. A fierce and solitary predator, it feeds on bream, roach and even tiny bleak.

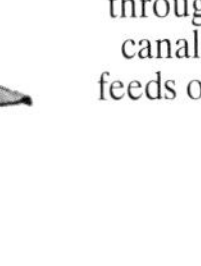

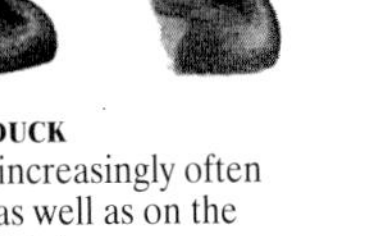

Tufted duck

These ducks are seen increasingly often on London's canals as well as on the capital's park lakes.

Bream

Roach

London woodlands

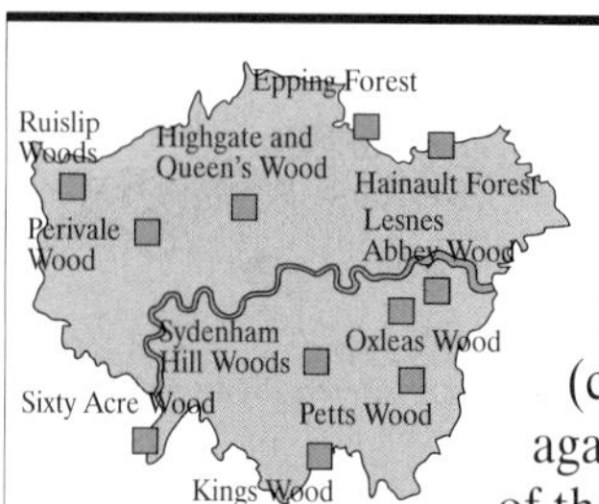

The walker who is tired of the relentless noise of the West End will find oases of calm in woodland areas, such as Epping Forest. The trees are often coppiced (cut to their bases and allowed to grow again) or pollarded (cut back to the tops of their trunks), both signs of traditional management. Few woods are managed today but at least they have survived and in summer they are filled with rich greenery and birdsong.

Jay

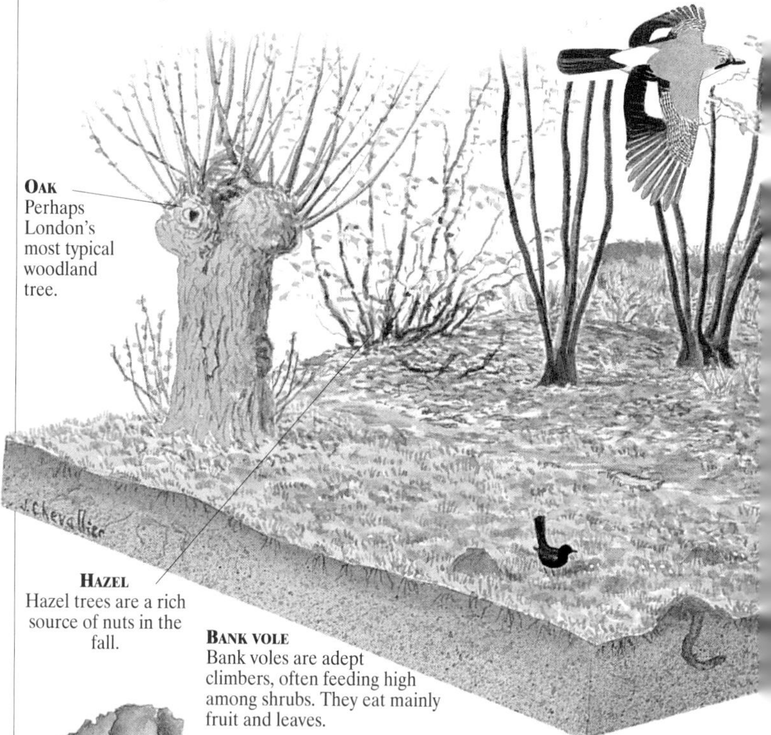

Oak
Perhaps London's most typical woodland tree.

Hazel
Hazel trees are a rich source of nuts in the fall.

Bank vole
Bank voles are adept climbers, often feeding high among shrubs. They eat mainly fruit and leaves.

Broad buckler fern
This common fern prefers a shady environment.

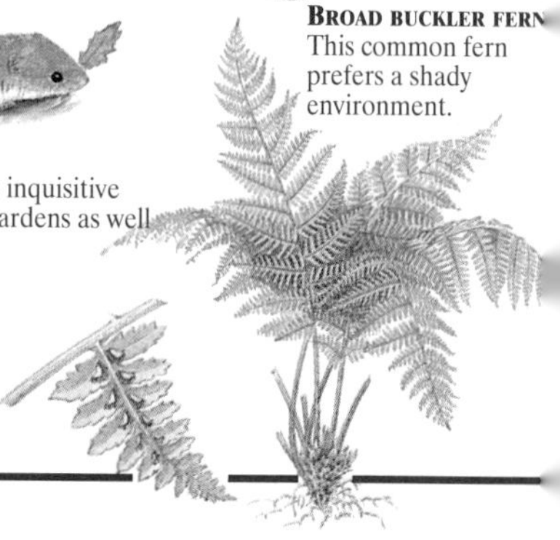

Wood mouse
A nocturnal animal, it is inquisitive and bold, and inhabits gardens as well as woodland areas.

Mole
Found in fields, gardens and woodland. Although molehills are a familiar sight, the animals are rarely seen above ground.

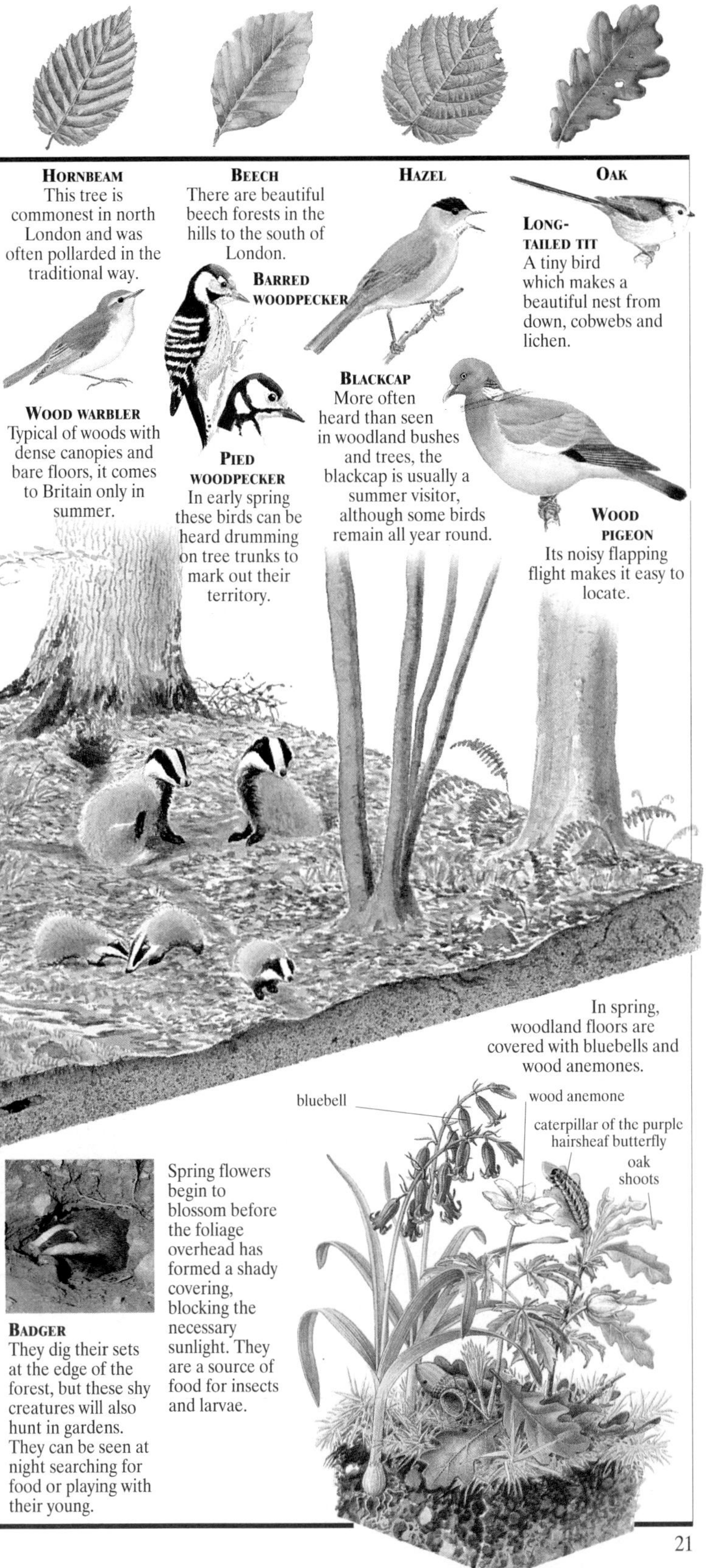

Hornbeam
This tree is commonest in north London and was often pollarded in the traditional way.

Beech
There are beautiful beech forests in the hills to the south of London.

Hazel

Oak

Long-tailed tit
A tiny bird which makes a beautiful nest from down, cobwebs and lichen.

Barred woodpecker

Wood warbler
Typical of woods with dense canopies and bare floors, it comes to Britain only in summer.

Pied woodpecker
In early spring these birds can be heard drumming on tree trunks to mark out their territory.

Blackcap
More often heard than seen in woodland bushes and trees, the blackcap is usually a summer visitor, although some birds remain all year round.

Wood pigeon
Its noisy flapping flight makes it easy to locate.

In spring, woodland floors are covered with bluebells and wood anemones.

Badger
They dig their sets at the edge of the forest, but these shy creatures will also hunt in gardens. They can be seen at night searching for food or playing with their young.

Spring flowers begin to blossom before the foliage overhead has formed a shady covering, blocking the necessary sunlight. They are a source of food for insects and larvae.

When land is neglected for a long time, it is gradually invaded by bushes and shrubs, followed, in time, by more substantial trees. In just a few decades, a small wood will grow up on a suitable site such as an abandoned cemetery. Vegetation gradually begins to dominate grassy spaces between the gravestones. Sycamores and ash trees are among the most common species found on such land. This type of environment also suits fauna that adapt readily to change, such as sparrows and small rodents.

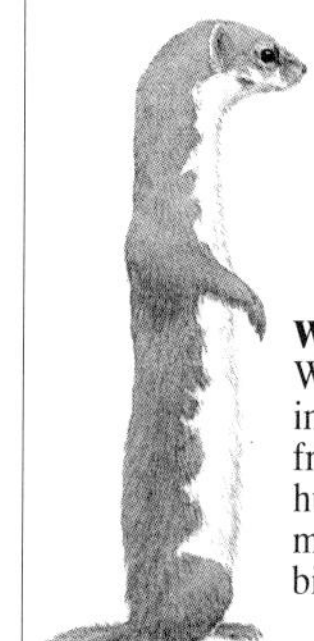

WEASEL
Weasels are found in London's rural fringes, where they hunt small mammals and birds.

HEDGEHOG
The hedgehog's snuffling nocturnal activities and apparent fearlessness make it a familiar mammal.

IVY
Commonly found growing up old walls, this evergreen climber thrives in the shade.

Young birch

Rosebay willowherb

Young sycamore

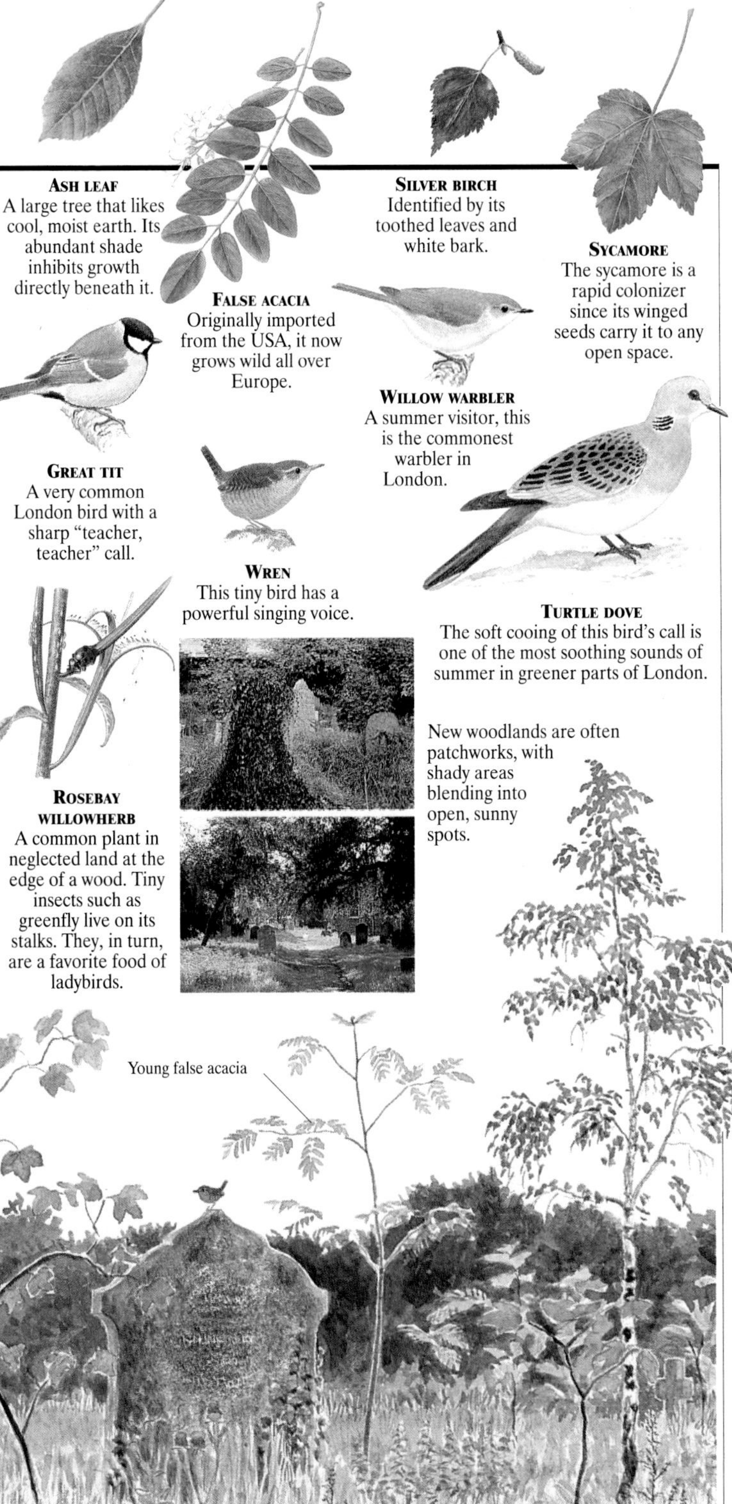

Ash leaf
A large tree that likes cool, moist earth. Its abundant shade inhibits growth directly beneath it.
Silver birch
Identified by its toothed leaves and white bark.
Sycamore
The sycamore is a rapid colonizer since its winged seeds carry it to any open space.
False acacia
Originally imported from the USA, it now grows wild all over Europe.
Willow warbler
A summer visitor, this is the commonest warbler in London.
Great tit
A very common London bird with a sharp "teacher, teacher" call.
Wren
This tiny bird has a powerful singing voice.
Turtle dove
The soft cooing of this bird's call is one of the most soothing sounds of summer in greener parts of London.
New woodlands are often patchworks, with shady areas blending into open, sunny spots.
Rosebay willowherb
A common plant in neglected land at the edge of a wood. Tiny insects such as greenfly live on its stalks. They, in turn, are a favorite food of ladybirds.
Young false acacia

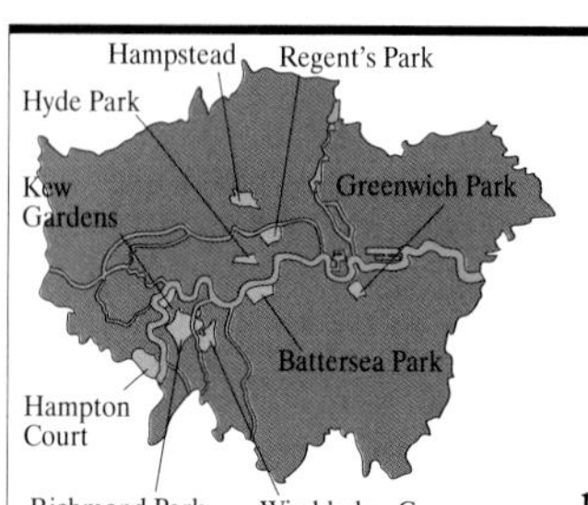

London is known as the green city, largely because of its superb parks. They are lovely spots for people to relax in but expanses of closely mown grass and avenues of trees are not so attractive to animals as they do not provide shelter. Where there is a more varied landscape, the less shy species such as ducks, geese and squirrels can be found. Some parks are set aside for nature, such as Camley Street Natural Park at the back of King's Cross station.

Geese often graze the grass at the edges of London's park lakes, leaving it as neat as if the park-keeper had cut it with a lawnmower.

GRAY SQUIRREL Cursed by foresters, who accuse it of harming trees, the gray squirrel is friendly and inquisitive.

LONDON PLANE
LIME
ROSE-RINGED PARAKEET
A surprising bird to see in London, this tropical parakeet is well established in some suburbs.
HORSE CHESTNUT
Many of the trees in London parks are of foreign origin: the horse chestnut comes from southern Europe.
TAWNY OWL
Even in the most urban areas, the mournful hooting of the tawny owl may be heard.
CANADA GOOSE
The Canada goose was introduced from North America several centuries ago and is now common throughout London, especially in the parks.
CARRION CROW
The hoarse call of this dark bird is often heard around the city.
MAGPIE
A relative of the crow and similarly intelligent, it has become a city bird in this century.

The British are very fond of birds, and in the past introduced several exotic species into habitats such as parks. This rarely happens today.

With its hedges, lawns, vegetable patches and pond, the London garden is home to a surprising amount of wildlife. Some animals are welcomed and encouraged by gardeners, while others find their own way, welcome or not. The robin perching in the shrubbery, the swallows swooping round the eaves, the caterpillars eating the cabbage, the butterflies and moths sipping nectar from the garden flowers, and the frogs and toads of the garden pond all share the garden with its human owners.

Privet
These hedges are the home of the privet hawkmoth caterpillar, which turns into a magnificent pink and brown nocturnal moth.

Dandelion
This is a bright, pretty and common garden weed.

Now that unpolluted farm and field ponds are rarely to be seen in the countryside, garden ponds are important nature reserves.

Common toad
Toads breed in ponds and are popular with gardeners for their slug-eating habits.

Town pigeon
Londoners call them "rats with wings" because of the mess they make.

Robin
A most confiding bird, the robin is often seen perching in gardens looking for insects and grubs.

Pipistrelle bat
London's commonest bat, seen flitting around houses, especially in summer.

House mouse
This tiny creature is one of the few wild mammals that will enter houses in search of food.

Swift
Swifts swoop screaming high over London's rooftops and nest under the eaves of houses.

Swallow
When swallows arrive, Londoners say that summer has come.

Captive countryside

Green woodpecker
This bird is most often seen on the ground. It feeds on ants.

Totteridge Fields
Walthamstow Marshes
Wanstead Flats
Yeading Valley
Hampstead Heath
Chare Nature Reserve
Richmond Park
Wimbledon Common
Bushy Park
Keston
Hutchinson's Bank

As London has grown and expanded over the centuries, so it has surrounded patches of open countryside. Some have survived because their owners refused to build on them, some because of their beauty, and some purely by chance. They are varied in nature but all have an expanse of grassland and in the past many were grazed. Today some still are, by horses, ponies, cattle, sheep and – in some places such as Richmond Park – deer.

Greenfinch
They eat weed seeds and chase smaller birds from garden bird-feeders.

Chaffinch
These are more frequent in countryside at the edge of the capital.

Grey partridge
The grey partridge lives in small groups in grassy places and feeds on leaves, seeds and insects.

Flower-rich grasslands with scattered trees are classic English landscapes.

Wild rabbit
These familiar animals flourish where there is plenty of short grass and herbs to feed on.

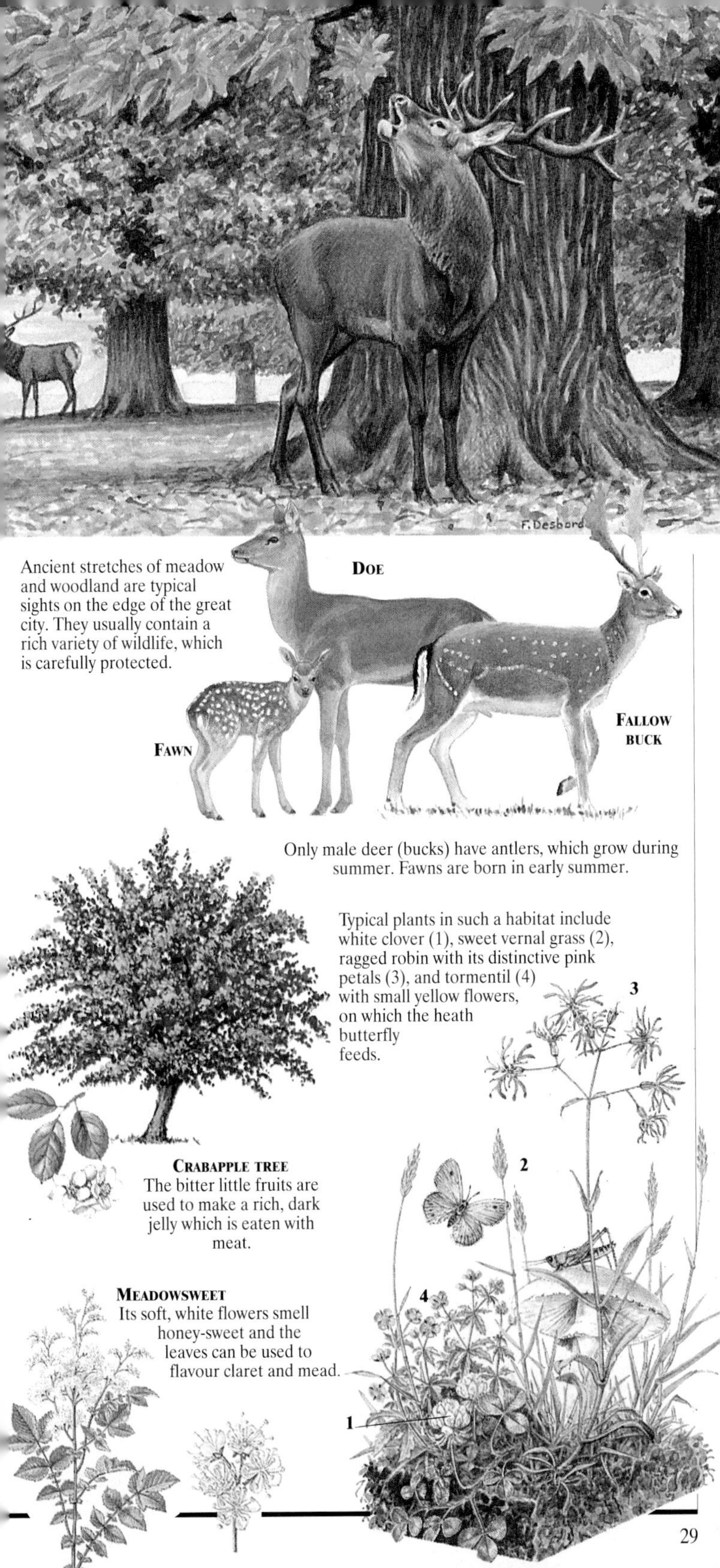

Ancient stretches of meadow and woodland are typical sights on the edge of the great city. They usually contain a rich variety of wildlife, which is carefully protected.

Only male deer (bucks) have antlers, which grow during summer. Fawns are born in early summer.

Typical plants in such a habitat include white clover (1), sweet vernal grass (2), ragged robin with its distinctive pink petals (3), and tormentil (4) with small yellow flowers, on which the heath butterfly feeds.

CRABAPPLE TREE
The bitter little fruits are used to make a rich, dark jelly which is eaten with meat.

MEADOWSWEET
Its soft, white flowers smell honey-sweet and the leaves can be used to flavour claret and mead.

Nature invades an environment wherever it can, refusing to be conquered even by concrete or tarmac. The seeds of weeds are borne on the wind and then take root in the most barren patches of ground. These are soon followed by insects, which in turn are followed by birds and small mammals if the area is large enough to contain them. Given time, this wasteland can become a haven for wild creatures and constitute a true – if temporary – wilderness in the capital.

Common blue butterflies

Red admiral butterfly

These migratory butterflies are seen in London almost every year.

BUDDLEIA
Butterflies flock to the nectar-rich flowers of the buddleia.

COMMON LIZARD
Railway banks are typical habitats for this nimble, shy lizard.

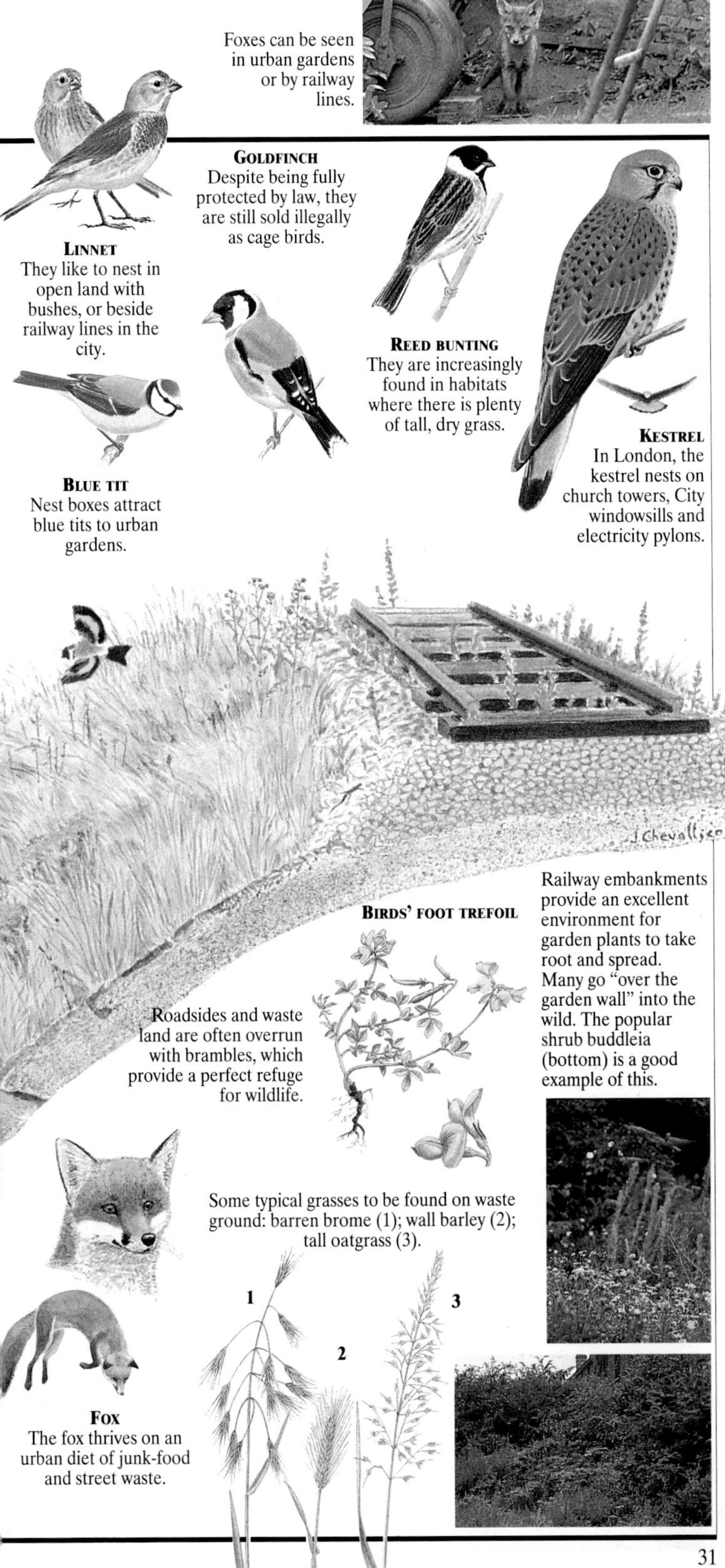

Foxes can be seen in urban gardens or by railway lines.

Linnet
They like to nest in open land with bushes, or beside railway lines in the city.

Goldfinch
Despite being fully protected by law, they are still sold illegally as cage birds.

Reed bunting
They are increasingly found in habitats where there is plenty of tall, dry grass.

Kestrel
In London, the kestrel nests on church towers, City windowsills and electricity pylons.

Blue tit
Nest boxes attract blue tits to urban gardens.

Birds' foot trefoil

Railway embankments provide an excellent environment for garden plants to take root and spread. Many go "over the garden wall" into the wild. The popular shrub buddleia (bottom) is a good example of this.

Roadsides and waste land are often overrun with brambles, which provide a perfect refuge for wildlife.

Some typical grasses to be found on waste ground: barren brome (1); wall barley (2); tall oatgrass (3).

Fox
The fox thrives on an urban diet of junk-food and street waste.

Garden walls

Ivy-leaved toadflax was first introduced east of London in about 1600 and is now common on walls over most of Britain.

London is an old city and it has old walls. Sun, rain, wind and frost nag at the bricks over the years, loosening the mortar that binds them. At last there is room for plants to get a hold and a habitat of small plants and insects begins. London has many exotic plants which arrived in the great days of sea trading and now thrive in exposed, sunny walls.

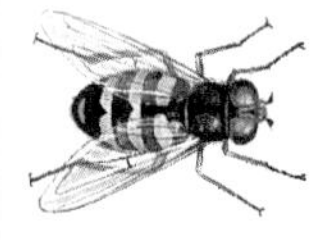

Hoverfly
Its wasp-like appearance deters would-be predators but it is actually harmless.

House sparrow
Once a very common bird in London, nesting in holes in walls, it is now rarely seen in the center of town.

Starling
Huge flocks arrive in central London on winter evenings, drawn by the warmth.

Red valerian grows wild, mainly in the south of London.

Dunnock
A quiet little bird which is often seen hopping along picking for food.

Oxford ragwort thrives in the dry, dusty environment of walls and waste ground.

Canadian fleabane is very common in London.

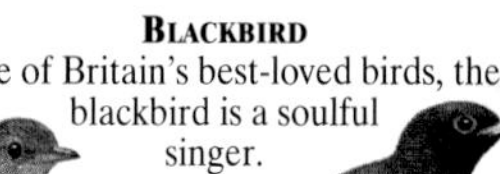

Blackbird
One of Britain's best-loved birds, the blackbird is a soulful singer.

Brown rat
These animals flourish in sewers and on waste land. They are true urban survivors.

HISTORY

1ST–10TH CENTURIES: THE FOUNDATIONS

55–4 BC
The first Roman expeditions to Britain.

70–84 AD
Wales, the North and most of Scotland fall to the Romans.

Medal from the end of the 3rd century showing the Emperor Constantine.

409–10
Britain rebels and puts an end to Roman domination.

Roman mosaic excavated in the City (right).

c. 450
The Saxons invade Britain and settle in Kent.

LONDINIUM. The name is of Celtic origin, and was probably that of a Roman stronghold established soon after the conquest of Britain by the armies of Claudius (r. 41–54 AD). The site was chosen in 43, upstream from the Thames estuary, where the river was fordable. In approximately 50 the construction of a bridge across the river made London an important junction, which expanded to become a busy administrative and commercial settlement. This first period ended in 60–1, when the warrior-queen Boudicca from East Anglia attacked London, burned it and slaughtered up to seventy thousand Romans.

THE BIGGEST CITY IN BRITAIN. The important business and mercantile center of London was quickly rebuilt after the revolt had been put down. It became the seat of the garrison (inside a large fort), of the procurator (tax collector) and of the governor of Britain. It contained the only mint in the country. The city was surrounded by a wall more than 2 miles long; at its peak in the 3rd century there were almost forty thousand inhabitants. Raw materials and luxury goods from all parts of the empire arrived on the quays lining the Thames, while London exported corn, wood, silver and slaves. In the 4th century London gradually declined, thanks to British uprisings against the Romans and invasions from abroad. But when the Roman legions finally left Britain in 410, London managed to survive.

LUDENWICK. Around 500 the city appeared largely deserted as the Saxons, its new conquerors, were installed outside the old Roman fortifications. In 604 the first Saxon bishop Mellitus founded St Paul's Cathedral in London, which was part of the kingdom of Essex; by the 8th century the city had recovered much of its former importance, and its troubles diminished. In spite of Danish invasions in the 9th and 10th centuries, it continued to expand as a trading center, and took advantage of the lack of a centralized monarchy to acquire the first shoots of a civic administration, the City. Around 1050 the Anglo-Saxon King Edward the Confessor (r. 1042–66) began the construction of Westminster Abbey, consecrated in 1065. His royal residence was nearby.

Charles of Orleans in the Tower of London.

11TH–15TH CENTURIES: THE RISE OF THE CITY

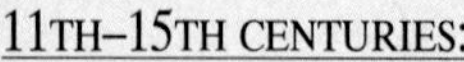

The Norman Conquest reinforced the power of London. After the victory of 1066, William the Conqueror (r. 1066–87) kept guard over the City using three fortresses: the Tower, Castle Baynard and Montfichet Tower. But royal power soon became centered at Westminster, where it was to remain for the next five hundred years, separate

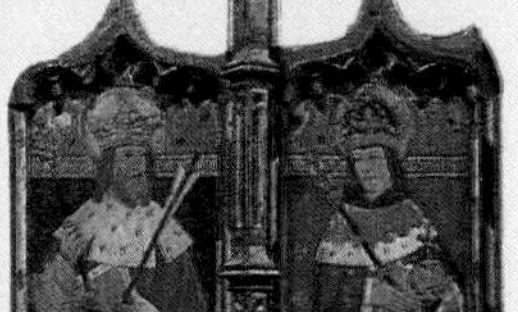

Henry VI (1422–71) and St Edmund.

from the power of the City. The tools of government were all concentrated in London: the royal palace, parliament and the law courts in Westminster, the law schools at the gates of the City and the Mint in the Tower.

PRIVILEGES. With commerce now flourishing, the City sought a means of keeping itself as separate from the Crown as possible. It took advantage of political difficulties in the 12th and 13th centuries to obtain greater control over its own affairs. In 1191 the future King John gave it the status of a self-governing community and in 1215 (when he was king) the right to elect its own mayor. In 1319 Edward II recognized the City's autonomy, and from 1351 it elected its own council. By the end of the 14th century London had attained such independence that the sovereign himself could go there only with the consent of the municipality.

HARD TIMES. Between 1348 and 1375 the Black Death killed half the population of London. It was followed by a period of grave social unrest, and in 1381 the imposition of a poll tax led to the Peasants' Revolt led by Wat Tyler. One hundred thousand men marched on London, sacked the town, murdered the archbishop of Canterbury and won concessions from Richard II before Tyler was seized and put to death. The badly prepared uprising then fizzled out.

THE CAPITAL CITY. During the 15th century London became the uncontested capital of England. Only the spiritual leadership lay outside, in Canterbury, but high-ranking clerics built homes in and around London in imitation of the nobility. In 1450 London was shaken by an insurrection led by Jack Cade, who entered the capital with forty thousand men from Kent and Sussex and submitted his demands. But the insurgents eventually dispersed, and Cade was killed trying to escape. The Wars of the Roses (1455–85) hardly touched London, but the accession of Henry VII (Henry Tudor) in 1485 was the beginning of England's Golden Age.

864–99
The start of the Danish Conquest and the reign of Alfred the Great.

1066
The Norman Conquest.

1190
Richard the Lionheart leaves for the Crusades. His brother Prince John becomes regent.

Effigy of Richard II (r. 1377–1400).

1199
Richard's brother, John Lackland, succeeds to the throne.

1215
Civil war. King John signs the Magna Carta.

1348
The Black Death.

1492
Christopher Columbus discovers America.

THE 16TH CENTURY: THE AGE OF THE TUDORS

THE PORT OF LONDON. London had relatively poor maritime connections with great mercantile ports such as Venice, Lisbon and Genoa. But in the 16th century the port of London expanded, forging new links with the Americas and east coast of India. Merchants evolved sophisticated trading

1517
Martin Luther and the Reformation.

View of old London Bridge before 1760.

1509–47
Reign of Henry VIII. The break with Rome, precipitated by the king's insistence on nullifying his marriage in 1533, splits the church in England.

1553–8
Reign of the Catholic Mary Tudor. Persecution of the Protestants.

1603–25
Reign of James VI of Scotland as James I of England.

Queen Elizabeth I (right).

1605
The Gunpowder Plot led by Guy Fawkes, the last important Catholic conspiracy.

Southwark Cathedral in 1647.

techniques, forming companies with shares and privileges given by royal charter. The first was the Muscovy Company of Merchant Adventurers in 1555; the Virginia Company of London was created to colonize and develop lands discovered by Sir Walter Raleigh in 1585. The East India Company was formed in 1600. It dominated the subcontinent for two hundred years and played a major role in the developing port of London. New-found prosperity brought a dramatic rise in population, which grew from 50,000 inhabitants at the start of the century to 200,000 in 1600. London spread out principally to the northwest, and to the east beyond the port as far as Wapping and Limehouse.

THE DISSOLUTION OF THE MONASTERIES. Two acts of Dissolution passed by parliament on the orders of Henry VIII in 1536 and 1539 brought in money, most of which was spent fighting the French. King and City took over the two main services provided by the monasteries, namely hospitals and education.

THE GOLDEN AGE OF QUEEN ELIZABETH. The growth of learning received a great boost when William Caxton set up the first printing press in 1477, near Westminster Abbey. The reign of Elizabeth I (1558–1603) saw great developments in the arts, particularly music, with such composers as William Byrd, John Bull and Orlando Gibbons; and also the theater, with William Shakespeare (1564–1616), Christopher Marlowe (1564–93) and many other dramatists. Even in its Golden Age, England was vulnerable to threats from abroad: in 1588 it defended itself against the Spanish Armada, which was defeated by a combination of bad weather and the navy under the command of Sir Francis Drake.

THE 17TH CENTURY: GOOD TIMES AND BAD

1611
Authorized Version of the Bible published.

1649
Execution of Charles I.

Great Fire of London in 1666.

THE CIVIL WARS. During the civil wars (1642–6 and 1648) London sided with the anti-royalist Puritans, who favored parliament and the Commonwealth. The City was suspicious of Charles II at the Restoration of the Stuarts in 1660, and after James II lost his throne in the revolution of 1688 it welcomed William III and Queen Mary's acceptance of the Bill of Rights.

LONDON'S MISFORTUNES. In 1665 London was ravaged by bubonic plague, which claimed 100,000 lives between April and November and led to a serious economic crisis. The capital was abandoned: the king moved to Oxford, and grass grew in the streets. The next year, the city was still recovering when it was destroyed between the September 2 and 6 by the Great Fire, which wiped out all the ancient buildings. Gradually the capital was rebuilt under the direction of Sir Christopher Wren, but many projects had to be abandoned in favor of less costly developments. The City never recovered its former density of population, for wealthier inhabitants moved to areas in west London where the aristocracy lived. To the east, new districts grew up as the docks expanded. By the end of the century London had some 600,000 inhabitants.

THE FINANCIAL CAPITAL OF THE WORLD. In the 17th century London finally overtook Amsterdam as the biggest financial and commercial center in the world. Thanks to the return of the Jewish community, authorized by Oliver Cromwell (1599–1658) in 1655, and the installation of the French Huguenot refugees at Spitalfields, London was able to ensure its supremacy. Its new status was symbolized by the founding of the Bank of England in 1694.

The coronation of George IV in 1821.

1653–8
Oliver Cromwell becomes the Lord Protector of England.

1757
Victory at Plassey in Bengal ensures British supremacy in India.

1763
The Treaty of Paris cedes Canada to the British, who had taken possession of Quebec in 1759.

1773
The Boston Tea Party. American colonists protest at the duty on imported tea which favors the East India Company.

THE 18TH CENTURY: GEORGIAN LONDON

EXPANSION. The Hanoverian period was the great age of urban development. London grew at an astonishing rate, most of all around the West End. There were three phases of development. In the first half of the century the great squares such as Hanover, Cavendish, Grosvenor and Berkeley Squares were laid out. After 1763 the West End underwent further development at the hands of two rival architects, William Chambers and Robert Adam. Between 1812 and 1830 the prince regent (the future George IV) embarked on a series of developments that gave the West End some of its finest buildings, such as those around Regent's Park. The construction of further Thames bridges between 1750 and 1819 boosted developments south of the river. The population continued to increase (though it only passed the one million mark around 1815), and social inequality became more apparent. While the West End was the center of the fashionable world, living conditions for the majority of Londoners remained precarious. A system of street lighting with oil lamps was introduced in 1750, and major renovations were carried out around Westminster in 1762. Sewers and the public water supply were extended, the streets and sidewalks were paved, statues were erected in public places, and houses were systematically numbered. But there was much unrest: the anti-Catholic Gordon Riots of 1780 and the French Revolution of 1789 brought the possibility of a bloody uprising uncomfortably close to London society.

The prince regent in 1815 (opposite).

1776
American Declaration of Independence.

1793–1815
Wars with France.

The opening of Tower Bridge in 1894.

1824
Legalization of trade unions. Opening of the first railway line in Britain, between Stockton and Darlington.

Fleet Street in the early 1900's (right)

Queen Victoria (reigned from 1837 to 1901).

THE VICTORIAN ERA

POPULATION EXPLOSION. The population of London, which was 900,000 in 1801, passed 2.4 million in 1851 and had reached 6.5 million by the time Queen Victoria died in 1901. The capital attracted immigrants from all over the British Isles and Europe, in particular Jews from central Europe who settled in the East End.

BUSINESS CAPITAL OF THE WORLD. The establishment of the great banks, the Stock Exchange, Corn Exchange and insurance companies all helped to maintain the City of London as the world center of capitalism. The port of London imported raw materials and food from all over the world, and in turn exported vast quantities of manufactured goods. Much of this industry too was based in London.

THE GREAT EXHIBITION. The brainchild of Queen Victoria's husband, Prince Albert, the Great Exhibition opened on May 1, 1851. The Crystal Palace, a glass and iron "cathedral" erected in Hyde Park, was designed by Joseph Paxton as a symbol of Britain's success. Six million visitors came to see the wonders displayed by almost 14,000 exhibitors from all over the empire.

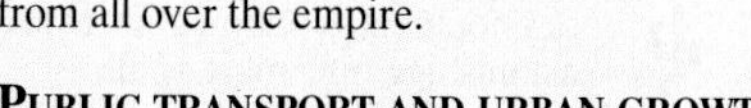

PUBLIC TRANSPORT AND URBAN GROWTH. The expansion of the railway system began to link London to the provinces in 1836. Then from 1863 the London underground railway (the "tube") provoked further growth of the capital. Victorian suburbs stretched in every direction: long terraces of two-story brick houses, each with its own little patch of garden.

St Pancras Station after 1869.

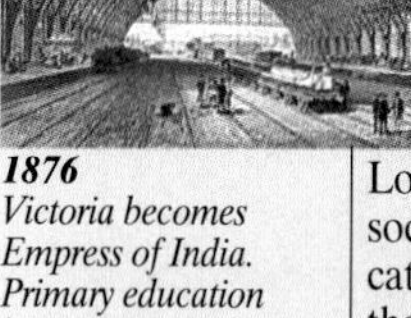

TWO FACES OF LONDON. The West End and the East End became the two opposite poles of London. The West End was the fashionable London of high society, with its fine houses for the rich and luxury shops that catered to their every need. The other face of London lay on the far side of the City in the East End, a poor and squalid area. The trade union movement held its first big rally, in Hyde Park, in 1884; and in 1886 a mass meeting of the unemployed in Trafalgar Square sparked off a riot. The first major strike took place in the docks in 1889. The creation that same year of the London County Council, elected by the people and dominated by Fabian socialists, resulted in many reforms that improved living standards of the poor and underprivileged in the capital.

Harrods, the world-famous store (right).

1829
The Catholic Emancipation Bill grants civil rights to Roman Catholics.

1832
The Great Reform Bill extends the franchise.

1833–4
Abolition of slavery. Introduction of workhouses.

1876
Victoria becomes Empress of India. Primary education becomes compulsory (free after 1891).

1899–1902
The Boer War.

1906
Birth of the Labour Party.

1918
Votes for women over the age of thirty.

THE 20TH CENTURY: FROM RUINS TO RICHES

World War One hardly touched London at all, although the city suffered its first air raid in 1915. The inter-war period that followed was marked by considerable further growth. The population of Greater London grew from 7.5 million in 1921 to 8.7 million in 1939. The suburban areas doubled in size. At the same time, the City was actually getting smaller: in 1931 it had only 11,000 residents. London also suffered from the effects of the economic depression during this period, with the General Strike of 1926, the Fascist rallies in the East End led by Sir Oswald Mosley, and hunger marches, of which the most famous was from the naval dockyards at Jarrow in 1936.

WORLD WAR TWO AND THE BLITZ. London suffered two separate phases of bombardment during World War Two. After the Battle of Britain (August–September, 1940), the bombing raids in the winter of 1940–1 inflicted some terrible damage. Then, in 1944–5, the capital sustained some prolonged attacks, greatly increasing the number of casualties; and the docks, the City, the East End and Westminster were all partially destroyed. From June 1940 to December 1941 Britain was the last line of defence against Nazi Germany, and throughout the war it remained a refuge for foreign governments in exile.

POST-WAR DEVELOPMENTS. By the 1950's, London's days as the capital of an imperial power were numbered, although it kept a brave face by staging the Festival of Britain in 1951. But life became more pleasant in the capital, as prosperity increased, and the 1956 Clean Air Act banished the smog that had once blighted it. The 1950's and 60's also saw an upsurge in immigration and the emergence of London as a multiracial city. The sixties really swung for Londoners, as the capital became the focus of a cultural revolution, with a thriving music and fashion scene. The 1970's, on the other hand, were marked by industrial strikes and dubious fashion sense; it was also the decade that saw an increase in car ownership in the capital and greater tourism. The Thatcher years saw the decline of the country's heavy industry, to be replaced by modern service industries. While this led to economic hardship elsewhere, London benefited from the change, especially with the growth of financial services and new technology, and the fruits of mass privatization and foreign investment were recouped with a number of development projects such as Canary Wharf in the Docklands. The city was becoming more affluent: new buildings were being constructed, people were buying their own homes and disposable incomes increased, allowing people to dine out more frequently in new, trendy restaurants.

INTO THE 21ST CENTURY. Today London remains the financial capital of Europe. The regeneration of some of the most deprived areas and the creation of huge housing developments are well underway. London has also benefitted from a number of cultural projects, the most popular being the creation of the Tate Modern. The election of a Mayor in 2000 was a big boost for London, and it looks set to establish a lucrative cultural and urban infrastructure.

1921
Independence and partition of Ireland.

1931
Creation of the Commonwealth.

1939–45
At war since 1939, Britain is led by Winston Churchill from May 1940.

Churchill in the debris of the Blitz.

1952
Accession of Queen Elizabeth II.

1969
Sectarian violence in Northern Ireland.

1972
Britain joins the Common Market.

1982
The Falklands War.

1990
Margaret Thatcher (Conservative Party), prime minister since 1979, resigns.

1997
Tony Blair (Labour Party) elected prime minister. Death of Diana, Princess of Wales.

2000
Ken Livingstone (independent) becomes the first directly elected mayor of London.

Samuel Pepys (1633–1703).

The Great Fire of London began on Sunday, September 2, 1666, at 2 o'clock in the morning and continued burning until the following Thursday afternoon. With the exception of a small area in the northeast, the whole City center was devastated; St Paul's Cathedral was destroyed, along with 88 parish churches, 13,200 houses and countless works of art. But curiously this disaster claimed only twelve lives, and had the effect of finally ridding London of the Great Plague that had haunted it since the 14th century. Samuel Pepys, the cheerful and observant chronicler of London life, recorded the events in his *Diary*: "The wind mighty high, and driving [the fire] into the City; and everything, after so long a drought, proving combustible, even the very stones of churches."

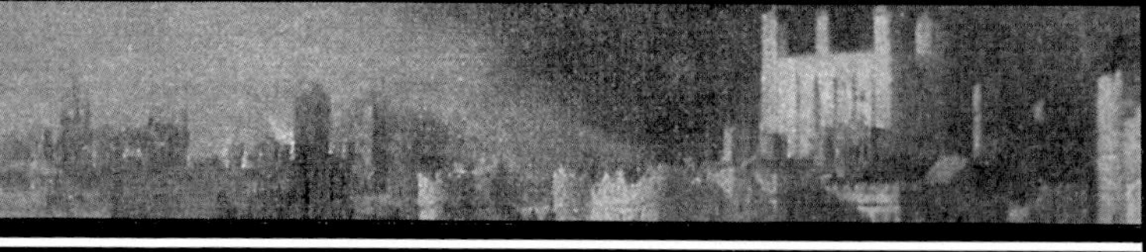

Samuel Pepys
This great Londoner attained high government office, but the *Diary* he kept from 1660–9 was not intended for publication; written in shorthand it was not deciphered until 1825. It is a very personal record, as well as being a unique sourcebook for the events of the period, among them the Great Fire: "The fire . . . as it grew darker, appeared more and more; and in corners and upon steeples, and between churches and houses, as far as we could see up the hill of the City, in a most horrid, malicious, bloody flame. . . . We stayed till, it being darkish, we saw the fire as only one arch of fire from this to the other side of the bridge, and in a bow up the hill of above a mile long; it made me weep to see it."

Around 5p.m. on September 7, 1940, the Blitz hit London. (The word comes from the German *Blitzkrieg*, meaning "lightning war".) The attack began quite suddenly. Within twelve hours a thousand aeroplanes had bombed the capital and dropped shells with parachutes, starting more than a thousand fires: once again, London was burning. For the next two months more than two hundred bombers continued to harass and maim the capital. The Blitz finally came to an end with the most terrible raid of all on the night of May 10, 1941.

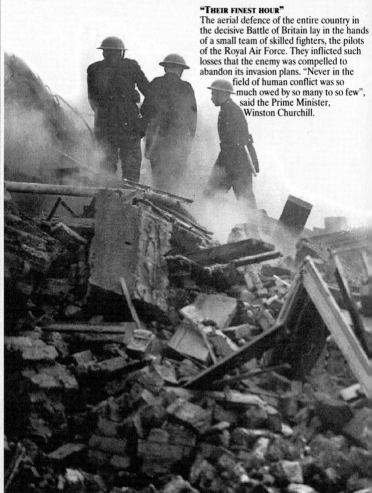

"Their finest hour"
The aerial defence of the entire country in the decisive Battle of Britain lay in the hands of a small team of skilled fighters, the pilots of the Royal Air Force. They inflicted such losses that the enemy was compelled to abandon its invasion plans. "Never in the field of human conflict was so much owed by so many to so few", said the Prime Minister, Winston Churchill.

The biggest target in the world
«We shall not flag or fail. We shall go on to the end... We shall defend our island whatever the cost may be. We shall fight on the beaches, we shall fight on the landing grounds, we shall fight in the fields and in the streets, we shall fight in the hills; we shall never surrender.»
Winston Churchill, 1940

Braving the bombing
During the Blitz, in spite of the black-out, German planes dropped more than 100,000 high-explosive bombs and over one million incendiary devices. The terrible damage inflicted inspired a communal feeling of patriotic unity, and Londoners organized themselves to deal with the danger and hardship brought by the air raids. Fifteen thousand lives were lost, a relatively small figure in comparison with the 3.5 million houses that were destroyed or damaged.

"CROSS READINGS NEAR CHARING CROSS"
"To be read from top to bottom", recommends the caption to this illustration.

"A beggar works by standing out of doors in all weathers and getting varicose veins, chronic bronchitis, etc. It is a trade like any other; quite useless, of course – but then many reputable trades are quite useless. And as a social type a beggar compares well with scores of others. He is honest compared with the sellers of patent medicines, high-minded compared with a newspaper proprietor, amiable compared with a hire-purchase tout – in short, a parasite, but a fairly harmless parasite."
George Orwell, *Down and Out in Paris and London*

"The pre-1939 East End as a whole was rough, polyglot, noisy and in parts criminal. Courage, toughness and sometimes aggression were needed to survive. It never lacked vitality, even exuberance. Poverty undermined people but did not extinguish their spirit."
Peter Vansittart, *London, A Literary Companion*

Following the Norman Conquest of 1066, French began to usurp the national language in Britain, though its influence on the different dialects was slow to take effect. The spelling of Middle English changed to resemble the spoken language rather more closely, for 11th and 12th-century scribes were strongly influenced by French models. By the 14th century, English had become a respectable written language as well as a spoken dialect; and for political, demographic and economic reasons the language spoken in London gradually evolved into the standard English which is in use today.

"COKENEY". This Middle English word originally meant "a cock's egg", a malformed egg sometimes laid by young chickens. By extension it could also be used to refer to a fool, an effeminate man, or a feeble-bodied townsman in contrast to a brawny peasant. During the course of the 17th century, *Cockney* came to be an affectionately pejorative word used to describe Londoners. By the 18th century it had become even more specific in application, meaning a working-class Londoner; in more snobbish society it was now being used in a way that was anything but affectionate. The expression "to be born within the sound of Bow Bells," means to be born within earshot of the City church of St Mary-le-Bow in Cheapside (which is not in fact all that close to the East End), and this is the one essential qualification for being a real Cockney. Formerly London grew up around two different nuclei, the commercial center of the City, and the political capital of Westminster. These two separate entities were only linked together during the 16th century. After the Great Fire, the more wealthy residents began to leave the City, whose population had formerly been drawn from all walks of life; they preferred instead the more exclusive surroundings of the

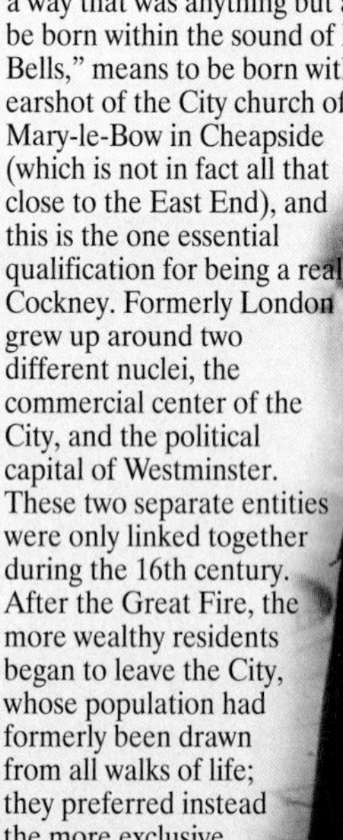

West End. The boundary beween the East End and West End in the 18th century occured around Soho Square: Regent Street was in part conceived as a *cordon sanitaire* between these two areas, a distinction that remained evident until well into the 19th century. After 1800 the construction of the docks brought a large working-class population into districts that then became collectively known as the East End. The character of the area was further defined by the increasing number of refugees and immigrants who created a class of artisans and tradesmen. The City remained as something of a little kingdom apart, retaining its own aristocracy, gentry and small businessmen. Thus, many different accents and dialects contributed towards the language of London.

STANDARD ENGLISH AND COCKNEY. The Liberal statesman WE Forster's Elementary Education Act of 1870 stressed the importance of teaching "correct English" as well as the traditional "three Rs" (reading, writing and arithmetic). It also encouraged the building of primary schools, where the children of the poor at last began to acquire some of the rudiments of an education. At the beginning of the 20th century, "Cockney" referred exclusively to a working-class Londoner, though for many the word is inseparable from the London that is described in Charles Dickens' novels. The novelist and critic JG Lockhart first coined the term "Cockney School" for some 19th-century writers (among them Keats and Shelley!) whose language in his opinion lacked the necessary classical purity. Then as now, the middle classes spoke what is known as "standard English". But a large percentage of Londoners do still talk with a mixture of accents (those of Essex and south-east London being particularly distinctive) together with a

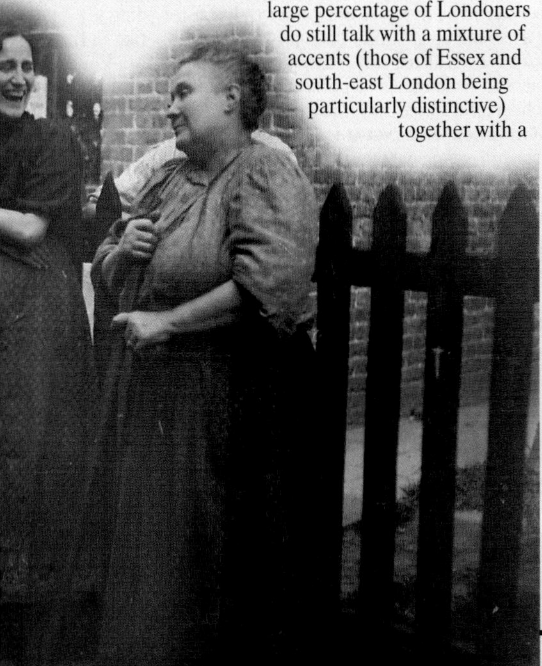

A PUBLIC SCHOOL EDUCATION

"The low rich purr of a Great Western express is not the worst background for conversation, and the journey passed pleasantly enough. Nothing could have exceeded the kindness of the two men. They raised windows for some ladies, and lowered them for others, they rang the bell for the servant, they identified the colleges as the train slipped past Oxford, they caught books or bag-purses in the act of tumbling on to the floor. Yet there was nothing finicky about their politeness; it had the public school touch, and, though sedulous, was virile."

E.M. Forster, *Howards End*

" 'My dear fellow,' said Sherlock Holmes . . . 'life is infinitely stranger than anything the mind of man could invent. . . . If we could fly out of that window, hover over this great city, gently remove the roofs, and peep in at the queer things going on, the strange coincidences, the plannings, the cross-purposes, the wonderful chains of events, working through generations, and leading to the most outre results, it would make all fiction with its conventionalities and foreseen conclusions most stale and unprofitable.' "

A Conan Doyle, *A Case of Identity*

RHYMING SLANG Market traders evolved this curious language as a secret means of communication; a dealer could use it to offer a low price to a colleague, for example, without announcing it to his other customers. The rhyming tags often contain a punning reference to the word they conceal, as in "Edward Heath" for "teeth", an allusion to the British ex-Premier's broad grin.

variable amount of Cockney. The polished tones of what has become known as "BBC English" still predominate on the radio, although in recent years broadcasters with regional or American accents have become increasingly popular. The distinction between the West End and East End has also diminished, with the gradual redistribution of the population. Before World War Two, the middle classes rarely set foot in the East End of London, but now many parts of the area have become "gentrified" and the 18th-century houses have become the homes of those with some money to spend. Even though the cheerful Cockney way of life is still associated with the East End, the accent has penetrated other social layers. And though the "working classes" do still predominate in the area to the east of the City, London is now a much greater mix of social groups.

THE COCKNEY REGION AND ACCENT. The present-day East End begins at Aldgate and runs the length of Commercial and Whitechapel Roads, taking in the districts of Stepney, Limehouse, Bow, Old Ford, Whitechapel and Bethnal Green in the process. One of the accent's most distinctive features is the "dropped aitch", ("half" becomes "arf"). "Th" is pronounced as "f" or "v", and sometimes even as "d"; the double t as in "butter" changes to a glottal stop or sometimes to a double d ("better" becomes "bedder"). The final t of a word can be dropped altogether ("didn'" for "didn't"). The "a" sound as in "take" changes to a long "i" ("tike"). But Cockney is also a state of mind as well as simply a London accent: its language is packed with whimsical word-plays and a cheerful disregard for the rules of grammar.

THE COCKNEY LANGUAGE. Cockney's best-known feature is its rhyming slang, which first appeared at the end of the 19th century and has been evolving ever since. Typical examples include "plates of meat" for "feet", "trouble and strife" for "wife", "bees and honey" for "money", "pleasure and pain" for "rain", and so on. To add to the confusion, half of the rhyming tag is sometimes omitted: thus "tit for tat", meaning "hat", is shortened to "titfer"; and "Lilian Gish" for "fish", becomes simply "Lilian" or "Lil". It is quite incomprehensible to the uninitiated, and, though less common now than before World War Two, remains a perfectly normal means of communication for market porters and stall-holders, who formerly used it when they didn't want their conversation to be understood by the police. Some of the most adept speakers of cockney today are traders in such places as Chapel Market in Islington, who sell china tea services or household linen at knock-down prices to the accompaniment of their own high-speed patter. These monologues, virtually incomprehensible to the tourist, rarely fail to work their good-humored magic on the gullible crowds who gather to listen.

London life

336 R.J.KNAPMAN. 336
Baker
HOVIS BREAD
PREVENTS INDIGESTION
DAREN
DAREN

Despite the much-publicized problems that it has undergone in recent years, the royal family remains for the vast majority of people the cornerstone of Britain. It is so much a part of the national life that interested visitors cannot fail to appreciate the stabilizing effect of the Crown upon the country as a whole. As head of the Anglican church, the queen has responsibilities that go beyond presiding at official ceremonies. She also has a part to play in the political life of the country. Nominally at least she chooses the prime minister and will dissolve Parliament at his request. This is a useful safety valve in times of political unrest. Queen Elizabeth II has been on the throne for more than 50 years.

THE CORONATION OF ELIZABETH II
The elder daughter of George VI, Princess Elizabeth married Philip Mountbatten, later Duke of Edinburgh, in 1947. She was crowned on June 2, 1953.

PRINCE OF WALES
The title is reserved for the future monarch. Right: Edward, prince of Wales (later Edward VIII), stands behind his father, King George V.

QUEEN ELIZABETH II AND PRINCE PHILIP
The royal couple has four children: Charles (b. 1948), Prince of Wales; Anne (b. 1950), the Princess Royal; Andrew (b. 1960), Duke of York, and Edward (b. 1964), Earl of Wessex. In 1960 the queen changed the family name from Windsor to Mountbatten-Windsor.

THE REIGN OF QUEEN VICTORIA
In 1837 the young Princess Victoria (1819–1901) succeeded her uncle William IV and became queen. In 1876 she also became empress of India. She was immensely popular for most of her long reign, a time when the British empire was at its height.

● The Royal Guard

The Royal Guard consists of seven regiments: two of them are Household Cavalry (the Blues and Royals, and the Life Guards), and the other five are infantry (the Grenadier, Coldstream, Scots, Irish and Welsh Guards). The guards are equally at home on a tank or in the saddle on Horse Guards Parade riding in the ceremony of Trooping the Colour ● *53*.

The Horse Guards
1. *Blues and Royals*: blue tunic with red plume.
2. *Life Guards*: scarlet tunic and white plume.

The Foot Guards
They all wear scarlet tunic, dark blue trousers and a bearskin, but have different insignia.
3. *Grenadier Guards*: white plume on the left of the bearskin, and evenly spaced buttons.
4. *Coldstream Guards*: red plume on the right of bearskin, buttons in pairs.
5. *Irish Guards*: blue plume on the right, buttons in fours.
6. *Welsh Guards*: green and white plume on the left, buttons in fives.

Grenadier Guards entering Ambassadors' Court in St James's Palace for the Changing of the Guard.

The standard (left) of the first battalion of the Welsh Guards (founded in 1915), and that of the Life Guards: the sovereign's standard (below).

The Scots Guards
Opposite, above: The Scots Guards bearing their standard (regimental colors) at the Battle of Alma (1854). The regiment of Scots Guards was created in 1642 by Charles I. Their scarlet tunic differs from the other Foot Guards by having buttons grouped in threes and the thistle of Scotland on the collar. Unlike the other regiments of the Brigade of Guards, there is no plume on their bearskin, a helmet that came into use in 1831 and which was modeled on those of Napoleon's Imperial Guard.

The London year is punctuated with ceremonies and celebrations that demonstrate the British love of tradition. Among the biggest public celebrations are Trooping the Colour, which takes place in June; the annual congregation of the Pearly Kings and Queens, at St Martin-in-the-Fields on the first Sunday in October; the Lord Mayor's Show, held on the second Saturday in November; and the Beating of the Bounds, which takes place every three years on Ascension Day.

PEARLY KINGS AND QUEENS
These costermongers wear costumes stitched with thousands of tiny pearl buttons. Every year since 1880 they have been elected by their borough, originally to help their fellow traders' relations with the police.

THE BEATING OF THE BOUNDS
The Beefeaters (Yeomen Warders of the Tower ▲ *183*) escort a group of children (including choirboys), led by an almoner. The procession walks round the walls of the Tower of London, while the children strike the thirty-one ancient boundary marks with willow wands.

ROYAL BIRTHDAY
The sovereign's official birthday (not the Queen's actual birthday) is celebrated by Trooping the Colour on Horse Guards Parade, when the monarch reviews the seven regiments of the Royal Guard ● *50*.

LORD MAYOR'S SHOW ▲ *146*
In former times the procession used to take place on the Thames (above), with brightly decorated boats and barges. Today the incoming lord mayor reviews the troops at Mansion House before riding in his golden coach to be sworn in at the Royal Courts of Justice in the Strand.

TROOPING THE COLOUR
The "colours" are the regimental standards of the guards. The queen arrives from Buckingham Palace in a phaeton built for Queen Victoria and reviews the troops. The ceremony is a marvelous display of dazzling color and pageantry.

THE CITY CELEBRATES
The procession from the Mansion House to the Strand is magnificent, with pikemen in armor accompanying the lord mayor's coach (1757), drawn by six horses. The parade is led by the historic painted wooden effigies of Gog and Magog, the mythical giants who are supposed to have founded London.

London has some of the best theaters in the world, and theatergoing is one of the city's favorite pastimes. With plays ranging from classical to modern, and with opera, ballet and an abundance of musical comedy, a hundred different theaters cater for all tastes: there is something for everyone. Much of London theater's high standard and eclecticism is due to the training the actors undergo, following a system that is observed closely by other countries and is seen by many as one of the wonders of the modern theatrical world.

THE PALACE THEATRE
This enormous Victorian Gothic building opened in 1891 as the Royal English Opera House. The venture failed, so Augustus Harris took it over and opened it as a music-hall the following year as the Palace Theatre of Varieties. Pavlova and Nijinsky danced here. Too big for the production of straight plays, since 1924 it has been used for musical comedies, such as *Jesus Christ Superstar* (1972) *and Les Miserables* (1985).

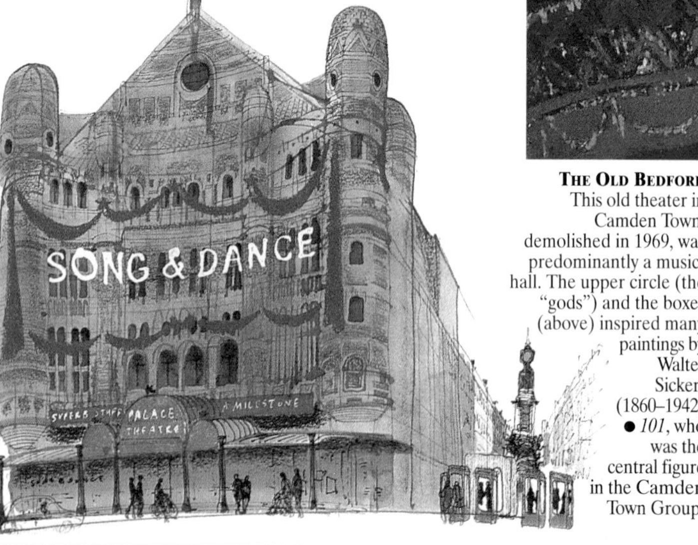

THE OLD BEDFORD
This old theater in Camden Town, demolished in 1969, was predominantly a music-hall. The upper circle (the "gods") and the boxes (above) inspired many paintings by Walter Sickert (1860–1942) ● *101*, who was the central figure in the Camden Town Group.

“I sat in the dingy box absolutely enthralled. I forgot that I was in London and in the nineteenth century.”

Oscar Wilde

THE WEST END: THEATRELAND

Shaftesbury Avenue (top right) is lined with theaters. Like church architecture, West End theaters are mostly Victorian buildings designed for effect: imposing façades, immense pillars, and interiors decorated with statues, stucco and wrought ironwork. The Albery Theatre (right), built in 1903 and therefore not strictly speaking Victorian, is nevertheless typical of the style. Inside these older theaters is a wealth of fascinating history, and many are open to the public during the day.

A NEW SHAKESPEARE THEATER: THE GLOBE THEATRE ▲ *322*

On the south bank of the Thames, near Southwark Bridge, this replica of the famous round theater is more than just a reconstruction of one of the first formal open-air theaters. The new Shakespearean complex offers the public interesting experimental interpretations of the works of the “Great Bard”.

NATIONAL THEATER

This is the most important theater complex in Britain. The concrete fortress with terraces overlooking the river was built on the South Bank by architect Denys Lasdun. The National, currently being redeveloped as part of the ongoing South Bank project, houses three separate theaters, the largest of which is named The Olivier after the company’s first artistic director Sir Laurence Olivier. The public can go backstage and see behind the scenes.

The English sport of cricket has its roots in the Middle Ages, and over the years has gradually turned into a national obsession that many Englishmen discuss endlessly all through the summer months. The name may come from *crice*, an ancient word for "stick", or from the French *cricquet*, a stick used in the game of boules. Cricket is a part of life in Commonwealth countries as well as in England, where the level of competition is extremely high and there are many important international Test matches.

THE FIELD
Two teams of eleven players meet on a large field in the center of which is the pitch, a carefully mown grass rectangle, 66 feet long and 10 feet wide and with a wicket at each end defended by a batsman.

FAIR PLAY
The behavior of players on the cricket field, like their respect for the rules of the game, is supposed to reflect the English temperament: there should be no swearing, no displays of temper and no arguments. The game itself is simple, but the rules are complicated.

HOME OF CRICKET
Lord's Cricket Ground has been the home of the MCC (Marylebone Cricket Club) since 1787.

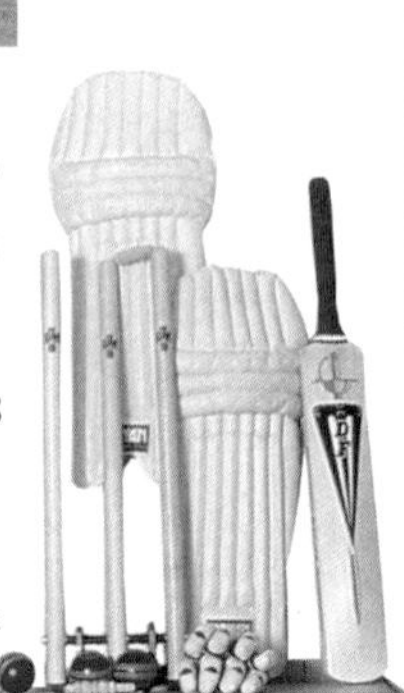

THE EQUIPMENT
The wooden bat is 38 inches long and the blade is made of willow. The ball is covered in hard leather. The batsman wears pads and protective gloves.

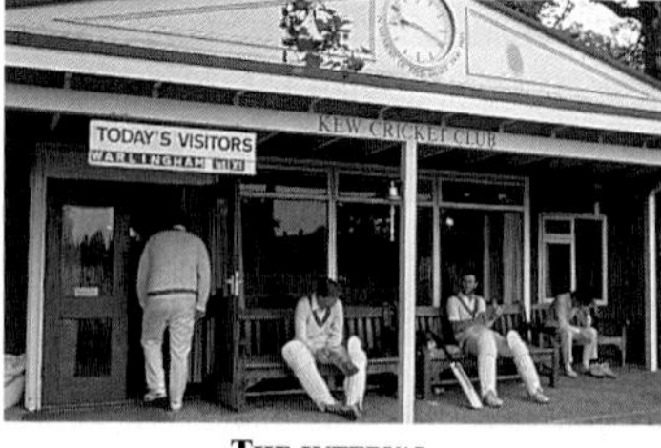

THE INTERVAL
The British politician Lord Mancroft was a great lover of cricket, though he once described it as "a game which the English, not being a spiritual people, have invented in order to give themselves some conception of eternity."

Headgear
A special cap completes the cricketer's outfit, while umpires and spectators often favor the traditional Panama.

They're off
Weather permitting, the cricket season opens in the second week of April and finishes in September on the hallowed turf of Lord's Cricket Ground in London, the Mecca of cricketers everywhere.

Uniform
Cricket clothes are distinctive and elegant, in white or off-white. Only the V-neck and waistband of the jumper (with or without sleeves) have bands of color. Modern protective headgear is needed to cope with the speed and force of today's bowling.

Beginning and end of the game
The bowler sends the ball down to the opposite wicket; the batsman tries to stop it and hit it as far as he can. In the time it takes for a fielder to retrieve the ball, the batsmen run back and forth between the wickets. Each "run" counts as one point. To win, a team must score as many runs as possible and get the opposing team's batsmen "out" for as few runs as possible.

Penalties
A batsman is "out" if the bowler succeeds in knocking off the bails placed horizontally on top of the wicket that the batsman guards. He is also out if a fielder catches the ball once he has hit it and before it touches the ground.

Learning the game
Cricket is taught at many English schools.

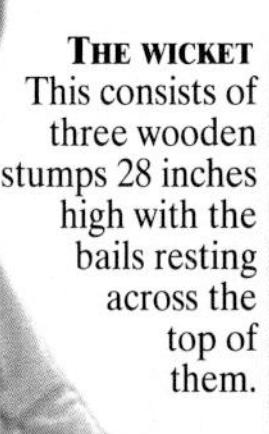

The wicket
This consists of three wooden stumps 28 inches high with the bails resting across the top of them.

One of the most characteristic features of English social life is the public house, the traditional meeting place for a pint of beer and a chat. Sport, politics and other issues of the day are freely discussed over a drink in a friendly and comfortable setting. In central London, the traditional pub, usually partitioned into different areas, is increasingly giving way to refurbished, open-plan "superpubs" selling beers from around the world and "gastropubs" where the focus is as much on the quality of the food as on the drink.

THE LAW
Former regulations restricting pubs' opening hours are gradually being liberalized. Most pubs now open from around 11am to 11pm. The minimum age for buying and drinking alcohol is 18. Under-16s must be accompanied by an adult, and sit in areas away from the bar.

ATMOSPHERE
During the Victorian era pubs offered a more luxurious environment than the working man could hope to find at home. Left, the Queen Victoria, built around 1860. Far left, the Princess Louise. Today's modern city pub is more likely to feature an airy, minimalist décor and to be controlled by a large brewery or other corporation.

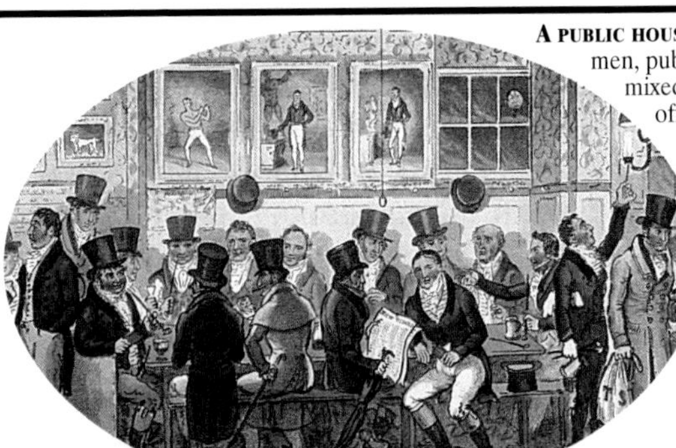

A PUBLIC HOUSE. Once the preserve of men, pubs now thrive on a diverse, mixed clientele: in the city, office workers pop in for lunch, and colleagues stop off for a chat before heading home; later, friends meet up there for a night out in town.

DRAFT BEER
The most common drink is bitter ale (bitter), a flat, unpressurized beer flavored with hops and served at room temperature. It is an acquired taste, and many visitors prefer lager, a pale fizzy beer, bland in flavor but sometimes deceptively strong. Dark Irish beers such as Guinness stout have greatly increased in popularity over the last twenty years.

PUB NAMES
Many pubs have names linked to local history or trades: the Carpenters' Arms, the Coach and Horses, the Ferry-boat Inn, the Waggoners and the Narrow-boat all evoke the character of a city now irrevocably changed by the invention of the motor car.

In the second half of the 17th century England developed a passion for a new drink that came from China. "I did send for a cup of tee (a China drink) of which I had never drank before," wrote Samuel Pepys in his diary in 1660. By the 18th century tea had become a fashionable refreshment, drunk in public by both sexes in the pleasure gardens of London such as Vauxhall and Ranelagh. It was celebrated in verse by Edmund Waller, Alexander Pope, and William Cowper, who borrowed his famous phrase, "the cups that cheer but not inebriate", from Bishop Berkeley.

THE TEA PLANT
Camellia sinensis is an Asiatic evergreen shrub, pruned for several years before being harvested to obtain the maximum number of buds. Different varieties, such as green teas (China), black fermented teas (India and Ceylon) or semi-fermented oolong (Taiwan), all come from the same plant: the difference between them lies in the way the leaves are treated after picking. Each tea has a distinctive color and aroma, determined by the climate (ideally hot and humid), the altitude (6,500 feet) and the season in which it is harvested (spring is best). Quality also varies according to the leaves: the smallest and youngest leaves nearest the tip of the plant produce the finest teas, while the oldest and biggest leaves are used for teas of an inferior quality.

VITAL INGREDIENTS
Like wine, tea has regions renowned for producing leaves of outstanding flavor and fragrance. Darjeeling produces a fruity brew that goes well with cake, while Ceylon is excellent at breakfast. The teapot is silver, pewter, china or earthenware. Water must be free of lime and iron (which precipitates tannin).

Tea time

Some time in the 19th century Anna, Duchess of Bedford, began to serve tea and cake between luncheon and dinner in order to stave off what she called "that sinking feeling". Subsequently the ritual of afternoon tea was popularized, if not initiated, by Queen Victoria. It soon became a favorite British institution, conventionally presided over by the lady of the house and ideally situated at the fireside in winter or in the garden in summertime. The ritual establishes "tea time" as a time to relax and make civilized conversation. Henry James thought the day held no more pleasant period than the hour given over to afternoon tea. Small sandwiches, perhaps filled with thinly sliced cucumber, buttered scones with strawberry jam and thick or "clotted" cream, and a range of different cakes are traditional teatime accompaniments.

Making tea

Care taken in the preparation will result in a brew which is bright and fragrant. Use freshly boiling water. Warm the teapot beforehand, and put in one teaspoon of leaves for each person plus what the British call "one for the pot". Carefully pour the boiling water onto the leaves, stir, cover and leave to stand for five minutes (a minute or two less for tea-bags, which easily become bitter). Pour and serve with milk or lemon and sugar. Some maintain that the milk should be put in the cup before the tea, claiming it makes a richer brew; but milk is generally handed round with the sugar after the tea has been poured.

Christmas pudding is the traditional way of rounding off the festive dinner on December 25. It is usually made several weeks in advance, and then stored in a cool place, in order to give the flavor plenty of time to mature. The quantities of dried fruit and sugar used in its preparation allow it to keep for a long time, perhaps up to a year or more. It is served hot, usually with brandy butter.

2. Finely chop ½ cup blanched almonds.

3. Mix in 1 cup plain flour, sifted with a teaspoon of powdered ginger.

6. Add the chopped almonds and one grated carrot. Stir again.

7. Beat six eggs with a whisk.

10. Put the bowl in boiling water, which should come half-way up the side.

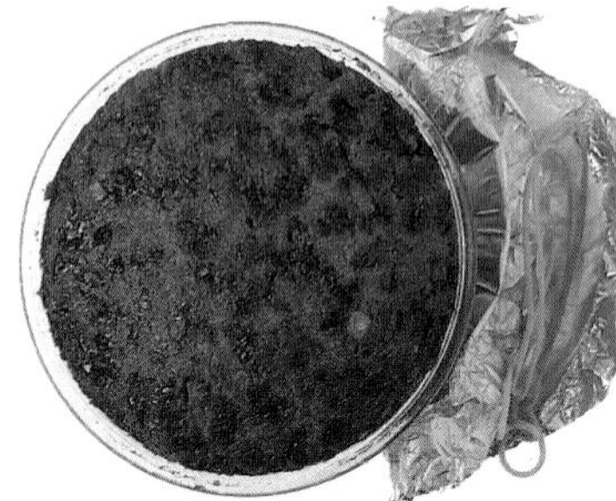

11. Cover and simmer for 8 hours. Allow to cool, remove and store in a cool, dry place. Reheat in the same way for 2 hours to serve.

Making Christmas Pudding is a lengthy process. First assemble all the ingredients, before mixing them together in successive stages.

1. Into a large bowl put 2 cups stale breadcrumbs, 1 cup soft brown sugar, a teaspoon of chopped preserved ginger and a teaspoon of grated nutmeg. Then mix well.

4. Add the following chopped crystallized fruit, well mixed together: ½ cup cherries, ¼ cup lemon peel, ½ cup orange peel and 2 tablespoons lime.

5. To this add 1 cup currants, 1 cup sultanas and 1 cup raisins, mixing thoroughly.

8. Add the eggs to the mixture, stirring continuously, then add 2 tablespoons of molasses, mix in 1 cup grated beef suet, and stir in ¾ cup dark beer (Guinness is ideal).

9. Turn the mixture into a buttered ovenproof bowl, cover with greaseproof paper and seal with aluminium foil or a cloth, tied firmly around beneath the rim with string.

12. To make brandy butter, cream together 1 cup granulated sugar and ¾ cup unsalted butter, then gradually stir in ½ cup of brandy.

COOKIES
The English may have a cookie (or biscuit) whenever it is time for a cup of tea. Among the most popular are Digestive Biscuits (sometimes with chocolate on one side), and Ginger Snaps (above).

DESSERTS
Gelatine (English jelly) is a very popular dessert with the young: it comes in a variety of colors and flavors, such as lime (above), and is also used in making trifle. Also popular is Treacle Tart, an open pastry case baked with a filling of golden syrup and breadcrumbs.

Potato chips (crisps) are sold in pubs: they are an ideal snack with a pint of beer. There are many flavors, such as Salt and Vinegar, Cheese and Onion, or Smoky Bacon.

London would not be London without its famous red double-decker buses: above, a miniature version to take home as a souvenir of your visit.

NEWSPAPERS
The British national press has a worldwide reputation for excellence. The quality broadsheet papers (*The Times,* the *Guardian,* the *Independent,* the *Financial Times* and the *Daily Telegraph*) are side by side on news-stands with the popular tabloids, such as the *Sun* and the *Daily Mirror.* The *Evening Standard* is the only daily evening paper in London. The British press pioneered weekend color supplements, now standard in many countries.

BEER
Even in the 14th century Chaucer's Canterbury pilgrims sang the praises of London ale. Among the great breweries are Fuller, Smith & Turner at Chiswick, Young's of Wandsworth (whose beers are still delivered by horse and dray), and Courage's Anchor Brewery in Southwark. The traditional product is unpasteurized, drawn from a cask without carbon dioxide pressure.

ARCHITECTURE

Londinium was the name given by the Romans in the 1st century AD to the settlement that originally consisted of a Thames crossing – later a bridge – and a garrison. It was surrounded with a stout wall ● *34*. Devastated in the 5th century by Anglo-Saxon invaders, it was gradually rebuilt to become the capital of the kingdom of Essex in the 7th century. On a piece of land to the west the Anglo-Saxons built a palace and an abbey of Westminster (the abbey in the west) as the nucleus of another town. Houses for high-ranking clerics, shops and taverns occupied the space between these two buildings. London also extended south of its bridge, but in a haphazard fashion.

The wall was raised and strengthened in the Middle Ages when the upper part of the Roman wall was replaced by brick fortifications.

LONDON WALL ▲ *178*
The wall enclosing London, built by the Romans between 190 and 220 AD.

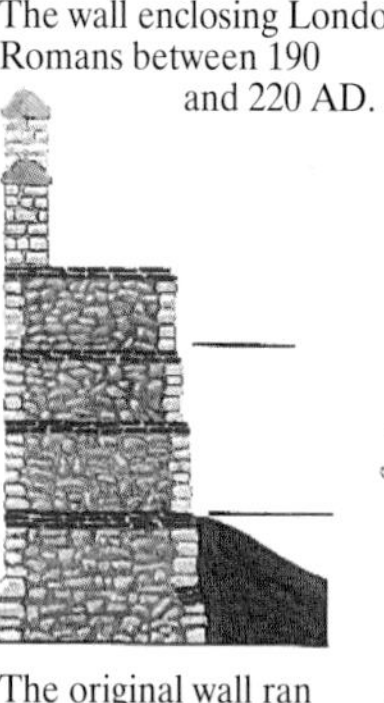

The original wall ran round the Tower to Cripplegate ▲ *181*, under the Old Bailey and back down to the Thames. The ground level was constantly rising (see above); this was the reason for the medieval additions to the wall and explains why much of it is now buried beneath the ground.

GUILDHALL ▲ *148*
Of the original medieval building constructed between 1411 and 1440, the vaulted crypt and porch plus much of the masonry remain to show the city's pride in its commercial success.

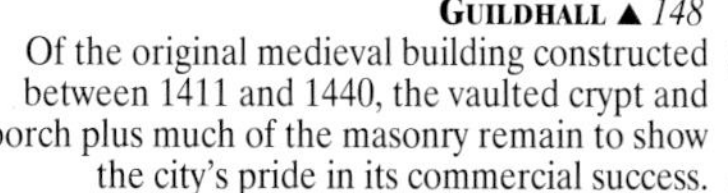

Temple Church ▲ *169*
The Templars' churches were always round, hence the design of the Temple Church in London (1160–85). The new Gothic arches of the period are interspersed with Romanesque ones. The choir is an early 13th-century addition.

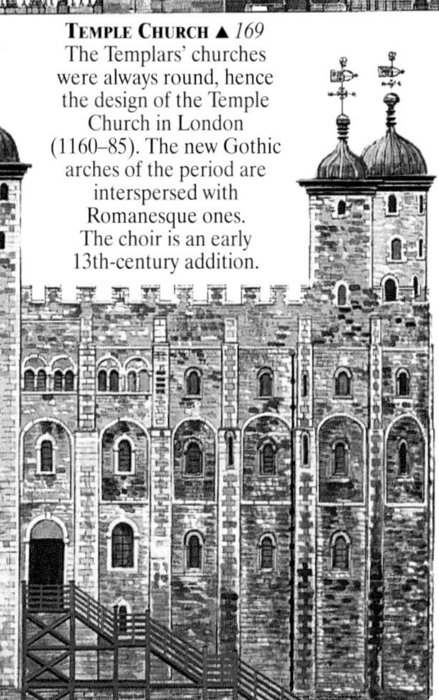

White Tower ▲ *182*
Part of the Tower of London, this was built to keep a wary eye on Londoners, and not for their protection. It was constructed on the orders of William the Conqueror between 1077 and 1097, and is the most important Norman fortified building in Britain. Built of Caen stone with walls 12 feet thick at the base, its heavy Norman solidity contrasts with the charming pepper-pot cupolas, which are a later addition.

St Bartholomew the Great ▲ *176*
St Bartholomew's was part of an Augustinian Priory founded in 1123. It is the most impressive Romanesque survival in London.

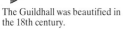

The Guildhall was beautified in the 18th century.

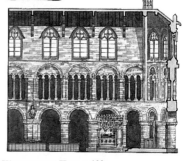

Westminster Hall ▲ *133*
Its hammer-beam roof was constructed by Henry Yevele in the late 14th century. Never before had such a framework been built on so large a scale.

MIDDLE TEMPLE HALL ▲ *162.* The rose window is an example of the Gothic style surviving into the 16th century.

There are surprisingly few surviving buildings from the period 1500–1666 in London. The most important Tudor buildings, such as the Palace of Whitehall, were to the west of the City and therefore missed the Great Fire ● *40*, but many disappeared in subsequent blazes. Wealthy merchants of the early 17th century built houses outside the City walls, and took pride in their design. These buildings are a fascinating blend of classicism and Jacobean Mannerism.

QUEEN'S CHAPEL, ST JAMES'S PALACE ▲ *241*
Inigo Jones' elegant Italianate design adapts well to the sober formality of this Catholic chapel, built in 1625 for Charles I's French wife, Henrietta Maria.

LINCOLN'S INN ▲ *165*
One of the entrance gates (1518), showing the unusual decoration of blue brickwork on a red background.

CHARLTON HOUSE, GREENWICH
Sir Adam Newton was tutor to Prince Henry, the eldest son of James I. His house, built between 1607 and 1612, has the finest Jacobean façade in London. This detail shows the ornate entrance to the substantial E-shaped building, which has an unusually large window on the top floor.

STAPLE INN, HIGH HOLBORN
These houses are the only surviving examples of 16th-century domestic architecture in central London. Their half-timbered frames, projecting upper stories and strip windows are typical Elizabethan features. They were heavily restored in 1937.

QUEEN'S HOUSE ▲ *327*
Inigo Jones' earliest building (1616–37) was also England's first house in the Palladian style.

MIDDLE TEMPLE HALL ▲ *162*
Built between 1560 and 1570, Middle Temple has many medieval elements in its Elizabethan design. The hall has a spectacular double hammer-beam roof. The magnificent carved oak screen at the east end was carefully re-assembled after being hit by a German bomb during the Second World War

THE BANQUETING HOUSE ▲ *144*
Built between 1619 and 1622, this was Inigo Jones' second royal commission. Its façade was remarkable for its dignity, further enhanced in 1829–30 when Sir John Soane recovered it in Portland stone.

ST JAMES'S PALACE ▲ *240.* Henry VIII commissioned this building as a "goodly manor" for one of his illegitimate children, the Duke of Richmond. The apartments, chapel and tall gatehouse form a continuous sequence of Tudor building in red brick with a blue diaper pattern.

PRINCE HENRY'S ROOM FLEET STREET
(1610–11) The Prince of Wales' three feathers and the letters PH are on the ceiling.

In the Middle Ages London had more than a hundred churches, eighty-eight of which were destroyed or damaged in the Great Fire of 1666 ● *40*, along with Old St Paul's Cathedral. Sir Christopher Wren (1632–1723) set out to redesign the entire City after the fire. This grand scheme was never entirely realized, but he rebuilt St Paul's ▲ *171, 174* and designed fifty-one new London churches.

ST MARY ALDERMARY ▲ *157*
Completed in 1682 in Gothic style; Wren may have copied the early-17th-century church destroyed in the fire but probably felt free to take liberties with the design of the original.

VAULTING OF ST MARY ALDERMARY ▲ *157*
Wren's superb plaster rosettes and fan vaulting of the interior roof seem more Baroque than Gothic.

ST MARY LE BOW ▲ *157*
The elegant spire of Wren's church (1670–83) projects forward of the main building. The interior was largely rebuilt after wartime bomb damage.

ST MARY WOOLNOTH ▲ *149*
Hawksmoor's ▲ *312* highly original interior has groups of Corinthian columns supporting a clerestory with large lunettes.

ST BRIDE'S, FLEET STREET
The tower composed of successively diminishing octagonal figures is Wren's tallest spire (226 feet). A City baker of the time copied the new spire for a wedding cake, and the tradition has stuck.

ST STEPHEN WALBROOK ▲ *149*
While building this church, Wren was also working on St Paul's Cathedral, with which it shares the same centralized interior plan as well as the cupola. Inside, the dome is supported on Corinthian columns set in a square.

ST MARY WOOLNOTH ▲ *149*
Hawksmoor broadened the west tower of the church (1716–27) in his design to almost the full width of the building. This bold stroke is accentuated by the rusticated stonework around the entrance. St Mary's was one of the few City churches to remain undamaged during the Second World War.

CHRIST CHURCH, SPITALFIELDS ▲ *311*
Soaring above the arched pediment of the portico, Hawksmoor's spire dominates his whole design for the church (1714–30). Inside is a flat ceiling with barrel-vaulted side aisles.

It is uncertain whether the Venetian-style east window shows Palladian influence, or whether it is simply echoing the arched pediment at the entrance.

Much of London's distinctive character derives from the fact that it is quite visibly a collection of separate villages. Some of its parish churches are medieval buildings, although the majority have been rebuilt in more recent times. They display a rich variety of styles, and some of them are still surrounded by ancient graveyards. Most are little known to the general public.

HOLY TRINITY, CLAPHAM
Built between 1774 and 1777, the church has an elegant neo-classical design.

ST JOHN, HAMPSTEAD ▲ *261*
The 14th-century church was rebuilt 1744–7 by John Sanderson when Hampstead was becoming a popular spa. In 1872 it was enlarged by F.P. Cockerell to make room for the rapidly increasing population of the borough. John Constable is buried within the tree-shaded churchyard.

ST MARY, ISLINGTON
The graceful slim steeple is all that remains of the original church (1751–4) in Upper Street. The porch was added in 1903.

ST MARY THE VIRGIN, WANSTEAD
Built in 1790 by Thomas Hardwick, the church has an exceptionally fine interior, with slender Corinthian columns, box pews and a pulpit with columns modeled as palm trees. In the churchyard is the "Watcher's Box", a safeguard against grave robbers.

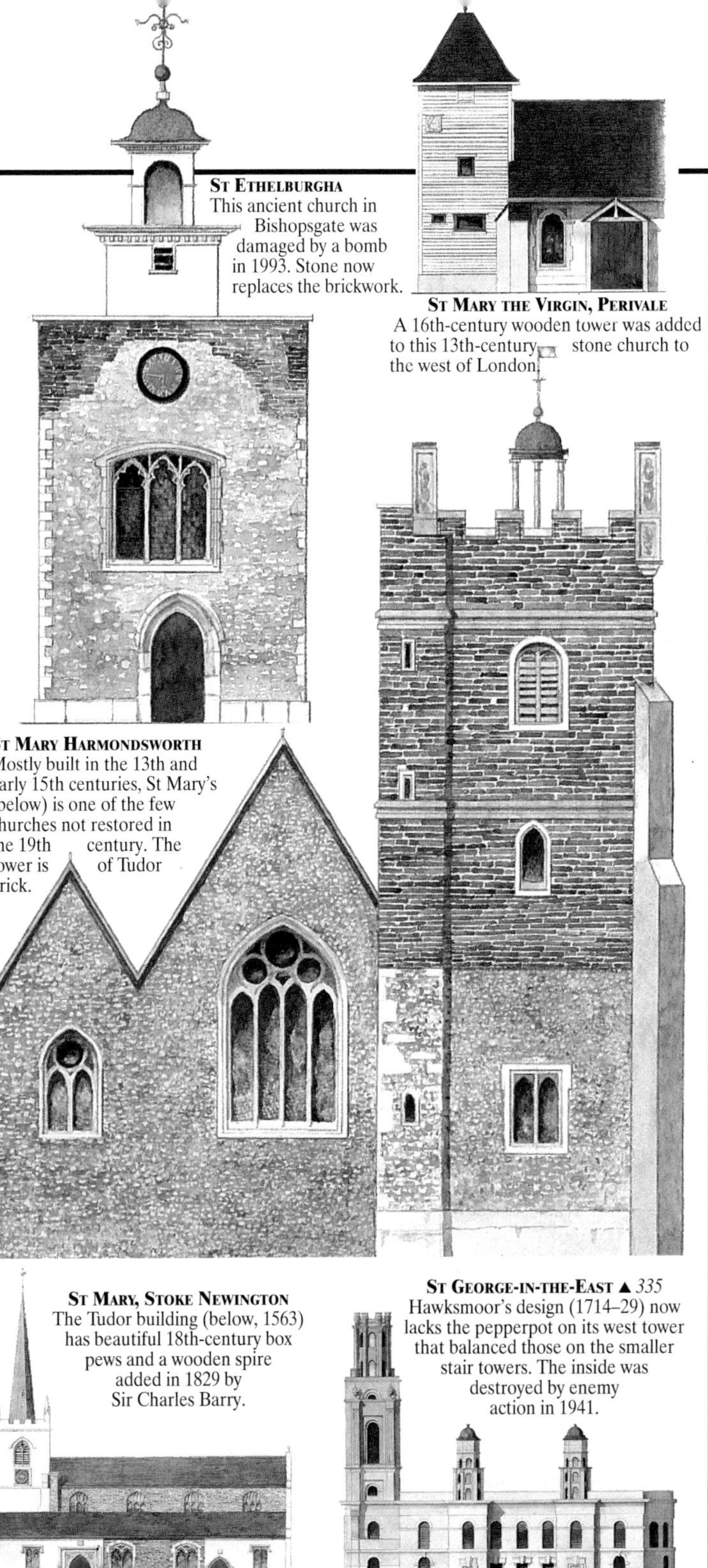

St Ethelburgha
This ancient church in Bishopsgate was damaged by a bomb in 1993. Stone now replaces the brickwork.

St Mary the Virgin, Perivale
A 16th-century wooden tower was added to this 13th-century stone church to the west of London.

St Mary Harmondsworth
Mostly built in the 13th and early 15th centuries, St Mary's (below) is one of the few churches not restored in the 19th century. The tower is of Tudor brick.

St Mary, Stoke Newington
The Tudor building (below, 1563) has beautiful 18th-century box pews and a wooden spire added in 1829 by Sir Charles Barry.

St George-in-the-East ▲ *335*
Hawksmoor's design (1714–29) now lacks the pepperpot on its west tower that balanced those on the smaller stair towers. The inside was destroyed by enemy action in 1941.

ALBURY STREET, DEPTFORD
Built by a local mason between 1706 and 1714 in a district inhabited by wealthy shipowners, Albury Street has some splendid ornamental carved doorways.

After the Great Fire of 1666 legislation was passed in the Georgian period requiring houses to be built in terraces, which served as models for the later expansion of London. New features introduced in the late 17th century included the widespread use of brick, and sash windows with a metal counterbalance suspended over a pulley. As a precaution against fire, laws passed in 1707 and 1709 restricted the use of wood on building façades.

FENTON HOUSE, HAMPSTEAD ▲ *262*
This magnificent residence was built in 1693. Its graceful hipped roof was a popular feature of the time. The colonnade on the side facing the street was added later.

NEWINGTON GREEN, ISLINGTON
Numbers 52–5 (1658) are among the oldest surviving houses in London.

39–43 OLD TOWN, CLAPHAM
The high roof and busy façade of the Queen Anne terrace seem old-fashioned for its date (1707). Top-heavy doorways and cornices under the eaves fell out of use after 1709.

QUEEN ANNE'S GATE
This superb group of regular houses was begun in 1704 near St James's Park.

57–60 LINCOLN'S INN FIELDS ▲ *165*
No. 57–8 (far left) was built in 1730 to complement its 17th-century neighbor Lindsey House (left, 1640). Both houses were later divided into two separate dwellings.

The Rugby Estate, Holborn
The district has many surviving houses from the period 1680–1720. The "area", a small courtyard beneath the façade admitting light to the kitchens in the basement, was an early Georgian innovation, as were the double roof built on a single façade and the decoration concentrated on the entrance.

Doorways in Rugby Street
Classical design and elaborate decoration are typical of the 1720's.

36 Elder Street
Columns and pediment introduced a more neo-classical style around 1760–80.

Princelet Street
Consoles supporting a flat architrave are another characteristic feature of the 1720's.

75 Elder Street
This unusual doorway of 1726 combines Doric and rustic elements.

A note of austerity entered architectural design around 1760. In 1774 a law was passed further restricting the use of timber and requiring the counterweight mechanism of sash windows to be concealed within the fabric. Formality of design was accompanied by a fashion for grey or yellow brickwork, moving away from warm brown tones. Rendered façades became popular too, painted to resemble stone; and the terraces, particularly those of John Nash, became monumental in scale.

BEDFORD SQUARE ▲ *300* (c. 1775) The center house on each side is stuccoed, and doorways are decorated with Coade stone ● *82*.

FITZROY SQUARE ▲ *308* Designed by R. Adam in 1792.

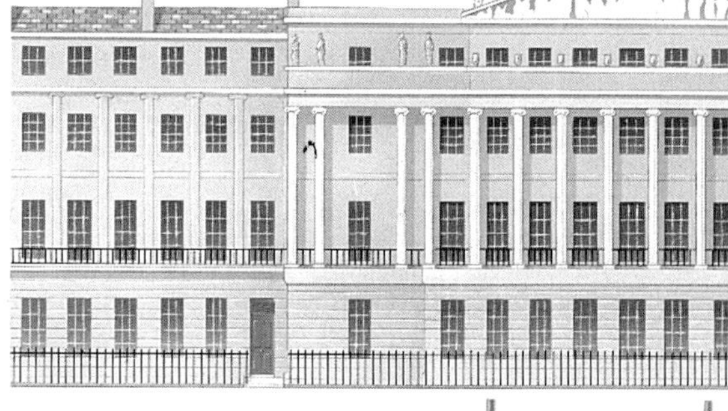

CUMBERLAND TERRACE ▲ *256* The most magnificent of John Nash's Regent's Park terraces was built in 1826–7 in three linked groups, the center one having Corinthian columns and a decorated pediment. It is 800 feet long.

DOUGHTY STREET ▲ *298* Late Georgian terraces line either side of the street. They are of simple but pleasing design with brick façades (some of them have unfortunately been painted). Charles Dickens completed *Oliver Twist* and *Nicholas Nickleby* at number 48, his home from 1837 to 1839.

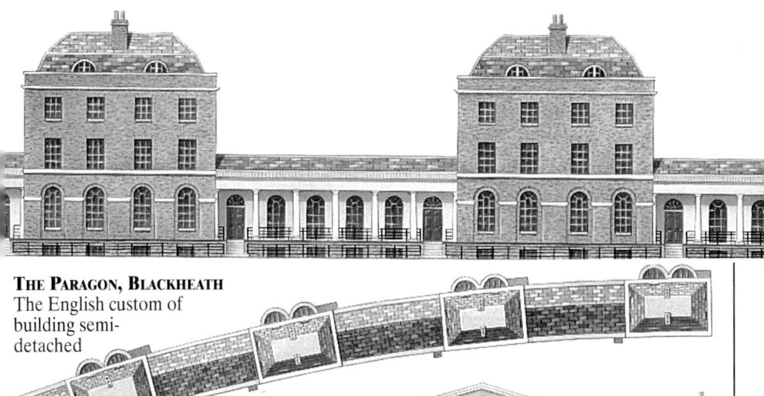

The Paragon, Blackheath
The English custom of building semi-detached

houses dates back at least to the 18th century. The fourteen huge houses that make up this group, designed by Michael Searles around 1790, are linked by Tuscan colonnades. It is one of the finest Georgian housing developments in London.

Chester Terrace (1825) ▲ *258*
Wings at either end of John Nash's longest Regent's Park terrace (940 feet) are connected to the main building by graceful arches.

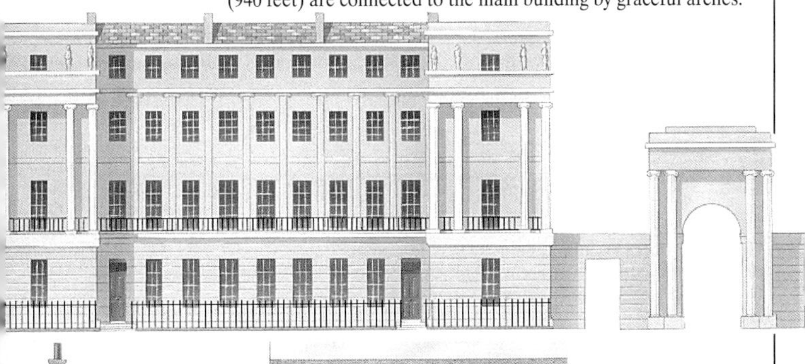

Lonsdale Square
In the 1840's many architects and builders abandoned the neo-classical style, and under the influence of the Romantic movement began to favor mock-Tudor design. R.C. Carpenter was one who adapted the Tudor style to this charming square, designed for the Drapers' Company.

Milner Square
The unique design of this Islington square dates from about 1843. The houses are now apartments. Each has three bays separated by thin pilasters which, with the continuous attic floor at the top, give the houses a curiously elongated appearance. Like other squares in the borough, its entrances are in the middle of the sides rather than at the corners.

BUTLER'S WHARF AND COURAGE'S BREWERY
The immense riverside façade of Butler's Wharf adjoins the distinctive outline of the Courage Brewery.

The docks along the River Thames, once the largest port complex in the country, closed in the late 1960's–early 70's. The 1980's saw the beginnings of the complete regeneration of the area, with the addition of an airport, a university, a light railway system, and development of the old warehouses into housing, restaurants and shops. Life is breezing back on both sides of the Thames, but these gaunt, tall buildings still present a spectacular industrial landscape.

SHAD THAMES
At the back of Butler's Wharf on the western side are the remains of an 18th-century brewery. The street has preserved much of its character, with high gabled roofs and the latticed ironwork of its footbridges evoking the 19th-century engravings of Gustave Doré.

WEST INDIA DOCK ▲ *330, 337*
The severely functional-looking façade of these bonded warehouses (1802–3) has a wealth of detail, with stair towers for shifting goods between floors, lunettes on the top floor and round windows in the central bays. The building now houses the Museum in Docklands.

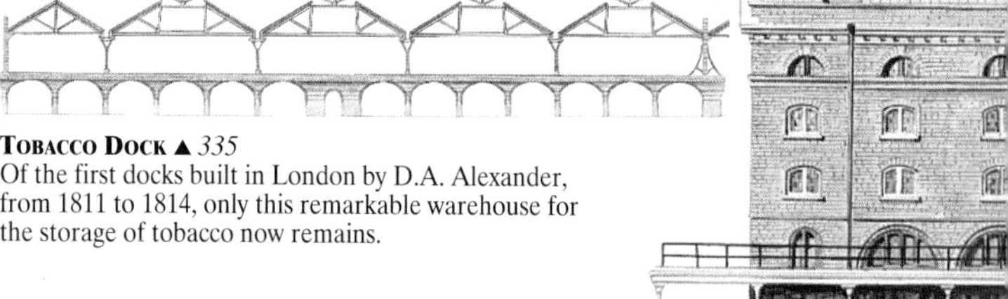

TOBACCO DOCK ▲ *335*
Of the first docks built in London by D.A. Alexander, from 1811 to 1814, only this remarkable warehouse for the storage of tobacco now remains.

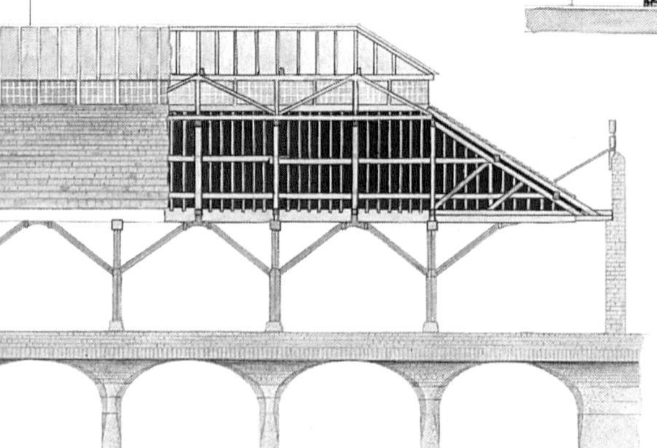

STONE, IRON AND WOOD
The complex structure using all three materials is also known as the "Skin Floor": imported furs were stored here too. The sophisticated cast-iron framework of Tobacco Dock, which supports a timber-framed roof, is set on a brick and stone system of wine cellars.

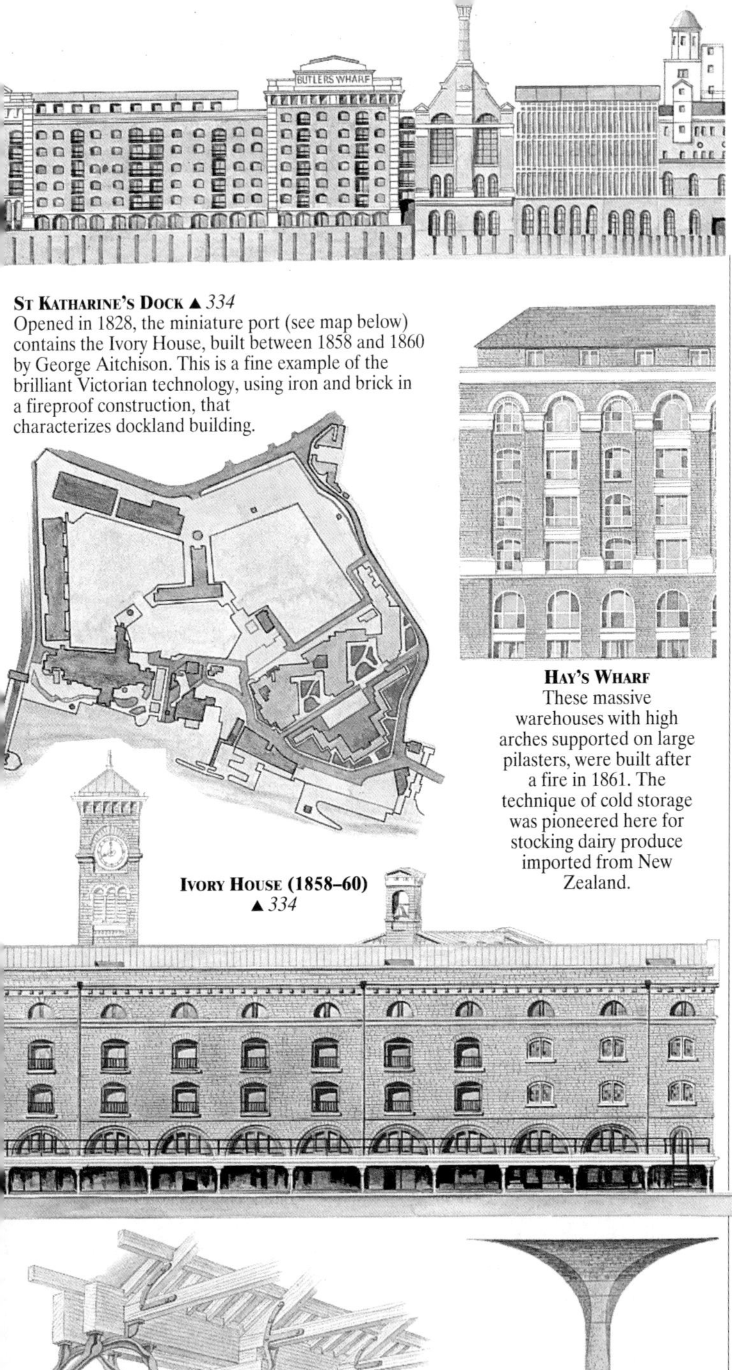

St Katharine's Dock ▲ *334*
Opened in 1828, the miniature port (see map below) contains the Ivory House, built between 1858 and 1860 by George Aitchison. This is a fine example of the brilliant Victorian technology, using iron and brick in a fireproof construction, that characterizes dockland building.

Hay's Wharf
These massive warehouses with high arches supported on large pilasters, were built after a fire in 1861. The technique of cold storage was pioneered here for stocking dairy produce imported from New Zealand.

Ivory House (1858–60)
▲ *334*

Cast-iron supports
Cast-iron pillars branch out at the top in tree-like formation to support the light timber frame of the roof.

Foundations
The bevelled corners of the stone pillars are continued in the brickwork to stabilize a structure supported on massive stone bases with wooden piles beneath.

Railway motif on the capital of a column at St Pancras Station.

Around 1820 there was a revival of interest in medieval architecture. But it was the religious revival of the 1840's that was responsible for the reintroduction of the Gothic style. An important pioneer in the field was Augustus Pugin (1812–52), a Catholic architect, writer and propagandist. He worked with Barry on the new Houses of Parliament. Anglican architects such as Butterfield, Scott and Street went on to adapt his ideas using the medium of brick. Before long, mock-Gothic factories and houses were springing up everywhere.

TOWER HOUSE
The neo-Gothic architect William Burges built himself this house in Kensington 1876–81. In the tower is a circular staircase.

NEW RIVER PUMPING STATION
With its tower-shaped chimney, battlements, and windows like loopholes, this industrial building in Green Lanes looks like a medieval castle. Built 1854–6 by W. Chadwell Mylne, it has been replaced by a miniscule plant alongside.

ST PANCRAS HOTEL
The ultimate in neo-Gothic design, the Midland Grand Hotel (1868–74) at St Pancras is as extravagant inside as out. Its colorful façade is made up of bright red Nottingham brick, red and grey granite and beige stone. Scott's huge building was considered by many to be the finest hotel in England (it boasted the first ever Ladies' Smoking Room). It was closed in 1935, but is due to be reopened as part of a comprehensive development plan of the station and its area.

ST PANCRAS STATION
George Gilbert Scott designed the splendid façade (1866–8) for the Midland Railway at the same time as he was working on the Albert Memorial. The station is being redeveloped to become the new terminus for the Eurostar trains (from 2007).

ROYAL COURTS OF JUSTICE ▲ *163*
Architect George Edmund Street was worn out by this huge project and died in 1881, before the completion of his masterly Gothic design (1874–82). Its style is pure 13th-century, and it was the only major government-funded building erected in the Gothic style.

HOLY TRINITY, SLOANE STREET
Designed in 1890 by John Dando Sedding, the church (right) is a virtual memorial to the Arts and Crafts movement of the period.

T JAMES THE LESS This raceful Pimlico church 1861) has superb iron rick decoration inside and out.

As St Pancras Station (below) shows, Victorian architects were principally concerned with applying the styles of the past to the latest technology.

ST PANCRAS STATION: THE GLASS ROOF
The huge glass and iron terminal, designed by the engineer William Henry Barlow, was for years the widest span in the world (245 feet). The ties binding this brilliant design are concealed underneath the platforms.

● Terracotta and Artificial Stone

Gallipoli Baths
A decorated oriental-style kiosk (1895) provides the entrance to these sumptuous public baths.

In the 1770's the fashion emerged for decorating brick façades with moulded ceramics. London has no stone quarries of its own, so encouraged the manufacture of interesting artificial materials like Coade stone. Terracotta manufactured by such firms as Doulton and Company became a distinctive feature on Victorian buildings. Ceramics were much used for creating historical designs, while in the early 20th century these clean bright surfaces were popular for decorating the exteriors of theaters and picture palaces.

Mount Street
Pink terracotta virtually covers this delightful 1893 terrace.

The Palace Theatre, Cambridge Circus ● *54–5*
Thomas Collcutt built this enormous theater on an imposing corner site in 1890. Its extravagant decoration features bands of pale faience separating the red brick of the façade.

Hackney Empire
Frank Matcham's dignified façade for this famous variety hall (1901) features a pair of remarkable terracotta domes.

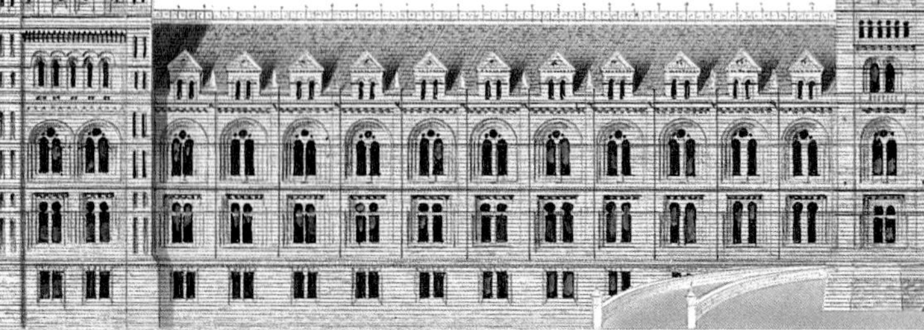

Natural History Museum ▲ *234*
Architect Alfred Waterhouse covered his palatial design in decorative patterns of terracotta. The museum took almost nine years to build, and opened in 1881. Its inspiration is Romanesque rather than Gothic, and the interior resembles a giant cathedral. The huge façade is 675 feet wide.

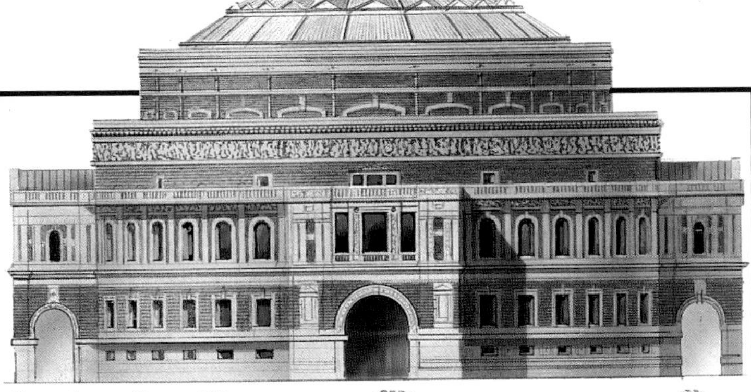

ROYAL ALBERT HALL ▲ *235*
The huge domed concert hall (1867–71) is a memorial to Prince Albert, who worked so hard at making South Kensington a center for the advancement of learning. The fundamental design is simple: it is the intricate terracotta ornamentation that gives the building its festive air.

DEBENHAM HOUSE, 8 ADDISON ROAD
Architect Halsey Ricardo covered the exterior of this millionaire's residence (1905–7) with ceramic tiles.

DOULTON FACTORY
The building was expressly designed by architect R. Stark Wilkinson to show the range of building products manufactured by Doulton and Co., which explains its curious polychrome appearance.

CARLTON CINEMA
George Coles designed this 1929 cinema in the Egyptian style, using luridly colored tiles known as Hathernware. The result is novel and arresting, ideal for a picture palace.

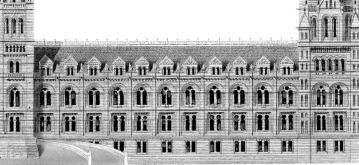

London needed many markets to provision its enormous population and to supply its commercial needs. Smithfield for meat, Billingsgate for fish, Covent Garden, Spitalfields and Borough for fruit and vegetables, and numerous others were established in the Middle Ages and enlarged in more recent times. The elegant West End arcades cater predominantly for luxury goods.

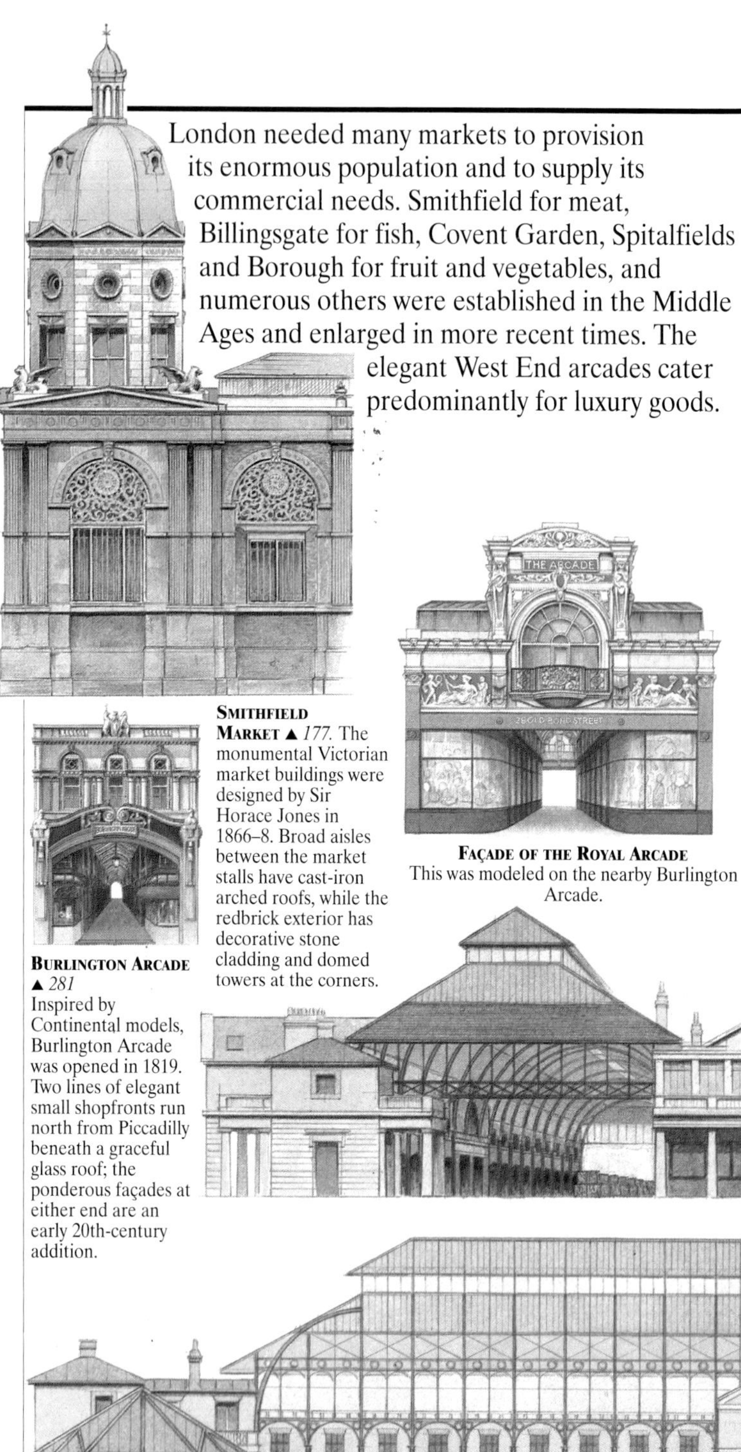

SMITHFIELD MARKET ▲ *177.* The monumental Victorian market buildings were designed by Sir Horace Jones in 1866–8. Broad aisles between the market stalls have cast-iron arched roofs, while the redbrick exterior has decorative stone cladding and domed towers at the corners.

FAÇADE OF THE ROYAL ARCADE This was modeled on the nearby Burlington Arcade.

BURLINGTON ARCADE ▲ *281* Inspired by Continental models, Burlington Arcade was opened in 1819. Two lines of elegant small shopfronts run north from Piccadilly beneath a graceful glass roof; the ponderous façades at either end are an early 20th-century addition.

Royal Arcade, Old Bond Street
Linking the fashionable Brown's Hotel to Bond Street, "The Arcade" (1879) became "Royal" three years later with the permission of Queen Victoria, who patronised Bretell's at number 12. Each shop has its own bay rising up to the glass roof at the top, which is supported by delicately molded hollow pediments (top).

Leadenhall Market ▲ *154*
The ornate and beautifully proportioned design (1881) is the work of Sir Horace Jones, architect also of Smithfield.

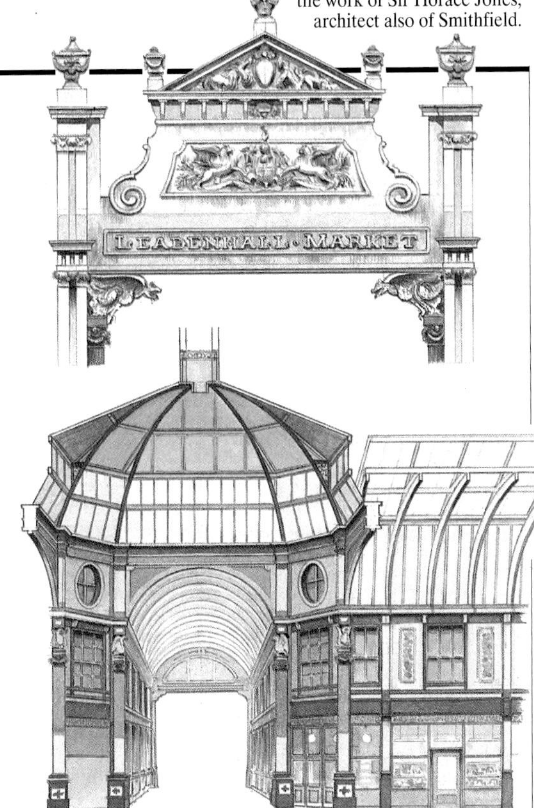

The decorative design of Leadenhall Market features a majestic central dome with florid ornament in red, silver and gold. It is a retail as well as wholesale market, traditionally supplying specialty foods and poultry.

Covent Garden
▲ *272*
Set in one of London's oldest squares, the market's present buildings were designed by Charles Fowler between 1828 and 1831. Its beautiful central arcade is flanked by two halls with iron arches. Surrounding it is a colonnade of Scottish granite, with square pavilions at each corner.

THE MAYFLOWER INN
This Rotherhithe pub celebrates the ship of the Pilgrim Fathers, moored nearby in 1620.

ENGLISH COUNTRY ALES

In the late 19th century competition from the large breweries proved too much for their smaller, less prosperous rivals and led to the construction of immense and palatial pubs. Just about every London street has one of these garish façades, with ornate frosted-glass windows and gilded calligraphy extolling the quality of the drink inside. The rich brewers spared no expense to attract the custom of the working man, making him comfortable in a setting much more luxurious than he could find at home.

THE GEORGE, BOROUGH HIGH STREET
Last London coach stop on the road to Canterbury, the George is the only surviving galleried inn in London. Built in 1676, it is little altered, though missing one side of the courtyard.

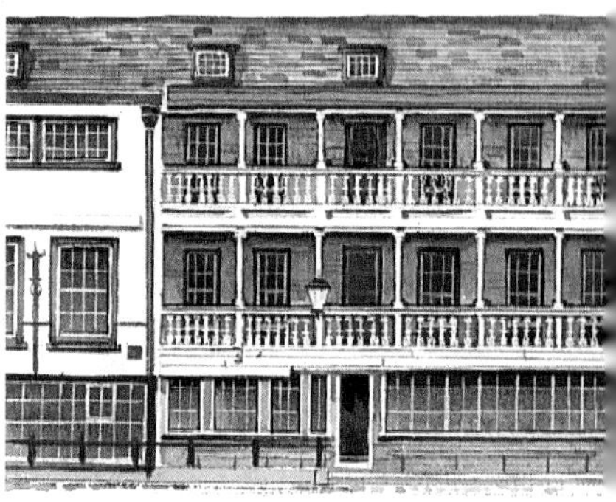

THE SALISBURY, GREEN LANES
The center of a property development by the builder J.C. Hill, this grandiose "gin palace" opened in 1899. Inside is a concert hall and billiard room, as well as a suite of comfortable drinking parlors. The Art Nouveau decorations in glass, carved wood and wrought iron are a delight.

THE PRINCE ALFRED
A notable feature of this pub built around 1890, is its series of tiny bars or 'snugs', now a rare survivor from times when pubs were not always 'fit' places to be seen in.

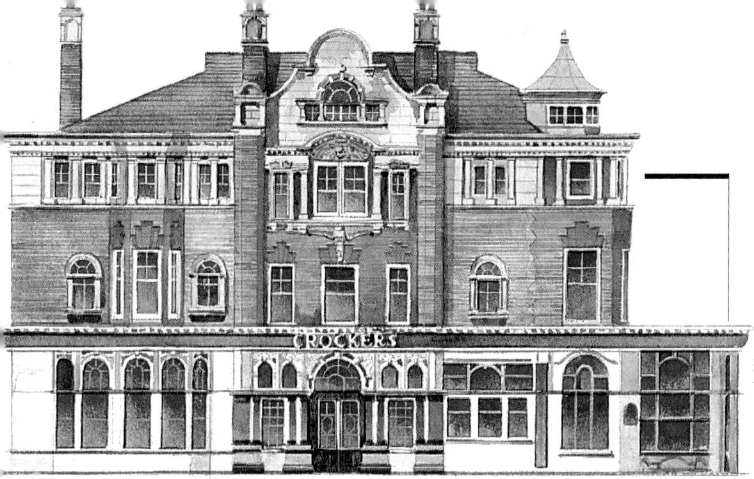

Crockers, Aberdeen Place
Formerly called the Crown, it was built by the successful publican, Frank Crocker, in 1898. It combined the facilities of a bar and lounge with a billiard hall and suite of meeting rooms. The interior decor remains a masterpiece of late Victorian fantasy.

The Princess Louise
The interior of this pub was redesigned in 1891 by the firm of Simpson and Son, who decorated it with ornamental panels and friezes. Morris and Son supplied the gilded and engraved mirrors, creating a sumptuous design which has been well preserved.

The Black Friar, Blackfriars Bridge
Built around 1875, the pub interior was created in 1904, with its cheerful friezes of merry friars in marble, brass, copper, wood and mosaic.

The grotto of the Black Friar
In 1917 a grotto-like addition was built into the vaults of the neighboring railway, and moral inscriptions such as "industry is all" were at odds with the jocular pub atmosphere.

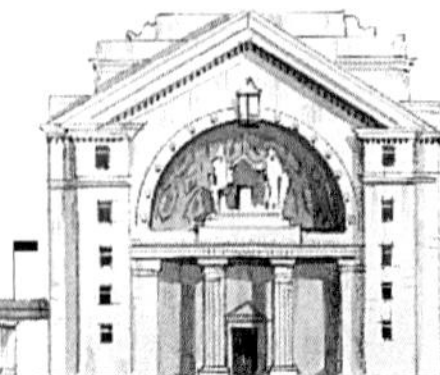

BUSH HOUSE
The huge building (1925–35) at the Aldwych is in the style known as American Corinthian.

At the beginning of the 20th century the Crown and the Grosvenor Estate, which between them owned most of the West End, redeveloped much of the land in order to exploit their property to the maximum. At about the same time less prestigious areas were also opened up with new streets that soon became popular. Department stores and office blocks were built on a grand scale, completely transforming London's shopping streets.

27–30 WIGMORE STREET, FORMERLY DEBENHAMS
Opened in 1909, this old department store was covered with Carrara tiling.

INVERESK HOUSE
At the west entry to the Aldwych is one of London's first steel-framed buildings (1906–7), built in the French style and clad with granite. Its original appearance is marred by the addition of two extra top floors. Inveresk House was formerly the home of the now defunct daily, the *Morning Post*.

SELFRIDGES ▲ *297*
Built between 1907 and 1928, this giant among department stores has a steel frame, with massive Ionic columns along its immense façade.

REGENT STREET ▲ *283*

John Nash's original Regency design was considered inadequate at the turn of the century, and was rebuilt on a monumental scale by Sir Reginald Blomfield in the French Baroque style.

LIBERTY'S ▲ *283*

The father and son team of architects E.T. and E.S. Hall designed this new Marlborough Street building in 1924 in mock Tudor style, complete with hand-made roof tiles and oak timbers from two old British warships.

HARRODS, KNIGHTSBRIDGE ▲ *225*

London's most exclusive department store is also the biggest in Europe. The façade is covered in red terracotta tiles that give the building its distinctive appearance. It was designed by C.W. Stephens and built 1894–1911.

THE COTY FACTORY
One of the great Art Deco designs was built for the Coty cosmetics company on the Great West Road around 1932.

London more than doubled in size between 1914 and 1938. The slump of the period hit heavy industry that relied on coal but, with the recovery, industries powered by electricity sprang up to replace these works along the arterial roads out of London. New suburbs developed to house skilled workers for the factories, and extensions to the underground railway assisted the growth of these so-called dormitory towns. The new Art Deco style was reflected in pubs, cinemas, apartment blocks and even churches.

ODEON, WOOLWICH
George Coles' 1937 design for this cinema is a particularly fine example of a style derived from German models, composed of white rectangular shapes.

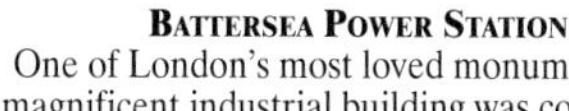

BATTERSEA POWER STATION
One of London's most loved monuments, this magnificent industrial building was constructed between 1929 and 1955 by Sir Giles Gilbert Scott. Affectionately described as an upside-down billiard table, it was closed in 1983 and is now in a sorry half-demolished condition. There are plans to develop the building into a multi-purpose center available for a wide range of entertainment, spectator events and cultural activities.

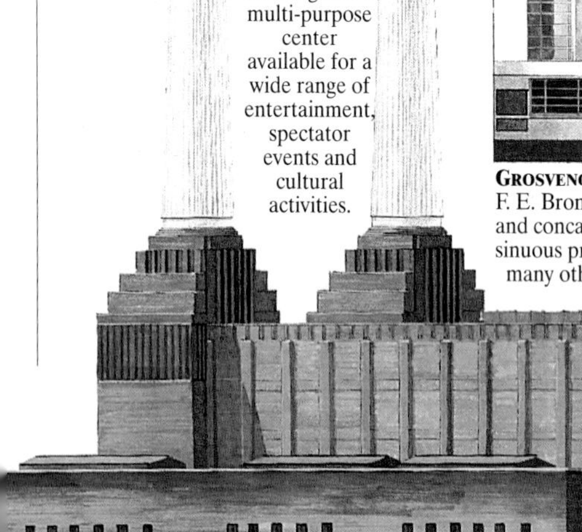

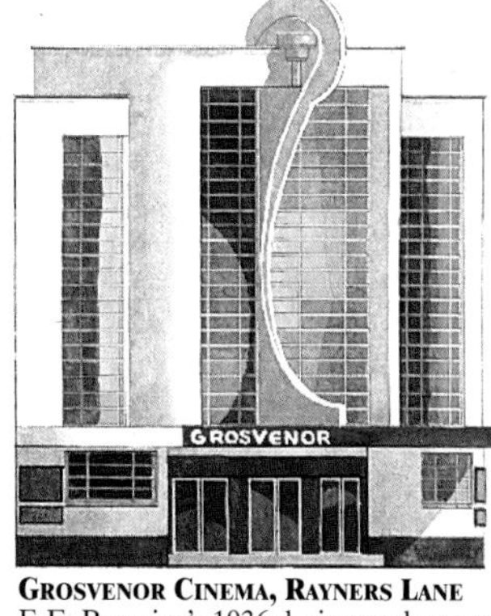

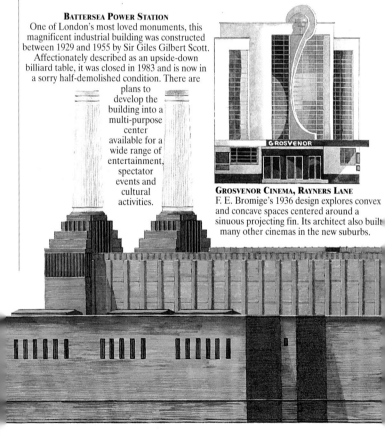

GROSVENOR CINEMA, RAYNERS LANE
F. E. Bromige's 1936 design explores convex and concave spaces centered around a sinuous projecting fin. Its architect also built many other cinemas in the new suburbs.

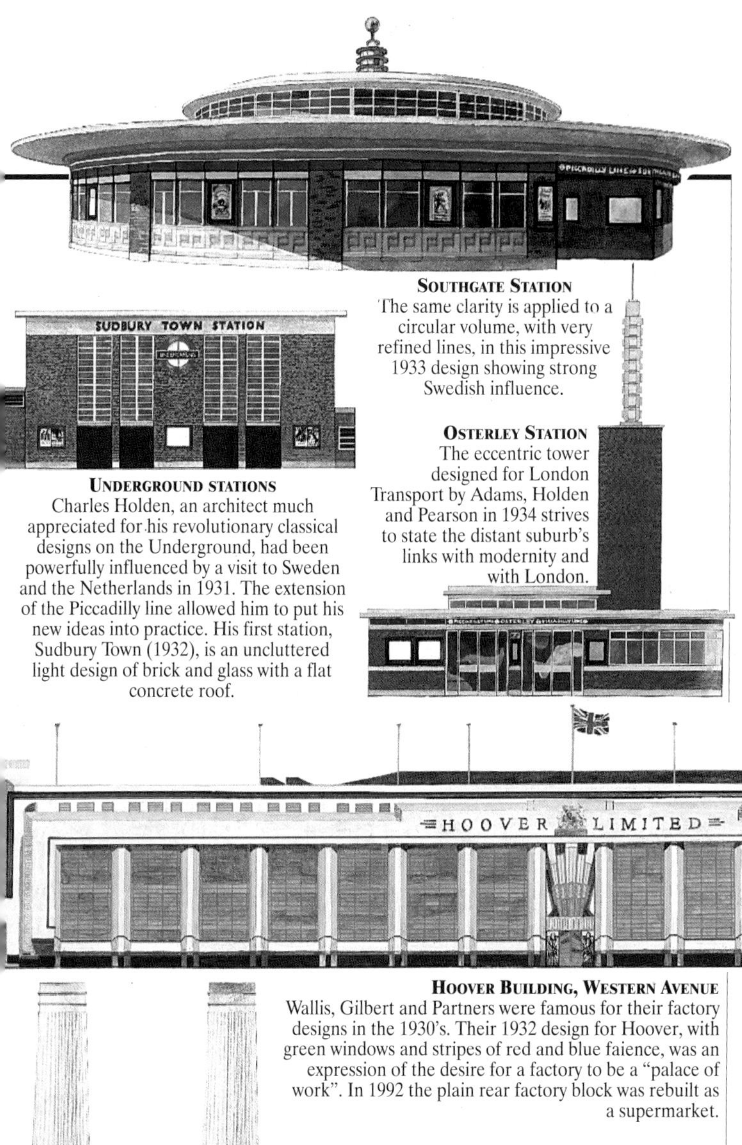

SOUTHGATE STATION
The same clarity is applied to a circular volume, with very refined lines, in this impressive 1933 design showing strong Swedish influence.

OSTERLEY STATION
The eccentric tower designed for London Transport by Adams, Holden and Pearson in 1934 strives to state the distant suburb's links with modernity and with London.

UNDERGROUND STATIONS
Charles Holden, an architect much appreciated for his revolutionary classical designs on the Underground, had been powerfully influenced by a visit to Sweden and the Netherlands in 1931. The extension of the Piccadilly line allowed him to put his new ideas into practice. His first station, Sudbury Town (1932), is an uncluttered light design of brick and glass with a flat concrete roof.

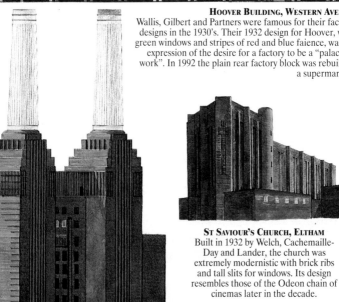

HOOVER BUILDING, WESTERN AVENUE
Wallis, Gilbert and Partners were famous for their factory designs in the 1930's. Their 1932 design for Hoover, with green windows and stripes of red and blue faience, was an expression of the desire for a factory to be a "palace of work". In 1992 the plain rear factory block was rebuilt as a supermarket.

ST SAVIOUR'S CHURCH, ELTHAM
Built in 1932 by Welch, Cachemaille-Day and Lander, the church was extremely modernistic with brick ribs and tall slits for windows. Its design resembles those of the Odeon chain of cinemas later in the decade.

DAILY EXPRESS BUILDING, FLEET STREET
Completed in 1932, this gleaming black-glass block has gracefully curved corners.

Few cities have suffered as much as London at the hands of property speculators, resulting in a great many office blocks of no architectural interest whatever. But there are some buildings, mostly private commissions, which show great originality and imagination. In the late 1980's came some impressive high-tech constructions and American post-modernist buildings (a style much appreciated in London).

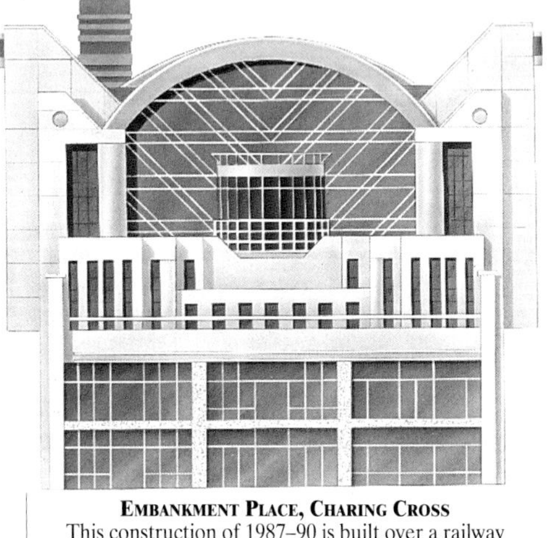

EMBANKMENT PLACE, CHARING CROSS
This construction of 1987–90 is built over a railway station – the inspiration for its arched form. Terry Farrell's glass walls and fat columns accentuate the design.

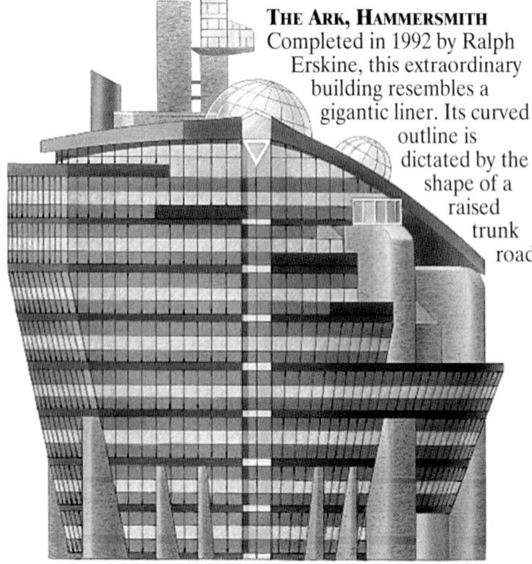

THE ARK, HAMMERSMITH
Completed in 1992 by Ralph Erskine, this extraordinary building resembles a gigantic liner. Its curved outline is dictated by the shape of a raised trunk road.

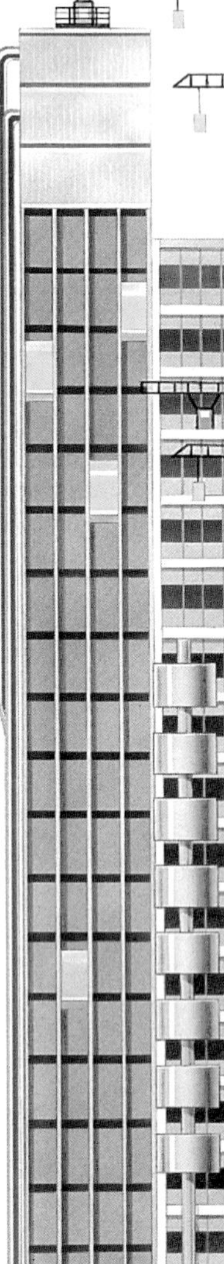

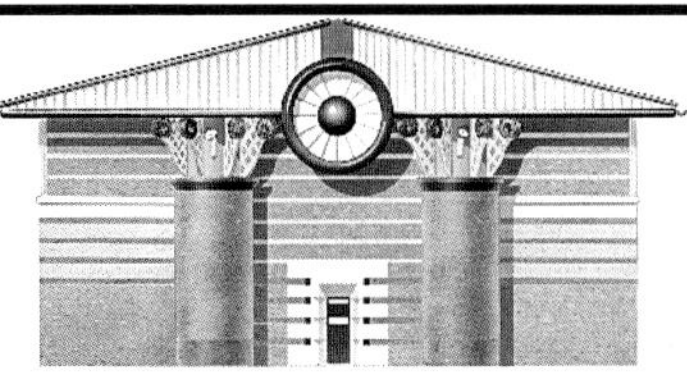

STORMWATER PUMPING STATION, ISLE OF DOGS ▲ *336*
Between 1986 and 1988 John Outram built this eclectic, brightly colored construction incorporating Hollywood-style Egyptian columns.

CHINA WHARF, MILL STREET
The partnership of Campbell, Zogolovich, Wilkinson and Gough were among the first to introduce post-modernism to London. This concrete, brick and glass building with mock-oriental arches (1986–8) is a housing development of seventeen apartments.

LLOYD'S BUILDING ▲ *153*
Richard Rogers is the best known and most controversial architect in Britain. The dramatic building he designed for Lloyd's (1978–86) is his biggest project in London. Lifts, lavatories and other services are installed on the outside, with the twelve-story glass atrium supported on columns in the center, giving the building a fortified appearance.

CANARY WHARF TOWER, ISLE OF DOGS ▲ *338*
At 800 feet, this is Britain's tallest building, its distinct pyramidal top visible even from the distant Kent countryside.

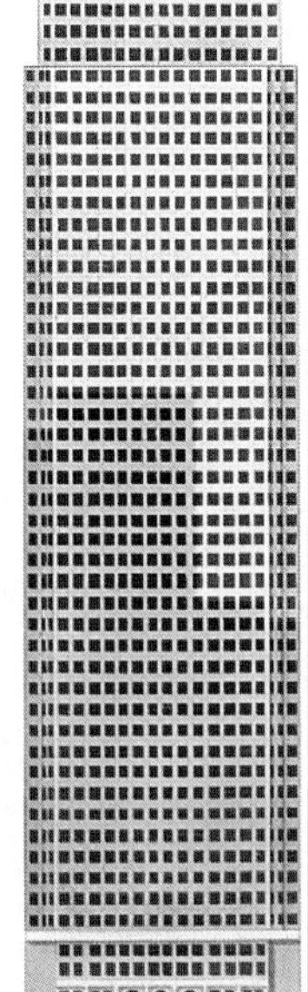

CANARY WHARF TOWER
Completed in 1991, the clean, unfussy outline of Cesar Pelli's monumental tower is the centerpiece of a new commercial district. Very high buildings such as this make the greatest impact with minimum decoration.

THE CLATTERN BRIDGE, KINGSTON
Built in the 12th century, this is the oldest bridge in the London area.

BLACKFRIARS RAILWAY BRIDGE
Built 1862–4, the bridge is supported on massive red granite columns. The railway's insignia are on the monumental stone piers.

Until 1738 London Bridge was the only one spanning the Thames in the city itself, which helped to ensure that river traffic was a lot busier then than it is now, with crowds of ferryboats. Today London has thirty-two bridges, the most recent being the Millennium bridge. Some of the most elegant of the bridges are 19th-century iron constructions.

COLUMN FROM BLACKFRIARS RAILWAY BRIDGE

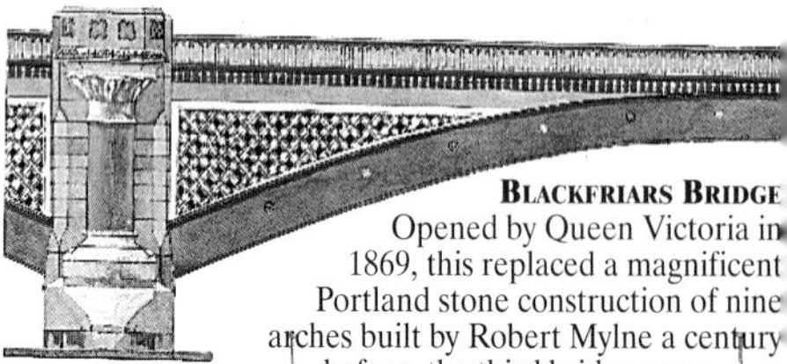

BLACKFRIARS BRIDGE
Opened by Queen Victoria in 1869, this replaced a magnificent Portland stone construction of nine arches built by Robert Mylne a century before, the third bridge over the Thames in London.

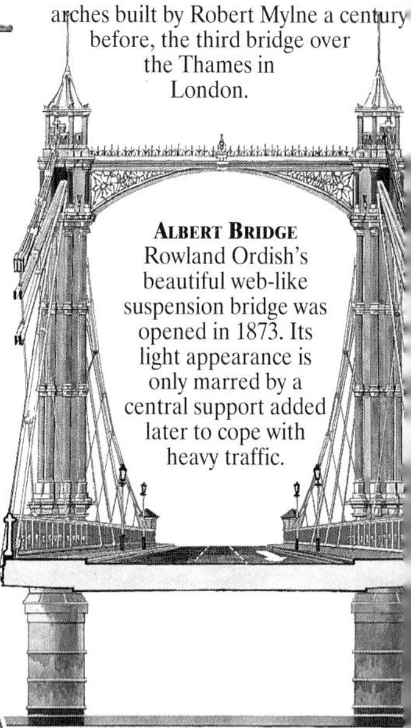

ALBERT BRIDGE
Rowland Ordish's beautiful web-like suspension bridge was opened in 1873. Its light appearance is only marred by a central support added later to cope with heavy traffic.

TOWER BRIDGE ▲ *189*
The world-famous outline of Tower Bridge shows its two functions: the lowe span opens in the center to let tall ships through, while pedestrians climb the stairs in the towers to cross the river by the high walkway.

LONDON AS SEEN BY PAINTERS

The Houses of Parliament had just been built when Claude Monet (1840–1926), taking refuge in London from the war of 1870 and the Commune which followed it, painted his famous picture of 1871, *The Thames at Westminster* (2). The way Monet treats the misty atmosphere with subtle gradations of color is typical of his visual preoccupations at this time. When he came back to London, in 1899, he painted a series of views of the Houses of Parliament from the balcony of his room in the Savoy Hotel. In the 18th century Canaletto (1697–1768) had likewise drawn inspiration from the banks of the Thames. In his picture *The Thames and the City of London from Richmond House* (1747) (1, detail) he captures the majestic sweep of the Thames toward St Paul's Cathedral with the magical lightness we recognize from his views of Venice. His style was to influence many English artists: Samuel Scott, for example, adapted it in his painting *An Arch of Old Westminster Bridge* (1750) ● *95*, in which the human figures are eclipsed by the immense scale of the bridge.

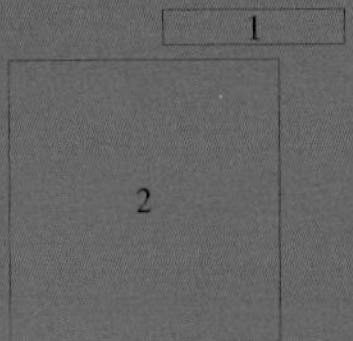

1

2

DAILY NEWS

In his picture *Saint Pancras Hotel and Station from Pentonville Road: Sunset* (1884) (4) the Irish painter John O'Connor (1830–89) selected one of the most characteristic sights of Victorian London. The station, with its vast glass roof (ultra-modern and quite without precedent when it was built) looks more like some Gothic palace from the distant past. In this view of St Pancras, looking down from the hill above, O'Connor has contrasted the romantic sunset and foggy landscape with the busy street in the foreground. The *View of Greenwich* (2) by Henry Pethers (1828–65) has a disturbing, almost surrealist, quality. Its grandiose scale suggests one of Claude Lorrain's harbor scenes at sunset. Atkinson Grimshaw (1836–93) specialized in nocturnal river landscapes. His views of the Thames (1 & 3) have a rather sinister air about them, recalling the writer Arthur Conan Doyle's more mysterious tales.

	1
2	3
4	

OXFORD
CREMORNE

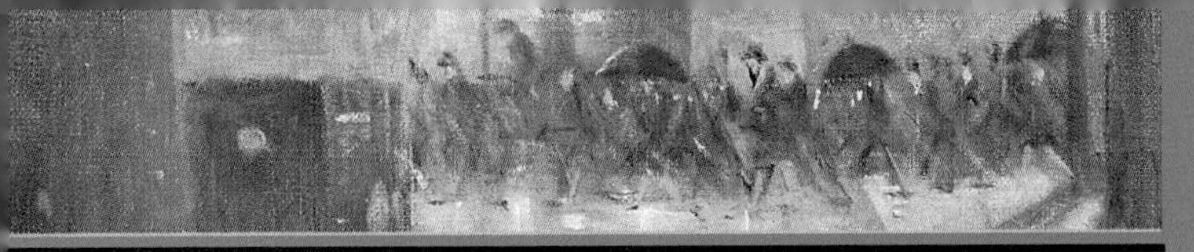

Walter Greaves (1846–1930), in his picture *Hammersmith Bridge on Boat Race Day* (c. 1862), has filled the canvas with a forceful throng of figures. The Boat Race between Oxford and Cambridge Universities has been an annual event since 1829, held on the Thames between Putney and Mortlake. Greaves' naïve style, with its exaggerated perspective, is a highly original view of a crowd waiting to watch the race. Scenes portraying daily life became more common in the 20th century with the emergence of schools like the Camden Town Group, whose members shared the influence of French Impressionism and a fascination with the commonplace details of everyday events.

Malcolm Drummond (1880–1945) peopled his painting *St James' Park* (1912) (3) with Londoners in an extraordinary variety of poses that comes close to caricature. In *Piccadilly Circus* (1912) (4) by Charles Ginner (1878–1952), the technique of composition recalls photography, as well as the influence of Degas and Sickert. The density of the painting's surface, composed of a mosaic of tiny brush spots, intensifies the frantic activity of this busy intersection. The same air of hustle and bustle infects *The Strand by Night* (1, detail) by Christopher Nevinson (1889–1946) with figures hurrying through the rain. The influence of the Futurists is clearly apparent in the jagged geometrical shapes.

1
2
3 4

In his watercolor *The White House at Chelsea* (1800) (2) Thomas Girtin (1775–1802) shows a rural view of the Thames, at a time when Chelsea was still a country village. Girtin evolved a distinctive style very early in his career, his talent being widely acclaimed in his short life. The lyrical atmosphere which dominates Girtin's picture is recalled a century and a half later in *The Quiet River: The Thames at Chiswick* (1943–4) by Victor Pasmore (b. 1908) (1, detail). An altogether more eventful day on the river was captured by J.M.W. Turner (1775–1851) in his painting of the *Houses of Parliament on Fire* in 1834 (3), which he watched from a boat on the Thames. The dramatic effect of this watercolor is heightened by the orange reflections in the water, which add an extra dimension to this awesome, historic moment. Watercolor is the perfect medium for capturing the immediacy of this kind of scene, where buildings, water and fire merge into a whirl of color. Turner later exhibited two much more characteristic oil canvases of the same event, and neither of them captured the vivid drama of this little sketch.

1

2

3

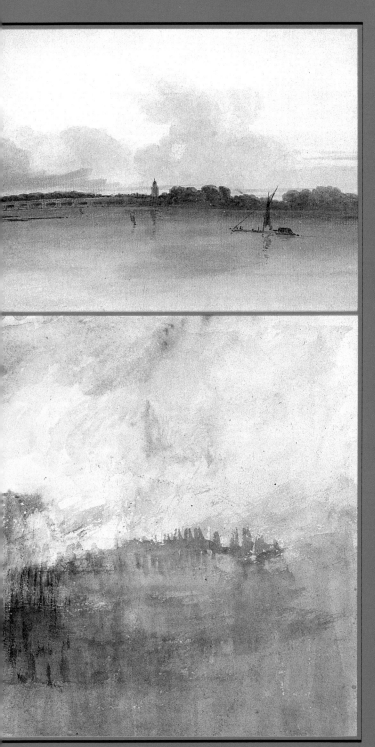

London as seen by painters

The American James Abbott McNeill Whistler (1834–1903) settled in London in 1859 and painted a series of pictures featuring misty twilight scenes of the Thames. *Nocturne in Blue and Gold: Old Battersea Bridge* (1872) is heavily influenced by Japanese art, and the work's abstract quality is underlined by its title, which relegates the actual subject of the painting to second place in favor of music and color.

LONDON AS SEEN BY WRITERS

A collection of villages

Where will it all end?

Daniel Defoe (1660–1731) was a prolific writer of novels, poetry, satire, journals and political pamphlets and he produced 560 books in his lifetime. He was a particularly good observer of the tiny detail that sums up a scene and this skill, along with his plain, unadorned prose, made him an excellent reporter. His three-volume guidebook to the British Isles is an account of the state of the country and in the passage below he bemoans the steady growth of London.

“London, as a city only, and as its walls and liberties line it out, might, indeed, be viewed in a small compass; but when I speak of London, now in the modern acceptation, you expect I shall take in all that vast mass of buildings, reaching from Black-wall in the east, to Tot-Hill Fields in the west; and extended in an unusual breadth, from the bridge, or river, in the south, to Islington north; and from Peterburgh House on the bank side in Westminster, to Cavendish Square, and all the new buildings by, and beyond, Hannover Square, by which the city of London, for so it is still to be called, is extended to Hide Park Corner in the Brentford Road, and almost to Marybone in the Acton Road, and how much further it may spread, who knows? ... We see several villages, formerly standing, as it were, in the country, and at a great distance, now joined to the streets by continued buildings, and more making haste to meet in the like manner; for example, Deptford, this town was formerly reckoned, at least two miles off from Redriff, and that over the marshes too, a place unlikely ever to be inhabited; and yet now, by the increase of buildings in that town itself, and the many streets erected at Redriff, and by the docks and building-yards on the riverside, which stand between both, the town of Deptford, and the streets of Redriff, or Rotherhith (as they write it) are effectually joined.... The town of Islington, on the north side of the city, is in like manner joined to the streets of London, excepting one small field, and which is in itself so small, that there is no doubt, but in a very few years, they will be entirely joined, and the same may be said of Mile-End, on the east end of the town.... That Westminster is in a fair way to shake hands with Chelsea, as St Gyles's is with Marybone; and Great Russel Street by Montague House, with Tottenham-Court: all this is very evident, and yet all these put together, are still to be called London. Whither will this monstrous city then extend? and where must a circumvallation or communication line of it be placed?”

Daniel Defoe,
A Tour through the Whole Island of Great Britain, 1724–6

Anonymity

Henry James (1843–1916)lived in London for more than twenty years, during which he wrote most of his novels.He also wrote several volumes of travel sketches. His impressions of London, although written from the point of view of a foreigner, would probably strike a chord with many born and bred Londoners.

“It is, no doubt, not the taste of every one, but for the real London-lover the mere immensity of the place is a large part of its savour. A small London would be an abomination, as it fortunately is an impossibility, for the idea and the name are beyond everything an expression of extent and number. Practically, of course, one lives in a quarter, in a plot; but in imagination and by a constant mental act of reference the accommodated haunter enjoys the whole – and it is only of him that I deem it

worth while to speak. He fancies himself, as they say, for being a particle in so unequalled an aggregation; and its immeasurable circumference, even though unvisited and lost in smoke, gives him the sense of a social, an intellectual margin. There is a luxury in the knowledge that he may come and go without being noticed, even when his comings and goings have no nefarious end. I don't mean by this that the tongue of London is not a very active member; the tongue of London would indeed be worthy of a chapter by itself. But the eyes which at least in some measure feed its activity are ... solicited at any moment by a thousand different objects. If the place is big, everything it contains is certainly not so; but this may at least be said, that if small questions play a part there, they play it without illusions about its importance. There are too many questions, small or great; and each day, as it arrives, leads its children, like a kind of mendicant mother, by the hand. Therefore perhaps the most general characteristic is the absence of insistence. Habits and inclinations flourish and fall, but intensity is never one of them.”

HENRY JAMES,
ENGLISH HOURS, 1905

A CHANGING NEIGHBORHOOD

Evelyn Waugh (1903–66) was born in Hampstead, the son of a publisher; his autobiographical "A Little Learning" covers this period. As a novelist, he became famous for his satirical digs at the frivolity of the inter-war generation.

“I was four years old when my father built his house in what was then the village of North End, Hampstead. He was, in fact, the first of its spoliators. When we settled there the tube reached no further than Hampstead. Golders Green was a grassy cross-road with a sign pointing to London, Finchley and Hendon; such a place as where "the Woman in White" was encountered. All round us lay dairy farms, market gardens and a few handsome old houses of brick or stucco standing in twenty acres or more; not far off there survived woods where we picked bluebells, and streams beside which we opened our picnic baskets. North End Road was a steep, dusty lane with white posts and rails bordering its footways. North End, the reader may remember, was the place where Bill Sikes spent the first night of his flight after the murder of Nancy.... Soon after ours other new houses sprang up alongside us. Opposite us stood a large late Victorian villa named Ivy House (whrer Pavlova spent her last years) with wooded grounds. Soon these were built on, leaving only the garden and a pond for the ballerina's privacy. Then the tube emerged into the open at Golders Green and round the station grew shops, a theatre, a cinema and a dense spread of new brick and rough cast dwellings not unlike our own. Eventually (I think soon after the first war) our postal address was altered from Hampstead to Golders Green. My father deplored the change. and, as far as was possible, ignored it, because Hampstead had historic associations, with Keats and Blake and Constable, while Golders Green meant, to him, merely a tube station.”

EVELYN WAUGH, *A LITTLE LEARNING*, 1964

THE BLITZ

London suffered its worst damage since the Great Fire of 1666 in the Blitz of World War II. The great 20th-century English novelist Graham Greene (1904-91) used it as the setting for one of his finest thrillers "The Ministry of Fear". In the excerpt below Greene describes how the very real threat of the terrifying bombing raids changed Londoners' lives.

"Rowe had breakfast in an A.B.C. in Clapham High Street. Boards had taken the place of windows and the top floor had gone; it was like a shack put up in an earthquake town for relief work. For the enemy had done a lot of damage in Clapham. London was no longer one great city: it was a collection of small towns. People went to Hampstead or St John's Wood for a quiet week-end, and if you lived in Holborn you hadn't time between the sirens to visit friends as far away as Kensington. So special characteristics developed, and in Clapham where day raids were frequent there was a hunted look which was absent from Westminster, where the night raids were heavier but the shelters were better. The waitress who brought Rowe's toast and coffee looked jumpy and pallid, as if she had lived too much on the run; she had an air of listening whenever gears shrieked. Gray's Inn and Russell Square were noted for a more reckless spirit, but only because they had the day to recover in."

GRAHAM GREENE,
THE MINISTRY OF FEAR, 1943

WAPPING

William Wymark Jacobs (1863-1943) is best remembered as a writer of short stories. These were of two basic types: the macabre, exemplified by his gruesome tale "The Monkey's Paw"; and an altogether jollier type of yarn, comic adventures set among the seafaring community of the Port of London at the turn of the century.

"As a residential neighbourhood Wapping is perhaps undesirable, though a considerable population contrives to exist in the narrow streets hemmed in between the dock walls and the warehouses bordering the river. For the river itself is completely hidden, except where the swing-bridges, which give entrance to the docks, afford a passing glimpse. From a picturesque point of view Wapping was no doubt much better in the days when docks and swing-bridges were unknown; when the bow-windows of its ancient taverns projected quaintly over the river and the waterman's stairs inspired the muse of the songwriter. Then the raucous bellowings of the hurrying steamers were unheard, and sailing craft thoughtfully waited for tides, while master mariners sat drinking in the bow-windows aforesaid. The old church and the charity school, with the overgrown graveyard opposite, with its rank grass and dingy trees, are the remains of those days. The green of the churchyard is a relief to the bricks and mortar, for trees are scarce in Wapping, though there are a few others in front of the old-fashioned houses on the breezy pier-head hard by – trees which, having been coaxed to grow in that uncongenial spot, conscientiously endeavour to indicate the seasons, and make very few mistakes considering. High Street, Wapping, the principal thoroughfare, realising, possibly, that High Streets are apt to adhere too slavishly to one pattern, appears to have determined to be original. It sternly eschews the drapers and hatters, the bootmakers and tailors of other High Streets.... One window is much like another – herrings, rejoicing in their strength, competing for favour with bacon of guaranteed mildness and eggs of blameless exterior."

W.W. JACOBS,
WAPPING ON THAMES, 1926

LONDON BRIDGE

Thomas Stearns Eliot (1888–1965) was born in St Louis but moved to London in 1914. The following excerpt is from "The Waste Land", a poem which quickly came to be seen as representing the inter-war frustrations of his generation. Eliot claimed that it was not so much a piece of social criticism as "a piece of rhythmical grumbling". This section describes City clerks unwillingly traveling to work.

Unreal City,
Under the brown fog of a winter dawn,
A crowd flowed over London Bridge, so many,
I had not thought death had undone so many.
Sighs, short and infrequent, were exhaled,
And each man fixed his eyes before his feet,
Flowed up the hill and down King William Street,
To where Saint Mary Woolnoth kept the hours
With a dead sound on the final stroke of nine.

T.S. ELIOT, *THE WASTE LAND*, 1922

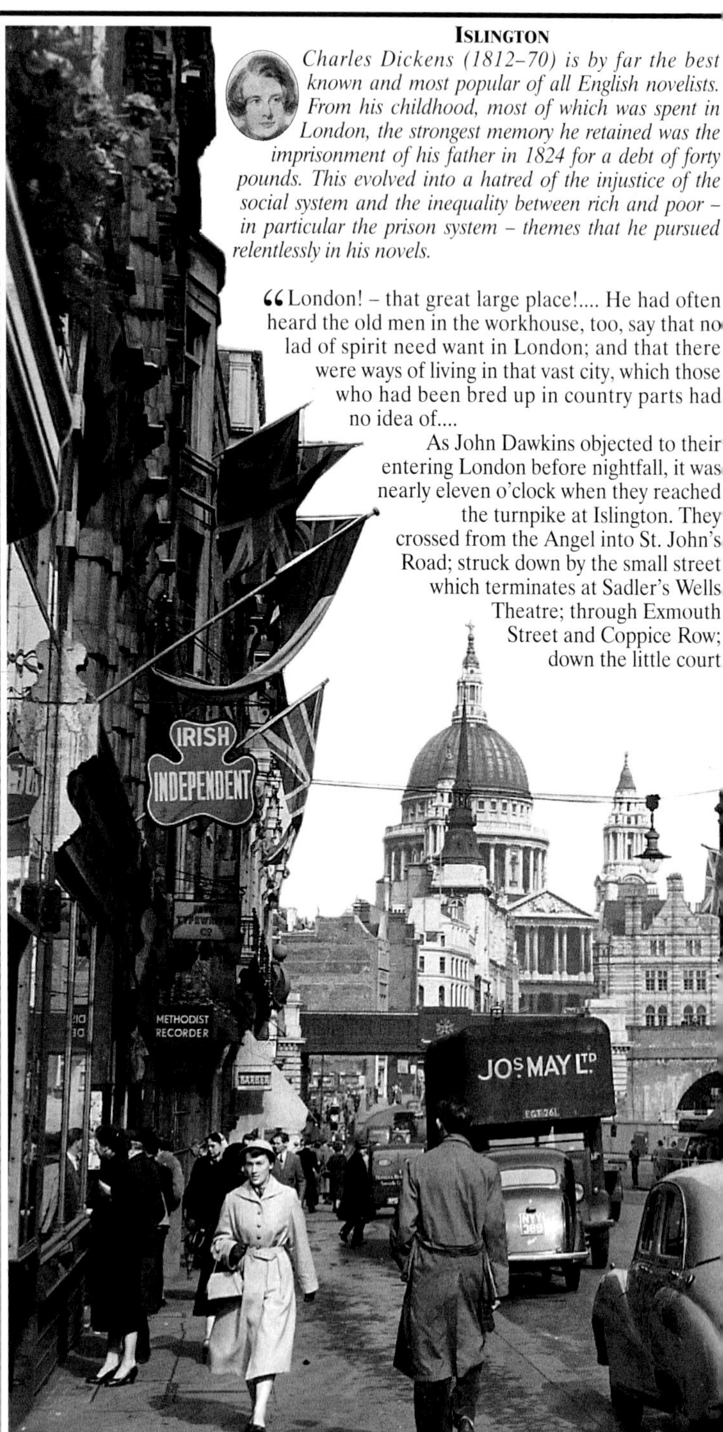

ISLINGTON

Charles Dickens (1812–70) is by far the best known and most popular of all English novelists. From his childhood, most of which was spent in London, the strongest memory he retained was the imprisonment of his father in 1824 for a debt of forty pounds. This evolved into a hatred of the injustice of the social system and the inequality between rich and poor – in particular the prison system – themes that he pursued relentlessly in his novels.

"London! – that great large place!.... He had often heard the old men in the workhouse, too, say that no lad of spirit need want in London; and that there were ways of living in that vast city, which those who had been bred up in country parts had no idea of....

As John Dawkins objected to their entering London before nightfall, it was nearly eleven o'clock when they reached the turnpike at Islington. They crossed from the Angel into St. John's Road; struck down by the small street which terminates at Sadler's Wells Theatre; through Exmouth Street and Coppice Row; down the little court by the side of the workhouse; across the classic ground which once bore the name of Hockley-in-the-Hole; thence into Little Saffron Hill; and so into Saffron Hill the Great: along which the Dodger scudded at a rapid pace, directing Oliver to follow close at his heels.

Although Oliver had enough to occupy his attention in keeping sight of his leader, he could not help bestowing a few hasty glances on either side of the way, as he passed along. A dirtier or more wretched place he had never seen. The street was very narrow and muddy, and the air was impregnated with filthy odours. There were a good many small shops; but the only stock in trade appeared to be heaps of children, who, even at that time of night, were crawling in and out of the doors, or screaming from the inside. The sole places that seemed to prosper amid the general blight of the place, were the public-houses; and in them, the lowest orders of Irish were wrangling with might and main. Covered ways and yards, which here and there diverged from the main street, disclosed little knots of houses, where drunken men and women were positively wallowing in filth; and from several of the door-ways, great ill-looking fellows were cautiously emerging, bound, to all appearance, on no very well-disposed or harmless errands.

Oliver was just considering whether he hadn't better run away, when they reached the bottom of the hill. His conductor, catching him by the arm, pushed open the door of a house near Field Lane; and, drawing him into the passage, closed it behind them.❞

CHARLES DICKENS,
OLIVER TWIST, 1837

COVENT GARDEN

Oscar Wilde (1854–1900) is best known for his society comedies and for his homosexuality. In 1895 he was sentenced to two years' hard labour for having homosexual relations with the son of the Marquis of Queensberry. While in prison he was made bankrupt and on his release he moved to France and lived out the rest of his life in exile. In his one novel "The Picture of Dorian Gray", against a London setting he recounts the adventures of a beautiful young man in search of pleasure but haunted by the effects of the passage of time.

❝As the dawn was just breaking he found himself close to Covent Garden. The darkness lifted, and, flushed with faint fires, the sky hollowed itself into a perfect pearl. Huge carts filled with nodding lilies rumbled slowly down the polished empty street. The air was heavy with the perfume of the flowers, and their beauty seemed to bring him an anodyne for his pain. He followed into the market, and watched the men unloading their waggons. A white-smocked carter offered him some cherries. He thanked him, and wondered why he refused to accept any money for them, and began to eat them listlessly. They had been plucked at midnight, and the coldness of the moon had entered into them. A long line of boys carrying crates of striped tulips, and of yellow and red roses, defiled in front of him, threading their way through the huge jade-green piles of vegetables. Under the portico, with its grey sun-bleached pillars, loitered a troop of draggled bare-headed girls, waiting for the auction to be over. Others crowded round the swinging doors of the coffee-house in the Piazza. The heavy cart-horses slipped and stamped upon the rough stones, shaking their bells and trappings. Some of the drivers were lying asleep on a pile of sacks. Iris-necked, and pink-footed, the pigeons ran about picking up seeds.❞

OSCAR WILDE, *THE PICTURE OF DORIAN GRAY,* 1890

HYDE PARK

At the age of seventeen Joseph Conrad (1857-1924) left his native Poland to go to sea. Before getting his master's certificate he worked on British coasters, using his spare time to learn English and read Shakespeare. He wrote his first novel "Almayer's Folly" in English, and in 1896 settled in England where in spite of indifferent health he devoted himself to writing. Of "The Secret Agent" he remarked, "I have just finished a novel without a single drop of water in it (except for the rain); this is natural enough because all of it is set in London."

"Through the park railings these glances beheld men and women riding in the Row, couples cantering past harmoniously, others advancing sedately at a walk, loitering groups of three or four, solitary horsemen looking unsociable, and solitary women followed at a long distance by a groom with a cockade to his hat and a leather belt over his tight-fitting coat. Carriages went bowling by, mostly two-horse broughams, with here and there a victoria with the skin of some wild beast inside and a woman's face and hat emerging above the folded hood. And a peculiarly London sun – against which nothing could be said except that it looked bloodshot – glorified all this by its stare. It hung at a moderate elevation above Hyde Park Corner with an air of punctual and benign vigilance. The very pavement under Mr. Verloc's feet had an old-gold tinge in that diffused light, in which neither wall, nor tree, nor beast, nor man cast a shadow. Mr. Verloc was going westward through a town without shadows in an atmosphere of powdered old gold. There were red, coppery gleams on the roofs of houses, on the corners of walls, on the panels of carriages, on the very coats of the horses, and on the broad back of Mr. Verloc's overcoat, where they produced a dull effect of rustiness. But Mr. Verloc was not in the least conscious of having got rusty. He surveyed through the park railings the evidences of the town's opulence and luxury with an approving eye."

JOSEPH CONRAD,
THE SECRET AGENT, 1907

CHELSEA

Thomas Carlyle (1795–1881), the English scholar and historian, moved to Cheyne Row in 1834 with his wife Jane. While still house-hunting, he described Chelsea in a letter to Jane, obviously attracted by the peace and quiet.

"A broad highway with huge shady trees, boats lying moored, and a smell of shipping and tar. Battersea Bridge (of wood) a few yards off; the broad river with white-trowsered, white-shirted Cockneys dashing by like arrows in their long canoes of boats; beyond the green beautiful knolls of Surrey with their villages – on the whole a most artificial green-painted, yet lively, fresh, almost opera-looking business, such as you can fancy. Chelsea is a single heterogeneous kind of spot, very dirty and confused in some places, quite beautiful in others, abounding in antiquities and the traces of great men – Sir Thomas More, Steele, Smollett, etc."

THOMAS CARLYLE,
LETTER, 1834

LONDON TRANSPORT

THE HANSOM CAB

Jerome Klapka Jerome (1859-1927) achieved a kind of immortality with his comic novel "Three Men in a Boat", a hilarious chronicle of a boating holiday on the Thames at the turn of the century. Jerome was a prolific journalist, and joint editor of a humorous magazine, "The Idler", for some years. The excerpt below is from his autobiography.

"It was a picturesque vehicle, the old hansom: there was that to be said for it....But to ride in, they were the most uncomfortable contrivances ever invented. To get into them, you grabbed at two handles, one jutting out from the splash board and the other just over the wheel, and hauled yourself up on to a small iron step. If the horse made a start before you got further, you were carried down the street in this position, looking like a monkey on a stick. If you had not secured a firm hold, you were jerked back into the gutter: which was safer, but even less dignified. Getting out was more difficult. A false step landed you on all fours, and your aunt or your sister, or whatever it might happen to be, stepped on you. To enter or alight without getting your hat knocked off by the reins was an art in itself. The seat was just big enough for two. It was high, and only long ladies could reach the floor. The others bobbed up and down with their feet dangling. The world always thought the worst, but as often as not, one put one's arm round her purely to prevent her from slipping off. There was a trap-door in the roof. Along dim-lit roads, one noticed the cabman holding it open, and driving with his head bent down... I have no regrets for the passing of the hansom.

The old two-horse bus, one is glad had disappeared, if only for the sake of the horses. It had straw inside and a little oil lamp that made up in smell what it lacked in illuminating power... There was no bell. Passengers stopped the bus by prodding the conductor with their umbrellas. The driver wore a mighty coat with flapping capes, and wrapped a rug round his legs before strapping himself to his seat. He was a genial soul, not above accepting a cigar, and had a tongue as clever as his hands. Wit and sarcasm dropped from him as he drove. The motor has silenced the humour of the streets."

JEROME K. JEROME,
MY LIFE AND TIMES, 1926

RAILWAY STATIONS

Edward Morgan Forster (1879–1970) born in Tonbridge, England, went to Cambridge University before devoting himself to a life of journalism, literary criticism and fiction. In his books, which generally deal with characters drawn from genteel society, Forster explores social differences set against the different environments of urban and country life. This is particularly true of "Howards End", for example in this passage about the great London termini, which are described as necessary evils to be endured in effecting the transition from town to the country house.

"Like many others who have lived long in a great capital, she had strong feelings about the various railway termini. They are our gates to the glorious and the unknown. Through them we pass out into adventure and sunshine, to them, alas! we return. In Paddington all Cornwall is latent and the remoter west; down the inclines of Liverpool Street lie fenlands and the illimitable Broads; Scotland is through the pylons of Euston; Wessex behind the poised chaos of Waterloo. Italians realise this, as is natural; those of them who are so unfortunate as to serve as waiters in Berlin call the Anhalt Bahnhof the Stazione d'Italia, because by it they must return to their homes. And he is a chilly Londoner who does not endow his stations with some personality, and extend to them, however shyly, the emotions of fear and love.

To Margaret – I hope that it will not set the reader against her – the station of King's Cross had always suggested Infinity. Its very situation – withdrawn a little behind the facile splendours of St. Pancras – implied a comment on the materialism of life. Those two great arches, colourless, indifferent, shouldering between them an unlovely clock, were fit portals for some eternal adventure, whose issue might be prosperous, but would certainly not be expressed in the ordinary language of prosperity. If you think this is ridiculous, remember that it is not Margaret who is telling you about it; and let me hasten to add that they were in plenty of time for the train....”

EDWARD MORGAN FORSTER,
HOWARDS END, 1910

TRAMS

Born in Bradford, John Boynton Priestley (1894–1984) settled in London in 1922 and quickly made a name for himself as a journalist and critic. He wrote stories of ordinary, unremarkable men and women with remarkably sharp and humorous observation. "Angel Pavement", a saga of clerical staff in a dreary City office was a grim "Realist" novel of London life which became an instant best-seller when it appeared.

“Before he reached the High Street and his tram, the bottom of his trousers were unpleasantly heavy, his boots gave out a squelching sound, and the newspaper he carried was being rapidly reconverted to its original pulp. The tram, its windows steaming and streaming, was more crowded than usual, of course, and carried its maximum cargo of wet clothes, the wearers of which were simply so many irritable ghosts. After enormous difficulty, Mr. Smeeth succeeded in filling and lighting his morning pipe of T. Benenden's Own, and then – so stubborn is the spirit of man – succeeded in unfolding and examining his pulpy newspaper. Before he had reached the end of City Road, he had learned that the cost of a public school education was too high, that the night clubs on Broadway were not doing the business they had done, that a man in Birmingham had cut his wife's throat, that students in Cairo were again on strike, that an old woman in Hammersmith had died of starvation, that a policeman in Suffolk had found six pound notes in the prisoner's right sock, and that bubonic plague is conveyed to human beings by fleas from infected rats.”

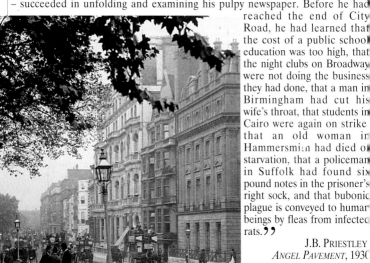

J.B. PRIESTLEY
ANGEL PAVEMENT, 1930

A NIGHT IN WESTMINSTER ABBEY

When the French writer and politician Chateaubriand (1768-1848) arrived in London on May 21, 1793, it was as an exile from revolutionary France. There he became familiar with poverty and hunger, keeping body and soul together with some private teaching and translating. But it was in London that he wrote his first book "An Historical, Political and Moral Essay on Ancient and Modern Revolutions, and Their Relation to the French Revolution" (1797), which brought him to the attention of other refugees in exile. During his years in London, dealt with in volume 10 of his "Memoirs from Beyond the Grave", he relates the extraordinary episode when, accidentally locked in Westminster Abbey, he was compelled to spend the night there.

"On one occasion it happened that towards the end of day, having wished to view the Abbey at dusk, I completely lost myself in admiration of such lofty and fanciful architecture. Awed by the 'dark immensity of Christian churches' (Montaigne), I wandered slowly about till I found myself overtaken by the night: the doors were closed. I tried to find a way out; I shouted for the usher, I banged on the doors: but all the noise I made was scattered and lost in the silence, so I resigned myself to settle down and sleep with the dead. After some deliberation in the choice of my lodging I stopped by the tomb of the Earl of Chatham, at the foot of the rood screen and by the two floors of the Knights' Chapel and that of Henry VII. At the foot of these stairs, the shelter they offered barred by metal gates, a tomb set into the wall opposite a marble figure of the Grim Reaper offered some refuge. A draped marble shroud formed a little niche, and like Charles Quint before me I resigned myself to my entombment.

It was the perfect place from which to see the world for what it really is. What glories are enclosed within these vaults! But what remains? Vain are their sorrows, vain are their joys; the wretched Lady Jane Grey is no different now from the once happy Adela of Salisbury (only her skeleton is less ghastly because it lacks the skull: her mortal remains are the lovelier thanks to her fate and the absence of all that once made her beautiful). The tournament of the victor at Crecy, or Henry VIII's Field of Cloth of Gold will never be seen again in this mausoleum. Bacon, Newton, Milton too are all deeply buried, gone just as surely as all their unknown contemporaries. And I, an exile, outcast and poor, would I wish to cease from being the small, forgotten, miserable creature that I am, to have been one of these dead souls, famous, powerful and sated with pleasures? But that's not what life is! Should we be surprised when we peer into the beyond that we glimpse no sign of divinity? Time is a veil that separates us from God just as an eyelid will shut out the light from an eye.

Crouching on my marble coverlet I come down from these lofty thoughts to find my anxiety tinged with a certain pleasure at my predicament. When the wind used to howl round my tower-house at Combourg it was much the same: a shrieking gale and a disembodied spirit have much in common.

As my eyes got used to the darkness, I began to make out the shapes of figures on top of the tombs. Gazing at the gothic corbelling round the tomb of the English St Denis it seemed to me that all the past years and all that has happened hung from it like ancient lanterns: the whole edifice was a monument of petrified history.

I heard the clock strike ten and then eleven. The hammer that rose and fell upon the bell was the only other living thing there with me. Outside now and then I could hear a passing carriage or the call of a watchman, nothing more. These far-off sounds seemed part of another world. Mist from the river mingled with smoke had penetrated the Abbey, adding to the Stygian gloom inside.

At length the faint sign of dawn began to grow in a distant corner: I stared at this slowly growing light that seemed to emanate from the two little sons of Edward IV, murdered by their uncle. 'Thus lay the gentle babes,' says the Bard, 'Girdling one another within their alabaster innocent arms: Their lips were four red roses on a stalk, Which in their summer beauty kissed each other.' But God wasn't sending me these sweet, sad litle souls, instead I could make out the faint apparition of a young girl carrying a lantern shaded with a twist of paper; it was the little bell-ringer. I heard the sound of a kiss, and the bell tolled daybreak. The poor girl was scared out of her wits when I emerged to leave through the cloister door with her. I told her of my adventure, and she told me she was standing in for her father who was sick; neither of us mentioned the little kiss I had heard.”

CHATEAUBRIAND,
MEMOIRS FROM BEYOND THE GRAVE, 1849–50

THE QUEEN IN BOND STREET

London, where Virginia Woolf (1882-1941) was born, played a prominent role in her life and her novels. In fact it was in her London house behind the British Museum that the so-called Bloomsbury Group was founded, bringing together writers, historians, economists and critics in one of the key movements of modern English thought. In London too, together with her husband Leonard Woolf, she founded the Hogarth Press, taking on the duties of a publisher as well as an author. In the novel "Mrs Dalloway" we follow society hostess Clarissa through the streets of London getting ready for a large party at her house that evening.

“The motor car with its blinds drawn and an air of inscrutable reserve proceeded towards Piccadilly, still gazed at, still ruffling the faces on both sides of the street with the same dark breath of veneration whether for Queen, Prince, or Prime Minister nobody knew. The face itself had been seen only once by three people for a few seconds. Even the sex was now in dispute. But there could be no doubt that greatness was seated within; greatness was passing, hidden, down Bond Street, removed only by a hand's-breadth from ordinary people who might now, for the first and last time, be within speaking distance of the majesty of England, of the enduring symbol of the state which will be known to curious antiquaries, sifting the ruins of time, when London is a grass-grown path and all those hurrying along the pavement this Wednesday morning are but bones with a few wedding rings mixed up in their dust and the gold stoppings of innumerable decayed teeth. The face in the motor car will then be known.

It is probably the Queen, thought Mrs. Dalloway, coming out of Mulberry's with her flowers; the Queen. And for a second she wore a look of extreme dignity standing by the flower shop in the sunlight while the car passed at a foot's pace with its blinds drawn. The Queen going to some hospital; the Queen opening some bazaar, thought Clarissa.

The crush was terrific for the time of day. Lords, Ascot, Hurlingham, what was it? she wondered, for the street was blocked. The British middle classes sitting sideways on the tops of omnibuses with parcels and umbrellas, yes, even furs on a day like this, were, she thought, more ridiculous, more unlike anything there has ever been than one could conceive; and the Queen herself held up; the Queen herself unable to pass. Clarissa was suspended on one side of Brook Street; Sir John Buckhurst, the old Judge on the other, with the car between them (Sir John had laid down the law for years and liked a well-dressed woman) when the chauffeur, leaning ever so slightly, said or showed something to the policeman, who saluted and raised his arm and jerked his head and moved the omnibus to the side and the car passed through. Slowly and very silently it took its way.

Clarissa guessed; Clarissa knew of course; she had seen something white, magical, circular, in the footman's hand, a disc inscribed with a name, – the Queen's, the Prince of Wales's, the Prime Minister's? – which, by force of its own lustre, burnt its way through (Clarissa saw the car diminishing, disappearing), to blaze among the candelabras, glittering stars, breasts stiff with oak leaves, Hugh Whitbread and all his colleagues, the gentlemen of England, that night in Buckingham Palace. And Clarissa too, gave a party. She stiffened a little; so she would stand at the top of her stairs.”

VIRGINIA WOOLF,
MRS DALLOWAY, 1925

MORMONS IN WHITECHAPEL

George Orwell (1903–50) worked in a series of ill-paid jobs in London and Paris while struggling to have his writing accepted by a publisher. He describes this period in "Down and Out in Paris and London", published in 1933, from which the following description of London street life is taken.

“All day I loafed in the streets, east as far as Wapping, west as far as Whitechapel. It was queer after Paris; everything was so much cleaner and quieter and drearier. One missed the scream of the trams, and the noisy, festering life of the back streets, and the armed men clattering through the squares. The crowds were better dressed and the faces comelier and milder and more alike, without that fierce individuality and malice of the French. There was less drunkenness, and less dirt, and less quarrelling, and more idling. Knots of men stood at all the corners, slightly underfed, but kept going by the tea-and-two-slices which the Londoner swallows every two hours. One seemed to breathe a less feverish air than in Paris. It was the land of the tea urn and the Labour Exchange, as Paris is the land of the *bistro* and the sweatshop.

It was interesting to watch the crowds ... Here and there were street meetings. In Whitechapel somebody called The Singing Evangel undertook to save you from hell for the charge of sixpence. In the East India Dock Road the Salvation Army were holding a service. They were singing 'Anybody here like sneaking Judas?' to the tune of 'What's to be done with a drunken sailor?' On Tower Hill two Mormons were trying to address a meeting. Round their platform struggled a mob of men, shouting and interrupting. Someone was denouncing them for polygamists. A lame, bearded man, evidently an atheist, had heard the word God and was heckling angrily. There was a confused uproar of voices.

'My dear friends, if you would only let us finish what we were saying – ! – That's right, give 'em a say. Don't get on the argue! – No, no, you answer me. Can you *show* me God? You *show* 'im me, the I'll believe in 'im. – Oh, shut up, don't keep interrupting of 'em! – Interrupt yourself! – Well, there's a lot to be said for polygamy. Take the – women out of industry, anyway. – My dear friends, if you would just – No, no, don't you slip out of it. 'Ave you *seen* God? 'Ave you *touched* 'im? 'Ave you shook *'ands* with 'im? – Oh, don't get on the argue, for Christ's sake don't get on the *argue*!' etc. etc.

I listened for twenty minutes, anxious to learn something about Mormonism, but the meeting never got beyond shouts. It is the general fate of street meetings.

In Middlesex Street, among the crowds at the market, a draggled, down-at-heel woman was hauling a brat of five by the arm. She brandished a tin trumpet in its face. The brat was squalling.

'Enjoy yourself!' yelled the mother. 'What yer think I brought yer out 'ere for an' bought y' a trumpet an' all? D'ya want to go across my knee? You little bastard, you *shall* enjoy yerself!❞

GEORGE ORWELL,
DOWN AND OUT IN PARIS AND LONDON, 1933

IMPRESSIONS OF THE CITY

LONDON'S BRIDGES

Many of Dickens' novels were originally published in weekly or monthly instalments in magazines and periodicals, and they proved immensely popular with the public. "The Old Curiosity Shop" first appeared in a new weekly called "Master Humphrey's Clock", which was launched in 1840 and written wholly by Dickens.

❝Then, the crowds for ever passing and repassing on the bridges (on those which are free of toll at least), where many stop on fine evenings looking listlessly down upon the water, with some vague idea that by-and-by it runs between green banks which grow wider and wider until at last it joins the broad vast sea – where some halt to rest from heavy loads, and think, as they look over the parapet that to smoke and lounge away one's life, and lie sleeping in the sun upon a hot tarpaulin, in a dull, slow, sluggish barge, must be happiness alloyed – and where some, and a very different class, pause with heavier loads than they, remembering to have heard or read in some old time that drowning was not a hard death, but of all means of suicide the easiest and best.❞

CHARLES DICKENS
THE OLD CURIOSITY SHOP, 1840–1

POETS AND PHILOSOPHERS

One of the last great German Romantics, Heinrich Heine (1797–1856) won recognition and acclaim with the publication in 1827 of a collection of poems "The Book of Songs". At this time he also published two volumes of "Travel Sketches", and a further two volumes were completed between 1826 and 1831. In them, drawing on his travels in Italy, Great Britain and other countries, Heine gave rein to his imagination, sometimes developing his political theories, which were liberal and which resulted in the banning of his works in several German states.

❝I have seen the most astonishing thing that the world has to show: I have seen it and I marvel at it still....I see it now, this forest of bricks bisected by a river and filled with a teeming horde of people who cherish a thousand different passions rent by love, hunger and hate.... I mean London.

Send a philosopher to London by all means, but for the love of God don't send a poet! Take a philosopher there and set him down at the corner of Cheapside, and he will learn more than ever there was in all the books at the last Leipzig Book Fair put together; and while this tide of humanity goes babbling round him there will rise a sea of thoughts before him too, the eternal spirit which hovers overhead will touch him with its breath and the darkest secrets of humanity will be revealed in an instant, quite clearly shall he see and hear the vital pulse of the world...for if London is the world's right hand, strong and vigorous, this highway with the Stock Exchange at one end and Downing Street at the other must be its artery.

Never send a poet to London! The serious business of putting a price on everything leaves nothing untainted; there is a dreadful uniformity as of a clockwork motor even pleasure wears a gloomy face. The very pressure of the place stifles th

magination and destroys the heart; and if by chance you were to send a German poet, a dreamer who stands and stares at anything from a ragged beggar-woman to a gleaming goldsmith's shop, then he'd be trampled underfoot! Jostled and buffeted on all sides, swept off his feet with a friendly curse. Curse those confounded crowds!"

HEINRICH HEINE,
TRAVEL SKETCHES, 1826–31

NOSTALGIA

Charlie Chaplin (1889–1979), the film actor and director, harbored a secret nostalgia for the London of his childhood, which he revealed in his autobiography of 1964.

"This was the London of my childhood, of my moods and awakenings: memories of Lambeth in the spring: of trivial incidents and things: of riding with mother on top of a horse-bus trying to touch lilac trees – of the many coloured bus-tickets, orange, blue, pink and green, that bestrewed the pavement where the trams and buses stopped ... of melancholy Sundays and pale-faced parents and children escorting toy windmills and coloured balloons over Westminster Bridge: and the maternal penny steamers that softly lowered their funnels as they glided under it. From such trivia I believe my soul was born."

CHARLIE CHAPLIN,
MY AUTOBIOGRAPHY, 1964

A LAND OF PRIVACIES

Paul Theroux has written about several countries around the world in works of fiction and non-fiction. His view of London, as an American, is one shared by many visitors to the city.

"It had been a mistake to walk from my hotel to this reception. My hotel was in Chelsea, near the Embankment; the party was at Horton's, Briarcliff Lodge, in Kensington. London is not a city. It is more like a country, and living in it is like living in Holland or Belgium. Its completeness makes it deceptive – there are sidewalks from one frontier to the other – and its hugeness makes it possible for everyone to invent his own city. My London is not your London, though everyone's Washington, DC, is pretty much the same. It was three miles from my hotel to Horton's, and this was only a small part of the labyrinth. A two-mile walk through

any other city would take you inevitably through a slum. But this was unvarying gentility – wet narrow streets, dark housefronts, block upon block. They spoke of prosperity, but they revealed nothing very definite of their occupants. They were sedate battlements, fortress walls, with blind windows, or drawn curtains. I imagined, behind them, something tumultuous. I had never felt more solitary or anonymous. I was happy. The city had been built to enclose secrets, for the British are like those naked Indians who hide in the Brazilian jungle – not timid, but fantastically private and untrusting. This was a mazy land of privacies – comforting to a secretive person, offering shelter to a fugitive, but posing problems to a diplomat.”

PAUL THEROUX,
THE LONDON EMBASSY, 1982

CHRISTMASTIME

Martin Amis has become something of a commentator on late-20th-century manners and morals in his novels. "Money" was the first of his books to achieve best-seller status, but others have followed since.

“It is Christmastime in London.
In London, Christmastime is the time when cabbies' change feels as hot as coins coughed from the bowels of fruit-machines, when office duds try their hands as wits in the pubs and on the long tables of cheap bistros, when in the dead days before New Year people show their presents to the world in buses and tube trains: collars grip the neck like a cold compress, gloves lie on the lap as stiff as pickled octopi, watches and fountain pens flash their signals in the hired light. Christmastime is the time when all girls talk about things being lovely and warm.

The first annual snowfall caused dismay, breakdown, anarchy, as it does every year. All week I've been walking though the London streets and wondering what they look like. They look like something terribly familiar. People are wiggling on their faulty gyroscopes. Whoops! we all go on the hoof-marked brocades. We stare at the pavements to find our footing but we can't tell what the pavements look like. For fifteen minutes the snow was crispy white and squeaky clean. Then no colour at all – no colour, not even grey. What does it look like? With its murky scurf and banked channels of glint and scum, it looks like washing-up, it looks like the London skies. London summer skies: that's what they look like. And so is everything the same?
The second annual snowfall caused dismay, breakdown, anarchy, as it does every year. This second snow stayed white and hard for a lot longer. It was better-quality stuff: it obviously cost more. The snow surprised everyone, as it does every year. It surprised me. But then, snow surprises. Snow is surprising! It is the element of surprise. For a while the world was lunar. It was silent. It was snowjobbed. It was hushed the next morning until at last you heard the apologetic sounds of whispering cars. We all tiptoed out of doors and blinked at the world. Everyone seems to think that everything is all their fault. But we give ourselves credit too sometimes.”

MARTIN AMIS
MONEY, 1984

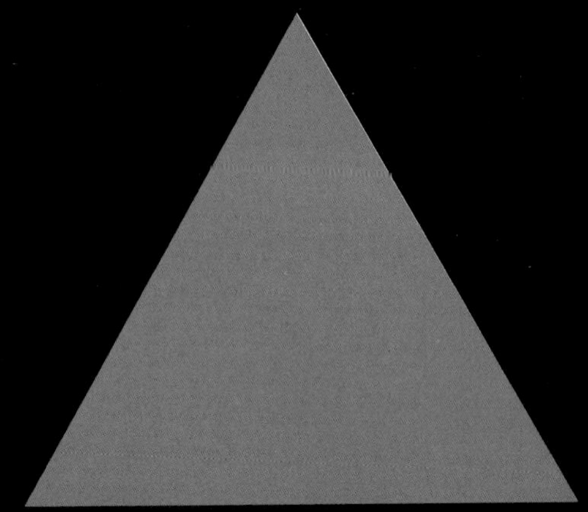

A journey through London

▲ *HMS Belfast* and Tower Bridge.

▲ Christmas lights in Regent Street.

▼ The Isle of Dogs and Canary Wharf

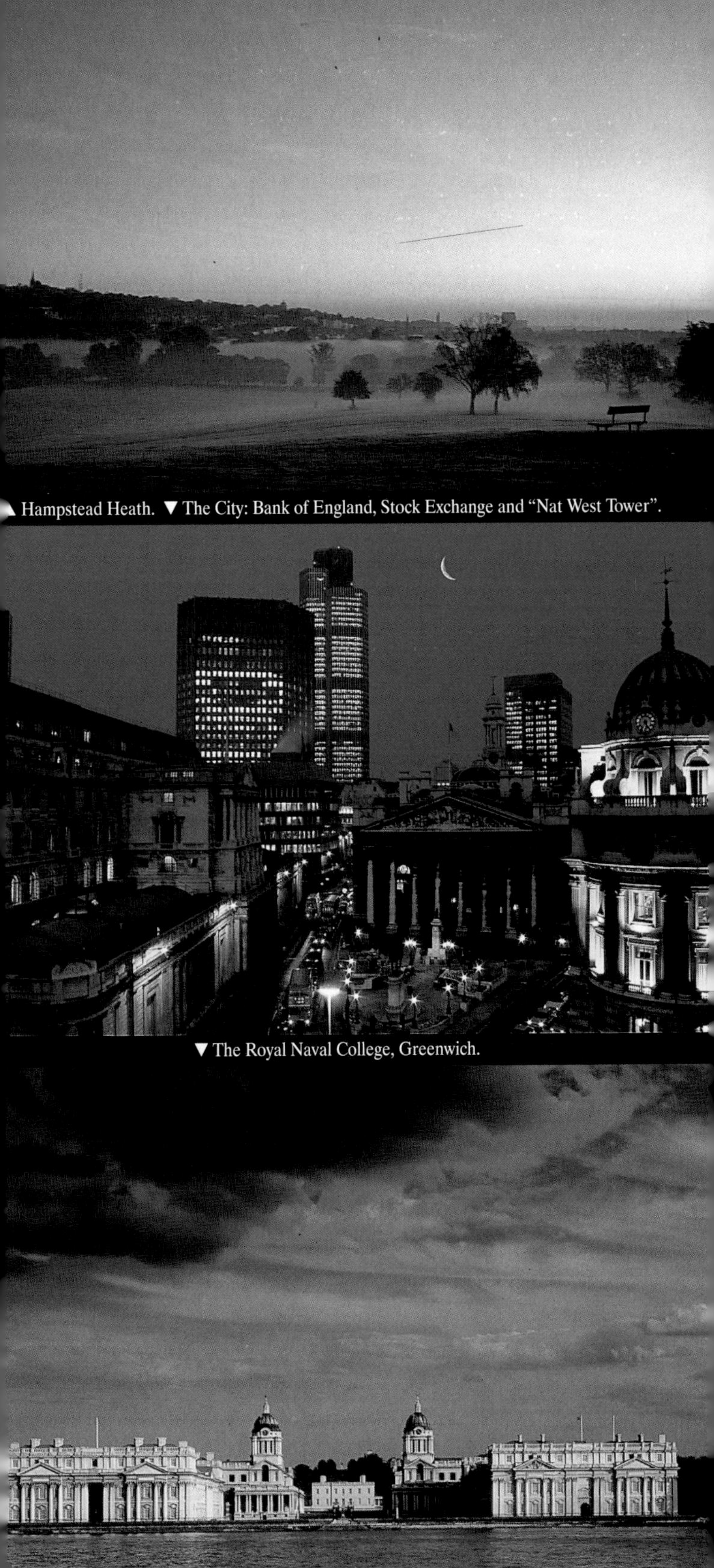

▲ Hampstead Heath. ▼ The City: Bank of England, Stock Exchange and "Nat West Tower".

▼ The Royal Naval College, Greenwich.

▲ Trooping the Colour.

▼ Horse Guards Parade.

A walk in Grovelands Park. ▲ A garden party at Buckingham Palace.

▲ The residential district of Highgate has preserved its village atmosphere.

▲ Syon House.

▼ The gardens at Hampton Court Palac

THE SIGHTS OF LONDON

▲ From Westminster to Victoria Station

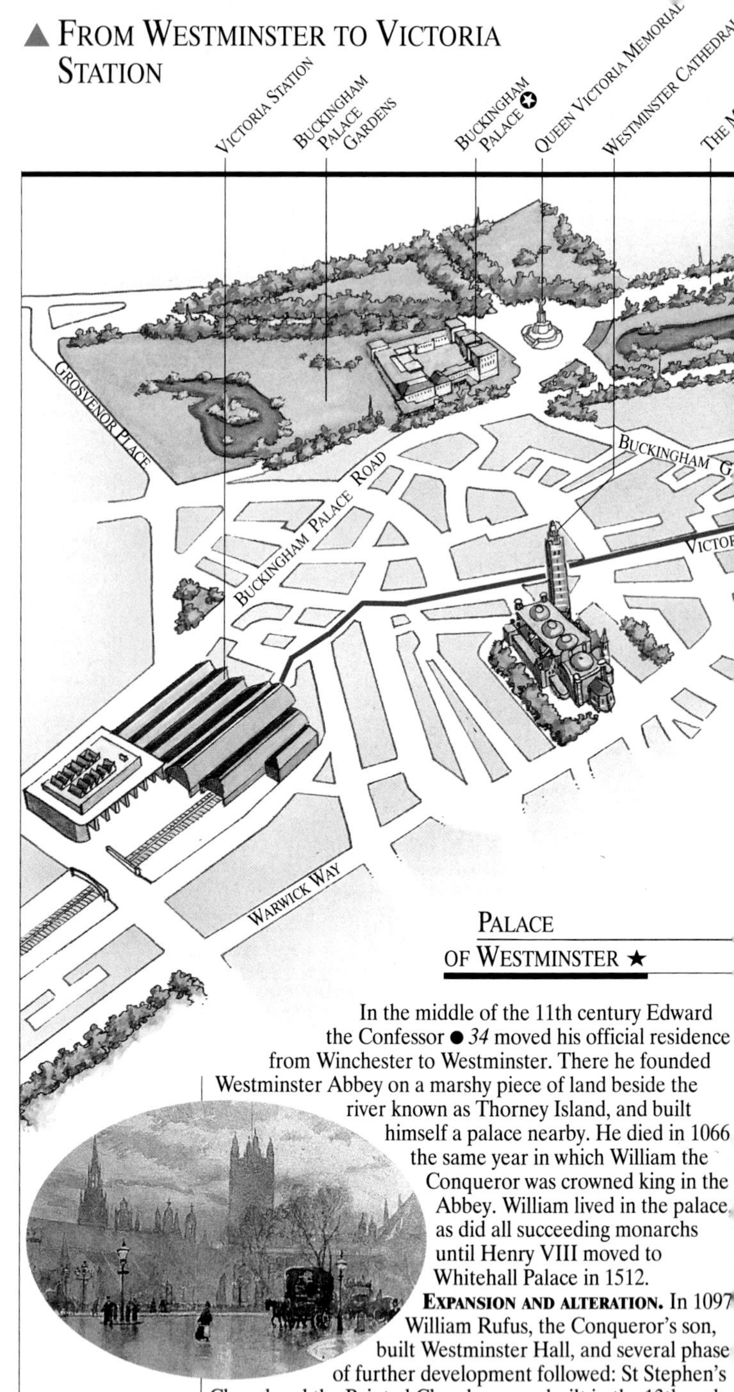

Palace of Westminster ★

In the middle of the 11th century Edward the Confessor ● *34* moved his official residence from Winchester to Westminster. There he founded Westminster Abbey on a marshy piece of land beside the river known as Thorney Island, and built himself a palace nearby. He died in 1066 the same year in which William the Conqueror was crowned king in the Abbey. William lived in the palace, as did all succeeding monarchs until Henry VIII moved to Whitehall Palace in 1512.

Expansion and alteration. In 1097 William Rufus, the Conqueror's son, built Westminster Hall, and several phase of further development followed: St Stephen's Chapel and the Painted Chamber were built in the 13th and 14th centuries, and the Jewel Tower was built to the south west of the palace near Westminster Abbey in 1364–6. The sovereign's treasures and jewels were kept here until the reign of Henry VII, and from 1621 to 1864 it housed the official archives of the House of Lords. The Jewel Tower is now a museum of the history of Parliament. After 1547 the Palace o Westminster ceased to be an official royal residence, and became the home of both upper and lower Houses of

"The palace of Westminster reclines – it can hardly be said to stand – on the big parliamentary bench of its terrace."
Henry James

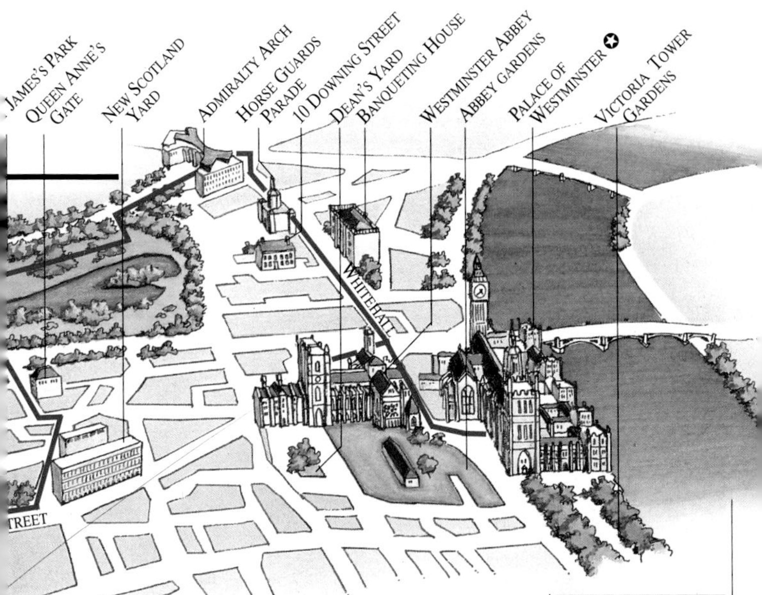

James's Park
Queen Anne's Gate
New Scotland Yard
Admiralty Arch
Horse Guards Parade
10 Downing Street
Dean's Yard
Banqueting House
Westminster Abbey
Abbey Gardens
Palace of Westminster ✪
Victoria Tower Gardens
Whitehall
treet

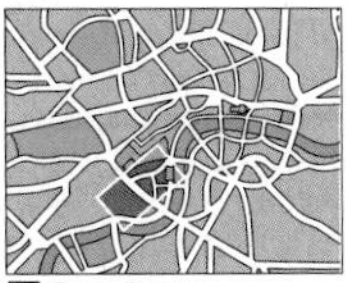

Parliament. Until it was destroyed by fire in 1834, the palace towered over a great maze of little streets that were filled with lodging houses, taverns, coffee-houses and shops.

Rebuilding: Barry and Pugin. Out of ninety-seven designs that were submitted for the rebuilding of Parliament, the eventual success of Sir Charles Barry's project was largely due to his collaboration with another architect, Augustus Pugin (1812–52). Pugin was one of the great neo-Gothic stylists of his day, and assisted Barry with his designs from 1836 until his death. The contrasting temperaments of the two men resulted in a design that was both elegant and highly original. Barry provided the building with its classical balance and symmetry, while Pugin supplied the ornamentation and asymmetrical elements, such as the Victoria Tower and the Clock Tower. Pugin was also responsible for much of the interior decoration and furnishings. Albert ▲ *228*, prince consort since 1840, was a keen amateur follower of the arts and was

One day

◆ **F** C1-C2-D1

WESTMINSTER AND BIG BEN ✪

At the heart of Westminster is Parliament Square. Big Ben is at the northeast corner of the square. This 320-foot tower with a four-faced clock contains a 14-ton bell that chimes the hours. Next to Big Ben are the Gothic-Revival-style Houses of Parliament, seat of government since 1582. When Parliament is in session onlookers are admitted to the visitors' gallery. In the southwest corner of the square is Westminster Abbey, the coronation venue for the majority of England's monarchs since 1066 and where many are buried. Visit the 13th-century French Gothic nave and Henry VII's Tudor-style chapel. You should also visit the museum and Chapter house in the grounds of the Abbey.

"The famous Abbey, standing like a pale ghost in the smoke-ridden city, has no memory of the pious king who built it."
Paul Morand, *London*

devoted to the medieval style in particular. In 1841 he formed a selection committee in order to decide which artists should design the frescoes, statuary and ironwork for the Houses of Parliament: Dyce, Maclise and Gibson were among those to be selected. The rebuilding process began in 1839 and was finally completed in 1860, when the roof was put on the Victoria Tower.

WESTMINSTER HALL ★. The hall was built by William Rufus between 1097 and 1099, as an extension of Edward the Confessor's palace. At the time it was probably the largest building of its type in Europe, measuring 240 feet long and about 40 feet high. During the last decade of the 14th century it was altered by Richard II's architects, the walls being raised and a fine porch added. The most significant alteration however was the addition of the magnificent hammer-beam roof, which was 92 feet high in the center. Parliaments were held here, and many famous trials took place, among them those of Anne Boleyn (1536), Guy Fawkes ● *36* (1606) and King Charles I (1649). After the Restoration of Charles II, the head of Oliver Cromwell was displayed on the roof of the hall , and in more recent years the bodies of Gladstone, Edward VII and Winston Churchill have all lain in state here. Westminster Hall is now part of the House of Commons, linked to it by St Stephen's Hall.

PARLIAMENT. The United Kingdom Parliament is composed of two Houses: the House of Lords, which was for many years

THE FIRE OF 1834
The fire blazed through the night of October 16–17, and several painters hurried to the Palace of Westminster in order to capture the scene. Constable took up a position on Westminster Bridge, while Turner set off in a boat on the Thames with another artist from the Royal Academy, Clarkson Stanfield, and painted several watercolors from there ● *102*. By dawn on the morning of the 17th, nothing was left of the ancient royal palace except for Westminster Hall, the cloisters and the crypt of St Stephen's Chapel.

exclusively made up of hereditary peers; and the House of Commons, the members of which are elected by the people. In former times when Parliament sat in Westminster Hall, the two chambers sat together. They finally separated at the beginning of the 14th century.

The House of Lords. More than a thousand peers sit in the House of Lords. They are divided into three categories: hereditary peers, who have around 90 seats since a bill was passed in 1999 abolishing the hereditary principle; life peers, who have been the largest group in the Lords since the political reform of 1958; and the spiritual peers, all bishops of the Anglican church. The power of the House of Lords was curtailed by two Acts of Parliament passed in 1911 and 1949: the Upper House cannot refuse the passage of a bill, though it can suspend it. It frequently alters clauses of a bill coming before it, which then necessitates a further reading in the House of Commons. The Lord Chancellor presides over the House of Lords, sitting beneath the throne on the Woolsack, a legacy from the days when England's economy was founded on the wool trade. One more important function of the Lords is a judicial one: it is the highest court of appeal in the land.

The House of Commons. The fight against absolute rule of the monarch was a long one, and began with King John in 1215 when the barons forced him to sign the Magna Carta. In 1642 Charles I stormed Parliament with four hundred soldiers to arrest five MPs (Members of Parliament) only to find "the birds had flown": since then the monarch has never been admitted to the House of Commons. The last battle was won in 1689 when William and Mary signed the Bill of Rights ● *36*. In 1701 Parliament drew up the rules of royal succession, and from that time sovereignty has been in its control. Over the centuries the Commons has become increasingly democratic, suffrage being extended by numerous parliamentary reform bills in the 19th century, and women gaining the right to vote in two acts passed in 1918 and 1928. When MPs vote in the Commons, they leave the Chamber either by the "Aye" corridor or the "No" corridor which lead off from either side of the Speaker's chair. Outside, counting the votes, are the party "whips", a term derived from the whipper-in of hounds in the hunting field.

Destruction. On May 10, 1941, at the height of the Blitz ● *42*, the House of Commons was destroyed by incendiary bombs and by a high-explosive bomb near the Victoria Tower. Between 1945 and 1950 it was rebuilt by Sir Giles Gilbert Scott to a plainer version of Barry's original design, but

The political heart of the country
When Henry VIII left to take up residence in Whitehall, the Palace of Westminster became one of the chief political and administrative centers of the kingdom. The law courts were here from the 13th century until 1882, first in Westminster Hall and then in a building designed by Sir John Soane. For centuries the palace has also been home to the Houses of Parliament: its name has become synonymous with theirs.

"I have worn my knees by writing on them on the old back-row of the old Gallery of the old House of Commons; and I have worn my feet by standing to write in a preposterous pen in the old House of Lords, where we used to be huddled together like so many sheep – kept in waiting, say, until the woolsack might want re-stuffing."
Charles Dickens (1865)

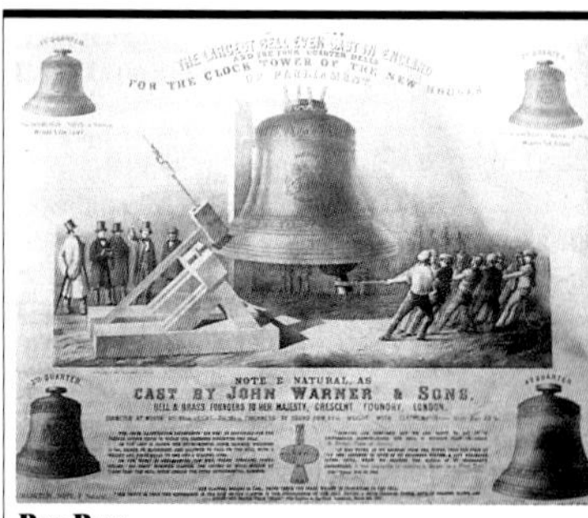

BIG BEN
The great bell in the Clock Tower was cast in 1858 in the famous Whitechapel Foundry. It weighs 13½ tons and is 7 feet high. It may be named after a famous boxer popular at the time, Benjamin Caunt, or after the chief commissioner of works, Sir Benjamin Hall. The light above the clock is switched on when Parliament is sitting.

DESIGN FOR THE CLOCK BY SIR CHARLES BARRY
The clock was completed only after heated competition between Barry's protégé Benjamin Vuillamy and another clockmaker E.J. Dent. Dent was awarded the contract in 1852, but died before he could complete the project. The clock faces are 22½ feet in diameter and the minute hands are 14 feet long. It began working on May 31, 1859.

THE SPEAKER
The Speaker presides over the House of Commons, being elected at the beginning of each government's term of office. Should the government change before the period has elapsed, the Speaker generally retains his office. Right, George Thomas, Speaker from 1976–83.

1. Clock Tower
2. Westminster Hall
3. House of Commons
4. Commons Lobby
5. Central Lobby
6. Peers' Lobby
7. House of Lords
8. Prince's Chamber
9. Royal Gallery
10. Victoria Tower
11. Robing Room

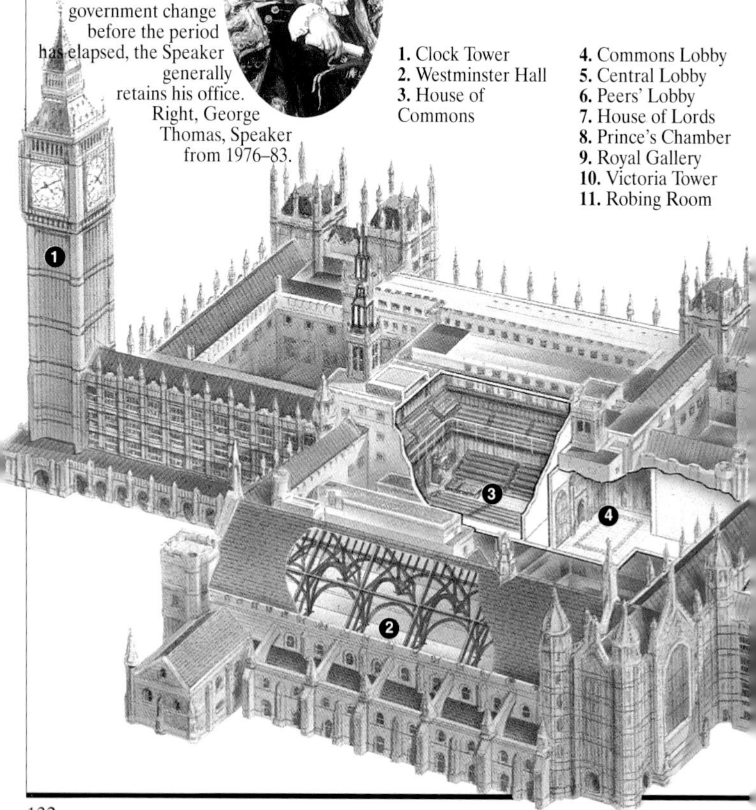

ISTORY IN THE HOUSE OF COMMONS
op, William Pitt the Younger (1759–1806) naking a speech in the House of Commons. Ie was only twenty-four when he became rime minister, and in the last years of his hort life he did much to save England from nvasion by the French. The lower painting hows Prime Minister W.E. Gladstone ▲ *139* ntroducing the Irish Home Rule Bill to the Iouse of Commons.

THE HOUSE OF COMMONS
The House of Commons initially met in the Chapter House or the refectory of Westminster Abbey. It moved to St Stephen's when the latter was secularized in 1547. The Speaker's chair was in the space formerly occupied by the altar.

THE HOUSE OF LORDS
The finest achievement of its architect Augustus Pugin, this "magnificent and gravely gorgeous chamber" is decorated in gold and scarlet. At the far end is the throne, beneath a highly ornate Gothic canopy. Above left, Queen Anne on the throne in the House of Lords.

ST STEPHEN'S HALL
The House of Commons sat here from 1547 until the fire of 1834.

THE HOUSE OF COMMONS
The government and opposition sit facing each other, divided by a space (the Floor).

without Pugin's neo-Gothic decoration. Instead, exotic timber was presented from all over the Commonwealth to decorate the Chamber, which did, however, retain the traditional green leather-covered benches. The comparatively bland result can be seen every day on British television, since the cameras were first allowed in, in 1989.

PARLIAMENTARY SESSIONS. Members of Parliament assemble in the House of Commons under the chairmanship of the Speaker. The session opens when the Speaker sits down in front of the table on which the sergeant-at-arms has placed the golden mace, symbol of the sovereignty of Parliament. The Speaker is in control of the day's business, choosing who will speak: those selected never speak to another Member directly, but always address the Speaker.

THE VICTORIA TOWER. The huge, square neo-Gothic tower at the southwest corner of the palace is 336 feet tall. The arch at the foot of it is the royal entrance to the palace. The tower is the repository of the parliamentary archives (more than three million documents).

BIG BEN ★. The Clock Tower at the north end of the palace is 320 feet high. The first of the clock's great bells to be known as Big Ben was cast in Stockton-on-Tees in 1856 and reached London by boat up the river. It cracked the following year and was replaced in 1858 by another cast at the Whitechapel Foundry ▲ *316* weighing 13½ tons. The clock mechanism proved remarkably reliable for 117 years, until 1976 when extensive repairs were carried out. When the palace was bombed in 1941, the clock became temporarily inaccurate by 1½ seconds! It stopped three times during the war, once when a hammer was accidentally jammed in the works, again in 1945 when a spring broke, and a third time when the striking mechanism froze in the cold weather. The clock's hourly chime is copied from St Mary's Church in Cambridge. There are words to its simple melody: "All through this hour, Lord be my guide; And by Thy power, no foot shall slide."

THE STATE OPENING. Each year in November the sovereign comes to Westminster to open the parliamentary session. Coming in

by the Royal Entrance, the queen puts on her robes and the Imperial State Crown in the Robing Room. Accompanied by the Prince of Wales, she is greeted in the House of Lords by the Lord Chamberlain and the Peers in their robes. Once she is seated on the throne, the Members of Parliament are invited by a herald to come to the House of Lords and hear the queen's speech. This outline of government policy for the coming year is always drafted by the prime minister. Only after this ceremony can Parliament get down to business. The ceremony is preceded by an annual inspection of the palace cellars, a legacy from the Gunpowder Plot of November 5, 1605, when Guy Fawkes and his fellow conspirators attempted to blow up the palace during King James I's speech.

St Margaret's Church

This church in Parliament Square was founded in the 12th century and rebuilt between 1486 and 1523. It is the parish church of the Houses of Parliament, and has innumerable important links with the past. The window was made in honor of Prince Arthur's engagement to Catharine of Aragon, though Arthur died before the wedding, and Catharine married his younger brother, Henry VIII. Also married here were Samuel Pepys ● *40* (1655), John Milton (1656) and Winston Churchill ● *42* (1908). Among historical figures buried in the church are William Caxton (1491), and Sir Walter Raleigh (1618) after his execution in Old Palace Yard.

Westminster Abbey ★

Coronations and burials. With two exceptions (Edward V and Edward VIII), the monarchs of England from William the Conqueror to Elizabeth II have been crowned in Westminster Abbey. It is also the burial place of most of them, from Harold Harefoot (1040) to George II (1760).

Uncertain origins. A church was probably built on this site in the 7th century, followed by a Benedictine abbey between 730 and 740. When Edward the Confessor

Big Ben
The astronomer royal, George Biddell Airy, was appointed to oversee the

accuracy of the new clock in 1846. He specified that the first stroke of each hour should be correct to the nearest second, and that its exactness should be checked by telegraph twice each day at the Royal Observatory, Greenwich.

Central Lobby
This octagonal room (left) in the center of the palace separates the Lords from the Commons. Members of Parliament receive the press here.

Invitation to the coronation of George IV in Westminster Abbey.

FRENCH INFLUENCE
Henry III greatly admired the cathedrals of Rheims and Amiens, as well as the Sainte-Chapelle in Paris, and Westminster Abbey reflects these influences. The apse and its radiating chapels derive from Amiens, together with the recessed portals in the north transept. The tall windows in the chapels of the apse derive from Rheims; and there are many other features imported from France, such as the flying buttresses, rose windows and immensely tall nave.

ascended the throne in 1040, he rebuilt the abbey and added a Norman church. The church was dedicated on December 28, 1065: a week later the king died and was buried inside it. When he was canonized in 1139, successive kings gave rich endowments to the church, keen to have their names linked with Edward's.

GOTHIC REBUILDING. In 1220 Henry III began to rebuild the abbey. He started by adding the Lady Chapel (demolished in the construction of the Henry VII chapel), and the foundation stone of the new building was laid on July 6, 1245. The old building was gradually demolished as construction work continued westward: the east end, choir, transepts and the first bay of the nave were all complete by the end of the century. The first master builder to work on the rebuilding was Henry de Reynes, possibly brought back by Henry when he visited Rheims in 1243. There is certainly much French influence in the abbey's design, though the style was not simply copied from Continental models. The ribbed vaulting is a typically English feature, as are the galleries, the long nave, wide transepts and the polygonal Chapter House.

ENTER HENRY YEVELE. In 1269, in order to celebrate the completion of the transepts, the north façade, part of the cloisters and the Chapter House, the abbey was consecrated and the remains of Edward the Confessor were moved to the newly built St Edward's Chapel before the high altar: before the Dissolution of the monasteries, its upper part was decorated with gold and jewels, and sick people would spend the night in the recesses at the base praying for recovery. Henry III died in 1272 and was also buried in front of the high altar, having paid for the rebuilding with all his private fortune. His death brought building work to a halt, to begin again 104 years later in 1376 under the supervision of master mason Henry Yevele, who had redesigned Westminster Hall and built the nave of Canterbury Cathedral. Yevele undertook

"PROCESSION OF KNIGHTS OF THE ORDER OF THE BATH"
This painting by Canaletto (1697–1768) shows the knights leaving Westminster Abbey. The Bath is the second oldest order of knighthood in England, and in 1725 the Henry VII Chapel became the chapel of the order. Their carved stalls divide the aisles from the nave, each bearing their arms engraved on a copper plaque with their standards displayed above.

the construction of the nave, working as far as possible to the former plans of Henry de Reynes, and also built the Jerusalem Chamber in the dean's lodgings, where Henry IV died in 1413 after collapsing while at prayer before the shrine of St Edward. Yevele's devotion to the 13th-century designs gave the abbey a remarkable unity of style, which was in due course respected by his successors. With the exception of the towers on the west front, which were added by Hawksmoor ▲ *311* in the mid-18th century, the abbey was complete by 1532. Apart from looting during the Dissolution of the monasteries ● *36* royal protection has saved this magnificent building from either damage or alteration.

Mausoleum of the Great and Good. The sheer number of monuments inside it has all but transformed Westminster Abbey into a museum of English sculpture. There are the tombs of no fewer than fifteen monarchs located here, together with a great many other members of the British royal families. They are scattered around the abbey chapels, two of which are of outstanding importance: those of Edward the Confessor and Henry VII. Altogether, Westminster Abbey contains more than five thousand tombs, monuments and memorials. Over the centuries many of the greatest Englishmen and women have been interred here: Isaac Newton, Handel, Charles Darwin, Oliver Cromwell, Cecil Rhodes, Henry Purcell, David Livingstone and literally thousands more.

Resting places. The tombs and memorials are sometimes grouped together in different parts of the abbey. Part of the north aisle and transept is devoted to statesmen: there are statues here of Benjamin Disraeli (1804–81), his despised rival William Ewart Gladstone (1809–98), Lord Palmerston (1784–1865) and many more. The great radical Charles James Fox (1749–1806) has a statue depicting him dying in the arms of Liberty. In the south transept is the famous Poets' Corner, which was named after the first two poets to be buried here, Geoffrey Chaucer and Edmund Spenser. Many more writers are commemorated than are actually buried here, but John Dryden, Samuel Johnson, Sheridan, Robert Browning and Tennyson are some of those whose remains lie within the abbey. Ben Jonson was buried upright at his own request, so as to take up as little space as possible. Westminster Abbey also has memorials to the two world wars: the Unknown Soldier was interred in the nave in 1920, at the front of which is a memorial plaque to Winston Churchill, with another to the memory of US President Franklin Delano Roosevelt near the west door.

The north transept
Its splendid façade overlooks Parliament Square. A large rose window is framed by elegant flying buttresses over a triple entrance.

The Henry VII Chapel in 1828
Situated at the east end behind the altar, it contains the tomb of the first Tudor king. This was carved by the Florentine Pietro Torrigiano, who left Italy after he broke Michelangelo's nose in a fight.

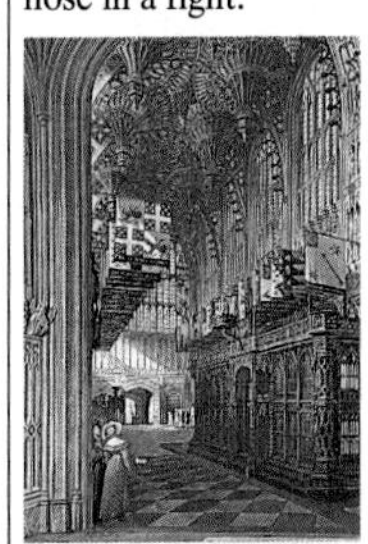

Westminster Abbey choristers
The abbey has its own choir, composed exclusively of men and boys who sing "with the greatest ease imaginable".

THE CHAPEL OF EDWARD THE CONFESSOR AND THE CORONATION CHAIR ★. The tomb of the royal saint is in the middle of the chapel. Also here is the Coronation Chair, made around 1300 and used for every coronation since 1308. Beneath it is a block of brown sandstone, the Stone of Scone: the kings of Scotland had been crowned on this piece of rock for as long as anyone can remember, and it was symbolically brought to London by Edward I in 1297 after his conquest of Scotland. Legend also associates the stone with Jacob's pillow at Bethel. In almost seven hundred years the Coronation Chair has only left the abbey four times: once when Cromwell was made Lord Protector in Westminster Hall, twice for safekeeping during the two world wars, and once in 1950–1 when it was stolen by Scottish nationalists. At the east end of the chapel is the oak effigy (once coated with silver) of Henry V (1387–1422). His beloved "Kate", Catharine de Valois (1401–37), whom he married in 1420, is interred above him in the king's chantry chapel. For three hundred years after her death, Catharine's embalmed body lay here in an open coffin.

THE HENRY VII CHAPEL ★. The reign of the first Tudor king, Henry VII (1485–1509), was an important one in the abbey's history. Henry embarked on the construction of a chapel to contain the remains of his murdered uncle Henry VI (1421–71), whom he wished to have canonized. The pope demanded an extortionate fee for this service, so the chapel was dedicated to the Virgin Mary instead. It was finally completed in 1512, three years after Henry's death and in the reign of his son Henry VIII. This enormous chapel at the east end of the abbey is a masterpiece of Tudor building. In the words of the American writer Washington Irving: "Stone seems, by the winning labor of the chisel, to have been robbed

EFFIGY OF WILLIAM DE VALENCE (D. 1296)
William was Henry III's French half-brother, and earl of Pembroke. He fought for Henry at the Battle of Lewes, and went on the last crusade to Palestine with Prince Edward (later Edward I).

The coronation of William IV in Westminster Abbey.

THE NAVE
The dimensions of the nave are exceptional for an English cathedral: 102 feet high and 72 feet wide, including the aisles. It is the highest Gothic nave in England. The central section is separated from the aisles by graceful columns of grey Purbeck marble, which accentuate its height. The interior light comes from the large 15th-century window above the west door.

of its weight and density, suspended aloft as if by magic, and the fretted roof achieved with the wonderful minuteness and airy security of a cobweb." There are many royal tombs in the chapel: Elizabeth I (1558–1603) shares one with her sister Mary I (1553–8), not far from their brother, the boy-king Edward VI (1547–53). In the south aisle is the effigy of Mary, Queen of Scots (1542–87); most poignant of all, at the end of the chapel known as "Innocents' Corner" are the bones of the two princes murdered in the Tower in the 15th century.

ROYAL AIR FORCE CHAPEL. This lies at the far end of the Henry VII Chapel, with a window commemorating the Battle of Britain in 1940 and a roll of honor with the names of the 1,497 Allied airmen killed in the battle. Here too is the tomb of Oliver Cromwell. At the Restoration, his body was exhumed and hanged at Tyburn. His head was left on the roof of Westminster Hall for twenty-five years until it fell down.

KINGS AND COMMONERS. Coronations take place in the choir of the abbey and follow a strict procedure laid down in the 14th century. But the abbey has had its share of political life as well. The early House of Commons met in the CHAPTER HOUSE until 1547, to the great annoyance of the monks, who complained about the noise. Access to the Chapter House is through the cloister: it is a beautiful octagonal room with six large windows and 14th-century frescoes including a frieze of animals. Its vaulted roof springs outward from a central column of Purbeck marble. The Chapter House was bombed in World War II and has been carefully restored. The tiled floor (c. 1250) is the finest of its kind to survive from the 13th century. The ABBEY MUSEUM in the Norman undercroft beneath the Chapter House has wax and wooden effigies of historical figures. Most spectacular are those of Charles II, in his Garter robes, and of Lord Nelson: "It is as if he were standing there," said a contemporary. Nearby is the PYX CHAMBER (c. 1070), originally a Norman chapel, with the oldest altar in the abbey. It was converted in the 13th century to a royal strongroom (note the locks on the double door). Gold and silver coins were brought to be tested against standard pieces, kept in a special box called a pyx. There is a display of church plate.

POETS' CORNER
Geoffrey Chaucer's monument in the south transept was the original landmark that was responsible for the institution of Poets' Corner (he also lived in a house on the site of the Henry VII Chapel). It should be remembered that many of the monuments are merely retrospective and do not mark actual burial places. But among the many notable figures interred here are David Garrick, with a monument representing him making his final bow; Handel, with a fine statue by Roubiliac; Samuel Johnson, with a noble bust of the great Englishman by Nollekens; and John Gay, author of *The Beggar's Opera* and author too of his own epitaph, "Life is a jest, and all things shew it; I thought so once, and now I know it."

TOMB OF QUEEN ELIZABETH I

TOMB OF EDWARD THE CONFESSOR
Only the lower part is original (left). The gilded wooden upper section (1557) replaces a precious shrine decorated with gold and jewels which was vandalized and looted at the time of the Dissolution of the monasteries.

DOWNING STREET
Number 10, one of the most famous addresses in London, is connected to numbers 11 and 12. George II presented it to Robert Walpole (then First Lord of the Treasury) in 1732, but the latter only accepted in his professional role. When the post of prime minister was created, the house became the premier's official residence. The substantial interior of the house was altered by William Kent, 1732–5, and by Sir John Soane in 1825. The famous Cabinet Room is on the ground floor. Number 11, next door, is the home of the Chancellor of the Exchequer.

HORSE GUARDS AND HORSE GUARDS PARADE
The building on the left, the Horse Guards, was completed in 1758 by John Vardy to the designs of William Kent, who died ten years before. On the Whitehall side this Palladian building forms three sides of a square, while on the other side is Horse Guards Parade (right), reached by the three arches at the back. Only the monarch is allowed to use the central arch.

DEAN'S YARD

In this peaceful square is the entrance to one of Britain's most famous public schools, Westminster. Formerly a monastic school attached to the Benedictine abbey, it was refounded by Elizabeth I in 1560, after the Dissolution ● *36*. Famous old boys include Ben Jonson and Christopher Wren.

ASHBURNHAM HOUSE. Built around 1662 for the Ashburnham family (possibly by John Webb, son-in-law of Inigo Jones), the house is now part of Westminster School. The interior has a fine staircase around a square well and lit by a lantern in the roof. It has been called the finest 17th-century domestic interior in London.

AROUND WHITEHALL

Whitehall links Westminster with Trafalgar Square and Charing Cross. It is a wide road, and around it are ministries, government offices and the official residence of the prime minister.

WHITEHALL. York Place, the London residence of the archbishop of York, formerly stood on the site of Whitehall. It was built in 1245, and extensively refurbished in the early 16th century by Cardinal Wolsey. When Wolsey fell into disgrace in 1530, Henry VIII confiscated the Renaissance palace Wolsey had built for himself and chose it for his own London residence, abandoning the old-fashioned Palace of Westminster. He changed its name to Whitehall and embarked on an ambitious building project, purchasing more land to the west of the palace. But in Henry's reign the palace was never more than a disparate collection of buildings, of which none remain today. It was left to the Stuart dynasty to make the greatest changes to the palace. James I

Horse Guards
The guard is kept here every day from 10am until 4pm by two mounted troopers on the Whitehall side, and by two foot soldiers on Horse Guards Parade ● *50*.

commissioned Inigo Jones (1573–1652) and Jones' son-in-law John Webb (1611–72) to redesign and enlarge Whitehall, which resulted in plans for a palace of around two thousand rooms, extending for half a mile along the river and reaching back almost as far as Horse Guards Parade. This grandiose scheme was inspired by the Escorial in Spain and the Tuileries Palace in Paris, but it was soon abandoned. Only the Banqueting House was ever completed. After 1685 it was Wren who left his mark on Whitehall, building a Privy Gallery and Catholic chapel for James II. (When William of Orange landed in England in 1688, the king "stole away from Whitehall by the Privy Stairs".) England's new rulers, William and Mary, deserted Whitehall for Kensington Palace, which suited the king's asthma better. Whitehall was damaged by fire in 1691, and when in 1698 it burned to the ground leaving only the Banqueting House, it was not rebuilt.

Downing Street. This narrow street derives its name from the diplomat Sir George Downing (1623–84), who built a cul-de-sac of terraced houses here. Numbers 10, 11 and 12 are the only surviving original buildings. On the south side of the street is the Foreign and Commonwealth Office, while number 10 is known the world over as the prime minister's residence. The street is now blocked off by large security gates, commissioned by Margaret Thatcher.

The Old Treasury. The Treasury Building in Whitehall, below the Horse Guards and on the same side, was built by Sir Charles Barry ▲ *129* in 1844, replacing an earlier one designed by Sir John Soane which had become too small. Barry retained Soane's columns and frieze however.

Admiralty and Admiralty House. The last large official building on the west side of Whitehall before Trafalgar Square is the Admiralty. Admiralty House was built between 1786 and 1788 by Samuel Pepys Cockerell as the home of the First Lord of the Admiralty. Access to it is through a

Whitehall
The road connecting Westminster to Charing Cross was already residential in the 16th century: the poet Edmund Spenser had a house here, and so did Oliver Cromwell in the following century. Most of the buildings now are government offices built in the 19th century.

Cabinet War Rooms
These rooms, preserved as a memorial to Winston Churchill, are in King Charles Street, which runs parallel to Downing Street. You can see the spartan room Churchill occupied during the Blitz, part of the underground HQ of the armed forces. Another great attraction is the famous map room, busy day and night, which charted the progress of the British campaign.

Officer of the Life Guards
The Trooping of the Colour first took place in 1755 and has been a regular event since 1805. The ceremony originates in the practice of parading the colors in front of the troops, so that each regiment would recognize its rallying point on the battlefield ● *50*.

wing of the Admiralty. The graceless façade of Thomas Ripley's Admiralty (1722–6) is masked by an elegant stone screen (1759–61), an early work by Robert Adam.

BANQUETING HOUSE ★. Situated on the east side of Whitehall opposite the Horse Guards, this is the only surviving building of Whitehall Palace. In 1581 Elizabeth I approved plans for a reception building here in which to entertain envoys of the Duke of Alençon, her projected fiancé. It was to be a temporary affair made of wood and canvas, but even so it had almost three hundred glass windows. The next banqueting house on the site was built on the orders of James I in 1608, and until its destruction by fire in 1619 it was frequently used as a theater. In the same year, James commissioned the architect Inigo Jones ▲ *272, 326* to replace it.

BANQUETING HALL ★. Jones built a vast double cube, the interior dimensions of the hall itself, on the first floor, being 115 feet long, by 60 feet wide and 55 feet high. There are two stories of seven windows, separated by Ionic half-columns below and Corinthian pillars above. In 1630 Charles I commissioned Rubens to paint the ceiling: installed in 1635, the panels were executed in Brussels, and glorify the union of England and Scotland under the wise rule of Charles' father, James I. The Banqueting House is used for all kinds of state occasions, such as the ritual washing of the commoners' feet by the monarch on Maundy Thursday, and the annual dinner for the Knights of the Garter on St George's Day. In 1649 Charles I was executed on a scaffold set up outside one of its windows, and in 1689 William and Mary consented to become joint sovereigns of Britain in the hall of the Banqueting House. A few years later Wren converted it into a chapel, which it remained until Queen Victoria decided to hand it to the Royal United Services Institute in 1890 to be used as a museum. It was extensively restored in 1963, and the paintings were returned to their correct positions (Rubens' allegorical story begins at the far end of the hall).

THE MALL

Running from Admiralty Arch down to Buckingham Palace, the Mall was formerly a leafy avenue laid out in St James's Park at the Restoration. Its name, like Pall Mall, comes from the game of Pell Mell that was once played here with balls and mallets. The present road was constructed as a processional route beside the old Mall in the first decade of the present century.

WESTMINSTER CATHEDRAL ★

At the far end of Victoria Street from Parliament Square, on the lefthand side in Ashley Place, stands Westminster Cathedral, the headquarters of the Roman Catholic church in

CEILING OF THE BANQUETING HOUSE
These huge canvases by Rubens, depicting the *Apotheosis of James I*, so pleased Charles I that he knighted the artist.

ADMIRALTY ARCH
Sir Aston Webb's monumental arch (below right) was built in 1910 as part of the national memorial to Queen Victoria. It is a massive, pompous Edwardian construction, framing a fine view down the Mall to the Victoria Memorial with Buckingham Palace in the background.

CARLTON HOUSE TERRACE
The elegant terraces that overlook the Mall were built between 1827 and 1832 by John Nash on the site of Carlton House, where George IV lived before Buckingham Palace was completed. The short pillars at the base of the façade are an early use of cast iron. Prime ministers Palmerston and Gladstone both had houses here.

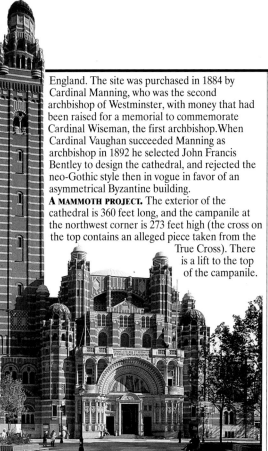

England. The site was purchased in 1884 by Cardinal Manning, who was the second archbishop of Westminster, with money that had been raised for a memorial to commemorate Cardinal Wiseman, the first archbishop. When Cardinal Vaughan succeeded Manning as archbishop in 1892 he selected John Francis Bentley to design the cathedral, and rejected the neo-Gothic style then in vogue in favor of an asymmetrical Byzantine building.

A MAMMOTH PROJECT. The exterior of the cathedral is 360 feet long, and the campanile at the northwest corner is 273 feet high (the cross on the top contains an alleged piece taken from the True Cross). There is a lift to the top of the campanile.

The nave is the widest in the whole of England, with seating for twelve hundred people, not counting the side-aisles which can hold several hundred more. The walls, columns and domes are all covered with mosaics made from more than a hundred different varieties of marble. The overall effect is mystical and sumptuous. The dark green marble columns in the nave are made from stone taken from the same quarry that provided the marble for St Sophia in Istanbul. Note the *Stations of the Cross*, which was executed by Eric Gill between 1913 and 1918, and also a 15th-century statue of the Virgin and Child. The decoration is still incomplete, with some rough brick exposed on many of the cupolas.

VICTORIA STATION

This formless building is really two stations joined into one. In the 1860's the London, Brighton and South Coast Railway's terminus at the junction of Victoria Street and Buckingham Palace Road was joined on its east side by the London terminus of the London, Chatham and Dover Railway. The latter handled boat trains to the Continent, and has been the arrival and departure point of more visiting heads of state than any other London terminus. In the First World War troops bound for the trenches in France left from Victoria Station.

SOUTHERN RAILWAY
In 1923 it took over the stations at Victoria and handled Britain's Continental travel.

WESTMINSTER CATHEDRAL
In order to avoid unfavorable comparison with the Gothic masterpiece at the other end of Victoria Street, architect John Francis Bentley searched around for a different style. On a trip to Italy in 1894 he explored early Christian buildings, the medieval architecture of Siena and Venice, and visited Constantinople. The final building (left) was constructed in red brick (12½ million bricks were needed) with bands of white Portland stone. The cupola was modeled on that of St Sophia in Constantinople, while the immense campanile was derived from models in Venice and Siena.

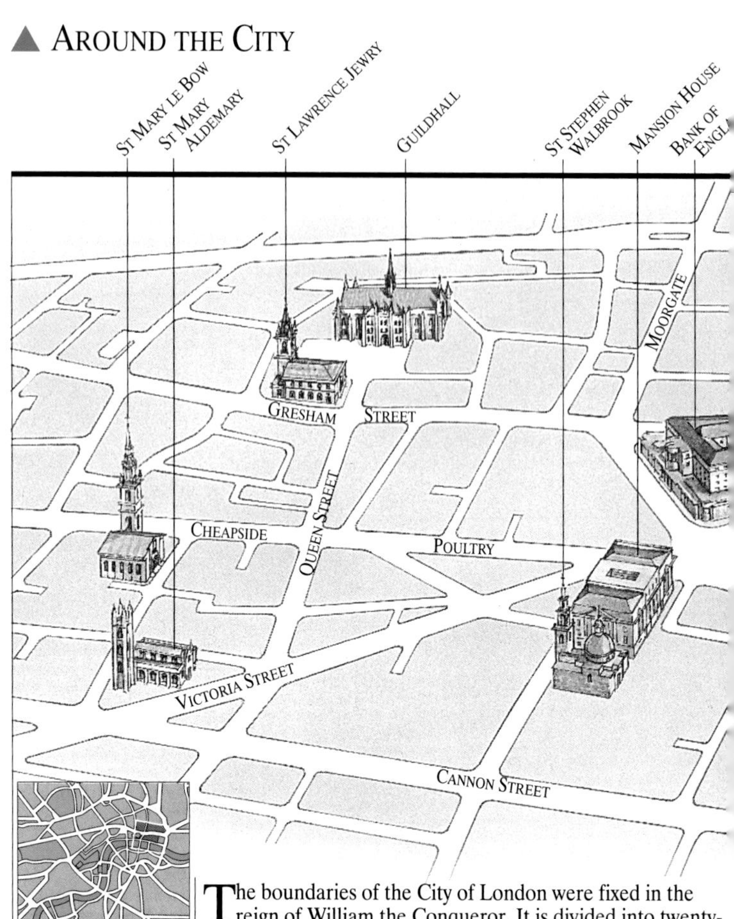

Half a day
◆ **C** D2-D3 **G** A1-A2

The boundaries of the City of London were fixed in the reign of William the Conqueror. It is divided into twenty-five districts, called wards. The City has its own system of government, independent of the crown and Westminster, a privilege that it acquired when the monarchy was weak: in 1191 and again in 1215 King John granted London its commune, or status as a self-governing corporation, with the right to elect its own mayor.

LIVERY COMPANIES. The Livery, or uniformed, Companies, whose name derives from the distinctive uniform which their members wear at banquets and on official occasions, took on the role of governing the City in the 12th century. Although they have now lost the power they wielded in the Middle Ages, Liverymen still have a role to play in City government: each year they elect the Lord Mayor and sheriffs. An order of precedence for the twelve principal guilds was established in 1514: Mercers, Grocers, Drapers, Fishmongers, Goldsmiths, Skinners, Merchant Taylors, Haberdashers, Salters, Ironmongers, Vintners and Clothworkers – an order that is still jealously preserved. The hundredth company, that of Information Technicians, was created in 1992.

ELECTING THE LORD MAYOR. Every year since 1189 or 1192, the approximate date on which the event first took place, a new Lord Mayor is elected at the Guildhall. This is an important event, since within the City the Lord Mayor takes precedence over everyone except the sovereign, and is

THE QUEEN VISITS THE LORD MAYOR
Queen Victoria arriving at the Guildhall in November 1837. As head of the world's oldest corporation, the Lord Mayor has privileges within the City and precedence over everyone except the sovereign, with whom he has the right of audience.

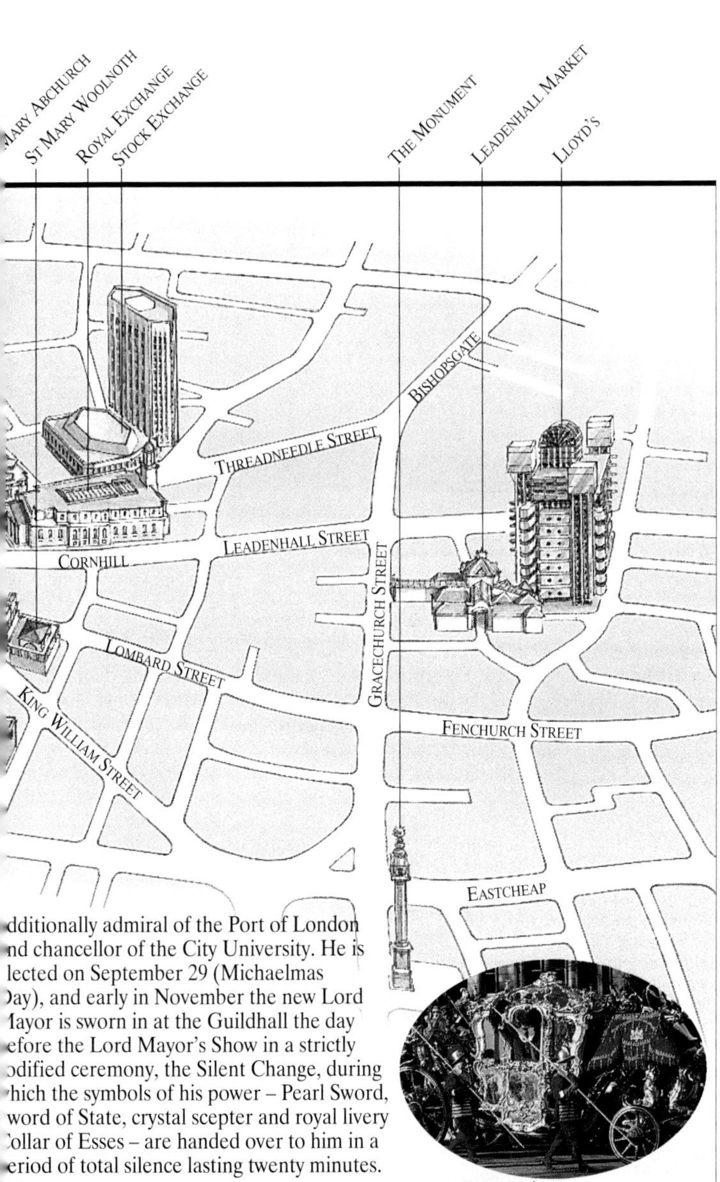

dditionally admiral of the Port of London nd chancellor of the City University. He is lected on September 29 (Michaelmas Day), and early in November the new Lord Mayor is sworn in at the Guildhall the day efore the Lord Mayor's Show in a strictly odified ceremony, the Silent Change, during hich the symbols of his power – Pearl Sword, word of State, crystal scepter and royal livery Collar of Esses – are handed over to him in a eriod of total silence lasting twenty minutes.

THE LORD MAYOR'S SHOW
A great parade like a carnival escorts the new Lord Mayor on his way to swear allegiance to the sovereign. It accompanies him as far as the Mansion House, his official residence. In the 17th century poets wrote pageants to be performed at the celebrations. The coach has been in use since 1755 and is drawn by six dapple-grays. The panels are by Giovanni Cipriani.

THE LORD MAYOR'S BANQUET
The new Lord Mayor used to host a banquet after the Lord Mayor's Show. The tradition goes back to 1501, though now it is held on the Monday following the show. After dinner, in front of seven hundred guests, the prime minister makes an important speech.

ST LAWRENCE JEWRY
This church has a square stone tower. Between the columns of the portico, niches alternate with windows under a superb frieze showing fruit and flowers, the work of Wren ▲ *171, 174.*

THE GUILDHALL ★

The Guildhall has been the seat of municipal power since 1192. Construction of the present building began in 1411 and was practically complete in 1439. Its cost was defrayed by the guilds. Of the 15th-century fabric, largely destroyed in the Great Fire of 1666 ● *40* and in December 1940, there remain only the porch, the walls of the hall, and the crypts. The façade into which the medieval porch is set was altered by George Dance the Younger in 1788.

THE HALL. Sir Giles Gilbert Scott rebuilt the roof and ceiling of the hall in stone (for the arches) and steel. The walls are decorated with the arms of all the Livery Companies and the standards of the twelve principal ones. The names of the Lord Mayors and the arms of the sovereigns are represented in the windows.

THE CRYPTS. There are two crypts beneath the Guildhall: the later one, on the eastern side, with nave and side-aisles separated by graceful pillars of Purbeck marble, dates from the beginning of the 15th century. The one on the western side is probably from the late 13th century, and in spite of the fine vaulting supported by heavy octagonal pillars, is in an altogether more primitive style.

THE LIBRARY. The Guildhall is fortunate to have a magnificent library, founded in 1423 by a bequest in the will of Richard Whittington. It was the first public library, but it was seized in 1549 by the Duke of Somerset. It was restored in 1828 and opened to the public in 1873, and houses the finest collection of artifacts, prints and maps of London, as well as documents relating to the office of Lord Mayor. It also contains one of the most valuable collections of clocks in the world. In 1974 a new library was opened in the west wing.

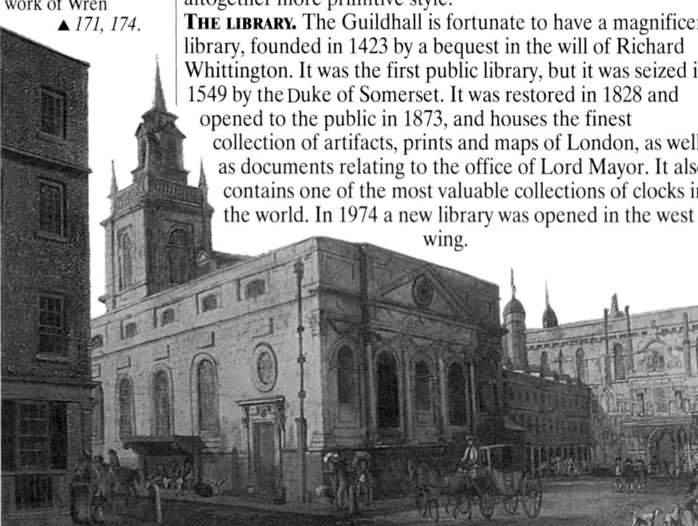

St Lawrence Jewry

St Lawrence Jewry is opposite the Guildhall, within the ancient Jewish quarter from which it gets its name. **The official church of the Corporation of London.** The Lord Mayor and aldermen all have their own pews, and there is a chapel consecrated to the Commonwealth commemorating the part played by the City merchants in the creation of the empire. The original 13th-century church was destroyed in the Great Fire and replaced with a new one to Wren's design between 1670 and 1687. The interior was again destroyed in 1940 and restored by Cecil Brown, who altered it slightly to create more space.

St Mary Woolnoth ★

At the corner of Lombard Street and King William Street is St Mary Woolnoth. The church antedates the Norman Conquest, and was rebuilt by William the Conqueror. Wren ▲ *171, 174* was content to patch up the damage it sustained in the Great Fire; in 1716 the work of reconstruction was given to one of his pupils, Hawksmoor ▲ *311*, who in ten years built the most original church in all the City. The Baroque elegance of the interior is a delight, with four rows of three slender Corinthian pillars forming a square. Among the monuments are those of Edward Lloyd ▲ *153*, founder of the famous insurance company, and John Newton, a former slave trader who repented and preached here.

Mansion House

Mansion House stands at the financial heart of the City. The work of George Dance the Elder, it is a heavy building of Portland stone in Palladian style. Its façade bears a portico of six immense Corinthian columns on a rusticated base. On top is a pediment carved with allegorical figures of London and the Thames. At the end of the 18th century the building was altered by George Dance the Younger, who raised the inside staircase and redecorated the Egyptian Hall (the Lord Mayor's reception room) in Roman style. Barrel vaulting allowed the ceiling to be lowered, and high windows and carved niches were added.

St Stephen Walbrook

The church of St Stephen, built by Wren between 1672 and 1679, seems like a sketch for St Paul's Cathedral ▲ *171*.

Watery pageants
Sometimes the new Lord Mayor used to make his way from the Lord Mayor's Show to Westminster by barge in a colorful display, recalling the pageantry at Venice in the ceremonial wedding of the Doge to the sea.

The Lord Mayor's residence
The palace of the Mansion House was built between 1739 and 1753 on the site of Stocks Market, a fish and meat market started in the 13th century at the end of Poultry. Dance the Elder had to cope with the problems such a site presented. The Lord Mayor's associates and officers work in the Mansion House, and one of the two City courts is held there. In the cellars are ten prison cells for men and one for women (known as the "birdcage"). The suffragette Emmeline Pankhurst was imprisoned here.

Interior of St Stephen Walbrook
The rectangular space, divided by four rows of pillars into five aisles, supports a cupola with a lantern on top. Light comes from three different sources: the lantern, the east-facing windows and those of the nave.

Ingots in the Bank of England
The bank continues to hold the country's gold reserves in its strongrooms.

A City street at the turn of the century
This photograph is an illustration (showing the Mansion House and Cheapside) from the time when the City was still the undisputed financial center of the world.

The Bank of England
By stages, Soane finally completed the bank's neo-classical building. Behind the large blank wall decorated with Corinthian columns are the Stock Office (1792), the Rotunda (1796) and the Dividend Office (1818–23), showing how light and graceful neo-classical design can be. In the bank's museum is a model showing the originality of Soane's design.

The City

Built on the site of Roman London, the City of London was largely destroyed in World War Two and since the 1950's has presented an ever-changing face to the world. New buildings erected during the 1950's have given way to ultra-modern blocks of glass and steel which have been put up by property developers cheek by jowl with the few carefully preserved "listed" buildings.

The Bank of England ★

A national bank enabling the government to raise money as it needed to was conceived by a Scotsman, William Paterson, in order to fund William of Orange's war against Louis XIV of France. It came into existence in 1694. Then, in 1766, Prime Minister Pitt the Elder placed the bank directly under government control. A law passed in 1844 divided the bank into two, separating its note-issuing function from its general banking functions and its responsibility for guarding the country's financial reserves.
"The Old Lady of Threadneedle Street". What the playwright and politician Sheridan called "The Old Lady of Threadneedle Street" was nationalized in 1946. It is the bankers' bank, overseeing the highly complicated British banking system which was first laid down in the 18th century (with clearing houses that exchange checks and bills, and accepting houses, or merchant banks). It is run by a board of governors who are chosen by the crown, and is the only bank in England with the right to issue notes.
Soane's building. The bank was originally housed in the Mercers' Hall, then in the Grocers' Hall in Poultry, and in 1734 it finally moved to Threadneedle Street. In 1788 Pitt the Younger entrusted the building of new premises to John Soane ▲ *166*, but producing a practicable design proved to be fraught with problems due to the lack of ground space. In addition the fear of riots led to the construction of a solid blank wall on its exterior. The building was greatly enlarged and altered between the wars by Sir Herbert Baker, who retained only a few of Soane's architectural features, such as the outside wall.

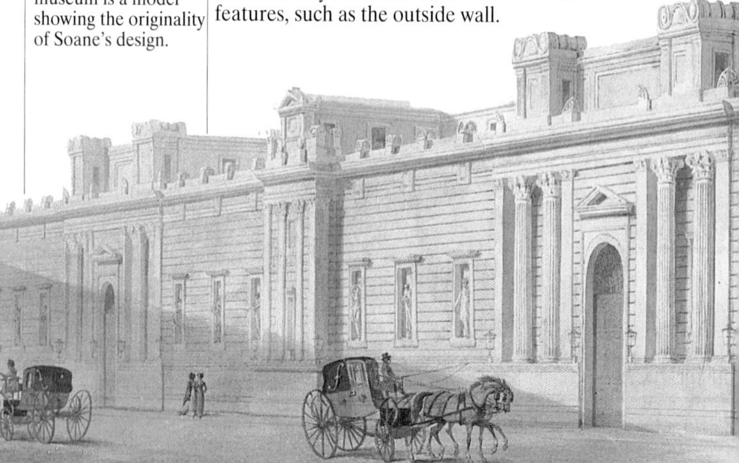

THE ROYAL EXCHANGE

Opposite the Bank of England is the Royal Exchange, the oldest mercantile institution in the City, founded by Sir Thomas Gresham. The Exchange, built on Cornhill by Flemish craftsmen using materials imported from Flanders, opened for business in 1567. Modeled on those at Antwerp and Venice, the Exchange consists of a piazza surrounded by galleries with dealers' premises above. It was officially opened in 1570 by Queen Elizabeth I, who granted permission for the Exchange to call itself "Royal". The building was destroyed in the Great Fire, replaced by a larger one designed by Jarman which was again destroyed in 1838, and finally rebuilt by Sir William Tite to be officially opened by Queen Victoria in 1844. It is in neo-classical style, and its façade has a portico of eight large Corinthian columns supporting a carved pediment. The figure in the center represents Commerce. It ceased trading in 1939. From the 1980's it was used by the London International Financial Futures Exchange (LIFFE) for the sale of forward transactions, then underwent renovation and was reopened in 2001 as a high-class shopping complex.

WELLINGTON'S STATUE. In front of the Royal Exchange is an equestrian statue of the duke of Wellington ▲ *246*, cast in bronze from French cannons captured at the Battle of Waterloo. It was unveiled in 1844 in the presence of the duke, and is the work of Sir Francis Chantrey.

"DIVIDEND DAY"
This picture of 1859 depicts Dividend Day, one of the four annual Quarter Days when stockholders on the London Exchange receive their dividends.

THOMAS GRESHAM
The son of a merchant who became Lord Mayor, Thomas Gresham (1519–79) was the first to lead a double career – in the service of the crown and amassing great wealth as a merchant in his own right. While working as a "king's merchant" on the Exchange in Antwerp, he conceived the idea of building a similar establishment in London for the merchants of Lombard Street. His emblem of a gold grasshopper with a crown still adorns the façade.

THE STOCK EXCHANGE

The Stock Exchange came into being to supply capital needed by the share-issuing companies and the demands of rapidly developing commerce and industry.

THE AGE OF COFFEE HOUSES. Up until the 17th century shares were bought and sold outside the Royal Exchange. But the dealers within were bothered by the noise the brokers made and chased them away. The latter shifted their business to the coffee houses of Change Alley, between Lombard Street and Cornhill. There, at JONATHAN'S COFFEE HOUSE, which opened around 1680, or at GARRAWAY'S, which opened ten years earlier, prospective buyers would go to see how the shares were moving, and stockbrokers dealt with their clients. Then in 1773, when Jonathan's ceased to be available, they opened their own premises in Threadneedle Street and called it the Stock Exchange. For sixpence per day, anyone was free to deal there. In 1801 a group of disaffected brokers built a new exchange in Capel Court that housed more than five hundred members, soon including most of those from the former premises. Expansion necessitated a new building in 1888 and again in 1972: there are now several thousand members of the Stock Exchange.

BROKERS AND JOBBERS. Apart from the admission of women to the floor in 1973, the workings of the Stock Exchange had hardly changed since the 18th century, until October 1986, when the "Big Bang" removed the distinction between *jobbers* and *brokers*. Until then, its members had been of two kinds: jobbers sold stocks, making their profit from the difference between the buying price and the selling price, though they were not allowed to sell stocks directly to clients outside the Exchange.

EXPERIENCING THE CITY LIFE
It is best to explore the City on a weekday during office hours, when the streets are swarming with up to half a million men and women who work there. In the evenings the district is deserted. Gone is the old Victorian look of the place that dominated until the 1950's. The bowler-hatted "city gent", with black waistcoat, striped trousers, white shirt, stiff collar and tightly rolled umbrella is a thing of the past. There is now a substantial proportion of women in the workforce, which was for long a masculine preserve. Customs have also changed: people now call each other by their Christian names in the office, and lunch in a wine or sandwich bar.

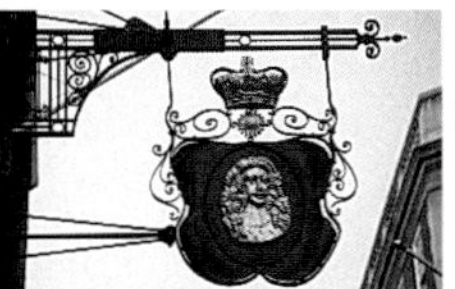

Accordingly, for each deal, prospective buyers needed a broker who, in exchange for a fixed commission, negotiated with the jobber.

The private banks. The majority of the large private banks have their headquarters within the City. In 1930 the Midland Bank (founded in Birmingham in 1836) moved to an imposing Portland stone building that had been commissioned from Sir Edwin Lutyens (1869–1944). Its construction was not completed until 1936. You have to stand well back to glimpse the dome on its top, which resembles one that Lutyens had earlier put on the Viceroy's House in New Delhi. Nearby are the head offices of the National Westminster Bank, a company formed in 1968 from the amalgamation of three other banks. The main building of the so-called "NatWest" is its 600-foot tower between Bishopsgate and Old Broad Street, beside the City of London Club which was founded in 1832 by a group of wealthy bankers. The contrast between the latter's Palladian exterior (built in 1833–4) and the fifty-two-story tower block beside it has with some justification been called "architectural schizophrenia".

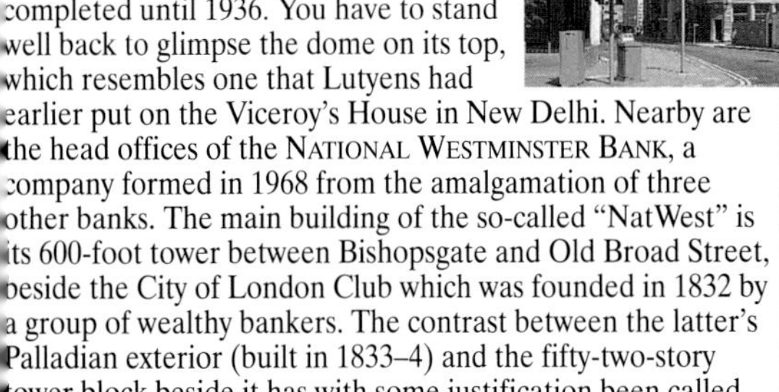

Lloyd's: a cathedral of glass and metal
The new building which opened in 1986 is a testament to the company's modern approach to business. Designed by Richard Rogers, co-designer of the famous Pompidou Center in Paris, it is a glass and metal rectangle with six satellite towers, built round a central atrium culminating in a vast arched roof 190 feet high. In 1991 Lloyd's had 26,500 members. In its museum can be seen the Underwriting Room and the *Lutine*, a bell which is still rung to announce either bad or good news according to whether it is struck once or twice.

Lloyd's ★

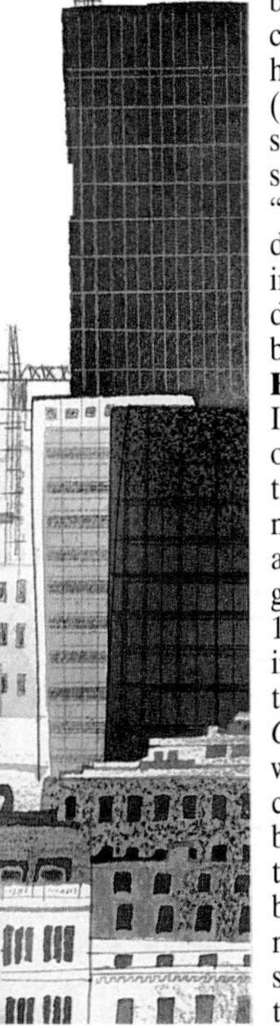

Lloyd's is not an insurance company but a stock exchange for insurance contracts. Two types of people work here: the Lloyd's members (underwriters) have the sole right of selling risk insurance, and the annual subscribers (Lloyd's names) are "invited" to stand surety. Contracts are drawn up between a company or individual and a member, who then distributes both the dividends and risks between a number of subscribers.

From an inn to Leadenhall Street. In the late 1680's, Edward Lloyd opened a tavern in Abchurch Lane at the corner of Lombard Street, where merchants used to buy and sell ships and underwrite their insurance, a growing market in the 18th century. In 1769 a group of underwriters primarily interested in maritime insurance left the tavern to open the *New Lloyd's Coffee House* in Pope's Head Alley, where ships were bought and sold "by candle" (in a candle auction the last bid before a small candle expires secures the property). The coffee house soon became too small and in 1771 Lloyd's moved to the Royal Exchange, where it stayed until 1928. From there it transferred to Leadenhall Street.

"Lloyd's Coffee House"
The origins of Lloyd's are now a legend, and have grown over the years since Edward Lloyd first opened his coffee house for business in the late 17th century.

THE CITY'S OWN MARKET
The present Leadenhall Market was built in 1881 by Sir Horace Jones.

The metal arches painted maroon and cream, the glass panels and the central cupola all contribute to its charm. High-quality produce from here goes to supply the banquets of the Livery Companies ▲ *146*. Now the market's cafés, wine bars and sandwich bars do flourishing business at lunchtime.

LEADENHALL STREET

The corn and hay markets were here in the Middle Ages. Leadenhall Market is on the north side of the street, an odd place in the heart of the City. The City acquired the land at the end of the 13th century, and later the right to open a market here, which has continued to the present day.

ST ANDREW UNDERSHAFT. This Gothic church, which has undergone much alteration, contains the tomb of John Stow (1525–1605). A Cornhill tailor turned publisher, he was an avid collector of manuscripts and was the first real chronicler and historian of London. On his death his widow placed a terracotta bust of her husband holding a quill pen in St Andrew's: in 1905 the guild of Merchant Taylors replaced it. Each year a ceremony takes place in the presence of the Lord Mayor, when a new goose-feather pen is put in place and the old one presented, together with a copy of *Stow's Survey of London* (first published in 1598), to the schoolchild who has written the best essay on London. Hans Holbein the Younger may also be buried here. Nearby is the SWISS RE TOWER a tubular skyscraper built in a series of glass spirals by Norman Foster and partners. The "gherkin", as it has been nicknamed, was built on the site of the former Edwardian Baltic Exchange, which had been irreparably damaged by an IRA bomb in 1992.

THE LEADENHALL MARKET TRADESMEN
After the Great Fire, Leadenhall Street became a general market selling meat, game, fish, fruit, vegetables and flowers.

CHEAPSIDE AND CORNHILL

In the Middle Ages Cheapside was one of the most important streets in London. Its many fine buildings were completely destroyed in the Great Fire ▲ *40*. London's principal market used to be here, a place of ceaseless activity, always with plenty to see, whether a uneral, state procession or even a public xecution. The Cheapside pillory was otorious. Different sections of the narket specialized in different types of roduce, and have given their names to he streets that cross it. Bread Street was vhere the bakers were, Milk Street was he dairy produce market, ironmongers nce worked in Ironmonger Lane, and oldsmiths in Goldsmith Street.

HE STREET OF PUBLISHERS. The grain market was on Ornhill, the highest point of the City. It also boasted a otorious prison and pillory. It was on Cornhill too that Thomas Guy (philanthropist and founder of Guy's Hospital) ad his bookshop and printed Bibles. From 1816 to 1868 the irm of Smith and Elder were at number 32, publishers of Thackeray, Mrs Gaskell and the Brontë sisters, and Leslie Stephen (Thackeray's son-in-law and father of Virginia Woolf ▲ *114*) was a frequent visitor. Now banking and insurance are he businesses of Cornhill. At the corner of Lime Street, East ndia House once stood, home of the East India Company 1600–1862). Until the Indian Mutiny of 1857 the Company njoyed the monopoly of Indian trade and acted as the overnment's agent there.

ORNHILL CHURCHES. Two churches on the south side of Ornhill are worth visiting: St Michael's, the tower of which urvived the Great Fire, was rebuilt by Hawksmoor 1715–22 n neo-Gothic style; and St Peter-upon-Cornhill, where Mendelssohn played the organ in 1840 and 1842.

THE GREAT HIGHROAD OF CHEAPSIDE
Rebuilt in 1720 after the Great Fire, the new Cheapside was said to be "a beautiful wide street, bordered with tall houses".

OMBARD STREET

After the expulsion of the Jews in 1290, the Lombards, who ad already settled in this street in the previous century, took ver the business of banking.

HE BANKERS' STREET. Nearly all the large British banks are ased in Lombard Street, and foreign banks have their main ondon agencies there. Some have their roots way back in the ast: Barclay's, for example, developed from a goldsmith's usiness set up in Lombard Street around 1694. Between 736 and 1896 the firm of Barclay took over numerous other

ALEXANDER POPE (1688–1744)
The great poet lived in Lombard Street as a child. This was where his father worked as a linen-draper.

FENCHURCH STREET

BILLINGSGATE MARKET
This has been in existence since the 13th century, and in 1699 a royal charter granted it the monopoly of selling fish. Before World War Two 400 tons of fish used to change hands at Billingsgate every day.

A MEMORIAL TO THE GREAT FIRE
This column of Portland stone has 331 steps leading up to a balcony, with good views over the Thames and the London skyline.

banks, some of which had formerly been goldsmiths themselves. Barclay's presented to the City the fountain of Poseidon in George Yard, the work of Sir Charles Wheeler.
CHARLES DICKENS' FIRST ROMANCE. In 1829 the seventeen-year-old Dickens fell in love in Lombard Street. He was living at number 2, near the bank of Smith, Fayne & Smith, and the object of his affections was Maria Beadnell, the daughter of an employee there.

FENCHURCH STREET

This is a continuation of Lombard Street. Its name may come from the old hay market (from the French word *foin*) in Gracechurch Street.
FOUNTAIN HOUSE. The fountain that stands at the corner of the street was erected 1954–7. It is a copy of the one at Lever House in New York.
LLOYD'S REGISTER OF SHIPPING. This is at number 71, an Art Nouveau building decorated with columns, turrets and friezes. This is where all documentation concerning merchant shipping is registered and classified. Differences had arisen over the standards of classification, and at the end of the 18th century this led a group of shipowners to set up their own organization. Since 1834 the ties between the insurance company and Lloyd's Register have strengthened.
PLANTATION HOUSE. The Rubber Exchange and the London Commodity Exchange are housed in this building constructed between 1934 and 1937 on a large quadrilateral set among narrow lanes. In nearby Mincing Lane is the neo-Georgian Clothworkers' Hall that was opened in 1958.

AROUND THE MONUMENT

THE MONUMENT. Christopher Wren and Robert Hooke submitted several designs for a memorial to the Great

Fire ● *40* before building this tall Doric column, 202 feet high, which is the precise distance from the base of the monument to the place where the fire started in Pudding Lane. Opened in 1677, it was erected when Parliament had decided to commemorate the Great Firc in suitable fashion. On the monument's pedestal are four panels which describe the extent of the disaster and also tell the story of the rebuilding of London. If the dry weather and a strong wind were thought to be the prime causes of the fire, other explanations were offered in the 1670's, when there was powerful anti-Catholic feeling: agents of the pope were blamed, as was the baker in whose shop it began. The Latin inscription on the north side of the pedestal was rounded off in 1681 with a few words denouncing the fanatical Catholics. When James II ascended the throne these words were removed, only to be restored when William of Orange became king. They were finally taken off in 1830 when the Catholics were at last given their civil rights.

BILLINGSGATE MARKET. "Each morning the hall in Billingsgate takes in its scaly harvest . . . there are always salmon for Belgravia and herrings for Whitechapel", commented the 19th-century French writer Jules Vallès. Billingsgate, once the biggest fish market in London, was famous for its smell, its noise and its foul-mouthed fishwives. After centuries of activity, the market finally closed in 1982. A new fish market has since opened at West India Dock on the Isle of Dogs, keeping at least the name of Billingsgate.

AROUND CANNON STREET

In the Middle Ages Cannon Street was the district where candlemakers lived: the street's name is a corruption of its earlier name of Candlewick Street. Most of its interesting buildings were destroyed in the Blitz, such as the fine 18th-century Cordwainers' Hall, which stood on the site of St Paul's Garden. In the wall of the Bank of China is the London Stone, probably a Roman milestone, which stood on the other side of the road in the wall of St Swithin's church, until that beautiful Wren building was destroyed in 1941.

ST MARY ABCHURCH ★. This church, begun in 1681, is the most graceful of all Wren churches and the one that has best withstood the ravages of time. Square in plan, it is flanked by a red-brick and stone tower topped with a perforated lantern and an elegant lead spire. The square nave, without side-aisles, is underneath a cupola pierced with oval windows that sits on eight arches. The cupola was painted by William Snow. The church also has a reredos, the only one that can be attributed with confidence to Grinling Gibbons ▲ *173*.

ST MARY ALDERMARY. Near Queen Victoria Street is the oldest church consecrated to the Virgin, rebuilt in 1681–2. Here Wren appears to have experimented with the Gothic Perpendicular style ● *70* almost to the point of parody, using fan vaulting with surprising additions.

OLD LONDON BRIDGE
This was built on the site of an ancient Roman bridge. Peter the Bridgemaster began work on the first one in 1176; it was the first stone bridge to be built in Europe since Roman times, and London's only bridge until 1749. Set on nineteen piles with arches of unequal size, it was lined with houses and shops. In 1758 the sheer weight of traffic necessitated its demolition, and a new bridge was built between 1823 and 1831, the work of John Rennie. The present bridge dates from 1973.

ST MARY-LE-BOW (1670–80)
This church, restored 1956–64 by Laurence King, has the most beautiful porch and spire that Wren ever built. The porch, inspired by one of the entrances to Mansart's Hôtel de Conti, is adorned with Doric columns. The graceful way in which the round bell-tower rises from its square base lends the church a unique elegance. It is much loved by all who live in the City. A true Cockney must be born within hearing of Bow Bells. It is one of the thirteen churches that come under the direct jurisdiction of the archbishop of Canterbury.

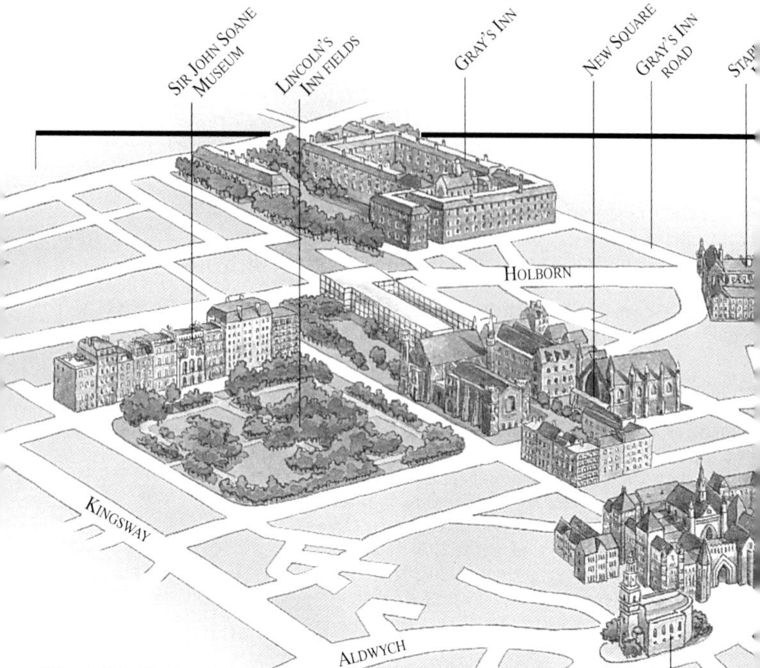

Sir John Soane Museum
Lincoln's Inn Fields
Gray's Inn
New Square
Gray's Inn Road
Holborn
Kingsway
Aldwych
St Clement Dane's

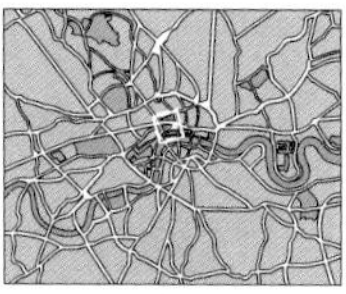

One day

◆ **F** A3-A4

Fleet Street

Fleet Street runs east from the Royal Courts of Justice as far as Ludgate Circus. It takes its name from the Fleet river, which used to follow the route where Farringdon Road now stands. At that time traffic had to cross over the Fleet Bridge in order to reach the cathedral.

The first press barons. Fleet Street's associations with printing go back to the end of the 15th century, when the pioneer publisher Wynkyn de Worde moved here from Westminster. Between 1500 and his death in 1535, from his premises *At the Sign of the Sun*, he printed and published hundreds of books, many on legal and religious subjects (the Inns of Court and Blackfriars Monastery were both nearby). Other printers working in the area included Richard Pynson, printer to the king after 1508, whose office was at the corner of Fleet Street and Chancery Lane. In 1530 Sir Thomas More's nephew William Rastell began printing and selling books from premises in St Bride's churchyard, bringing out an edition of his uncle's works in 1557. It was clear that the publishing

"Fleet River" This painting by Samuel Scott (1702–72) shows the mouth of the Fleet River as seen from the Thames. On the left is the spire of Wren's St Bride's Church ● *171*, ▲ *174*.

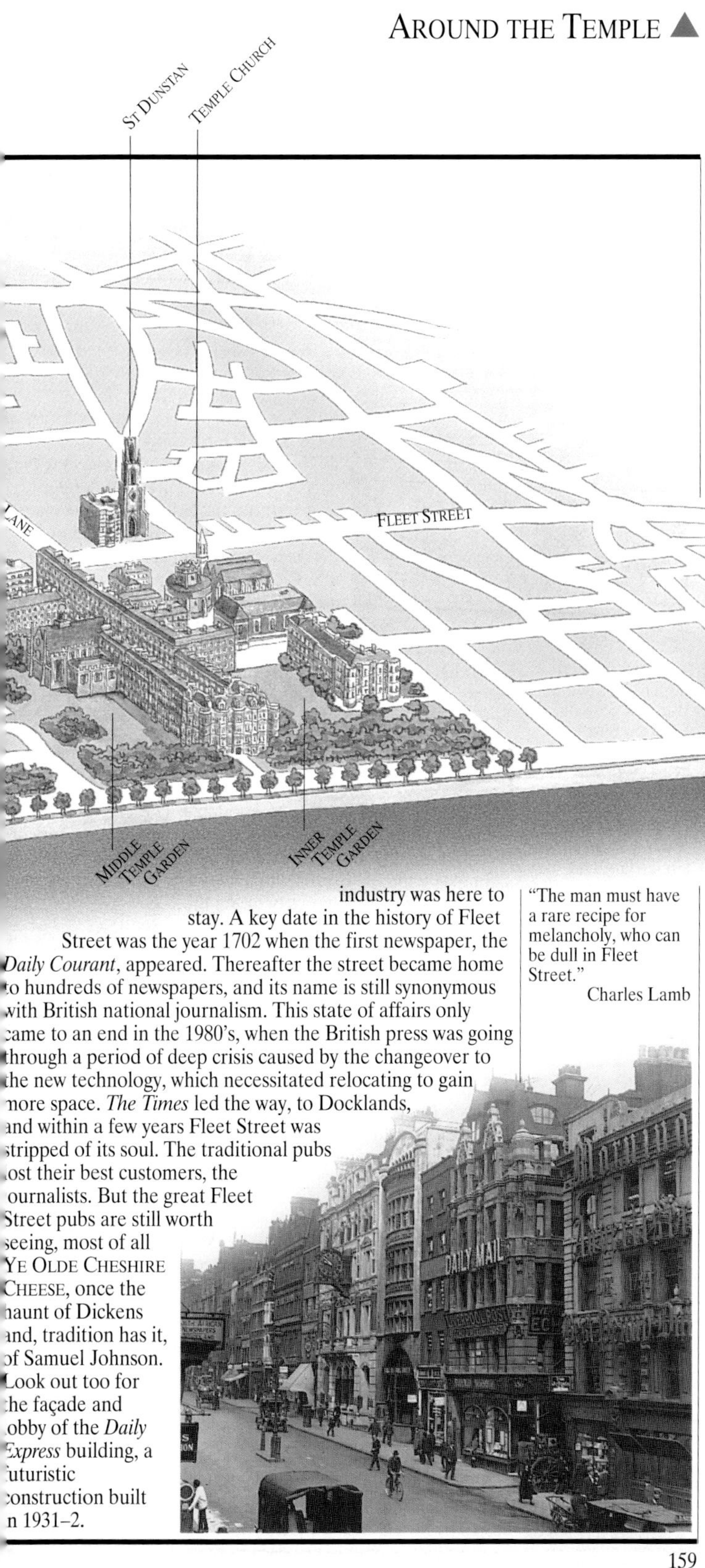

industry was here to stay. A key date in the history of Fleet Street was the year 1702 when the first newspaper, the *Daily Courant*, appeared. Thereafter the street became home to hundreds of newspapers, and its name is still synonymous with British national journalism. This state of affairs only came to an end in the 1980's, when the British press was going through a period of deep crisis caused by the changeover to the new technology, which necessitated relocating to gain more space. *The Times* led the way, to Docklands, and within a few years Fleet Street was stripped of its soul. The traditional pubs lost their best customers, the journalists. But the great Fleet Street pubs are still worth seeing, most of all Ye Olde Cheshire Cheese, once the haunt of Dickens and, tradition has it, of Samuel Johnson. Look out too for the façade and lobby of the *Daily Express* building, a futuristic construction built in 1931–2.

"The man must have a rare recipe for melancholy, who can be dull in Fleet Street."
Charles Lamb

ST CLEMENT DANE'S

There has been a church of St Clement on this site at the eastern end of the Strand since Harold, king of Wessex (known as "Harefoot"), was buried there in the 11th century. At that time a stone church was constructed to replace the original wooden building. Rebuilt in 1682 by Christopher Wren, it was his only design to incorporate an apse. In 1719 it was altered by the architect James Gibbs, who raised the height of the belfry and added a domed vestry.

"ORANGES AND LEMONS". Sometimes you can hear the bells of St Clement Dane's chime the notes of the old rhyme: "Oranges and lemons say the bells of St Clement's". This tuneful little verse imitates the bell-peals of the old London churches. There is a tradition that once a year after service the children of St Clement Dane's primary school each receive an orange and a lemon.

THE RAF CHURCH Damaged in World War Two, St Clement Dane's was restored by W.A.S. Lloyd between 1955 and 1958 thanks to contributions from the Royal Air Force. A war memorial lists airmen killed on active service. Together with the insignia of the various units and squadrons and other memorabilia, it serves as a reminder that the church is now dedicated to the RAF.

RUGBY AND THE RECTOR. Another tradition claims that William Webb Ellis, rector here in the 19th century, while a pupil at Rugby School was the boy who picked up and ran with the ball during a game of football and so originated the game of rugby.

TEMPLE BAR

From 1191 to 1319 the City of London ▲ *170*, enclosed within walls, asserted its independence from the neighboring City of Westminster, the seat of royal power. Temple Bar, situated just outside the old fortifications, has been one of the boundaries between the two cities since 1222. Originally it was just a chain between two posts barring the entrance to Fleet Street; in 1351 a great gate with a jailhouse in its upper part was built. This was replaced at the start of the 1670's with a design by Wren. In 1877–8 traffic flow necessitated its demolition, and in 1880 the present memorial was erected in its place.

FELON'S GATE. Until 1772 the heads of executed criminals were exhibited at Temple Bar, near a pillory where, among others, Daniel Defoe, the author of *Robinson Crusoe*, passed a nasty few minutes in 1703.

TEMPLE BAR TODAY Horace Jones' monument of 1880 is surmounted by a dragon, the symbol of the City of London.

AROUND THE TEMPLE

A little to the west, between Fleet Street and the River Thames, is the Temple, a haven of tranquillity. The Templars, established in London in the first half of the 12th century, were granted this piece of land on the bank of the river. There they built a church, consecrated in 1185, and then a monastery. Several monarchs, among them John Lackland, have since stayed there. After the Dissolution of the monasteries between 1536 and 1539, the Temple became crown property, and in 1609 James I granted the land in perpetuity to the members of the MIDDLE and INNER TEMPLES. After the Second World War it was rebuilt to a design by Sir Edward Maufe partly in neo-Georgian style.

The Inns of Court. Lawyers and law schools have been concentrated in the area of Temple Bar since the Middle Ages. At first, lawyers who came to London for the sessions of the Royal Courts of Justice used to put up in local taverns, the Inns. The schools, also called Inns, were founded around the 13th century when the need arose to teach the subject, which was not then a university discipline. Studies took seven or eight years, and faculty members, lawyers, probationers and students were all fed and lodged there, minimizing contact with the outside world. Of the ten inns that existed in the 14th century, only four remain: LINCOLN'S INN (1422), the MIDDLE and INNER TEMPLES (1501 and 1505), and GRAY'S INN (1569). Each of these Inns has its own hall (where students are obliged to eat a certain number of dinners to qualify for call to the Bar), its own church, library, cloister and gardens, all going to make up a little world apart.

TEMPLE CHURCH ★

● 67

The Temple Church, all that remains from the age of the Templars, is rare among English churches in having a circular plan modeled on the Church of the Holy Sepulcher in Jerusalem. It was built in the transitional period between the Norman and Gothic styles, with elements of each side by side.

Paper Buildings of the Inner Temple
In the southern part of the Inner Temple, these were designed in the 19th century by the Smirkes, father and son.

Samuel Johnson
17 Gough Square, a late 17th-century house, was Dr Johnson's home from 1746 to 1759. Here he compiled his *Dictionary of the English Language*, containing definitions of more than 40,000 words and with 114,000 quotations. The house is now a museum, where a first edition of the dictionary can be seen.

The Temple Church rotunda
The Temple Church rotunda is supported by columns of Purbeck marble and houses the stone tombs of nine Templars, dating from the 12th and 13th centuries. There are figures lying with their feet crossed, carved from Purbeck marble on top of these: (above) the effigy of William Marshal, first earl of Pembroke and brother of King John Lackland, who died in 1219.

TEMPLE CHURCH
Temple Church has been altered many times. Above left is the exterior as it was after 19th-century alteration; above right shows the roof structure after damage sustained during World War Two.

Between 1220 and 1240 the church was completed with a Gothic choir, with nave and side-aisles of the same height. The building has been altered many times, notably at the end of the 17th century by Wren ▲ *171*, who designed the reredos carved by William Emmett in 1682. Removed in 1840 by Sydney Smirke, it was returned to its place in the post-war restoration.

MIDDLE TEMPLE ★

MIDDLE TEMPLE GATEWAY. The brick entrance, built in 1684 by Roger North, lawyer and bencher (senior member) of the Inn, has four Ionic pilasters and a pediment fronting on to Middle Temple Lane.
MIDDLE TEMPLE HALL. The Tudor-style Middle Temple Hall (1562–73) is the main building of the Middle Temple, just above FOUNTAIN COURT. Its ornate carved-oak roof in Perpendicular style ● *68* is the finest extant. At the end of the room is an Elizabethan rood screen with a gallery above supported by caryatids.
TWO TABLES. The resplendent "benchers' " table, presented by Queen Elizabeth I and made from Windsor Forest oak trees, is a prominent exhibit in the Middle Temple. Nearby is a smaller table known as the Cupboard, on which newly qualified lawyers sign their names when they become members of the Inn. Legend has it the Cupboard is made of hatch-covers from the ship in which Sir Francis Drake sailed round the world, the GOLDEN HIND: Drake was a member of

ROYAL COURTS OF JUSTICE
These are usually known as the law courts. The task of designing the new buildings was given to George Edmund Street (1824–81). Work was begun on the new courtrooms in 1874, and they were duly opened in 1882 by Queen Victoria. They represent what is probably the most extreme example of the neo-Gothic style that was so dear to the Victorians, at the start of its decline.

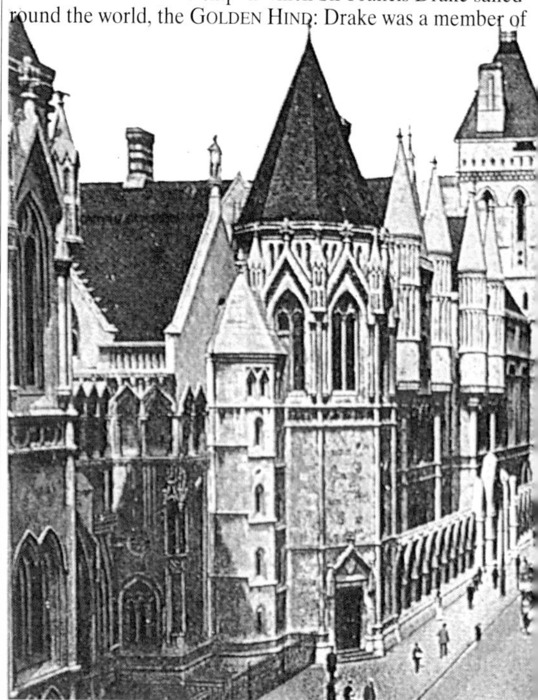

the Inn. For a long time the hall was used as a theater: it was here in 1601 that Queen Elizabeth I attended the first performance of *Twelfth Night*.

The library. Rebuilt in neo-Georgian style in 1956 the library possesses, in addition to a fine pair of globes made by Molyneux in 1600, an important collection of works on American law.

The Wars of the Roses. Middle Temple Gardens, to the south of Fountain Court, was the birthplace of the Wars of the Roses, a civil war that ravaged England from 1455 to 1485 and inspired two of Shakespeare's tragedies, *Henry IV* and *Richard III*. It is here, in *Henry IV*, that Somerset picks a red rose, the symbol of the House of Lancaster, and Warwick picks a white one, the symbol of the House of York.

Window display of a law bookshop in New Square.

Inner Temple ★

As there are few historic buildings remaining in the Inner Temple, which was badly damaged in the Blitz, go down King's Bench Walk with its view over the Thames and Inner Temple Gardens. Numbers 4 and 5 were built in 1677–8 to designs by Christopher Wren. Number 7 dates from 1685, number 8 (1782) was the home of novelist George Moore, and adventure-story writer Rider Haggard lived at number 13.

The Tudor Inner Temple Gateway. Opening on to Fleet Street, it dates from 1610, and in spite of reconstruction at the beginning of the 19th century, remains one of the best-preserved buildings of the period in London.

Wigs and gowns
Judges and lawyers wear these wigs in court. Barristers wear black gowns too, made of silk if they are Queen's Counsel (senior barristers). High Court judges wear scarlet robes.

The law courts ● *81*

The law courts are the Royal Courts of Justice. They used to be housed in Westminster Hall, until they were moved in the second half of the 19th century to be close to the Inns of Court. The brick façade skirts Bell Yard as far as the

The law courts
Looking up Fleet Street from St Clement Dane's. Middle Temple and Inner Temple are behind the houses on the righthand side of the picture.

LINCOLN'S INN
Its name comes from the Earls of Lincoln, owners of the land whose arms – a lion rampant gules – are on both buildings.

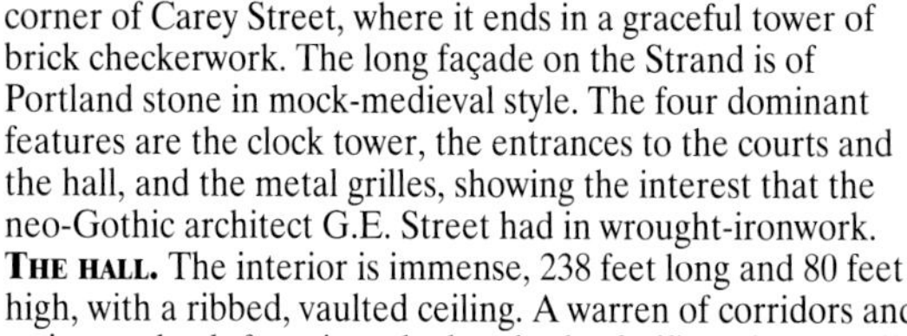

corner of Carey Street, where it ends in a graceful tower of brick checkerwork. The long façade on the Strand is of Portland stone in mock-medieval style. The four dominant features are the clock tower, the entrances to the courts and the hall, and the metal grilles, showing the interest that the neo-Gothic architect G.E. Street had in wrought-ironwork.
THE HALL. The interior is immense, 238 feet long and 80 feet high, with a ribbed, vaulted ceiling. A warren of corridors and staircases leads from it to the hundreds of offices that are all part of the thirty-five courts of the Supreme Court of Justice.

ST DUNSTAN-IN-THE-WEST

Leaving Johnson's Court in the direction of Fleet Street, you pass in front of this octagonal church, built between 1829 and 1833, where Catholic, Anglican and Orthodox services are held. It is an early example of the 19th-century Gothic Reviva ● *80*, replacing an earlier 12th-century church demolished in the widening of Fleet Street ▲ *158*.
THE GIANTS' CLOCK. A token of thanksgiving erected in 1671 by members of the parish who escaped damage in the Great Fire, this was the first public clock in London to have a minute hand and two dials. On the quarters of the hour, two giants strike a bell: the clock was much admired by David Copperfield, the hero of Dickens' ▲ *106* eponymous novel.

STAPLE INN AND LINCOLN'S INN
Staple Inn (top) and Lincoln's Inn (above) were established in the 14th century. Since 1884 the former has been the Institute of Actuaries, and the latter is an important barristers' college.

CHANCERY LANE

Chancery Lane is on the right as you leave the church. Its name dates back to 1377, after Edward III had bestowed the CONVERTS' HOUSE (a refuge for Jews who had renounced their faith and their money) on the Lord Chancellor. This wa demolished in 1896, and on its site stands the PUBLIC RECORI OFFICE, the British national archives. The museum contains a wealth of rare documents such as the 1129 *Pipe Roll*, medieva records, state papers before 1782, legal archives, volumes of the *Domesday Book* (a land census ordered by William the Conqueror), a copy of the *Magna Carta* dated 1225, Shakespeare's will, and many more treasures.

LINCOLN'S INN ★

Undamaged in the Second World War, Lincoln's Inn is the only one of the four Inns of Court to have preserved its original character. The huge entrance in Chancery Lane, with its arch and square towers, dates from 1518. It opens on to OLD BUILDINGS, dating from the Tudor period and built of brick except for the chapel. It forms an irregular square.

FAMOUS ALUMNI. Cromwell studied here, and among its other famous members the Inn boasts Sir Thomas More (1478–1535), who in his role as bencher contributed toward the construction of the Chancery Lane entrance; John Donne, chaplain to the Inn, the writer on jurisprudence Jeremy Bentham, and the founder of Pennsylvania, William Penn.

THE OLD HALL ★. On the west side and built between 1485 and 1492, the hall contains a large Hogarth painting *Paul before Felix* (1748). The arch-braced roof, carved wooden screen, panelling and bay windows are impressive. Dickens set the suit of Jarndyce v. Jarndyce from *Bleak House* in Old Hall.

THE CHAPEL. The stone façade is in Gothic style and was built between 1619 and 1623. The foundation stone was laid by John Donne; another poet, Ben Jonson, took part in the building armed with trowel in one hand and book in the other. The chapel, with a barrel-vaulted roof and mullioned windows in Perpendicular style, has a low gallery used by students as a meeting place. Eighty Members of Parliament held a meeting there in 1659 with the intention of restoring the monarchy. It was renovated by Wren ▲ *171, 174* in 1685, by Wyatt in 1791, and in 1882 by Salter. In December there is a sung service here with lessons read by the senior judges.

LINCOLN'S INN FIELDS ★. This contains some magnificent architecture from the 17th to 19th centuries. In the 1930's the south and west sides were built to William Newton's designs.

LINDSEY HOUSE. Long thought to be the work of Inigo Jones, this house is a fine example from the Stuart period of the search for a national style of architecture, inspired by Palladio. It owes its sense of lightness to the use of brick, now covered in stucco, and tapering pilasters bearing fine Ionic capitals. The purity of design is apparent by comparison with the weighty appearance of the adjacent house, number 57–8, built around 1730 by Henry Joynes in Portland stone, and decorated with pilasters and an architrave.

LINCOLN'S INN FIELDS
In the Middle Ages there were two fields here, used by Londoners (particularly the inhabitants of Lincoln's Inn) for walks and recreation. Their owners, St John's and St Giles' Hospitals, rented them out for grazing. From the time of Queen Elizabeth I public executions were carried out here.

"A Lincoln's Inn beggar was a proverb. The whole fraternity knew the arms and liveries of every charitably disposed grandee in the neighbourhood, and as soon as his lordship's coach and six appeared, came hopping and crawling in crowds to persecute him."

Lord Macaulay, *History of England*

A barrister in Lincoln's Inn Fields.

▲ The Sir John Soane Museum

In 1790 the architect Sir John Soane (1753–1837) began to collect all manner of objects, and he spent thirty-two years building a house in Lincoln's Inn Fields to contain them. This three-story house (actually three houses converted into one) is of a complicated design and full of surprises. Preserved just as it was when Soane died, this is one of the most remarkable museums in London.

Illustration of the Corinthian order, used in Soane's Royal Academy lectures in 1819.

Library of the Sir John Soane Museum
Soane collected an astonishing number of books and manuscripts, including the entire library of Robert Adam. He also amassed a fine collection of drawings and engravings.

Sir John Soane
Under the influence of the Romantic age, this stonemason's son collected classical and Renaissance carvings and casts, fragments of Roman architecture, funeral monuments, bronzes, vases and much more besides.

his space, with a glass
ome above, creates a
ell of light in the
iddle of the house.

CTIONAL VIEW OF E DOME IN THE R JOHN SOANE USEUM ane's friend eorge Bailey did is drawing showing e collection of ssical casts ranged on three ors. The museum s remained much it was when Bailey ade this illustration in 10.

"IMAGINARY VIEW OF PUBLIC AND PRIVATE DESIGNED BY SIR JOHN SOANE." Soane's colleague J.M. Gandy drew this odd landscape of buildings designed by Soane between 1789 and 1815.

THE GARDENS OF GRAY'S INN
The gardens were a fashionable meeting place in the 17th century. Samuel Pepys liked to walk there, as did Charles Lamb, who thought them "the most beautiful gardens of the Inns of Court", and the young Charles Dickens, who at the age of fourteen was apprentice clerk to a lawyer's office there.

THE ROYAL COLLEGE OF SURGEONS. The Royal College of Surgeons is on the south side of the square. The surgeons left the Barber-surgeons in 1745 and founded their own separate institution which became a royal college in 1800. The Lincoln's Inn Fields premises, opened in 1797, were designed by George Dance Jr (1741–1825), and were superseded in 1835 by Barry's ▲ *129* building which integrated Dance's huge Ionic portico and which was again enlarged in 1888. In the college is the HUNTERIAN MUSEUM, named after the famous 18th-century Scottish surgeon. John Hunter is considered the founder of scientific surgery. Fascinated by the concept of surgical transplantation, he amassed an enormous collection of anatomical specimens for comparative study. This was acquired by the government in 1799 and gradually expanded until the Second World War, when the collection was greatly diminished in the air raids.

NEW SQUARE ★. Built at the end of the 17th century around a central lawn, New Square is just to the west of Lincoln's Inn Fields, and consists of terraced four-story houses. An archway from New Square leads to Carey Street. On the north side are STONE BUILDINGS, built in Palladian style between 1774 and 1780 by Robert Taylor. These are in sharp contrast to Philip Hardwick's brick-built neo-Tudor buildings of 1843–5: the New Hall, the Treasury and the Library. The latter, established in 1497, has seventy thousand volumes and forms an important collection of legal works. In the New Hall is an immense allegorical mural painted by G.F. Watts in 1859, in a style that mixes Pre-Raphaelite and Romantic elements.

GRAY'S INN

To the north of Lincoln's Inn is the last of the Inns of Court, Gray's Inn. During the 14th century the Inn became a hotel for lawyers and took the name of Sir Reginald de Grey, the Chief Justice of Chester, whose London residence it had formerly been. In 1594 Shakespeare (whose patron, the earl of Southampton, was a member of the Inn) gave the first performance in the hall of *The Comedy of Errors*. The interior of the hall, destroyed during World War Two and rebuilt by Sir Edward Maufe, has retained some parts dating from the 17th, 18th and the early 19th centuries. An old rood screen carved from the wood of a Spanish galleon survived the damage and is now on view. The gardens are the only ones of the four Inns of Court that are open to the public. They were a notorious dueling ground in the 17th century.

THE PHILOSOPHER'S GARDEN
The gardens are the most beautiful part of Gray's Inn. They were laid out in 1606 by Sir Francis Bacon (1561–1626), who wrote a famous essay about them. The great philosopher was first a student (1576), then a bencher (1586) and finally treasurer of Gray's Inn in 1608. It is said that he planted the catalpa tree behind number 4 Raymond Buildings.

Historical Journey

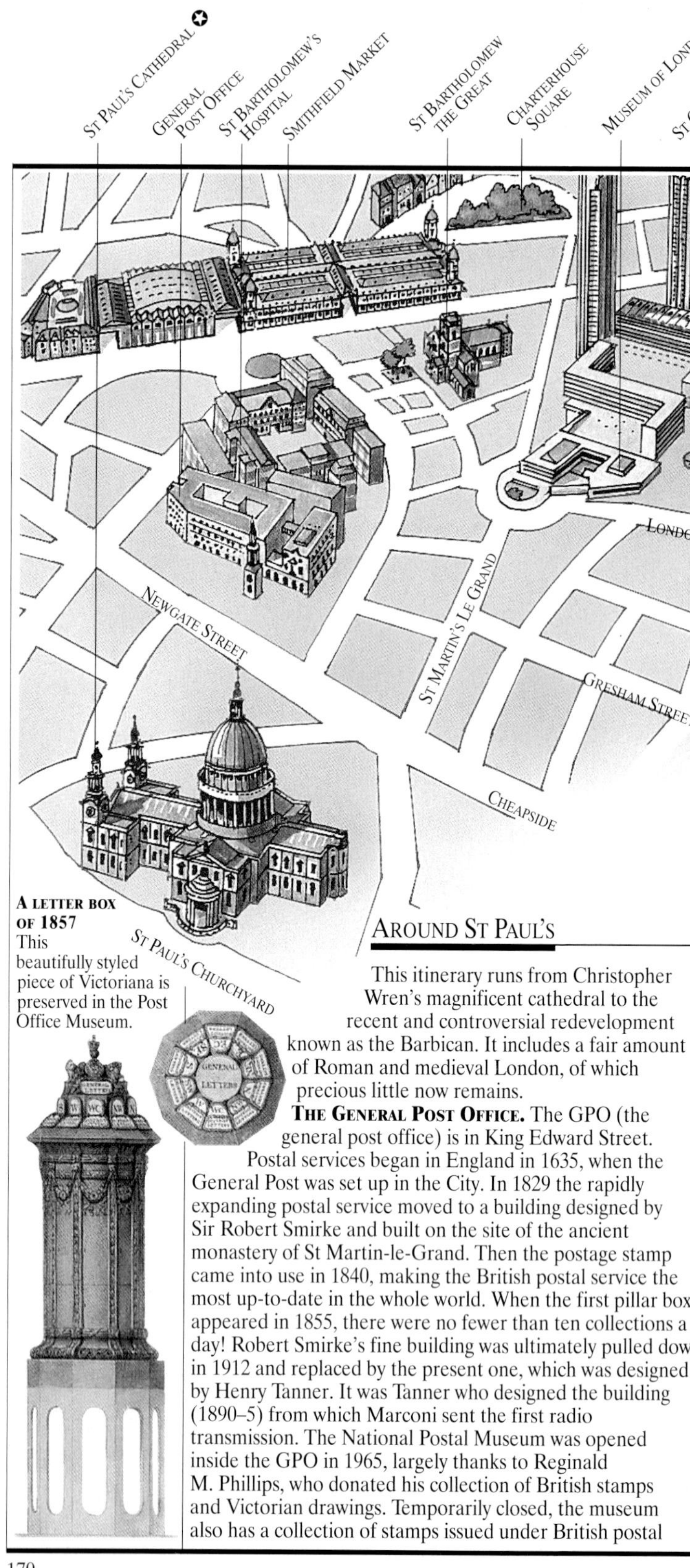

A LETTER BOX OF 1857
This beautifully styled piece of Victoriana is preserved in the Post Office Museum.

AROUND ST PAUL'S

This itinerary runs from Christopher Wren's magnificent cathedral to the recent and controversial redevelopment known as the Barbican. It includes a fair amount of Roman and medieval London, of which precious little now remains.

THE GENERAL POST OFFICE. The GPO (the general post office) is in King Edward Street. Postal services began in England in 1635, when the General Post was set up in the City. In 1829 the rapidly expanding postal service moved to a building designed by Sir Robert Smirke and built on the site of the ancient monastery of St Martin-le-Grand. Then the postage stamp came into use in 1840, making the British postal service the most up-to-date in the whole world. When the first pillar box appeared in 1855, there were no fewer than ten collections a day! Robert Smirke's fine building was ultimately pulled down in 1912 and replaced by the present one, which was designed by Henry Tanner. It was Tanner who designed the building (1890–5) from which Marconi sent the first radio transmission. The National Postal Museum was opened inside the GPO in 1965, largely thanks to Reginald M. Phillips, who donated his collection of British stamps and Victorian drawings. Temporarily closed, the museum also has a collection of stamps issued under British postal

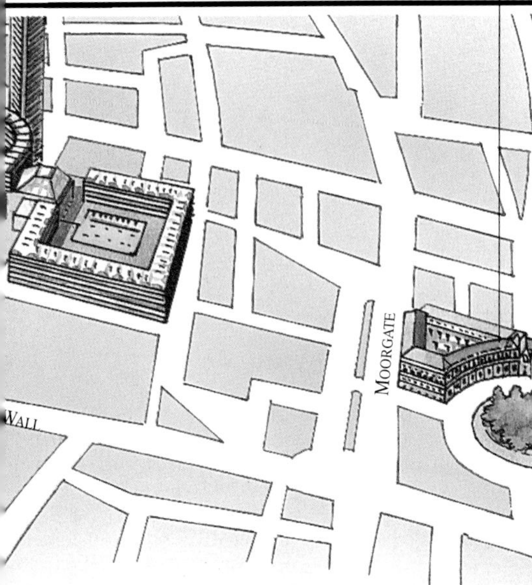

One day
◆ C C1-C2-D1-D2-D3

ST PAUL'S CATHEDRAL AND THE CITY ✪
The views from St Paul's Golden Gallery are stunning, as are the acoustics in the aptly named Whispering Gallery. The crypt includes the tombs of Wellington and Nelson along with designer Christopher Wren's Great Model. The City itself covers a relatively small area and is packed full of varied architecture ranging from Roman remains to stunning new constructions. The best time to wander around the city is at weekends, when it is quiet.

SIR CHRISTOPHER WREN (1632–1723)
The genius of English Baroque architecture was responsible for rebuilding London after the Great Fire of 1666 ● *40*, a commission which included St Paul's Cathedral.

control since 1840, in Britain and overseas. The collections includes the famous Penny Black (left), the first adhesive stamp in the world, as well as a fascinating collection of objects connected with the postal service, such as stamp-boxes, rubber stamps and letterboxes. In the courtyard of the General Post Office, near to St Bartholomew's
ospital, is a part of the medieval London Wall as well as a ection of a Roman wall.

T PAUL'S CATHEDRAL

ISTORY. The cathedral is built on top of ne of the hills in the City, where in oman times ● *34* there was once a mple in honor of Diana. The first athedral to be built on the site, in 604, as destroyed by fire in 1087. Rebuilt etween the 11th and 13th centuries, the ew Norman and Gothic structure was aid to be the biggest medieval church in e whole of Europe, and it boasted the llest spire ever built. The spire burned own in 1561. The old cathedral was at e center of a complex of religious uildings: there was the chapter house, e bishop's palace and the free-standing esus Bell Tower, for example. After the nglish Reformation, the cathedral was bandoned for a while and became a arket-place, to be restored by Inigo ones around 1634 by order of King

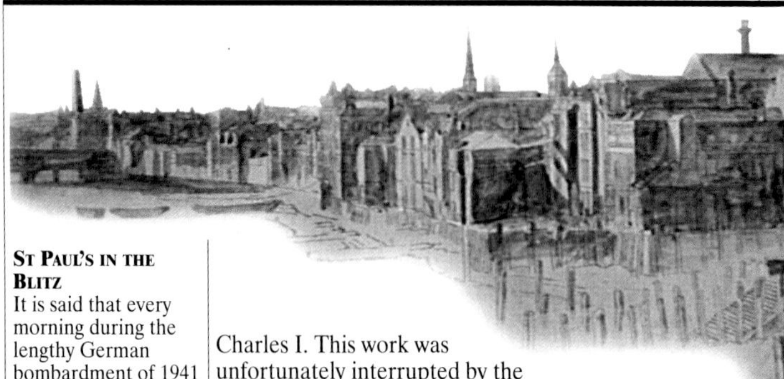

ST PAUL'S IN THE BLITZ
It is said that every morning during the lengthy German bombardment of 1941 Winston Churchill would ask if St Paul's was still standing. Miraculously, the building sustained very little damage during the war.

Charles I. This work was unfortunately interrupted by the outbreak of the English Civil War ● 35.

WREN'S PROJECTS. Soon after the Restoration of 1660, Christopher Wren was given the job of restoring St Paul's Cathedral, which he planned to do by encasing the Gothic structure in a classical shell and then replacing the spire with a dome. His plan was finally approved on August 27, 1666, just one week before the Great Fire ● 40 razed it to the ground. So a new cathedral had to be built. Wren was appointed as director of works by the king in 1669, and the architect submitted several different designs: his first and favorite one, which Charles II also liked, featured a Greek cross plan with a dome. But the high-ranking clergy rejected it as being too untraditional. His "Great Model" of 1673 sought to overcome the clerical resistance by the addition of a portico and a vestibule topped with a dome. That too was rejected, so in 1675 Wren came up with the "Warrant Design", which had the "Norman English" Latin cross shape with a long nave and transepts, and a long choir with narrow ambulatories ending in an apse.

ST PAUL'S CATHEDRAL
LONDON
IT'S QUICKER BY RAIL
FULL INFORMATION FROM ANY L·N·E·R OFFICE OR AGENCY

THE DOME OF ST PAUL'S. The building is crowned with a massive dome which is 107 feet in diameter and whose top is 365 feet above the ground. The dome is supported on eight pillars. Its weight was a problem that Wren eventually solved by building a stone cone between an inner and an outer dome to take the weight of the lantern. The view over London from the Golden Gallery above the dome is quite superb.

THE EXTERIOR. Apart from the lead-covered dome of the cathedral, on to which all the main lines of the building seem to converge, the cathedral's exterior has three other important features: the great tambour of the dome, which is surrounded by a colonnade with alternate niches and loggias; a screen wall which serves as a buttress concealing the supporting arches and enhances the majestic overall effect (an impression that is further heightened by the semicircular colonnaded porticoes of the north and south transepts); and finally the west front, which was a predominantly Baroque inspiration. It features two graceful towers that frame a double portico with columns surmounted by a carved pediment.

THE DOME OF ST PAUL'S
When his model, with dome, was rejected as too revolutionary, it is said that Wren burst into tears.

VIEW OF ST PAUL'S FROM THE RIVER
Among the great men buried in St Paul's is Lord Nelson, whose sarcophagus of black Italian marble was meant for Cardinal Wolsey. Henry VIII took it from him.

HE INTERIOR. The athedral's impressive interior is icking in warmth and fails to inspire the ame wonder as the exterior. Between 1690 and 1720 Vren employed many different artists to decorate it. There 'as Sir James Thornhill ▲ *326*, who painted the cupola with 'escoes illustrating the life of St Paul, and nearly fell to his eath in the process. Grinling Gibbons ▲ *157, 198* carved the ıagnificent choir-stalls, the bishop's throne and the organ ase; the French artist Jean Tijou executed the wrought-iron rilles of the choir and the balustrade leading up to the brary. The best view of the interior (certainly of the hornhill frescoes) is probably from the Whispering Gallery.

OMBS. The cathedral interior was all but free of tombs until 790. Since then, like Westminster Abbey, it has become a ɔrt of Pantheon. Great men buried here include Lord Ielson, the duke of Wellington and, fittingly, Wren himself.

THE MORNING CHAPEL

THIRTY-FIVE YEARS TO BUILD
The length of this job gave rise to a popular saying: "As slow as the builders of St Paul's!"

"Si monumentum requiris, circumspice." ("If you seek his monument, look around you.") That is the inscription over the interior of the North Door, said to have been composed by the son of Sir Christopher Wren for his father, the architect of St Paul's, a rare example of a cathedral completed during its builder's lifetime. The plans, which bear witness to lengthy wrangles between Wren and the royal commission responsible for overseeing the project, show how the design evolved. In fact Wren, once he had the royal seal of approval, changed the design during construction. Some of the modifications were the work of his assistant Nicholas Hawksmoor ▲ *311*.

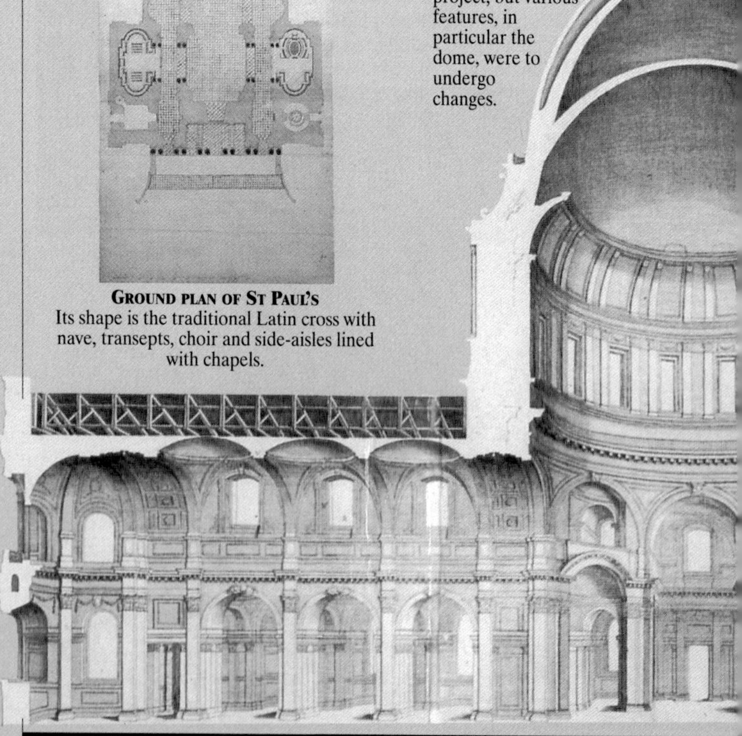

LONGITUDINAL SECTION THROUGH THE CATHEDRAL
Preliminary drawings made around 1675 show the massive scale of the project, but various features, in particular the dome, were to undergo changes.

GROUND PLAN OF ST PAUL'S
Its shape is the traditional Latin cross with nave, transepts, choir and side-aisles lined with chapels.

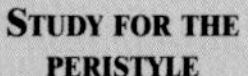
Study for the peristyle

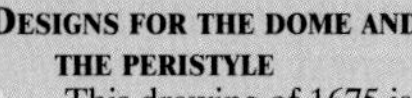
Designs for the dome and the peristyle
This drawing of 1675 is headed "definitive plan" but this was not to be the case: Wren had not yet conceived the intermediary stone cone or the drum-shaped peristyle.

Study for the west front
In Baroque style, the design has an elegant two-storied portico. At this stage the plan still lacked the two turrets which balance the mass of the dome.

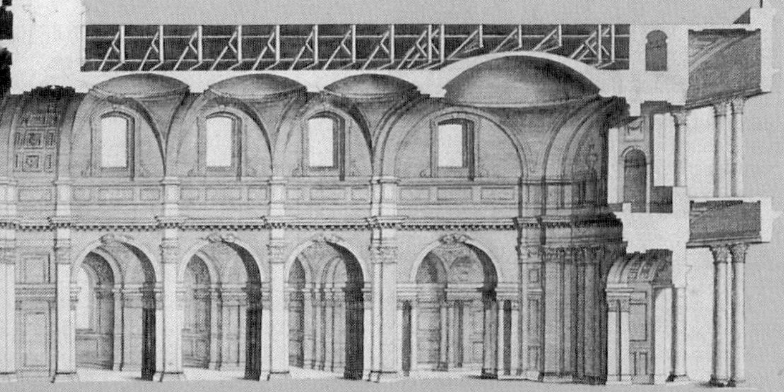

ST BARTHOLOMEW THE GREAT
This is the oldest church in London and is a rare example of Norman architecture in the capital. Other examples include St John's, Clerkenwell, the Tower Chapel and the Temple Church. The elegant porch was built in 1893 by Sir Aston Webb. The original portal of the vanished nave still exists, in the gatehouse to the west.

STATE OCCASIONS AT ST PAUL'S CATHEDRAL. A great many state funerals have been held here over the centuries, including those of Lord Nelson (1805), the duke of Wellington (1852) and Winston Churchill (1965). Queen Victoria celebrated her Golden Jubilee here in 1887, and in 1981 Prince Charles chose to marry Lady Diana Spencer in St Paul's Cathedral.

SMITHFIELD

This was a suburb to the north of London that has gradually been absorbed into the city. Smithfield gets its name from "smooth field", since it was originally a vast stretch of grassland at the edge of London. Today the area is home to many fashionable restaurants and bars, notably along St John's Street.

ST BARTHOLOMEW'S HOSPITAL ★. This is London's oldest hospital. Together with a priory, it was founded in 1123 by Henry I's jester, Thomas Rahere, and then refounded in the 16th century by Henry VIII following the Dissolution of the monasteries before being again rebuilt between 1730 and 1759 by James Gibbs. Nothing now remains of the hospital's original buildings. Above the entrance is a statue of Henry VIII by Francis Bird, a sculptor who also worked for Christopher Wren ▲ *171*. William Harvey, who discovered the principle of the circulation of the blood, was chief physician here 1609–33. In the 18th century one of its governors was the painter William Hogarth ▲ *210*, who donated two pictures, *The Pool at Bethesda* and *The Good Samaritan* (1735–6), now hanging on the main staircase.

ST BARTHOLOMEW-THE-LESS. This church was originally built around 1184 as the hospital chapel. When the hospital was refounded in 1547, it became a parish church. Damaged during World War Two, it was restored in the 1950's. Many famous surgeons and physicians of the hospital are buried here. The square tower with turret is of 15th-century origin.

ST BARTHOLOMEW-THE-GREAT. The priory, which was founded in 1123 by Rahere, was bought in 1544 by Sir Richard Rich, and then remained in his family until 1862. If the church escaped damage during the Great Fire, down the centuries it suffered in a number of different ways: for instance, the Lady Chapel became a house and then a printer's office, the cloisters became stables, and the north transept was turned into a blacksmith's forge. By the middle of the 19th century the church was no more than a ruin. Its restoration began in 1858; only a part of the nave now remains, although the Norman choir is still most impressive. The tracery of the high windows is from the 14th century, together with the eastern end of the choir and the Lady Chapel. The cloisters are 15th-century in origin, the tower was built in 1628, and the present porch in 1893. The church has undergone many changes over the centuries.

SMITHFIELD TODAY
Neither a museum nor a concrete monstrosity (as around St Paul's), Smithfield is an example of a successful fusion of tradition and modernity.

Smithfield Market. Crowds used to flock to this square located just beyond the City walls in the Middle Ages in order to watch the public executions (Smithfield was one of the main places of execution both for Scottish rebels and for Protestant martyrs), to see some jousting, or to attend the popular Cloth Fair, which lasted for three days and was held every year during August. There has been a cattle market in Smithfield since late Saxon times (the 11th century). By the 16th century the area around the market had developed into a considerable community, with its gates at the end of St John Street. The nuisances that an urban cattle market brings with it forced its closure in 1855, and it was then moved to Islington. But the meat market remained, in the new halls which were built to house it.

The London Central Meat Market. The four market halls ● *84* were the work of Sir Horace Jones. The future of Smithfield is now under threat from property developers, just like Covent Garden ▲ *272*, Billingsgate ▲ *157* and Spitalfields ▲ *312* before it.

Charterhouse Square ★. Within this peaceful, paved and gas-lit square is the old monastery of the Charterhouse, which was founded in the 14th century in order to house monks of the Carthusian order. Subsequently it became first a school and later a retirement home. Thomas More ▲ *197*, *320* lived here from 1499 to 1503, and Thomas Cromwell stayed here in 1535. The buildings are not open to the public, although the gardens may be visited by going through the gate.

The "Fat Boy". This chubby little figure in gilded wood stands at the corner of Giltspur Street and Cock Lane, on the site of an old tavern, marking the site where the Great Fire ended.

London Central Meat Market
As soon as it opened in 1868, the market was an immediate success. It still sells more than a thousand tons of meat per day. Behind the stone and red-brick walls are huge glass-roofed halls.

"The Old Smithfield Market"
This painting by Thomas Sydney Cooper shows the cattle market in the 19th century.

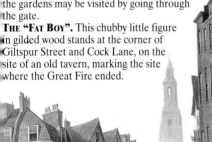

THE OLD WALL
Remains of a 3rd-century brick Roman rampart, incorporating pieces of medieval stone.

THE GOD MITHRAS
This 4th-century head discovered in 1954 in the Temple of Mithras, provides evidence of a flourishing Mithraic cult in Londinium.

THE MUSEUM OF LONDON

This enterprise opened on its present Barbican site in 1976. It is extremely popular with Londoners as well as with tourists, and is an amalgamation of the old London and Guildhall Museums.

HISTORY. The Guildhall Museum was founded in 1826 to display the remains of Roman and medieval London discovered in the City and surrounding areas or donated. The London Museum was founded by Viscounts Harcourt and Esher in order to give London an equivalent of the Musée Carnavalet in Paris, and it was intended to house all that could be found concerning the capital's history. It opened in 1912 in Kensington Palace, and then moved to Lancaster House. Archeologist Sir Mortimer Wheeler suggested a fusion of the two in 1927, but the plan was forgotten until after the Second World War, the City and the government having other, more important priorities. The decision was finally made in 1965, and the Museum of London was born. Adequate space was eventually found for it in 1971, and a modern building was constructed in the Barbican. Now it contains a number of superb and informative collections relating to the economic and social history of the capital. Whole buildings, houses and shops have been reconstructed here. The main entrance by the rotunda leads to the upper level. This is where to begin exploring the ten rooms tracing the history of London.

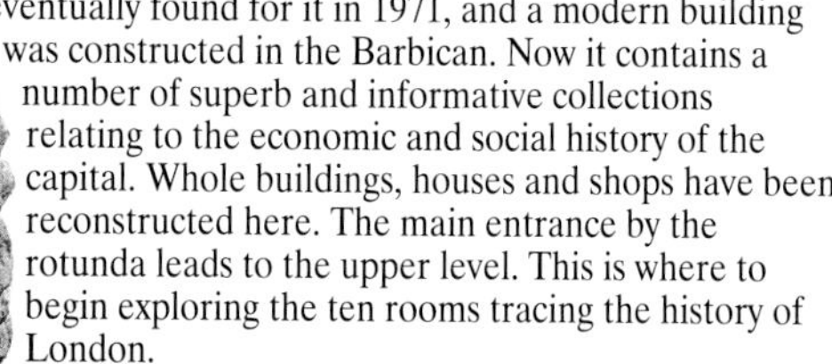

THE THAMES IN PREHISTORY. This room leads the visitor through prehistoric and protohistoric London, from its earliest recorded origins to 42 AD. There is paleolithic and neolithic silex, pottery which was found at Heathrow, and some bronze weapons.

ROMAN LONDON. This is the history of Londinium ● *34* from 43 to 410 AD. One of the remains from this period is the Temple of Mithras, which was unearthed in 1954 in Walbrook and moved to Temple Court, 11 Queen Victoria Street.

MEDIEVAL LONDON. This room covers a thousand years of history from 410 to 1484. Among the treasures from this period are some 11th-century Norman battleaxes, objects such as the carved-wood panel (left) from a chest dated 1400 and illustrated with scenes from the *Canterbury Tales*, and a heavy 6th-century gold brooch of Saxon origin (above right), found in an Anglo-Saxon necropolis at Mitcham, Surrey.

BARTHOLOMEW FAIR
Until it was suppressed in 1855, this annual fair on the site of Smithfield Market had been a popular attraction for seven hundred years.

TUDOR LONDON. This room shows the astonishing growth of the City, and the daily life of Londoners between 1485 (the year of Henry VII's accession) and 1603 (when Queen Elizabeth died and the first Stuart king, James I, ascended the throne). The room is filled with arms, jewelry and costumes of the period, and there are watches and clocks made by Flemish craftsmen living in the City.

EARLY STUART LONDON. The early Stuart period (1603–66), including the Commonwealth, is covered in this room. There are models of a Shakespearean theater and London Bridge, and a death mask of Oliver Cromwell, as well as a diorama of the Great Fire complete with sound effects.

THE LATER STUARTS. The history of the period 1667–1714 is illustrated in this room, which ends with the accession of George I. There is a fine example of a Londoner's costume of the time, a fascinating sectional model of the new St Paul's Cathedral ▲ *171*, and a gaming table for backgammon and chess.

GEORGIAN LONDON. The terrific expansion that went on in this period (1714–1800) is well covered here; there is also the reconstruction of a prison interior, a pillory, and arms.

NINETEENTH-CENTURY LONDON. In this room, covering the period 1801–80, there some excellent models, such as one of a barge dated 1807, one of the Crystal Palace (constructed in 1851 for the Great Exhibition), and a fire truck of 1862.

IMPERIAL LONDON. This room displays the late Victorian and the Edwardian eras from 1881 to 1910, with reconstructions of a street and a public house.

TWENTIETH-CENTURY LONDON. There are objects here from the period between the wars that will be familiar to many older visitors, such as a 1928 elevator from the big department store *Selfridges*, an air raid shelter and even a broadcasting studio.

This 13th- or 14th-century vase is of Venetian origin.

PLATE
Dated 1602, this earthenware tin-glazed plate is probably the work of a Flemish potter working in Aldgate. It bears an inscription celebrating Elizabeth I.

AROUND THE BARBICAN

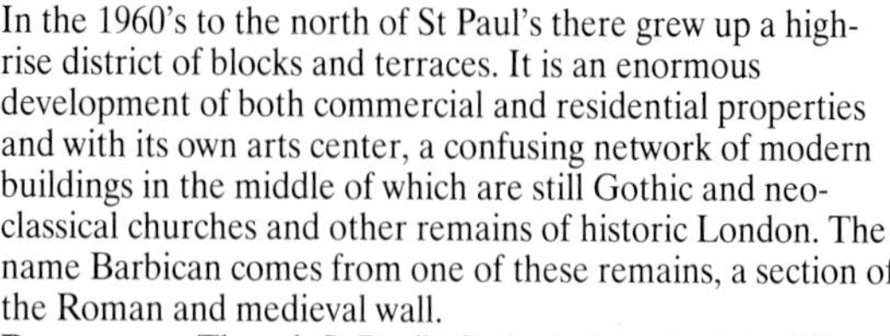

In the 1960's to the north of St Paul's there grew up a high-rise district of blocks and terraces. It is an enormous development of both commercial and residential properties and with its own arts center, a confusing network of modern buildings in the middle of which are still Gothic and neo-classical churches and other remains of historic London. The name Barbican comes from one of these remains, a section of the Roman and medieval wall.

REBUILDING. Though St Paul's Cathedral survived the Blitz ● *42* relatively unscathed, a third of the City was destroyed. The worst-hit area was around the Barbican. Post-war problems delayed the bulk of reconstruction work until 1955. It was decided to rebuild in a contemporary style and to make a clean break with the past, constructing new houses and flats, office blocks, recreation and cultural centers. The work was entrusted to three architects who shared the design and planning of the scheme: Chamberlain, Powell and Bon.

BARBICAN
This maze of tower blocks, courtyards, stairways, tunnels and passages was built on land flattened in the Blitz ● *42*.

A CONTROVERSIAL DEVELOPMENT. Work started in 1962 and went on for the next twenty years, to be finally completed on March 3, 1982. Derelict for many years, the Barbican now houses almost two-thirds of the City's population. With the traffic re-routed underground, it has the appearance of an area entirely dedicated to pedestrians. For the latter, there is a network of terraces, passageways, squares and fountains that are designed to link the various disparate features of the development. Critics say that the development is difficult to get to and easy to get lost in, a dreary concrete world that lacks the human touch appropriate for its cultural institutions. These include the GUILDHALL SCHOOL OF MUSIC AND DRAMA and the CITY OF LONDON SCHOOL FOR GIRLS.

THE BARBICAN CENTRE FOR THE ARTS AND CONFERENCES. Officially opened in March 1982, the Barbican, which has ten stories in all (some of them underground), is constantly diversifying its activities. Although no longer the seat of the prestigious Royal Shakespeare Company, it welcomes numerous other companies, and an annual international festival brings together the élite of the

"FINSBURY CIRCUS"
This 19th-century painting by an unknown artist shows the northern side, with the now demolished London Institution where there were lectures "by eminent scientific and literary men".

theater world. The Barbican remains the home of the London Symphony Orchestra, but all types of concerts are held here, from jazz to Latin-American rhythms. Cinemas, exhibitions and conferences all help to make it one of the most important socio-cultural complexes in the world.

St Giles Cripplegate The church, one of the few to have escaped the Great Fire of 1666 (although it was less fortunate in the Blitz), takes its name from one of the five Roman gates to the City: Cripplegate, Aldgate, Newgate, Bishopsgate and Ludgate. The present building dates from the mid-16th century, and the tower is 17th century. In the choir of the church are the tombs of the explorer and navigator Martin Frobisher (1535–94) and of the poet John Milton (1608–74). Oliver Cromwell (1599–1658) was married here in 1620.

The wall. Several remains of the old wall encircling the City are still visible in the street named London Wall, particularly in the garden of St Alfege and at West Gate. The wall is a mixture of Roman foundations, medieval sections with gray stone supports from the 14th century, and some 15th-century sections built with red brick.

All Hallows Church. Built between 1765 and 1767 in London Wall by George Dance the Younger ▲ *149*, this church is constructed in neo-classical style. The altar painting is by the architect's brother, Nathaniel Dance. A section of the original Roman fortifications is still visible in the church garden.

Finsbury Circus. This fine circular "square" is on the east side of Moorgate. Unfortunately none of George Dance the Younger's early 19th-century houses remain; but there are some imposing buildings, such as Lutyens House (1924–7, by Sir Edwin Lutyens), surrounding an attractive garden.

"St Botolph's, Aldersgate"
This Victorian painting shows the sub-tropical plants in the churchyard, which in 1880 became a most unusual garden, Postman's Park. It is in Noble Street, on the other side of the Barbican.

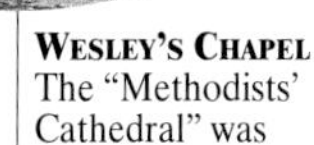

Wesley's Chapel
The "Methodists' Cathedral" was consecrated in 1778 by the evangelist and missionary John Wesley (1703–91).

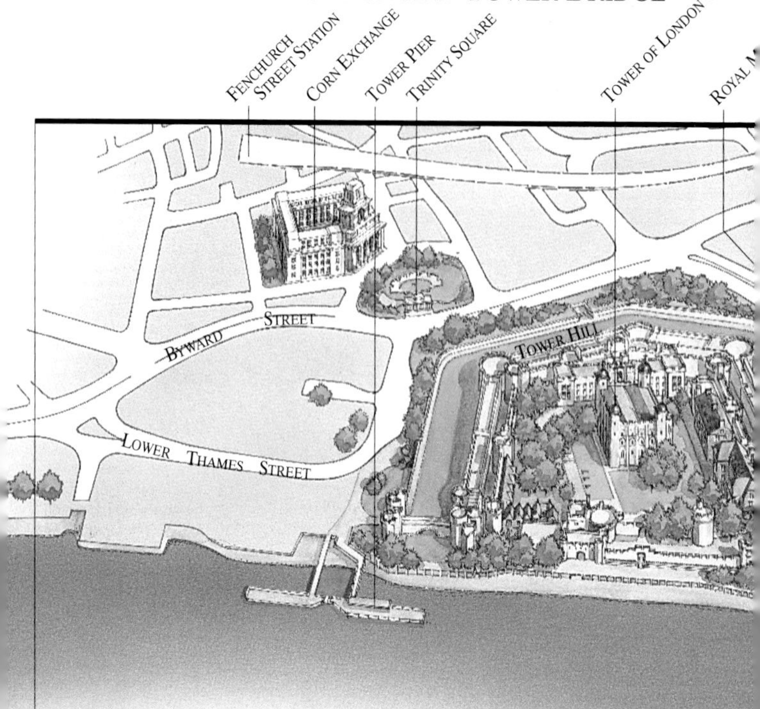

▲ The Tower of London and Tower Bridge ✪

Fenchurch Street Station
Corn Exchange
Tower Pier
Trinity Square
Tower of London
Royal M

Byward Street
Tower Hill
Lower Thames Street

Two hours

◆ **G** A3-B3

By the year 200 London had become one of the wealthiest cities in the Roman empire, surrounded by walls (traces of which are still to be seen in Trinity Square and inside the Tower). But in spite of its fortifications London was still taken by William the Conqueror in 1066. Ten years later he built the White Tower. His successors each added various features, Edward I adding the outer curtain wall and moat in the late 13th century. The White Tower was so called not from the Caen limestone and Kentish ragstone of which it was built, but because in 1240 Henry III had the entire building whitewashed. In the 17th century the Norman windows were enlarged by Christopher Wren ● *70*, ▲ *171, 327*. The White Tower now houses a magnificent collection of arms and armor, the Heralds' Museum, and St John's Chapel (the oldest church in London and a masterpiece of early Norman architecture).

The White Tower
The keep known as the White Tower is the oldest part of the Tower of London. Its only staircase spiraled clockwise to make it easier for defenders to fight with their swords in their right hands.

Royal palace and royal prison ★ The Tower first became a royal residence when Henry III (1216–72) built a palace to the south of the White Tower. It was partially rebuilt in the reign of Henry VIII, and in 1540 the half-timbered houses on Tower Green, including the Queen's House, were constructed. The palace was redecorated for the coronation of Henry VIII's second wife Anne Boleyn, but the Tower ceased to be a royal residence and became a prison for enemies of the crown. Many famous men and women were imprisoned and sometimes executed here on Tower Green, including the seventeen-year-old Lady Jane Grey, Anne Boleyn and Catharine Howard (second and fifth wives of Henry VIII). Execution on Tower Green instead of in public on Tower Hill was a privilege reserved for high-ranking prisoners, who also had the right to be buried in the 13th-century chapel of ST PETER AD VINCULA; this was destroyed by fire in 1512 and rebuilt three years later. Sir Thomas More ▲ *197* and John Fisher, bishop of Rochester, were also beheaded on Tower Green, the latter so weak he had to be carried to the block. They were executed for refusing to take the Oath of Supremacy (1534), which put the Church of England under the control of the sovereign. In 1413 Sir John Oldcastle (Shakespeare's Falstaff) was confined in the Tower to await execution, but he escaped the following year only to be recaptured and hanged. Shakespeare dramatized another incident which took place in 1483, when the boy-king Edward V and his brother were reputedly murdered in the Garden Tower (afterward known as the Bloody Tower). The skeletons of two children were found in 1674 under the stairs leading to St John's Chapel, and when the remains were exhumed in 1933 they were thought to be those of "the Little Princes". Other famous prisoners include Sir Walter Raleigh (who spent twelve years there), the Earl of Essex (beheaded on Tower Green), Guy Fawkes and his fellow conspirators, who were tortured in the basement of the White Tower, and the Duke of Monmouth after the failure of his rebellion in 1685. Two famous risoners in the 20th century include Sir Roger Casement hanged at Pentonville) and Hitler's deputy Rudolf Hess, fter his mysterious flight to Scotland in 1941.

HE RAVENS. Legend has it that the kingdom will fall if the avens leave the Tower. The origin of this superstition is not nown but may derive from Charles II, who wanted to get rid f the birds but was advised against it.

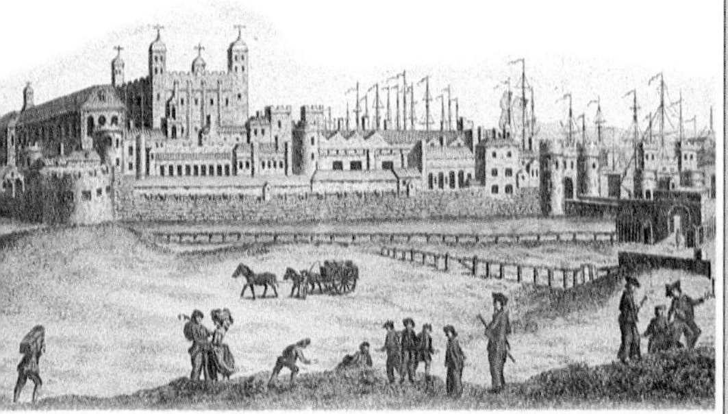

A Beefeater at the Tower of London.

TOWER OF LONDON AND TOWER BRIDGE ✪
The magnificent two-turreted Tower Bridge was first opened in 1894. A glass-enclosed walkway on the top of the bridge offers great views along the River Thames. Next to the bridge is the Tower of London, a former prison. Two of Henry VIII's six wives were among those executed here, and it was in the famous Bloody Tower that the two princes were reputedly murdered in 1483. The Crown Jewels are on display in the White Tower; they include crowns, rings, swords and the robes used in state occasions. The Royal Armouries contain 40,000 pieces of arms and sporting equipment. Look out for the "Beefeaters", in their distinctive red and black garb, and the resident ravens – rumor has it that if leave the Tower the "kingdom will fall".

▲ THE TOWER OF LONDON

1. MIDDLE TOWER
Built in the 13th century, the tower gives access to the stone bridge that crosses the moat.

2. BYWARD TOWER
This is the 'tower of the password' which gives access to the outer walkway. Be sure to admire its 14th-century wall painting.

3. BELL TOWER
Thomas Moore and the future Queen Elizabeth I were imprisoned here.

4. ST THOMAS' TOWER
Built in the 13th century, it houses models of the Tower.

5. BLOODY TOWER
It was here that the sons of Edward IV were allegedly murdered.

6. WAKEFIELD TOWER
Henry VI was killed here.

7. BEAUCHAMP TOWER
Built in the early 14th century, it houses objects found during excavations.

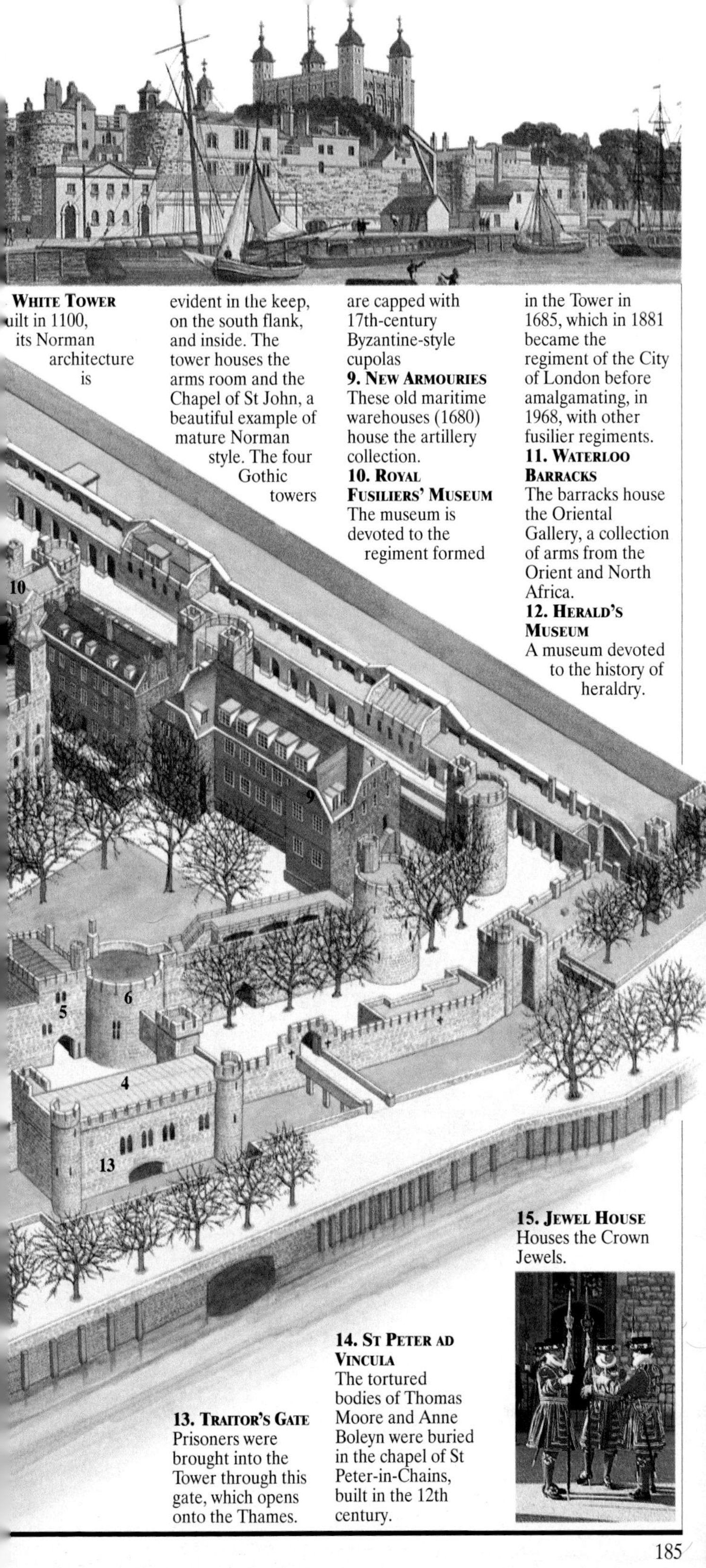

White Tower
uilt in 1100, its Norman architecture is evident in the keep, on the south flank, and inside. The tower houses the arms room and the Chapel of St John, a beautiful example of mature Norman style. The four Gothic towers are capped with 17th-century Byzantine-style cupolas

9. New Armouries
These old maritime warehouses (1680) house the artillery collection.

10. Royal Fusiliers' Museum
The museum is devoted to the regiment formed in the Tower in 1685, which in 1881 became the regiment of the City of London before amalgamating, in 1968, with other fusilier regiments.

11. Waterloo Barracks
The barracks house the Oriental Gallery, a collection of arms from the Orient and North Africa.

12. Herald's Museum
A museum devoted to the history of heraldry.

13. Traitor's Gate
Prisoners were brought into the Tower through this gate, which opens onto the Thames.

14. St Peter ad Vincula
The tortured bodies of Thomas Moore and Anne Boleyn were buried in the chapel of St Peter-in-Chains, built in the 12th century.

15. Jewel House
Houses the Crown Jewels.

The coronation ceremony, which dates back to the time of Edward the Confessor (1042–66), includes the important rituals of taking the oath, anointing with holy oil, receiving the tokens of royalty, and enthronement. Elizabeth II (left) wears the Imperial Crown of State, with bracelets and royal ring; she holds the scepter with the cross and the orb. The Crown Jewels are on view to the public in the Jewel House at the Tower of London; many of them were made for the Coronation of Charles II in 1661.

THE SCEPTER WITH THE CROSS
The Sovereign is given two scepters. The scepter with the cross is the ensign of power and justice: in 1910 it was set with the biggest cut diamond in the world, the Star of Africa, 530 carats. The scepter with dove symbolizes the spiritual power given to the sovereign.

THE AMPULLA AND ANOINTING SPOON
Using these, the archbishop of Canterbury anoints the sovereign's hands, breast and head with holy oil. The 12th-century spoon is the oldest of the royal insignia, and was first used at the coronation of John Lackland in 1199. The ampulla, in the form of an eagle, was used at the coronation of Charles II.

Before the archbishop of Canterbury placed St Edward's Crown on the head of Elizabeth II, on June 2, 1953, she wore this diamond circlet known as Queen Victoria's diadem.

The Imperial Crown of India (1911) and the State Crown of Queen Elizabeth the Queen Mother (1937)
The first crown (1) is set with more than six thousand precious stones from India: it was only worn once, when George V was crowned Emperor of India in Delhi. The second (2), made of platinum, contains the famous Koh-i-Noor diamond (Mountain of Light).

he Imperial State Crown
his crown (above) was made for the coronation of Queen Victoria in 38. Set with more than 2,800 diamonds, it also contains the Black ince's ruby, worn by Henry V at the Battle of Agincourt. Elizabeth II ore this for her coronation procession.

Saint Edward's Crown and Queen Mary's Crown
St Edward's Crown (3) weighs almost 5lbs. It was made for the coronation of Charles II in 1662: most of the Crown Jewels had been scrapped during the Commonwealth. This crown is only used for the crowning ceremony. Queen Mary's Crown (4) was worn by Mary at the coronation of George V.

The Coronation Ring and the Queen's Ring
After the crowning ceremony, the archbishop places the Coronation Ring on the third finger of the monarch's right hand. These rings were made for the coronation of William IV and Queen Adelaide in 1831.

▲ The Tower of London and Tower Bridge

The Prince of Wales unveiled this commemorative plaque on Monday June 21, 1886.

Formerly there was a menagerie within the Towerof London: in 1235 the Holy Roman Emperor presented Henry III with three leopards, as an allusion to the leopards which figured o the Plantagenet coat of arms, and it was this gift that began the royal menagerie. Next, in 1252 a polar bear arrived as a gift from the king of Norway; it was kept on a long chain which allowed it sufficient freedom to catch fish in the River Thames. Louis IX of France gave Henry an elephant; over th years a number of other animals were added, and the menagerie became a popular attraction. But by 1822 the roya collection had dwindled to just a grizzly bear, a single elephant and a few assorted birds. So a new royal keeper, Alfred Copps, was appointed and he enlarged it to include fifty-nine species. In 1835, when a lion attacked some soldier in the Tower, the animals were all transferred to the Zoological Gardens in Regent's Park ▲ *257*.

Tower Bridge ★

Tower Bridge has long symbolized the city of London to people from all over the world. It was the gateway to the capital for ships coming upriver to dock in the port, and it is the first bridge over the Thames coming upriver from the east. Its design and its brilliant engineering encapsulate the heart and soul of Victorian London. Today the bridge continues its threefold function, permitting the efficient movement of road vehicles, river vessels and pedestrians.

Construction. The construction of a new bridge across the Thames was necessitated by the density of traffic that was traveling over the river in the 1880s, particularly over London Bridge. As its site roughly corresponded with the City limits, the City's own architect, Sir Horace Jones, was commissioned to build it. His design was inspired by the lift bridges over the canals in Holland. His daring plan was to have a relatively low through bridge,

The Yeomen Warders and the Ceremony of the Keys

The Yeomen of the Guard have been part of the sovereign's personal guard since 1485 when they formed Henry VII's escort at his coronation. The ancient Ceremony of the Keys has taken place every evening for more than five hundred years, officially locking up the Tower for the

night. The ceremony lasts for exactly seven minutes. At 9.53pm, the Chief Yeoman Warder, dressed in a red and black Tudor costume, leaves the Byward Tower carrying the keys of the Tower and a lantern. At Traitor's Gate four armed soldiers fall into step behind him, and all five of them march through the Byward Tower gates to the entrance beyond Middle Tower. When this is locked they march back, and the gates of Byward Tower are locked behind them. A sentry at the Bloody Tower challenges them: "Halt, who goes there?" "The keys." "Whose keys?" "Queen Elizabeth's keys; God preserve Queen Elizabeth!" replies the Chief Yeoman Warder. "Amen," calls the entire guard, and the keys are taken to the Queen's Tower.

“Steel skeletons clothed with stone”, was how architect Sir Horace Jones described his towers at either end of the bridge.

ıly 30 feet above the water, with a double lift giving ships :cess to Upper Pool, the basin between Tower Bridge and ondon Bridge. Two other men of vision must also share the edit for this immense project: engineer John Wolfe-Barry he son of the famous architect Sir Charles Barry), and chitect G.D. Stevenson, who modified the plans after Jones ed in 1887.

HE ARCHITECTURE. Parliament and the ity both specified a neo-Gothic design r the bridge (at the request of Queen ictoria and the War Office), with towers at would conceal the hydraulic lifting achinery as well as blend in well with e nearby Tower of London. An lditional factor was that the neo-Gothic yle was at its height at this time. The fluence of Scottish castle architecture is ıe to Stevenson, who was a Scot himself, and this is apparent the decoration of the towers as well as in the use of steel r the superstructure of the bridge. The stone cladding over metal framework offered the best resistance to the stresses at were imposed by the two lifting bascules. The foundation one of the river’s “Gateway to the City” was laid by the ince of Wales in 1886. Its length is approximately 800 feet tween the two towers, and though today Londoners think Tower Bridge with considerable affection, it was the subject some harsh criticism at its opening in 1894.

HIPS UNDER THE BRIDGE. At any hour of the day or night, a ip with a superstructure or fixed mast that is more than 33 et in height can signal to Tower Bridge from the level of nerry Garden Pier that it requires to pass through. There is a similar procedure in operation for vessels that are going downriver.

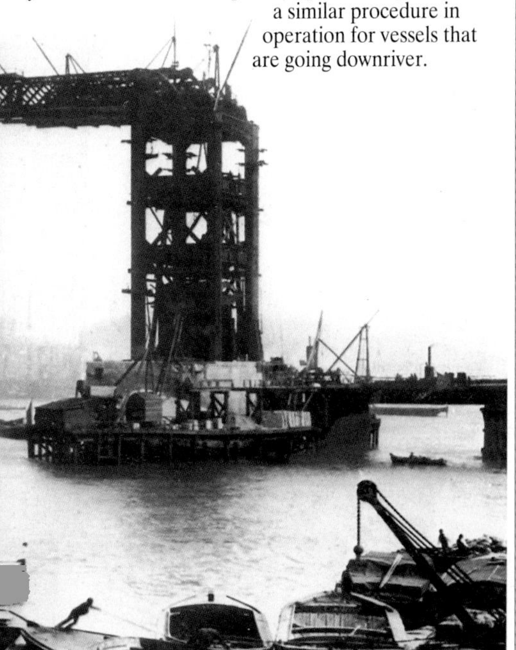

THE LAST BRIDGE OVER THE THAMES
Tower Bridge was specifically designed to facilitate the passage of river traffic.

DETAIL OF THE PARAPET
The metal parts of the bridge, painted red, white and blue, are decorated with royal insignia.

TOWER BRIDGE IN APRIL 1892
The bridge is a perfect example of the Victorian blend of architecture and engineering, historical detail combined with the latest technology. During its construction many people spoke out against covering a metal framework with stone.

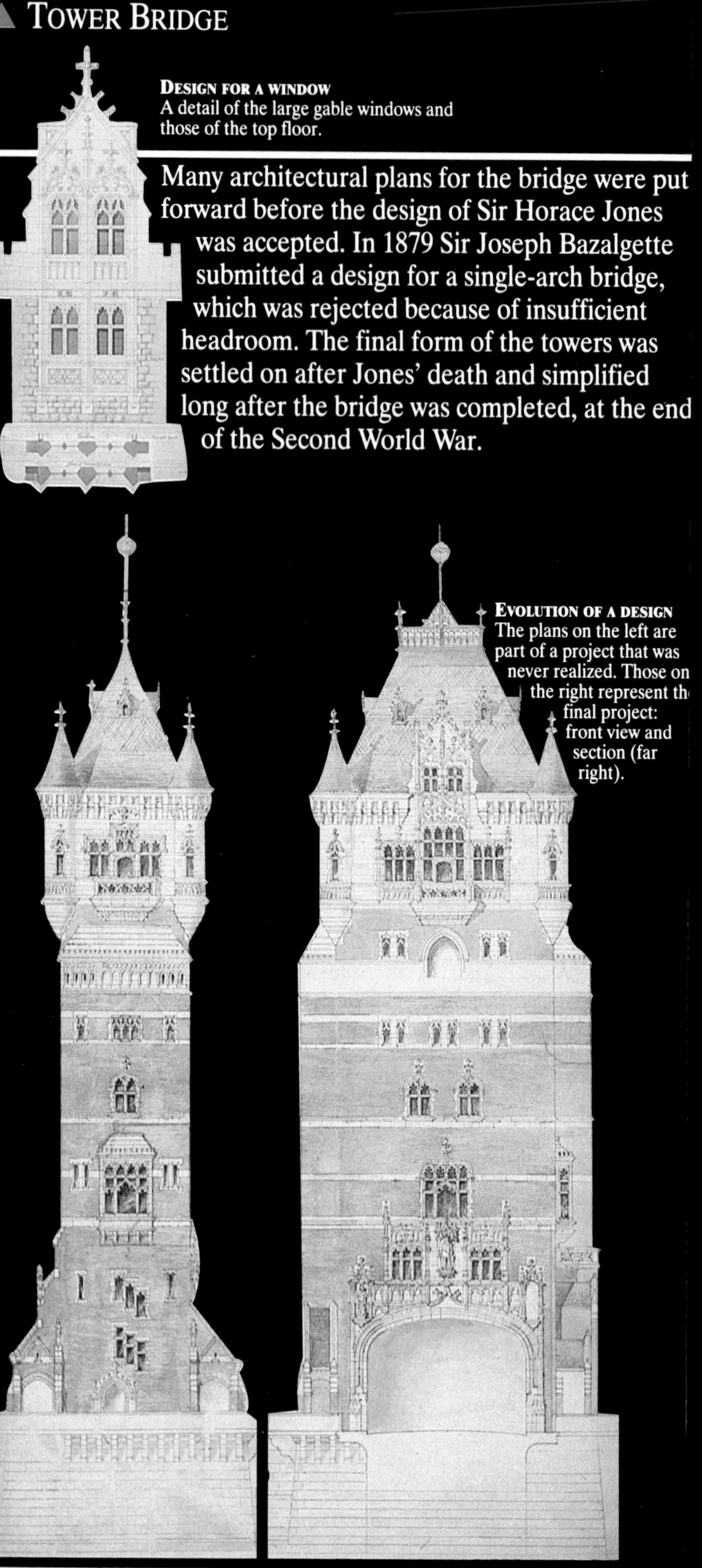

Design for a window
A detail of the large gable windows and those of the top floor.

Many architectural plans for the bridge were put forward before the design of Sir Horace Jones was accepted. In 1879 Sir Joseph Bazalgette submitted a design for a single-arch bridge, which was rejected because of insufficient headroom. The final form of the towers was settled on after Jones' death and simplified long after the bridge was completed, at the end of the Second World War.

Evolution of a design
The plans on the left are part of a project that was never realized. Those on the right represent th final project: front view and section (far right).

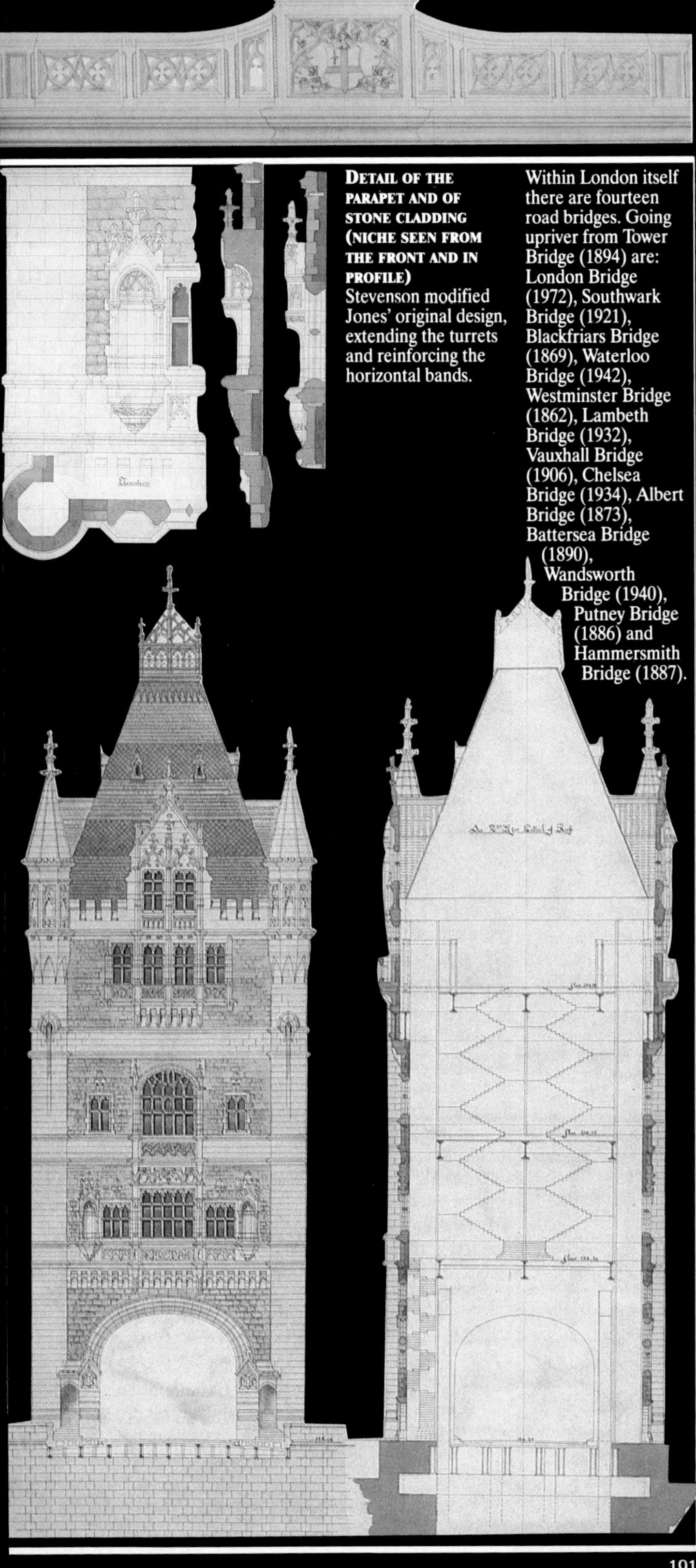

Detail of the parapet and of stone cladding (niche seen from the front and in profile)
Stevenson modified Jones' original design, extending the turrets and reinforcing the horizontal bands.

Within London itself there are fourteen road bridges. Going upriver from Tower Bridge (1894) are: London Bridge (1972), Southwark Bridge (1921), Blackfriars Bridge (1869), Waterloo Bridge (1942), Westminster Bridge (1862), Lambeth Bridge (1932), Vauxhall Bridge (1906), Chelsea Bridge (1934), Albert Bridge (1873), Battersea Bridge (1890), Wandsworth Bridge (1940), Putney Bridge (1886) and Hammersmith Bridge (1887).

The footbridge
Each tower has a lift to take pedestrians up to the walkway, necessary in the days when the bridge was opened very frequently. It was closed in 1911 because of the large number of suicides. But it was glassed in and reopened in 1982, and now offers superb views over the river.

A new City Hall
Facing the Tower of London from across the river and next to Tower Bridge's south side, is City Hall, home to the London Assembly and the office of the Mayor of London. The distinctive ten-story glass building, designed by Foster and Partners and opened in 2002, has a form derived from a geometrically modified sphere and leans back toward the south. The shape was designed to reduce heat gain (from the sun) and heat loss via the building's skin. Parts of City Hall are open to the public.

Note that the ships are not required to wait: rather, the road traffic must give way to the traffic on the river. A tugboat is always waiting at the ready at the northeast corner in order to assist the passage of sailing boats through the bridge.

The bridge at work. At one time there were eighty men at work on Tower Bridge. When it has to be opened, the look-out on duty warns the policeman in charge of the traffic on the bridge, which is then closed by the use of traffic lights. Careful synchronization between the river and road traffic is necessary at this point in order to prevent an accident: there are many stories of incidents that have happened here. There was the driver of a London bus who went through the red light and was caught on the opening bascules. The bus jumped a gap of several feet to land safely on the other side. When they reach the bridge, ships have to wait only one and a half minutes before they can pass through. The original hydraulic lifting machinery was made by the Newcastle firm of Armstrong-Mitchell Ltd, and never once failed to work. River traffic diminished in 1970 when the wharves in Upper Pool closed down. Scarcely any more large vessels came far enough upriver to use the bridge, whose running costs were extremely

high. There was talk of abandoning the lifting facility, or at least switching to new machinery that would be less costly to maintain. Tower Bridge was used almost exclusively by road traffic and as its once-revolutionary Victorian machinery became aged and impractical, it was in danger of becoming just another monument. But in 1976 the hydraulic system was replaced by electric motors, so that the bridge, although seldom called into use by passing ships, remains in working order.

Tower Bridge Museum and "HMS Belfast". A museum opened in the old power house on the south side in 1982. It traces the history of the bridge. Stevenson's original drawings are on display, and the original hydraulic lifting machinery is demonstrated. The old walkway high above the road has also been reopened. *HMS Belfast* (11,500 tons), which was opened as a museum in 1971, is moored nearby. It is the largest cruiser ever to have been built by the Royal Navy: it saw service in World War Two on the Arctic convoys.

VILLAGES AND MUSEUMS

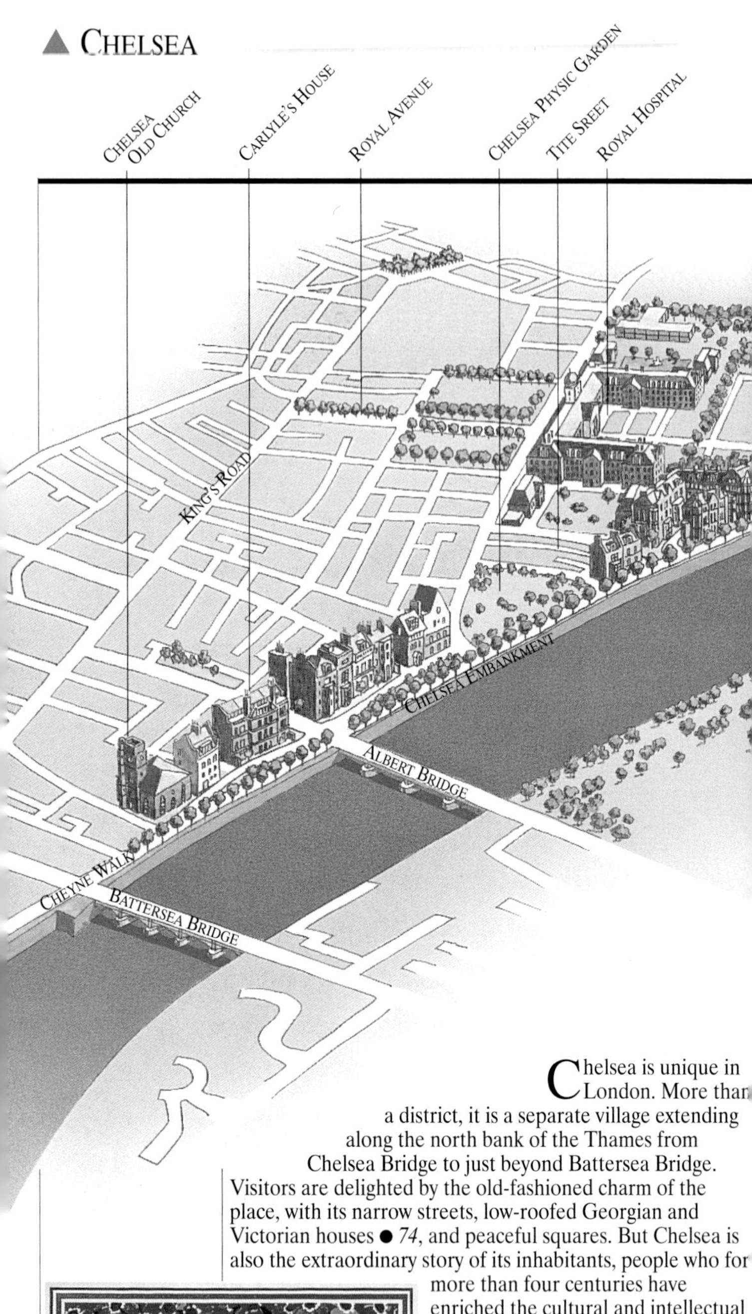

Chelsea is unique in London. More than a district, it is a separate village extending along the north bank of the Thames from Chelsea Bridge to just beyond Battersea Bridge. Visitors are delighted by the old-fashioned charm of the place, with its narrow streets, low-roofed Georgian and Victorian houses ● *74*, and peaceful squares. But Chelsea is also the extraordinary story of its inhabitants, people who for more than four centuries have enriched the cultural and intellectual life of England.

CHELSEA FLOWER SHOW
MAY 22-23-24
Station SLOANE SQUARE
BUS ROUTES 11 · 39 · 46

HISTORY

Once a simple fishing village, in the 16th century Chelsea became the home of courtiers. Sir Thomas More, Lord Chancellor, historian and humanist, had his house in Beaufort Street, where he lived from 1524 until his execution eleven years later. There he received such friends as Erasmus

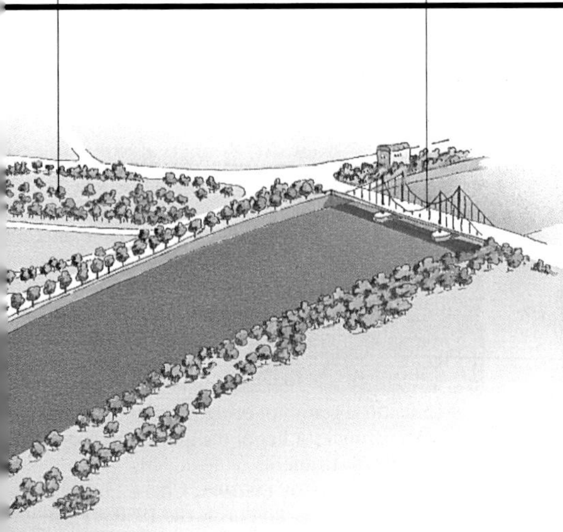

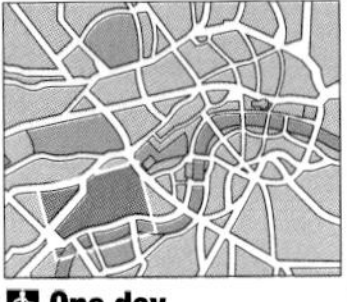

One day

◆ **H** A2-A3-A4-B2

(1469–1536) and the German painter Hans Holbein (1497–1543), who was to have a marked influence on English portrait artists after him. In 1537 King Henry VIII 36 built the NEW MANOR HOUSE ɛside the Thames, which in the 17th ɛntury came into the possession of the heyne family and was bought in 1712 y the celebrated physician Sir Hans loane ▲ *301,* who kept his famous abinet of Curiosities there.

HE HOME FOR OLD SOLDIERS. Over ıe years Chelsea changed a great deal ıd it was definitively put on the map ı the 17th century with the ɔnstruction of the Royal Hospital. etired soldiers, or "Pensioners", of e Hospital probably boasted about ıe fresh air and the peace they found ıere, far from the smoke and fog of e city, and from 1742 all London arted coming to Chelsea to take the r. Their favorite spot was RANELAGH ARDENS, to the east of the Royal ospital, where there were regular ɔncerts, balls, grand dinners and ɛework displays.

OHEMIA. Artists, writers and intellectuals of all kinds started move to Chelsea at the beginning of the 19th century, duced by the peace and quiet they found there. The poet ıelley and the landscape painter Turner ● *102,* ▲ *215, 216* ɛre among the first. Word spread, and its popularity creased. Later in the century Chelsea could number among inhabitants the painters Dante Gabriel Rossetti ▲ *218,*

CHELSEA FLOWER SHOW

The Flower Show is a feature of the London social season. Below, the cover of a piano piece written to celebrate the famous event attended by high society from the Royal Family downward.

CHELSEA'S CHARM
The unity of style in Chelsea buildings derives partly from its use of mellow red brick and the Flemish-style houses (right and below).

Holman Hunt and James Abbott McNeill Whistler ● *104*; and the writers George Eliot, Henry James and Oscar Wilde ● *111*. It was not long before Chelsea acquired a reputation as a cultural Bohemia, and then followed famous men from the worlds of science and beyond, such as the historian Thomas Carlyle and that extraordinary architectural genius of bridges and tunnels, Sir Marc Brunel (father of the great Isambard Kingdom Brunel).

THE TEMPLE OF FASHION. Chelsea became fashionable again during the 1950's. First of all the new generation of dramatists, the so-called "Angry Young Men", had their plays staged at the Royal Court Theatre. These were playwrights such as John Osborne and Arnold Wesker, who were reacting against what they called the "Establishment". Then, during the 1960's, Chelsea became the musical Mecca for rock music devotees, with the Rolling Stones leading the field, and for fashion too, with the young Mary Quant well up front. The media personalities and rock stars took over from the dreamy intellectuals who had gone before them, but Chelsea remains the lively little village it has always been, with its pretty cottages and landscapes, never getting bogged down in the past. Right through the 20th century it has continued to be a home for all manner of creative personalities, from the thriller writer Agatha Christie, philosopher Bertrand Russell and writer-director Peter Ustinov, to such unlikely figures as millionaire Paul Getty and the ex-prime minister Margaret Thatcher.

IN MEMORY
Some houses in London have blue ceramic plaques recording the name and dates of a famous personality who lived there.

SIR CAROL REED FILM DIRECTOR LIVED HERE 1948 - 1978

EXPLORING CHELSEA

Invaded as it has been since 1970 by trendy boutiques, the commercial parts of Chelsea at least have changed, yet somehow without relinquishing all links with the past. A walk around will reveal an attractive jumble of fashion shops, traditional pubs (some with their own little theaters attached), delightful statues, good restaurants, antique shops and historic gardens.

A HOST OF CELEBRITIES
Among the famous people who settled in Chelsea are (below, left to right): Whistler (1834–1903), an American painter celebrated for his riverscapes; George Eliot (1819–80), author of *Middlemarch* and *Silas Marner*; Oscar Wilde (1854–1900), dramatist and wit; and Algernon Charles Swinburne (1837–1909), English poet and critic.

RED BRICK AND WHITE STUCCO
Detail of a typical 19th-century Chelsea house.

LOANE SQUARE. This extremely busy square, with the Royal 'ourt Theatre on the east side (which reopened its doors in 000 after two years exile in the West End because of estoration work) opposite the famous *Peter Jones* department tore, marks the boundary between northern Chelsea and the tart of Belgravia. It is named after Sir Hans Sloane ▲ *301,* he 18th-century physician and benefactor of Chelsea.

ING'S ROAD. This road was laid out during the 17th century t the orders of Charles II as a link between the Palace of Vhitehall ▲ *142* and Hampton Court ▲ *352.* It was a private oad until 1830, and a special pass was needed to use it. ing's Road, which became fashionable in the 1960's, is today ne of the busiest roads in Chelsea, with its numerous shops, ubs and restaurants, and the colorful crowd of people rronging the pavements: hippies in the past, then punks, ow whatever the latest trend is, to which are added the ourists. On Saturdays the pavements are swarming with eople, because King's Road is the essential hang-out or young Londoners, the place where you come to see nd be seen. King's Road is also lined with antique shops, e best known of them being the Antiquarius Centre at umbers 131–141; an arcade of antique shops at number 31; and the Chelsea Antiques Market at umbers 245–253.

HE OLD TOWN HALL. This building was onstructed between 1885 and 1907 in the nglish neo-Baroque style. Every year ere is an important antique fair held ere that attracts a large number of sitors from all over the world.

UMBER 152 KING'S ROAD. Only the açade remains of THE PHEASANTRY with s portico supporting a quadriga. This as once a magnificent private house, built in 1881 for the rtist Amédée Joubert.

RGYLL HOUSE. Opposite the new Chelsea College of Art is a roup of listed 18th-century buildings. Argyll House is at umber 211, built in 1723 by the Venetian Giacomo Leoni. r Thomas Augustine Arne (1710–78), composer of *Rule, ritannia*, and the writer-director Peter Ustinov have both ved here.

HE ROYAL AVENUE. This elegant space, bordered with lime ees and lined with rows of fine houses, is all that remains of ambitious urban development that was initiated by William I, who wanted to build an avenue from the Thames up to ensington Palace. The Royal Avenue bisects the grassy wns of Burton's Court and finishes up outside the central uilding of the Royal Hospital.

HE ROYAL HOSPITAL ★

he hospital was built in 1682 by King Charles II a retirement home for old soldiers of his lately constituted army. Sir Stephen Fox, the army's aymaster general, was entrusted with the job of ising the money. The diarist and courtier John Evelyn ughed out the plans for the hospital, whose design nd construction was the work of Sir Christopher ren ● *70,* ▲ *171, 276.* It was only completed in

STENDHAL IN CHELSEA
"I loved London for its beautiful walks along the Thames to Little Chelsea. The tiny cottages wreathed in roses brought tears to my eyes," said the French novelist Stendhal, author of *Scarlet and Black*.

SIR THOMAS MORE
This statue of England's great Lord Chancellor was erected in 1970 opposite Chelsea Old Church in Cheyne Walk.

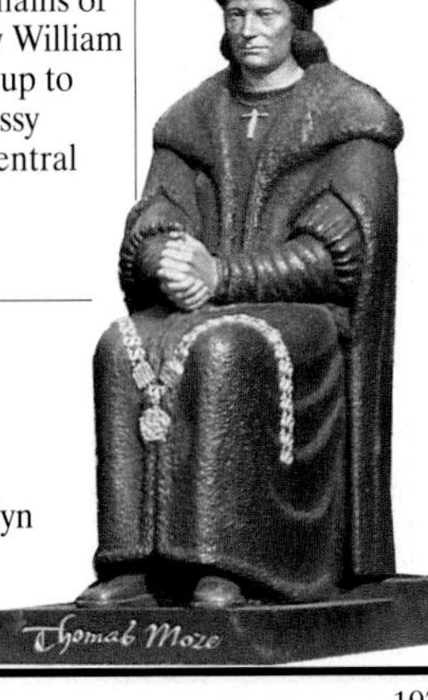

A haven of tranquillity
In this painting by Peter Tillemans (1684–1734) the buildings of the Royal Hospital, set among lawns and the Ranelagh Gardens (right), rise above the Thames to show the classical severity of their architecture – which prompted the historian Thomas Carlyle to call it: "Quiet and dignified and the work of a gentleman".

A harmonious effect
This canvas by Edward Haytley dates from 1746 and captures the building's elegant proportions. Its geometric simplicity is enhanced by the bright red brickwork contrasted with white stone. Before the construction of Chelsea Embankment, the hospital gardens ran right down to the Thames.

1692 in the reign of William III, though 476 Pensioners were admitted in 1689. The number of inmates has changed little i the time since then. Between 1765 and 1782 Robert Adam ● *76*, ▲ *256*, *263* made some alterations. Between 1819 and 1822 some additional buildings in a severe neo-classical style were erected to the east and west. They were designed by Sir John Soane ▲ *150*. The Royal Hospital was seriously damaged by enemy action during the Second World War and has been largely rebuilt since then.

A tour of the Royal Hospital. The Royal Hospital is constructed of red brick and white Portland stone and it consists of a central building with a lantern turret. The two long wings that house the Pensioners form courtyards on either side, with additional wings on each side of them. In the middle of the central courtyard is a statue of Charles II, depicted as a Roman emperor, by Grinling Gibbons ▲ *173*. The main portico, with its Doric columns, divides the chapel from the Great Hall. The chapel was consecrated in 1692. Its fine woodwork was carved by William Emmett and Renatus Harris, while the apsidal vaulting was decorated 1710–15 with a fresco by the Venetian artist Sebastiano Ricci. Both Pensioners and visitors come to worship in this chapel every Sunday. On the other side of the portico, the Great Hall was used as a refectory until the end of the 18th century In 1852 it was used for the lying-in-state of the Duke of Wellington ▲ *246* and many Londoners came here to pay their last respects to the great soldier. Replicas of the flags that were captured from the French during the revolutionary and Napoleonic wars hang from the refectory walls. On the front wall is an allegorical fresco by the Italian Antonio Verri (1639–1707), which was begun around 1667. It, too, represents Charles II. On the eastern side of the buildings, in an annex near the Royal Hospital's cemetery, is a small museum which traces the history of the institution. Here ther is a fascinating collection of medals and decorations that belonged to the Pensioners.

The Chelsea Pensioners. The old soldiers are easily recognizable by their distinctive uniform, which has not changed since the end of the 18th century. During the

A celebration
On special occasions during the summer, and when they go out, the Chelsea Pensioners wear a tricorn hat, trimmed with gold braid, and a scarlet coat bearing their medals.

summer they wear red to go out, and also on festival days. Summer here begins on May 29, which is known as Oak Apple Day, the birthday of King Charles II. Pensioners must be at least sixty-five years old; and they receive an allowance "for beer and tobacco", pocket money, and are fed and lodged at the expense of the state. In exchange they are bound to attend military church services and parades. Custom dictates that in the refectory these old soldiers from the ranks are served before officers. It is a common sight to see Chelsea Pensioners walking down the King's Road or in one of the local pubs.

Chelsea Flower Show. The Royal Hospital Gardens slope down toward the bank of the river, and each May the Chelsea Flower Show is held here, opened by the queen in person. It is organized by the Royal Horticultural Society, whose members provide the exhibits. The show is also a competition and lasts for four days; the winner's picture appears in *The Times* the following day. The show attracts thousands of visitors, some from as far away as the United States.

Ranelagh Gardens. Redesigned around 1860, Ranelagh Gardens are now on the east side of the Royal Hospital Gardens. They are on the site of what was once the estate of Lord Ranelagh, paymaster general to the Forces until his death in 1712. For more than half a century, from 1742 to 1804, the gardens were a fashionable walking and recreation place for Londoners.

National Army Museum. This museum was opened in 1971, in modern buildings to the west of the hospital in Royal Hospital Road. It displays the history of the British Army and its regiments from 1485 until the outbreak of World War One.

A home for old soldiers
The Royal Hospital is still a working hospice for approximately four hundred ex-servicemen of the British Army. They

are predominantly veterans of World War Two. Only some parts of the hospital are open to the public: the chapel, a small museum, the Great Hall (above), and also the huge gardens (below).

Around Cheyne Walk

Leaving King's Road and the Royal Hospital, the visitor also leaves Old Chelsea, toward less opulent but perhaps even more attractive sights. There is a subtle charm to be found in the maze of little residential streets such as Oakley Street, Old Church Street and Upper Cheyne Row; and in the elegant Georgian ● *74* town houses of Cheyne Walk, facing the river. Ceramic blue plaques ■ *373* on some façades give the name and dates, together with a few other details, of various famous men and women who have lived in Chelsea; they are a satisfying stimulus to the imagination.

Winter uniform
The heavy, dark blue outfit worn in winter keeps the Pensioners warm, but is duller than the summer one.

Chelsea Physic Garden ★. With the exception of the one at Oxford, this is the oldest botanical garden in England. It was founded in 1673 by the Apothecaries' Company, which wanted a collection of medicinal plants for educational and scientific study. The land it occupies was originally the gift of Sir Hans Sloane. One of the greatest horticulturalists of the day, Philip Miller, was put in charge of it and he made the Physic Garden the envy of his contemporaries. The first cedar trees in England were planted here in 1683, and here also were raised cotton plants from the South Seas which went to found an industry in the colony of Georgia in 1732. Behind the Physic Garden's wrought-iron railings, there is still a horticultural and botanic study center of the highest quality. There are many trees that are more than a hundred years old and more than seven thousand varieties of herbs, fruits and vegetables. The garden is open to the public during the summer, and visitors can enjoy the benefit of an expert and dedicated staff, as well as a number of books and leaflets available from the information bureau. From the entrance gate, an avenue leads to the imposing statue of Sir Hans Sloane. This is a copy of the one that was carved by Rysbrack in 1737. From this point, there is a magnificent view over the whole of the rest of the garden.

Cheyne Walk ★. Facing the river bank is Cheyne Walk, an extremely pleasant and shady street that is lined with a row of fine Georgian ● *74* brick houses. The most beautiful of these buildings are gathered at the beginning of the street, and perhaps the most remarkable of them all is Crosby Hall, a much earlier house, which was built between 1466 and 1475 by the wool merchant Sir John Crosby. This street has been much involved with painting and poetry: the Pre-Raphaelite Brotherhood was founded here, since this was where several of its members also lived.

Famous residents. Mary Ann Evans, who, writing under the pseudonym of George Eliot, was a famous novelist of the realist school, died in 1880 at 4 Cheyne Walk. At number 16 lived Dante Gabriel Rossetti. He was an eminent poet and painter, the son of an Italian immigrant teacher and the leader of the Pre-Raphaelite movement. He lived here from 1862 until his death. The poet Algernon Charles Swinburne (1837–1909), novelist George Meredith (1828–1909) and the

The Physic Garden
The illustrations above show the garden as it was in the 19th century.

A ceramic plaque
This type of ornament (right) is often seen on houses in Chelsea.

Sloane's tomb
In the graveyard of All Saints, Chelsea (known as Chelsea Old Church), is a great urn marking the grave of Sir Hans Sloane (1660–1753), the Chelsea physician, botanist and collector. His museum and library helped to found the British Museum.

critic John Ruskin (1810–1900) were among the frequent visitors to his house (which was built in 1717). The American novelist Henry James (who became a British citizen in 1915) died at 21 CARLYLE MANSIONS in Cheyne Walk. During the 1920's, the historian Arnold Toynbee (1889–1975), author of a controversial ten-volume *History of the World*, and the poet T.S. Eliot (1888–1965) also lived here for a while.

LINDSEY HOUSE. At 95–100 Cheyne Walk is Lindsey House, which was built around 1674 by the earl of Lindsey. In the late 18th century it was divided into a number of separate dwellings: the American painter James Abbott McNeill Whistler (1834–1903) ● *104* lived at number 96. He believed in "art for art's sake" and disliked the quasi-literary approach of the members of the Pre-Raphaelite movement. The paintings he made of Battersea Bridge, together with his portraits of his mother and of Thomas Carlyle, are probably among his most famous works. J.M.W. Turner (1775–1851) ● *102* spent the last ten years of his reclusive life at 118–19 Cheyne Walk, living under the name of Booth. Turner was one of the greatest English landscape painters, and he derived much of the inspiration for his work from the River Thames. He was a precursor of Impressionism. Within the Tate Gallery, the Charles Clore Gallery is entirely devoted to Turner's work ▲ *207*.

THE PRE-RAPHAELITES ▲ *218*. The originators of the Pre-Raphaelite Brotherhood were three Royal Academicians: William Holman Hunt (1827–1910), John Everett Millais (1829–96) and Dante Gabriel Rossetti. Reacting against the academic painting of the period, they affirmed the social and religious duties of art. They were the forerunners of Symbolism, and of naturalism too, for their work is characterized by a precise and minute attention to detail.

18TH-CENTURY ELEGANCE
Many of the houses in Cheyne Walk date from this period, and are first-rate examples of the Georgian style.

CARLYLE SQUARE
Its yellow brick houses ornamented with stucco are typical of the period 1830–40. Charles Dickens found the style ugly, and in his novel *Nicholas Nickleby* (1839) he spoke out against the design of prosperous Belgrave Square houses as well as what he called "the barbaric chaos of Chelsea".

CHEYNE WALK
One of the most attractive streets in London, it has the Thames on the south side and fine 18th-century houses on the north.

PAULTON'S SQUARE
This attractive Georgian square was built in the 1830's. It faces onto the King's Road near the area known as World's End.

The movement only survived into the 1870's, but its influence on 20th-century Symbolism remained important.

CHELSEA OLD CHURCH. This is Chelsea's old village church. Although it is partly medieval, most of the church was built during the 17th century, and it was again heavily restored following the bombing of 1941. The SIR THOMAS MORE CHAPEL, which was rebuilt by the man himself in 1528, now contains a monument to him. After More's execution, however, his head was buried at Canterbury. Popular legend has it that Henry VIII married his third wife Jane Seymour here in 1536.

CHELSEA AND SIR THOMAS MORE. Before the King's Road ran through Chelsea, its main road was Old Church Street, which was lined with little cottages. Sir Thomas More was Henry VIII's Lord Chancellor ▲ *197, 320*, and also the author of the fantasy *Utopia* and some other philosophical writings. But after Henry's divorce and the consequent rejection of the Catholic church, More felt himself unable to recognize the sovereign as the head of the newly formed Anglican church, and he was accordingly beheaded in the Tower of London. He was beatified in 1886 and then made a saint in 1935. The Irishman Jonathan Swift (1667–1745), author of *Gulliver's Travels*, lived for a time in Old Church Street. The many friends who came to visit him there included John Gay (1685–1732), William Congreve (1670–1729) and Alexander Pope (1688–1744).

CHEYNE ROW ★. The Scottish historian Thomas Carlyle (1795–1881) lived at 24 Cheyne Row for almost fifty years, from 1834 until his death ▲ *112.* His writings, among the most famous of which were the *History of the French Revolution* and a six-volume *Life of Frederick the Great*, were tremendously influential. Carlyle loved the sense of history and the bohemian disorder that he found in Chelsea. His house has now become the Carlyle Museum.

RIVERSIDE PUBS
The pubs around Cheyne Walk have carefully preserved their traditional atmosphere. The *King's Arms* at number 114 is still a village inn, likewise the *King's Head and Eight Bells* at number 50.

TITE STREET. The Irish writer Oscar Wilde ● *111* (1854–1900) settled at 3 Tite Street in 1880 and a few years later he moved 'nto a different house in the same street, at number 34. Born in Dublin, Wilde was friends with James Abbott McNeill Whistler ● *104*, the art critic John Ruskin (1842–1900), the French poet Stéphane Mallarmé (1842–98), Sarah Bernhardt (1844–1923) and Mark Twain (1835–1910). Wilde made himself the darling of society thanks to his brilliant wit and his dandified elegance. It was at number 34 that he wrote his only novel, *The Picture of Dorian Gray*, the homosexual mplications of which were to cause a scandal when the work appeared in 1890. Four years later its creator caused an even bigger scandal when he was arrested in the Cadogan Hotel, Sloane Street, and charged with having homosexual relations with Lord Alfred Douglas, son of the Marquis of Queensberry. Wilde was found guilty and sentenced to two years' hard labor, which he served at Reading ail; after his release he became an impoverished alcoholic exile in France, where he died. The American painter John Singer Sargent (1856–1925) ived at number 31 from 1885 until his death. In his work he was much influenced by two of his friends, Monet and Whistler. His painting fell into disfavor after his death but he is now recognized as a great portrait artist of the Edwardian era. Finally, two Art Nouveau houses designed by architect E.W. Godwin are well worth a look: number 44, built in 1878 for Wilde's friend the painter Frank Miles; and number 46, built a couple of years later and consisting of four artists' studios one on top of the other.

CHELSEA EMBANKMENT ★. The Embankment was completed in 1874 and runs parallel to Cheyne Walk. It is lined with houseboats and barges that continue to attract the attention of tourists.

Cheyne Walk now overlooks scores of houseboats and converted barges.

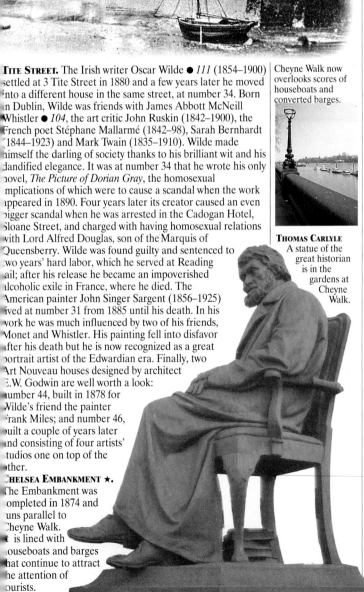

THOMAS CARLYLE
A statue of the great historian is in the gardens at Cheyne Walk.

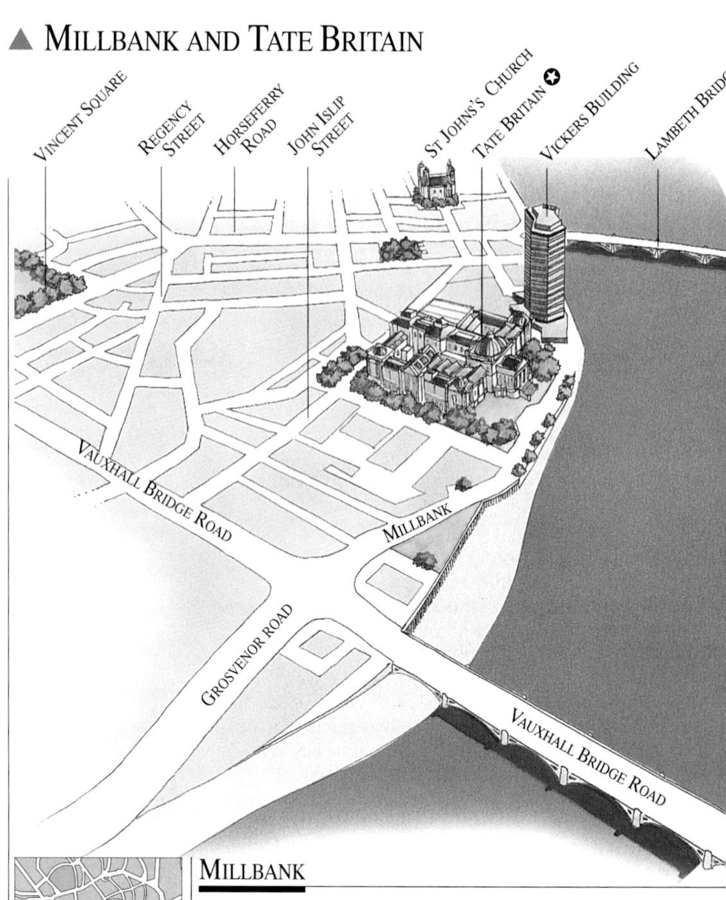

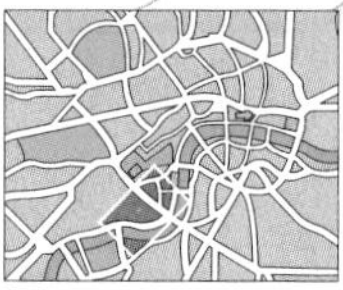

Half a day
◆ F D2

MILLBANK

Until the early 18th century Millbank was an ordinary road that crossed fields full of crops and water meadows linking Westminster and Chelsea. Its name derives from the mill of Westminster Abbey, which stood at the end of what is now Great College Street; this was pulled down by Sir Robert Grosvenor in 1736 so that he could build himself a manor house.

MILLBANK PENITENTIARY. In 1809 the seat of the Grosvenor family was demolished to make way for the Millbank Penitentiary, which was to be London's biggest prison in the 19th century. Liberal thinker Jeremy Bentham's ideas for prison reform were the motivating force behind its construction. He thought the prison should be circular, with the warders in the middle. Prisoners should learn to enjoy work through sharing in the profits of the goods they made

THE PRISON WALLS
Inside the walls was a maze of corridors three miles long. It is said there was one warder who had to mark his way with a piece of chalk even after working there for seven years.

(boots and mailbags). In 1794 Bentham persuaded the government to finance the building of a model prison, putting up some of the money for the project himself. The penitentiary was completed in 1821, a star-shaped building with six arms extending over seven acres of marshland on the bank of the river. Bentham's reforming ideas were never adopted, and in 1843 the penitentiary became an ordinary prison, to be closed in 1890 and demolished soon after. The Tate Gallery was built on the site.

MILLBANK CONVICTS
The prisoners each had their own cell, where they used to make boots and sew mailbags. All communication between them was strictly forbidden for the first half of their sentence.

PIMLICO

The district of Pimlico is bounded to the east by Vauxhall Bridge Road, to the west by Chelsea Bridge Road and by Ebury Street in the north.

THE ORIGINS OF THE NAME. Where the district of Pimlico's name actually comes from remains obscure. Some say it was the name of a drink for which the recipe is lost, others associate it with the Pamlicos, a tribe of North American Indians who exported timber to London during the 17th century. It may alternatively have been the name of a bird that used to make its home in these parts, or it may have referred to a 16th-century publican called Ben Pimlico. The earliest traces of occupation in the area date from 1626. These were the NEAT HOUSES, some cottages that were built on land belonging to Westminster Abbey. The land where Pimlico now stands was composed mainly of vegetable gardens, willow coppices and untenanted ground that in 1830 belonged to the Grosvenor family. They leased it to Thomas Cubitt (1777–1855), who pursued his policy of developing the area as he had already done successfully in both Bloomsbury and Belgravia.

THE PENITENTIARY IN 1876
"The Millbank Penitentiary covered at least seven acres of land, and was roughly in the shape of a wheel, with six wings each extending out from the common center and terminating in a tower as the spokes. The governor's house at the center was the hub. . . . The authorities were obliged to relax the harsh discipline in the cells early on, in response to numerous cases of madness induced by solitary confinement. Man is a social animal who needs his fellow creatures, even if they are rogues."
Louis Enault,
London

THOMAS CUBITT. He started his career as a carpenter, before advancing to become a contractor of public works whose influence on urban development in London was probably as profound as that of Christopher Wren ▲ *171–4* and John Nash ▲ *257* before him. He built houses on the Russell lands in Bloomsbury, and then became a property developer in Belgravia. Pimlico always lacked the fashionable cachet of Belgravia: it was respectable, but never really smart. Yet if this district lacks the real elegance of some of Cubitt's other developments, there are still some exceptionally fine terraces of stuccoed 19th-century houses to be seen here.

ECCLESTON SQUARE. Begun by Thomas Cubitt in 1835, this square is named after one of the duke of Westminster's country properties. Winston Churchill lived at number 33 from 1908 to 1911. The same house was later to become the headquarters of the Workers' Party during the General Strike of 1926.

EBURY STREET. This road crosses some of the most attractive residential streets to be found just south of Belgravia. The eight-year-old composer Amadeus Mozart wrote his first symphony at number 180. Across the road is a fine example of tenement dwellings, which were built in 1871, the COLESHILL FLATS.

THE TWO TATES ✪
The Tate Gallery has an international reputation for the quality of its sometimes extremely daring modern art exhibitions. The Tate is also home to the Turner prize, awarded each year to an "outstanding" young artist. With the opening of the seven-floor Bankside site (Tate Modern) in 2000, which concentrates exclusively on modern art, the original Tate (now renamed Tate Britain) has now reverted to the original intention of its founder, Sir Henry Tate, and holds the world's best collection of British art, from Hogarth to Constable, Turner and Hockney. Work is planned at Tate Britain over the next few years with the addition of new galleries to extend the exhibition space by more than 35 percent, refurbishment of the pre-war buildings, and external landscaping.

PIMLICO ROAD. This is the area's main shopping street, and it has some first-class antique shops. The small Victorian Gothic church of St Barnabas was built between 1847 and 1850 by Thomas Cundy. St Saviour's is in George Square, a rectangle between Grosvenor Place and Lupus Street. It was built in 1864 to a design submitted by Thomas Cundy the Younger.

CHURCHILL GARDENS. This prize-winning housing development for 6,500 people was built by Westminster Council between 1952 and 1960. The architects responsible were A.J.P. Powell and J.H. Moya.

Sir Henry Tate.

THE TATE GALLERY (NOW TATE BRITAIN) ★

The Gallery of Modern British Art, which has become under the name of the Tate Gallery, one of the most famous museums in the world, was opened in 1897 on Millbank facing the Thames.

SIR HENRY TATE. The museum is named after the businessman, sugar merchant and art collector Sir Henry Tate. He gave his private collection of British art to the nation (sixty canvases and three sculptures), which became the nucleus of the museum, and he financed the construction of the building.

EARLY DEVELOPMENTS. Lord Duveen, another benefactor, financed the

"VAUXHALL GARDENS, THE GRAND WALKABOUT 1751"
Canalettto ● 97 painted several views of Vauxhall Gardens (left) then known as New Spring Gardens. Laid out in 1660 on the south bank of the Thames, they were embellished with statues, Gothic "ruins", rotundas of antiques, Chinese pavilions and even concert halls and music halls.

A NEO-BAROQUE BUILDING
Sydney Smith designed the museum in a neo-Baroque style: the imposing façade consists of a portico with Corinthian pillars approached by a staircase from the embankment.

ving built to house the collection that Turner bequeathed o the nation, previously hung in the National Gallery. n 1926 a first extension was built to house the foreign ollections; a second followed in 1937, both financed y Lord Duveen's son. Other extensions were built n 1971 and 1979, before the opening of the Clore Gallery in 1987.

THE CLORE GALLERY. This gallery (opposite), pened by the Queen, was designed to house he Turner collection: three hundred oil aintings and more than nineteen thousand rawings and watercolors, the pride of he Tate Gallery.

HE TATE MODERN. The original museum vas able to display only about one tenth f the museum's actual holdings, so a econd site was therefore constructed in rder to maximise the richness of the ollection. Opened in May 2000, the new ate Modern, which is built on an xpanded site at Bankside, offers seven evels dedicated to modern art from round the world, while the Tate at Millbank, renamed "Tate Britain", emains dedicated to English painting nd sculpture from the 16th entury onward.

In one of London's most significant projects for the new millennium, the Tate collection of art, which was formerly housed at the Tate Gallery at Millbank, has now been divided into two distinct collections. Renamed Tate Britain, the site at Millbank holds the world's best collection of British art from 1500 to the present day. International works and contemporary art are now housed in the heart of London, in the transformed Bankside Power Station. First opened in May 2000, this exciting new branch, named Tate Modern, was an instant hit with Londoners and tourists alike.

Joseph Mallord William Turner (1775-1851)
This British painter is famous for his watercolors, drawings and engravings. He produced an enormous amount of paintings, mainly landscapes. His work has influenced a large number of Impressionists. Since 1987, the Clore Gallery has housed the prestigious Turner Collection of more than 19,000 drawings and watercolors, as well as 300 oil paintings. The gallery was designed by James Stirling.

"Self-portrait" (1797),
Joseph Mallord William Turner. On display in Tate Britain.

"Pompeii"
Hans Hofmann (1880–1966). This German painter, who lived in the USA from 1931, founded a school of art in New York in 1933. Until 1940 his work remained figurative in the Expressionist tradition. Then he developed an abstract style, represented by this canvas of 1959. Works by Hofmann are now on display in Tate Modern.

"Faa Iheihe"
The Tahitian title of this work has been translated as "Pastoral Symphony": it was painted by Paul Gauguin (1848–1903) during his last stay on Tahiti. It portrays a vision of Paradise, a hymn to the harmony existing between man and nature, and was painted after a period of profound creative pessimism. It is one of the landmarks in the collection of modern European and American art from Impressionism to the new avant-garde of the 1970s which the Tate Gallery began to assemble between 1910 and 1920. Gauguin's paintings are now on display in Tate Modern.

"THE FORGE"
Joseph Wright (1734–97), known as "Wright of Derby", started out as a painter of the Industrial Revolution in the Midlands. In a uniquely recognizable style influenced by Caravaggio, Wright combined realism with sentiment, and made much use of the effects of light.

"THE ARTIST AND HIS DOG"
This self-portrait of 1745 by William Hogarth (1697–1764) is resting on works of Shakespeare, Swift and Milton: from now on, painting took its place beside literature as a noble art form. X-ray examination reveals that Hogarth originally painted himself dressed like a gentleman.

"In my best room is a choice collection of the works of Hogarth, an English painter of some humor."

Charles Lamb

"Captain Thomas Lee"
Captain Lee, officer of the County of Essex, took part in the conquest of Ireland. Estimating that he lacked the means to continue the war, he returned to England in 1594 to plead his cause before Queen Elizabeth I, and had his portrait painted by Marcus Gheeraerts the Younger (c. 1561–1636). Lee is richly dressed, but has bare feet like a poor soldier. He is standing in an Irish landscape under an oak tree, symbol of courage. He was executed at Tyburn for his part in the conspiracy of 1601.

"The Saltonstall Family"
This painting by David des Granges (c. 1611–75) is a fine example of 17th-century family portraiture. At first glance it seems to be simple enough: a husband congratulating his wife who has just borne him a third child. In fact, as was often the case during the Elizabethan era, the living and the dead are painted together. Saltonstall is depicted here with his two wives: his deceased first wife holds out her hand toward her two children. His second wife is holding her new baby.

"Three Daughters of Sir William Montgomery as Graces Adorning a Statue of Hymen"
Joshua Reynolds (1723–92), first president of the Royal Academy, elevated relatively unimportant genres of painting, especially the portrait, by introducing elements of Grand Genre. His painting of the three sisters (1773) bears witness to his efforts. At the request of the gentleman who commissioned the painting, Reynolds incorporated symbolic features derived from classical antiquity and the Old Masters. The sisters are seen praising the god of marriage in poses used by Poussin and Rubens. To the right of Elisabeth is Anne, dressed in white and already married; on the left is Barbara, who married the following year.

"The Harvesters"
The self-taught painter George Stubbs (1724–1806) became during his lifetime the most famous animal painter in England, working for the aristocracy and adapting the grand style to his pictures of animals. Above all, he was famous for painting horses; but he also produced some delightful scenes of English country life. In an age when peasants were held to have a merely decorative value in paintings, Stubbs shows them in a more sympathetic light, making them real personalities. This painting (1785) is nevertheless composed in a severely classical style. A girl is in the center, while a horseman on the right balances a couple binding corn. Men bent at their work link the two groups.

"Giovanna Baccelli" Thomas Gainsborough (1727–88) is unusual in that he never left England, having arrived in London fairly late in life, in 1774. It was there that the duke of Dorset, who was also the ambassador to Paris, commissioned Gainsborough to paint a portrait of his mistress Giovanna Baccelli, the prima ballerina at the Haymarket Theatre. She had started her career at the Opéra in Paris, and is depicted executing a dance step. Here the artist's technical mastery and his feeling for line result in a composition where exceptional grace and lightness combines with fresh colors to produce a portrait of great subtlety and beauty. The picture was exhibited at the Royal Academy in 1782.

"BEATRICE ADDRESSING DANTE FROM THE CAR"
William Blake (1757–1827) believed himself entrusted with the mission of preserving the Divine Vision in a troubled age. This watercolor, painted between 1824 and 1827, is from a series of a hundred illustrations to Dante's *Divine Comedy*. It represents a scene from the *Purgatorio,* describing Dante's first sight of Beatrice.

"THE BLIND FIDDLER"
David Wilkie (1785–1841) was a Scottish artist who enjoyed an immense success in England during the early 19th century. Early in his career he painted scenes of rustic life that were derived from Dutch and Flemish models. His influence later extended all over Europe.

"THE OPENING OF WATERLOO BRIDGE". In this scene depicting the opening of the bridge on June 18, 1817, the English painter John Constable (1776–1837) makes a direct reference to one of Canaletto's paintings as a symbol of England's superiority over other nations.

"THE BRIDGE OF SIGHS, THE DUCAL PALACE AND THE CUSTOM-HOUSE, CANALETTI PAINTING". When Joseph Mallord William Turner (1775–1851) visited Venice for a second time in 1832, he became obsessed with painting the city. This bold sunlit canvas was in homage to Canaletto, the great Venetian painter; and there is also an underlying desire on Turner's part to make himself part of the great artistic tradition.

"THE DOGANO, SAN GIORGIO, CITELLA, SEEN FROM THE STEPS OF THE EUROPA" Painted in 1842 after his third visit to Venice, this returns to Turner's more subdued range of colors, a testament to his emotions at the collapse of the great republic.

"PETWORTH, SUNSET IN THE PARK". Turner had a studio at Petworth, the country seat of his friend and patron Lord Egremont. This watercolor dates from around 1830, and is one of more than a hundred that he painted there.

"**SNOWSTORM – STEAMBOAT OFF A HARBOR'S MOUTH MAKING SIGNALS IN SHALLOW WATER AND GOING BY THE LEAD. THE AUTHOR WAS IN THIS STORM ON THE NIGHT THE ARIEL LEFT HARWICH.**" Snowstorms and storms at sea are recurrent themes in Turner's work. This picture, where the tempest's power is centered on the frail mast at the heart of a whirling mass of paint, was exhibited in 1842, after the artist had spent four hours lashed to the mast of a boat crossing from Harwich in such a storm that he did not expect to survive.

"BEATE BEATRICE"
Dante Gabriel Rossetti (1828–82) was, together with Hunt and Millais, a founder of the Pre-Raphaelite Brotherhood. Their principal aim was to paint only serious subjects, and to portray them with the utmost realism. The title of this work, painted in 1863, refers to the death of Dante's beloved Beatrice. Rather than paint a corpse, Rossetti chose to treat his subject symbolically, undergoing a spiritual transfiguration. The painting is in homage to the artist's wife, Elizabeth Siddal, who died from a drug overdose in February 1862, and he used her face for the figure of Beatrice.

"THE AWAKENING CONSCIENCE"
The young mistress of a wealthy man remembers the innocent days of her childhood and turns toward the light from the garden, reflected in a mirror. Holman Hunt (1827–1910) uses the effects of light and the room's decoration to reflect the state of mind of the young woman.

"THE GOLDEN STAIRS"
Edward Burne-Jones (1833–98) belonged to the late Pre-Raphaelite period. He was influenced by Rossetti and then by the Italian Old Masters. The sinuous curved lines in this painting of 1880 are characteristic features of the artist's later work.

"OPHELIA"
The inspiration for this picture by John Everett Millais (1829–96) comes from the death of Ophelia described in Act IV of *Hamlet*. The background was painted between July and October 1851 during a visit to the village of Ewell in Surrey. Back in London that winter, the artist used Rossetti's wife Elizabeth Siddal as his model, as did many other Pre-Raphaelites. The detailed vegetation in the picture includes plants and wild flowers with particular symbolic significance: the poppy, for example, is a symbol of death.

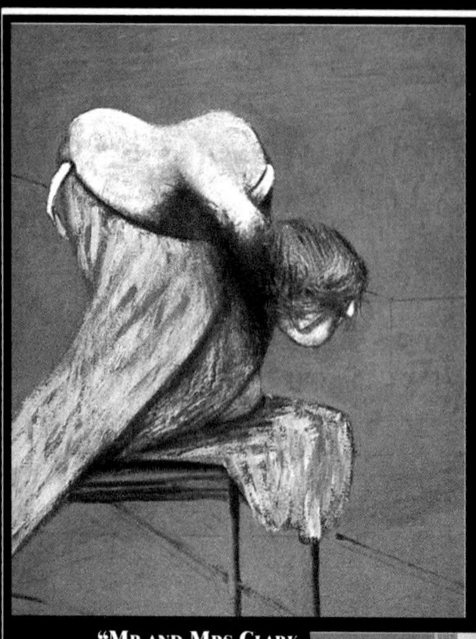

"MR AND MRS CLARK AND PERCY"
David Hockney (b. 1937) studied at the Royal College of Art from 1959, and then exhibited at the Whitechapel Art Gallery. His early work reflects the influence of Francis Bacon and of Jean Dubuffet. After a period of abstract painting Hockney evolved a naturalistic approach from 1965. The subjects in this picture, painted between 1970 and 1971, are the famous dress designers of the period Ossie Clark and Celia Birtwell.

"WHAAM!"
The American master of Pop Art Roy Lichtens (b. 1923) painted many pictures in the early 19 that were inspired by strip cartoons. This one, da from 1963, exemplifies his use of bright colors exaggerated shapes that tend toward abstracti

"LIGHT RED OVER BLACK"
An American painter of Russian origin, Mar Rothko (1903–70) was initially influenced by t Surrealists. In the 1950's he evolved an original of his own, using rectangular bands of color Up to the middle of the decade his palette wa mainly bright, but it gradually darkened, dominated by black or dark red on a brown background (left, a work of 1957).

"Three Studies for Figures at the Base of a Crucifixion" Francis Bacon (1909–92) exhibited these three studies in 1945 after a period of eight years of silence. They show the influence of Picasso's work in the 1920's; the figures have become the Eumenides, the Furies who pursue Orestes in the *Oresteia* of Aeschylus. The zoomorphic shapes have shrieking human mouths, an obsessive image in Bacon's work.

"Weeping Woman" On April 26, 1937, during the Spanish Civil War, German aeroplanes bombed Guernica. Pablo Picasso (1881–1973) began his famous painting *Guernica*, in which a weeping woman carries a dead child in her arms, two days later. Picasso took up the theme again in June 1937, making three sketches and painting four canvases, of which this is the last of the series. His model was the photographer Dora Maar, who was also his mistress.

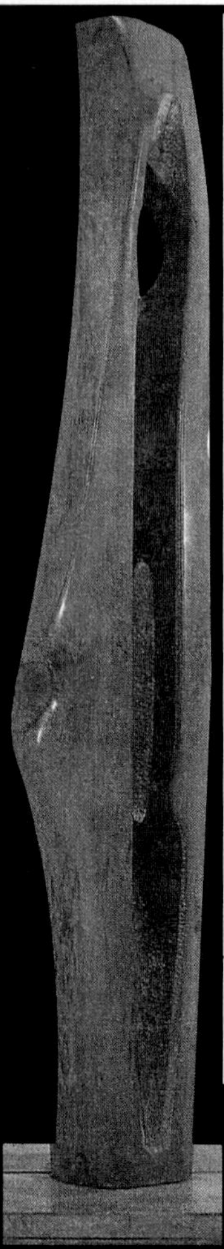

"THE MATADOR"
"For me a shape is never abstract: it always signifies something – a man, or a bird or something else," said the Spanish Surrealist Joan Miró (1893–1983). He painted this work toward the end of his life, modifying its abstract elements with thick black strokes to define the figure.

"FIGURE, NANJIZAL"
Barbara Hepworth (1903–75) drew her inspiration for this wooden sculpture of 1958 from the landscapes of Cornwall, where she had settled in 1939. She was among the first British abstract sculptors, attempting to express the soul of the material she used by the form she gave it.

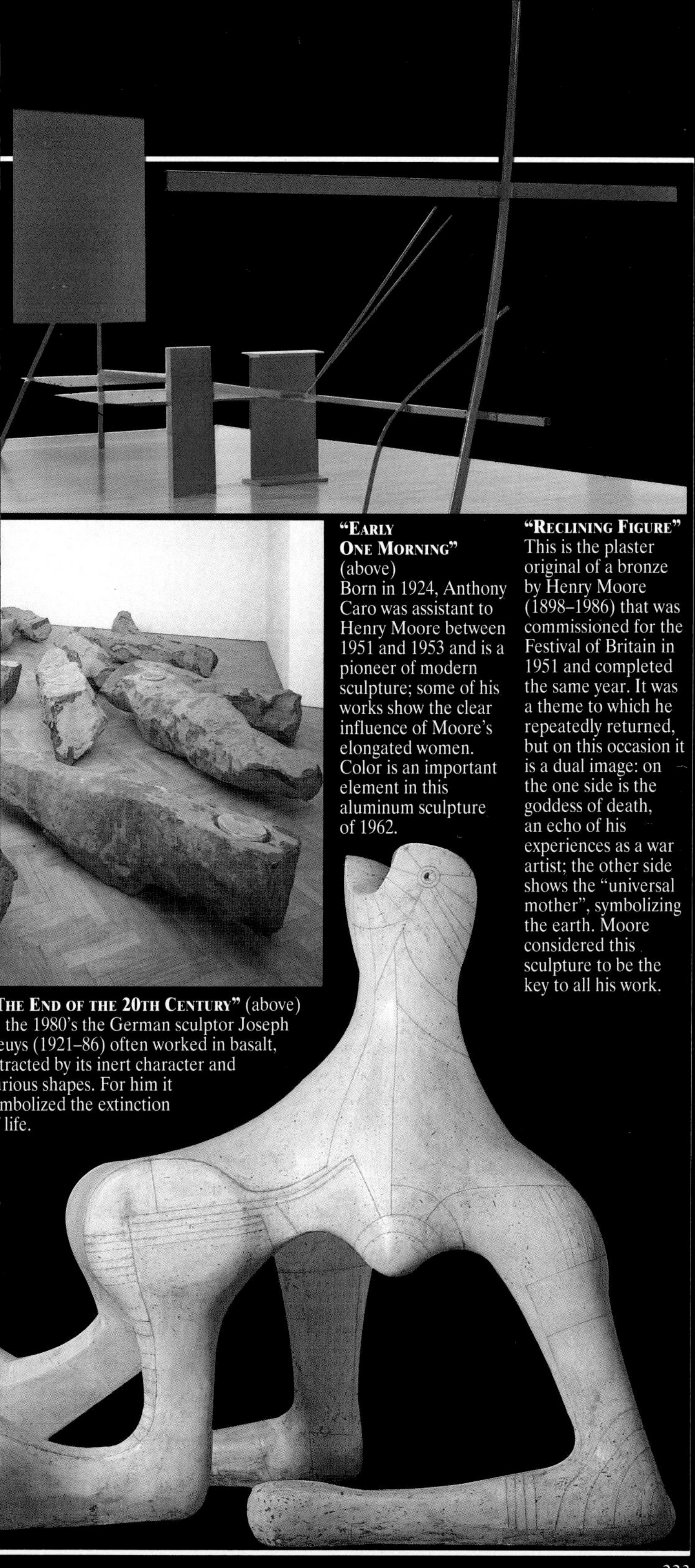

"Early One Morning" (above)
Born in 1924, Anthony Caro was assistant to Henry Moore between 1951 and 1953 and is a pioneer of modern sculpture; some of his works show the clear influence of Moore's elongated women. Color is an important element in this aluminum sculpture of 1962.

"Reclining Figure"
This is the plaster original of a bronze by Henry Moore (1898–1986) that was commissioned for the Festival of Britain in 1951 and completed the same year. It was a theme to which he repeatedly returned, but on this occasion it is a dual image: on the one side is the goddess of death, an echo of his experiences as a war artist; the other side shows the "universal mother", symbolizing the earth. Moore considered this sculpture to be the key to all his work.

[T]he End of the 20th Century" (above)
[In] the 1980's the German sculptor Joseph [B]euys (1921–86) often worked in basalt, [at]tracted by its inert character and [va]rious shapes. For him it [sy]mbolized the extinction [of] life.

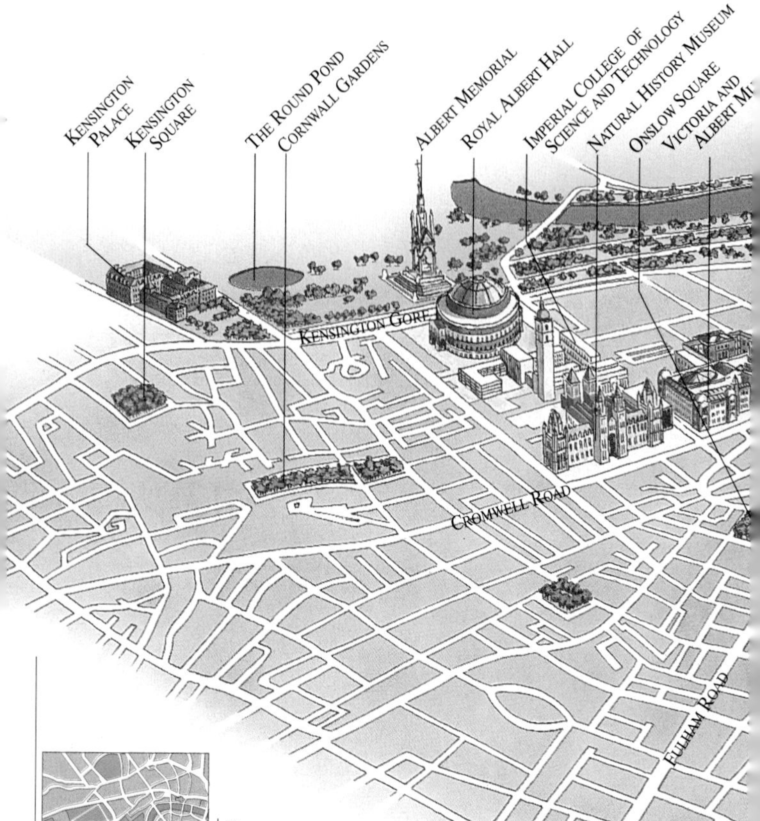

KENSINGTON PALACE
KENSINGTON SQUARE
THE ROUND POND
CORNWALL GARDENS
ALBERT MEMORIAL
ROYAL ALBERT HALL
IMPERIAL COLLEGE OF SCIENCE AND TECHNOLOGY
NATURAL HISTORY MUSEUM
ONSLOW SQUARE
VICTORIA AND ALBERT MU
KENSINGTON GORE
CROMWELL ROAD
FULHAM ROAD

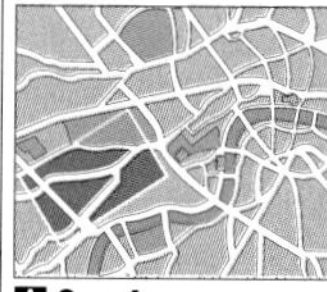

One day
◆ **E** B1-C1-C2-C3-C4

THE VICTORIAN TERRACE
Painted stucco below yellow London brick is typical of Belgravia's Victorian terraces and also of those in Islington. Islington terraces often have arched front windows with stucco surrounds.

BELGRAVIA

The fashionable district of Belgravia was once a stretch of land known as "Five Fields". It was a notorious haunt of robbers right up to the time that development started, with the first houses being built in Grosvenor Place in 1747. When George III acquired Buckingham House (now Buckingham Palace) in 1762, the area's future was assured, although large-scale development only began in the 1820's when Lord Grosvenor engaged the builder and town planner Thomas Cubitt (1777–1855) to help him increase the value of his property. Cubitt, who had excavated St Katharine's Dock ▲ *334* near the Tower of London, used the earth and rubble from the excavations to raise the level of the marshy land of Belgravia. Then he laid out squares and terraces lined with large elegant houses. The finest of all is BELGRAVE SQUARE, a central square

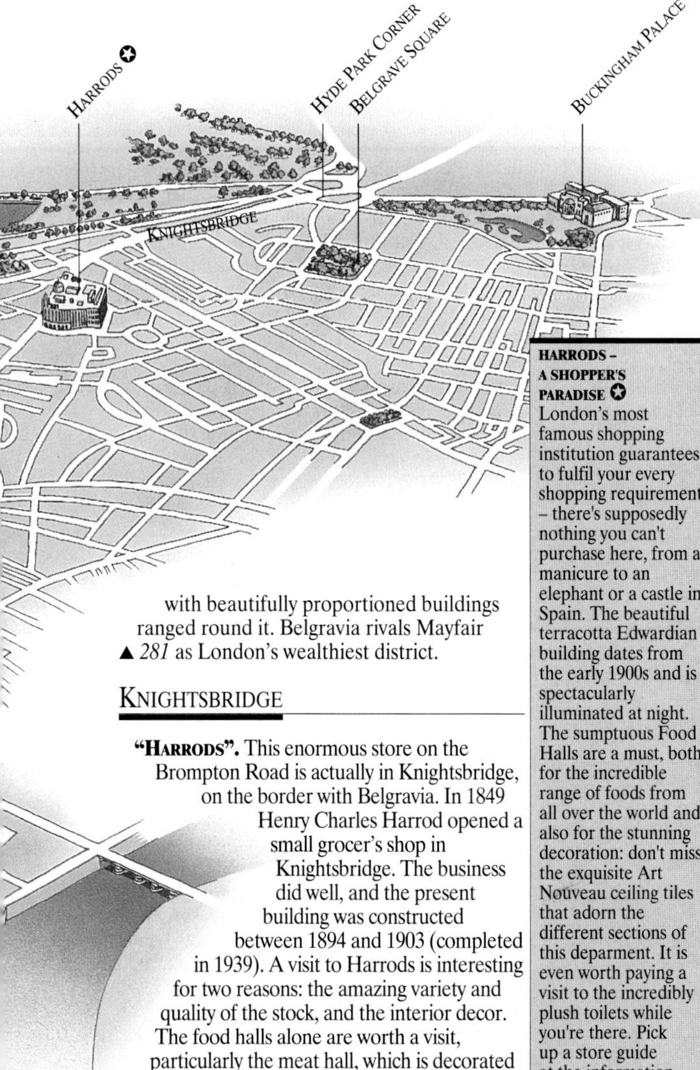

with beautifully proportioned buildings ranged round it. Belgravia rivals Mayfair ▲ *281* as London's wealthiest district.

KNIGHTSBRIDGE

"HARRODS". This enormous store on the Brompton Road is actually in Knightsbridge, on the border with Belgravia. In 1849 Henry Charles Harrod opened a small grocer's shop in Knightsbridge. The business did well, and the present building was constructed between 1894 and 1903 (completed in 1939). A visit to Harrods is interesting for two reasons: the amazing variety and quality of the stock, and the interior decor. The food halls alone are worth a visit, particularly the meat hall, which is decorated with tiles depicting hunting scenes, the work of W.N. Neatby.

HARRODS – A SHOPPER'S PARADISE ✪
London's most famous shopping institution guarantees to fulfil your every shopping requirement – there's supposedly nothing you can't purchase here, from a manicure to an elephant or a castle in Spain. The beautiful terracotta Edwardian building dates from the early 1900s and is spectacularly illuminated at night. The sumptuous Food Halls are a must, both for the incredible range of foods from all over the world and also for the stunning decoration: don't miss the exquisite Art Nouveau ceiling tiles that adorn the different sections of this deparment. It is even worth paying a visit to the incredibly plush toilets while you're there. Pick up a store guide at the information desk.

KENSINGTON

Until the 17th century Kensington was a village on the outskirts of London. In 1689, King William III bought Nottingham House, Kensington, and commissioned Christopher Wren ● *70, 171, 250* to turn it into a royal residence, known as Kensington Palace ▲ *250*. Nottingham House and Holland House between them transformed Kensington into a much sought-after residential district.

KENSINGTON SQUARES. Kensington Square was the first of the district's distinctive squares to be built (Thomas Young, 1681). It was originally named King's Square in honor of James II, and until 1840 it remained entirely surrounded by

HARRODS, THE MEAT HALL
This hall is decorated with hunting scenes, by W.J. Neatby.

Kensington and Queen Victoria
When Queen Victoria died in 1901, Kensington was made a royal borough in her honor, the only one in London. Later this was extended to include Chelsea, and the district is now called the Royal Borough of Kensington and Chelsea.

Kensington houses
Queen Victoria was born in Kensington Palace and spent the first eighteen years of her life living there, until she ascended the throne in 1837. Her long reign was also a period of intense urban development. The enormous houses of Kensington were replaced by squares and crescents ● *76* such as Edwardes Square, Trevor Square, Montpelier Place, Pelham Crescent and many more.

fields. The population of London had doubled by the first half of the 19th century, and Kensington expanded along with it. Onslow Gardens and Onslow Square are both in typical early Victorian style. They were built around 1846 by Charles James Freake. Their name comes from the then owner of the land, the earl of Onslow. The elegant houses in Onslow Square are covered in white stucco. Hereford Square is also a typically Victorian design, a peaceful little place that was built in 1847 by Edward Blore. The residential district of Kensington extends behind either side of the busy Kensington High Street. Kensington Palace Gardens (1843) is a long private road bordering Kensington Gardens ▲ *247* and lined with many magnificent houses that were built between 1844 and 1870. Many of them are now used as embassies. Parallel with this street, to the west, is Kensington Church Street, which was once a country lane linking Kensington to Notting Hill Gate. There are some fine 18th-century properties to be seen along it.

Fine families and fine art. Kensington has some exotic and extravagant 19th-century houses, particularly those located around Holland Park, which were built by newly rich Victorians. Their owners bought many pictures – though not usually with much discernment. The artist Frederick Leighton (1830–96) was so successful that he made a fortune and built himself a studio-house at 12 Holland Park Road, called Leighton House. This palatial dwelling includes an Arab Hall (1879) that gives a good idea of the 19th-century taste for exotica. Like the rest of the house, the hall was the work of George Aitchison, and it is an ingenious blend of all kinds of decorative elements, but pays little heed to their artistic quality. The other rooms are hung with a number of pictures by Lord Leighton and his friends. Nearby, at 29 Melbury Road, is Tower House. This is a strange medieval-style house that was constructed by the architect William Burges between 1876 and 1881.

In Queen's Gate (formerly Albert's Road) the houses were built in an Italianate style in the latter part of the 19th century. Some of these have been converted into flats or hotels, and though many more have since disappeared, the street retains a genteel late Victorian air.

South Kensington

To the south of Kensington Village is the residential district of South Kensington, an area that is notable for some interesting mews streets. These were formerly alleys consisting of stables and coach houses which were located behind the streets. These alleyways have now become delightful cobbled lanes, and the stables have been converted into some charming town cottages. The Great Exhibition of 1851 set in motion the building of museums and colleges in this district, projects that were initiated by Prince Albert: the Albert Memorial and the Royal Albert Hall were both built in his memory. Taking a walk down Cromwell Road, with its imposing porticoed houses, or down into "South Ken", the visitor can hardly fail to notice the French flavor of the area. This is hardly surprising since located here are the French Lycée, the French Institute, the French Consulate and the cultural department of the French Embassy. Around these institutions have sprung up several French bakers, patisseries, butchers and bookshops to cater for the substantial expatriate population living here.

Around the beginning of the 20th century the middle classes began to reject the showy opulence of their houses in favor of comfort. Interior décor quietened down, and they evolved the neo-Georgian style in imitation of the old Georgian. And as fewer families had servants, gradually the houses were broken up into flats. It became a familiar sight to see a front door with fifteen bells on it, where formerly there had been only one.

"Before reaching Knightsbridge, Mr Verloc took a turn to the left out of the busy main thoroughfare, uproarious with the traffic of swaying omnibuses ... and ... marched now along a street which could with every propriety be described as private. ... The only reminder of mortality was a doctor's brougham arrested in august solitude close to the curbstone. The polished knockers of the doors gleamed as far as the eye could reach, the clean windows shone with a dark opaque lustre. And all was still."

Joseph Conrad, *The Secret Agent*

"ALBERTOPOLIS"
This aerial view shows the Royal Geographical Society, Albert Hall Mansions, the Royal Albert Hall and, in the foreground, the Albert Memorial.

MUSEUM LAND

The southern part of Kensington, between Chelsea and Kensington Gardens, might be seen as a separate center of learning devoted t the study or appreciation of science and the arts In this one relatively small area is a concentrated group of museums, colleges and learned societies that is quite unique in London. The area is sometimes known as "Albertopolis", a symbol of the 19th-century middle-class reverence for learning anc a general thirst for knowledge. And no-one was more active in this movement for self-improvement than Prince Albert, the husband of Queen Victoria.

THE HIGH POINT OF THE VICTORIAN ERA. The first Great Exhibition ● *38* in London was held in 1851. It was considered a huge success, the apogee of Victoria's reign, and attracted some six million visitors. The vast Crystal Palace, built in Hyde Par by Joseph Paxton to house the exhibition, drew the attention of the government and of Prince Albert to the need for a cultural center in the west of London, an area which was then expanding rapidly. From 1856 onward, museums and teaching institutions for science and the arts began to spring up in an area north of the Cromwell Road, the thoroughfare opened up in 1855 in imitation of Louis-Napoleon's new Paris boulevards.

PRINCE ALBERT. For long confined to the role of a roy figurehead, the German prince Albert (left) devoted himself to the education of his and Victoria's nine children. This then developed into an obsession with educating the British nation, scientifically and

culturally. He was determined that the people should have specialized schools, colleges and museums. His friend Sir Henry Cole shared this view and and helped him to organize the new South Kensington developments. A collection of artifacts purchased during the Great Exhibition was put on display at MARLBOROUGH HOUSE, and this was such a huge success that the two of them decided to add to it and build a museum to house it. From 1852 to 1856 a museum of arts and sciences was moved from one temporary location to another, but it was only in 1859 that the home for the collection was finally built, providing the germ of what would subsequently become the Victoria and Albert Museum. Oddly enough, Prince Albert's premature death in 1861 had the effect of hastening the realization of this enormous project.

THE MUSEUMS. Two monuments were erected to the memory of the prince consort: the Albert Memorial (1863–72) and the Royal Albert Hall (1867–71). Less ostentatious, though of incalculable value, were the museums, colleges and institutes that opened, creating a form of living encyclopedia of science and art. This has never stopped growing: from 1873 up to the present such institutions as the NATURAL HISTORY MUSEUM, the ROYAL GEOGRAPHICAL SOCIETY, the ROYAL COLLEGE OF ORGANISTS, the ROYAL COLLEGE OF MUSIC, the GEOLOGICAL MUSEUM and the SCIENCE MUSEUM have opened here. The IMPERIAL COLLEGE OF SCIENCE AND TECHNOLOGY and the ROYAL COLLEGE OF ART have rounded off this extraordinary area of learning. The museums are astonishing.

THE VICTORIA AND ALBERT MUSEUM ★

The masterpiece of Museum land. It opened in 1852 as the Museum of Manufactures, to become the South Kensington Museum in 1859; and finally in 1899 the Victoria and Albert Museum.

FIFTY YEARS OF CONSTRUCTION. This extraordinary building is the result of no fewer than six quite unrelated architectural designs, successively assembled by Francis Fowke, and after his death in 1866 by Henry Young Darracott Scott and Aston Webb ▲ *243*. The result is something of a muddle, with decoration only on certain parts of the edifice. In a rather haphazard way it is centered round a rectangular courtyard, the QUADRANGLE, inspired by the Italian Renaissance. The oldest wing is the one lying to the east of the Quadrangle, built between 1856 and 1858 to house the collection of English painting donated by a rich Yorkshire industrialist, John Sheepshanks; its façade is rather later, dating from 1901. The west wing was designed by Geoffrey Sykes and his assistants in 1864, and set the style that was used for the rest of the museum (and for many other buildings in Museum land as well), i.e. brick with terracotta and mosaic decoration. The north building was constructed (1856–9) as the museum's main entrance. Between 1877 and 1884 the Quadrangle was closed to the south by a wing holding the National Art Library. Last of all, the main façade was added by Aston Webb between 1899 and 1909. The decoration on the great bronze doors is a reminder that the "V & A" is devoted to science as well as the arts. A new extension is now planned, due to be completed in 2006; Daniel Libeskind's radical "decentered spiral" design is generating much public debate.

THE "V & A"
In 1899 Queen Victoria laid the foundation stone of a new building that finally completed the Victoria and Albert Museum. It was her last appearance in public. Construction work on the museum continued until 1909, when the "V & A" (as Londoners usually call it) was finally opened by her son King Edward VII.

ASTON WEBB'S FAÇADE
Aston Webb went on to design the façade of Buckingham Palace. For his long façade (over 800 feet) of the Victoria and Albert Museum on Cromwell Road, he drew inspiration from early 16th-century French and Flemish designs. In addition there are statues executed by Alfred Drury.

"CHRIST'S CHARGE TO PETER"
For this design, Raphael (1483–1520) drew on the Gospel according to St John. Peter is depicted receiving the keys, on his knees before Christ. The cartoon underlines the primacy of St Peter, and by extension affirms the supremacy of the pope.

"FLATFORD MILL"
Together with Turner, John Constable (1776–1837) is one of the greatest English landscape painters. The artist's "light and shade of nature" is everywhere in the painting, which also shows his fascination with painting the sky.

AN ELIZABETHAN MEDALLION
This miniature of a courtier was painted by Nicholas Hilliard (c. 1547–1619).

A MUSEUM OF FINE ARTS AND THE APPLIED ARTS. The museum is an extraordinary assembly of collections taken from all over the world. There are no fewer than 145 rooms: to see them all would represent a walk of more than 5 miles! Three rooms in particular encapsulate Victorian taste: the "Green Dining Room" decorated by William Morris; the Gamble Room or central dining room, which is covered in ceramic tiles; and the Grill Room, decorated by Edward Poynter. Finally the visitor should make a point of seeing the ceramic staircase, completed in 1871 by students to the designs of F.W. Moody.

THE MUSEUM'S COLLECTIONS

THE RAPHAEL CARTOONS ★. These are the most important large-scale works of Renaissance art in the whole of England. In 1623 the future Charles I, then in Genoa, bought seven of ten cartoons by Raphael (the remaining three have never been found), depicting scenes from the lives of St Peter and St Paul. They were designs for tapestries originally commissioned by Pope Leo X to decorate the Sistine Chapel on special feast days. From Rome the cartoons went to Brussels, where they were cut into strips and copied in the workshops employed to fulfil the commission. When Charles bought them, he sent them to one of the great English tapestry-makers at Mortlake that had recently been founded by Charles' father, James I. Centuries later the reassembled cartoons were loaned by Queen Victoria to the V & A. Since tapestries are woven from the back, the cartoons are really mirror images of the intended effect and so should be read from right to left. They are shown in chronological order, beginning with *The Miraculous Draft of Fishes*. The same room has a tapestry woven at Mortlake to this design.

THE INDIAN COLLECTIONS ★. The presence of these artifacts in the V & A is the result of the demolition in 1956 of the Indian Museum that was situated on the other side of Exhibition Road. From the end of the 18th century India became the object of serious study by a number of British

"It was worthwhile to come here, if only to see Raphael's cartoon in pencil of . . . Julius II. It has all the immense power of . . . the oil painting, and . . . verifies Mr Power's assertion, that colour is not needful to expression."

Sophia Hawthorne

"St Paul Preaching at Athens"
This cartoon was executed for the *Acts of the Apostles*; Raphael shows St Paul preaching the Word of God.

"The River Goddess Yamuna"
The V & A has Indian sculptures dating from 2000 BC up to the 19th century AD, depicting such figures as gods of the earth and nature, and scenes from the life of Buddha. Below: a Hindu sculpture from central India, c. 900 AD.

cholars. In 1801 the East India Company opened a private nuseum in London in order to display antiquities, curios and istorical souvenirs that were sent home by the company's mployees working out there. When the company was issolved in 1858, following the Indian Mutiny, the sub-ontinent came directly under the control of the crown, and he collection was then moved to the India Office. Public nterest in Indian art and civilization, which had already been roused by the Great Exhibition of 1851, now grew even more apidly. The South Kensington Museum received the main ody of the India Office collection in 1880, and it was greatly xpanded during the second half of the 19th century with ieces that were brought back by British manufacturers to opy and sell over here, undercutting the Indian market. An xploration of the collections on display gives the visitor an xcellent overview of religious, ceremonial and domestic life n India, and demonstrates what can be learned from the tudy of other civilizations.

'HE ENGLISH COLLECTIONS ★. The V & A is the only museum o offer the visitor a survey of five centuries of British art. 'here are two different categories in which to trace the istory of British art over this period: decorative arts and ainting. Two decorative artists who each embody important novements are well represented here: Robert Adam ▲ *256*, vho was one of the initiators of neo-classicism, and William Aorris, who originated the Arts and Crafts movement. Both hese men wanted to create a style that was modern (one in he late 18th century, and one in the late 19th century) and at

"Prince on Horseback"
Gouache on paper; Moghul art, c. 1720.

"The Tippoo Tiger"
Made in 1790 for the sultan Tippoo Sahib, this tiger devouring an Englishman has a mechanism that emits groans and roars. The sultan had recently been defeated by the English at the siege of Seringapatam.

The V & A has costume collections too. Above is an evening gown made by the Callot sisters around 1922.

THE SCULPTURE GALLERY
This displays European sculpture from the 15th to the 19th centuries.

THE CAST ROOM
This houses casts of sculptures and bas-reliefs. Opposite: a cast of the Roman emperor Trajan's column.

the same time to reinvent a historical style, both were bold experimenters, using new industrial techniques and at the same time placing great importance on traditional methods. The V & A was partially conceived as a museum of industrial and artisanal design, which included the responsibility for inspiring contemporary British artists and decorators, as well as educating the common man: a look round the exhibition galleries will make this intention quite apparent. Last of all, English painters are very well represented thanks to numerous legacies and donations made between 1857 and 1908. Works donated by the textile magnate John Sheepshanks include two remarkable collections: there are a total of 233 oil paintings by such masters as Mulready, Landseer, Etty, Turner, Gainsborough and Reynolds; and there is also Sheepshanks' huge collection of watercolors, to which have been added some Pre-Raphaelite paintings and early 20th-century pictures. The most important collection of paintings by Constable is also on display in the V & A: no fewer than 95 canvases and 297 drawings and watercolors were the gifts of his daughter Isabel, of Sheepshanks and of Henry Vaughan. The latter left *The Hay Wain* and *The Jumping Horse* to the museum. Constable is now regarded as the leader of the English landscape school.

THE MINIATURES ★. The V & A has the most important collection of English miniatures, allowing the visitor to follow the development of an art form that began with Hans Holbein the Younger and Nicholas Hilliard, and continued up to the early Victorian age.

THE JONES COLLECTION ★. The Jones Collection has works in several different departments. John Jones (1799–1882) was actually a military tailor who bequeathed to the museum a collection that he started around 1850, when he retired from business. This was predominantly composed of works of French decorative art from the time of Louis XIV to Louis XVI. Jones was one of those collectors who was shrewd enough to take advantage of the sale and dispersal of the contents of châteaux and other noble houses after the French Revolution, and he acquired some first-class pieces in this way. All of this material bears witness to the taste and the bargaining skill of a quite exceptional Victorian collector. Jones managed to acquire a collection of 18th-century French furniture, with works signed by André-Charles Boulle (1642–1732) and Martin Carlin, as well as some English pieces, such as this cabinet designed by Crosse and built in the workshops of Wright & Mansfield in London for the Paris Exhibition of

Snuff box (1775–7)
Made by Pierre-François Drais, and decorated with miniatures of the French royal family: Louis XVI, Marie-Antoinette and the children (Jones Collection).

"L'Alarme, ou la Gouvernante Fidèle" (c. 1785)
Originally attributed to Watteau, this painting from the Jones Collection is now considered the masterpiece of Jean-François de Troy (1679–1752).

1867 (below right). The latter pieces bear witness to the limits of Jones' knowledge, for he bought them as 18th-century work when in fact they were from the 19th century. He also had a fine porcelain collection, chiefly of Sèvres but also with a few rare specimens of Vincennes and Chelsea. His collection of miniatures was a particularly important bequest, both for its quantity (more than 160 pieces, including an interesting selection by the 17th-century artist Jean Petitot) and its diversity: the earliest examples are Renaissance. Jones also collected French sculpture of the 18th century, such as Houdon's bust of *Voltaire*, a *Cupid and Psyche* by Clodion, and *Perronet* by Pigalle; as well as contemporary English sculpture such as John Gibson's *Grazzia Puella Capuensis*. Last of all, paintings, watercolors and drawings are all well represented in this collection: there are French works (Boucher, Lancret, Pater, de Troy) hanging side by side with paintings by Guardi and Jones' English contemporaries (Turner, Mulready, Etty, Frith and Landseer), painters whose charms were also working their magic on Sheepshanks at the time. The appeal of the Jones rooms has been enhanced by the restoration of certain pieces, such as the boudoir of Mme de Serilly, a music desk and table decorated with Sèvres porcelain that once belonged to Marie-Antoinette, and the Italian Oval Salon.

The Tippoo vase
This Sèvres vase was a gift to Sultan Tippoo of Mysore from Louis XVI in grateful recognition of his alliance against the English.

THE WORLD OF SCIENCE

The Natural History Museum ★ ● *82*. In 1860 it was decided to move the natural history department of the British Museum to a base in South Kensington. Most of its contents had been collected by the physician Sir Hans Sloane (1660–1753) ▲ *200, 301*, president of the Royal Society. At his death he

THE CENTRAL HALL AND DINOSAUR GALLERY ★
The Natural History Museum was built with exceptional symmetry. The huge central hall resembles the nave of a vast cathedral, vaulted in glass and metal and decorated with terracotta panels. Among other displays there is an impressive dinosaur skeleton, and off the hall is the dinosaur gallery.

POST-WAR RESTORATION
Several of the museum's galleries were destroyed by enemy action in World War Two. They were rebuilt in the late 1950's and early 1960's; a new wing housing laboratories was added on the Exhibition Road side between 1971 and 1975.

bequeathed his collection of some eighty thousand objects to Parliament in exchange for a suitable pension for his daughters. From then until the middle of the 19th century, the collection was repeatedly enlarged by numerous donations, and in particular by those of Captain Cook. In 1866 the commission to design a new museum was awarded to Alfred Waterhouse. Construction began six years later, and the first departments were opened in 1881. The interior layout was the work of the museum's first director, the zoologist Richard Owen. It was decided to divide the layout of the museum into five sections: Paleontology, Zoology, Entomology, Botany and Mineralogy. The west and east halls were devoted to birds, fossils and geology. In 1990 the east gallery was rearranged in order to accommodate a new Ecology section, and 2002 saw the opening of the Darwin Centre, which holds 22 million zoological specimens. The Natural History Museum now operates as both a museum and a research center, and it is endowed with a magnificent library.

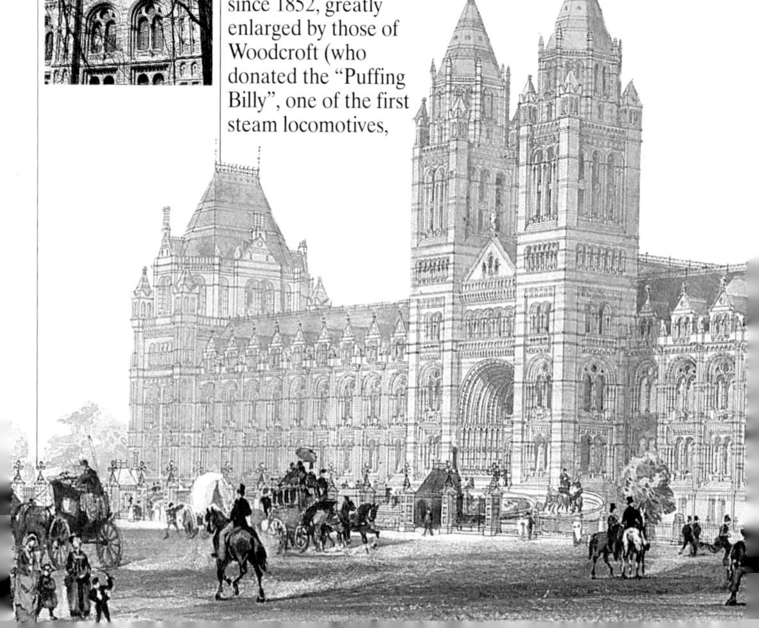

THE SCIENCE MUSEUM. The collections assembled since 1852, greatly enlarged by those of Woodcroft (who donated the "Puffing Billy", one of the first steam locomotives, uilt in 1813) and Maudsley (who presented a great number f machine tools and marine engines), were installed in ne present building, begun in 1913 by Allison and finally ompleted in 1977. The five floors are laid out along an nstructive route displaying instruments and models (some of hem working), to give a general overview of the discoveries nd inventions that assured Britain's industrial and scientific re-eminence from the late 18th century onward. Here too re the great inventions of the 20th century from all over the vorld, with displays of their use and applications. A new wing vas opened in 2000, dedicated to science and modern echnology, and included among its ttractions are an IMAX cinema and nteractive exhibitions.

HE GEOLOGICAL MUSEUM. This museum ates back to 1835, when it was housed in Craig's Court, Whitehall. It has been in its resent home since 1933. It connects to the cience Museum by means of a covered assageway. Originally it was devoted to British minerals and geology, and mining nd oil prospecting in the North Sea are horoughly explained. The museum has about one million nineral specimens, including fossils and precious stones.

HE IMPERIAL COLLEGE OF SCIENCE AND TECHNOLOGY. The College initially consisted of three institutions, including the Royal College of Chemistry, founded in 1845 by Prince Albert. Building work began in 1953 to enable it to double the umber of students. This involved the demolition of old uildings such as the Imperial Institute: only the Renaissance ower was left. Today Imperial College, which onsists of several engineering departments, s one of the leading colleges in the world.

HE ROYAL ALBERT HALL ★ ● *83*

he idea of building a cultural enter and concert hall on the site f Gore House was first mooted n 1853, but it was not until ıst after Prince

A GRIMY SPECTACLE
A few years ago the cleaning of the Natural History Museum's façade removed a century's worth of soot, dust and pollution, restoring the building to its former splendor, enhanced by the fine terracotta decorations.

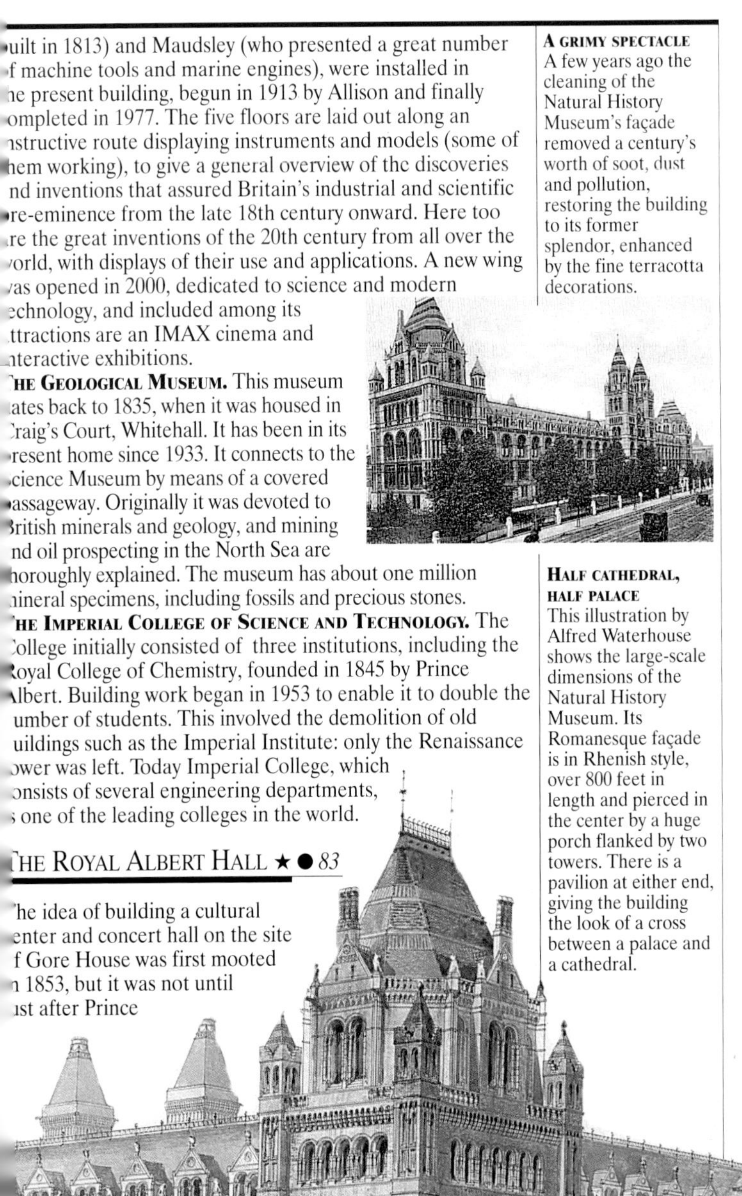

HALF CATHEDRAL, HALF PALACE
This illustration by Alfred Waterhouse shows the large-scale dimensions of the Natural History Museum. Its Romanesque façade is in Rhenish style, over 800 feet in length and pierced in the center by a huge porch flanked by two towers. There is a pavilion at either end, giving the building the look of a cross between a palace and a cathedral.

THE AUDITORIUM
The Albert Hall can seat more than five thousand people in its auditorium, which is 680 feet in circumference, topped with a glass cupola.

THE ALBERT MEMORIAL
It took twelve years, from 1861 to 1872, to compete this monument, built at the request of Queen Victoria. Situated opposite the Albert Hall, it was designed by the architect George Gilbert Scott and has recently been completely renovated.

BROMPTON ORATORY
This picture by Herbert Gribble (1847–94) perfectly captures the impressive character, with all its excessive decoration, of the church's interior. It was designed in Baroque style, with unusual additions of polychrome marble.

Albert's death that the plan finally came to life. A friend of Prince Albert, Sir Henry Cole, who initiated the project, also came up with the idea of selling 999-year leases on the seats to help finance the construction. The architect Henry Darracott Scott was responsible for the final building, which has rather unkindly been likened to the lid of a Wedgwood soup tureen. Queen Victoria laid the building's foundation stone in 1867, and the hall was opened on March 29 1871, in the presence of the Prince of Wales. The exterior is predominately of red brick, and the façade is relieved by a terracotta frieze which illustrates the theme of the Triumph of Arts and Letters. Just about every one of the world's great conductors has performed here at some point in his or her career, but the hall's popularity soared to even greater heights after 1941. Until then, the famous London "Proms" (the Henry Wood Promenade Concerts, begun in 1895), an annual summer season of music that combines popular symphony concerts with a broad range of other less fashionable works, were held in Queen's Hall. This was bombed by the Germans in 1941, and the Proms were then transferred to the Royal Albert Hall, where they have continued to take place during an eight-week season starting in July each year.

THE ROYAL GEOGRAPHICAL SOCIETY. Founded in 1830, the society moved to LOWTHER LODGE in 1913. This is a large house built between 1873 and 1875 by Norman Shaw. It organized and financed a number of major expeditions, such as those of Livingstone to Africa and of Captain Scott to the South Pole. The society's library contains 130,000 books, to which the 7,500 members have ready access.

THE ALBERT MEMORIAL. This giant neo-Gothic monument is 175 feet high. It is built from a dazzling variety of materials (among them different colored marbles, Portland stone, mosaic and bronze) and is decorated with detailed allegorical figures. It illustrates the gulf that was separating Victorian art from the industrial achievements of the age.

BROMPTON ORATORY ★

When he converted to Roman Catholicism in 1845, Cardinal John Henry Newman (1801–90) introduced to Britain a branch of the brotherhood of St Philip Neri (founded in Rome in the 16th century). They settled at Brompton in 1847. The Baroque church was built between 1878 and 1884 to the designs of Herbert Gribble. Inside, visitors are often surprised at the size of the enormous nave. Round the sides of the building is a series of chapels. The life-sized statues of the twelve Apostles are the work of Guido Mazzuoli (1644–1725), and were purchased at Siena in 1895. In 1896 a monument to Cardinal Newman was erected in front of the Oratory.

LONDON'S PARKS

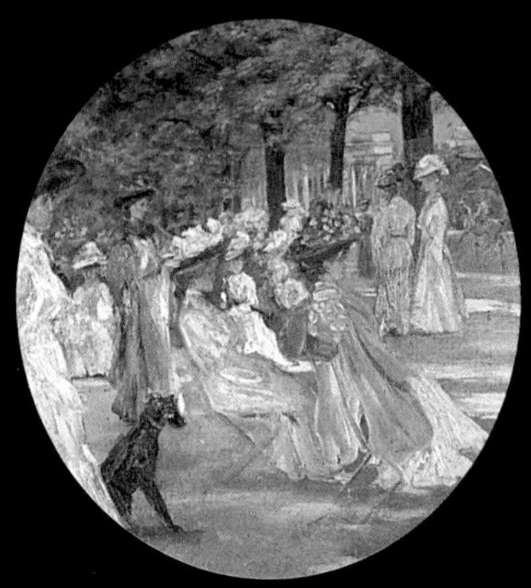

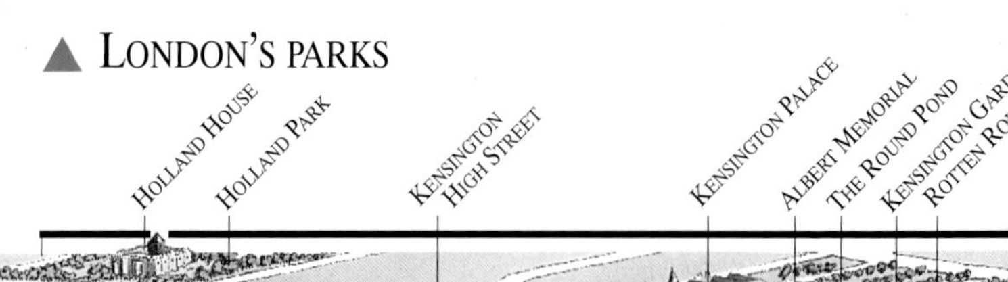

The park in summer
The green and white striped deck chairs are ideal for dozing in the sunshine. A small fee is charged for use.

"It is a park of intimacy. . . . There are few hours of the day when a thousand smutty children are not sprawling over it, and the unemployed lie thick on the grass and cover the benches with a brotherhood of greasy corduroys."
Henry James, *English Hours*

Seen from the air, London appears as a spacious town dotted with sizeable patches of green (parks, football pitches, cricket grounds and thousands of private gardens) set around a long and meandering river. The Englishman's love for his garden prompted Emerson to remark in his *English Traits*: "England is a garden. Under the sooty sky, the fields, combed and rolled, appear to have been created with a brush instead of a plough". Whitehall, home of the Horse Guards and just to the east of St James's Park, is an ideal starting point from which to explore the great parks of London: St James's Park, Green Park, Hyde Park, Kensington Gardens and Holland Park.

St James's Park

This, the oldest of the royal parks, is also the smallest, and the most ornamental. The Mall cuts it off from the district called St James's.

Reclaiming marshland. In 1536 Henry VIII decided he wanted a park on the boggy lands between the palaces of St James and Whitehall, so he had the marsh drained and stocked the land with deer, for decorative purposes rather than for hunting. Dotted with trees and with leafy avenues (of which the Mall is the only one to admit traffic), it was opened to the public in 1662 during the reign of Charles II, who aske

"St James's "
Watercolor by Benjamin Read (c. 1838).

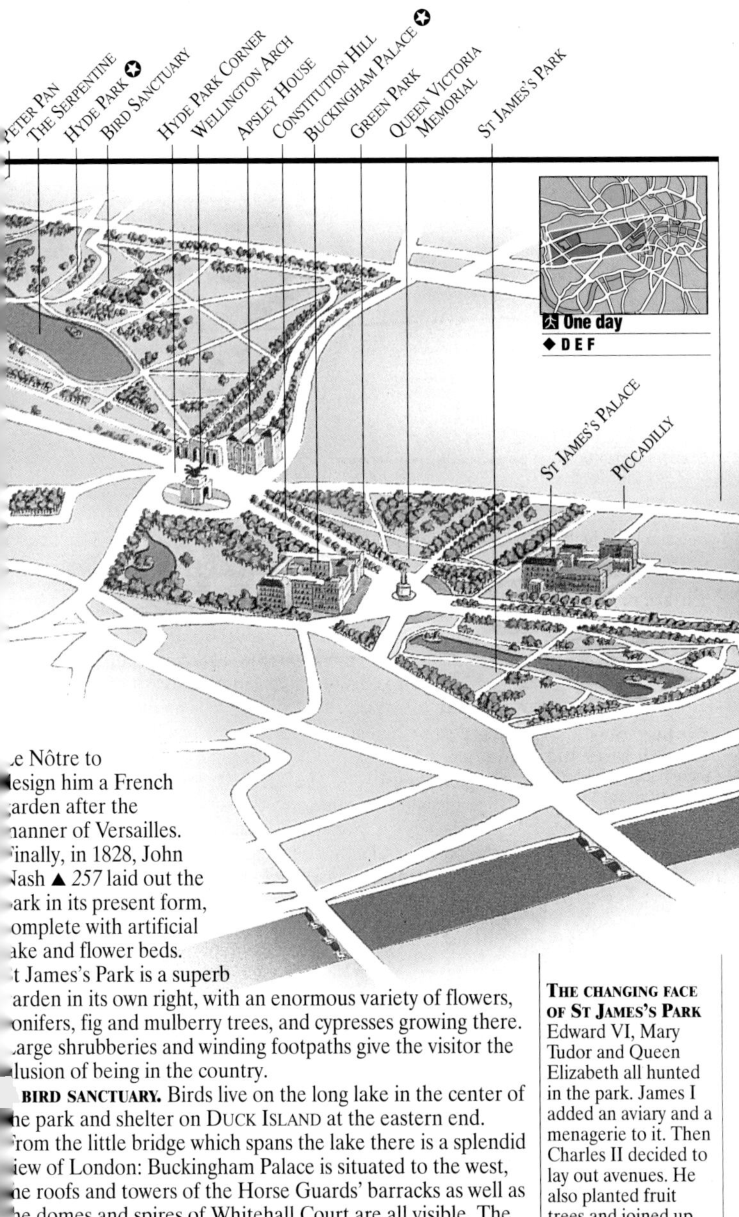

.e Nôtre to lesign him a French ;arden after the nanner of Versailles. 'inally, in 1828, John Vash ▲ *257* laid out the ›ark in its present form, omplete with artificial ake and flower beds. t James's Park is a superb arden in its own right, with an enormous variety of flowers, onifers, fig and mulberry trees, and cypresses growing there. .arge shrubberies and winding footpaths give the visitor the lusion of being in the country.

BIRD SANCTUARY. Birds live on the long lake in the center of ne park and shelter on DUCK ISLAND at the eastern end. 'rom the little bridge which spans the lake there is a splendid iew of London: Buckingham Palace is situated to the west, ne roofs and towers of the Horse Guards' barracks as well as ne domes and spires of Whitehall Court are all visible. The ›ark gates open at 5am each day; this is an ideal time for bird-vatchers, who come here before going on to the ›ffice. After the World War One, many new vaterbirds had to be introduced, for the ake had been drained in an attempt to top the gleam of the water acting as a andmark for Zeppelins, guiding them o nearby Buckingham Palace. Pink amingoes, pelicans, swans (the property f the queen), gulls, geese and ducks – thirty ifferent species of bird now perch round the edge of ne lake. BIRDCAGE WALK, which borders the park to the outh, is named after the aviary that James I had installed ear this tree-lined avenue. During the summer, in fine veather, there is live music in the bandstands, usually played

THE CHANGING FACE OF ST JAMES'S PARK
Edward VI, Mary Tudor and Queen Elizabeth all hunted in the park. James I added an aviary and a menagerie to it. Then Charles II decided to lay out avenues. He also planted fruit trees and joined up a series of pools to form a canal. He left the romantic Rosamond's Pool (above) intact.

by military brass bands. It is extremely pleasant to visit the park in the calm of the evening: after dark, the lake is floodlit and the air becomes full of the scents of trees and flowers, while the lights of the city twinkle brightly in the background.

THE QUEEN'S CHAPEL
This was built for Queen Henrietta Maria, King Charles I's Catholic wife. It was the first church in England to be built in classical style.

THE KITCHENS
Above right: a 19th-century impression.

THE GATEHOUSE
The main entrance to the palace, in Tudor style, is reached from Pall Mall or St James's Street.

ST JAMES'S PALACE

AN ANCIENT ROYAL PALACE. Construction of this Tudor building began in 1532 on the orders of Henry VIII, and it became a permanent royal residence in 1698. The English court is still known as "The Court of St James". Queen Victoria preferred to live in Buckingham Palace when she acceded to the throne in 1837. Now St James's Palace houses the Yeomen of the Guard (the royal bodyguards), and also the Gentlemen at Arms ● *50* (the sovereign's personal guard), the Lord Chamberlain and other court officials.
A MIXTURE OF STYLES. The incongruous medley of buildings that makes up St James's Palace is the result of several centuries of alterations. Of the original building there is still the guardhouse left, constructed in brick with crenellated walls and octagonal towers. Another old part of the palace is the GATEHOUSE, the main entrance to the palace and a fine fortified Tudor building, which opens into COLOUR COURT, one of the palace's four courtyards. The three others are: AMBASSADOR'S COURT, FRIARY COURT and ENGINE COURT. Located off the latter is the Chapel Royal, which was built by Henry VIII and then altered in the early 1800's. Friary Court was rebuilt in neo-Tudor style after a fire in 1809. The accession to the throne of a new monarch is always proclaimed from a balcony overlooking this courtyard.

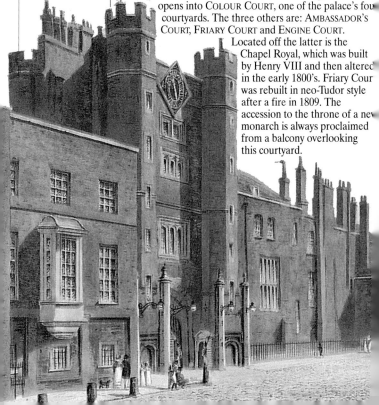

HE GUARDHOUSE. This old building is easily identified 'om Pall Mall thanks to its distinctive octagonal towers. It ɔntains the THRONE ROOM (the carved mantelpiece of which signed by Grinling Gibbons), the TAPESTRY ROOM and also ıe ARMS ROOM, designed by William Morris (1867).

'HE CHAPEL ROYAL. The Chapel Royal, where the queen's ıoristers sing, is between 'olour Court and Ambassador's 'ourt. George IV, George V nd Queen Victoria were all ıarried here.

HE QUEEN'S CHAPEL AND 'LARENCE HOUSE. The Queen's 'hapel was built using Portland tone between 1632 and 1635 by ıigo Jones ▲ *69, 325*, and was ttached to the palace before Iarlborough Road was driven ırough. Inside there are some fine English Baroque eatures, among them a sculpture by Grinling Gibbons. ɔ the west of the chapel is Clarence House, which was ɔmpleted by John Nash in 1827. It was the London home f the Queen Mother until her death in 2002, and is now the fficial London residence of Prince Charles, who undertook large program of refurbishments. Parts of the house are pen to the public (August to mid-October, pre-booked ckets only, see Places to Visit ◆ *386*).

'HE HORSE GUARDS' BARRACKS. This was built in the mid-8th century in Palladian style, which lends it a rather palatial ppearance. Its U-shaped design was the work of William ent just before his death in 1748, and it was completed y John Vardy; it is a curious mixture of arches, ediments and eaves. The "U" encloses a ɔurtyard on the Whitehall side, while on ıe side of St James's Park are three rches giving access to the piece of land nown as HORSE GUARDS PARADE. The uilding has an imposing clock-tower that mes the changes of the guard every hour etween 10am and 4pm. There are two uardsmen posted in front on Horse Guards arade, and two mounted troopers of the Household Cavalry n the Whitehall side. The latter are quite unruffled by the rowds of tourists constantly clicking cameras. The barracks ɔuses the forty mounted sentries of the Royal Guard ● *50* responsible for protecting the royal residences of London. There are two regiments of Horse Guards: the Life Guards (scarlet coat, white-plumed helmet, and horse with black or white saddlecloth), and the Blues and Royals (blue coat, red-plumed helmet and horse with black saddlecloth).

HORSE GUARDS PARADE
From the entrance to the barracks an arched passageway leads to a large patch of ground where the ceremony of the Changing of the Guard takes place during the summer; in winter it is held in the inner courtyard. This square, known as Horse Guards Parade, is flanked by statues of Generals Wolseley and Roberts and there are two cannons.

BUCKINGHAM PALACE SEEN FROM ST JAMES'S PARK
The palace is on the site of Buckingham House, which was built on the edge of London at the start of the 18th century for John Sheffield, first duke of Buckingham and Mulgrave. This in turn replaced thousands of mulberry trees that were planted here by James I to promote the silk industry.

Buckingham Palace ✪
Originally built as a house by the Duke of Buckingham and later turned into a palace by George III, this has been the home to Britain's monarchs since Queen Victoria's ascension to the throne in 1837. The palace, built to designs by John Nash, is open to the public in August and September (state rooms only). The Royal Standard is flown when royalty is in residence. The nearby Royal Mews with its collection of carriages is open to visitors throughout the year. The Changing of the Guard takes place at 11.30am each day April to July and alternate days August to March.

The Picture Gallery
The present appearance of the Picture Gallery owes much to Queen Mary, wife of George V. She changed the lighting, reduced the number of paintings on display and replaced the great crimson carpet with smaller rugs.

The Green Drawing Room
The Green Drawing Room (center) is so called because of the color of the silk chair covers and the brocade wall-panels.

The Music Room
The Music Room (right) has hardly changed since the days of Queen Victoria. It is now used only at royal baptisms and for receiving official visitors.

Buckingham Palace

In 1762 King George III, who was not over-fond of the neighboring St James's Palace, bought Buckingham House, which became the home of Queen Charlotte in 1775.

John Nash rebuilds it. Soon after his accession to the throne, in 1820, George IV (who had been regent since 1811) decided to commission John Nash ▲ *257* to transform the house into a royal palace. But the cost of the works far exceeded the money that was made available by the government, and on the king's death in 1830 the palace, which included the shell of Buckingham House, remained incomplete. Nash was dismissed and replaced by Edward Blore. Building started once again in 1837, when Victoria ascended the throne: Blore replaced Nash's dome with an attic, and in 1847 he enclosed the courtyard with an Italianate east wing. He also removed Marble Arch from outside the palace and moved it to the top of Park Lane. In 1913 Aston Webb added the present façade constructed of Portland stone. The ground floor and the two upper floors of the palace have more than six hundred rooms, which are linked by several miles of corridors. The finest parts of the palace are those designed by Nash.

The Great Hall. The Grand Staircase rises up from here to the next floor and the state apartments. It is decorated in white marble with bas-reliefs. The stairwell was designed by Nash, and is topped with a dome. The richly gilded walnut balustrades are blended with one of the finest examples of Regency wrought-ironwork. The north wing of the quadrangle, housing the queen's apartments, overlooks Constitution Hill. The state apartments, also by Nash, are in the south and west wings on either side of the Picture Gallery.

The Picture Gallery. This was completed in 1914 and hung with many paintings from the royal collection, started in the reign of Henry VIII, who put Holbein the Younger in charge of it. Charles I purchased works by Titian and Raphael, George III added Canalettos and Gainsboroughs, and George IV bought pictures by Van Dyck, Rembrandt and Vermeer. Queen Victoria further enriched the collection with paintings by Constable, Turner, Hogarth and Reynolds.

The State Dining Room. This is used for official balls, diplomatic receptions and royal weddings. The original interior was designed by John Nash, but Edward Blore changed it and added the three

Buckingham Palace in the 19th century
The watercolour painted by John Nash in 1846 (top) shows Marble Arch in its original position at the entrance to the courtyard of Buckingham Palace.

Music at the palace
This is the invitation that guests received to a soirée held on Friday June 13, 1890.

The king is ill
When Edward VII was confined to his bed in 1902, an anxious crowd gathered outside Buckingham Palace.

"SUMMER DAY IN HYDE PARK"
This picture by John Ritchie, a genre painter who exhibited at the Royal Academy from 1858 to 1875, looks north from the Serpentine toward Marble Arch.

"Walked up to Hyde Park. . . . The South Middlesex Volunteers were to be inspected by Lord de Grey on the site of the old Crystal Palace, one of the dearest and most sacred spots in this neighbourhood to me."
A.J. Munby, *Diaries*

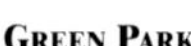

GREEN PARK
To the east of the park, between Piccadilly and the Mall, is Queen's Walk. Notable among the buildings on the east side of Green Park is the Palladian Spencer House, designed by John Vardy and James Stuart and built for the 1st Earl Spencer in 1756–66. Spencer House's splendid terrace and garden overlook the park. It has a number of state rooms that can be hired for private functions.

cupolas. The walnut dining table can seat sixty people. On the other side of the Picture Gallery, next to the Green Drawing Room, is the Throne Room. On this wing and overlooking the Mall is the famous balcony, which was first used in 1854 by Queen Victoria. The royal family ● *48* still come out on to it on important occasions. The state rooms are open for visits during the summer.

THE QUEEN'S GALLERY. Opened in 1962, the Queen's Gallery is on the site of the chapel that was built by John Nash and destroyed by a bomb in 1940. The Gallery displays a changing selection from the royal collection's 9,000 paintings.

THE ROYAL MEWS. Until the National Gallery was built, the Royal Mews used to be near Charing Cross. Nash's 1826 buildings are virtually a small village inside Buckingham Palace. The name Mews comes from buildings that used to house falcons in moult. The Master of the Queen's Horse is the head of the Royal Mews, a title that dates from 1391. His house is located at the entrance to the buildings. In former days the Royal Mews used to hold only the state coaches (the Gold State Coach of 1762, used for coronations, and the Irish State Coach of 1851, which is used for the opening of Parliament), the State Landau, used for state visits, other carriages, and also the royal horses.

BANDSTAND IN GREEN PARK
Around 1900 bands, protected from the weather by bandstands, were a great favorite with the public.

HYDE PARK ✪
This oasis of greenery, once Henry VIII's private hunting ground, is the largest of the city's central parks and has much to offer visitors and locals alike. You can take a walk in the formal gardens on the south side of the park, watch the Household Cavalry Brigade exercise their horses on Rotten Row, or go for a row on Serpentine lake (if you're brave enough you can even take a dip in the lake). The Serpentine Gallery holds exhibitions of contemporary art, and concerts are held in the park in summer. Speakers Corner (at the northeast corner of the park) has drawn inquisitive crowds every Sunday for over a hundred years with its numerous "soap-box orators".

THE PALACE GARDENS. Buckingham Palace has a park of some 45 acres, with fine gardens laid out in the 19th century by W.T. Aiton: the lake on the west side of the park is named after him. In February 1841 Prince Albert had an involuntary bath in it while skating on deceptively thin ice.

GREEN PARK

To get to this attractive park, well furnished with cast-iron benches, all the visitor has to do is cross the Mall. There are great stretches of lawn to walk on, and in season there is the heady scent of the lime trees. The avenue called Broad Walk is covered with grass and lined with plane trees. Picnics are popular here in fine weather: people who work around Piccadilly, as well as schoolchildren, take advantage of the shade under the trees.

HYDE PARK

Hyde Park Corner and WELLINGTON ARCH mark the southeast corner of Hyde Park. The arch was designed in 1825 by the architect John Nash as a grand entrance to Buckingham Palace. It is open to the public, and its rooftop balcony affords excellent views of

This publicity postcard of the British Overseas Airways Corporation (now British Airways) shows Wellington Arch.

ROTTEN ROW
Of all the London parks, Hyde Park is probably the least formal.

Buckingham Palace and Hyde park, the largest of the royal parks. Hyde Park and its adjoining neighbor Kensington Gardens have between them a total of 615 acres of parkland in the heart of London. Hyde Park was first opened to the public in the 17th century by Charles I, and at once it became extremely popular. People loved walking along its country paths, though duels were frequently fought in the more secluded corners. The gibbet at Tyburn in the northeast corner of the park attracted huge crowds. Fashionable beaux and ladies used to walk along here wearing masks, a practice which led to so many unseemly excesses that it was ultimately forbidden by royal edict in 1695. George II added the Serpentine in 1730 and then the famous Rotten Row seven years later.

THE SERPENTINE. This artificial lake was constructed for Queen Caroline. The damming of the river Westbourne began in 1730. When this was finished two boats were moored here for the express use of the royal family. A great fair was held in Hyde Park in 1814, which included a reconstruction of the Battle of Trafalgar on the Serpentine. The lake is also associated with the death of Shelley's first wife Harriet Westbrook: pregnant by the husband who had left her, she drowned herself here. Today boats can be hired and there is public bathing. There is also an old tradition of bathers who come here for a dip on Christmas Day, come wind or snow, and even if the ice has to be broken. The Serpentine Gallery is an old tearoom built in 1908 by Sir Henry Tanner. Today it is used for exhibitions of contemporary art organized by the Arts Council.

SPEAKERS' CORNER. At the northeast corner of Hyde Park, near Marble Arch ▲ *252*, is Speakers' Corner. In 1855 at least 150,000 people gathered here to demonstrate against Lord Robert Grosvenor's Sunday Trading Bill, authorizing shops to open on Sundays. Mobs like this were illegal, but when police appeared to arrest the ringleader they were too late. Then, in 1872, after many demonstrations of similar

THE DUKE OF WELLINGTON (1769–1852)
He is best known for his defeat of Napoleon on June 18, 1815, at Waterloo. He was a High Tory of the old school, and he played a leading role on the domestic and international political stage for many years. He was prime minister from 1828 to 1830.

HYDE PARK CORNER
On the left of the photograph are the three arches linked by columns known as the Hyde Park Screen, designed by Decimus Burton in 1825 as the southeast gate to the park. Beyond it is Apsley House, formerly Wellington's home and now open to the public.

Riding in Rotten Row
High society went riding here in the 19th century. In Rotten Row fashionable people drove up and down in carriages to look at each other and to make sure of being seen themselves.

›roportions, the right to hold meetings here vas finally granted, and the area became :nown as Speakers' Corner. ⁝veryone has the right to ,tand up here and to say vhatever he or she thinks, ›rovided that it is not ›bscene, blasphemous ›r slanderous.

ᴀPSLEY HOUSE. This was ›riginally a house built of 'ed brick by the Adam ›rothers between 1771 and .778 for Henry Bathurst, the Lord ⊃hancellor of England (Baron Apsley and second earl of ⁝athurst). It later became the London home of the duke of Vellington, with the impressive address of Number One, ,ondon. In 1829 Wellington commissioned Benjamin and ᵓhilip Wyatt to put a Bath stone cladding on the walls, and to ıdd the Corinthian portico and build the Waterloo Gallery. ⁝ach year on June 18 a great banquet is held at Apsley House ›o celebrate the famous victory at the Battle of Waterloo. The radition is still upheld of using the silver Portuguese dinner ervice that is on display in the Waterloo Gallery. Apsley Iouse is now also the magnificent WELLINGTON MUSEUM, vith pictures by Goya, Murillo, Velásquez, Rubens and many ›thers.

ROTTEN ROW. The name comes from the French *route du roi* King's Way), which was gradually corrupted into its present orm. It links Kensington Palace to St James's, and was the irst road in England to have street lighting. It was William III vho ordered three hundred lanterns to be hung from the rees that lined it as a precaution against the footpads who nade it a dangerous place at night. In 1687 a malefactor was ıanged for killing a lady who had wallowed her wedding ring to prevent its heft. But it remained a haunt of cut-hroats: in 1749 Horace Walpole, on his vay home from Holland House, was ıttacked by two men who held him up vith a blunderbuss, relieving him of his vatch and eight guineas. Today there are ›lenty of horsemen and children on ›onies from the riding school at the Serpentine exercising here. This is also the road that the Horse Guards ● *50* use every morning. Some Londoners know this road as "The Mile".

"The Crinoline Equestrian"
"No one can fail to admire the elegant simplicity of my dress!", ran the caption to this mid-19th-century lithograph.

The Crystal Palace
Joseph Paxton designed the building, a metal framework with panes of glass, that housed the Great Exhibition of 1851. In 1854 the Crystal Palace was taken down and reassembled at Sydenham. Once much larger and divided into separate galleries, the Crystal Palace now became an entertainment center with plays, concerts, exhibitions and even circuses staged inside it. Statues and fountains ornamented the surrounding park, where firework displays were regular features. Eventually there were football matches here. The palace was destroyed by fire in 1936.

KENSINGTON GARDENS

Sir Christopher Wren replanned the private gardens of Kensington Palace before the joint monarchs William and Mary took it over as their London residence. Queen Anne, who disliked the formal Dutch gardens, had most of them dug over. During the 1720's Henry Wise and Charles Bridgeman embarked on a new layout.

"AUTUMN IN KENSINGTON GARDENS"
A painting by the landscape artist James Wallace (1872–1911). Queen Mary, wife of William III, took a great interest in the arrangement of the park and summoned the royal gardeners Henry Wise and George London to create Dutch gardens: beds bordered with low box hedges and yew bushes. George II opened Kensington Gardens to the public (by which he meant the genteel public), and its main avenue Broad Walk soon became as fashionable a place to be seen in as the Mall ▲ *144*.

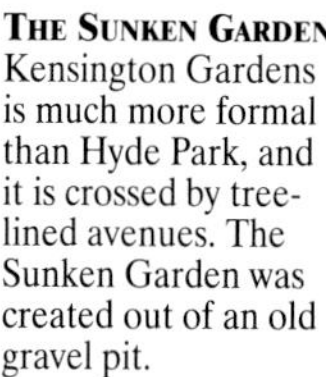

THE SUNKEN GARDEN
Kensington Gardens is much more formal than Hyde Park, and it is crossed by tree-lined avenues. The Sunken Garden was created out of an old gravel pit.

THE MONUMENTS IN THE GARDENS. It was probably William Kent who in 1726–7 built the small temple at the southeast end of the gardens, which later became part of Temple Lodge King William IV first opened the park to the public, and a Flower Walk was planted here in 1843. The ALBERT MEMORIAL was unveiled in 1863, and then enlarged in 1872. A granite obelisk was erected here in 1864 commemorating the discovery of the source of the Nile by John Hanning Speke, followed by the statues of Queen Victoria in 1893 and then of William III in 1907. The statue *Physical Energy* by G.F. Watts dates from 1904, while the *Elfin Oak* by Ivor Innes is a treetrunk carved with woodland creatures. It is close to the children's playground on the north side of the park, near Black Lion

> "Mrs Cheveley is one of those very modern women of our time who find a new scandal as becoming as a new bonnet, and air them both in the park every afternoon at five-thirty."
>
> Oscar Wilde

Gate. The bronze does and fawns decorating the Queen's Gate are the work of P. Rouillard (1919).

THE PETER PAN STATUE. This is one of London children's avorite statues, and has been so ever since it was irst put here in 1912. George Frampton's bronze depicts the boy who was first created by J.M. Barrie in *The Little White Bird*, a story set in Kensington Gardens. The character was mmortalized in the eponymous play which still egularly thrills young audiences in London and lsewhere. Nina Boucicault, who created the role of Peter, sat for the sculptor. He is depicted here playing the pipes, while fairies, mice and rabbits rolic round his feet.

THE ROUND POND. In the middle of the park is a small lake hat also attracts London children (especially on Sundays), who sail their model boats here. There are even some old ailors too, dressed in navy blue and a white cap, who come to aunch some exquisitely fashioned models.

THE SUNKEN GARDEN. This garden, which was laid out in 909, is on the east side of the park. Rows of flowers are planted on the three terraces to form a rectangle round a

THE QUEEN'S CHAMBER IN KENSINGTON PALACE
One of the magnificent interior designs created by Sir Christopher Wren around 1690, and altered in the 1720's.

KENSINGTON GARDENS
Seen from across the Round Pond.

"We walked out to Kensington and strolled through the delightful Gardens. It is a glorious thing for the King to keep such walks so near the Metropolis, open to all his subjects. We were very calm and happy. Our conversation was most agreeable."
James Boswell, *Diary for May 21, 1763*

pool, and with a delightful walk under a vault of lime trees. Leaving the park on the left by the northwest gate, the road then leads west into Notting Hill, a lively and extremely cosmopolitan quarter. It then proceeds down to Holland Park. On the lefthand side is the beautiful Campden Hill Square, which was built on a slope, making it a magical sight, particularly at Christmas time, when all the occupants put lighted candles in the bow windows of these early Victorian houses.

KENSINGTON PALACE. This manor house was first built for Sir George Coppin, before being bought by the earl of Nottingham, who duly called it Nottingham House. Following the 1689 revolution, it became the home of the young royal couple William III and Mary, since the king suffered from asthma which was greatly exacerbated when he lived beside the Thames. In addition, the setting of Kensington delighted him, for he loved the countryside. He commissioned Sir Christopher Wren ● *70*, ▲ *171* to enlarge and transform the house into a palace, and employed Nicholas Hawksmoor ▲ *311* to supervise construction. Wren added a new façade and royal apartments to the building. He also designed a magnificent wrought-iron staircase (executed by Jean Tijou) and built new stables. Queen Anne added the Orangery in 1704, probably to plans drawn up by Hawksmoor that were then modified by Vanbrugh. Under George I, three of the state rooms were rebuilt in Palladian style. George II and Queen Caroline moved here in 1727. After his death in 1760, his grandson, who was now King George III, decided to live instead at Buckingham House. Kensington Palace, as it was now called, was therefore abandoned for a time, before some of the royal children took apartments here. At the beginning of the 19th century James Wyatt made some extensive alterations to the palace in neo-classical style. Princess Victoria was born here in 1819, and it was here too that news came to her in 1837 that she was queen. Today Princess Margaret has apartments in the palace, and it was also the residence of Diana, Princess of Wales. Still open to the

"MY LADY'S GARDEN"
This picture by John Young Hunter, painted in 1899, shows the walled Dutch Garden in Holland Park very clearly in the background. It was laid out by Buonaiuti in 1812, and consisted of flower beds in geometric shapes edged with low box hedges. It is still there today. One feature is not in the picture: the niche in the northeast wall known as ROGERS' SEAT, above which is an inscription by Lord Holland in tribute to his friend the banker and Romantic poet Samuel Rogers.

ublic, the palace contains a fine collection of costumes that ɿere worn at court after 1750. The state apartments are ecorated with paneling and Old Master paintings dating rom the 17th and 18th centuries. In the queen's apartments here are mirrors with carved and gilded frames by the amous Grinling Gibbons ▲ *173, 276*, and also William Kent's upola room, while in the king's apartments the Privy Council hamber was created by the same architect.

IOLLAND PARK

Surrounded by imposing Victorian houses, Holland Park is a most delightful retreat from the busy world outside its walls, with squirrels, peacocks, Australian emus and many other rather less exotic birds. It was once part of the land belonging to Holland House, which was built in 1607 and almost entirely destroyed by enemy action in 1941 during the Second World War. There are three gardens laid out around it, namely the ROSE GARDEN, the DUTCH GARDEN and the IRIS GARDEN. The flowers are a ıixture of the exotic and indigenous, among them catalpas, amboos, yuccas, lime trees, holly, oaks, poplars and ash trees *24*. There are also several statues, including a monument to ord Holland (1872) by Watts and Boehm, *The Boy and the ear Cubs* (1902) by John MacAllan Swan, and also a work by ric Gill. The small conical 18th-century stone construction as once an ice house. There are refreshments for sale at the afé, which makes a perfect spot in which to get away from e crowded city. Last of all there is the magnificent ɔrangery, built together with the stables in 1638–40, where ere are bronze copies of statues. Art exhibitions and ɔncerts are also held here.

OLLAND HOUSE. Only parts remain of e original building, which was called ope Castle and built for Sir Walter ope, who was Chancellor of the xchequer under James I. All that emains are the east wing, some arcades the courtyard, and a gateway that is tributed to Nicholas Stone and Inigo ɔnes. The property was for a long time the family of Charles James Fox, who ecame a Member of Parliament at just nineteen years of age nd then leader of the Whig party. In the first part of the 19th ntury Lady Holland had a salon here, attended by such mous names as Sheridan, Sir Walter Scott, Lord Byron, ɿordsworth and Dickens, and all the great Whig politicians ho opposed the war with France. After the 1941 bombing olland House was abandoned until 1952, when the London ɔunty Council took control of it.

RELAXING IN HOLLAND PARK
In common with the other London parks, Holland Park is an ideal place to relax in, whatever the season. To the south the park slopes gently down, giving visitors a fine view over the roofs of the town.

HOLLAND HOUSE, THEN AND NOW
The engraving below shows the original Holland House, while in the oval picture (above left) is the house as it appears today. In summer there are plays, ballets and operas given in front of the façade. This open-air terrace is called the Court Theatre.

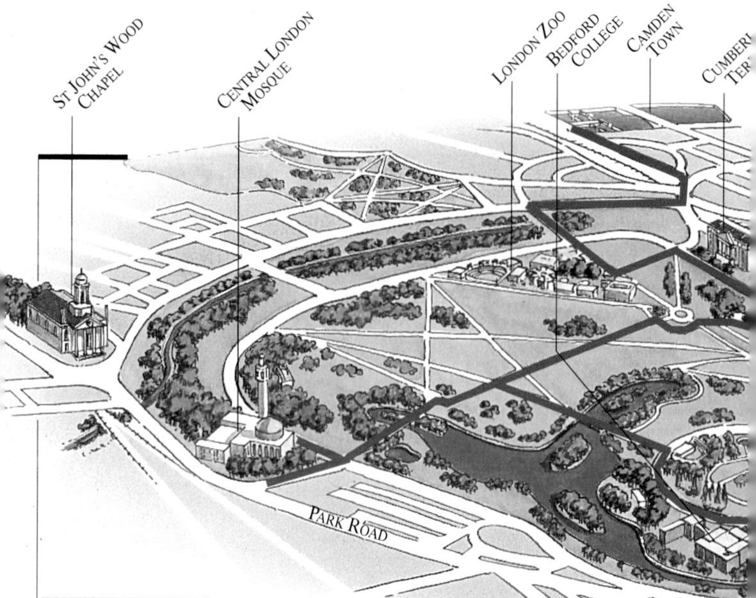

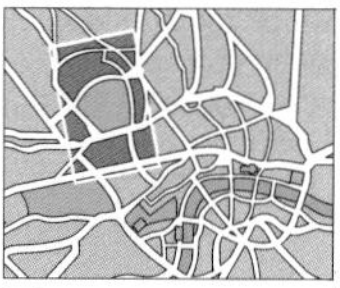

St John's Wood Chapel

Central London Mosque

London Zoo

Bedford College

Camden Town

Cumberl… Ter…

Park Road

A stroll through Marylebone from Marble Arch to Regent's Park will remind you of London as it was at the beginning of the 19th century, a residential quarter with squares and gardens, the streets lined with opulent houses.

One day
◆ **A** B3-B4-C4
B A1-B1-C1-D1 **C** A3

Around Marylebone

Marble Arch. At the top of Park Lane, which runs up the eastern side of Hyde Park, is Marble Arch roundabout. The triumphal arch which stands there is of white Italian marble. It was executed in 1828 by Decimus Burton (1800–81). Originally intended as a ceremonial gate for Buckingham Palace ▲ *242*, Marble Arch was moved to its present position in 1851 as its wrought-iron gates proved too narrow to let the state coach through. At the beginning of the present century became apparent that Marble Arch was insufficient to meet the needs of the new motor traffic, so it was placed on an island around which the traffic now flows.

Marble Arch
Just a few steps from Marble Arch, a stone triangle set into the road marks the site of Tyburn, where, for six centuries, criminals and martyrs from the Tower of London were publicly executed.

Marylebone. The district extend from both sides of Marylebone Lane and Marylebone High Street. In the middle of the 18th century many important building projects were initiated in the village of Marylebone, which rapidly became incorporated into London with the construction of new streets, squares and grand town houses. These improvements were partly the work of Robert Adam (1728–92) assisted by his three brothers ▲ *268*. Adam brought a freedom of movement into architecture, reacting against the suffocating restraints of the noble Palladian style, in a great variety of private houses which can still be seen.

Harley Street. Laid out in 1820, Harley Street has been the preserve of the medical profession since the middle of the 19th century. Eighteenth-century houses jostle with Victorian and Edwardian dwellings. In buildings that date from 1765 at

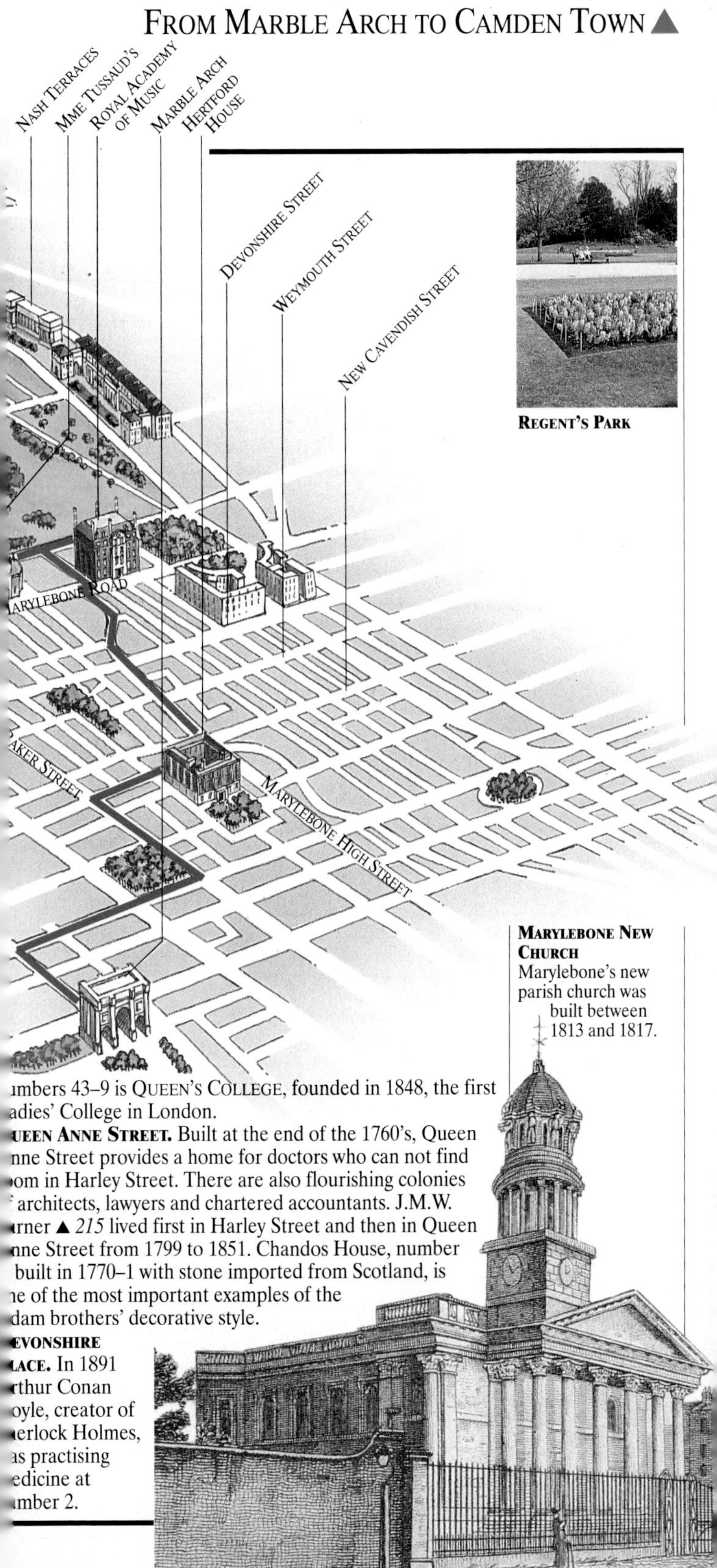

REGENT'S PARK

MARYLEBONE NEW CHURCH
Marylebone's new parish church was built between 1813 and 1817.

ımbers 43–9 is QUEEN'S COLLEGE, founded in 1848, the first adies' College in London.

UEEN ANNE STREET. Built at the end of the 1760's, Queen nne Street provides a home for doctors who can not find oom in Harley Street. There are also flourishing colonies ' architects, lawyers and chartered accountants. J.M.W. ırner ▲ *215* lived first in Harley Street and then in Queen nne Street from 1799 to 1851. Chandos House, number built in 1770–1 with stone imported from Scotland, is ıe of the most important examples of the dam brothers' decorative style.

EVONSHIRE LACE. In 1891 rthur Conan oyle, creator of ıerlock Holmes, as practising edicine at ımber 2.

Hertford House in Manchester Square houses the famous Wallace Collection. Assembled by the four first Marquises of Hertford and the illegitimate son of the last Marquis, Sir Richard Wallace (1818–90), the collection was bequeathed to the nation by Sir Richard's widow, and opened in 1900. It has a magnificent collection of French art (Fragonard, Boucher, Watteau), as well as works by Italian (Guardi), Spanish (Velásquez, Murillo), Flemish and English artists. For its centenary, the Wallace Collection has been beautifully restored. It has acquired new underground space for watercolor, reserve and temporary galleries, as well as for a host of educational facilities, including a library and lecture theater.

"VENUS ARISING FROM THE WAVES" This majolica (glazed Italian ceramic ware) tablet wa executed in 1553 by Francesco Xanto Avell

"THE LAUGHING CAVALIER" This familiar portrait was painted in 1624 by the Dutchman Frans Hals (c.1585–1666). The brushwork was a great influence on 19th-century painters, notably Manet.

CLOCK WITH ASTRONOMICAL DIAL This clock in gilded, patinated bronze, the work of Michel Stollerwerck (c.1746–75), is just one example from a substantial collection of clocks.

"MADAME DE POMPADOUR"
This painting of Louis XV's mistress by Francois Boucher (1703–70) is part of a collection of French art that was assembled by the Marquis of Hertford during the Revolution.

MILANESE GORGETS (C.1610)
These pieces of armor protected the soldier's neck and throat. It is part of a collection of armor purchased from the Count of Nieuwekerke.

"Regent's Park" This painting by John Knox (1778–1845) shows a general view of London and Regent's Park from Primrose Hill to the north.

The Nash Terraces Their splendid Regency façades line Regent's Park on the east and west.

The Planetarium Next door to *Madame Tussaud's*, the Planetarium's dome is a screen for the visitor to observe the movement of the stars and planets.

Portland Place. One of the grandest urban development schemes of the 18th century, begun in 1773 by the Adam brothers. Only ten of the original houses are still standing, near the BBC Broadcasting House.

Marylebone High Street and Thayer Street. The main road and the very heart of old Marylebone, it still retains something of a village atmosphere, and is lined with shops.

Town squares. Portman Square was laid out between 1764 and 1784 on land belonging to the Portman family. At numbe[r] 30 is Home House, Robert Adam's finest town house and witness to his genius for combining different elements in one harmonious whole. Manchester Square contains the Wallace Collection; and though it is in no sense a square, this is the place to mention Stratford Place (just off Oxford Street), an elegant little impasse dating from 1774.

Baker Street. Baker Street's most celebrated tenant lived a[t] number 221b. This was Sherlock Holmes, whose museum is i[n] the *Sherlock Holmes* pub in Northumberland Avenue, south of Trafalgar Square. The upper part of the street is one of the best preserved sections in the area.

Marylebone Road

Marylebone New Church. From 1813 to 1817, on land donated by the duke of Portland, Thomas Hardwick built a new parish church, the third, with a heavy Corinthian portico and a domed tower supported by caryatids.

The Royal Academy of Music. The present red-brick English Baroque building was built in 1910–11. When the Academy first opened in 1823, an early pupil was Charles Dickens' sister Fanny.

Madame Tussaud's. In 1802 Marie Tussaud (1761–1850) arrived in London from France with thirty-five wax figures and death masks of famous revolutionaries who had fallen victim to the guillotine. By 1884 the museum boasted four hundred figures. Today, among many other features, it contains a Hall of Fame, Chamber of Horrors, relic[s] of the old London prisons and many historical tableaux. It is one of the most popular tourist attractions in London, attracting millions of visitors every year.

The London Planetarium. This opene[d] in 1958. With optical lenses supplied by

he Zeiss laboratories, the sky is projected on to a great ·opper dish. On certain evenings the space is used as a .aserium, and sometimes concerts are held here.

ꞮEGENT'S PARK ★ ● 24

'or the French historian Hippolyte Taine, who came to London n 1864, Regent's Park appeared "a solitary place with no noise of traffic; London is forgotten and you are quite alone". The .ewest of London's parks is also the most splendid and varied. 'his giant green space of more than five hundred acres was ormerly a hunting ground of King Henry VIII. In 1811 the 'rince Regent (the future George IV) gave his favorite .rchitect John Nash the job of developing the land. The plan alled for no fewer than fifty six villas, a summer residence for he Regent, and a Pantheon dedicated to England's greatness, vhile the park was to be ringed with gracious terraces of houses. Nash dreamed of creating a new, idealized garden city landscape. The project never came to completion thanks to lack of funds and customers, but over the years the park became a delightful and original environment. Nash began work on the park in 1812, and worked on it with is assistant Decimus Burton until 1827 ▲ 278. But Regent's 'ark was not opened to the public until 1838.

'ISITING THE PARK. Except for the northern area, occupied by he zoo, and the lawns in the center, most of the park is given ver to sports, such as cricket ● 56. There are long, tree-lined venues for walks, refreshing lakes and flowerbeds. Regent's 'ark has undergone something of a transformation recently, nd some gardens have been completely redesigned, such as 'roadwalk, which is now embellished with statues of lephants. To see the park, it is best to set out from the emicircular PARK CRESCENT, with its magnificent Ionic olonnade. The west side of the park is centered around the OATING LAKE; but the most beautiful part is the middle or NNER CIRCLE. It contains QUEEN MARY'S GARDEN and rose ardens (as fine as any in England), and the OPEN-AIR HEATER, where each summer performances of one of hakespeare's plays are held against a backdrop of greenery.

T JOHN'S LODGE. On the southwest side of Regent's Park tands this 18th-century villa (above, inset) with a wing that 'as added in the 20th century, surrounded by a delightful arden that is open to the public.

"The Crescents and gardens alike had a faint Regency character, partly, perhaps, because they faced remote light blue distances, such as one sees in watercolors of the period."

Edith Sitwell, *I Live under a Black Sun*

CUMBERLAND TERRACE
The most grandiose of the Nash terraces in Regent's Park looks like a palace.

THE REGENT'S PARK MOSQUE
On the west side of Regent's Park, the mosque is next to Winfield House, the residence of the American ambassador.

THE NASH TERRACES ★ ● *76.* These are the fruits of Nash's town-planning project. They are made up of gracious town house in Regency style, each terrace forming a substantial palace with long stuccoed façade. Among the most remarkable terraces on the west side are YORK TERRACE and CORNWALL TERRACE (which was the first one to be built, in 1820–1), and Sussex Place, decorated with Corinthian columns and domed towers. Perhaps the two most imposing terraces on the eastern side are CHESTER TERRACE, 325 yards long and decorated with Corinthian columns, and CUMBERLAND TERRACE, Nash's most accomplished work built in 1825. This has the grandest façade of all of them, with an arrangement of Ionic columns surmounted by a pediment carved by G.H. Bubb and topped by three statues. After the Second World War, these delapidated terraces were tempting investments for property developers, and have since been converted to luxury apartments.

ST KATHARINE'S HOSPITAL. The northeast entrance to the park, by Gloucester Gate, faces the old hospital of St Katharine. The neo-Gothic complex of buildings includes the old church of St Katharine, which is now the Danish church in London, and houses built in 1826 by Ambrose Poynter. St Katharine's, a charitable foundation, was moved here from its original site near the Tower when the land was taken over for the construction of St Katharine's Dock ▲ *334*.

THE CENTRAL LONDON MOSQUE. London's new central mosque is beside Hanover Gate on the west of the park. With its minaret and copper dome, it is an impressive building built between 1972 and 1978 by Frederick Gibberd, a testament to the importance of the Islamic religion in London.

ZOO LIFE
Each new birth in London Zoo is announced on a noticeboard at the main gate.

LONDON ZOO

Today the zoo covers 37 acres in the northern part of Regent's Park. Sir Stamford Raffles founded the Zoological Society in London in 1826, and in 1828 its members opened a zoological garden to plans laid out by Decimus Burton. It was immediately popular, and two years later the collection of animals from the Tower was added. Within the next few years came giraffes, lions, snakes and apes, and the famous African elephant, Jumbo.

THE CANAL
Regent's Canal runs along beside the zoo in lush green surroundings before turning off toward the East End.

London Zoo in the 19th century
The animals lived in cages then, separated from the public by bars as shown in the illustration.

modern zoo. London Zoo was a real pioneer when it pened the Mappin Terraces in 1913. For the first time ever, eople could see animals in captivity in something resembling ieir natural habitat. The remarkable penguin enclosure, pened in 1934, was followed 1962–5 by the elephant and iinoceros houses. A more general reorganization of the zoo ɔok place during the 1960's to plans laid down by Sir Hugh 'asson. Lord Snowdon, at that time the husband of Princess Iargaret, designed the giant aviary in 1967 with the intention f giving the birds at least a modicum of freedom. Finally, in 976, the New Lion Terraces allowed the great beasts to ielter or take advantage of an open-air green space as they ished. London Zoo also has a Twilight House (the Charles 'lore Pavilion, home of nocturnal ıammals), an Institute of Comparative hysiology, and an animal hospital. The ɔo has thousands of animals, covering ıore than a thousand species. It has ːcently undergone a transformation: the nce-famous Lion House no longer exists, hile in 1999 the Web of Life was pened, a center for preservation and ɔnservation. A library with more than 00,000 volumes enables visitors to understand or improve ıeir knowledge of the habits of the zoo's inmates.

Camden Lock
Artists, sellers of bric-à-brac and secondhand clothes have been coming to set up shop here at weekends for the last twenty-five years, on the old quays beside the locks of the Regent's Canal. A favorite destination for tourists, Camden Lock should be visited in the morning, when the crowds are not too huge and it's still possible to walk around.

ROUND CAMDEN LOCK

egent's Park is bounded on the north by the Regent's Canal, ith its picturesque locks which create an attractive backdrop ɔ the craft and antique stalls of Camden Lock.

rimrose Hill ★. This dominates the Thames valley beyond ıe canal: being 203 feet high, it offers some splendid views ver London. Covered with grass and set with groups of iestnut and plane trees, Primrose Hill was once a favorite ace for duelists. At the bottom of the hill is Regent's Park oad with trendy shops and cafés, one of the prettiest and ıost sought-after streets in the area.

egent's Canal. The prettiest parts of the canal are just ːside the zoo and near Macclesfield Bridge. The Regent's anal was opened in 1820, linking the Thames to Paddington and thence, via the Grand Union Canal, to Birmingham and beyond. In contrast to its earlier days, the canal is now used relatively little. Walkers and anglers enjoy the towpath, and the old horse-drawn barges have been replaced by pleasure craft.

Camden Lock. This is now the location of an excellent antique market beside the Regent's Canal. It is situated in former commercial premises (stables or warehouses) that were used by the canal and the nearby railway. Camden Town has traditionally been an old-fashioned working-class district, but the area has seen much redevelopment and building of upmarket housing, bars and restaurants, especially along the canal.

Stiff competition
Camden Lock now rivals the famous Portobello Road flea market and the antique shops of Camden Passage in popularity.

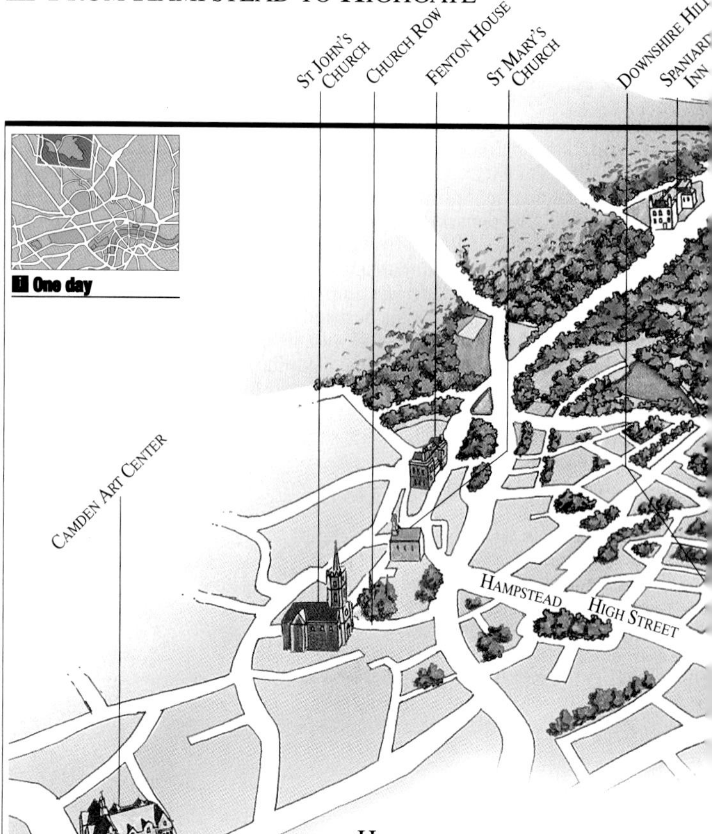

St John's Church
Church Row
Fenton House
St Mary's Church
Downshire Hill
Spaniard Inn
Camden Art Center
Hampstead High Street

One day

HAMPSTEAD ★

Hampstead is the perfect place for a fascinating stroll. Its streets are lined with houses like country cottages, with neat front gardens. The area is enormous fun to explore on holiday, rain or shine. The High Street is packed with interesting shops: some are open on Sunday too. Hampsteac was once woodland, but a lot of it was cut down to rebuild tł City after the Great Fire ● 40. Well-to-do Londoners built their country houses here in the 18th century near the heath which was well known for its fresh air and spring water. The water used to be sold in the taverns: it was bottled in Flask Walk. There used to be a thermal spring in Well Walk; and i the same street once lived John Keats and the landscape painter Constable ▲ *214*. (Formerly he lived for a while at 2 Lower Terrace.) Many media personalities still live here today. To see more of the history and architecture of Hampstead, go to Church Row and marvel at its magnificen Georgian houses, just before you reach St John Street.

HAMPSTEAD FROM PARLIAMENT HILL FIELDS, WITH THE BATHING POND
This ancient bathing place, a mixture of Georgian and Victorian styles perched on the side of a hill, has attracted many famous people to its waters: Keats, Shelley, Lord Byron, Kipling, D.H. Lawrence, H.G. Wells, and Sigmund Freud.

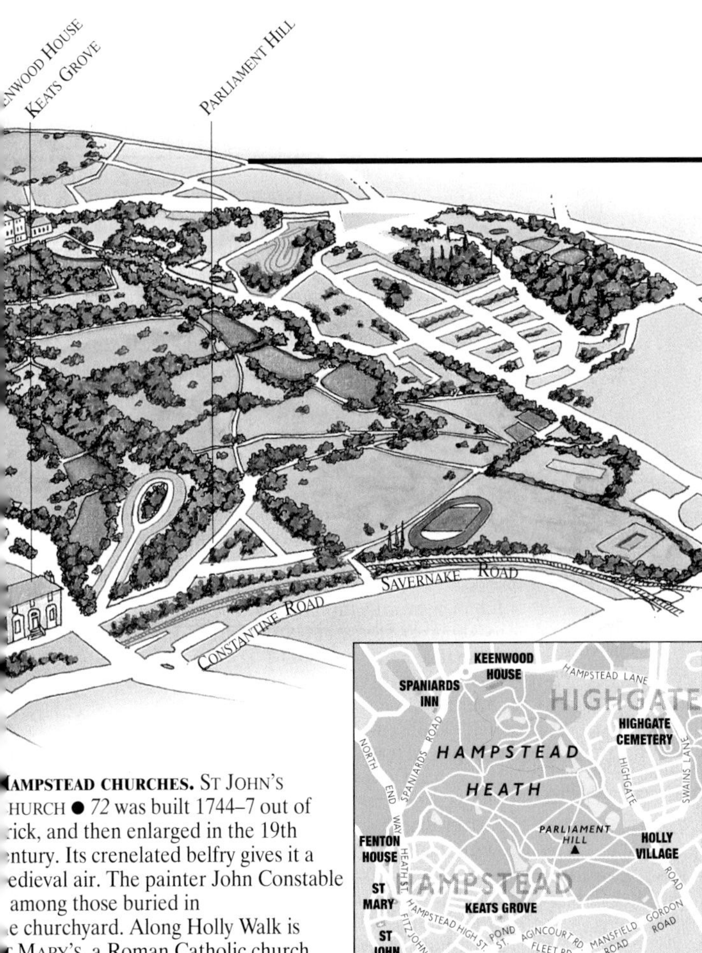

AMPSTEAD CHURCHES. ST JOHN'S HURCH ● *72* was built 1744–7 out of rick, and then enlarged in the 19th ntury. Its crenelated belfry gives it a edieval air. The painter John Constable among those buried in e churchyard. Along Holly Walk is T MARY'S, a Roman Catholic church unded by a Frenchman, Abbé Morel. Its hite walls form an attractive contrast ith the brown brick of Hampstead houses. There are some teresting 20th-century mosaics to be seen inside its two apels. Skirting the National Institute of Medical Research uilt in 1880), you come to Mount Vernon. On Holly Bush ill is a timber-built house which was constructed in 1797 for eorge Romney, a portrait artist whose work was very opular with the nobility of that time.

EATS' HOUSE, KEATS GROVE. From 1818 to 1820 John eats (1795–1821) lived in Wentworth Place (as it was en called), in a double-fronted house built for his friends harles Armitage Brown and Charles Wentworth Dilke. eats first came to Hampstead in 1816 to meet the urnalist and poet Leigh Hunt, who lived in the Vale of ealth, and it was through his connections that Keats came to ow Shelley, William Hazlitt, Wordsworth and Charles amb. In 1817 he moved to Well Walk with his brothers eorge and Tom; then, when he was left by himself (George d emigrated to America and Tom had died from a chest fection), he accepted his friend Brown's invitation and nt to live in the lefthand part of this house. Dilke rented half to a Mrs Brawne, whose daughter Fanny was later become Keats' fiancée. Keats' House, like so many others the suburbs, boasts a luxuriant garden. Inside the house n be seen autograph manuscripts and personal effects

"London is indeed a thousand villages; remove them and all that is left is a vast hulk peppered with spectacular buildings . . . ."
Ian Nairn

"ADMIRAL'S HOUSE"
This landscape was painted by Constable in 1820 and captures the village atmosphere of Hampstead.

that belonged to the poet. Not far awa and still in Keats Grove, is the courtya of an old brewery surrounded by 17th-century buildings, Old Brewery Mews.
FENTON HOUSE ● *74.* Built in 1693, th house is named after the merchant wh bought it in 1793. Inside there is a collection of early keyboard instrumen including a magnificent harpsichord th Handel used to play. There is also a fi collection of porcelain that once belonged to Lady Binning, who bequeathed the house to the National Trust in 1952 along with some pictures Constable and Breughel the Elder. HAMPSTEAD GROVE and ADMIRAL'S WALK are lined with some early 18th-century houses and cottages. The nove John Galsworthy (author of *The Forsyte Saga*) lived next do to Admiral's House at GROVE LODGE from 1918 until his death in 1933.

JOHN KEATS (1795–1821)
The poet lived in Hampstead for three years. His *Ode to a Nightingale*, the longest of his odes, was written on a May evening in the garden at Wentworth Place.

HAMPSTEAD HEATH. This grassy common, covering 420 acres, includes Parliament Hill Fields and Kenwood, and separates Hampstead from Highgate. Until the 13th century its only inhabitants were wolves; it was not until late in the 17th century that the medicinal qualities of its spring waters were discovered, when the place suddenly became extremely popular. Today Londoners use this beautiful spot with its open spaces, lakes and wooded groves for picnics and walks. Music lovers will be pleased to learn that at Concert Pond there are frequent open-air concerts held in summer. The view over London from Parliament Hill Field most impressive. There are also severa famous pubs in the area. The 18th-century Kit-Kat Club used to meet in *Upper Flask Inn* in Flask Walk. This wa basically a club of Whig politicians ▲ 2 but it had some illustrious members including the writers Alexander Pope ▲ *155*, Richard Steele and Joseph Addison, the painter Sir Godfrey Kne and many others. Keats and Shelley drank here too. The club took its nam from the pastrycook Christopher Katt, whose house the first meetings were h On top of the heath, near Whitestone Pond, is JACK STRAW'S CASTLE, a histo pub frequented by Charles Dickens ● *110,* ▲ *299.* You can make your way Kenwood House along Spaniards Roa and stop at the *Spaniards Inn*, which is four hundred years old and was the Spanish ambassador's residence durin the reign of James II. In 1780 the landlord got the Gordon Rioters drun

HOME, SWEET HOME
The name Hampstead derives from "*homestead*". It is said that long ago a Saxon cut down part of the forest here and built himself a farm.

ere, and attempted to stop them burning Kenwood House. he inn was also a meeting place for writers such as Keats, helley, Byron and Dickens.

ENWOOD HOUSE ★. Bought by the chief justice of the King's ench, Lord Mansfield, in 1754, fifty years after it was built, arts of the original brick house can be seen today. Mansfield ommissioned Robert Adam to transform the place: e resulting parts added by the young architect on e south façade overlooking Hampstead Heath are naginative and beautifully proportioned. The finest oom in the house is undoubtedly the LIBRARY. After Mansfield's death in 1793, his nephew added the two ings on either side of the north façade, where the ain entrance is, with a portico by Adam. Lord eagh (grandson of the founder of the brewing ynasty, Arthur Guinness) purchased Kenwood in 925 and filled it with his collection of paintings ncluding Rembrandt's *Self Portrait*, Vermeer's *Guitar ayer*, and notable works by Gainsborough and ubbs). He bequeathed the house and all its contents the nation on his death in 1928. The east and west wings of enwood house have recently been refurbished with 18th- ad 19th-century-style décor that complements its collection masterpieces and splendid original furniture.

ADAM AT KENWOOD
The south façade of Kenwood House (above) is decorated with ornate pilasters in classical style.

At each end of the library (above) is an apse guarded by two Corinthian pillars. Robert Adam was particularly proud of the curved ceiling.

IGHGATE

ighgate High Street crosses Highgate Hill and was built in 386 on the order of the bishop of London, for the route und the hill was proving difficult in winter. Travelers used to ay a toll at the top of the hill in front of a large gateway, ter which both hill and street are named. At the foot of the ll, the Whittington Stone commemorates the spot where ichard Whittington, while he was a poor apprentice turning s back on London, is supposed to have heard the bells of Mary-le-Bow (Bow Bells) calling him to return and become ord Mayor. He was to be Lord Mayor four times, and at his eath in 1423 he left his fortune to finance the building of the uildhall ▲ *148*.

THE PARK AT KENWOOD
In the 18th century there was a decorative "English" garden here. Today, open-air symphony concerts are given regularly at Kenwood in what is a beautiful rustic setting.

THE KINGDOM OF SHADES
Many famous people lie buried in this romantic Victorian cemetery: Karl Marx,

Christina Rossetti, Michael Faraday, George Eliot and Ralph Richardson are just a few of them.

THE FREUD MUSEUM
Fleeing from the Nazi invasion of Vienna in 1938, Sigmund Freud, the father of psychoanalysis, took refuge at 20 Maresfield Gardens in Highgate, and died there the following year. His daughter Anna lived there until her death in 1982.

CROMWELL HOUSE
This magnificent dwelling, built of brick in 1637–8, is on the east side of the summit of Highgate Hill.

LAUDERDALE HOUSE. Highgate grew up around a group of grand country houses that had been built by the nobility in an attempt to escape from the ever-increasing noise and bustle of London. The place has managed to retain its village atmosphere ever since. An example is Lauderdale House, a 16th-century dwelling that was remodeled in the middle of the following century by the duke of Lauderdale. In 1871 it was bought by the philanthropist Sir Sidney Waterlow, who let it to St Bartholomew's Hospital as a rest home. In 1889 he gave the house and gardens to the London County Council. The house is now used for exhibitions and concerts. There is also museum and restaurant.

HIGHGATE SCHOOL. This famous school is situated on North Road. In 1565 Queen Elizabeth I authorized Sir Roger Cholmley to open a school that would offer the best education to children of good families, and also serve the needy of the village. In 1571 the school had just forty pupils; in 1993 the school numbered 930 boys. Its French-style neo-Gothic buildings date from 1865 to 1868. POND SQUARE, in the middle of the village, owes its name to a pool (filled in in 1864) formed by the repeated removal of gravel from the spot to mend the roads. The poet Samuel Taylor Coleridge and the violinist Yehudi Menuhin lived at numbers 3 and 2 THE GROVE, a road that is well known for its elegant houses. In South Grove there is a fine group of 18th-century houses. At the foot of Swain's Lane is HOLLY VILLAGE ★, a group of eccentrically designed cottages that were built in 1865 by Henry Darbishire. Among the more modern buildings should be mentioned Highpoint 1 and 2, which were built on North Hill in 1938 by Lubetkin and Tecton. Filled with admiration, Le Corbusier called them "a vertical garden city".

HIGHGATE CEMETERY ★. ST MICHAEL'S CHURCH, a neo-Gothic building, was constructed by the architect Lewis Vulliamy in 1830 on the site of the old home of Sir William Ashurst, who was Lord Mayor of London in 1694. Soon afterwards the rest of the land was bought by Stephen Geary, who then founded the London Cemetery Company and laid out the cemetery. As soon as it was opened in 1839 it proved to be an incredible success. Everyone wanted to be buried there, and since then visitors have flocked to explore the place. In fact, so great was Geary's success that in 1857 he had to create an extension in Swain's Lane. On the west side are Egyptian Avenue and the catacombs, housing the remains of rich families, which have lost nothing of their magnificence.

The West End

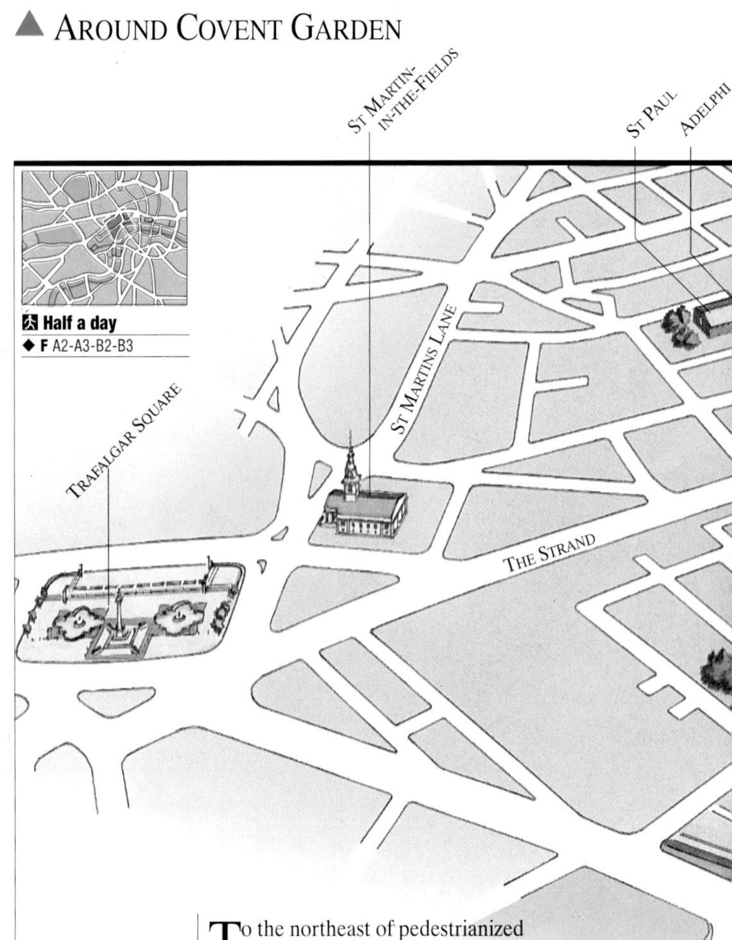

Half a day
◆ **F** A2-A3-B2-B3

To the northeast of pedestrianized Trafalgar Square, just a few steps from the City, is the very heart of London. The route leads from the Strand to Covent Garden, past theaters and along the river. It is a district packed with history, but unfortunately heavily redeveloped in the 20th century.

ST MARY-LE-STRAND
Like its neighbor, St Clement Dane's, this church has the distinction of sitting in the middle of the Strand, which widens here to form a sort of square.

THE STRAND

This broad main road runs between Fleet Street and Charing Cross Station, linking the City of London to the City of Westminster. It is one of the busiest streets in the whole of the capital, packed with traffic and with many thousands of commuters hurrying to and from the station. Already by the middle of the 19th century, when Charlotte Brontë came to London to see her publishers, she found that crossing the road here was a hazardous affair.

HISTORY. The street started out as a track running east above the riverbank, hence its name. During the 16th centur courtiers wanting to live near the royal palace of Whitehall built themselves large town houses along the road, with

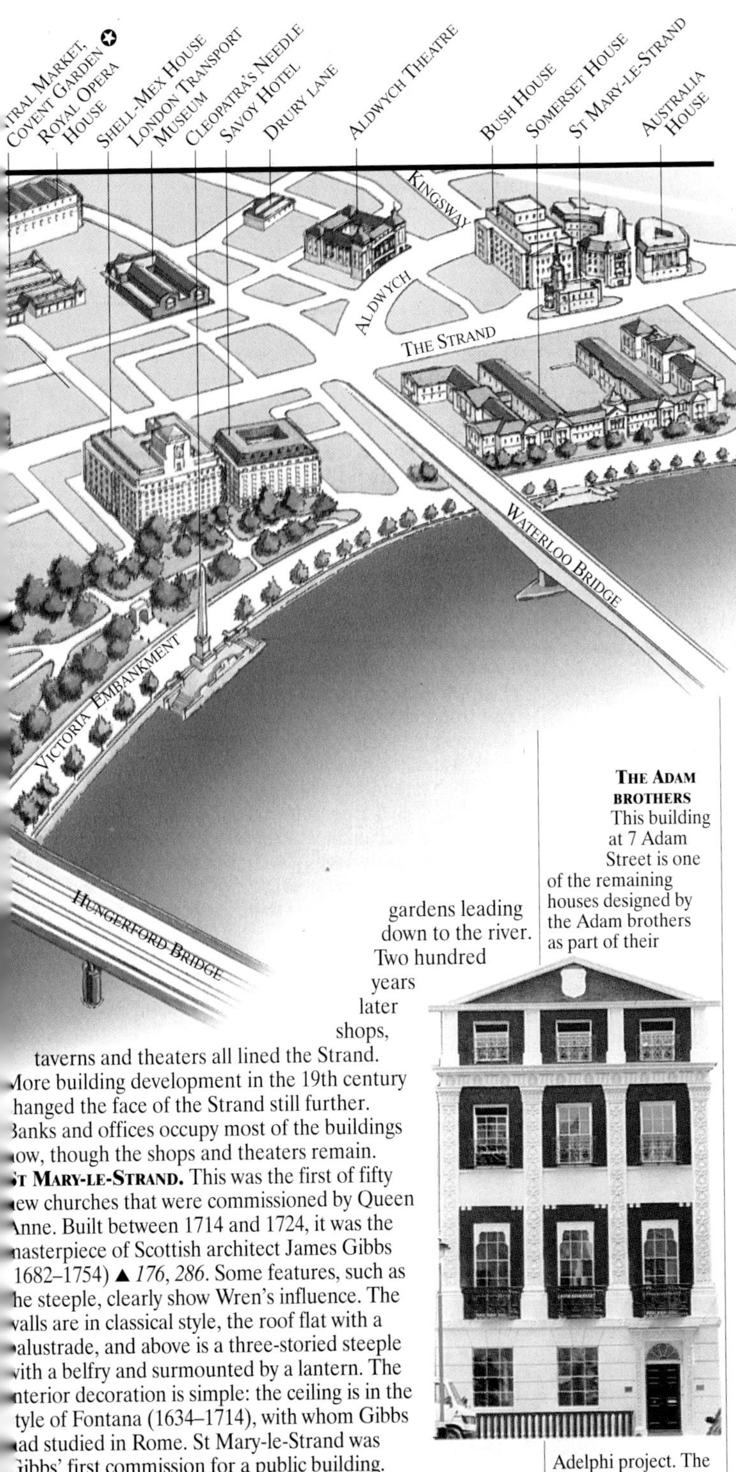

The Adam brothers
This building at 7 Adam Street is one of the remaining houses designed by the Adam brothers as part of their Adelphi project. The façade is typical of their work, its stiff classical lines softened by exterior decoration and delightful ironwork.

gardens leading down to the river. Two hundred years later shops, taverns and theaters all lined the Strand. More building development in the 19th century changed the face of the Strand still further. Banks and offices occupy most of the buildings now, though the shops and theaters remain.

St Mary-le-Strand. This was the first of fifty new churches that were commissioned by Queen Anne. Built between 1714 and 1724, it was the masterpiece of Scottish architect James Gibbs (1682–1754) ▲ *176, 286*. Some features, such as the steeple, clearly show Wren's influence. The walls are in classical style, the roof flat with a balustrade, and above is a three-storied steeple with a belfry and surmounted by a lantern. The interior decoration is simple: the ceiling is in the style of Fontana (1634–1714), with whom Gibbs had studied in Rome. St Mary-le-Strand was Gibbs' first commission for a public building.

The Adelphi. In Adam Street and John Adam Street are the remains of one of the most ambitious urban redevelopments in London, and indeed in all of Europe as far as neo-classical architecture is concerned. This was the Adelphi, brain-child of Robert, John and James Adam ▲ *252*, begun in 1772. This

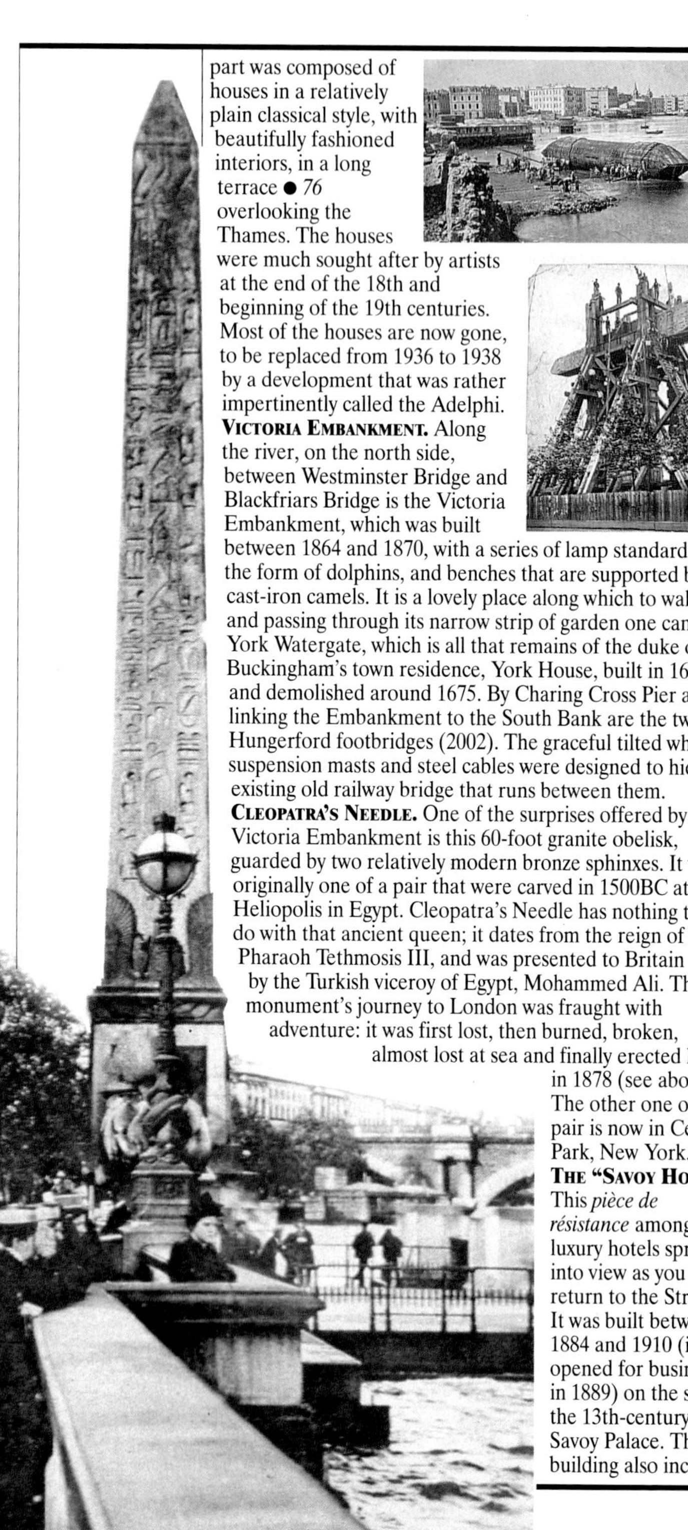

part was composed of houses in a relatively plain classical style, with beautifully fashioned interiors, in a long terrace ● *76* overlooking the Thames. The houses were much sought after by artists at the end of the 18th and beginning of the 19th centuries. Most of the houses are now gone, to be replaced from 1936 to 1938 by a development that was rather impertinently called the Adelphi.

VICTORIA EMBANKMENT. Along the river, on the north side, between Westminster Bridge and Blackfriars Bridge is the Victoria Embankment, which was built between 1864 and 1870, with a series of lamp standards in the form of dolphins, and benches that are supported by cast-iron camels. It is a lovely place along which to walk, and passing through its narrow strip of garden one can see York Watergate, which is all that remains of the duke of Buckingham's town residence, York House, built in 1625 and demolished around 1675. By Charing Cross Pier and linking the Embankment to the South Bank are the two Hungerford footbridges (2002). The graceful tilted white suspension masts and steel cables were designed to hide the existing old railway bridge that runs between them.

CLEOPATRA'S NEEDLE. One of the surprises offered by the Victoria Embankment is this 60-foot granite obelisk, guarded by two relatively modern bronze sphinxes. It was originally one of a pair that were carved in 1500BC at Heliopolis in Egypt. Cleopatra's Needle has nothing to do with that ancient queen; it dates from the reign of the Pharaoh Tethmosis III, and was presented to Britain by the Turkish viceroy of Egypt, Mohammed Ali. The monument's journey to London was fraught with adventure: it was first lost, then burned, broken, almost lost at sea and finally erected here in 1878 (see above). The other one of the pair is now in Central Park, New York.

THE "SAVOY HOTEL". This *pièce de résistance* among luxury hotels springs into view as you return to the Strand. It was built between 1884 and 1910 (it opened for business in 1889) on the site of the 13th-century Savoy Palace. The building also includes

the Savoy Theatre, which was built in 1881 for performing the comic operas of Gilbert and Sullivan. One of the hotel's most famous guests was Claude Monet, who painted his finest views of London from the balcony of his room ● *96*.

FORMER SHELL-MEX HOUSE. Built in 1931, this giant building has a proportionally large clock on its façade, from which it is much easier to tell the time if looking from across the river. It was once the Hotel Cecil, at the time the largest in Europe with eight hundred bedrooms, and was then the headquarters of the Shell-Mex company. The Austrian painter Oskar Kokoschka was given permission to paint from its flat roof. In around 2000 the building was redeveloped as a normal office block, with a refurbished courtyard and new glass canopy, and is now officially named "80 Strand".

CHARING CROSS STATION. "The full tide of human existence is at Charing Cross", said Samuel Johnson (1709–84), long before the great railway terminus serving southeast England was built here. The building incorporates the Charing Cross Hotel, and was opened in 1864. In the forecourt is Queen Eleanor's Cross, which was erected in 1865 by Edward Middleton Barry, and is a copy of one of the twelve crosses put up by King Edward I to commemorate his wife Eleanor of Castile, who died in 1290.

COUTTS BANK. The old building of this famous bank located opposite the station was redeveloped in the 1970's, with a spacious modern atrium but retaining the elegant Nash ▲ *257* façade. Coutts and Co. are the queen's bankers.

SOMERSET HOUSE
This great neo-classical building on the banks of the Thames once extended right down to the water's edge.

80 STRAND (FORMER SHELL-MEX BUILDING) AND SAVOY HOTEL
These buildings dominate the skyline above Victoria Embankment.

SOMERSET HOUSE

It is a good idea to view Somerset House from Waterloo Bridge before exploring the inside. This immense Georgian residence is the sole remaining example of the great houses that once lined the Strand. Built on the site of a Renaissance palace, the present Somerset House was constructed between 1776 and 1786 by the Scottish architect Sir William Chambers (1723–96) ▲ *280, 348* to house government offices, as well as the Admiralty, the Royal Academy, the Royal Society and the Society of Antiquaries. Two additional wings were added in the 19th century: the west wing in 1856, designed by Sir James Pennethorne; and the east wing (1835), designed by Robert Smirke. In the magnificent courtyard, surrounded by four wings with bases of Portland stone, is a bronze statue (1778) of King George III. Somerset House contains part of the National Archives and the Courtauld Institute Galleries. After extensive restoration, Somerset House reopened in 2000 and now also houses the Gilbert Collection of decorative arts and the Hermitage Rooms. Open-air events are held in the courtyard, which features a large, walk-through fountain in which jets of water shoot up out of the ground, perfect for cooling down on hot summer days; at the back is the River Terrace, a public promenade, on which an ice-skating rink is set up in winter.

SOMERSET HOUSE
This illustration shows the ornate porch of the great palace.

TREASURES AT THE COURTAULD INSTITUTE GALLERIES Among the most famous works at the galleries are Manet's *A Bar at the Folies-Bergère* (top), *A Quack Addressing a Crowd at a Fair* (above), an ink-and-wash sketch by Rembrandt (1606–69) and *Adam and Eve* (bottom right) by Lucas Cranach the Elder (1472–1553).

KING'S COLLEGE. The east wing of Somerset House is occupied by King's College (founded in 1828 by the duke of Wellington), part of the University of London since 1908.

GILBERT COLLECTION. In 1996 Sir Arthur Gilbert gifted to the nation his large collection of English and European decorative arts objects, now housed on the south side of Somerset House. The more than 800 remarkable items include silver objects, gold snuff-boxes and Italian mosaics.

HERMITAGE ROOMS. On the ground floor of the south wing are rooms housing a changing exhibition of works usually found in the Hermitage Museum of St Petersburg.

COURTAULD INSTITUTE GALLERIES ★. The collections of the Courtauld Institute were moved in 1990 from cramped premises in Woburn Place to Somerset House. The pictures are now to be seen hanging in the eleven elegant rooms on the upper floor of the east wing that were once occupied by the Royal Academy and other learned societies. As well as the main collections of canvases, painted panels, gold, Venetian glass and Italian ceramics are displayed here. The Courtauld Institute's worldwide reputation rests chiefly on its collection of French Impressionist and Post-Impressionist paintings. The heart of the institute's collection is composed of a series of paintings belonging to textiles magnate Samuel Courtauld (1876–1947), which he presented to London University in 1932.

THE ITALIAN AND FLEMISH SCHOOLS. The collections of Lord Lee, of Mark Gambier-Parry and the Prince's Gate collection of Count Antoine Seilern are principally of Flemish and Italian Old Masters from the Renaissance period to the 17th century. The best pieces are an Italian triptych and a polyptych from the

"The Conversion of St Paul"
This painting by Peter Paul Rubens (1577–1640) is typical of the Flemish master's colorful style. He was the greatest master of the Baroque style in northern Europe.

century, a Botticelli *Trinity with John the Baptist and Mary Magdalene* (15th century) and a painting by Breughel the Elder (16th century). There are some fine 18th-century portraits too, notably by the English masters Romney and Gainsborough ▲ *213*. Count Seilern bequeathed to the Institute a total of thirty-two paintings by Rubens from the 16th and 17th centuries. These are displayed in the first rooms and include three sketches for a *Descent from the Cross* from Antwerp Cathedral, a painting depicting the *Placing of Christ's Body in the Tomb*, and six sketches for the Jesuit church in Antwerp. There are also some fine canvases by Rubens' pupil Van Dyck.

A wealth of French Impressionists. The pictures which Samuel Courtauld acquired include just about all of the leading names of French Impressionism: there are works by Manet (*A Bar at the Folies-Bergère*), and by Monet (*Autumn at Argenteuil*), by Renoir (*La Loge*), Pissarro (*Lordship Lane Station*), two of Gauguin's Tahiti pictures and two Van Goghs, including his self-portrait with his ear cut off. There are also some fine pictures by Sisley, Boudin, Degas, Berthe Morisot and many more. One of the rooms is devoted exclusively to the French Post-Impressionists, such as Seurat (*Jeune Femme se poudrant*), Utrillo (*A Street in Sannois*), Cézanne (*Mont Sainte-Victoire*), Toulouse-Lautrec (*Jeanne Avril*) and a *Nude* by Modigliani.

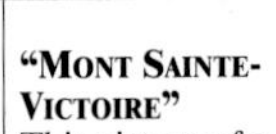

"Mont Sainte-Victoire"
This picture of a mountain near Aix-en-Provence was painted by Paul Cézanne (1839–1906) around 1886–8, when he had married and finally settled in his native Provence.

Contemporary art. As well as the above-mentioned material, the Courtauld Institute collections have received bequests and donations of more recent works, particularly from the English artist and critic Roger Fry (1866–1934), including works by Bonnard, Browse, Derain, Hunter and Fry himself, gouaches by Rouault, African sculptures and a number of pieces from the Omega Workshops that Fry founded in 1913.

COVENT GARDEN ✪
Once the site of London's fruit and vegetable market, the Covent Garden piazza now houses various arts and crafts stalls, a range of small shops, boutiques, bars and restaurants, and is the venue for an array of street performers and musicians. To the west of the piazza is the actors' church (St Paul's) whose walls are lined with memorials to famous theatrical personalities including Charlie Chaplin and Vivien Leigh. South of the piazza is the Jubilee Market with stalls ranging from antiques and crafts to food and clothing. To the east of the piazza is the newly refurbished Royal Opera House, home to the Royal Opera and the Royal Ballet – drop in and see the breathtaking Floral Hall, and maybe catch a free lunchtime concert.

COVENT GARDEN ★

The market and the theater were the two dominant features of Covent Garden for almost three hundred years. The area's restoration in 1980 then gave it another lease of life.

A MONASTERY GARDEN. Covent Garden was originally the vegetable garden of the monks of Westminster Abbey ▲ *137*. With the suppression of the monasteries in the reign of Henry VIII ● *36* it came into the possession of the Russell family, earls of Bedford. In 1631 the fourth earl decided to construct a piazza on the spot and he entrusted the project to the royal architect Inigo Jones ▲ *328*. Jones incorporated features from the Place des Vosges in Paris and also the piazza at Livorno into his designs, which were built between 1631 and 1635 on a rectangular space backing on to the Russells' property ▲ *298*, Bedford House. Because of the considerable cost, the square was lined with arcades on only two sides; the south side was bordered by the gardens of Bedford House, and the west by St Paul's Church. With its terraces of matching houses and elegant right-angled streets, Covent Garden was London's first "square". It was predominantly a residential district inhabited by courtiers, but in 1661 it was partially restored to its old purpose when the Russells decided to start a fruit, flower and vegetable market there. This was such a success that it was soon the principal market of its kind in England. In an attempt to keep

COVENT GARDEN IN TIMES PAST
This 1737 picture (top) by Balthazar Nebot shows the piazza's arcades and the façade of St Paul's Church ▲ *328*. The watercolour by John Wykeham Archer (opposite) gives a good idea of Covent Garden market in the 19th century, as portrayed by G.B. Shaw in the play *Pygmalion* (1913), later brought to the big screen as the musical *My Fair Lady* (1963).

this colorful but chaotic market under control, in 1829 and 1833 architect Charles Fowler built the market halls ● *85*. These were three long, parallel buildings in the center of the piazza. They were divided into stalls with iron colonnades and with a glass roof. Nothing remains of Jones' original piazza, though the arcades on the north side of the square give some idea of how it must once have looked.

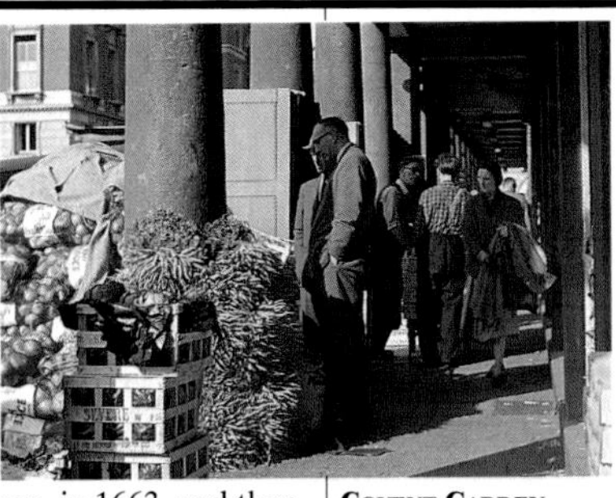

COVENT GARDEN MARKET IN 1950
The market continued working in the halls built by the duke of Bedford in 1829 right up to the 1970's, and was a familiar part of the London scene.

THE MUSES GO TO MARKET. The opening of the Theatre Royal, Drury Lane, in 1663, and then of Covent Garden Theatre in 1732, transformed the area and brought in crowds of theatergoers. But it was in the 19th century that the district found its greatest theatrical vocation, with the construction of forty new theaters in an area that was already famous for its liveliness and fun.

A SUCCESSFUL FACELIFT. The market retained its cheerful and somewhat scruffy appearance until 1974. When it finally moved to Nine Elms on the other side of the river, the character of the quarter was quickly lost, and plans were made to redevelop the site as offices. Thanks to the determination of the people who lived there, such as artists and architects, the authorities were eventually persuaded to restore Covent Garden. The work was successfully completed in 1980, with a central pedestrian area and NEAL STREET, a lively collection of small shops, contributing to a new lease of life for the old market.

THE FLOWER MARKET. Opposite the main halls, the Jubilee Market (1904) is still in business, with a flea market operating on Mondays. The old Flower Market beside it, which was built in 1891, houses a fascinating theater museum, and there is also the LONDON TRANSPORT MUSEUM to be visited, where horse-drawn ancestors of the famous red London buses are on show. A substantial collection of buses, trams, models, paintings, posters, tickets and other ephemera all help to tell the story of the history of public transport in the capital city.

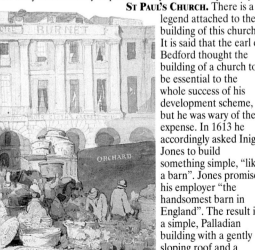

ST PAUL'S CHURCH. There is a legend attached to the building of this church. It is said that the earl of Bedford thought the building of a church to be essential to the whole success of his development scheme, but he was wary of the expense. In 1613 he accordingly asked Inigo Jones to build something simple, "like a barn". Jones promised his employer "the handsomest barn in England". The result is a simple, Palladian building with a gently sloping roof and a

COVENT GARDEN MARKET TODAY
When the market moved away to new premises south of the Thames, its elegant old buildings were saved from demolition and subsequently restored. Since 1980 they have been home to a range of craft and antique stalls, restaurants, fashion boutiques and a host of other ventures.

THE ACTORS' CHURCH
St Paul's is the church of artists and actors. In its crypt and adjoining graveyard are buried the writer Samuel Butler, the woodcarver Grinling Gibbons, the composer Thomas Arne, court painter Sir Peter Lely and dramatist William Wycherley. The painter J.M.W. Turner was baptized here.

pillared porch, in front of a blind façade looking on to the piazza. St Paul's was badly burned in 1795, and then faithfully restored by Thomas Hardwick.

THEATERLAND

● 54

There are a number of major theaters in the neighborhood of the Strand, including the Savoy Theatre, the Vaudeville Theatre, the Fortune Theatre, the Adelphi, the Strand and the Aldwych. With the addition of the two big ones in Covent Garden, the Theatre Royal, Drury Lane, and the Royal Opera House, the area has long supplied the very lifeblood of the London stage.

THE DRURY LANE THEATRE. The present theater in Drury Lane is the work of Benjamin Dean Wyatt (1755–1850), and it was actually the fourth theater to be built on the site. It was opened in 1812. The second theater had been designed by Wren ▲ *171* in 1672–4, but this was demolished in 1791. Here the actor Edmund Kean (1789–1833) performed many of his great Shakespearean roles, such as Shylock, Iago and Richard III. The auditorium, which was rebuilt in 1922, is the largest in all of London with a seating capacity for three thousand people.

THE ROYAL OPERA HOUSE. This building first opened its doors in 1732 as the Covent Garden Theatre. The present building, which was constructed between 1856 and 1858 by Edward Barry, was the third theater to be built on the site. The previous ones were both destroyed by fire. Its façade is decorated with a Corinthian portico shielding reliefs and a frieze by John Flaxman (1755–1826). The acoustics of the auditorium, which seats two thousand, are famous throughout the opera world. A new west wing was added in 1982. The foundation of the Royal Opera Company in 1946 and of the Royal Ballet 10 years later helped to enhance the theater's reputation as one of the finest opera houses in the world. In 1999 the building of a spectacular new foyer, auditoriums and creative workshops has helped to rejuvenate this prestigious institution.

COVENT GARDEN THEATRE
This engraving shows the interior of the old theater in 1809. Mrs Siddons and Edmund Kean acted here, and the German composer Weber was musical director in the 1820's.

This is a fascinating street for anyone wishing to study the ladies doing their

ɿopping, as the shops and other establishments are close together, and the

isplays in the shop windows are such that the emotions proper to the gentler sex

re forever in danger of being undermined." Henry Mayhew, *The Shops and*

ompanies of London and the Trade and Manufactures of Great Britain, 1865.

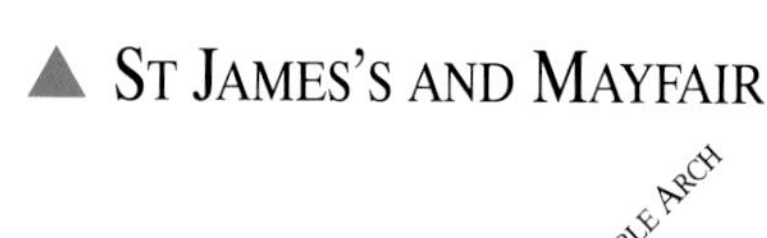

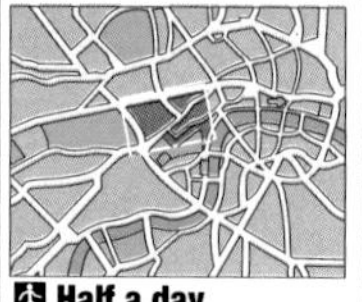

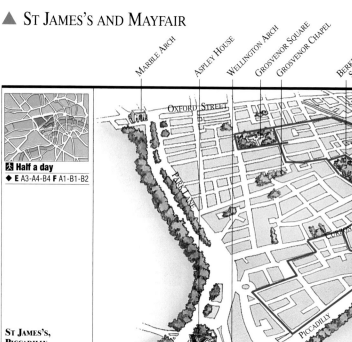

Half a day

◆ **E** A3-A4-B4 **F** A1-B1-B2

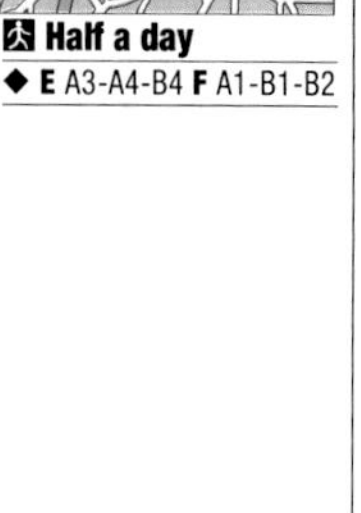

St James's, Piccadilly
The church, constructed of brick and Portland stone, was built in 1674 by Wren ▲ *172* and restored after the Second World War by Sir Albert Richardson. It has a gallery and a vaulted ceiling ornamented with plaster molding. The organ was made for the Chapel Royal in Whitehall; its case is decorated with gilded figures, the work of Grinling Gibbons ▲ *157, 173, 198*, who also decorated the marble fonts and the limewood reredos.

Around St James's

The exclusive district of St James's is at the very center of fashionable London. Peaceful and opulent, it is an area of gracious town houses and gentlemen's clubs, bounded on the north side by Piccadilly, by Haymarket in the east, with St James's Park on its southern boundary and Green Park to the west side. Its links with royalty go back as far as the 17th century, but today many of its fine, original houses are gone, replaced by commercial developments of the 19th and 20th centuries.

A royal district. Ever since Charles II moved into St James's Palace ▲ *240* the surrounding district has acquired

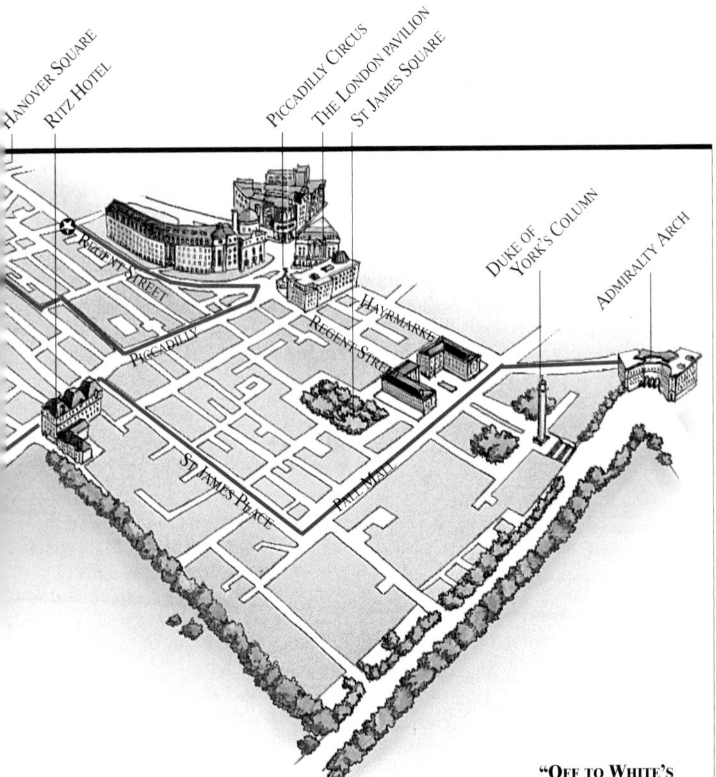

HANOVER SQUARE
RITZ HOTEL
PICCADILLY CIRCUS
THE LONDON PAVILION
ST JAMES SQUARE
REGENT STREET
PICCADILLY
HAYMARKET
REGENT STREET
DUKE OF YORK'S COLUMN
ADMIRALTY ARCH
ST JAMES PLACE
PALL MALL

touch of royal glamor. Henry Jermyn, earl of St Albans was ıe first to develop the area: he took advantage of the king's ːsidence nearby to build houses on land that was granted ım by Charles II. Then he sold the elegant town houses that ıe St James's Square to a number of wealthy noblemen who anted to be as near to the court as possible. The district took ff again during the 18th century, with government ministries ıd foreign embassies settling in St James's. Numerous ɔffee-houses and shops also opened up, notably in St James's treet, to cater for the needs of such a high-class clientèle. In ɔite of the young Queen Victoria's decision to move to uckingham Palace in 1837, St James's continued to be the ɔme of high society.

HE AGE OF ELEGANCE. Dandyism was born in England at the art of the 19th century. Dandies were young men of high rth who expressed their contempt for political democracy ıd social equality by their exquisite dress, affected speech, ĸaggerated manners and refined taste. The dramatist ichard Brinsley Sheridan (1751–1816) and the Romantic ɔet Lord Byron (1788–1824) were among the founding ıthers of the fashion, whose unchallenged leader was George rummell (1778–1840), known as "Beau". Brummell's iendship with the Prince Regent, the future George IV, ɔened the doors of society for him, and he soon became the biter of good taste and the king of fashion. He even chose ıe clothes that his manservant wore, and would spend hours ing his cravat. A break with the prince obliged Beau rummell to take refuge from his creditors in France, where e died in Caen, destitute, dirty and mad.

LUBLAND. The gentlemen's clubs of St James's are some of ıe pillars of the English establishment. They are descendants

"OFF TO WHITE'S CLUB"
This silhouette of 1819 by Richard Dighton shows William Archer strolling to his club, recalling the observation by a French visitor to London that "a dandy should have a victorious, carefree and insolent air, and take immense pains with his toilette . . ."

NINE HUNDRED CLUBS
There used to be around nine hundred clubs in London. Billiards (below: the billiard room in Brooks's Club) was a typical activity, as was conversation.

of the coffee-houses where the fashion-conscious used to gather to sip either this new drink from Arabia or else chocolate imported from the Americas. These gradually evolved into meeting-places for discussions about politics, literature and the pressing topics of the day. The clubs have a series of strict rules and restricted membership policies, but members can relax, meet each other (on condition that they never talk "shop"), drink, dine and stay overnight. All rules are carefully observed by the club members, who are still almost exclusively men.

PALL MALL

On turning into Cockspur Street or Pall Mall East, one can see at the end the featureless façades of Pall Mall, which takes its name from an old game, somewhat resembling croquet, that was once played there. Now these large, plai buildings house many of the famous gentlemen's clubs.

THE ATHENAEUM. The most famous of al London clubs was founded in 1823, and it has long been the preserve of the British cultural élite. Past members have included the naturalists Thomas Huxley (1825–95) and Charles Darwin (1809–82), and the writers Charles Dickens (1812–70) ● *110–11, 118,* Joseph Conrad (1857–1924) ● *112*, and Rudyard Kipling (1865–1936). The club has also been popular with many politicians and bishops. Membership of the Athenaeum, which carries great kudos in certain circles, is by application, followed by a ballot where members vote with white or black balls. If a member expresses his objection by the use of a black ball, the candidate is said to be "blackballed" or turned down. Bertrand Russell ▲ *308* had to wait forty years after being blackballed before he was finally admitted to membership of the club. Naturally enough the building is in quasi-Grecian style, built in 1828–30 by Decimus Burton ▲ *257*. It is a most spectacular affair, with a majestic hall dominated by a statue of Apollo, reading room, dining room, games room and a magnificent library where the walls are lined with precious books. Members' private apartments are situated on the uppe floors. Certain rules must be observed. For example, it is forbidden to discuss business or to take any paper out of your pocket in the dining room: a lady dining there once with her husband was called to order by the club steward when she took a sample of wallpaper out of her bag.

The Marquis of Hertford in 1818.

THE TRAVELLERS' CLUB. This club was founded in 1819 for travelers to meet, exchange experiences and possibly tell a few tall tales. It is at 106 Pall Mall in a clubhous

lesigned by Charles Barry ▲ *131* in 1829–32. To be eligible or membership, a candidate must have traveled at least a housand miles from London. Many diplomats are members.
THE REFORM CLUB. The "Italian palazzo" at numbers 104–5 s the home of the Reform Club, traditionally the preserve of vealthy radicals. It was built in 1837 by Charles Barry.
THE ROYAL AUTOMOBILE CLUB. The present building at 30 Pall Mall was built 1908–11 by the architects of the *Ritz Hotel* ▲ *280*, and now has fifteen thousand members up and lown the country. The clubhouse incorporates a much older building, Schomberg House (1698), where the artist Gainsborough ▲ *213* lived from 1774 to 1778.
THE OXFORD AND CAMBRIDGE CLUB. This was founded by Lord Palmerston in 1830. The building, at 71 Pall Mall, was he work of the Smirke brothers, who were also the architects of the British Museum ▲ *300*. Membership is open to those who have studied at one or other of the wo universities.

ST JAMES'S STREET

Pall Mall leads to St James's Street, which is one of the most elegant and aristocratic in London. An atmosphere of luxury and quiet refinement rules here, among the old businesses for which the treet is world-famous.
THE CLUBS. Boodle's (number 28) together with Brooks's and White's (number 37) are some of the oldest clubs n the street. The Carlton Club, in a building dating from 1827, is another Tory institution, founded in 1832 by the luke of Wellington.
"BERRY BROTHERS AND RUDD". This family business founded in the 17th century is at 3 St James's Street. It is renowned for its excellent clarets and whisky. The large scales inside have been used to weigh famous patrons since 1765, the results being recorded in nine leather-bound volumes.
"LOCK'S". The famous hatter's shop has been at 6 St James's Street since 1759. High society still comes to *Lock's* for top hats and bowlers. Before Lord Nelson ▲ *284* left for his final victory at Trafalgar, he came here and ordered a hat specially fitted with an eyeshade.
"LOBB'S" BESPOKE BOOTMAKERS. "The world's finest bootmaker" is at 9 St James's Street. He makes boots and shoes for the royal feet, and among his many other famous customers have been Winston Churchill, Katharine Hepburn and Frank Sinatra.
BYRON HOUSE. This was built in 1960 on the site of Lord Byron's house where, as he said, he awoke one beautiful morning in 1812 after the publication of his poem *Childe Harold's Pilgrimage* to find himself famous.

BROOKS'S CLUB
Situated at the corner of Park Place, Brooks's Club (above, in 1825) was founded in 1764 by William Almack, and later became the rendezvous of the Whig party. The 1778 clubhouse was the work of Henry Holland.

JOHN LOBB
The wooden lasts of each client are kept here. The shop is virtually a museum.

Hugh Johnson, a wine merchant's shop in St James's Street also sells everything, new and old, connected with the subject of wine.

WHITE'S CLUB
The rival of Brooks's Club, White's started out in 1693 as *White's Chocolate House*. It is an exclusively Tory institution. Beau Brummell and many prime ministers have been members. Prince Charles held his stag party here.

The luxurious "Ritz"
The hotel's many features include an arcade, copied from the rue de Rivoli in Paris, its Louis XV décor, and excellent afternoon tea.

Regent Street in 1820
This view looking down Regent Street from Oxford Circus shows the carriages and elegant dress of passers-by, typical of Mayfair early in the 19th century.

Jermyn Street

The world-famous perfumier *Floris* (above) is here. Founded in 1730, the shop is noted for its pots-pourri, its stephanotis scent and its rose geranium bath salts. Famous clients have included Queen Victoria, the Duke of Windsor, Oscar Wilde and Queen Elizabeth II. Other notable establishments on Jermyn Street are the famous cheese shop *Paxton & Whitfield* the cigar merchant *Davidoff*, hatters *James Lock & Co* and *Bates*, shoemakers *J. Lobb* and several fine shirtmakers.

Piccadilly

This broad avenue was laid out in the 18th century. It runs from Hyde Park Corner to Piccadilly Circus, separating the district of St James's from Mayfair. Today it is lined with first-class hotels, expensive shops, majestic old town houses and other splendid dwellings converted into clubs.

The "Ritz Hotel". This is the biggest hotel in London. Built of Norwegian granite on a steel frame by Mewes and Davis at the corner of Green Park, it opened in 1906.

Burlington Arcade. In 1819, to protect his garden from passers-by, who tended to throw rubbish into it, Lord Burlington asked the architect Samuel Ware to construct a roof above the little street that today joins Piccadilly and Burlington Gardens. This Regency-style gallery has about 40 little shops where gentlemen, sheltered from onlookers, could buy presents for their mistresses. Today, the shops sell luxury articles, particularly cashmere and jewelry. The arcade Britain's first shopping mall, was copied throughout the British Empire.

The Royal Academy of Arts. Burlington House, opposite Shepherds Market, has been home to the Royal Academy for more than a century. The actual building was altered and enlarged between 1867 and 1874 by Banks and Barry, and again more recently by Norman Foster but it retains its Palladian interior. The academy was founded in 1768 to teach fine arts, and holds an exhibition every summer to which many thousands of artists send their work for selection. Other exhibitions also take place throughout the year. Each elected academician is obliged to donate one of his or her works. The list of donors includes Gainsborough ▲ *213*, Benjamin West, Sir William Chambers ▲ *269, 348*, Turner ▲ *215–217*

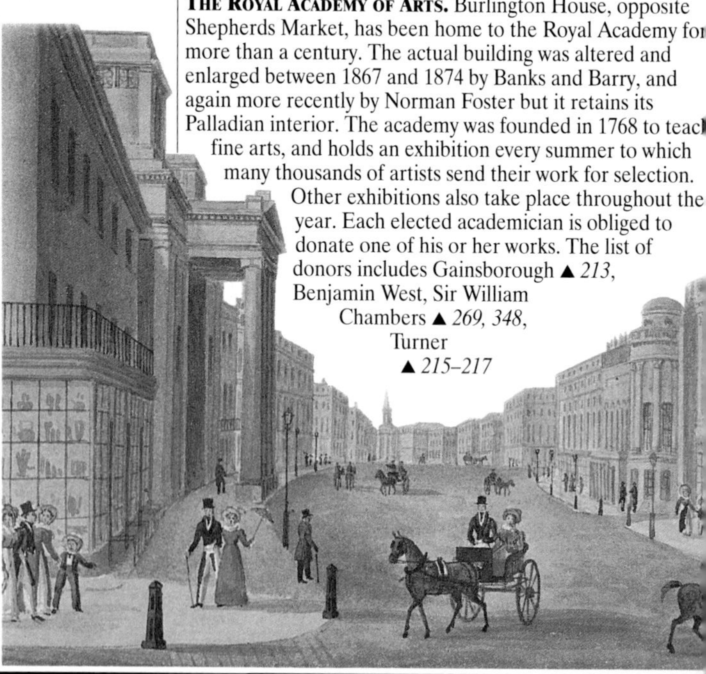

“To be English is to belong to the most exclusive club in the world.”

Ogden Nash

nd Constable ▲ *214*. Acquisitions have also enriched the ermanent collection, which boasts a lovely marble tondo by Aichelangelo: *Madonna and Child with the Infant St John*. Redevelopment works, which will double the premises' size by ncluding the building behind, are planned to be completed in 007; the Academy will remain open throughout.

FORTNUM & MASON'S". This superb rocery store restocks the royal larders. ts orange marmalade is much in lemand, likewise its pickles and tea.

HATCHARDS" BOOKSHOP. The oldest ookshop in London, opened by John Iatchard in 1797, it soon began to esemble a club, attracting famous ustomers such as Lord Byron, Wellington, Gladstone and Oscar Wilde.

THE ROYAL ACADEMY
The diarist Samuel Pepys and scientist Isaac Newton were presidents in the 17th century.

MAYFAIR

The little district of Mayfair, on the edge of Hyde Park, is bounded by Oxford Street, Regent Street and Piccadilly. The ame comes from the “May Fairs”, local ivestock and grain markets that from 688 were held in the first week of May. The area was first developed in the 18th entury by the Grosvenor family, the lukes of Westminster, then grand houses nd numerous squares were added. Mayfair is the wealthiest part of London. It divides fairly eatly into two: the area around Bond Street with its prosperous businesses, and west toward Hyde Park, which is he elegant residential quarter. Many celebrated people have ived here, such as Lord Byron, the historian Macaulay and prime minister Gladstone in the 19th century; and more ecently the novelist Graham Greene and former Conservative premier Edward Heath.

BURLINGTON ARCADE
This private thoroughfare is supervised by “beadles” in coats and bowler hats. By day they watch over the behavior of passers-by (singing is not allowed); and at night they close the gates ● *84*.

CURZON STREET. This street still has some 18th-century ouses such as Crew House (number 15), built in 1730 for Edward Shepherd. The shop of *Geo. F. Trumper* (number 9), perfumier and hairdresser, is well worth a look. His shaving creams in such scents as rose, violet and almond, as well as his goats' milk soap and other items, are a delight.

SHEPHERD MARKET. The site of this market, designed by Edward Shepherd in 1735 and altered in 1860, was, up to the 17th century, where the May Fair was held. Around the pedestrian areas and paved courtyards are old-fashioned shops selling food and antiques. There are interesting restaurants too.

BERKELEY SQUARE. This was laid out in 1737–47 to designs by William Kent (1685–1748), the protégé of Lord Burlington. Queen Elizabeth II was born at 17 Bruton Street in Berkeley Square House on the east side of the square.

NAMES DOWN THE AGES
The noble families who developed Mayfair in the 18th century, with its beautiful houses and elegant squares, have their memorials in many street names. They include Thomas Bond, Lord Dover, Sir Nathaniel Curzon, Hugh Audley, Lord Chesterfield, Lady Berkeley of Stratton and the Grosvenor family.

THE "CAFÉ ROYAL" This famous restaurant is on the curve of the Regent Street Quadrant. It opened in 1865 and was the haunt of notable writers and artists, such as Oscar Wilde (1854–1900), and the artists Aubrey Beardsley (1872–98), James Abbott McNeill Whistler (1834–1903) ● *104* and Augustus John (1878–1961).

"LIBERTY'S" This enormous store, renowned for its cottons and silks, is at the corner of Regent Street and Great Marlborough Street ● *89*. The building dates from 1924–5. Behind it is another section in mock-Tudor style, leading on to Great Marlborough Street.

GROSVENOR SQUARE. This was built between 1720 and 1725 a the end of Upper Brook Street. In 1785, John Adams, future president of the USA, moved to number 9 when he was ambassador here. Ever since, the area has been known as "Little America".

BROOK STREET. Along Brook Street toward Hanover Square is the Savile Club with its French 18th-century-style interior. The composer George Frederick Handel (1685–1759) spent the last thirty years of his life at number 25. Just before Bond Street is the famous *Claridge's Hotel*, which since 1860 has enjoyed the reputation of being one of London's best hotel.

SAVILE ROW. The great tradition of British tailoring is centered here: there is *Henry Poole* (tailor to Emperor Napoleon III), *H. Huntsman & Sons*, *J. Dege & Sons*, *Gieves & Hawkes*, *Ozwald Boateng*, and many others.

BOND STREET

This is the main street in Mayfair. It runs down to Piccadilly under the name of Old Bond Street, and up to Oxford Street as New Bond Street. Lord Nelson ▲ *286* once lived here with his mistress Lady Hamilton; Beau Brummell and Lord Byron are among other famous residents of Bond Steet.

SUPPLIERS TO THE COURT. Bond Street is also the home of luxury shops such as *Beal & Inman* and *Herbie Frogg* for clothes, *Church & Co.* for shoes, and *Asprey's*, which sells leather goods and jewelry as well as antiques. Above certain shops gleams the sign *By Appointment to Her Majesty*; these re suppliers to the court, a guarantee of high uality and the best workmanship.

REGENT STREET

Regent Street runs from the Athenaeum in Pall Mall up to the north of Oxford Circus, and was built to designs by John Nash ▲ *257* between 1813 and 1823. This majestic road, lined with gracious stucco-faced houses linked the Prince Regent's home of Carlton House in St James's Park to Regent's Park in the north. The street was entirely rebuilt between 1898 and 1928, and along it are large luxury shops such as *Liberty's*, *Aquascutum*, and *Hamley's*, one of the biggest and most celebrated toyshops in the world.

LIBERTY'S". *Liberty's* was founded in 1875 by Arthur Liberty, whose fabrics were all the rage in the days of Art Nouveau *89*. Today the printed fabrics have become classics of the English style and some can be reordered in exactly the same design from year to year. But this is a department store too, selling men's and ladies' fashions and household goods.

THE QUADRANT. This is the name of the impressive curve made by Regent Street as it sweeps down toward Piccadilly Circus. In the façades, rebuilt at the beginning of the century, no trace remains of Nash's original work.

PICCADILLY CIRCUS. This road junction has come to represent the heart of London for millions of tourists. But it is in fact only a busy intersection. At night it is brightly illuminated by giant neon signs, the first of which was erected in 1890. The little statue in the middle does not in fact depict Eros, as is generally thought, but the Angel of Christian Charity. It was put up in 1893 in memory of the Victorian philanthropist Lord Shaftesbury.

ST JAMES'S STREET, REGENT STREET, BOND STREET ✪
Mahagony, brass, thick carpets and a velvet atmosphere: the Mayfair shops are the height of luxury. Many display the words "By Appointment of Her Majesty", distinguishing them as suppliers to the court. The prices here are high, but even if you don't buy anything this is a great place to go window shopping. Other pretigious shops are found close by on Curzon Street and Jermyn Street, while elite tailors are found on Savile Row. More touristy, Burlington Arcade, a luxury temple of shopping , is very busy around sales periods.

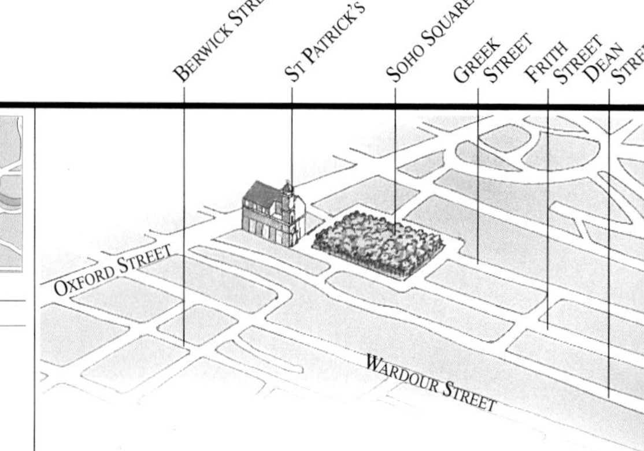

One day
◆ **F** A1-A2-B2

TRAFALGAR SQUARE

CHRISTMAS CAROLS IN TRAFALGAR SQUARE
The Christmas tree is decorated with lights, and around it the singing is led by a number of different choirs who collect money for charity.

CHRISTMAS IN TRAFALGAR SQUARE
An enormous Christmas tree has been erected here every year since 1947. This gift from the people of Norway is in recognition of the refuge that Britain gave to the Norwegian royal family during World War Two.

In 1820 it was the architect John Nash's idea to lay out a square at the top of Whitehall on the site of the former Royal Mews. The only existing constructions to antedate Trafalgar Square in this area are the church of St Martin-in-the-Fields, and the equestrian statue of Charles I, which was made by Le Sueur in 1633 and erected on its present site around 1767. The construction of this famous square began in 1829: the sloping land was leveled and then paved in 1840 by Sir Charles Barry, who also added the north terrace below the National Gallery. There are statues of George IV and Generals Havelock and Napier at three corners of the square. The fountains by Sir Edwin Lutyens were added in 1939. In 2003, the north side of the square was pedestrianized, providing a traffic-free North Terrace linking the National Gallery and the square for the first time, and opening up a splendid vista. From North Terrace, a grand central staircase was built to link the National Gallery to the square below, which now features an open-air café and other public facilities, greatly enhancing enjoyment of one of the city's most famous spots for Londoners and visitors alike.

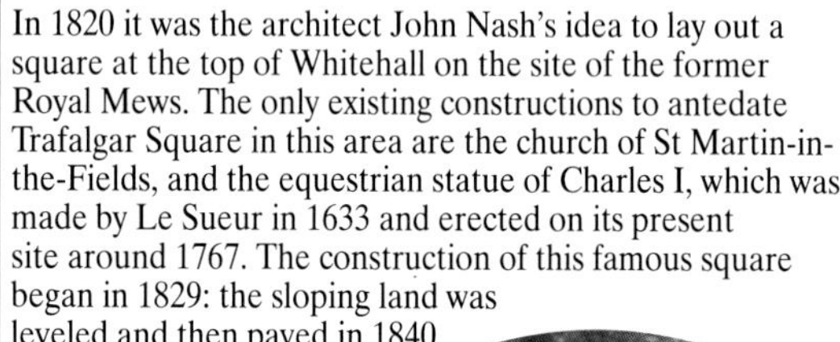

MEETINGS IN TRAFALGAR SQUARE. The square has been a traditional place for public meetings ever since the time of the Chartists in 1848. Many political marches end here with rallies, at which speakers usually address the crowds from the base of the column. Every year at Christmas there is a huge illuminated fir tree, the gift of the Norwegian people in memory of World War Two. The tradition is for huge crowds of Londoners to flock here on New Year's Eve in order to hear Big Ben chime midnight and then to wish each other a Happy New Year. The gatherings can get extremely noisy and boisterous. Another celebration, which takes place at the beginning of October each year, is the gathering of the Pearly Kings and Queens

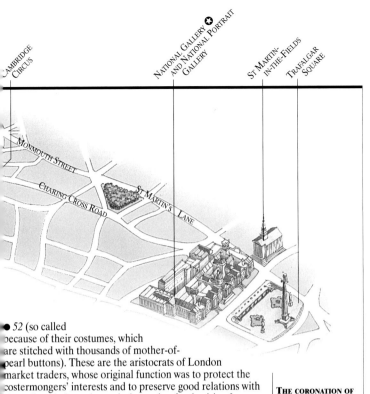

Cambridge Circus

National Gallery and National Portrait Gallery ✪

St Martin-in-the-Fields

Trafalgar Square

Monmouth Street

Charing Cross Road

St Martin's Lane

● *52* (so called because of their costumes, which are stitched with thousands of mother-of-pearl buttons). These are the aristocrats of London market traders, whose original function was to protect the costermongers' interests and to preserve good relations with the police; their work now is devoted to fund-raising for various charities.

Nelson's Column. A statue of Lord Nelson over 17 feet tall dominates the square. It was erected in 1843 on a granite column that is 185 feet high, the base of which is ornamented with four bronze lions (1867) by the artist Sir Edwin Landseer. The pedestal of the monument has a number of bas-reliefs, cast from French cannons, which depict the great admiral's naval victories at Cape St Vincent, the Battle of the Nile, Copenhagen, and Trafalgar. It was during the latter, on October 21, 1805, that Nelson was killed.

South Africa House. Sir Herbert Baker (1862–1946) designed this seven-story building in 1935 on the site of the former *Morley's Hotel* (1831). There is a striking sculpture

The coronation of Queen Victoria
Victoria (b. May 24, 1819) became queen on June 20, 1837. Her coronation the following year, and the jubilees in 1887 and 1897, were scenes of great celebration. Her reign (she died in 1901) was also the high point in Britain's status as a world power.

Horatio, Lord Nelson (1758–1805)
An unsigned picture (above) of Edward Baily (1788–1867) at work on his statue of Nelson, which surmounts the column. Portrait of the admiral by Sir William Beechey (right).

of a springbok at the entrance; the building's portico echoes the design of the portico of the adjacent church of St Martin-in-the-Fields.

Canada House. Sir Robert Smirke's original building (1824–7), on the west side of the square, was intended for the Royal College of Physicians. The original exterior has been much altered since, but the magnificent interior is well preserved, in particular the fine staircase and library.

Admiralty Arch. Sir Aston Webb's triumphal arch was completed in 1911 at the southwest corner of Trafalgar Square. It was erected in memory of Queen Victoria. The central arch is only opened on a few state occasions, as it stands on the royal route from Buckingham Palace to St Paul's Cathedral. Named after the adjacent Admiralty buildings, it stands on the site of the 17th-century Spring Gardens.

St Martin-in-the-Fields.
The unusual design of this church, built between 1722 and 1726 by James Gibbs ▲ *176, 267*, is a curious mixture of styles. It rather resembles a rectangular Roman temple, with a Corinthian portico and high steeple. Many famous people are buried here, including the actress Nell Gwyn, Charles II's mistress, the artists William Hogarth and Sir Joshua Reynolds, the cabinet-maker Thomas Chippendale and the highwayman Jack Sheppard. By tradition it is also the royal parish church: Charles II was one of the many royal babies to be christened here.

The church attracts many people for its lunchtime and evening concerts. There is a fine café in the crypt.

National Gallery ✪
This splendid gallery, on the northwest corner of Trafalgar Square, houses one of the world's best selection of paintings from the leading European schools – Italian, Dutch, Flemish, French, Spanish and British, all arranged chronologically. Be sure to visit to the Sainsbury wing and its superb collection of Renaissance paintings. There are also free concerts in the foyer on Wednesday evenings. Next door is the renovated National Portrait Gallery to which a new wing was added in 2000. The top-floor restaurant affords great views over the West End.

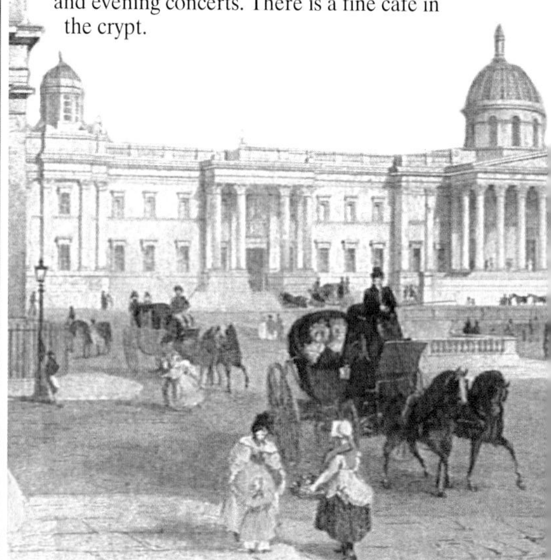

"Thank God, I have done my duty."

Nelson, on board the *Victory* after the Battle of Trafalgar, October 21, 1805

NATIONAL GALLERY ★

In 1824 the government purchased thirty-eight paintings from the estate of the wealthy merchant John Julius Angerstein, including works by Titian, Raphael, Rembrandt and Rubens, for £57,000. They were first exhibited in Angerstein's Pall Mall house, until the construction of a new gallery was entrusted to William Wilkins, who built it on the north side of Trafalgar Square between 1832 and 1838. It is a long and repetitive low structure in classical style which has been much enlarged, with mock-Grecian colonnades, and a dome separating the two wings. One wing formerly housed the Royal Academy before its removal to Burlington House in 1869 ▲ *280*. Since it was opened in 1838, the original shallow design has greatly increased in depth, the latest addition being the Sainsbury wing on the west side, built by Robert Venturi in 1975. A regular grant for the acquisition of pictures was voted by Parliament in 1855. The interior is much more successfully designed and holds one of the greatest collections of paintings in the world. Its marvels were more than enough to depress the frustrated young artist Branwell Brontë (1817–48), brother of Charlotte and Emily: "When after several days of desultory wandering through the streets . . . he eventually visited the National Gallery and saw the work of the great masters after which he had yearned all his life, his reaction was one of despair. He saw their perfection and realized his own incapacity, in the same horrible moment of truth."

THE CHANGING FACES OF TRAFALGAR SQUARE
The north side of the square is occupied by the National Gallery, with its colonnades and cupola. Below, to the right of the picture, is the tower of St Martin-in-the-Fields. The photograph above shows the square as it was before the north side was pedestrianized, and features Nelson's Column, St Martin-in-the-Fields, South Africa House and the National Gallery.

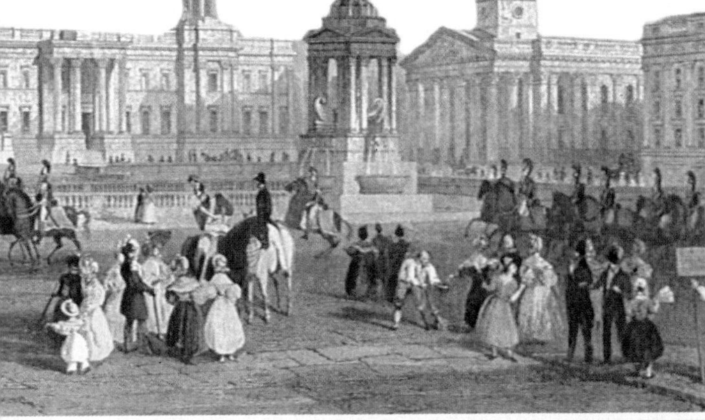

The National Gallery is one of the most important art galleries in the world. Altogether there are more than two thousand works here, including the finest collection of Italian art to be found outside Italy (particularly Primitive and Renaissance paintings). There is also a superb collection devoted to the work of Dutch and Flemish artists.

"VIRGIN AND CHILD"
Duccio di Buoninsegna (c. 1260–c. 1318) was one of the greatest masters of the Sienese school. His work is among the oldest in the possession of the National Gallery. This piece shows the influence of Byzantine art on the school of Siena, but the depth of color against the gold background shows the evolution toward the Gothic style.

"THE BATTLE OF SAN ROMANO"
Paolo Uccello (c. 1397–1475) painted four versions of this battle for the Medici family. San Romano (1432) was a celebrated victory for the Florentines over their Sienese neighbors: in the foreground the knight without armor represents the Florentine commander Niccolò da Tolentino. Except for the two white horses, the overall color scheme is very dark; but the eye clearly discerns Uccello's experiments in perspective.

"The Virgin and Child with St Anne and St John the Baptist"
Leonardo da Vinci (1452–1519) executed this cartoon around 1503 in Florence. It represents an experiment in creating a unified compositional form out of two figures with children. It was one of a series: there is another in the Louvre.

"The Doge Leonardo Loredan"
Loredan was doge of Venice from 1501 to 1521, nd Bellini's magnificent portrait seems to have been painted in the year he took office. The Venetian Giovanni Bellini (c. 1430–1516) was ery much influenced by Mantegna, who became his brother- in-law. Mantegna's influence is apparent in the neutral background to the picture, adding to its feeling of austerity.

"The Madonna of the Meadow"
"He is very old, but still the best painter there is," Dürer wrote home from Venice. Giovanni Bellini was around seventy-five when he painted this serene and colorful Madonna. Its pose resembles that of a Pietà, of which he executed several that show the influence of his artist father Jacopo.

Dual maternity
Sigmund Freud was fascinated by this cartoon, from which he made a psychological study of the role of the mother in the artist's work. Leonardo was the illegitimate son of a twenty-three-year-old lawyer called Piero da Vinci and a young peasant girl, Caterina. Piero married the daughter of a noble family the year after Leonardo was born, and they adopted the boy, who always retained a great affection for his stepmother. Freud thought that in making the Virgin and her mother St Anne appear the same age, Leonardo was actually reflecting the dual maternity in his own life.

"YOUNG MAN HOLDING A SKULL"
The greatest gift of the Dutch artist Frans Hals (c. 1585–1666) was for portraiture. If his portraits lack the psychological depth of his contemporary Rembrandt, no-one else's come to life more vividly. It is hard to think of another artist who could use oil paint with such virtuosity. This particular portrait is a Vanitas,

a popular genre in the 16th and 17th centuries derived from a passage in *Ecclesiastes*: "Vanity of Vanities ...". These images incorporated symbolic features such as hour-glasses with the sand running out, guttering candles and skulls to represent mortality. The model, with thick sensual lips and an irregular nose, also appears in other portraits by Hals.

“The Ambassadors”
Hans Holbein the Younger (c. 1497–1543) was born in Augsburg, Germany, but settled in England in 1532. The next year he painted *The Ambassadors*, which probably helped his appointment as court painter by Henry VIII in 1536. This double portrait depicts Jean de Dinteville, French ambassador from February to November 1533, on the left; and Georges de Selve, bishop of Lavaur, who arrived to visit Dinteville at 10.30am on April 11, indicated by the globe and clock. The shape in the foreground is a distorted skull, which assumes correct proportions when viewed from a certain angle. Other Vanitas symbols include the broken lute string and the brooch in the ambassador’s hat.

“The Marriage of the Arnolfini”
The Flemish artist Jan van Eyck (c. 1385–1441) painted the Bruges-based Italian merchant Giovanni Arnolfini and his wife Giovanna Cenami in their home. The picture is charged with symbols such as the single candle in the candelabra representing the unity of marriage.

Self-portrait of the artist, aged thirty-four
Throughout his life, Rembrandt (1606–1669) observed the effects of age and care upon his own face. This canvas, although apparently destined for a patron, does not seem to have been commissioned, and would rather seem to be a studio version of a type of artists’ self-portrait painted for public appreciation.

"THE ROKEBY VENUS"
Diego Velásquez (1599–1660) probably painted this picture of the Toilet of Venus in Italy. It is his only existing nude, and a rare example of a female nude in Spanish painting, with rich, warm colors inspired by Titian. Before the National Gallery acquired it, the picture was in Rokeby Park, Yorkshire, hence its name.

"LES GRANDES BAIGNEUSES II" (1900–5)
Toward the end of his life Paul Cézanne (1839–1906) painted many nude figures

"AVENUE AT MIDDELHARNIS"
Meindert Hobbema (1638–1709) was last in the line of great Dutch landscape painters. This, his most famous work, is dated 1689; and though the artist was never very successful during his lifetime, his work became highly prized in England in the 18th and 19th centuries: Hobbema was to prove a great influence on the English landscape painters.

"THE MARRIAGE CONTRACT"
The first in a series of six paintings *Marriage à la Mode* by William Hogarth (1697–1764), executed between 1743 and 1745. It is a comment on decadent society, with the artist satirizing marriages founded on money and snobbery. An impoverished nobleman is arranging the marriage of his son to the daughter of a wealthy merchant. Engravings of *Marriage à la Mode* were very popular.

in a landscape, though his reluctance to use nude models caused problems. This picture is a key work in art history, pointing the way to Cubism.

"Bathers at Asnières"
Georges Seurat (1859–91) was concerned with the static quality of his pictures rather than the flickering play of light favored by the Impressionists. This is an early example of Pointillism, where the colors are mixed in the viewer's eye rather than on the artist's palette, supposedly giving a cleaner and brighter effect.

Left to right: Samuel Cooper's portrait of Oliver Cromwell; George IV by Sir Thomas Lawrence; William Blake by Thomas Phillips.

The first directors made important acquisitions, particularly of Italian Renaissance and Flemish and Dutch masters. Today the Gallery has a well-balanced collection of more than two thousand pictures, representing five hundred years of painting, from the Italian Primitives to the French Impressionists.

THE NATIONAL PORTRAIT GALLERY ★

Since 1896 this gallery has been in a specially constructed building behind the National Gallery on its east side. It is a history of England in pictures, with more than nine thousand portraits (paintings, etchings, drawings, photographs and sculptures) of kings, statesmen, musicians, writers and artists from the time of Henry VIII to the present day. It was founded in 1856, to represent "a Gallery of the Portraits of the most Eminent Persons in British History". Precedence was given to politicians, writers, artists and musicians. The result is a unique, wonderful panorama of British history rather than an art gallery, and though the overall quality may be uneven, the gallery houses great treasures such as Holbein's portrait of Henry VIII, a self-portrait by George Stubbs, and the "Chandos" portrait of William Shakespeare. The new Ondaatje Wing, opened in May 2000, includes a gallery for the Tudor portraits and a modern space for the

SIR EDWIN LANDSEER (1802–73)
John Ballantyne painted this picture around 1865 of Landseer at work on a model of one of the four bronze lions that were placed round the base of Nelson's Column in 1867.

most recent portraits, as well as a lecture room and rooftop restaurant with stupendous views.

A GUIDED TOUR. The works of art in the National Portrait Gallery are exhibited chronologically, beginning on the second floor, which contains the Tudor Galleries. There are some magnificent portraits of Elizabeth I in all her finery, of Shakespeare (the best authenticated likeness), Mary Queen of Scots, Sir Walter Raleigh, Ben Jonson, John Donne and many others.

THE STUART PERIOD. This section of the gallery features a miniature portrait of Oliver Cromwell, which has been signed by Samuel Cooper (1609–72), a portrait of Samuel Pepys depicted wearing an Indian robe by John Hayls, and also a beautiful painting of Louise de Keroualle, the universally loathed duchess of Portsmouth who was a mistress of Charles II. The actress Nell Gwyn was another of the king's beauties, and she is painted here by Sir Peter Lely, together with a lamb.

THE GEORGIAN AGE. This fascinating collection includes Hudson's portrait of Handel, a self-portrait by William Hogarth, Reynolds' portraits of Johnson and Boswell, and Captain Cook, painted at the Cape of Good Hope in 1776. Two rooms are given over to Kneller's portraits of members of the 18th-century Kit-Kat Club ▲ *262*, including Congreve and Vanbrugh. A more unlikely portrait is the one of Charles Lamb by the writer William Hazlitt. In Room 15 there is an amateurish miniature of Jane Austen by her sister Cassandra, which is the only known likeness of the novelist.

THE ROMANTIC ERA. On display here is a portrait of Robert Burns, painted by his friend Alexander Nasmyth, Sir Walter Scott by Landseer, Byron in Albanian dress (1813) by Phillips, Wordsworth by his friend the eccentric Benjamin Robert Haydon, and Keats by Joseph Severn, who accompanied him on his last journey to Rome.

VICTORIANS AND EDWARDIANS. These portraits occupy the upper floor of the gallery. Look out in particular for the Brontë sisters, painted by their brother Branwell, and for Sargent's portrait of Ellen Terry as Lady Macbeth, as well as the likenesses of Oscar Wilde, Gilbert and Sullivan, Max Beerbohm and many of the Pre-Raphaelite painters. The ground floor is crowded with literally hundreds of famous faces from the 20th century.

Jerry Barrett painted Florence Nightingale (1820–1910) among the soldiers she nursed at Scutari in the Crimean War around 1856 (top of page). Vanessa Bell (above left), a painter herself, sat for this picture by Duncan Grant c. 1918. There are many contemporary portraits of Henry VIII (above center): this one is by an anonymous artist. Sir Peter Lely painted this portrait of Nell Gwyn (c. 1650–87) around 1675. Left, a photograph of the illustrator Aubrey Beardsley (1872–98) taken in 1894 by Frederick Henry Evans.

GEORGE BERNARD SHAW (1856–1950)
A watercolor by the Punch cartoonist Bernard Partridge.

CHINESE NEW YEAR IN SOHO
The Chinese community is based around Gerrard Street. Their New Year celebrations are a great attraction, with parades, dragons and firecrackers. There are a great many Chinese restaurants here, and gourmets should look out for the places where the Chinese themselves eat.

LEICESTER SQUARE

Just a few yards down Pall Mall from Trafalgar Square on the righthand side is the Haymarket, where there are situated two famous theaters with beautiful façades: the HAYMARKET THEATRE, and directly opposite, HER MAJESTY'S THEATRE ● *54.* On the righthand side of the Haymarket, Panton Street leads directly into Leicester Square, a pedestrianized thoroughfare which is usually crowded. The square is lined with souvenir shops, amusement arcades and the garish fronts of discotheques. On the west side is a booth (generally with a long line of people outside it) selling theater seats for West End productions at reduced prices. Formerly Leicester Square was a garden, developed in the 17th and 18th centuries: Hogarth and Joshua Reynolds had houses here. It has recently been extensively cleaned and renovated. There are several large cinemas in the square, which is at the heart of THEATERLAND ▲ *274*, close to St Martin's Lane, Monmouth Street, Shaftesbury Avenue, the Haymarket, Charing Cross Road and the Strand. The shows are of all kinds: musical comedies, classic plays, and whodunnits such a Agatha Christie's *The Mousetrap,* which has been playing without interruption for more than thirty-five years.

SOHO

The busy little district of Soho lies within a clearly defined square bounded by Oxford Street, Charing Cross Road, Coventry Street and Regent Street. It is a fascinating and cosmopolitan part of London, which has become famous for its sleazy strip-tease clubs, high-class foreign restaurants and food shops. By day, the district of

THE OTHER SIDE OF SOHO
Soho has long been associated with prostitution, though the girls are no longer permitted on the streets. Strip clubs and pornographic bookshops abound, although what they sell is mild in comparison to the equivalent in Hamburg, Copenhagen or Amsterdam.

“If you get Sohoitis, . . . you will stay there always day and night and get no work done ever. You have been warned.”

Julian Maclaren-Ross

oho is primarily a business center, especially WARDOUR TREET, which is the heart of Britain’s film industry. Parallel › this, and one street to the west, lies Berwick Street, the ›od market for local restaurateurs and gourmets from all ver London. There are a number of lively pubs all around oho, although they are probably best visited at lunchtime: in ıe evening, theatergoing crowds are replaced by those in earch of erotica, though the restaurants still do good usiness. CARNABY STREET is also part of ıe Soho legend, though the “swinging ixties” and its extravagant fashions now elong to the past. However, the street as recently been done up, and there are ow attractive boutiques side by side with ›urist shops.

BERWICK STREET
Most of the food shops in Soho are Continental, but Berwick Street Market is pure Cockney.

)XFORD STREET

tretching for 1½ miles from Marble Arch › Tottenham Court Road, Oxford Street ; the longest shopping street in London. None of the shops found here is articularly original, but all the famous British trademarks and chain stores are vell represented: *Marks & Spencer*, *Boots*, *he Body Shop*, *Littlewoods* and many, ıany more. There are also some igh-quality department stores as well, ıch as *Selfridge’s* ● *88*, *John Lewis*, and *)ebenham’s* ● *88*. The visitor really hould not miss a visit to the little shops in ST CHRISTOPHER’S LACE, access to which is via a narrow passage beside number 50 (almost opposite Bond Street Underground Station). *iberty’s* ● *88* ▲ *283* is a store famous for its scarves and abrics. It is situated on the corner of Great Marlborough treet (from where one can observe the shop’s impressive udor façade) and Regent Street ▲ *283*.

OXFORD STREET

“He found a place just off Oxford Street, one of those humble teashops with tall urns or geysers on the counter, a slatternly girl in attendance, a taxi-driver or two sitting at the first table and three Italians sitting at the back. He had a poor tea and it cost him fourpence-halfpenny more than he thought it would. When he went out again, it was drizzling, and miserably cold and damp. The queues for the pictures were enormous. All the cheaper seats were probably filled for the night.”
J.B. Priestley,
Angel Pavement

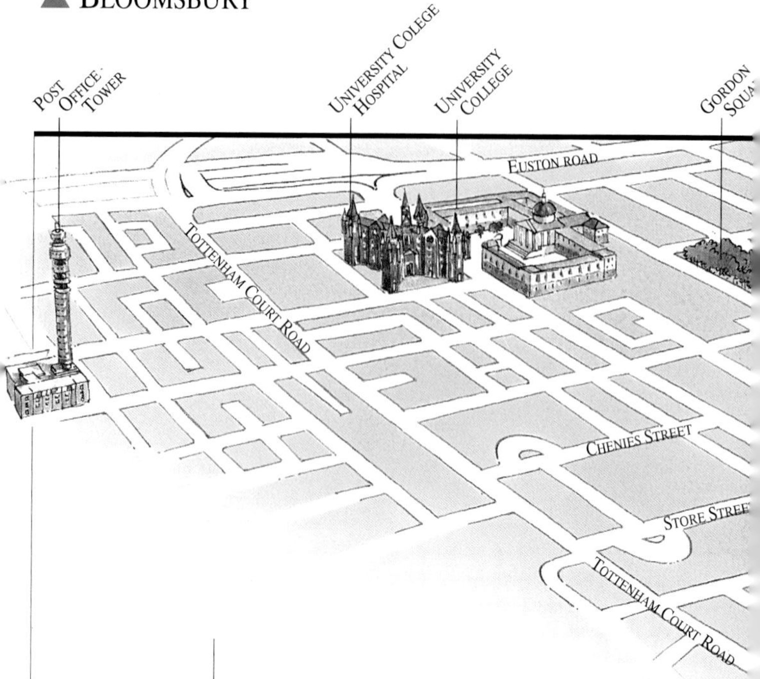

Post Office Tower
University College Hospital
University College
Gordon Squa
Euston Road
Tottenham Court Road
Chenies Street
Store Stree
Tottenham Court Road

Bloomsbury squares
Bloomsbury was a fashionable place to live in the 18th century. Most of its handsome squares were built then, such as Russell Square (below) and Bedford Square (foot of page) ● *76*, and in spite of the traffic they retain much of their old-world charm.

Bloomsbury

This part of the city is an echo in stone of Georgian and Victorian London. There are quiet streets and squares lined with lovely houses. Naturally enough, the gracious district of Bloomsbury has strong cultural traditions too, since it is set in the shadow of the British Museum. Bloomsbury's attractive streets and squares were first laid out in the late 17th century by the earl of Southampton, but its real expansion came later when celebrities moved in, such as John Constable (1776–1837), Dante Gabriel Rossetti (1828–82), and writers Charles Dickens (1812–70) and George Bernard Shaw (1856–1950). Then, early in the 20th century, the intellectual status of Bloomsbury was boosted again by the novelist Virginia Woolf, who, together with her talented friends, formed what is now known as the Bloomsbury Group.

Tavistock Square. This long, rectangular square has an attractive garden at its center, and was laid out in the early 19th century. The Woolfs, the composer Charles Gounod and Charles Dickens have all lived here; on the north side is a Jewish Museum with an interesting collection of Jewish historical items.

Dickens' House ● *76.* From 1837 to 1839, Charles Dickens ● *110–11, 118,* lived at 48 Doughty Street, where he wrote *The Pickwick Papers*, *Oliver Twist* and *Nicholas Nickleby*, his first three novels. The house is now a museum containing many souvenirs such as autographs, furniture and first editions of his books. In the basement is a reconstruction of the Dingley Dell kitchen from *The Pickwick Papers*.

Russell Square. This enormous square is at the top of Bedford Place. It was built in 1800, and at the beginning of the 20th

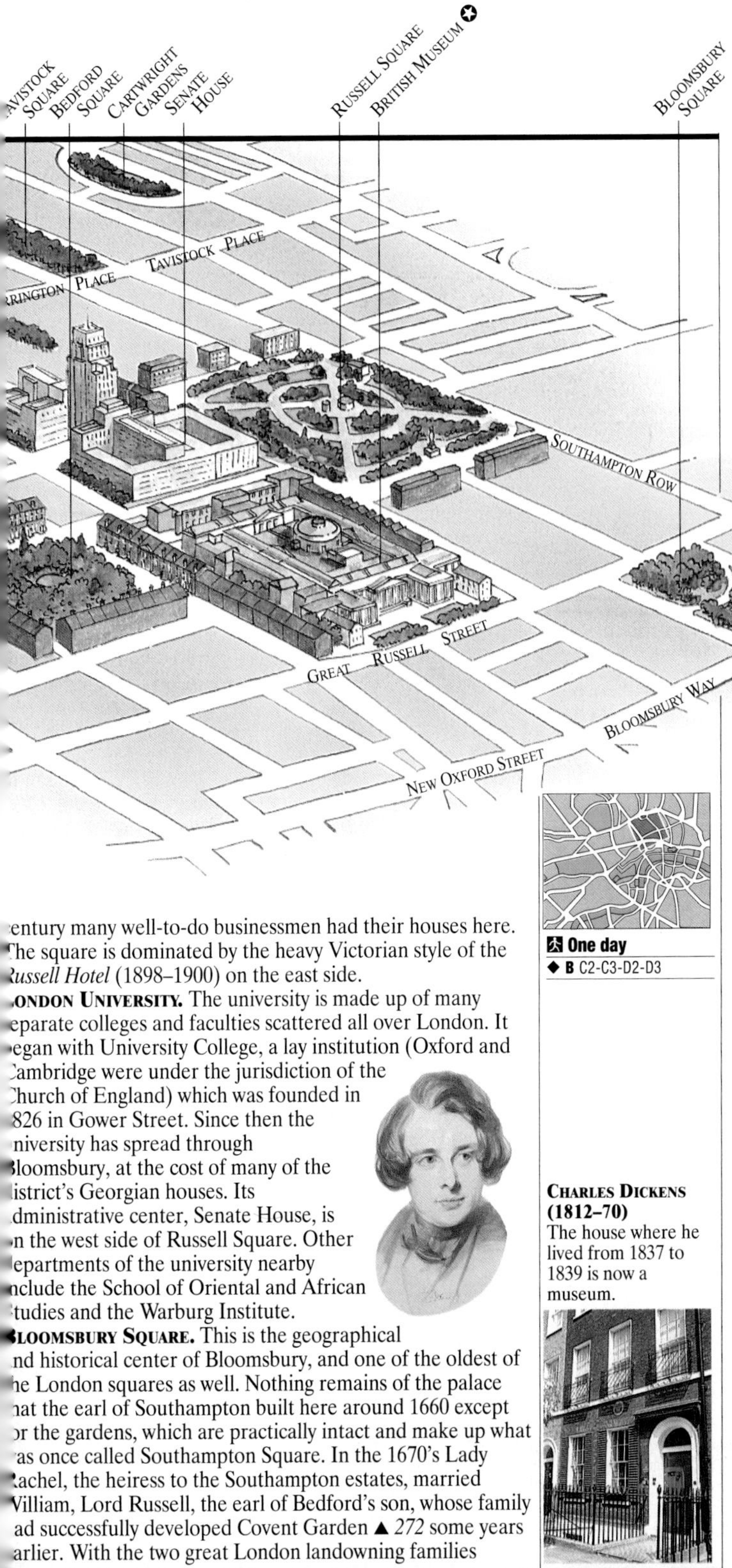

entury many well-to-do businessmen had their houses here. The square is dominated by the heavy Victorian style of the *Russell Hotel* (1898–1900) on the east side.

ONDON UNIVERSITY. The university is made up of many eparate colleges and faculties scattered all over London. It egan with University College, a lay institution (Oxford and Cambridge were under the jurisdiction of the Church of England) which was founded in 826 in Gower Street. Since then the niversity has spread through Bloomsbury, at the cost of many of the istrict's Georgian houses. Its dministrative center, Senate House, is n the west side of Russell Square. Other epartments of the university nearby nclude the School of Oriental and African tudies and the Warburg Institute.

LOOMSBURY SQUARE. This is the geographical nd historical center of Bloomsbury, and one of the oldest of he London squares as well. Nothing remains of the palace hat the earl of Southampton built here around 1660 except or the gardens, which are practically intact and make up what as once called Southampton Square. In the 1670's Lady Rachel, the heiress to the Southampton estates, married William, Lord Russell, the earl of Bedford's son, whose family ad successfully developed Covent Garden ▲ *272* some years arlier. With the two great London landowning families

One day

◆ **B** C2-C3-D2-D3

CHARLES DICKENS (1812–70)
The house where he lived from 1837 to 1839 is now a museum.

UNIVERSITY COLLEGE The north wing of University College houses the Slade School of Art.

united, Southampton House was renamed Bedford House and Southampton Square became Bloomsbury Square. Elegant Georgian terraces surround the gardens, which were laid out in 1800 by Humphrey Repton. Bloomsbury soon became a fashionable place in which to live, and expanded northward across fields in the direction of Hampstead ▲ *260*.

ST GEORGE'S CHURCH, BLOOMSBURY WAY. This church was completed in 1731 after fifteen years of construction work, to plans by Nicholas Hawksmoor ▲ *312*. Its majestic portico is Corinthian, and its remarkable pyramidal steeple derives from Pliny's description of the mausoleum at Halicarnassus; on top of this is a statue of George I dressed as a Roman. It may have been this which led Horace Walpole to call St George's "a masterpiece of absurdity".

BEDFORD SQUARE. Bedford House was demolished in 1800 by the 5th Duke of Bedford as part of a process of urbanization that anticipated the later streets and squares to the north of Bloomsbury Square. These elegant terraced houses, designed by the architect James Burton, are a good example of the Georgian style ● *76*. The statue of the great statesman Charles James Fox (leader of the Whigs at the end of the 18th century) is by Sir Richard Westmacott (1775–1856), and has stood on the north side of the square since 1816. To the south in Southampton Place, are houses dating from 1740 that have classical portals of different designs. The ARCHITECTURAL ASSOCIATION at numbers 34–36 has exhibitions of works of contemporary architects – such avant-garde masters as Rem Koolhaas (Euralille), Bernard Tschumi (Parc de la Villette) and Richard Rogers (Lloyds, Pompidou Center) all began their careers at this celebrated architectural school.

BRITISH MUSEUM: THE WORLD'S GREATEST STOREHOUSE OF TREASURES ✪
This magnificent neo-classical building with its Ionic-columned portico and collections amounting to more than six million objects (including the Rosetta Stone and the Elgin Marbles) is one of London's finest attractions. Of the many exhibitions here those relating to ancient cultures (Greece, Rome, Egypt) are particularly impressive. In December 2000, the museum inaugurated the transformed Great Court, with its spectacular glass roof. The Court, now the largest covered public square in Europe, encompasses the meticulously restored former Reading Room.

THE BRITISH MUSEUM ★

It would take more than a week to see all the British Museum and its collections of treasures (six or seven million objects). Internationally, it is one of the best-known British institutions. Work began on the present building in 1823, to replace Montagu House, Bloomsbury, which had become too small to hold

THE EGYPTIAN GALLERY
This wonderful collection is in three sections: a sculpture gallery, a mummies' gallery, and the collection of papyri.

the 120,000-volume library of George III. The architect Robert Smirke vorked on the building from 1823 to 1847, designing it in neo-:lassical style with an imposing portico of Ionic columns. His rother Sydney Smirke built the famous Reading Room 1852–7) ▲ *308* on the central courtyard. Between 1884 and 938 the museum was enlarged by adding the King Edward VII Galleries (1914) to the north, and the West Gallery for Greek sculpture.

THE ORIGINS OF THE MUSEUM. The museum grew around the rivate collection of Sir Hans Sloane (1660–1753) ▲ *197*, the Chelsea physician and botanist. He had many thousands of pecimens of minerals, corals, insects, shells and birds' eggs, is well as some 32,000 antiquities, all housed in his home at 3 Bloomsbury Square. It eventually became too cramped for iim to live in, so he bought the house next door. After his leath the State organized a public lottery to raise funds for urchasing Sloane's collections. To these were added the :ollection of manuscripts belonging to Robert and Edward Harley, 1st and 2nd Earls of Oxford. In 1756 George II resented the Royal Library with 17,000 manuscripts. These vere assembled into the British Museum, which first opened ts doors in 1759, the doors being those of Montagu House. At that time it was not easy to go and see the collections: a letailed written application had to be made, and only ten ickets were initially issued for any one day. The museum :ontinued to expand throughout the 19th century, especially he world-renowned archeological collections. In addition, he British Museum has notable collections of Asiatic, Islamic and European medieval art, and an important department of lrawings and engravings. The natural history collections were ransferred to South Kensington in 1870; the ethnography exhibits, which from 1970 to 1997 were in the former Museum of Mankind, are now in the main building of he British Museum.

"SEATED MAN", BY MICHELANGELO
A study from the priceless collection of drawings in the British Museum.

THE GREAT COURT
This vast space, refurbished to a design by Norman Foster, was opened at the end of 2000. An immense glass roof covers the court, and several levels feature galleries, bookshops and restaurants around the newly restored Reading Room ▲ *308*.

One of the most famous of the British Museum's collections is its Greek Antiquities section, which started with its acquisition of the Elgin Marbles. At the beginning of the 19th century Greece was occupied by the Turks, and the Parthenon in Athens, which had been severely damaged by a Venetian bomb, was left to decay. The British ambassador in Constantinople, Lord Elgin, loved classical architecture and, between 1802 and 1804, with authority granted to him by the sultan of Turkey, he removed various fragments from the Parthenon and shipped them back to London. The total sent was twelve statues, twenty slabs from the building's Ionic frieze and fifteen metopes. The rightful ownership of the Elgin Marbles is still disputed by the Greek government.

"HEAD OF APHRODITE" (GREEK ANTIQUITI
This bronze from the 2nd or 1st century BC found at Sadagh in northeastern Turkey

"THE NEREID MONUMENT" (GREEK ANTIQUITIES)
This reconstructed façade is from a funeral monument, which dates from around 400 BC. It was found at Xanthos in Lycia, Asia Minor. Statues of Nereids, sea nymphs who accompanied souls to the other world, stood between the Ionic pillars.

"THE HORSE OF SELENE" (GREEK ANTIQUITIES)
This horse's head is from the 4th century BC. It would have been one of four drawing the goddess Selene's chariot, and comes from the Parthenon's east pediment.

THE ELGIN MARBLES
ɩemoved from the temple of Athena (Parthenon) on the Acropolis in Athens, the Marbles include twenty sections of the frieze around the building, which depicts a great procession during one of the feasts in honor of the goddess.

THE MUSIC LESSON" (ROMAN ANTIQUITIES)
. wall painting from the 1st century AD ıat was brought back from ɬerculaneum, Italy.

BOXERS AND WRESTLERS (GREECE)
An amphora dating from 550–525 BC. On the neck are wrestlers watched by teachers and referees. The main body of the vase shows youths boxing, and carries the painter's signature, Nikosthenes. The black-figure technique was developed in the 7th century BC; red-figure vases became common a century later.

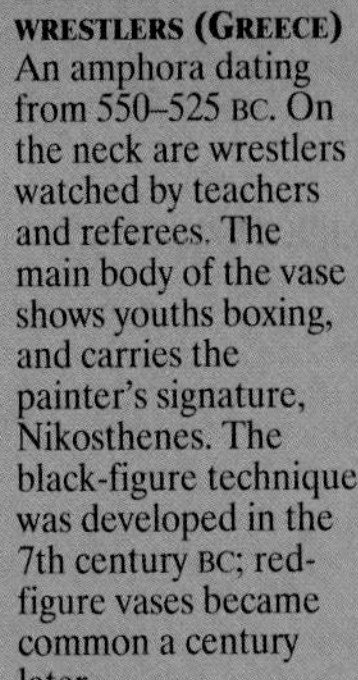

HERAKLES, OR DIONYSUS" (GREECE)
he figure is lying on a lion or panther ɩin. This is a sculpture from the 5th ɩntury BC originally on the east pediment f the Parthenon, which was the best-reserved section. It was with other ɩulptures such as *Helios Driving the hariot of Oceanus* and *Hebe earing the Cup of Zeus.*

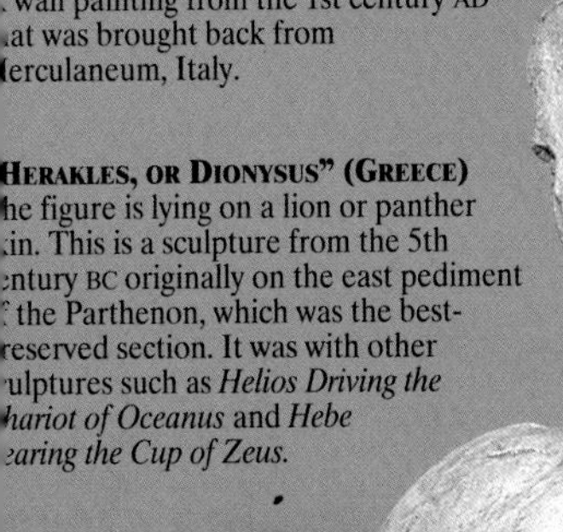

THE EGYPTIAN COLLECTION
This is one of the most important in the world outside Egypt, and has the museum's most spectacular exhibits. Initially it was assembled from pieces collected by the French expedition to Egypt, which were lost to the English after the Treaty of Alexandria in 1801. Since 1882 the collection has grown, largely thanks to excavations by the Egypt Exploration Fund.

"THE HUNT IN THE MARSH" (EGYPT)
This scene was discovered in the tomb of the scribe Nebamun (18th Dynasty, c. 1400 BC). It shows Nebamun and his family out hunting birds in a flimsy reed boat.

THE ROSETTA STONE (EGYPT)
This remarkable stone, carved in 196 BC, was found at Rashid (Rosetta) in the Nile Delta in 1799. The text is a decree of Ptolemy V written in Egyptian, in hieroglyphics (the language used by priests), in Demotic (the common language), and in Greek. A comparative study of the writing led the Frenchman Jean-François Champollion (1790–1832) to find the key to the written language of ancient Egypt.

THE "GAYER-ANDERSON" CAT (EGYPT)
This bronze (after 30 BC) dates from the Roman occupation of Egypt. It was offered to the museum by John Gayer-Anderson and Mary Stout. The cat was worshipped in ancient Egypt as the goddess Bastet incarnate.

The Near East collections
These superb pieces rival the museum's Greek collection for pride of place. They consist of Sumerian, Persian, Babylonian, Hittite, Assyrian and Phoenician works. The Anglo-Turkish alliance was a great help to British excavations in the Near East.

[A]ssurbanipal Killing a Wounded Lion" [A]ssyria). King of Assyria from 669 to 627 BC, [A]ssurbanipal was the ruler who subjugated [B]abylon and conquered Egypt. This bas-[r]elief of 645 BC was found in his palace [a]t Nineveh. The excavations at [N]imrud, Nineveh and Assur in Iraq [w]ere the work of Sir Austin Henry [L]ayard (1817–94), whose [d]iscovery of Assurbanipal's library [at] Nineveh laid the foundations for [A]ssyriological studies.

"The Lion of Nimrod"
The Nimrud Gallery is mainly devoted to the reign of the Assyrian king Assumazirpal II, ruler in the 9th century BC.

Menophis III (Egypt)
Amenhotep, the favorite architect of Amenophis III (1408–1372 BC), built him a magnificent palace and grandiose mausoleum in Thebes. The great temple at Luxor was also built during his reign.

Tutanhamon (Egypt)
This red granite lion was carved in the reign of Amenophis III and bears the name of Tutanhamon. It comes from the temple of the goddess Ishtar, at Nimrud on the River Tigris.

A VARIETY OF COLLECTIONS
The museum's possessions are by no means limited to classical antiquity or any specialized field: there are all kinds of artifacts from all over the world such as coins, engravings, fans, bookplates and playing-cards.

THE BODHISATTVA TARA (SRI LANKA)
Found near Trincomalee in Sri Lanka (Ceylon), this gilded 12th-century bronze is from the Oriental collections, which include South-East Asia and the Far East.

SAXON CUP (BRITISH ANTIQUITIES)
A 4th-century iridescent glass goblet, discovered in tomb at a Saxon cemetery in Mucking, Essex.

BRACELET (PERSIA)
This gold bracelet with two griffins' heads is just a small reminder of the splendor that passed with the Persian empire. Together with other finely worked gold ornaments, hairpins, combs and coins, it comes from the Oxus Treasure (c. 500–300 BC), a horde discovered near the River Oxus in central Asia. The Oxus is now called the Amou-Daria, and flows into the Aral Sea.

Bas-reliefs (Assyria)
These vigorous carvings depict the feats of King Assurbanipal's warriors (c. 645 BC).

"A Cart from the Oxus" (Persia)
This solid gold model of the cart of a high-ranking official comes from the famous treasure found by the River Oxus.

"Goat on a Tree" (Sumeria)
Covered with metallic leaves, gilt and lapis lazuli (which gives the blue color), this Sumerian model of a goat that dates from 2500 BC was found at Ur, near Babylon in southern Iraq.

Ming porcelain (China)
One of the loveliest pieces in the museum's huge collection of Chinese porcelain, this decorated vase is from the Ming dynasty, in the reign of Ch'eng hua (1465–87).

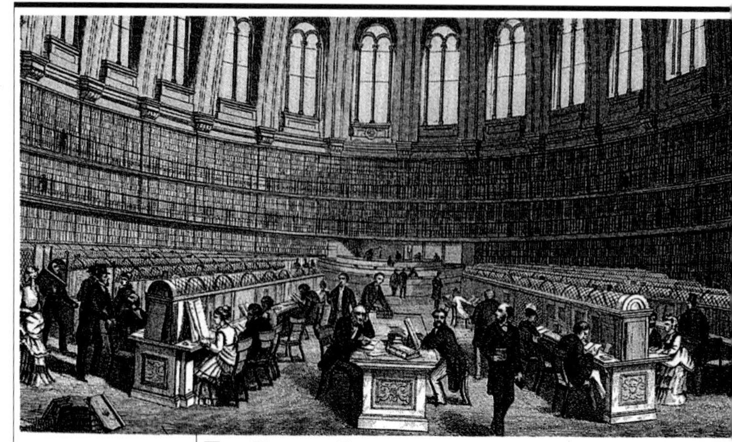

THE READING ROOM
The former Reading Room of the British Library, built by Sydney Smirke (1857), has been restored to its former glory. Its imposing dome (105 feet high), accommodates a multimedia library and has become the centerpiece of the Great Court, the new cultural complex of the museum.

THE BRITISH LIBRARY

In 1998, the British Library, one of the largest and richest in the world, was moved from the British Museum to new premises beside St Pancras station. The Library contains more than eighteen million books, some of which are unique or extremely rare, such as the *Lindisfarne Gospels* (c.700, in manuscript), the *Magna Carta* of 1215 (England's first charter of democracy), and first editions of Shakespeare (1623) and the Gutenberg Bible (1453). Many famous scholars have worked under the immense dome of its former Reading Room in the British Museum, including Karl Marx and Vladimir Lenin, and the writers Bernard Shaw and Rudyard Kipling.

THE BLOOMSBURY GROUP

This was the name given to a group of renowned artists, writers and intellectuals who lived in Bloomsbury early in the 20th century and used to meet at the house of the novelist Virginia Woolf. Along with her husband, the publisher and writer Leonard Woolf, and her sister, the painter Vanessa Bell, members included artist Duncan Grant, economist John Maynard Keynes, art critics Quentin Bell and Roger Fry, the poet T.S. Eliot and the novelist E.M. Forster. Even if their ideas sometimes clashed with one another, they were united in their desire to reject the conformity of the age. Their way of life was as great an influence on the younger generation as anything that they wrote. At the same time there was another group of intellectuals who used to meet at the salon of Lady Ottoline Morrell near Fitzroy Square, across Tottenham Court Road. The Fitzrovians included novelist Aldous Huxley, painter and designer Leon Bakst, the great dancer Nijinsky and philosopher Bertrand Russell ▲ *278*.

FITZROY SQUARE ● *76*
One of the finest London squares, it is now a pedestrian precinct.

VIRGINIA WOOLF (1882–1941)
In 1917 she and her husband founded the Hogarth Press to publish new and experimental work, as well as her own. Their "discoveries" included Katherine Mansfield and T.S. Eliot.

Around the East End

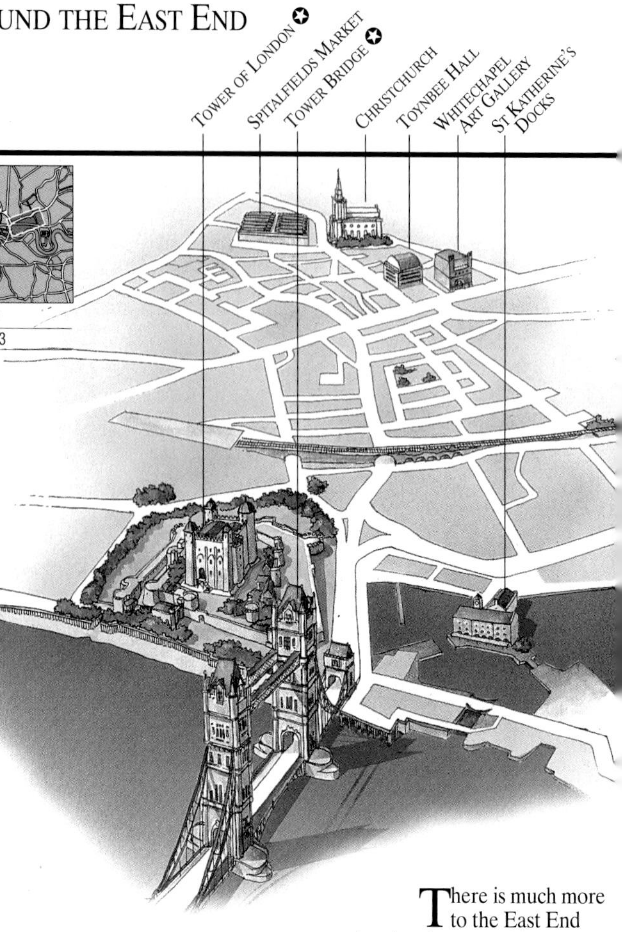

▲ Around the East End

Tower of London ✪
Spitalfields Market
Tower Bridge ✪
Christchurch
Toynbee Hall
Whitechapel Art Gallery
St Katherine's Docks

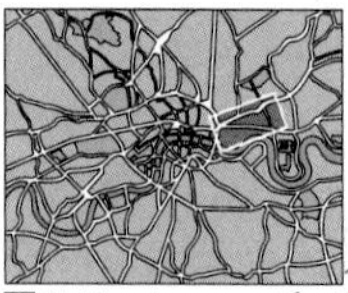

Half a day
◆ **C** C4-D4 **G** A3

There is much more to the East End than its often repetitive architecture. It is a microcosm of the real London, where the poor have lived for centuries, cheek by jowl with immigrants from the four corners of the world.

History

Christ Church, Spitalfields
Early in the 18th century a tax was levied on charcoal to build fifty new churches in London. This was one of them, the masterpiece of its architect Nicholas Hawksmoor.

Early on, the jumble of roads leading east out of London had no clearly defined districts except for the area comprising Spitalfields, Stepney and Whitechapel. First and foremost the history of the East End belongs to the successive hordes of immigrants who landed here and made their homes.

The Huguenots. In the 16th century the French Calvinists (Protestants) sought refuge here, and their numbers increased by another forty thousand after the Edict of Nantes was revoked in 1685. The majority of them were skilled craftsmen or weavers, who lost no time in finding profitable work, and gradually moved further west when their fortunes were made.

A home for the poverty-stricken. Space left by the enterprising Huguenots was taken over in the 18th century by the poor and hungry from all over Britain and Ireland, who abandoned their overcrowded or destitute homes in search of work in the capital. Their plight has

“Christ Church was thronged by the mournful train, the waving light now glistening upon the sombre habilments of the bearers, and on their shrouded load.”

Charles Reade

een frankly and sympathetically described by Charles Dickens nd others, with its appalling overcrowding, alcoholism, disease nd starvation. The poor lived huddled together in street after treet of filthy, leaking houses, and so the East End acquired its nenviable reputation.

INETEENTH-CENTURY IMPROVEMENTS. During the reign of)ueen Victoria there were two more floods of immigrants ere: the Irish fleeing the potato famine of 1847, and then round 1880 thousands of European Jews escaping pogroms their homelands. Among the latter were many bakers and arment-makers who quickly found their place in the ommunity. Many attempts were made to improve the quality f life in this wretched part of London throughout the 19th entury. William Booth started his famous Salvation Army ere in 1878.

MMIGRANTS FROM THE BRITISH EMPIRE. The 1950's saw an nflux of thousands of dispossessed ptimists from former British olonies, particularly Pakistanis, ndians, and then families from angladesh who opened many lothing businesses. This influx of iverse peoples again transformed ne East End, though poverty emained a dominant trait. Today, ne extension of the City, property peculation and rocketing prices epresent more of a serious threat the traditions of the East End nan all the immigrations of past enturies.

“He went straight off to Stepney, where she lived, as soon as the ship was berthed. He walked all the way, so as to ’ave more time for thinking, but wot with being nearly run over by a cabman with a white ’orse and red whiskers, he got to the ’ouse without ’aving thought of anything.”

W.W. Jacobs

PITALFIELDS

HRIST CHURCH, SPITALFIELDS ★ 71. This church on the corner f Commercial Street and 'ournier Street was built between 714 and 1729 by Nicholas Iawksmoor. It owes its existence Queen Anne (1665–1714), who 'as trying to put a stop to what ne saw as a grave moral decline England. Of fifty new churches she commissioned, only welve were ever built (most of them by Hawksmoor), three f them in the East End. As well as Christ Church, there re St Anne's, Limehouse ▲ *336*, and St George-in-the-East *335*. The portico has an unusual central arch, and the spire octagonal.

ICHOLAS HAWKSMOOR. Christ Church is probably the nasterpiece of its architect Nicholas Hawksmoor (1661–1736) *71, 73,* ▲ *139, 149, 174,* who after Wren was the greatest enius of Baroque English architecture. Hawksmoor became lerk to Christopher Wren ▲ *171–5* at the age of eighteen, nd later assisted his master in substantial projects such as the ebuilding of St Paul's Cathedral ▲ *171*. Starting in 1699, Iawksmoor worked on designs for a series of churches ommissioned by Queen Anne, in collaboration with Sir John 'anbrugh (1664–1726) and Thomas Archer (1668–1743).

“Certain small fried fish are sold in the area for breakfast, and are said to be known as Spitalfield weavers.”

19th-century guidebook

The East End has been making garments since the 16th century. This silk coat was made in 1787. Below is an official document concerning the weaving industry in this part of London.

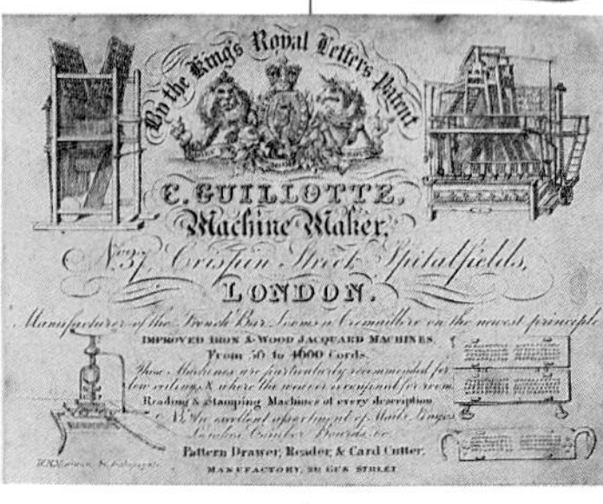

"I don't know what I expected, but I went out and wandered eastward, soon losing my way in a labyrinth of grimy streets and black, grassless squares . . . if I hadn't, I should have missed the greatest romance of my life."

Oscar Wilde, *The Picture of Dorian Gray*

FOURNIER STREET AND ELDER STREET ★ ● 7.

Among the French Protestant refugees fleeing the revocation of the Edict of Nantes in Spitalfields in the 17th century were a number of silk-weavers. Several c the houses they built can still be seen on either side of these two streets. The houses in Fournier Street (which was named after one of the Huguenot immigrants) and Elder Street have some fine doorways and large upper windows so as to admit as much light as possible for the weavers working inside. The houses, built between 1720 and 1750, have recently been restored.

SPITALFIELDS MARKET. In Elizabethan times this site was a renowned duelling place, and it is here that Jack the Ripper' first victim was found. This market in Commercial Street, founded in the 1600's, was moved in 1991. The early 20th-century buildings that housed it wer occupied by stalls selling fruit, organic vegetables and handicrafts before a "restoration" program was devised by developers. However, in 2002 and amid outrage from the loca residents and stall holders, the western end of the market wa demolished to make way for an office building. More than ha the stalls disappeared. The remaining half of the market, although listed, is also under threat.

COLUMBIA ROAD. This wonderful flower market takes place each Sunday morning behind Spitalfields. The road is also lined with little shops selling jewelry, antiques and designers' creations for the home and the garden.

PETTICOAT LANE ★. This unusual open-air market is held every Sunday in Middlesex Street. It resembles the English version of an oriental souk. Its name comes from all the skirt which the tailors and stallholders used to sell, along with other new and used clothes, at the start of the 20th century. Today the street is packed with several hundred stalls, attracting dealers and customers from many different communities: Bangladeshi, Pakistani, Indian and Arab. At 9(Whitechapel High Street the famous kosher restaurant *Bloom's* continues to cater for the long-established Jewish population. Middlesex Street also has an enormous variety o shops and restaurants, many of which are open on Sundays.

BRICK LANE. This old part of town was once famous for brewing and brickmaking. Truman's Brewery is set among a fascinating jumble of shops and garment factories in what is now the Bangladeshi quarter of London; it is the sole survivo of these traditional crafts. Around Brick Lane now are some of the finest Indian restaurants in London. Brick Lane Market sells a wide variety of cakes, fish, oriental spices and household goods, along with the ubiquitous ready-to-

BENGALI SARIS
Saris like these in a Spitalfields shop are still worn by Bangladeshi women.

/ear clothes. More surprisingly, there are also many political •amphlets and books on sale here. Behind all the bright olors and the enticing smells of this lively scene is the grim eality of the garment-makers' "sweat shops". In cellars and mall back rooms, there are more than thirty thousand Asian mmigrants making clothes for European boutiques, working n appalling conditions and for pitifully small wages. Poverty nd unrest seem always to have been endemic to this part of .ondon. In 1978 the Brick Lane Riots took place. These were series of pitched battles between the militant racists of the 3ritish National Front party and the immigrant community of 3rick Lane. They went on for several days.

COCKNEY SPECIALTY. In BETHNAL GREEN, a small green area ehind Vallance Road, they still sell jellied eels, an old ockney delicacy. These are prepared fresh every morning in uge enamel bowls, and then sold to the whelk-and-cockle talls or the old-fashioned eel-and-pie shops of the area. ellied eels are eaten cold, while pie and mash, covered with poonfuls of green parsley sauce ("liquor"), is a delicious and nexpensive hot meal.

THE HUGUENOT QUARTER
In Fournier Street (above) and Elder Street (below) there are still a number of houses built by Huguenot silk-weavers. These houses have been carefully restored, and are very rare in the capital.

VHITECHAPEL

Right at the heart of the East End, on the fringe of the City, is one of the busiest quarters of London. It gets its name from he white stone walls of St Mary Matfelon, a church that was built in the 3th century and which became the arish church of St Mary Whitechapel round 1338.

HE ROAD TO ESSEX. From Aldgate, Vhitechapel High Street was once the eparture point for the main road to the ields of Essex. Its former traffic of vagons and ox-carts explains the unusual vidth of Whitechapel Road and Mile End Road: the houses that line these ighways were built at a safe distance rom the mud and cow dung in the enter. Behind these busy main roads, Vhitechapel is actually filled with a ascinating maze of alleyways, courtyards nd narrow, winding, sunless streets.

SINISTER REPUTATION. For centuries Vhitechapel has been one of the most angerous parts of town. During the 9th century it was a refuge for gangs of narchists and communists, and in 1888 the famous Vhitechapel murders made Jack the Ripper a household ame all over the world. The poverty of the district also made it an attractive target for Victorian philanthropists.

JACK THE RIPPER. Whitechapel will always be associated with Jack the Ripper. On August 3, 1888, in a thick fog in

THE FORMER SPITALFIELDS MARKET
The sign is only for decoration, as the market was transferred to Leyton in 1991. The buildings almost disappeared, but a vast restoration programme will perhaps revitalise this area.

POVERTY AND SQUALOR
"Oh God, what I saw! People having no water to drink, hundreds of them, but the water of the common sewer which stagnated, full of dead fish, cats and dogs, under their windows. At the same time the cholera was raging, Walsh saw them throwing untold horrors into the ditch, and then dipping out the water and drinking it!"
Charles Kingsley

the heart of the busy East End, a prostitute was murdered an mutilated on a stairway in George Yard. Then, on September 8, the police found the body of another prostitute cut up in the same way. Panic ensued when a London press agency received a cheerful letter from the murderer, who announced his intention of continuing the killings and signed himself "Jack the Ripper". A large-scale hunt by Scotland Yard produced nothing. It certainly failed to stop the murder of two more prostitutes in the streets of Whitechapel on September 30. The last murder attributed to Jack the Ripper was the most horrible of all: on November 9 the body of a pretty young prostitute named Mary Jane Kelly was discovered in Hanbury Street cut up into pieces, and after thi the murders abruptly ceased. Eventually the police closed the file on Jack the Ripper, though rumors and speculation still continue as to the possible identity of the killer. But these killings, happening at a time when the social structure of England was fundamentally threatened, revealed to the privileged classes of London the grinding poverty that existec alongside them in the capital. The exposure consequently set in motion several programs of social welfare and reform.

THE MARKETS. From 1708 Whitechapel was one of the three great hay markets of London, along with Smithfield ▲ *177* and Haymarket. The capital's consumption of hay and straw was enormous, thanks to the size of its horse population. Huge trains of wagons loaded with hay arrived in the city every Tuesday, Thursday and Saturday from the farmland of Essex, Suffolk and Hertfordshire. Early in the 20th centur the hay was even being brought in by train and lorry. From 7am until lunchtime, Whitechapel

"It was said that the police went down Gallows Court in pairs. That is not true. They never went there at all, or only with the greatest circumspection, when bona fide cries of 'Murder!' called for their attention."

Edgar Wallace

Road and the streets running off it were packed with carts and swarming with people, and over everything hung the sweet, pervading odor of hay. The market finally closed in 1927, removing the last remnant of the countryside from the middle of London. But there are still some traditional markets operating in the area: the WASTE MARKET started in the middle of the 19th century, and further to the north there is MILE END WASTE.

A COSMOPOLITAN DISTRICT. Whitechapel was also famous for its many Jewish butchers and kosher slaughterhouses. They served the large Jewish community that was living here as far back as the 17th century, and an important food market grew up around them. Pakistani and Bangladeshi immigrants are gradually replacing the old Jewish community today, but they still keep up the traditional clothing industry.

REBUILDING THE EAST END. Attempts to improve the living conditions in the area were stepped up after 1888. But in spite of many new developments and the arrival of office blocks, Whitechapel retains its Victorian working-class atmosphere.

WHITECHAPEL BELL FOUNDRY. This famous bell foundry opened at 32–4 Whitechapel Road in 1738, though the foundry had already been in existence since the 15th century. It was established in 1420 in Houndsditch, then moved to Whitechapel in 1583, before transferring to its present site in the grounds of the 17th-century *Artichoke Inn*. The biggest bells in the world were cast here, and many of them

THE "PENNY"
Articles about the Whitechapel murders, like those in the *Penny Illustrated Paper*, struck fear into the hearts of the public all over London.

WHODUNNIT?
Three suspects for the identity of Jack the Ripper were George Chapman, hanged in 1902 for other offences; Montague John Druitt, the most likely suspect, who committed suicide in 1889; and the duke of Clarence, Queen Victoria's grandson, who had alibis that prove his innocence.

In the old buildings of the Whitechapel Bell Foundry (above right), a set of bells four hundred years old was discovered.

recast following World War Two. Big Ben ▲ *128*, the Liberty Bell (in Philadelphia, Pennsylvania, USA), the bells of Westminster Abbey and countless more were all created here. The foundry buildings and its 18th-century house form one of the most remarkable examples of pre-Industrial Revolution commercial sites in London.

ST DUNSTAN AND ALL SAINTS. The church is in Stepney High Street, south of Mile End Road. It was probably founded by St Dunstan, bishop of London in the 10th century. Its oldest part dates from the 13th century. The exterior was refaced in 1871–2; the church was heavily restored after a fire in 1901, and again after the bombardments of 1944. There is a large nave, and the glass in the windows is modern. The Renatus Harris organ of 1678 was sold to the Drury Lane Theatre.

WHITECHAPEL ART GALLERY
This holds many top quality exhibitions of modern art, as well as Old Master shows.

THE WHITECHAPEL ART GALLERY ★. The gallery was founded at the end of the 19th century by Canon Samuel Barnett, vicar of St Jude's Church, Whitechapel, "to bring the West End to the East End". In 1884 he opened the TOYNBEE HALL as a university for the common man, which grew into the Workers' Educational Association. This gave him the idea for the gallery, built at the corner of Commercial Street and Whitechapel High Street between 1897 and 1899 with private funds, notably from John Passmore Edwards. Already in the 1890's Barnett had organized several art exhibitions to get the locals used to the idea. It is a splendid Art Nouveau building designed by C.H. Townsend, with a mosaic over the door by Walter Crane. There are frequent exhibitions of modern art here, as well as exhibitions of local interest and an annual show each October.

A BUILDING IN COMMERCIAL ROAD
The front windows are decorated with fine moldings and medallions, all in white stucco.

WHITECHAPEL MARKETS. The WASTE MARKET, opposite the London Hospital, dates from the mid-19th century; fruit, vegetables and jewelry are sold here every day except Sunday. On Saturdays there is an additional market further north at MILE END WASTE; part of the Waste has been made into gardens, where there stands a statue of William Booth, founder of the Salvation Army.

ALDGATE. One of the six gates to the City in Roman times, Aldgate marked the entry point to London from the east. It was rebuilt between 1108 and 1147. The room above the gate was leased to Geoffrey Chaucer 1374–85. Again rebuilt 1606–9, the gate was finally demolished in 1761; the site is now covered by a corner of the street of the same name. In the 17th century this quarter was home to dressmakers and tailors, and it remained a center for this trade until the 20th century. A number of old buildings still stand, among them one of London's oldest inns, the *Hoop & Grapes*, at 47 Aldgate High Street.

MIDDLETON STREET
Among its many shops and stalls is the famous *Tubby Isaacs' Sea Food Kiosk*, where one can try all kinds of fish and seafood.

Along the Thames

FROM LAMBETH TO SOUTHWARK

BIG BEN ✪
WESTMINSTER BRIDGE
LAMBETH PALACE
ST THOMAS'S HOSPITAL
HUNGERFORD BRIDGE
COUNTY HALL
LONDON EYE
WATERLOO BRIDGE
ROYAL FESTIVAL HALL
ARCHBISHOP'S P
NATIONAL
THEA
LAMBETH PALACE ROAD
LAMBETH ROAD
LAMBETH BRIDGE

This stretch of the river commands an excellent view of the opposite bank and some of the City's historic buildings. The south bank was once all swamp as far as Blackfriars: the name Lambeth derives from *loam hithe*, "mud place". Its most important feature is Lambeth Palace, a rare surviving example of a 13th-century building.

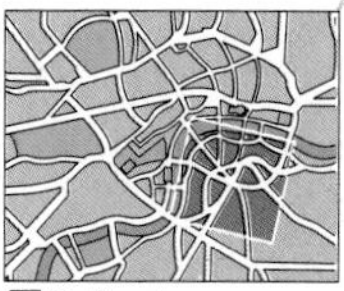

Half a day

◆ **F** B3-B4-C3 **G** A1-B1-B2

"YACHTS OF THE CUMBERLAND FLEET STARTING AT BLACKFRIARS"
A late 18th-century painting. River traffic acquired greater importance after Henry VIII had founded a naval shipyard at Deptford, near the palace of Greenwich.

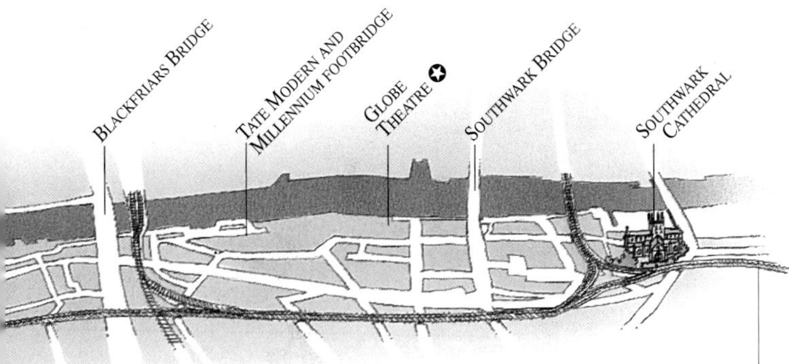

LAMBETH PALACE ★

Built between 1207 and 1229, the palace has been the residence of the archbishops of Canterbury for seven and a half centuries. The building shows signs of alterations made by many successive occupants.

THE CRYPT AND CHAPEL. The vaulted crypt beneath the chapel is the oldest part of the palace and dates from the beginning of the 13th century. Most of the archbishops were consecrated in the little chapel. In 1633 Archbishop Laud restored it, putting in a new altar, windows, throne and stalls. It was severely damaged during World War Two and had to be almost entirely rebuilt after the war.

THE MORTON TOWER. The massive red-brick gateway was built for Archbishop John Morton in the late 1400's.

THE GREAT HALL. This was rebuilt in 1663 in Gothic style by Archbishop Juxon. The hammerbeam roof is more than 50 feet high. The residential quarters were rebuilt in 1828 by Edward Blore, and the hall is now the library, founded thanks to a bequest from Archbishop Bancroft in 1610. The library has notable treasures, such as Queen Elizabeth I's prayer book and some fine illuminated manuscripts.

THE GUARD ROOM. It was here in 1534 that Thomas Cromwell and the Lords of the Council questioned Sir Thomas More ▲ *194, 197* when he refused to sign the Oath of Supremacy. There is a collection of portraits of archbishops hanging here, including works by Holbein, Van Dyck, Reynolds and Hogarth.

TRIALS AND REVOLUTIONS ● *36*. In 1378 the English reformer John Wycliffe, accused of heresy and depravity, was interrogated in the chapel. The palace has been the victim of attack on numerous occasions: in 1381 during the Peasants' Revolt, Wat Tyler's mob ransacked the place. The LOLLARDS' TOWER, actually a water tower built in 1435, is named after Wycliffe's followers who were imprisoned near this spot. From 1646 to 1658, during the Civil War and Cromwell's Commonwealth, Lambeth Palace was a prison. The poet Richard Lovelace was imprisoned here in 1648.

ST THOMAS'S HOSPITAL

Founded at the beginning of the 12th century, St Thomas's Hospital was once part of the Priory of St Mary Overie in Southwark. It was renamed St Thomas the Martyr in memory of Archbishop Thomas à Becket, who was murdered in 1170 and canonized three years later. During the 13th century it

ART AND INDUSTRY
In 1720, on the site where County Hall now stands, Richard Holt started a factory that made artificial terracotta for sculptures, which later became the Coade Artificial Stone Manufactory. Coade stone was an exceptionally hard and weatherproof material, and there are still many examples of it on London buildings, but when the company ceased trading in 1840 the formula for Coade stone disappeared as well. At the start of the 19th century the Doulton pottery company set up in business: its stoneware with relief decorations of hunting scenes was very popular.

LAMBETH PALACE AND ST MARY'S
A museum devoted to 17th-century landscape painters is in the 14th-century church tower.

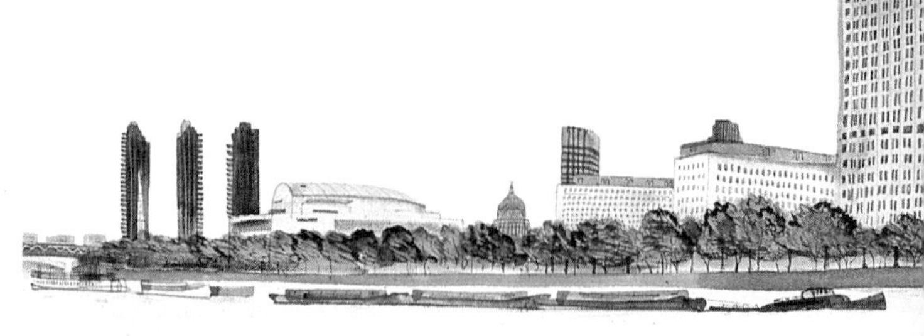

SHELL CENTRE AND COUNTY HALL
The immense power of industry is symbolized by the massive outline of the Shell Centre, built between 1953 and 1963. County Hall is easily identifiable from far away, thanks to its roof of Italian tiles. It was built on the site of a former brewery.

was moved to Borough High Street. At the Dissolution of the monasteries in 1540, Henry VIII decided to close the hospital. Edward VI reopened it in 1551 under the name of St Thomas the Apostle. Its land was purchased by the Charing Cross Railway Company in 1859 in order to build a new station; and so the hospital moved once more, to Lambeth Palace Road. The building was completed in 1871. Its design as a series of blocks was the work of Henry Currey. After World War Two, W. Fowler Howitt and then Yorke, Rosenberg & Mardall were commissioned to rebuild the hospital completely, a project that eventually had to be abandoned. Three of the seven original blocks remain as well as a chapel decorated with scenes in Doulton pottery.

THE FLORENCE NIGHTINGALE MUSEUM. In 1854, just before leaving for the Crimea, Florence Nightingale initiated numerous changes to the administration of this hospital. Then in 1860 she opened the first training school for nurses. Progress in the science of medicine led to the opening of a medical school here in 1871, and to the opening in 1900 of eleven specialist departments. The hospital also houses a museum that is dedicated to the memory and work of Florence Nightingale.

IMPERIAL WAR MUSEUM
Situated in Lambeth Road, the museum is devoted to military exploits involving Britain and the Commonwealth since 1914.

COUNTY HALL

The former city hall of London is an enormous building sitting beside Westminster Bridge and with a magnificent view across the River Thames to another formidable seat of power, the Houses of Parliament. Work on the foundations began in 1909, and it finally opened in 1922, although it was not actually completed until 1963. County Hall was designed by Ralph Knott in "Edwardian Renaissance" style ● *88*. The building, a concave arc with a tower and a rectangular wing on each side, is constructed around a series of interior courtyards and is clad in Portland stone (except for the base, which is made of granite, like the quayside wall). On the left-hand side is a lion that was carved from the famous Coade stone in 1837. It was once the symbol of the old Lion Brewery and is now the emblem of the whole South Bank Centre. County Hall now houses visitor attractions, including the multi-level LONDON AQUARIUM, with huge see-through tanks populated by sharks and other exotic fish, and smaller tanks where you can stroke rays, starfish and crabs. Also in County Hall are DALI UNIVERSE, which contains more than 500 works by the Spanish Surrealist artist Salvador Dalí (1904–89), and the SAATCHI GALLERY, exhibiting some of Britain's most important contemporary artists. The building is also home to the London Marriott hotel, which offers from its windows the most amazing views. The JUBILEE GARDENS, set beside

FLORENCE NIGHTINGALE
The nurses at St Thomas's are called "Nightingales".

County Hall, were opened in 1977 to celebrate the Silver Jubilee of Queen Elizabeth II.

The London Eye. The graceful 443-foot-high cantilevered observation wheel is also one of the capital's most popular attractions. It was designed by architects David Marks and Julia Barfield and built by British Airways, originally to function for the year 2000 only, but seems set to remain for years to come. A 40-minute "trip" in one of the capsules affords magnificent views of London.

The sculptures of County Hall
The exterior sculptures just above the first upper floor are the work of Ernest Cole and Alfred Hardiman.

Southwark

From the Roman occupation until the mid-1700's, Southwark was the only district of London on the south side of the River Thames. Linked to the City by a bridge, Southwark was not entirely under its domination. There were areas called "liberties", pieces of land that had formerly been church property, and which remained self-governing. This independence was ideal for the building of theaters.

A departure point. Southwark was the entrance to London for travelers coming up from the south, and its many inns and taverns had a wide reputation. Among them was the *Tabard*, from where Geoffrey Chaucer (c. 1340–1400) had his twenty-nine pilgrims set out for Canterbury. The *White Hart* is mentioned in Shakespeare's play *Henry VI* and Charles Dickens' novel *The Pickwick Papers.* Of these old places, only the *George Inn*, which was built in 1677 on the site of an earlier tavern, remains today.

Theaters. It was at Southwark (particularly Bankside, which runs just beside the river) that the first fixed London theaters were built (with the exception of the Theatre and the Curtain, which were both in the north of the City). The Rose Theatre opened in 1586. This was in the shape of a polygon, made of wood and plaster with a thatched roof over a section of it, and was destroyed in 1605. Until 1603 plays by Marlowe, Kyd and Shakespeare were performed here. Most famous was the

"The Thames at Lambeth"
This painting of 1706 shows the Horse Ferry crossing the Thames. Westminster Bridge was opened downriver in 1750, but the ferry continued to make the crossing until the 19th century.

A DOCK NEAR SOUTHWARK CATHEDRAL
This old three-master in an unlikely setting (below) seems to be waiting for her captain to return and take her away from all this . . .

Globe Theatre, and there were two others of less renown, the Swan and the Hope.

SHAKESPEARE'S GLOBE THEATRE ★. As well as acting here, Shakespeare was also a shareholder in the business. The name of the round wooden building (1598) comes from its sign, which showed Atlas bearing the world on his shoulders. At the start of *Henry V* the Chorus speaks of "this wooden O". In 1613 a cannon fired in a performance of *Henry VIII* started a fire that burned the theater down. Rebuilt the following year, it was lost from sight in 1644. In 1997, a replica of the Globe Theatre was completed, on the initiative of the American film director and Shakespeare-admirer Sam Wanamaker. As in Elizabethan times, the stage is in the open air, without stage lighting or sound amplification, and the audience can move around and mingle with the actors ● *55*.

TATE MODERN AND MILLENNIUM BRIDGE. The former Bankside Power Station, long disused, was reborn in 2000 as the Tate Modern, displaying the Tate's collection of international modern art ▲ *207, 220*. The brick-clad steel building, with a 325-foot-tall central chimney, was converted by the Swiss architects Herzog & de Meuron. Outside the museum is the Millennium Bridge, a footbridge which links the south and north banks of the river and provides a direct route to St Paul's Cathedral. The steel bridge, designed by Sir Norman Foster, was originally opened in 2000 but was found to sway disturbingly and was closed within a few days; after remedial work it was reopened, minus the "wobble", in 2002.

THE FIRST SOUTHWARK BRIDGE
This was built between 1814 and 1819 with three cast-iron arches and a span of 240 feet. It is mentioned by Dickens in *Little Dorrit*. The present bridge of five steel arches was designed by Sir Ernest George and built between 1912 and 1921.

THE SOUTH BANK CENTRE: A GREAT MULTIMEDIA COMPLEX. The revival of this area began in 1951, during the Festival of Britain, with the building of the Royal Festival Hall. Designed by Robert Matthew and Leslie Martin and developed further in 1962 by T.P. Bennett, the auditorium can seat three thousand people. The QUEEN ELIZABETH HALL, the PURCELL ROOM and the HAYWARD GALLERY (where art exhibitions are held) were completed in 1968. Ongoing refurbishment works are creating new foyers, visitor facilities and access stairways, and the Royal Festival Hall is due to close for a year from 2005. Also along the river are the National Theatre (1977), next to the National Film Theatre (transferred there in 1958) and, a little further to the east, the IMAX Cinema of the British Film Institute. This stretch of the river is a popular place to while away a sunny day, with many cafés, restaurants and bars, entertainers, and a second-hand book and print market under Waterloo Bridge.

Southwark Cathedral ★

The Augustinian monks of St Mary Overie built a Norman church on this site in 1106. The priory burned down in 1212, to be replaced by a Gothic building. After the Reformation it became the parish church of St Saviour, and was finally made a cathedral in 1905. The nave was rebuilt during the 19th century by A.W. Blomfield. Inside is an oak figure of a knight (1275), and an effigy of John Gower, the poet and friend of Chaucer. In the south aisle there is the tomb of the writer Edmund Shakespeare, brother of William. Above are stained-glass windows by Christopher Webb illustrating his plays. Not far from the cathedral is the operating theater of Old St Thomas's Hospital, which has been restored.

Southwark Cathedral and Pickford's Wharf
This is an incongruous setting for the cathedral, which is the most beautiful medieval building on the South Bank.

Bankside and Shakespeare's Globe Theatre ✪
On the riverfront, south of the river between Southwark and Waterloo bridges, is the Globe Theatre, a replica of Shakespeare's original 'wooden O', complete with thatched roof. Plays take place in the open-air main theater, and tours, talks and an exhibition are held inside the building. There are stunning views along the Thames and across to St Paul's and the City. Nearby, to the east are Southwark Cathedral, the Clink Prison Museum and the remains of Shakespeare's Rose Theatre. To the west is the Millennium Bridge and the new Tate Modern building.

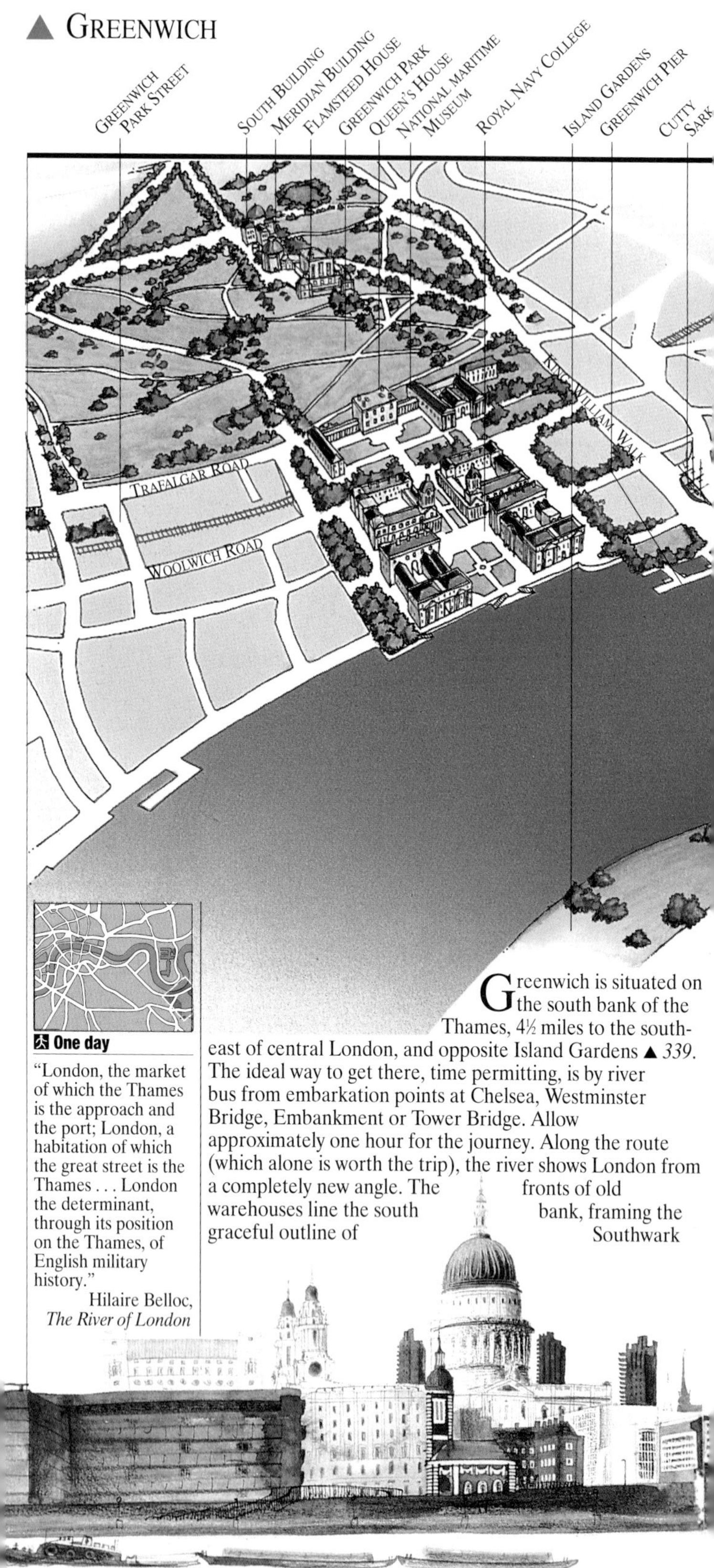

One day

"London, the market of which the Thames is the approach and the port; London, a habitation of which the great street is the Thames . . . London the determinant, through its position on the Thames, of English military history."

Hilaire Belloc,
The River of London

Greenwich is situated on the south bank of the Thames, 4½ miles to the south-east of central London, and opposite Island Gardens ▲ *339*. The ideal way to get there, time permitting, is by river bus from embarkation points at Chelsea, Westminster Bridge, Embankment or Tower Bridge. Allow approximately one hour for the journey. Along the route (which alone is worth the trip), the river shows London from a completely new angle. The fronts of old warehouses line the south bank, framing the graceful outline of Southwark

“The Thames is covered with small vessels, barges, boats and wherries, passing to and fro . . . such a forest of masts, for miles together, that you would think all the ships of the universe here realised.” Tobias Smollett

Cathedral ▲ *323* while, on the opposite side of the river, the City ▲ *146* appears as a succession of church towers, dominated of course by the dome of St Paul’s Cathedral ▲ *171*. Then comes the journey through Docklands ▲ *330,* and the great loop made by the river around the Isle of Dogs ▲ *336*.

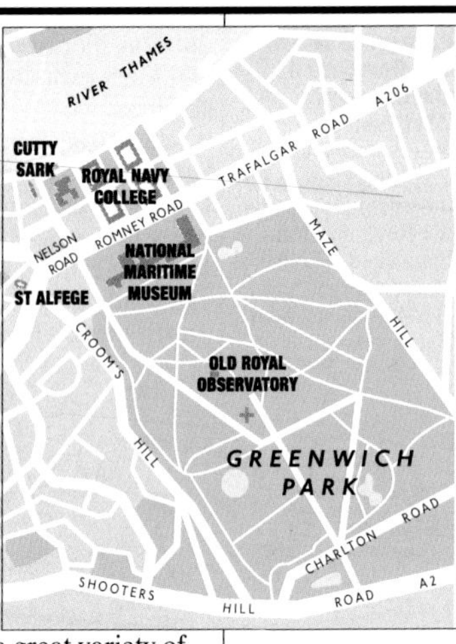

GREENWICH

The name of Greenwich is always associated with the zero Meridian, from which point longitude and world standard time (GMT, or Greenwich Mean Time) are measured. But Greenwich is filled with a great variety of other things to see, and has some magnificent buildings such as the Queen’s House and the Royal Naval College.

HISTORY. Greenwich (literally “green village”) was a fishing and agricultural settlement where in 1427 the duke of Gloucester, Henry V’s brother, built himself a sumptuous palace he called Bella Court, and later enclosed the 200 acres of Greenwich Park. After the Wars of the Roses the palace became the favorite resort of the Tudor monarchs: Henry VIII, Mary Tudor and Elizabeth I were all born here. Henry loved to go hunting in the park, and kept careful watch over the English fleet moored nearby in the royal dockyards. He enlarged the palace, adding a royal armory, banqueting hall and tiltyard. His son, the boy-king Edward VI, died here in 1553, and Elizabeth I made it her official summer residence on her accession in 1558. It was here that Sir Walter Raleigh is supposed to have laid his cloak over a puddle so that Elizabeth could keep her shoes dry. In 1615 James I commissioned Inigo Jones ▲ *269, 274* to build a house for his wife Anne of Denmark, now known as the Queen’s House. Work was interrupted by the queen’s death in 1619, but continued in the reign of Charles I. At the Restoration, Charles II decided to demolish and rebuild the palace, but

“The chief place of resort in the daytime, after the public-houses, is the park, in which the principal amusement is to drag young ladies up the steep hill which leads to the Observatory, and then drag them down again, at the very top of their speed, greatly to the derangement of their curls and bonnet-caps, and much to the edification of lookers-on from below.”
Charles Dickens, *Sketches by Boz*

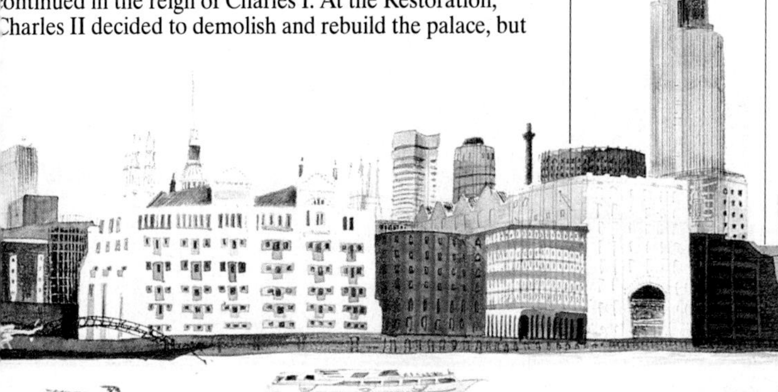

only one block was finished when he died. In 1694 William and Mary (who lived at Kensington and Hampton Court) commissioned Wren ▲ *171* and his assistant Hawksmoor ▲ *311* to transform the property into a Royal Hospital for Seamen (corresponding to the soldiers' institution at Chelsea), which in 1873 became the Royal Naval College.

TOUR OF GREENWICH. The little town has many elegant 17th- and 18th-century houses. The ancient Croom's Hill is a steep and winding residential road lined with some beautiful houses one of them, "The Grange", has 12th-century timbers. In the town center are some fine Georgian façades which are decorated with stucco, many good restaurants and historic pubs. The *Trafalgar Tavern* (1837) in Park Row was visited by Lord Macaulay, Thackeray and Dickens.

ST ALFEGE. This church in the center of Greenwich derives its name from Alfege, archbishop of Canterbury, taken hostage by the Danes and murdered at Greenwich in 1012 when he refused to allow himself to be ransomed. Henry VIII was baptized in the old church on June 28, 1491: the present building by Hawksmoor was completed in 1714. John James built the west tower in 1730. Inside are paintings by Sir James Thornhill ▲ *173*. The church was restored after being badly damaged in World War Two.

THE "CUTTY SARK". Launched in 1869 from the shipyards in Dumbarton in Scotland, this sailing ship was one of the most beautiful and fastest clippers ever built. Her speed enabled her to transport perishable cargos, such as freshly picked tea from China, but the opening of the Suez Canal in the

FLAMSTEED HOUSE AND GREENWICH OBSERVATORY
Wren built the observatory and Flamsteed House for the astronomer royal, the Reverend John Flamsteed. The Royal Observatory is now at Herstmonceux, near Battle, Sussex.

THE QUAYSIDE AT GREENWICH
The charm of the old port of Greenwich and its gracious houses was captured in this painting by John O'Connor (1850–89).

"Greenwich Hospital, seen from the Thames"
The fine buildings of Greenwich are clearly visible in the background of this painting by William Lionel Wylie (1851–1931).

same year dealt a decisive blow. The ship was sold to a Portuguese company in 1895, then bought back by the Cutty-Sark Preservation Society in 1954 and installed in a dry dock at Greenwich. Today it is a museum, illustrating life aboard the great sailing ships of the 19th century. Nearby, also in dry dock, is the little ketch *Gypsy Moth IV* in which Sir Francis Chichester sailed single-handed around the world in 1966–7 at the age of sixty-five.

Old Royal Observatory or Flamsteed House ★. The Royal Observatory owes its fame to the Greenwich Meridian. This was fixed as the standard zero meridian at an international conference held in Washington in 1884, all degrees east and west being measured from this point. The actual zero line is marked in the courtyard paving. King Charles II commissioned Wren to build the observatory in 1675 for his astronomer royal John Flamsteed (1646–1719), together with a house "for the observator's habitation and a little for pompe". The interior is now a museum, the present Royal Observatory having moved to Sussex largely because of the air pollution in London. The Meridian Building houses a fine collection of telescopes. Outside on the roof is a red time ball (1833), which still drops every day at 1pm as a time check for shipping on the river. Flamsteed House contains some elegant 17th-century furniture, and there is a superb panorama of London from the terrace.

Royal Naval College. Originally built as a naval hospital, on the banks of the Thames, the college consists of four symmetrical buildings with a central courtyard. Between the colonnades can be seen the back of the Queen's House. The north wing was designed as part of a palace for Charles II by John Webb between 1662 and 1669, and served as a model for the rest of the building. Wren ▲ *171–5* and Hawksmoor ▲ *149, 311* designed most of the new buildings, which include the magnificent Painted Hall, with its walls and ceiling, decorated in the Baroque style by Sir James Thornhill ▲ *173*, glorifying William and Mary (and successive monarchs). In 1805 the body of Lord Nelson lay in state in this beautiful room before its interment in St Paul's Cathedral. Opposite the Painted Hall is Wren's Chapel, which had to be rebuilt after a fire in 1779 by James "Athenian" Stuart (1713–88). His beautifully proportioned neo-classical design contains an altarpiece, *St Paul after the Shipwreck at Malta*, by the American painter Benjamin West (1728–1820), with statues of Faith, Hope, Charity and Humility by the same artist on display in the vestibule. In 1873 the empty buildings were turned into a university for naval officers.

The Queen's House. In 1616 James I commissioned Inigo Jones ▲ *269* to build a summer residence for his wife, Anne of Denmark. On her death three years later James gave the house to the future Charles I, whose wife Queen Henrietta Maria asked Jones in 1629 to complete it. It is a white double pavilion in the shape of an "H", built across the old road that ran from London to Rochester. It was the first Palladian building in England, "sollid, proporsionable to the rulles,

Scottish inspiration
The Scottish poem "Tam O'Shanter" by Robert Burns was the inspiration for the name Cutty Sark, which means a short vest, like that worn by the figurehead on the ship.

Ceiling of the Painted Hall
This domed room was built by Wren as a refectory, and is still used as a dining hall. James Thornhill and his assistants decorated it in rich Baroque style from 1708 to1727, being paid £3 per square yard for the ceiling, but only £1 for the walls.

masculine and unaffected", according to its architect. The queen was so pleased with the result that she called it her "House of Delights". Inside, the entrance hall is shaped as a perfect cube, with a gallery that is reached by the iron "Tulip Staircase". After some important restoration work the Queen's House reopened in 1999 with sixteen new galleries. Covered with a glass roof, Neptune's Court is used for exhibitions.

THE NATIONAL MARITIME MUSEUM. Established in the Queen's House in the 19th century, this is now one of the finest maritime museums in the world, illustrating the naval history of Great Britain with documents, paintings, models and other memorabilia. Rooms in the Queen's House are hung with naval paintings (opposite and left) as well as royal portraits and many other pictures. The West Wing is set on three floors: at the top are the sections devoted to the great maritime explorers and the Royal Navy up to 1700. On the middle floor are the James Cook Gallery and the Nelson Galleries. The most poignant exhibit displayed here is Nelson's uniform worn at Trafalgar, with the bloodstained bullet-hole visible in the left shoulder, through which he sustained the wound that was to kill him on October 21, 1805. The Navigation Room houses a superb collection of globes, charts and instruments. The East Wing of the museum houses a section that is devoted to the history of navigation from the earliest days of sail right through to the steam age. There is also the Arctic Gallery, devoted to the polar expeditions.

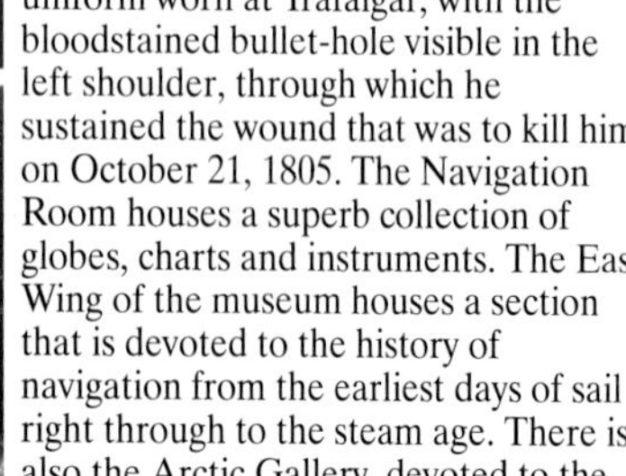

REENWICH PARK. This is the oldest royal park in London, nclosed by the duke of Gloucester in 1433 to be used as a unting ground. Its long avenues were first laid out for harles II by Louis XIV's landscape gardener Le Nôtre, who esigned the gardens of Versailles and who never even came the park. You can still admire the three-hundred-year-old hestnut trees, as well as a bronze by Henry Moore ▲ *223*. he view from the top of the hill over London and the hames is well worth the climb. On the southwestern dge of the park is the Ranger's House, a redbrick villa hat is home to the WERNHER COLLECTION, an exhibition f some 700 works of art purchased by mining magnate ir Julius Wernher (1850–1912). The collection brings gether paintings by Filippino Lippi, Pieter de Hooch and ther old masters, Renaissance jewelry, porcelain, silverware, urniture, woodcarvings and tapestries.

HE MILLENNIUM DOME. The Millennium Dome is at North reenwich, lying in a curve of the Thames a little upstream f the Thames Barrier. This gigantic structure, 3,280 feet circumference, was opened to the public admist much ontroversy on January 1, 2000, and was the centerpiece of he Millennium Experience. It now lies unused, although here are plans to develop it into a sports and entertainment rena, and for the surrounding area, a former dustrial site now called "Millennium Village", see the building of thousands of new homes, hops and offices.

LORD NELSON
Horatio Nelson ▲ *284* (1758–1805) is one of Britain's greatest heroes. He confounded Napoleon's invasion plans, and with the victory of Trafalgar (which cost him his life) assured Britain's maritime supremacy for one hundred years.

THAMES BARGE
On its way down river from London, the barge is seen passing through Greenwich.

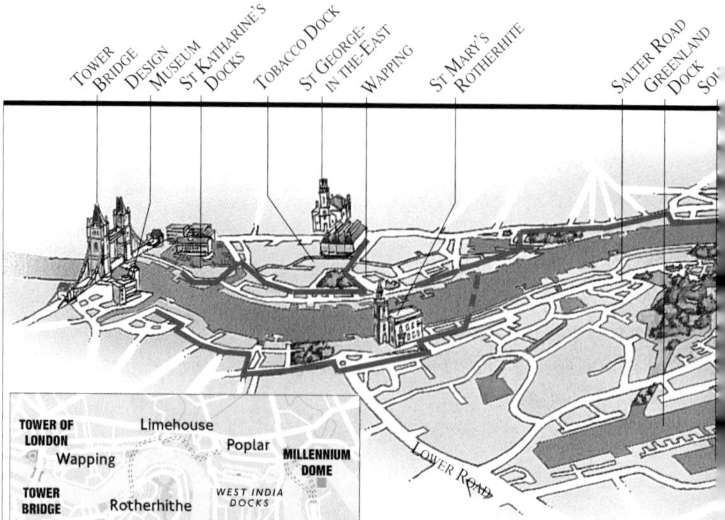

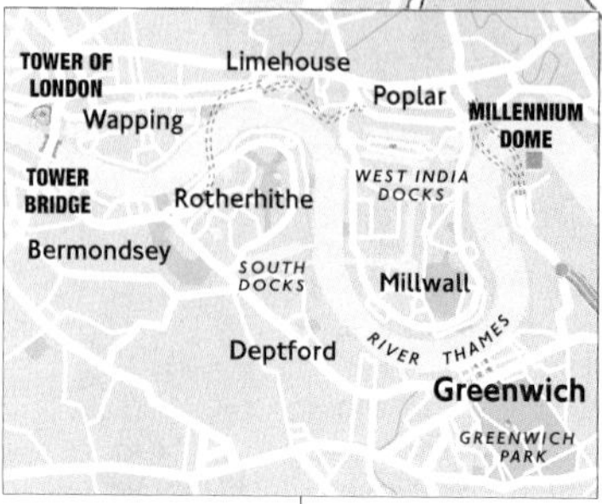

The Docklands are on the site of the old docks of the port of London. They were the biggest urban developmen of the late 20th century to be attempted in all Europe, but today they are running into trouble. The creation of a new town was meant to change the whole image of this old built-up area, covering several square miles, an area that was once a symbol of the commercial and industrial supremacy enjoyed by Britain and her empire. Five hundred years of history vanished with the redevelopment of the ancient port of London, and only a few traces remain of its former history, incorporated into a new Americanized landscape.

The history of the docks

By the 18th century the old docks and their equipment were proving inadequate to meet the needs of London and the economic expansion brought by the Industrial Revolution. The existing docks included Howland Great Dock at Rotherhithe, created in 1696 and later known as Greenland Dock, and the shipyard at Blackwall, constructed c. 1660, which were primarily used for repairing ships. By the end of

"West India Docks"
This view, looking from east to west across the Isle of Dogs from Blackwall, was painted in 1802 by William Daniell, when the docks were opened. They were finally closed in 1980: the new development of Canary Wharf occupies the whole area now.

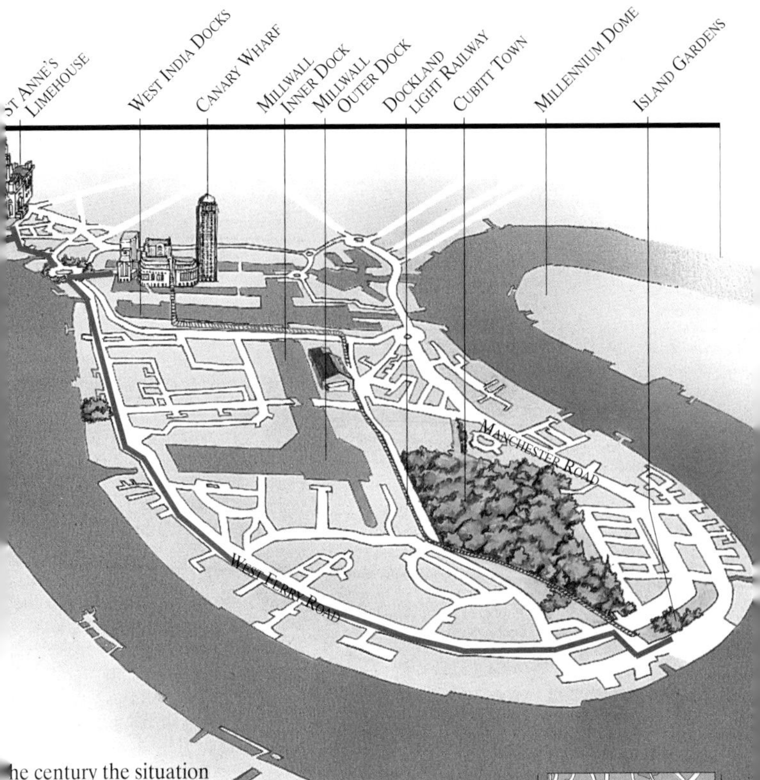

ST ANNE'S LIMEHOUSE
WEST INDIA DOCKS
CANARY WHARF
MILLWALL INNER DOCK
MILLWALL OUTER DOCK
DOCKLAND LIGHT RAILWAY
CUBITT TOWN
MILLENNIUM DOME
ISLAND GARDENS

MANCHESTER ROAD
WEST FERRY ROAD

he century the situation vas quite dramatic: each ear, 10,000 coastal vessels and ,500 ships moored near London at imehouse, Greenwich and Blackwall, all vaiting to load or unload their cargoes of harcoal, wood, grain or wool. Such a protracted delay nevitably had the effect of raising prices. In 1793 the owerful West India Company threatened to move elsewhere new accommodation were not provided.

HE NEW DOCKS. Matters improved quite rapidly after 1799. Vest India Docks ● *78*, opened in 1802 at Wapping, followed 1805 by London Docks. Built by D.A. Alexander and John Rennie, London Docks had two main basins with room for nore than three hundred ships. In the mid-19th century about two thousand vessels a year moored here. Imported goods from the tropics filled the warehouses, while in vaulted cellars beneath the level of the quays wine and brandy were laid down to mature. The tobacco warehouse, which the government rented out (Queen's Warehouse), was on one of the quays. East India Docks opened in 1806 at Blackwall, followed in 1812 by Regent's Canal Dock. The docks' success, the expansion of British trade, and the growth of London and of the empire all contributed to the area's continuing growth.

One day

A DOCKSIDE PUB
From St Katharine's in Bermondsey, the route is marked out with historic pubs. The first one, the *Dickens Inn*, is in St Katharine's Dock. In Wapping there is the *Town of Ramsgate*, where convicts were locked up awaiting deportation to Australia.

A WHARF NEAR LONDON BRIDGE
Until the early 19th century goods unloaded from ships could be stored on the quayside.

St Katharine's Dock opened in 1828, built by Thomas Telford (1757–1834). During Queen Victoria's long reign the Royal Victoria Dock opened in 1855, Millwall Dock in 1868, the West India Docks were rebuilt as the South West India Docks in 1870, and the Royal Albert Docks were opened in 1880. The complex was rounded off in 1921 with the completion of the King George V Dock.

NEW VENTURES. Around the wharves and warehouses, all kinds of service industries grew up during the course of the 19th century. Naval shipyards provided the motivating force during the Napoleonic wars, then there was the continued expansion of trade that flourished well into the 1860's. All this was responsible for the emergence of many other activities, such as mechanical and metallurgical industries, and food-processing factories. A hundred years later all this was in decline, with businesses having moved to the provinces or else disappeared altogether, largely as a result of the great post-war restructuring of London.

ISAMBARD KINGDOM BRUNEL (1806–59)
The son of Marc Brunel, who built the first tunnel under the Thames, Isambard Kingdom Brunel designed the *Great Eastern*, built at Millwall and launched in 1858. At the time, it was the largest steamship in the world.

A CHANGE IN POPULATION. With the opening of the docks and the rapid industrial growth that accompanied it, a new population arrived in the docks from all over Britain. Engineers, carpenters, mechanics, blacksmiths, coopers, ropemakers, stevedores, boatmen, lock-keepers, shopkeepers skilled and unskilled laborers all flocked here in order to wor at the new docks or in the new businesses that sprang up around them. A new and heterogeneous community grew up in the mid-19th century, with the poor in search of work living side by side with the more prosperous men in search of new investments. During the 1870's the wealthy and better-off members of the community began to move out of the district to make their homes elsewhere. The dockers and laborers who remained behind developed into a much more closely knit community with a shared socio-cultural background; and soon they settled into the domestic round of family life, work, school and recreation within some clearly defined geographical boundaries.

A CHANGE OF PACE. One half of all the dockland warehouses were damaged or destroyed by bombs during the Second World War, particularly St Katharine's and West India Docks They were rebuilt during the 1950's, but the increasing size of the new ships brought a gradual move downriver toward the Thames estuary, at the expense of those moorings nearer the City. Tilbury Docks, some 25 miles away, probably derived th most benefit from this shift of emphasis.

RECONVERSION. The docks began to close at the end of the 1960's, followed soon after by their redevelopment. This began in 1969 in St Katharine's Dock, and spread gradually to both sides of the river. But it was only in 1981, with the closure of the Royal Docks, that a vast redevelopment program to convert the entire area was launched by the

A view of the Docks in 1964
The docks begin just past Tower Bridge: to the left are St Katharine's Dock and London Docks in Wapping; to the right, in the bow of the river, are the Surrey Docks.

London Docklands Development Corporation (LDDC). This large-scale project first took shape with Canary Wharf on the Isle of Dogs. The tendency to relocate business centers in the east of London involved many significant moves. The great newspapers deserted Fleet Street, mostly in favor of Docklands: *The Times* went to Wapping, the *Financial Times* to Blackwall, the *Daily Telegraph* to Canary Wharf, the *Guardian* to Farringdon, and the *Daily Mail* to Rotherhithe. By the beginning of the 1990's the Docklands population had already risen to 65,000, and almost 70,000 people were

THE IVORY HOUSE AT ST KATHARINE'S DOCK
Engineer Thomas Telford and architect Philip Hardwick had an original idea in their 1828 design for St Katharine's Dock. The huge warehouses, built of brick and iron to reduce the risk of fire, were built right at the water's edge so that goods unloaded could be stored immediately in one manoeuver.

commuting here to work every day. But this enormous expansion was partially checked by the recession that hit Britain in the late 1980's and again in 1999 after the Dotcom crash; both times led to a steep decline in office space demand, and many commercial and residential blocks still remain empty, while the Canary Wharf project has run into serious financial difficulty.

FROM ST KATHARINE'S TO WAPPING ★

ST KATHARINE'S DOCK ★ ● *79*. The preliminary work at St Katharine's in 1826, to make way for the construction of the docks, was spectacular: a whole district with origins that went back to the Middle Ages was razed, and 1,250 houses were demolished. The ancient hospital and church of St Katharine ▲ *258*, founded in 1148 near the Tower of London ▲ *182* by Queen Matilda, in memory of her two sons who died at an early age, were just two casualties of this ruthless redevelopment. More than eleven thousand people who lived in the neighborhood of this royal institution, and who lacked the good fortune to be either homeowners or leaseholders, were made homeless because of these demolitions, despite ferocious protests. The authorities justified their actions by saying that the work was necessary in order to clean up an unhealthy part of town. The St Katharine's Foundation was awarded compensation from the St Katharine's Dock Company in the form of land by Regent's Park to build houses, a school and a church. After World War One the latter became the main Danish church in London. St Katharine's Dock was the first to be closed, in 1969, and has now been completely rebuilt as a business and recreation complex. Office blocks and a large hotel (the *Tower Thistle*), together with a number of craft shops, have been built in its place along with an international center of commerce, the World Trade Centre. The IVORY HOUSE ● *79*, an ivory warehouse built in 1854 of brick and cast iron, has been turned into flats. The *Dickens Inn* is located in an old wooden three-story warehouse here.

THE ENTRANCE TO THE DOCKS AT WAPPING

THE HISTORIC SHIP COLLECTION. One of the dock's basins has been converted into a marina with mooring space for a hundred yachts. Another, the eastern basin, now houses the Historic Ship Collection, which was opened in 1979. The collection of ancient ships on display includes the *Challenge*, a steam tugboat; the *Nore*, a 1931 lightship; and the *Cambria*, a sail-powered trading ship from 1906. The Royal Navy vessel *HMS Discovery* has also been converted into a maritime museum. This was the sail- and steam-powered three-master, built at Dundee, Scotland, which carried the explorer Captain Robert Falcon

Scott on his first expedition to the Antarctic, which took place between 1901 and 1904.

Wapping. Right beside St Katharine's Dock, the district of Wapping has an unsavory reputation. With its famous gallows and its wretchedly poor people, Wapping could once rival the worst parts of Whitechapel. Bomb damage during World War Two and the closure of many docks and warehouses brought further dereliction and neglect to the area. But with the building of new housing estates, the conversion of old warehouses into flats, and the creation of public gardens on waste land, Wapping is beginning to recover. Its modernization prompted French writer Claude Roy to comment in 1986: "Wapping Old Stairs, where for two hundred years there were thousands of jobless waiting to beg a shilling from passengers as they landed, were rotten when I last saw them. Now they're gone altogether."

Tobacco Dock
The main docks were linked by Tobacco Dock, which now contains some fine three-masted sailing ships open to the public.

Tobacco Dock ● *78.* The shopping center at Tobacco Dock is intended to be twice as large as the one already thriving in Covent Garden, once work on the *Highway* buildings is complete. Some of the original buildings have been protected and restored, showing the typical design of the old dockside warehouses. A case in point is the Skin Floor in the *Highway* at the corner of Wapping Lane. These buildings are metal-framed, and the 4 acres of space within them has ribbed or cradle vaulting in brick; this is now being converted in order to accommodate shops and cafés.

St George-in-the-East. This church, situated to the north of Tobacco Dock in Cannon Street Road, was built between 1714 and 1729 by Nicholas Hawksmoor ▲ *311*, and paid for by a levy on charcoal that was introduced in 1711. It was one of the fifty churches that were voted for by the Tory government and Queen Anne ▲ *311*, who did not want to leave the poverty-stricken parts of London bereft of some spiritual guidance. Although the exterior of the church, with its high tower (160 feet) of Portland stone, has maintained its original appearance, the interior, which was destroyed in 1941, was restored in 1960. There is a modern chapel in the nave.

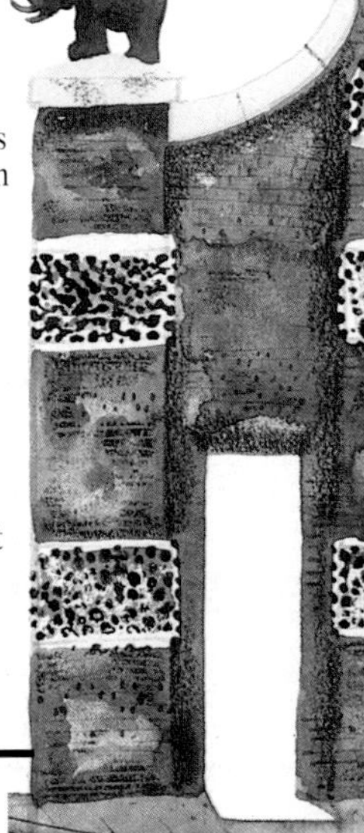

The entrance to St Katharine's Dock

Wapping High Street. There is a fine row of 18th-century houses and warehouses to be seen in Wapping High Street, which also houses the Metropolitan Special Constabulary. This is the name of London's river police, a force that was founded in 1798. In Wapping Wall is the *Prospect of Whitby* (left), the oldest of the Thames riverside pubs with roots going back to 1520. It was the haunt of smugglers and thieves, and also of the diarist Samuel Pepys (1633–1703) ● *40* and the artist J.M.W. Turner (1775–1851) ● *102*, ▲ *215–17*.

A HAWKSMOOR CHURCH
St Anne's, Limehouse, completed in 1730, boasts the highest church clock in London.

FROM LIMEHOUSE TO THE ISLE OF DOGS

LIMEHOUSE. In the Commercial Road at Limehouse, where charcoal used to be unloaded during the 18th century, is St Anne's, another church that was designed by Hawksmoor ▲ *311*. Built between 1714 and 1730 in a slum quarter of the town, St Anne's is a typical Protestant English Baroque structure virtually without any curved lines. The church's unusually high tower recalls the Gothic bell-tower in Boston. In Limehouse, *The Grapes* was a pub that Charles Dickens knew particularly well, for it appears in the first chapter of his novel *Our Mutual Friend* (1865).

POPLAR. This is another community that evolved with the opening of the docks and naval shipyards, growing from five hundred inhabitants in 1801 to some fifty thousand in 1881. Skilled craftsmen lived here side by side with the impoverished and jobless. Poplar played a leading role in the development of Socialism under the leadership of men like George Lansbury, who led the Labour Party from 1931 to 1935, when Poplar was the poorest part of London.

ST MATTHIAS. This church was completed in 1654 in Poplar Street and is one of the oldest buildings in Docklands. Originally a private chapel belonging to the East India Company, it was restored and rebuilt in 1776, and again in the middle of the 19th century in "medieval Victorian" style using Kent stone. Since the church was closed in 1977, it has been broken into and badly vandalized. Only the outside can now be seen.

THE ISLE OF DOGS ★ . In the 19th century the Isle of Dogs (especially Millwall and Cubitt Town) was a center of naval shipbuilding, first for sail and then for steam. The biggest

QUEENHITHE
Queenhithe is one of the few docks upstream from London Bridge. Only small boats and barges could tie up here.

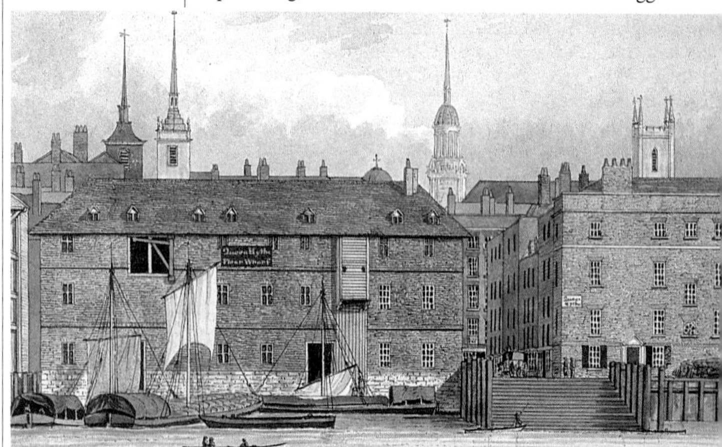

shipbuilders were all based here. In the mid-1860's Thomas Wright described the Isle of Dogs as the biggest naval shipyard on the whole river: "There are more than a dozen establishments. One of them, the giant Millwall Iron Works, employs around four thousand men and boys". This development is reflected in the population figures for the Isle of Dogs: this area was almost deserted at the beginning of the 19th century; by 1858 there were 5,000 inhabitants, and more than 21,000 from 1901 to 1939. In 1857 the Russell yards launched the *Great Eastern*, designed by Isambard Kingdom Brunel ▲ *332* and five times bigger than any other working steamship in the world.

Present developments. Since the middle of the 1980's the Isle of Dogs has again become the focal point of Docklands, and the area is right at the heart of its redevelopment. Forests of cranes no longer unload ships but instead help to build office blocks and luxury apartments on what has become one vast building site. Viewing the site as a whole, it is lacking in architectural unity and overall structure. Although some of the fine old warehouses have been preserved, the neighboring structures – glass and steel towers, and boat-shaped office buildings – are at odds with each other. As for the basins, these have now been turned into a marina. The transformation of the landscape has brought with it a radical change of employment. Any vacancies now are in the worlds of finance, newspaper publishing, or telecommunications, all beyond the reach of unqualified laborers and dockers, whose jobs are long gone. Without the ability to change their careers, and unable to afford homes, the laboring class has given way to the Yuppie class. The latter are the people best equipped to cope with the inflated prices of land speculators, who in turn are in business thanks to the generosity of a government that handed over Docklands to property developers without imposing adequate restrictions on them.

West India Dock
Two huge warehouses, rebuilt in 1824–5 by George Gwilt & Son, are all that remain from the great age of the docks.

The Isle of Dogs

"The river sweats
Oil and tar
The barges drift
With the turning tide
Red sails
Wide
To leeward, swing on
the heavy spar.
The barges wash
Drifting logs
Down Greenwich
reach
Past the Isle of
Dogs."

T. S. Eliot,
The Waste Land
(1922)

THE THAMES TUNNEL This was built in 1843 by a French immigrant, the engineer Marc Brunel (1769–1849), and was the first pedestrian underwater tunnel in the world. It is 1,200 feet long.

BILLINGSGATE MARKET. The famous fish market that used to be in Lower Thames Street in the City is now located on the Isle of Dogs, on the north quay of West India Quay. Billingsgate Market is set inside an enormous modern warehouse, which has been converted into a market hall equipped with huge cold stores.

CANARY WHARF. The best way to see the new Docklands developments is to walk the length of Canary Wharf to Heron Quays via West Ferry Road. The long pier is on an axis leading to West Ferry Circus. New office developments surround the 50-story Canary Wharf tower (officially named Canada Tower), which was the focus of the area when it was first developed. Beneath the tower is a huge shopping mall, complete with galleries and colonnades The Canary Wharf development, once faced with the threat of financial collapse, has enjoyed much success. It is the business and financial center of the new Docklands, and millions of square feet of offices have been created. Innovative architecture and infrastructure, such as the floating bridge by Future Systems, have given Canary Wharf a fresh, stimulating identity. This area has been made more accessible by the extension of the Jubilee Line, and it has been enlivened by many new restaurants in refurbished workshops and warehouses. In one of these warehouse complexes on West India Quay, just north of Canary Wharf, is the MUSEUM IN DOCKLANDS, which charts the history of the river, port and its peoples from Roman times to the present.

THE CANARY WHARF TOWER
Some Londoners are less than enthusiastic about this development. In 1988 Prince Charles considered the new Docklands a triumph of commercial opportunism over civic values. He thought it had too many mediocre new buildings, as well as a train that would be more suitable for a model village, all of which represented a poor contribution to the reconstruction of the capital.

THE DOCKLANDS LIGHT RAILWAY. This overhead railway, entirely operated by computer, was built to make the City only a matter of minutes away from Docklands. It serves the whole area, crossing the Isle of Dogs from the south and going almost as far as the Tower of London. But, in spite of all assurances, the space-age train has proved quite inadequate to cope with the number of passengers who use it.

MUDCHUTE PARK. It is interesting to visit Mudchute Park before you reach Island Gardens, and to see the farm that was opened in 1977 by Ted Johns. Visitors are usually surprised to find pigs, chickens and ponies, herds of cows, as well as a llama, so close to the urban development. There is also a riding school.

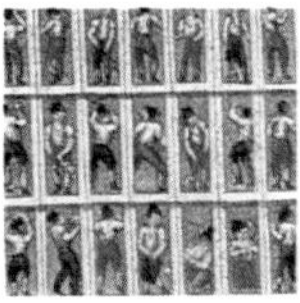

ISLAND GARDENS. This little park set on the south side of the Isle of Dogs has a beautiful view across the river to Greenwich and the Royal Naval Hospital (opposite, bottom right). In order to get there on foot, simply take the Greenwich Footway Tunnel, a pedestrian tunnel that was excavated under the river between 1897 and 1902.

THE SOUTH BANK

To get to the south bank and Rotherhithe from Island Gardens, walk through the tunnel that runs underneath the Thames and then catch a bus, or else go by boat. The south bank has not been spared the great urban alterations of Docklands. This is where London Bridge City was born in the 1980's, set between London Bridge and Tower Bridge.

SURREY DOCKS. These are the only docks on the south bank of the river, and they extend over 300 acres. The first basin opened in 1807. It had a monopoly of trade in Scandinavian timber, and it also dealt in wood pulp and grain. The various old docks on the south bank, faced with the expansion in coastal trade and in the railways, decided to merge in 1864, in imitation of the docks across the river, as the Surrey Commercial Docks Company. They finally closed in 1970. Since 1981 they have undergone radical alterations and have been transformed into a shopping and leisure center.

ROTHERHITHE ★. This was the old port from where the *Mayflower* set sail in 1620. On board were the first 102 colonists, 41 of them Puritans, who founded Plymouth in New England. The Howland Great Dock, ancestor of the future Surrey Docks, opened in 1696 in Rotherhithe for ship repairs and maintenance.

SURREY DOCKS FARM. To cover the distance from Rotherhithe to Bermondsey it is best to take a bus, stopping off first at Surrey Docks Farm, which sells only natural, chemical-free produce. The LAVENDER POND NATURE PARK was established in 1980–1 on the site of St Saviour's Dock.

BERMONDSEY. Two Victorian warehouses, at the boundary of Bermondsey and Southwark in Tooley Street, were built by Sir William Cubitt in 1857. They now

ST MARY'S, ROTHERHITHE
St Mary's (below left) was rebuilt in 1714. Its tower, erected around 1740, is the work of Launcelot Dowbiggin. Nearby, the street running through Shad Thames (below right) leads to the Design Museum ▲ 340.

THE "MAYFLOWER"
This ancient inn (bottom) was named after the ship moored nearby in 1620 that took the Pilgrim Fathers on their voyage to America. The ship's captain, Christopher Jones, is buried in St Mary's Church nearby.

"THE STEELYARD"
This painting of 1811 by George Shepherd depicts the old docks at work.

UNRECOGNIZABLE LONDON
The Czech painter Oskar Kokoschka (1886–1980) disliked the changes to London, which he painted so well. "If the face of London really is changing," he wrote in 1972, "to the point at which it will become unrecognizable, this is not simply the fault of two world wars, but above all it is the fault of speculators and builders. Thanks to them, Londoners will soon be completely ignorant of the organic growth of their city."

TOWER BRIDGE
seen from the docks.

house the shops of Hay's Galleria, under a cradle-vaulted roof of glass and steel. To the south, on Bermondsey Street, is the brightly colored building designed by Ricardo Legoretta to house the FASHION AND TEXTILE MUSEUM, created by designer Zandra Rhodes as the first museum in Britain dedicated to contemporary fashion and opened in 2003. Around Bermondsey Square is BERMONDSEY MARKET, full of fascinating antiques and bric-à-brac. The *Angel*, which was opened in the 15th century by the monks of Bermondsey, is an inn which was once the haunt of robbers and was frequented by the diarist Samuel Pepys (1633–1703), as well as by the navigator Captain James Cook (1728–79).

TOOLEY STREET. In the 13th and 14th centuries, rich merchants lived here. Some important clerics also had their London homes here, including the abbots of the Priory of St Augustine in Canterbury. St Olave's Grammar School was also founded here in 1560; one of the school's governors was Robert Harvard, the father of the man who subsequently founded the American university of that name. During the 19th century, between Tooley Street and the river, many groups of warehouses, such as Butler's Wharf, were built. ST OLAVE'S HOUSE is a remarkable Art Deco building (1831) on the site where the old church formerly stood. The young Keats lived in Dean Street, which is just off Tooley Street, while he was studying medicine at St Thomas's Hospital.

SHAD THAMES ● *78*. A huge renovation scheme has taken place in this area. The old warehouses have been completely refurbished and their façades carefully restored, with new buildings integrated. The result is a curious mixture of modern and 19th-century industrial architecture, with apartments, restaurants, shops and art galleries.

THE DESIGN MUSEUM ★. The world's second Design Museum (above) was opened by Terence Conran in 1989, between Shad Thames and the river. (The Cooper-Hewitt Design Museum in New York opened in 1976.) Its permanent collections are arranged in a clear, explanatory fashion, and among them is a collection of furniture ranging from classicism to Post-modernism. Temporary exhibitions are also held here. Beside the Design Museum is the BRANAM TEA AND COFFEE MUSEUM, which traces the history of two important London trades. There is also a collection of objects relating to tea and coffee ● *60*.

OUTSIDE THE CENTER

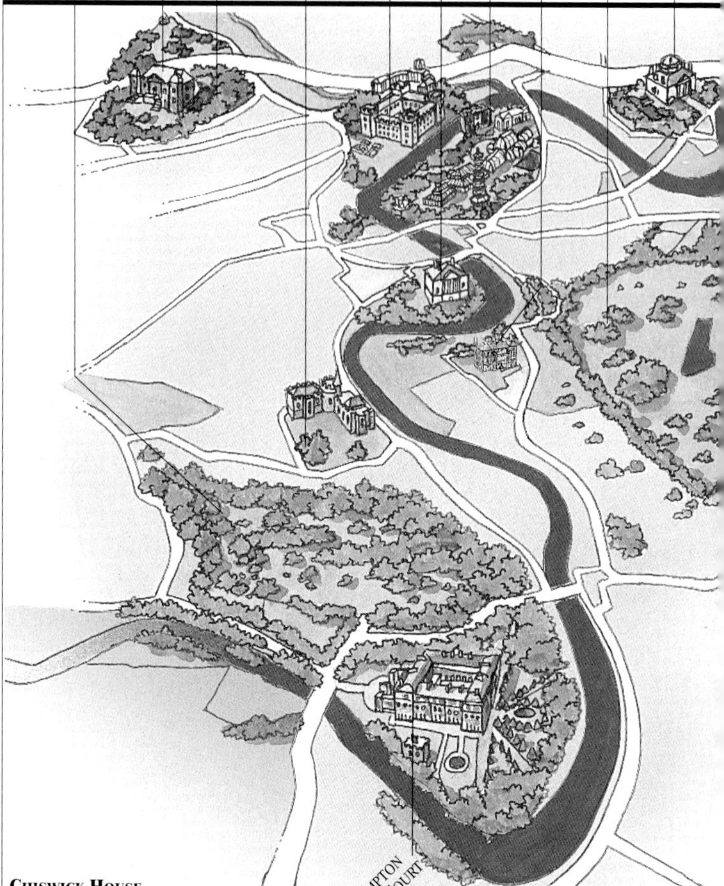

BUSHY PARK
OSTERLEY HOUSE
OSTERLEY PARK
STRAWBERRY HILL
SYON HOUSE
MARBLE HILL HOUSE
KEW PALACE
HAM HOUSE
RICHMOND PARK
CHISWICK HOUSE
HAMPTON COURT

CHISWICK HOUSE
Lord Burlington's elegant country villa was designed for entertaining rather than for living in, and the ground floor contained the earl's private apartments. At the foot of the monumental staircase are statues by Palladio and Inigo Jones.

PUTNEY

During the English Civil War ● *36*, in 1647, Oliver Cromwell held a council of war in this village southwest of London. It is a pleasant suburb on the south bank of the Thames, with streets of Victorian and Edwardian terraced houses.
PUTNEY BRIDGE. This bridge, which links Putney to Fulham, i also the starting point of the famous Boat Race: every year in March a rowing boat with a team of eight oarsmen from Oxford University (dark blue) races a boat with a team from Cambridge (light blue) over a 4½-mile course from here to Mortlake. The first race was held in June 1829 at Henley. There has only ever been one dead heat, in 1877; in 1912 bot boats capsized and the race had to be started again.

FULHAM

A 19th-century commentator described Fulham as "an orchard and kitchen garden on the north bank of the river". It remained largely working-class until the 1970's when it became a fashionable residential area.

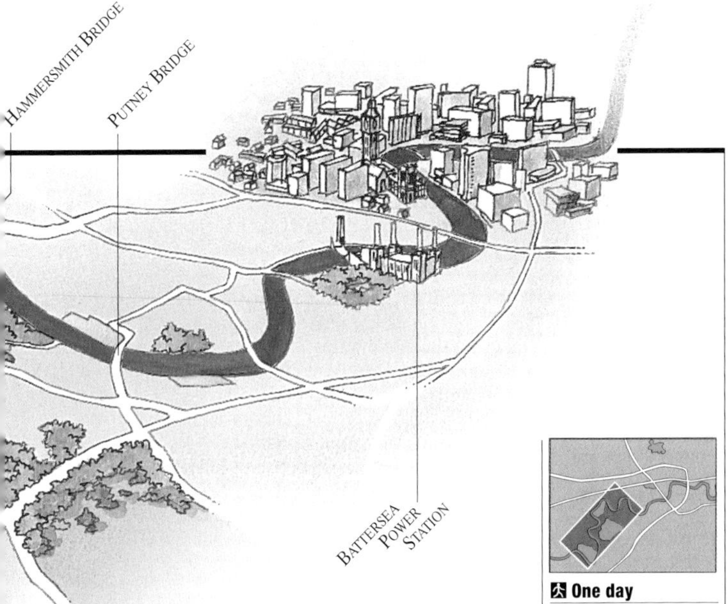

One day

ALL SAINTS CHURCH. The oldest part of this fine church is the 14th-century tower. Inside is a magnificent collection of monuments, most of them 17th-century. In the tower is a painting of 1690 showing a former beadle and sexton with his tankard of ale and churchwarden pipe. In the churchyard are eight tombs of former bishops of London.

BISHOP'S PARK. Once part of the land belonging to Fulham Palace, the residence of the bishops of London from the 7th century until 1973, this riverside park extends from Putney Bridge to Fulham Football Club.

CHISWICK

HOGARTH'S HOUSE. The artist William Hogarth ▲ *210, 292* bought what he called "a little country box by the Thames" in 1749. It became a museum in 1909, and contains a substantial collection of Hogarth prints and 18th-century furniture.

CHISWICK HOUSE. The 3rd earl of Burlington was an amateur architect and keen admirer of Palladio. He built this house between 1725 and 1729, modeled on Palladio's Rotonda (the Villa Capra) at Vicenza. Here he entertained such friends as Handel, Swift and Pope. Much of the interior decoration is the work of William Kent (1685–1748), like Burlington a disciple of Inigo Jones ▲ *272, 328*. On the ground floor is a series of engravings relating to the house. Upstairs are the elegant Blue and Red Velvet Rooms, and the central octagonal Dome Saloon, the ceiling of which forms the cupola which housed the earl's art collection.

SYON HOUSE ★

Situated on the bank of the Thames opposite Kew Gardens, this impressive house stands on the site of a 15th-century monastery. In the 16th century the

THE LONG GALLERY AT SYON HOUSE
Robert Adam designed this magnificent room, as well as some of its furniture. Its dimensions are unusual, 136 feet long and only 14 feet wide. It is decorated with landscapes by Zuccarelli.

Kew Gardens
In the background is the turreted Tudor façade of Syon House.

monastery became the property of the Duke of Somerset, Lord Protector in the reign of the boy-king Edward VI. It is now the property of the Percy family, the dukes of Northumberland, into whose hands it passed after Somerset's execution in 1552.

The house. Architect Robert Adam ▲ *268* was commissioned to improve the house in 1761. Though he retained the austere Tudor façade, the interior was redesigned on a grand and elaborate scale. The Great Hall has Doric columns, a black and white marble floor echoed in the diamond-patterned ceiling, and bronze copies of classical statues such as the Apollo Belvedere. The anteroom is heavily gilded and decorated in rich colors, with green marble pillars forming a screen at one end to create a square. The Long Gallery was intended as a "withdrawing room" for the ladies after dinner: pier-glass mirrors disguise the room's narrowness, and the ceiling has a crossline design. The Print Room contains family portraits and two fine 17th-century inlaid cabinets. There are many works of art in the house, principally by Lely, Van Dyck and Gainsborough.

The park. The gardens were laid out in the 18th century by "Capability" Brown. The Great Conservatory was completed in 1827; it contains exotic flowers, in particular orchids, and cacti. The west wing contains an aquarium. Also in the grounds is the London Butterfly House, a tropical conservatory where exotic butterflies are bred. The rose garden contains over four hundred varieties, and there are two mulberry trees planted by Somerset in the 16th century.

Kew Palace
Formerly known as the Dutch House, it was built by a 17th-century merchant of Dutch descent.

Royal Botanic Gardens, Kew ★

The world-famous botanical gardens at Kew, which face Syon across the Thames, have their root in a fondness for plants among members of the Hanoverian royal family. Augusta, dowager Princess of Wales, enjoyed "botanizing" and, in 1759, laid out some of her estate at Kew as a small botanic

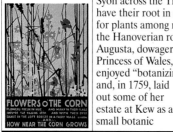

garden. She appointed William Aiton her head gardener, and Sir William Chambers to design some buildings in the grounds, including the lovely Orangery, and the striking ten-story, octagonal Chinese Pagoda. This last was apparently a "surprise" he conceived for her. The dowager princess's son and daughter-in-law, George III and Queen Charlotte, combined the neighboring estate of Richmond with Kew on her death in 1772. They encouraged Sir Joseph Banks, the naturalist, to superintend the botanic garden, and he, in turn, encouraged collectors to search out plants of interest all over the globe. "Capability" Brown directed the landscaping, at George III's request. The king and queen summered at Kew at the White House. Their thirteen children, tutors and governesses were lodged in houses round about, including some on Kew Green. The "Dutch House", or Kew Palace, built in 1631 by a merchant of Dutch extraction, was first an annex to the White House, then a favored residence of the king and queen when the White House was demolished in 1802. It was a domestic, and deliberately simple, existence, and Kew Palace is "plain as a dainty pikestaff" inside. (The Queen's Garden behind is now planted in 17th-century manner, with tulips, pleached hornbeams, lavender and bergamot.) The princesses kept their pets in a Royal Menagerie, while Queen Charlotte had a cottage orné with thatched roof built, where she often took tea, in the old Richmond grounds. In 1805 Princess Elizabeth designed the decorative scheme of the upper "Picnic Room" in Queen Charlotte's Cottage, where convolvulus and nasturtiums cling to bamboo on a leaf-green background. Framed Hogarth prints ▲ *210* decorate the Print Room below. Queen Victoria kept this cottage and the surrounding acres of woodland till 1897, when she gave it to the public to commemorate her Diamond Jubilee. The woods are a mass of bluebells in late spring. Meanwhile, the Royal Botanic Garden was growing apace, after the state acquired it in 1840. Sir William Hooker was the first appointed director, in 1841, and he established the museums and departments of Economic Botany (1847), the Herbarium and Library (1822). Hooker's son, Joseph, succeeded him as director, and opened the Jodrell Laboratory in 1876. The dowager princess of Wales' botanic garden had occupied 7 acres. The gardens now cover more than 300 acres, and the collection has over thirty thousand different types of plant.

A TOUR OF KEW GARDENS. You should begin at Decimus Burton's 1845 wrought-iron main gates, although the lion and unicorn which originally adorned them have been removed to a side gate. Among the trees in the Broad Walk leading into the gardens are some, including a maidenhair tree, which date from the dowager Princess of Wales' botanic garden. First comes Chambers' Orangery, then, on the river side, Kew Palace. The Rhododendron Dell, resplendent with oaks, was dug out by a company of Staffordshire militia in 1773, as part

QUEEN CHARLOTTE'S SUMMERHOUSE
Queen Charlotte loved to hold tea parties in this small, thatched cottage, built for her around 1771. It is reminiscent of Marie-Antoinette's "Petit Trianon" at Versailles.

THE CHINESE PAGODA
The pagoda (above and opposite), which is purely decorative in function, initiated a fashion for Chinese architecture. It may have been partly inspired by the Chanteloup pagoda constructed around the same time for the Duc de Choiseul near Amboise in the Loire

TEMPERATE HOUSE
Decimus Burton's glasshouse is more solidly built and conventional than the more ornamental Palm house.

of "Capability" Brown's landscaping scheme. The grassy paths past the artificial lake and through the Pinetum lead on toward a superb view across the Thames of Isleworth and Syon. Leaving the riverbank, go through the Diamond Jubilee woodland, past the cottage, to the southeast corner of the gardens and the pagoda. (Chambers, who took his inspiration for the folly from an earlier journey to Canton, made fashionable the use of Chinese motifs in garden architecture.) Before losing yourself in the series of glasshouses to come, visit a remarkable one-woman show, the Marianne North Gallery. Miss North, a redoutable Victorian, traveled the world to paint natural vegetation, and then presented 832 of her vivid botanical oil paintings to the gardens, together with a gallery to house them.

THE TEMPERATE HOUSE. Largest of all the glasshouses and the most spectacular, this houses plants from subtropical areas of the world – among them a Chilean wine palm, raised from seed collected in Chile in 1846, which threatens to raise the roof. The Temperate House, the late masterpiece of Decimus Burton, was built in stages between 1860 and 1899, and is planted in geographical sections. The northern wing of the Temperate House contains plants from Asia; the north octagon, from New Zealand and the Pacific Islands; the south octagon contains South African heaths and proteas. The central area is a veritable forest of trees, best seen by ascending the giddy heights to Burton's galleries above. The Temperate House becomes crowded in winter, on account of its delightfully effective heating system. The Australia House next door was built in 1952 of aluminum.

HOLLY WALK. North from the Temperate House lies the decorative Holly Walk, Berberis Dell, and King William's Temple, wherein are inscribed the names of British military victories – oddly, since William IV was known as the

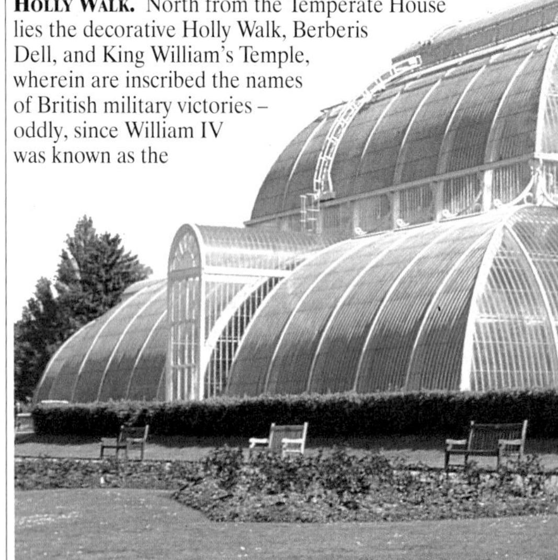

PALM HOUSE
Tropical plants are cultivated here. The atmosphere is kept at a constant 26 degrees centigrade.

"Sailor King". The British Columbia Loggers' Association donated the flagpole – made from a single piece of Douglas fir.

The Palm House. This amazed the Victorian public, with its ballooning ironwork and its exotic collection of plants from the tropical world. Rubber plants, banana trees, and a wealth of palms are still cultivated within, as are rare crops like cycads, in danger of extinction in their natural habitat. Decimus Burton and the engineer Richard Turner – who built the Waterlily House next door – collaborated to construct the house between 1844 and 1848. Condensation and heat conspired at last to endanger its fabric, and it was successfully dismantled and rebuilt between 1984 and 1989. An innovation is the display of tropical marine vegetation in a series of tanks beneath the Palm House.

The Waterlily House. To the north, steamiest of all the glasshouses, this was originally built in 1852 to house the giant Amazonian waterlily, now grown in the Princess of Wales Conservatory. Papyrus and the sacred lotus are grown here now, and curiosities of the cucumber family – the bottle gourd and loofah – climb the inner walls. The Palm House Pond in front of the Palm House boasts a fountain and statue (1826) of *Hercules and Achelous*, which makes an excellent evening perch for fishing herons. Behind the Palm House are the formal rose gardens.The area between the Palm House Pond and the main gate, completing the circular tour, is dense with research and display projects, ancient and innovative. The Princess of Wales Conservatory – the name of which honors also the dowager princess – makes use of the latest glasshouse technology to house plants from varied climes under one roof. The Alpine House (1981) is landscaped within a pyramidal structure. These two glasshouses jostle the Herbaceous Area, where Chambers' Temple of Aeolus (rebuilt by Decimus Burton in 1845) overlooks the Woodland Garden. Close to the Aquatic Garden

Campsis grandiflora
One of the thirty thousand species of plants at Kew Gardens.

A tropical environment
The heat and humidity of the Palm House favored the plants it contained, but damaged its structure, which was composed of a cast iron framework and sheets of glass.

Entrance to Osterley House.

and Grass Garden are the Order Beds, where students since Sir Joseph Hooker's time have been taught taxonomy, or how to identify, classify and understand plants. (The Herbarium on Kew Green, housing six million preserved specimens and the Jodrell Laboratory are complementary to the Order Beds.) Coming full circle back to the main gate – through the Duke's Garden with Cambridge Cottage, once the Duke of Cambridge's house, and the Kew Gardens Gallery – the Botanic Gardens honor the first of their enthusiastic superintendents with the Sir Joseph Banks Building and Landscape. This exciting, earth-covered, and energy-conserving building houses the Economic Botany Collection and Library. The building has a spectacular exhibition of the interdependence between man and plant life, which it is the work of the scientists and botanists at Kew to promote.

OSTERLEY PARK ★

Delightfully set among serpentine lakes, woodland walks, and arable land, Osterley House is itself an adornment to the landscape. (The noise from the nearby M4 motorway and Heathrow flight path overhead must be ignored.) The original four-turreted house was completed for Sir Thomas Gresham ▲ *151*, founder of the Royal Exchange, in 1575. The 16th-century stable block of soft red Tudor brick still stands. Robert Adam closed the front of Gresham's house in 1761 for another merchant prince, Robert Child of Child's Bank, with one of the finest porticos in England. The architect, Sir William Chambers ▲ *269*, *280*, had earlier advised Child on the landscaping which we see today, and erected the Doric Temple of Pan in the grounds. Robert Child died in 1763, but his brother, Francis, retained Adam to continue his remodeling of the 16th-century house, and to instal a great Orangery – burnt down in 1950 – and other buildings in the grounds. The resulting country villa is one of Adam's most pleasing schemes, as ever owing much to classical models and motifs, and employing his favorite master-craftsmen. The design and execution of a door-lock were as important to Adam as those of a ceiling. The State Bed, its dome crowned with silk flowers where once they were cut, is a masterpiece. The hall has a Roman vestibule as its model

'ohn Linnell carved the bookcases in the library; Pietro 3orgnis hand-painted the spidery decorations in the Etruscan Room. In the Long Gallery, fronting the Great Meadow, look out for a marigold, the symbol of Child's Bank, woven into he upholstery of a sofa. Francis Child was disappointed in his laughter, who eloped with Lord Westmorland to Gretna Green, where they were married without parental consent. The estate passed to her eldest daughter, Sarah Sophia, and hus into the Jersey family, when she married the earl. The ninth earl gave the house and furniture to the National Trust, and since then Osterley, with its 18th-century cedars of Lebanon, walks and lakes, has been a favorite weekend resort for Londoners.

STRAWBERRY HILL
A general view of Horace Walpole's remarkable Gothic creation.

THE GALLERY, STRAWBERRY HILL
Horace Walpole moved here in 1747. He called it "a little plaything of a house,

the prettiest bauble you ever did see". Its Gothic gallery has papier-mâché vaulting copied from Henry VII's chapel at Westminster, with niches modeled on a tomb in Canterbury cathedral.

TWICKENHAM ★

'ust across Richmond Bridge is the town of Twickenham, which has some fine 17th-century houses. The future King Louis Philippe (1830–48) of France (cousin to Louis XVI) took refuge here from Napoleon in the early 19th century, and again after the revolution of 1848, which deposed him.
A HIVE OF CULTURE. The country village of Twickenham on he outskirts of London became fashionable in the 18th century, and several members of the aristocracy built houses here. It also drew writers and painters such as the chronicler Horace Walpole, painters Godfrey Kneller and J.M.W. Turner, and the poet Alexander Pope (1688–1744) ▲ *155*. The latter lived on the bank of the Thames in Pope's Villa from 1719 until his death. It was later demolished. In 1876 Van Gogh lived at 160 Twickenham Road. Today Twickenham is best known as the home of rugby football.
STRAWBERRY HILL. An 18th-century house that is totally different from the classical buildings of the period, Strawberry Hill was created between 1749 and 1766 by the writer Horace Walpole (1717–97), fourth earl of Orford. He transformed a modest cottage into a miniature Gothic castle. The style is eclectic, reproducing ideas from Gothic buildings all over Europe: the fireplace in the Beauclerc Room is modeled on Edward the Confessor's tomb at Westminster ▲ *137*, and the staircase balustrade is copied from Rouen Cathedral. The house is now a teacher-training college, and has been kept in excellent condition.

MARBLE HILL HOUSE
Its design was influenced by Inigo Jones.

MARBLE HILL HOUSE

Built between 1724 and 1729 by Roger Morris to designs by Lord Herbert, Marble Hill House (above) was the home of the future George II's mistress, Henrietta Howard, who later became countess of Suffolk. The three-story Palladian building has been restored after falling into disuse, and there are paintings by Hogarth, Godfrey Kneller and others.

HAM HOUSE
One of the 17th-century doorways.

HAM HOUSE AND GROUNDS

Known as "Sleeping Beauty House", this 17th-century house is a classic example of the type of summer residence built on the outskirts of London by the nobility of that time. Its contents are skillfully presented by the Victoria and Albert Museum. The fabric, furnishings and decoration of the house have been little altered since the 1670's, when Elizabeth countess of Dysart and her husband, the duke of Lauderdale, first set their luxurious stamp on the house, built in 1610. They employed the joiner Thomas Carter to create the Grand Staircase. The balustrade is a marvel of carved and pierced panels, featuring trophies of arms. Franz Cleyn, director of the nearby Mortlake tapestry works, was probably employed to supervise the decoration of the North Front apartments. In the holiday atmosphere that followed Charles II's Restoration, the Lauderdales employed the architect William Sanwell to add a South Front, to include state apartments on the upper floor, decorated for the 1680 visit of Charles II's queen, Catherine of Braganza, and sumptuous private apartments for their own use on the ground floor. Elizabeth Lauderdale's son, Lyonel Tollemache, earl of Dysart, was at first hard pressed to make ends meet following her improvements, let alone make alterations. Later generations of Dysarts also chose to leave well alone, with happy results for the late 20th-century visitor. Almost all the paintings, including portraits by Lely and seascapes by Van der Velde, and furniture that is now on view including adjustable "sleeping chairs" – for the duke's gout – belong to the house. Woolen cut velvet upholstery survives from the 1630's in the Yellow Satin Dressing Room; in the Restoration Library Closet, the blue damask – brownish now – and the embroidered blue velvet frames date from the 1670's. (The library itself, including works that were printed by Caxton and Wynkyn de Worde, was sold in the 1930's.) In the Museum Room, a section of gilded leather hangings ornamented with flowers and cherubs is on show. The National Trust acquired the house and grounds in 1948. In one of the few later alterations to have been made, an avenue which led from the North Front entrance to a landing stage on the Thames was removed. While the V&A administers the house, it is the Trust which restored the Ham House gardens in 1975 to their appearance as created by the Lauderdales, with hornbeam arbors and lavender beds. The summerhouses in the Wilderness which forms a *patte d'oie* before the South Gates replicate those in a 1737 engraving.

STATUE IN THE GARDENS
The 17th-century garden of Ham House is a great rarity. Most formal gardens were destroyed when more natural garden landscapes became fashionable.

MEDALLIONS OF HAM HOUSE
Carved medallions decorate the façade on either side of the entrance.

HAM HOUSE
The house stayed in the family of the Earls of Dysart from 1637 until 1948. It is now in the care of the Victoria and Albert Museum ▲ *229*.

Richmond Bridge in 1780, three years after its completion.

RICHMOND-UPON-THAMES ★

The beautiful town of Richmond was the summer residence of the kings of England in Plantagenet times. Henry VII and Elizabeth I both died here. Today Londoners love its elegant buildings, attractive shops and peaceful riverside walks, and its green has been called the finest in England. Historic pubs such as *The Three Pigeons* (1735) at 87 Petersham Street, and *The Roebuck* (1738) at 130 Richmond Hill, enjoy fine views over the Thames valley; and at Richmond visitors should taste "*Maids of Honour*", a local specialty and a favorite cake of Henry VIII (the recipe remains a secret). Maids of Honour Row is an attractive terrace of four 18th-century red-brick houses built by the future George II to house his wife's personal attendants.

RICHMOND PARK ■ *24.* East of the town is this magnificent park (right), which was once a royal hunting ground enclosed by Charles I. It covers 2,470 acres, making it the largest park in Greater London. There are several lakes, medieval oak trees, and around six hundred red and fallow deer. From the top of the Henry VIII mound, the magnificent view extends from Windsor Castle to St Paul's Cathedral ▲ *170.*

RICHMOND BRIDGE. James Paine completed the five-arched bridge in 1777 to replace an earlier horse ferry. A toll was payable to cross it until 1859. It is the oldest bridge still standing across the Thames in Greater London, though it was widened in 1937.

WHITE LODGE. A former royal hunting lodge built in 1727 in Richmond Park, the Palladian-style White Lodge has housed the junior department of the Royal Ballet School since 1955. In 1894 the future Edward VIII (later Duke of Windsor) was born here to Queen Mary and George V.

RICHMOND HILL. From the top of the hill, the view of the Thames meandering in the valley below has been called the finest in all England. Several painters have been inspired by this superb landscape, among them Joshua Reynolds, who lived at Wick House on Richmond Hill for twenty years until his death in 1792. In the 19th century the view was painted by two of the greatest English landscape artists, Turner ▲ *215–17* and Constable ▲ *214.*

A REFUGE FOR FRENCH ÉMIGRÉS
During the French Revolution and the reign of Napoleon which followed it, a number of aristocrats managed to escape and find refuge here. The most important were the Duc d'Orléans and his family, which included the future King Louis Philippe.

RICHMOND
"We came to Richmond . . . our destination there was a house by the Green: a staid old house, where hoops and powder and patches, embroidered coats, rolled stockings, ruffles and swords, had had their court days many a time."
Charles Dickens, *Great Expectations*

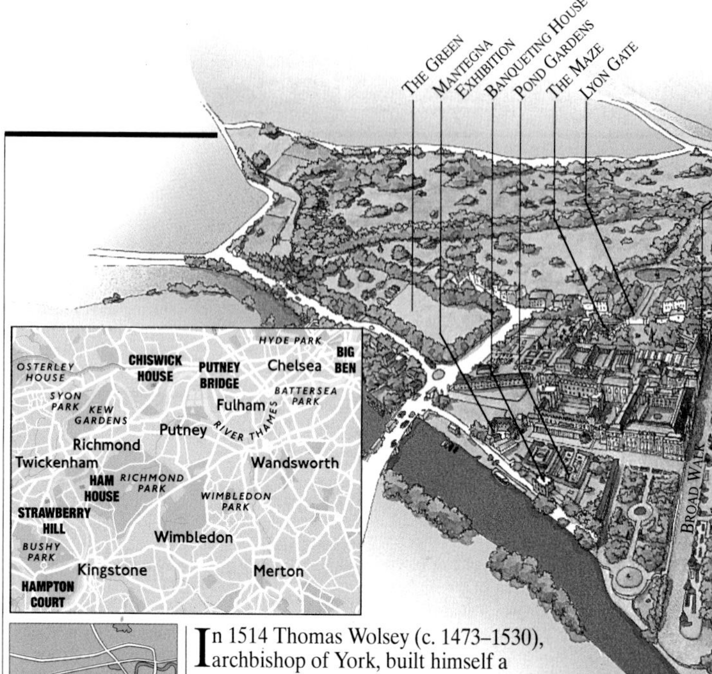

One day

The home of kings
Hampton Court is on the Thames about 14 miles southwest of London. It was a favorite residence of kings and queens from the 16th to the 18th centuries. Queen Victoria preferred Windsor Castle ▲ *356*, and opened Hampton Court to the public in 1838.

In 1514 Thomas Wolsey (c. 1473–1530), archbishop of York, built himself a magnificent palace at Hampton Court. In 1525, well aware of the delicacy of his position (Henry VIII had broken away from Rome and proclaimed himself head of the Church of England), Wolsey took the step of offering Hampton Court to the king. But it was too late: in spite of his generosity, all his property was forfeited to the crown and he died soon after.

Three palaces in one. Hampton Court is an English Renaissance building, initially constructed around two courtyards, Base Court and Clock Court. The Round Kitchen Court was added later. The red-brick building of the palace has white crenellation and lead-covered towers, and the interior decoration is magnificent, as witness the ceilings of the offices and apartments that Wolsey commissioned for his own use. Henry VIII decided to enlarge it. Between 1532 and 1535 Wolsey's original hall was rebuilt, the chapel was completed, and a suite of royal apartments was added (of which only the Great Watching Chamber remains). The kitchens too had to be enlarged to accommodate the royal household; and later the king added another room and a tennis court on the west side. In 1689 William of Orange and Queen Mary commissioned Wren ▲ *171–5* to rebuild the palace, which was then decorated by Englishmen James Thornhill, Caius Cibber, Grinling Gibbons ▲ *241, 274* and William Emmett, the Frenchman Louis Laguerre and the Neapolitan Antonio Verrio. After the demolition of Henry VIII's state apartments three major projects were built in the Baroque style: Fountain Court, replacing the former Green Court; the Cartoon Gallery, and the Queen's Wing in the

THE EAST FAÇADE
This is one of the grandiose alterations made by Sir Christopher Wren ● *70*, ▲ *171*. It is broken into two parts by a portico crowned with a pediment carved by Caius Cibber in 1696, and opens on to the gardens.

east and the north. The king's private apartments were altered, and finally the long façade on the east side was added.

THE TROPHY GATE. Constructed in the mid-18th century, the Trophy Gate is the main entrance to the palace.

THE GREAT GATEHOUSE. This majestic brick pavilion was built by Wolsey. The two wings leading back were added by Henry VIII in 1536. The mythical beasts beside the entry bridge date from 1950.

BASE COURT. The present palace still reflects Wolsey's original plans. This courtyard, with its crenellated walls, is where the servants' quarters once were.

CLOCK COURT. With the Great Hall on its north side, the courtyard gets its name from the Astronomical Clock that decorates the gateway. The Ionic colonnade on the south side is by Christopher Wren.

FOUNTAIN COURT. Wren drew upon the Château of Versailles for the design of this four-story court, combining Portland stone with pale orange brick. The bull's-eye windows on the façade are covered with monochrome medallions by Laguerre illustrating the Labors of Hercules.

THE ROUND KITCHEN COURT AND THE CHAPEL COURT. The first was built by Wolsey and the second by Wren. Chapel Court was altered in the 18th century.

THE KING'S APARTMENTS. The entrance is on the south side of

"Hampton Court is a great garden in the French style, laid out in the reign of William III . . . but the English taste is also apparent in the flower beds full of roses climbing slender trellises and the rows of flowers. Ducks and swans swim in the water and water-lilies open their satiny petals. The old trees are propped up in metal supports; when they die, so as not to lose them completely, great urns are made out of their trunks. Obviously they are loved and respected."
Notes sur l'Angleterre
Hippolyte Taine

▲ Hampton Court Palace

The Astronomical Clock
This is on the façade of Anne Boleyn's Gateway which leads into Clock Court, and was made by Nicholas Oursian. It tells the time, day, month, the number of days since the start of the year, the phases of the moon, and even the hours of high tide at London Bridge. Being made before Copernicus and Galileo, it also shows the sun revolving round the earth.

The Tudor chimneys
Hampton Court is topped with lead-domed towers as well as ornamental brick chimneys.

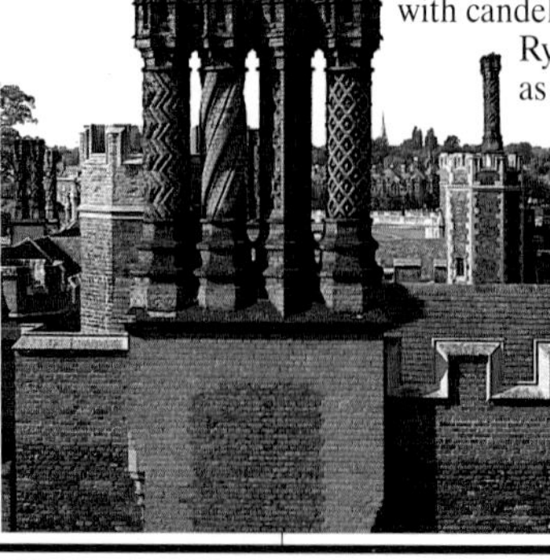

Clock Court, from where the visitor climbs the King's Staircase and crosses the guardroom. The ceiling of William III's State Bedroom is the work of Verrio. A corner staircase leads from the King's Study to the Queen's Gallery. Access from the king's apartments to those of the queen is by the Communication Gallery, running the entire length of Fountain Court, where *The Beauties of Windsor* by Sir Peter Lely are exhibited, eleven paintings of ladies of the court of Charles II.

The Cartoon Gallery. This is on the south side overlooking Fountain Court. Wren designed it expressly to house the Raphael cartoons (now in the Victoria and Albert Museum), purchased by Charles I in 1632. Access to the Queen's Wing, a suite of twenty rooms, partly decorated in the reign of Queen Anne (1702–14), is by the Queen's State Staircase, the work of Jean Tijou. The Queen's Gallery is decorated with a cornice by Grinling Gibbons. To the north is the Queen's Bedchamber with a ceiling by James Thornhill (1715), and the Queen's Drawing Room decorated by Verrio. Its large bay window looks on to Great Fountain Garden.

Wolsey's Closet. The ceilings of this room and also of Wolsey's apartments, which bear his coat of arms, as well as the carved "linen-fold" paneling, are a reminder of the refined and costly decoration the palace enjoyed under its first owner.

The Great Watching Chamber. The large guardroom is at the entrance to Henry VIII's state apartments, and is all that remains of them. Its cloisonné ceiling is decorated with carved oak pendants and the arms of the Tudor monarchs in papier-mâché. The Great Hall was built in the reign of Henry VIII and has a carved wood ceiling in English style by James Nedeham. Many other features of the hall, decorated with candelabra and acanthus leaves carved by R. Rydge, are in Italian Renaissance style. Just as they would have been in Henry VIII's reign, the walls are hung with tapestries, here illustrating the biblical story of Abraham. The 19th-century stained glass is by Thomas Willement.

The Tudor kitchens. In 1529 Henry VIII added another room to Wolsey's kitchen with three more fireplaces, as well as an additional one specially for cooking fish. An illuminated model shows the long route followed by those carrying the cooked food, which finally ascended an

THE SOUTH FAÇADE
The façade was decorated with the arms of Wolsey, still to be seen above Anne Boleyn's Gateway in Clock Court, and with terracotta medallions by the Florentine Giovanni da Maiano depicting Roman emperors. These were the first examples of the Italian Renaissance in England.

oak staircase to the HORN ROOM, where it waited before being served up in the Great Hall.

THE GARDENS. The gardens owe their present appearance to work done at the time of Charles II (r. 1660–85) and then William III (r. 1689–1702). Charles II had them landscaped after the French models of Le Nôtre: the goose-foot pattern and a canal in front of Wren's façade recall the Palace of Versailles. William III finished the canal by adding another semicircular section lined with lime trees specially imported from Holland. The PRIVY GARDEN is on the south side of the palace by the river, from which it is separated by twelve 17th-century wrought-iron grille panels by Jean Tijou. Beside the Privy Garden a conservatory houses the GREAT VINE, grown from a single root planted in 1768. The park also contains the famous maze and, at its northeastern end, an ice-house. The southern part is now a golf course.

THE BANQUETING HOUSE AND ORANGERY. These were both built by Sir Christopher Wren. The former, located near the site of the old Water Gallery (16th century) was decorated by Antonio Verrio, and in the latter are nine magnificent canvases painted by Andrea Mantegna in 1492, illustrating the *Triumph of Caesar*. These were collected originally by Charles I.

THE GOTHIC HALL
This gallery runs along the north and east sides of the Round Kitchen Court, and is supposed to be haunted by the ghost of Henry VIII's fifth wife, Catharine Howard, beheaded in 1542.

THE CHAPEL
In 1536 Henry VIII added a carved wooden ceiling to Wolsey's chapel. The rest of the decoration including the furniture is by Wren, except for the magnificent reredos by Grinling Gibbons.

THE KING'S STAIRCASE
This painting by W.H. Pyne (1819) shows Verrio's decorations glorifying William and Mary, and Tijou's fine staircase.

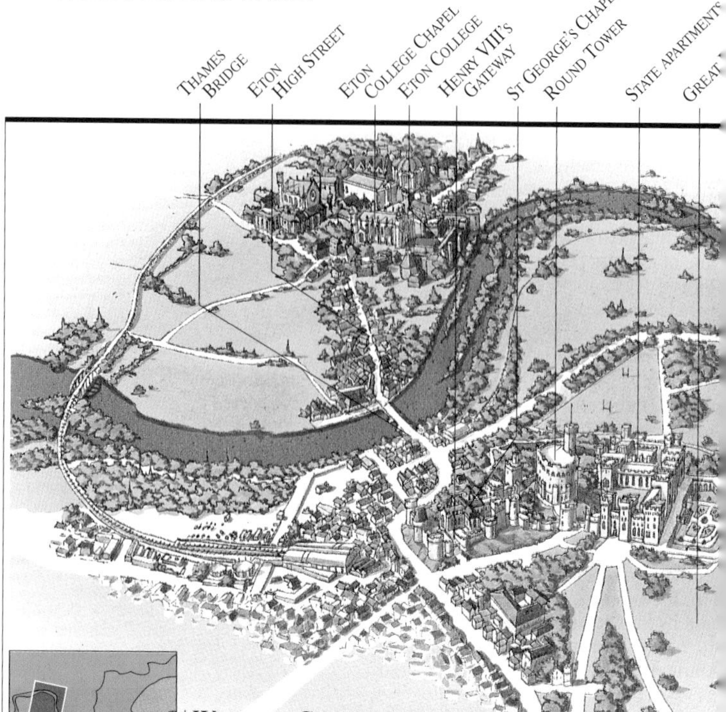

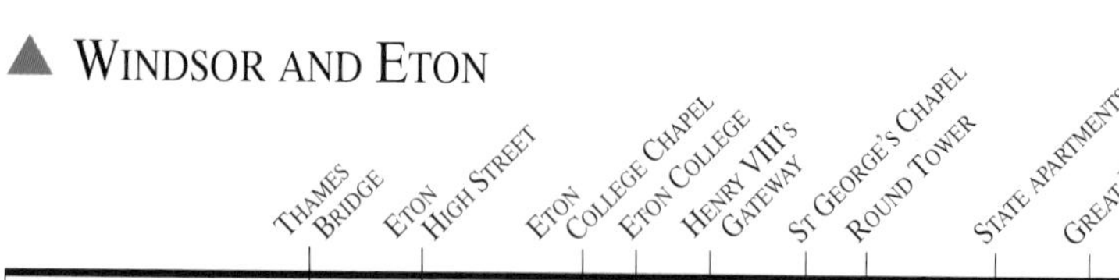

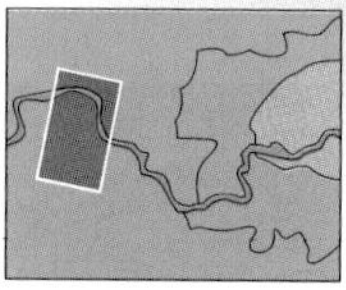

One day

CHANGING OF THE GUARD
Diverse regiments, including the Grenadier Guards raised by Charles II in exile, guard the castle and Queen Elizabeth II, just as Yeomen of the Guard used to guard Queen Elizabeth I. When the queen is in summer residence, the ceremony takes place in the Quadrangle. In the winter months the soldiers stamp to attention on the parade ground by the Henry VIII Gate.

WINDSOR CASTLE

Windsor Castle owes its distinctive castellated casing to George IV and his architect Jeffrey Wyatville, who homogenized the disparate medieval, Tudor and Stuart precincts in the 1820's. Among other bold flights of fancy, Wyatville added 30 feet in height and battlements to the Round Tower. (The royal standard flies from the tower when the queen is in residence; the Union Jack does so at other times.) The castle and precincts, however, maintain their medieval divisions of Lower Ward, Middle Ward and Upper Ward. William the Conqueror first selected the site for a wooden fortress in 1070; Henry II rebuilt his fortress in stone a century later, and added five rounded towers, including the Curfew Tower in Lower Ward, to the perimeter walls. Edward III, who founded the Order of the Garter, extended the royal apartments in Upper Ward to include St George's Hall (1362–5), where the Knights of the Garter banqueted. Edward IV founded St George's College and built St George's Chapel, which dominates Lower Ward, with Horseshoe Cloisters (1478–81), facing the Great West Door, to accommodate the clergy. The houses are occupied today by members of the staff of St George's Chapel, including the men of the choir. (The boy choristers come from

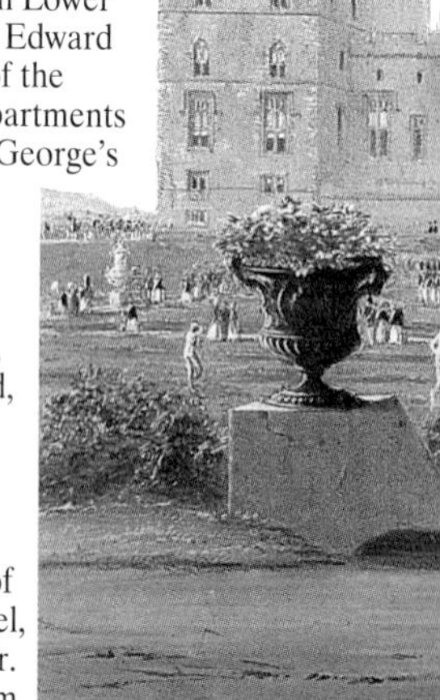

St George's Choir School, below the castle wall.) Henry VIII provided the castle entrance, or Henry VIII Gate, in 1511. His daughter Queen Mary added to the Military Knights' lodgings in Lower Ward, begun by Edward III. (The military, originally Poor Knights of St George, represent the absent Knights of the Garter in their choir stalls at church services.) Charles II remodeled the royal apartments (1675–83) in Upper Ward magnificently. George III (r. 1760–1820) rescued the castle from a period of neglect thereafter, and began, with James Wyatt, a Gothicizing process, which his son, George IV, and Wyatt's nephew, Jeffrey, pursued to dizzy heights. Windsor Castle is an incomparable treasure house. It houses the bulk of the Royal Collection, which includes the Royal Library, Print Room, Royal Archives, and paintings, furniture, armor, and hangings of inestimable value.

The fire of November 1992. The castle and its treasures were threatened with destruction in November 1992 when a fire began in the Queen's private chapel. It spread rapidly through the state apartments, and raged for twenty-four hours. Most moveable treasures were carried to safety, and the castle is today restored, but the damage was considerable.

A TOUR OF THE CASTLE

St George's Chapel. The burial place of ten monarchs, and spiritual home of the Order of the Garter. Here the queen and other members of the Order process, in Garter robes from the castle, for an annual June service. Above the stalls in the choir where the Knights of the Order take their places,

View of Windsor Castle from the river
"The most romantic castle in the world", according to Samuel Pepys. Salisbury Tower and Henry VIII Gate (below) have formed the principal entrance to the castle since the 16th century.

18th-century watercolors show the gate clogged by water-carts and chimney-sweeps.

The East Terrace Garden, by Joseph Nash c. 1840, showing Windsor in Victorian holiday mood. The 1992 fire swept through this section of the castle.

Shown above from left to right are the King's Audience Chamber, Old Guards' Chamber, the Ball Room and King's Drawing Room, from W.H. Pyne's *Royal Residences* (1819).

their individual banner, helmet and crest hang all year round. Edward IV founded St George's Chapel in 1475, probably in emulation of Eton College Chapel, that other jewel of Perpendicular Gothic. Henry VII completed the nave, and added the exquisite stone vaulted ceiling. A plate in the floor records the discovery of the tombs of Henry VIII, Jane Seymour and Charles I. Beneath the choir there also lies a vault, containing the coffins of many members of the Hanoverian royal family. Princess Charlotte, heir presumptive, who died in childbirth in 1817, is commemorated in a flowing marble tableau by the Great West Door. Among many other items of interest on show in the chapel is a rare "treacle" Bible, in which the word "balm" is rendered as "treacle".

ALBERT MEMORIAL CHAPEL. Following the death of Prince Albert, her consort, in 1861, Queen Victoria ordered Edward III's disused chapel of St George to be redecorated as a temporary resting-place for his tomb. (It was later moved to the Frogmore Mausoleum.) Sir George Gilbert Scott created the extravagantly decorated interior (1863–73), which now also houses Alfred Gilbert's tomb of the duke of Clarence, who died in 1892. Illustrated marble panels line the walls, the vaulted ceiling is decorated with

GEORGE III
He was known as the "Farmer King" because of his enthusiasm for agriculture. His equerries complained that he would ride 30 miles in a day to inspect a Berkshire neighbor's estate.

NORTH TERRACE, WINDSOR CASTLE

Venetian glass mosaic, and the stained glass in the south windows depict ancestors of Prince Albert.

Round Tower. William the Conqueror's wooden Round Tower originally stood on the mound of the Round Tower, which now houses the Royal Archives and Royal Photograph Collection. The mound itself is made of spoil dug in the 1070's from the moat, where there is now a Moated Garden, made in the 1910's by a governor of the castle. Above the Moated Garden may be seen the only two 17th-century windows in the castle to escape Hanoverian Gothicizing.

North Terrace. This was laid out by Henry VIII on a bluff above the Thames, commanding fine views of the river, Eton Chapel and the Chiltern hills. During the 18th century George III, Queen Charlotte, and their prodigious family used to walk on the castle terraces to provide an example to the nation of marital and domestic harmony. George III later occupied apartments overlooking the North Terrace, when his mind was deranged. His son acted as regent from 1811 until his death in 1820. On the North Terrace is the entrance to the gallery housing Queen Mary's Dolls' House and also to the state apartments.

State apartments. Charles II largely remodeled this area in the 1670's, employing the architect Hugh May, the master wood-carver Grinling Gibbons ▲ *274*, *355*, and the artist Antonio Verrio, to embellish the apartments. The King's Dining Room, of all the king's suite – otherwise comprising the King's Drawing Room, state bedchamber, Dressing Room, and closet – best display the work of Gibbons and Verrio. Charles II's queen consort, Catherine of Braganza, occupied the apartments known as the Queen's Drawing Room, the Ballroom, Audience, Presence and Guard Chambers. (Her state bedroom is now occupied by the Royal Library.) These lie on the southern, sunny side overlooking the Quadrangle, where the Changing of the Guard takes place when the queen is in residence. George IV confirmed the shifted focus of the castle when he linked the private apartments, first occupied by his mother and sisters, and still occupied today by the queen and royal family, by a Grand Corridor, on the eastern and southern side of the Quadrangle. Sir Jeffrey Wyatville also transformed many of

Castle views
The pictures below show a detail of a "Gothicized" window and the approach to the castle through the Henry VIII Gateway (1511). Notice the holes here for pouring boiling oil.

Inside the castle
The wards, towers and terraces accommodate many of the castle's 350-strong community.

the state apartments during the reigns of George IV and William IV. Among his alterations, he converted King Charles II's Presence Chamber, and part of his Audience Chamber, into the Garter Throne room. Here the queen invests new Knights of the Garter. The WATERLOO CHAMBER adjoining, where the queen lunches with the Knights of the Garter in June, houses portraits, which George IV commissioned Sir Thomas Lawrence to paint, of all the sovereigns, statesmen and soldiers who contributed to the Allied victory over Napoleon in 1815. King Charles II's Baroque chapel, greatly decayed, was demolished to make way for a new St George's Hall, where the Knights of the Garter assemble in June to process down to St George's Chapel for their annual service. This hall is to be restored, following its destruction in the fire of 1992.

THE GRAND STAIRCASE. This was rebuilt by the architect Anthony Salvin for Queen Victoria in 1866–7. (Beneath the statue of George IV by Sir Francis Chantrey is a suit of armor worn by Henry VIII.) Her taste, and that of Prince Albert, are apparent throughout the state apartments, as she lived and entertained here a great deal. The bed hangings in the KING'S STATE BEDCHAMBER, for instance, are of Napoleonic green and violet and embroidered with the arms of Louis Napoleon and the Empress Eugénie, for the latter's state visit in 1855.

QUEEN MARY'S DOLL'S HOUSE. Designed by Sir Edwin Lutyens on a scale of one to twelve and placed here, after exhibition, in a room of his own design in 1925, the display entrances children and adults alike. The palace exterior – in "Wrenaissance" style – is raised aloft by electricity to reveal over forty rooms on four floors, as well as working lifts, flushing lavatories, piped water and Crown Jewels behind a grille. Fifteen hundred companies and individuals contributed to make the Dolls' House a miniature showpiece of early 20th-century manufacturing and artistic standards and ingenuity. The library contains, apart from a pair of Purdey shotguns, a collection of minute prints and drawings by Paul

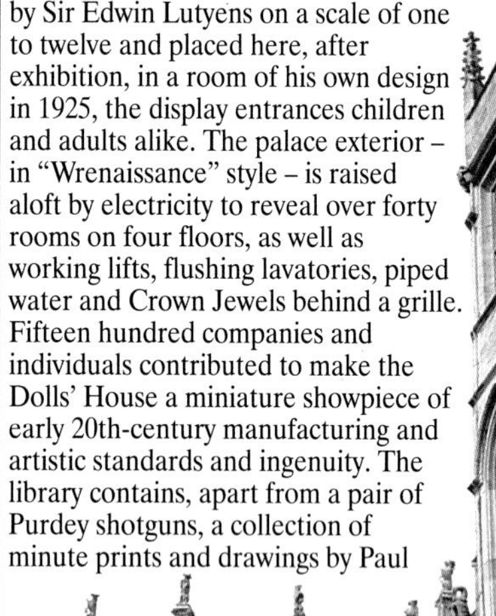

"HONI SOIT QUI MAL Y PENSE"
"Shame on him who thinks evil of it" is the motto of the Order of the Garter, which Edward III founded in 1348. These are the words with which Edward rebuked grinning courtiers when the countess of Salisbury's garter slipped to the ground, and he bound it chivalrously around his own leg.

The celebrated vista of Eton Chapel and the Chiltern hills from the North Terrace, across "a valley extended every way, and chequered with arable lands and pasture, cloathed up and down with groves, and watered with that gentlest of rivers, the Thames" (Hentzner, 1598).

ST GEORGE'S CHAPEL
The chapel and the buildings associated with this Royal Peculiar – no archbishop or bishop has authority within it – are rich in historical association. Shakespeare's *Merry Wives of Windsor* was first performed in what is now the Chapter Library.

On the walls at Windsor two angels support the royal arms, embossed with the motto of the Order of the Garter.

"Cricket match on the Green at Eton" by William Evans, c. 1843.

Nash and Mark Gertler among others, stories by Arthur Conan Doyle and poetry by Siegfried Sassoon. Gertrude Jekyll made the garden – contained, like the garage with its Rolls-Royce Silver Ghost, in a bottom drawer – Broadwood the grand piano, and Singer made the minuscule sewing machine in the linen room.

"Once admitted, the pupil must choose between rowing and cricket. Studying foreign languages, literature and music . . . are of secondary importance. Swimming, boats, oars, these are the magic formulae. Whoever plays well at football or cricket, plays well at life."
Paul Morand, *London*

Eton College

Eton College, the public school which has reared so many of England's great and famous men, lies across the river from Windsor, and is best reached by walking across Windsor Bridge – no cars – and sauntering past the ancient and motley buildings which crowd Eton High Street. In this way you are almost certain to bump into some Etonians, as the schoolboys are known, wearing their uniform of coat tails and striped trousers. You may even catch sight of a rarer bird than these penguins. (Their schoolmasters are called "beaks".) Twenty-four members of a select society, founded in the 1820's, called Pop, are entitled to sport fancy waistcoats. The annual Fourth of June celebrations is the time to view Eton from the river, when there are fireworks and processions of boats. Henry VI was only eighteen when he founded Eton College by charter in 1440. The founder, as he is still known, followed closely the model of Winchester College, founded by William de Wykeham in 1382, and poached his first master and scholars from there. As a college of secular priests with a provost and fellows, a charity school and an almshouse, Eton was to be "the first pledge" of Henry's devotion to God. Unfortunately, he was deposed in the wars of the Lancastrians and Yorkists in 1460, when the chapel, a superb example of Perpendicular Gothic, was only half-finished, and the college fortunes languished. Indeed, Henry's Yorkist successor, Edward IV, came near to suppressing Eton College. Today the founder's statue in School Yard stands surrounded by the 15th-century Lower School, cloisters and College Hall, with its octagonal kitchen, and by other buildings added piecemeal in later reigns. Lupton's Tower is of Tudor Gothic. In 1690 Sir Charles Wren ▲ *171–5*

M.R. James, provost of Eton, on Henry VI: "Looking back over fifty years and further, I wonder whether there has ever been any one who has made more boys – more lives – happy than King Henry the Sixth, our Founder, and I hope his ghost, too, crowned with content, sometimes walks among us."

Eton College Chapel
Stone from Caen, oak from Windsor forest, and bricks from Slough went to build the chapel (below left) which, but for the Wars of the Roses, would have been more than twice the length.

Cloisters Chapel
The cloister of Eton College (above right) was begun in 1443 and completed in the 18th century. It is still the center of the college.

enclosed the yard to the west with Upper School, later badly damaged in the Second World War. The original seventy King's Scholars of Henry VI's charter are now outnumbered by over a thousand *Oppidani*, or "townsmen" – so called because they live not in the college, but in the dense "town" of buildings which has grown up around it.

Windsor Great Park. George II's son, William, duke of Cumberland, created the lake of Virginia Water in the 1750's, when he was an exemplary ranger of the Great Park. The "ruins", or columns, of Lepcis Magna on the Ascot side of Virginia Water were presented to the Prince Regent in 1816, and were originally destined for the British Museum. A later ranger, Sir Eric Savill, was responsible in the 1930's for creating the garden close by, which bears his name, and also, after the war, the wondrous Valley Gardens, including the Kurume Punchbowl. There are wonderful rhododendrons and azaleas in May. Savill declared that his creations were "not botanic gardens, but should be thought of as private gardens accessible to the public". The Legoland theme park opened in the grounds of the former Windsor Safari Park in 1996.

The Long Walk. Laid out by Charles II, and brought up to the East Terrace of the castle by George IV, this is 3 miles long and connects the castle and Windsor Great Park.

Westmacott's 1831 equestrian statue of George III, known as the Copper Horse, is visible on the horizon. During Ascot week, the queen and her guests process down the Long Walk in carriages en route for the races.

FROGMORE. While Home Park immediately adjoining the castle is private, large stretches of Windsor Great Park are open to the public. Frogmore House and grounds, together with the royal mausolea, which lie between Home and Great Parks, are essential viewing when open for periods in the summer. Frogmore, a sprawling white mansion originally built in 1680 and much adapted since, was for generations of royal ladies an informal retreat from the rigours of castle life. The lake and grounds were landscaped by Uvedale Price's brother Richard. Queen Charlotte, consort to George III, was the first to enjoy Frogmore House. With her six daughters, she gardened, read, walked and painted here each morning.The Green Pavilion is restored to its appearance during her lifetime (she died in 1818). The flower painting in the Mary Moser room which she commissioned remains, and the Cross Gallery was painted by Princess Elizabeth, her most artistic daughter. Queen Victoria offered Frogmore to her mother, the duchess of Kent, in 1841, and twenty years later the duchess was buried in the grounds, in the mausoleum which she had wished to be built in her lifetime. The same Dresden architect, Grüner, designed the royal mausoleum nearby at Queen Victoria's request, following Prince Albert's death in the same year, 1861. The High Italianate interior reflects Prince Albert's reverence for Raphael. The tomb sculpture is somewhat pitiful, in that the figure of Queen Victoria, lying beside Albert, is so youthful. She was, of course, not interred until 1901. Queen Mary, consort to George V, loved Frogmore. In the early 20th century her sons, the future kings Edward VIII and George VI, had their schoolroom here. Queen Mary's Black Museum – a room housing her collection of papier mâché and mother of pearl – has been recreated from photographs in the Royal Photograph Collection.

FROGMORE HOUSE
The duchess of Kent, one of many royal ladies who lived at Frogmore House (above), has a mausoleum in the grounds. Her daughter, Queen Victoria, is entombed nearby with Prince Albert, her consort.

Eton School Library.

"Alas! regardless of
their doom
The little victims
play!
No sense have they of
life to come
Nor care beyond
today . . . ."

Thomas Gray,
Ode on a Distant Prospect of Eton College (1742)

"ST JOHN THE BAPTIST" (right, detail) by Guido Reni (1575–1642), a painter much influenced by Caravaggio.

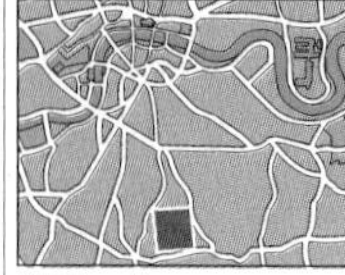

One day

DULWICH ★

This delightful suburb was once a village that grew up around Dulwich Manor, which originally belonged to Bermondsey Abbey in the Middle Ages and was demolished in the 19th century.

DULWICH COLLEGE. The school was founded in 1619 by the actor Edward Alleyn in Dulwich Manor. Alleyn purchased the manor in 1605 with part of a fortune he had made controlling theatrical licenses and as a partner in a bear-baiting pit. Childless himself, he conceived the idea of a charitable institution for the education of underprivileged boys, and spent the next six years transforming the manor into a school. After Alleyn's death the enterprise continued to expand, and eventually moved to its present buildings, which were designed by Charles Barry ▲ *129*, in the mid-19th century. Among the school's old boys are the novelists Raymond Chandler and P.G. Wodehouse. The latter used Dulwich as the setting in several of his books, calling it Valley Fields.

Dulwich Picture Gallery opened in 1814, six years before the National Gallery ▲ *287*, and was carefully restored after being hit by a bomb in 1944. Among its many rare treasures is a self-portrait of actor Richard Burbage, a friend of Alleyn and Shakespeare.

DULWICH PICTURE GALLERY. Reopened in May 2000 after eighteen months of extensive refurbishment and building works, this is one of the world's most beautiful small art galleries. The collection was started in 1626 when Alleyn bequeathed thirty-nine valuable paintings to Dulwich College, and was extended by a second legacy of 371 pictures in 1811 from the art dealer Noel Desenfans and Sir Francis Bourgeois. Sir John Soane ▲ *166* was then commissioned to build England's first public art gallery. Soane's five-roomed gallery is centered around a mausoleum that contains the tombs of Bourgeois and also of Mr and Mrs Desenfans, and houses many important works of art, such as Gainsborough and Lawrence's portraits of the Linley family, and works by Watteau, Murillo and Rembrandt.

A GALLERY OF MASTERPIECES
Dulwich Picture Gallery is largely composed of works by Old Masters such as Rembrandt, Rubens, Raphael, Van Dyck, Poussin (right, *The Triumph of David*), Veronese and many others. Many were purchased by Desenfans and Bourgeois from French aristocrats fleeing the French Revolution and the Emperor Napoleon. There is also a fine collection of English pictures by Gainsborough, Hogarth, Reynolds and others.

Practical information

USEFUL ADDRESSES

→ **IN THE US**

■ **British Embassy**
(Visa Office) 19 Observatory Circle, NW Washington D.C. 20008
Tel. 202 588 7800

■ **British Consulate General & British Tourist Authority**
845 Third Avenue New York NY 10022
Tel. 212 745 0200 (consulate)
Tel. 800 462 2748 (Tourist Authority)
www.britain-info.org

→ **IN THE UK**

■ **American Embassy**
24 Grosvenor Square London W1A 1AE
Tel. 020 7499 9000
www.usembassy.org.uk

→ **LONDON ON THE NET**

■ **www.londontown.com**
London Tourist Board website

■ **www.timeout.com**
Shows, events, outings.

■ **www.visitlondon.co.uk**
Website with valuable practical information, and addresses and opening times of London's main attractions.

ACCOMMODATION

→ **HOTELS**

London hotels are some of the most expensive in the world: in the center of town a double room with en-suite bathroom in an average hotel is seldom less than £70 per night. Hotels are often full so book well in advance. Continental breakfast is often included in the price, but a supplement may be required for the more substantial English breakfast.

■ **Central Reservations**
www.london-hotel.net
Tel. 020 7405 5500

→ **BED & BREAKFAST**

This type of accommodation has become very popular. Many London B&Bs are in fact guesthouses (family concerns) or small, reasonably-priced hotels. Advance bookings are recommended for any type of accommodation in the city center. A list of guesthouses is available from The British Tourist Board.

■ **Hosts and Guests Services**
103 Dawes Road London SW6
Tel. 020 7385 9922
www.host-guest.co.uk

■ **London B & B Agency Limited**
11 Fellows Road London NW3
Tel. 020 7586 2768
www.londonbb.com

■ **Uptown Reservations**
41 Paradise Walks London SW3
Tel. 020 351 3445
www.uptownres.co.uk

ANIMALS

Most mammals must be put in quarantine for 6 months when they arrive in the UK. Cats and dogs from certain countries may avoid quarantine under the "Pets Travel Scheme". See www.defra.gov.uk or contact your nearest British consulate for details.

CLIMATE

May–June and Sep–Oct are the most pleasant times (not as much rain).

FORMALITIES

→ **PAPERS**

US citizens need a valid passport; no visas are required for stays up to 6 months. EC members just need a valid passport or identity card. Authorization to leave the country of origin required for unaccompanied minors.

→ **HEALTH**

Private health care is very expensive. US visitors should check with their travel agents or insurance brokers for health coverage abroad. Form E111, issued by the authorities of EC countries, entitles EU members or residents to certain types of treatment on the British National Health Service (NHS).

→ **DRIVING**

Driving licence, car registration papers and green card.

MONEY

→ **CURRENCY**

The monetary unit is the Pound Sterling (£), divided into 100 pence.

→ **EXCHANGE**

£1 = $1.6
£1 = 1.44 euros at the time of printing.
***Warning**: Cash withdrawals by card are subject to charges. Traveler's checks are recommended.*

TIME CHANGES

→ **TIME DIFFERENCE**

In winter time (GMT) or summer time (BST), Britain is five hours ahead of New York and one hour behind Europe.

TELEPHONE

→ **FROM ABROAD**

Dial the international code, then 44, followed by 20 (020 when dialling from within London) and the eight digit number you require. Numbers beginning with **0800** are free.

TRAVEL

→ **BY AIR**

There are daily flights from New York, Chicago and Los Angeles to London Heathrow or Gatwick.

Airlines
United Airlines
Tel. 1 800 421 6522
www.unitedairlines.com
British Airways
Tel. 1-800-AIRWAYS
www.britishairways.com
Virgin Atlantic
Tel. 1 800 862 8621
www.virginatlantic.com

■ **New York–London**
Prices from $500, duration 7 hours.
Los Angeles–London
Prices from $700, duration 10–12 hours.
Chicago–London
Prices from $650, duration 9 hours.

→ **BY TRAIN (EUROSTAR)**

There are hourly trains from Paris (journey time: 2 hrs 35 mins) and Brussels (journey time: 2 hrs 20 mins) to London Waterloo.
To book in the UK: Tel. 08705 186186
To book in France: Tel. 08 36 35 35 39
www.eurostar.co.uk

→ **BY CAR AND TRAIN (EUROTUNNEL)**

From Calais, France to Folkestone, England via the Channel Tunnel.
To book in the UK: Tel. 08705 35 35 35
To book in France: Tel. 03 21 00 61 00

→ **BY CAR AND FERRY**

Ferry services operate from the European mainland.

■ **Hoverspeed**
Tel. 0870 240 8070

■ **P&O**
Tel. 08705 202020
Tel. 0825 013 013 from France

VOLTAGE

Voltage: 240 V, 75 MHz. Converters are necessary for foreign appliances (and are sometimes provided by hotels).

AIRPORTS AND AIRPORT LINKS

www.baa.co.uk

■ **Heathrow**
15 miles west of the city
Tel. 0870 000 0123

■ **Gatwick**
28 miles south of the city
Tel. 0870 000 2468

■ **London City Airport**
8 miles east of the city
Tel. 020 7646 0000

■ **Stansted**
33½ miles northeast of the city
Tel. 0870 000 0303

→ TO LONDON BY SUBWAY

■ **Heathrow**
Direct to Piccadilly (£3.80).

■ **London City Airport**
Airport Shuttle to Canary Wharf (15 mins, £3), then Dockland Light Railway or Jubilee Line to Waterloo.

→ BY TRAIN

■ **Heathrow**
HEATHROW EXPRESS
Approx. 15 mins to Paddington (£13; £2 premium if ticket purchased on train; children travel free if accompanying adult has bought ticket before boarding train).
Tel. 0845 600 1515

■ **Gatwick**
GATWICK EXPRESS
Approx. 30 mins to Victoria Station (£11)
Tel. 0845 850 1530
THAMESLINK
Approx. 30 mins to King's Cross (£10)
Tel. 0845 748 4950

■ **Stansted**
STANSTED EXPRESS
Approx. 40 mins to Liverpool Street (£13)
Tel. 0845 748 4950

→ BY BUS

National Express runs buses from all airports to the city center.
www.nationalexpress.com
Tel: 0870 580 8080

■ **Heathrow**
Shuttle every 30 mins (£6)
AIRBUS A1
Victoria Station £10 (approx. 40 mins) 7.30am–11.30pm
AIRBUS A2
Kings Cross £10 (1 hr) 4am–8pm

■ **Gatwick**
FLIGHTLINE N° 025
To Victoria Coach Station (£5)
7am–11.30pm

■ **Stansted**
AIRBUS A6
24 hrs £10 (1½ hrs) every 30 mins to Victoria Coach Station.

→ BY TAXI

■ **Heathrow**
Approx. 40 mins to 1 hr to the city center (around £50). Taxi rank outside each terminal.

■ **Gatwick**
From 1¼ to 2 hrs (£70–80)

■ **London City Airport**
Approx. 25 mins to the City (around £25)

→ AIRPORT-TO-AIRPORT LINKS

Jetlink Shuttle every 30 mins
Tel. 0870 580 8080

■ **Heathrow–Gatwick**
(1¼ hrs, £15)
2.05am–12.05am

■ **Heathrow–Stansted**
(1½ hrs, £19)
3.25am–11.40pm

■ **Gatwick–Stansted**
(3 hrs, £23)
2.05am–12.05am

BICYCLES

London is quite dangerous for cyclists. However, you can hire a bicycle for the weekend, when there is less traffic.

■ **On Your Bike**
52–54 Tooley St, SE1
Tel. 020 7378 6669

BOAT TRIPS

To Greenwich (50 mins), Richmond (3 to 4 hrs), or canal rides.

→ ON THE THAMES

The brochure *Discover the Thames* is available from the London Tourist Board

■ **Westminster Passenger Services**
Victoria Embankment
All year around
Tel. 020 7930 1661

■ **Circular Cruises**
Blackfriars Pier
Tel. 020 7936 2033

■ **Thames Leisure**
London Bridge
Tel. 020 7623 1805
www.thamesleisure.co.uk

→ ON THE CANALS

■ **London Waterbus Company**
Tel. 020 7482 2660
Little Venice–London Zoo–Camden Daily in summer, weekend only in winter.

■ **Jason's Trip**
Tel. 020 7286 3428
www.jasons.co.uk
Little Venice–Camden in summer.

BUSES

The typical double-deckers are cheaper than the subway, but they are not as quick or punctual.

→ LINES

Buses run from 5am until 11.30pm. Bus maps are available from major subway stations. Some buses do not run the whole length of their routes, so check the front of the vehicle for its destination.

→ BUS STOPS

Compulsory bus stops are indicated by white-colored signs; request stops by red-colored signs (you must signal to the driver to stop).

→ FARES

Ticket machines are found at most bus stops and single journey tickets are on sale for £1. A cheaper option is to buy a books of 6 tickets at newsagents (£3.90), or a travelcard (*see Subway*).

Note: *Tickets cannot be purchased on board anymore in central London.*

> **Visits by bus**
> More fun and cheaper than tour buses, London buses enable you to discover the city. **Line 11** (Victoria–Liverpool Street) and **Line 15** (Marble Arch–Tower of London) are the nicest routes.

→ NIGHT BUSES
From 11.30am–6am for certain routes (including the suburbs). Night buses are all indicated by the letter "N" and stop at request stops as well. The fare for a single journey is £1. ***Note**: the One-Day Travelcard is valid on night buses.*

DRIVING

→ RULES
Driving on the left-hand side with the wheel on the right (if your car is foreign, a right-hand side mirror is essential). Safety belts are compulsory. Speed restrictions are: 20 or 30 mph in town; 40 or 50 mph on main roads; 70 mph on freeways (motorways). Priority rules are complex, but pedestrians always have priority.

→ CONGESTION CHARGE
There is a £5 per day congestion charge payable for driving in central London Mon–Fri 7am–6.30pm excluding public holidays. Traffic signs indicate where the charge applies.

■ **When to pay**
You can pay in advance or on the day of travel. The charge is £5 if you pay before 10pm on the day of travel, rising to £10 if you pay 10pm–midnight on the day of travel. Penalty charges apply for non-payment.

■ **Paying the charge**
You can pay online, by telephone, by post, at selected shops, petrol stations and car parks, at BT Internet kiosks and by SMS text message from you mobile phone (register by phone or online first).

■ **Information and payments**
Tel. 0845 900 1234 (from the UK) or +44 207 649 9122 (from abroad)
www.cclondon.com

→ PARKING
Difficult and expensive (up to £2 for 15 mins in the center). It is illegal to park on double yellow lines and it is illegal to stop on "red routes", indicated by solid red lines. If you park illegally you will be fined and your car may be clamped or towed away.

■ **Car impounding**
Marble Arch (city center) and Vauxhall Bridge (south). Directions are indicated from the subway stations.

→ GAS (PETROL)
Sold by the metric liter, but Imperial gallon equivalents are also given.

SUBWAY

Opened in 1863, the London subway (commonly known as the Underground or Tube) is the oldest in the world and one of the most expensive. Some lines are rather slow, but the system is currently being modernized. It has recently been extended to Greenwich.

→ NETWORK
12 lines, as well as the Dockland Electric Railway. There are 6 zones covering Greater London, charging different fares.

→ OPERATING TIMES
Daily Mon–Sat 5am–midnight, Sun 5am–11.30pm.
Warning:
Some subway stations are closed at weekends or ouside office hours.

→ TICKETS
Tickets are expensive (the cheapest fare for an adult single journey is £2) and follow a complex fare classification system. Travelcards are better value.

> **Fines**
> Traveling without a valid ticket can result in a fine of £200, and possible prosecution.

■ **Travelcard**
One-day or Weekly Travelcards are valid on the subway, as well as on suburban trains and buses. On sale at ticket offices in subway stations (a passport photograph is necessary for a Weekly card).

■ **Visitor Travelcard**
This card works out much cheaper if you plan to use the public transport system a lot. It gives you unlimited access to the subway, buses and trains (including journeys to Heathrow Airport).
Cost (adult/child)
3 days: $33/$16
4 days: $44/$18
7 days: $65/$28
Warning:
This card can only be purchased outside Great Britain (through British Rail representatives, or British tourist offices).
www.raileurope.com

TAXIS

Slightly cheaper than their European counterparts. There are two types of cabs:

→ BLACK CABS
No cab driver knows its city as well as London's black cab drivers. Takes 4 passengers, 5 with the driver's consent.

■ **At taxi ranks**

■ **In the street**
By hailing them, or flagging them down. If a taxi is free to pick up a fare, its roof light will be on, indicating "For Hire" or "Taxi".

■ **By telephone**
A taxi will charge for driving over to the pick-up address.
Dial-a-Cab
Tel. 020 7253 5000

→ MINICAB
Far cheaper than black cabs, these are run by independent drivers who can be booked by telephone 24 hours a day.

■ **Fares**
Minicabs do not have meters so the fare must be agreed upon beforehand to avoid nasty surprises at the destination point. There is no extra charge for driving over to the pick-up address.

USEFUL ADDRESSES

→ TOURISM

■ **London Tourist Board (LTB)**
Victoria Station SW1 (outside the station) Open daily 8am–7pm.

■ **British Visitor Centre**
1 Regent Street
Open Mon–Fri 9am–6.30pm, Sat–Sun10am–4pm. For information on the whole of the UK.
www.visitbritain.com

→ PRACTICAL INFORMATION

■ **London Transport Information**
Tel. 020 7222 1234 for 24-hour information on the quickest routes by subway, bus and train for both Central London and the suburbs.
www.londontransport.co.uk

■ **Lost Property**
200 Baker Street NW1
Tel. 020 7486 2496
Mon–Fri 9.30am–2pm (wait at least 24 hours before reporting the loss).

DISTRICTS AND STREETS

The town is divided into districts, the initials of which appear in the address, such as EC (East Center), WC (West Center), N (North), E (East), SW (South-West), etc. These letters are followed by numbers which increase as the street runs further from the center.
As London is such a large city, we recommend that you use a map or a plan, such as the famous *London A–Z*.

EMERGENCIES

■ **Police, fire brigade, ambulances**
999 or 112
(24 hrs, calls are free)

Events

Chinese New Year
Jan or Feb.

The Boat Race
Last weekend in March. Famous boat race on the Thames, between Oxford and Cambridge rowing teams.

London Marathon
Mid-April.
Finishes on the Mall.
www.london-marathon.co.uk
Tel. 020 7620 4117

Chelsea Flower Show
End of May.
Floral show at the Royal Hospital.
Tel. 0870 534 4444

Trooping the Colour
2nd Sat in June.
Horse Guards Parade

Epsom Derby
June 9–10. The most popular horse race.

Grosvenor's House Art and Antiques Fair
Mid–June. Grosvenor House Park Lane W1
Tel. 020 7399 8100

Royal Ascot
End of June. Famous horse races – as famous for female spectators' hats as for the racing.

Wimbledon tennis tournament
End June–beg. July
Very difficult to find a hotel during this time.

City of London Festival
End June–mid July
Concerts, opera, theater in prestigious locations.
Tel. (Barbican office) 020 7638 8891
www.colf.org.uk

Notting Hill Carnival
Last weekend in Aug
Notting Hill Gate.
Europe's biggest street festival.
Very colorful.

■ **Dental emergencies**
Eastman Dental Hospital
Tel. 020 7837 3646

INTERNET

Access to Internet is available in some hotels, at Internet cafés and from street Internet kiosks.

■ **BT Internet kiosks**
Similar in appearance to the BT telephone kiosks, but colored blue, they allow you to access the Internet, send and receive emails, access local information including maps, travel, tourist information, restaurants and accommodation, send SMS text messages to mobile phones, pay for the congestion charge, and even make telephone calls. Kiosks accept cash and credit cards.

■ **Global Café**
15 Golden Square W1 (Soho)
Tel. 020 7287 2242
Open Mon–Fri 8am–11pm, Sat 10am–11pm, Sun 10.30am–10.30pm

■ **easyInternetcafé**
www.easyeverything.com
– 456/459 Strand WC2 (Trafalgar Square end)
– 160–166 Kensington High Street W8
–112–114 Camden High Street NW1

MAIL

→ POST OFFICES

Open Mon–Fri 9am–5.30pm, Sat 9am–1pm
The central post office in Trafalgar Square is open until 8pm on Sat.
24–28 William IV St London WC2

■ **Rates**
Two rates: First Class (more expensive, but usually delivered the day after), Second Class (cheaper and slower).

MEASURES

Although the UK has officially adopted the metric system, the Imperial system is still evident.

MEDIA

→ THE PRESS

■ **Dailies**
The Times
The Independent
The Guardian
The Daily Telegraph
The Financial Times
The Evening Standard
The Daily Mirror
The Sun
The Daily Mail

■ **Weeklies**
The Economist
Time Out
Plus all the Sunday supplements of the daily newspapers.

→ RADIO

BBC (FM 93,5 MHz) for broadcasting in foreign languages.
And . . .
Radio 1 (rock),
Radio 2 (popular),
Radio 3 (classical).

→ TELEVISION

5 public channels: BBC One, BBC Two, ITV, Channel Four and Channel Five.
www.bbc.co.uk

MONEY

→ EXCHANGE

Proof of identity is required for changing cash or Eurocheques at banks. Exchange points open daily at railway stations and 24 hours at airports.

→ BANKS

Open Mon–Fri 9.30am–3.30pm and sometimes Sat 10am–12.30pm.

PUBLIC HOLIDAYS (BANK HOLIDAYS)

■ Jan. 1
■ Good Friday
■ May Day (first Mon in May)
■ Spring Holiday (last Mon in May)
■ Summer Holiday (last Mon in Aug)
■ Christmas
■ Boxing Day (Dec. 26, or Dec. 27 and/or 28 if Christmas Day falls on a weekend).

SHOPPING

→ OPENING TIMES
Stores remain open during lunchtime but close earlier than in Continental Europe. Most stores are open Mon–Sat 10am–6pm (with a late opening on Thursday). Most supermarkets and many stores in central London open on Sunday 10am–4pm.

■ **7–Eleven stores**
These stores, which sell stationery, tobacco, newspapers and groceries, are, as their name indicates, open from 7am until 11pm.

Conversion table
Women's sizes
Size 38 = 28 or 6
Size 40 = 30 or 8
Size 42 = 32 or 10
Men's sizes (shirts)
Neck size 41 = 16
Neck size 42 = 16½
Neck size 43 = 17
Shoes
Size 38 = 5
Size 39 = 6
Size 40 = 7
Size 41 = 7½
Size 42 = 8
Size 43 = 9

SPORTS

■ **Athletics**
Crystal Palace
Ledrington Road
London SE19
Tel. 020 8778 0131
www.crystalpalacensc.co.uk

■ **Horse racing**
Ascot
Ascot, Berkshire SL5 7JN
(by train from Waterloo Station)
Tel. 01344 622 211
Epsom
Epsom Downs, Surrey KT18 5LQ
(by train from Waterloo Station)
Tel. 01372 470 047

■ **Golf**
SUNNINGDALE
Ridgemount Road
Sunningdale
Berkshire SLS 9RR
Tel. 01344 621681
www.sunningdale-golfclub.co.uk
(by train from Waterloo Station)
WENTWORTH
Wentworth Drive
Virginia Water
Surrey JU25 4LS
(by train from Waterloo Station)
Tel. 01344 842201

■ **Tennis**
ALL-ENGLAND LAWN TENNIS CLUB
(better known as Wimbledon)
Southfields Subway station, Church Rd
London SW19
Tel. 020 8946 2244
Museum open 10am–5pm (2–5pm on Sun).
See also Web pages for famous sports locations, such as Wembley (football), Lord's (cricket) and Twickenham (rugby).

TELEPHONE

→ FROM LONDON
■ **To the US**
Dial **00** followed by the country code (US: **1**), the area code and the number (omitting the initial 0).
■ **Operator:** Dial 100
■ **International operator:** Dial 155
■ Following changes in the regulations there are many numbers you can now call for national or international enquiries. Beware as each company charges differently. Calls from a landline will be much cheaper than from your mobile phone.
■ **Directory enquiries**
Dial 118 500 or 118 118 or 118 888
■ **International directory enquiries**
Dial 118505

→ PUBLIC TELEPHONES
■ **Coins**
20p, 50p and £1 coins
■ **Telephone cards**
Sold at post-offices, newsagents', supermarkets, etc. (check subway advertising).

→ Mobile phones
Mobiles can be hired for use in the UK (reserve in advance).

TIPS

Approx. 10% of your taxi fare.
In restaurants, a "discretionary service charge" is often automatically added to your bill. You do not have to pay it but it is often the only salary the waiters get when these charges are distributed at the end of the week.
No tipping in pubs.

TOURIST PASSES

→ LONDON PASS
Free admission to more than 50 attractions, plus free transport within London's 6 zones. Attractions include: Bankside Gallery; Courtauld Institute Gallery; Cutty Sark; Firepower! Royal Artillery Museum; Hampton Court Palace; HMS Belfast; Jewel Tower; Kensington Palace & The Orangery; Kenwood House; London Aquarium; London Zoo; London's Transport Museum; Old Operating Theatre, Museum and Herb Garret; Royal Botanic Gardens, Kew; Royal Mews; St Paul's Cathedral; The Tower of London; The Queens Gallery; The Wernher Collection at Ranger's House; Wellington Arch; Wimbledon Lawn Tennis Museum; Wimbledon Tour Experience; Windsor Castle.
■ **Cost**
Without/with transport: £23/£27 (£15/£16 for children) for 1 day; £44/£60 (£29/£38) for 3 days; £62/£94 (£41/£52) for 6 days.
■ **On sale**
on the Internet: www.londonpass.com or by phone: Tel. 0870 242 9988

VISITS

→ ON FOOT
■ **The Original London Walks**
Tel. 020 7624 3978
Fax 020 7625 1932
www.walks.com
Thematic walks with a tour guide, including a Jack-the-Ripper route (meeting point: 7.30pm daily outside Tower Hill subway station).

→ BY PANORAMIC BUS
Stops at most tourist sites.
■ **Golden Tours**
Tel. 020 7233 7030
■ **Original London Sightseeing Tour**
Tel. 020 8877 1722
www.theoriginaltour.com

- ⚀ < £75 per night
- ⚁ £75 to £140
- ⚂ £140 to £210
- ⚃ > £210

Note
Once you have chosen a hotel it is a good idea to search for it on websites such as travelocity.com, Orbitz.com *or* octopustravel.co.uk, *where substantial discounts can be had. The hotels' own websites also often offer special weekend rates.*

BLOOMSBURY

Arran House Hotel
◆ B C2
77–79 Gower St WC1
⊖ Euston Square
Tel. 020 7636 2186
www.arranhotel-london.com
Georgian house within walking distance of the West End and the British Museum, offering all comforts at reasonable prices. Round the clock Internet facilities in the lobby. Breakfast included.
⚀

Blooms Hotel
◆ B D3
7 Montague St WC1
⊖ Russell Square
Tel. 020 7323 1717
www.grangehotels.com
18th-century townhouse with private garden in a quiet street. Traditional style décor of wood-paneling and old paintings. Breakfast included.
⚂

Crescent Hotel
◆ B C3
49–50 Cartwright Gardens WC1
⊖ Russell Square
Tel. 020 7387 1515
www.crescenthotel oflondon.com
The same family has managed the Crescent Hotel since 1956 and the place has indeed a warm and friendly feel to it. Full English breakfast cooked to order; 27 rooms, access to the private garden square and the four recently renovated tennis courts at the front.
⚀⚁

The Generator
◆ B C3
Compton Place (off 37 Tavistock Place) WC1
⊖ Russell Square
Tel. 020 7388 7666
www.generatorhostels.com
Very unusual youth hostel, located in a former police station. Hi-tech décor. 837 beds (private single and double rooms available), a restaurant, 24-hour Internet café, 24-hour games room with pool tables and satellite TVs, luggage storage, safety deposit boxes and a Generator Shop with traveling essentials you may have forgotten. Booking essential in June–Aug. No membership to International hostels necessary.
⚀

Gower House Hotel
◆ B C2
57 Gower St WC1
⊖ Euston Square
Tel. 020 7636 4685
www.gowerhouse hotel.co.uk
Housed in a Georgian house so typical of the Bloomsbury area, the Gower House is a small family-run Bed & Breakfast. Friendly, very well situated, very reasonably priced.
⚀

Harlingford Hotel
◆ B C3
61–63 Cartwright Gardens WC1
⊖ Russell Square
Tel. 020 7387 1551
www.harlingfordhotel.com
Charmingly English hotel, recently redecorated enhancing its original Georgian features, with 43 very attractive bedrooms. Relaxed and friendly, a winner in the budget category. Ask for the key to the private gardens in front where you can also book one of the tennis courts.
⚁

John Adam's Hall
◆ B C2
15–23 Endsleigh St WC1
⊖ Euston Square
Closed for two weeks at Christmas.
Tel. 020 7387 4086
Students' hall of residence that accepts tourists during the holidays. Book well ahead.
⚀

Myhotel
◆ B D3
11–13 Bayley St Bedford Square WC1
⊖ Goodge St
Tel. 020 7667 6000
www.myhotels.co.uk
Opened in 2002, the sister of Myhotel Chelsea on p.374.
⚂

Ruskin Hotel
◆ B D3
23–24 Montague St WC1
⊖ Tottenham Crt Rd
Tel. 020 7636 7388
www.ruskinhotel.com
Well located, near the British Museum. Beautiful and reasonably-priced rooms. Breakfast included.
⚀

CITY

City of London Youth Hostel
◆ F A4
36 Carter Lane EC4
⊖ Blackfriars
Tel. 020 7236 4965
www.yha.org.uk
Particularly well-situated youth hostel in an area where there are very few hotels. Well-equipped double and triple rooms at unbeatable prices, with generous breakfast included. Friendly welcome.
⚀

COVENT GARDEN

Fielding Hotel
◆ F A2
4 Broad Court Bow Street WC2
⊖ Covent Garden
Tel. 020 7836 8305
www.the-fielding-hotel.co.uk
Amazingly quiet hotel in a historic pedestrian area, in the middle of Covent Garden and opposite the opera house. 24 large attractive rooms, all with ensuite showers. Book well in advance.
⚁

Royal Adelphi Hotel
◆ F B2
21 Villiers St WC2
⊖ Embankment
Tel. 020 7930 8764
www.royaladelphi.co.uk
Convenient location next to Somerset House and the Courtauld Galleries. Friendly welcome, attractive rooms, and reasonable prices (from £90 for a double room with ensuite bathroom). No elevator. Breakfast included.
⚁

Savoy
◆ F B2
Strand WC2
⊖ Temple
Tel. 020 7836 4343
www.savoygroup.com
One of the best-known and most beautiful hotels in London. Built toward the end of the 19th century, the Savoy is both large and luxurious. Special weekend rates with breakfast included. It is worth a visit just for breakfast or afternoon tea in the grand Thames Foyer, or, better still, for

lunch at the newly restored Savoy Grill (see p.381).

Swissotel Howard
◆ F A3
Temple Place
Strand WC2
Temple
Tel. 020 7836 3555
www.swissotel-london.com
Luxurious, very English hotel with splendid views of the Temple gardens.

FINSBURY
CLERKENWELL

Thistle City Barbican
◆ C C2
120 Central St
Clerkenwell EC1
Old Street
Tel. 0870 333 9101
www.thistlehotels.com
Large classical hotel with a good location for visitors interested in the East End's fashion stores. Attractive weekend rates on the Thistle website.

HAMPSTEAD
CAMDEN TOWN

Buckland Hotel
◆ A A2
6 Buckland Crescent NW3
Swiss Cottage
Tel. 020 7722 5574
www.bucklandhotel.co.uk
On a quiet tree-lined street, a very reasonably-priced guesthouse with a family atmosphere. Spacious, basic rooms and breakfast included.

Charlotte Guest House
195–197 Sumatra Road, NW6
West Hampstead
Tel. 020 7794 6476
www.charlotteguesthouse.co.uk
Well served by public transport (15 mins from Piccadilly by subway), this huge guesthouse has 49 single or double rooms, simply but tastefully furnished, some with kitchen facilities. Full English or continental breakfast (incl. in price) is served in the conservatory.

La Gaffe
107–111 Heath St
Hampstead NW3
Hamsptead
Tel. 020 7435 8965 or 7435 4941
www.lagaffe.co.uk
What a great location, high up on the streets of Hampstead. Quaint but cozy hotel with 18 rooms with ensuite bathroooms. Restaurant on the ground floor, and Louis Patisserie one of north London's best patisseries down the street.

Hampstead Village Guesthouse
2 Kempley Rd NW3
Hamsptead
Tel. 020 7435 8679
www.hampsteadguesthouse.com
There are only 8 rooms here (one with terrace, one with a free standing bath tub), and it feels like staying with friends, all the more so as the hosts are determined to make your stay as enjoyable as possible.This incredibly pretty Victorian guest-house, cluttered with antiques, stands in one of the prettiest street in North London, a few minutes away from Hampstead Heath. Book well in advance. Garden.

Holiday Inn
215 Haverstock Hill NW3
Belsize Park
Tel. 0870 400 9037
www.london-hampstead.holiday-inn.com
Comfortable rooms in a modern nondescript hotel, but whose distinct advantage is to be close to Hampstead and Camden Town, and with a fast link to the city center by subway. Excellent value for money.

Holiday Inn Camden Lock
28 Jamestwon Rd NW1
Camden Town
Tel. 7485 4343 or 0800 40 50 60
www.holidayinncamden.co.uk
Newly built hotel ideally placed in the middle of Camden Town, overlooking the locks. Ideal for those who want to spend their weekend shopping in the market, it is also a few stops away from the West End by subway. Very interesting rates on the website.

Sandringham Hotel
3 Holford Rd NW3
Hampstead
Tel. 020 7435 1569
Hotel set in pleasant surroundings and with many regular guests. Truly enormous English breakfast (not incl.).

Swiss Cottage Hotel
◆ A A2
4 Adamson Rd NW3
Swiss Cottage
Tel. 020 7722 2281
www.swisscottagehotel.com
Part of the Best Western chain. Discreetly luxurious hotel in a large Victorian house. Warm welcome and beautiful rooms with period furniture. English breakfast included.

HOLLAND PARK
NOTTING HILL

Holland House YHA
◆ D B3
Holland Walk W8
High St Kensington
Tel. 020 7937 0748
www.yha.org.uk
Very pleasant setting for this youth hostel in Holland Park, one o the plushest areas in London. Breakfast included.

Portobello Hotel
◆ D A3
22 Stanley Gardens W11
Notting Hill
Tel. 020 7727 2777
www.portobello-hotel.co.uk
Closed Dec 23–Jan 2
This little hotel is one of several elegant Victorian houses near the famous Portobello market. 21 rooms with an exquisite Victorian décor (some overlook a private garden) and the smallest have a nautical theme, resembling cabins in a boat; others are romantically decorated with muslin drapes. The basement bar and restaurant are more open and modern. It was here that Jimmy Hendrix died, and rock stars still come to drink at the bar.

MARYLEBONE
MAYFAIR

Bentinck House Hote
◆ B D1
20 Bentinck St W1
Bond St
Tel. 020 7935 9141
www.bentinck-househotel.co.uk
Situated between Hyde Park and the Wallace Collection. Breakfast included. Attractive prices for triple rooms and special weekend rates.

⚀ < £75 per night
⚁ £75 to £140
⚂ £140 to £210
⚃ > £210

Berkeley
◆ E C3
Wilton Place SW1
⊖ Hyde Park Corner
Tel. 020 7235 6000
www.savoygroup.com
Sumptuous rooms and suites, most with views over Hyde Park. Health and fitness center.
⚃

Durrants Hotel
◆ E A3
George St W1
⊖ Marble Arch
Tel. 020 7935 8131
www.durantshotel.co.uk
In a good location behind the Wallace Collection. Wood-paneled lounges with log fires.
⚁

Edward Lear Hotel
◆ E A3
28–30 Seymour St W1
⊖ Marble Arch
Tel. 020 7402 5401
www.edlear.com
Beautiful Georgian house with a Victorian décor. Breakfast included.
⚀

Hotel La Place
◆ A D4
17 Nottingham Place W1
⊖ Baker St
Tel. 020 7486 2323
www.hotellaplace.com
Good location near Oxford St and Marble Arch, with all modern comforts. Breakfast included.
⚁

Brown's Hotel
◆ F B1
30–34 Albemarle St W1
⊖ Green Park
Tel. 020 7493 6020
www.raffles.com
Established in 1837 by Byron's valet, this hotel has the atmosphere of a country house. Taking afternoon tea here is an opportunity to step into the past.
⚃

Claridge's
◆ E A4
Brook St W1
⊖ Bond St
Tel. 020 7629 8860
www.claridges.co.uk
Luxurious hotel with old-fashioned charm that has accommodated royalty and heads of state for more than two centuries. Faultless service.
⚃

Connaught
◆ E A4
16 Carlos Place W1
⊖ Bond St
Tel. 020 7499 7070
www.savoygroup.com
Small, supremely English hotel. Beautiful oak staircase and period furniture.
⚃

Grosvenor House
◆ E B4
90 Park Lane W1
⊖ Hyde Park Corner
Tel. 020 7499 6363
www.lemeridien-grosvenorhouse.com
Huge palace built at the turn of the century. Much more than just a hotel, it allows guests to sample the richness of a bygone age.
⚃

The Metropolitan
◆ E B4
19 Park Lane W1
⊖ Hyde Park Corner
Tel. 020 7447 1047
www.metropolitan.co.uk
There is no shortage of luxury hotels in London, or on Park Lane for that matter but the best, and by far, has to be the Metropolitan. All the surfaces are smooth, minimalist, glossy, curved and immaculate. So are the staff. Fashion-driven hotel that draws a continuous flow of celebrities and international high flyers. The Met Bar is also one of the most fashionable night spots in the capital.
⚃

Ritz
◆ E B4/F B1
150 Picadilly W1
⊖ Green Park
Tel. 020 7493 8181
www.theritz.com
The epitome of elegance and style. Book in advance for the famous afternoon tea.
⚃

PADDINGTON BAYSWATER

Delmere Hotel
◆ A D3
130 Sussex Gardens W2
⊖ Paddington
Tel. 020 7706 3344
www.delmerehotels.com
Attractive rooms, friendly welcome; continental breakfast included.
⚁

Garden Court Hotel
◆ D A4
30–31 Kensington Gardens Square W2
⊖ Bayswater
Tel. 020 7229 2553
www.gardencourthotels.co.uk
This is a type of hotel that one would like to find in every part of London. Situated in a peaceful, green Victorian square. Extremely friendly welcome. The 40 rooms have typically English charm; 14 have bathrooms. Tea, coffee, herbal teas and cakes are served in the lounge. Breakfast included.
⚀

Nayland Hotel
◆ A D3
132–134 Sussex Gardens W2
⊖ Paddington
Tel. 020 7723 4615
www.naylandhotel.com
Good location and excellent value. Breakfast included.
⚀

Rhodes House Hotel
◆ A D3
195 Sussex Gardens W2
⊖ Paddington
Tel. 020 7262 5617
www.rhodeshotel.com
Rooms with shower or bath. Breakfast included.
⚀

SLOANE SQUARE

Alison House Hotel
◆ E D4
82 Ebury St SW1
⊖ Sloane Square
Tel. 020 7730 9529
www.alisonhousehotel.co.uk
Pleasant, unpretentious hotel with generous breakfast included.
⚀

London Outpost
◆ E D3
Cadogan Gardens SW3
⊖ Sloane Square
Tel. 020 7589 7333
www.londonoutpost.co.uk
Beautiful English style guesthouse in the very smart and select Cadogan Gardens, with 11 tastefully decorated rooms. Peaceful and intimate, but rather expensive.
⚂

SOHO

Berners Hotel
◆ F A2
10 Berners St W1
⊖ Tottenham Crt Rd or Oxford Circus
Tel. 020 7636 1629
www.thebernershotel.com
Good location and very pleasant rooms. Special weekend rates.
⚂

Charlotte Street Hotel
◆ B D2
15 Charlotte St W1
⊖ Tottenham Crt Rd or Goodge St
Tel. 020 7806 2000
Sleek looking hotel; a blend of traditional old English and designer boutique. Elegantly

⚀ < £75 per night
⚁ £75 to £140
⚂ £140 to £210
⚃ > £210

furnished, with a 1930s feel and clear allusions to the Bloomsbury set. There is a bar and a restaurant adjacent to the hotel but that doesn't appeal Charlotte St isn't lacking in fine places to eat.
⚂

SOUTH KENSINGTON

Beaver Hotel
◆ **D** D3
57–59 Philbeach Gardens SW5
⊖ Earl's Court
Tel. 020 7373 4553
www.beaverhotel.co.uk
Quiet hotel (some rooms overlook a garden). English breakfast included.
⚂

Blakes Hotel
◆ **H** A1
33 Roland Gardens SW7
⊖ South Kensington or Gloucester Road
Tel. 020 7370 6701
www.blakeshotel.com
Designed by Anouska Hempel, this very stylish and very private hotel is a series of interconnecting houses. There are 50 individually decorated rooms, with all modern amenities such video and CD players, etc. Impeccable service.
⚁⚂

Gore Hotel
◆ **D** C4
189 Queen's Gate SW7
⊖ High Street Kensington
Tel. 020 7584 6601
www.gorehotel.com
Friendly welcome; impeccable service. Sophisticated decorations (rooms 101 and 211 are particularly pleasant). Special rates for long stays and weekends. Bar, two restaurants.
⚂

Myhotel
◆ **B** D3
35 Ixworth Place SW3
⊖ Goodge St
Tel. 020 7667 6000
www.myhotels.co.uk
Opened in 1999, Myhotel belongs to the first generation of "designer" hotels and advertises itself as "Brideshead Revisited meets Sex and the City". It is entirely decorated following feng shui principles and combines Western and Asian traditions, offering Oriental serenity in the midst of Western urban stress. You'll find cashmere bed throws, crisp linen sheets in the bedrooms, along with most hi tech extras such as plasma-screen TVs, Internet, piles of DVDs. A truly first-class hospitality.
⚂

ST JAMES'S

22 Jermyn Street
◆ **F** B1
22 Jermyn St SW1
⊖ Piccadilly Circus
Tel. 020 7734 2353
www.22jermyn.com
On one of the most select streets of London is this beautiful six-story townhouse dating back to 1870, when it was housing English gentlemen doing business in London. The hotel's entrance is a smart, deceptively narrow corridor but upstairs the luxurious rooms are spacious, furnished with soft carpets, antiques, silk fabrics on the walls, fresh flowers, modern bathrooms and plenty of toiletries. A haven of "Englishness". No restaurant or bar; impeccable service.
⚂

St Ermin's London Hotel
◆ **F** C1
Caxton St SW1
⊖ St James's Park
Tel. 020 7222 7888
www.jollyhotels.co.uk
Very good location. Attractive rooms and sumptuous lounges. Generous buffet breakfast not included.
⚃

TOWER BRIDGE
DOCKLANDS

Hilton Nelson Dock 265
265 Rotherhithe Street SE16
⊖ Rotherhithe
Tel. 020 7231 1001
www.hilton.co.uk
Located in a renovated 18th-century warehouse south of the river, in the new fashionable district opposite Canary Wharf. Shuttle bus and boat to the City. All amenities and facilities (swimming pool, fitness center, sauna, etc.). Free parking. Special weekend rates.
⚃

WESTMINSTER
BELGRAVIA

41
◆ **F** C1
41 Buckingham Palace Rd SW1
⊖ Victoria
Tel. 020 7300 0041
www.41hotel.com
Elegant townhouse overlooking Buckingham Palace Mews, 41 is a few minutes' walk away from St James's and Green parks and also close to Knightsbridge and Harrods. Small enough to feel like a highly selective club, where the service could not be more attentive. Fax/printer/scanner in every room. Quiet; very good breakfast.
⚂⚃

Corona Best Western Hotel
◆ **F** D1
87–89 Belgrave Rd SW1
⊖ Victoria
Tel. 020 7828 9279
www.coronahotel.co.uk
Bed & Breakfast with 50 rooms with every comfort. Good location (10 mins on foot from Victoria Station and 2 mins from Pimlico). Good value for money.
⚀

Goring Hotel
◆ **E** C4
15 Beeston Place Grosvenor Gardens SW1
⊖ Victoria
Tel. 020 7396 9000
www.goringhotel.co.uk
British elegance and friendly welcome. Some rooms have balconies over-looking the gardens. Bathrooms in wood and marble.
⚃

London Marriott County Hall
◆ **F** C3
The County Hall London SE1
⊖ Westminster
Tel. 020 7928 5200
In the long imposing building of the former County Hall, which also houses London's Aquarium and the new Saatchi Gallery, the Marriott has the best views of any London hotels with, across the Thames, the Houses of Parliament and Big Ben. Modern and reliable, with excellent service and amenities.
⚂

Windermere Hotel
◆ **E** D4
142–144 Warwick Way SW1
⊖ Victoria
Tel. 020 7834 5163
www.windermere-hotel.co.uk
Victorian décor and warm welcome. Spacious, well-equipped rooms. Good value for money. Breakfast included.
⚀

⚀ < £15 per person for two courses; not including drinks
⚁ £15 to £25
⚂ £25 to £45
⚃ > £45

BLOOMSBURY

Pizza Express
◆ B D3
30 Coptic St WC1
⊖ Tottenham Crt Rd or Holborn
Tel. 020 7636 3232
Open 11.30am–midnight
The Pizza Express chain has about 60 branches in London. The pizzas are generally very good. This branch is close to the British Museum.
⚀

Wagamama
◆ B D3
4 Streatham St
Off Coptic St WC1
⊖ Holborn
Tel. 020 7323 9223
Open Mon–Sat noon–11pm; Sun 12.30–10pm
A very popular Japanese noodle bar. Servings are generous and good value. You may have to queue in the evening. Non-smoking. Other branches:
▪ Soho at 10a Lexington St Tel. 020 7292 0990
▪ Camden Town at 11 Jamestown Rd Tel. 020 7428 0800
⚀

CAMDEN TOWN PRIMROSE HILL

The Engineer
◆ A A4
65 Gloucester Avenue NW1
⊖ Chalk Farm Rd
Tel. 020 7722 0950
Open Mon–Fri 9–11.30am, noon–3pm and 7–11pm; Sat 9am–noon, 12.30–3.30pm and 7–11pm; Sun 9am–noon, 12.30–3.30pm and 7–10.30pm.
www.the-engineer.com
Superb Modern British food in this gastropub favored by the trendy North London set. Immaculately cool clientele, simple but beautifully-presented décor and a stunning patio-garden if you're lucky enough to catch a spell of warm weather. Dishes range from the simple to the sumptuous, with the menu proudly stating that "all our meat is free-range or organic".
⚂

Marine Ices
◆ A A4
8 Haverstock Hill NW3
⊖ Chalk Farm Rd
Tel. 020 7482 9003
Restaurant open Mon–Fri noon–3pm, 6–11pm; Sat noon–11pm; Sun noon–10pm. Gelateria open Mon–Sat 11am–11pm (10pm Sun).
Opposite the Round House, 200 yards up from Camden Lock. Great pizzas and a few Italian dishes but above all, the best ice cream in London (which many restaurants buy to put on their menu). One of the child-friendliest place in London.
⚀

Lemonia
◆ B A1
89 Regent's Park Rd NW1
⊖ Camden Town or Chalk Farm Rd
Tel. 020 7586 7454
Open Mon–Fri noon–3pm, 6–11.30pm; Sat 6–11.30pm; Sun noon–3.30pm.
Highly reputable Greek restaurant. Warm and friendly atmosphere, albeit a bit noisy. Reasonable prices. Delicious mezedes (hors-d'œuvre), souvlaki (kebabs) and stufado (beef in wine sauce).
⚁

Odette's
◆ A A4
130 Regent's Park Road Primrose Hill NW1
⊖ Chalk Farm Rd
Tel. 020 7722 5388
Mon–Fri 12.30–2.30pm and 7–11pm; Sat 7–11pm; Sun 12.30–3pm
Slightly formal with long starch white tablecloths, silver cultery, candles – but very romantic if you have one of the cozy corner tables. The cellar houses an intimate, sophisticated wine bar.
⚁⚂

CHELSEA SLOANE SQUARE

Aubergine
◆ H A1
11 Park Walk SW10
Tel. 020 7352 3449
⊖ Sloane Square or South Kensington
Open Mon–Fri noon–2.30pm, 7– 10.30pm; Sat 7–11pm. Closed Sun.
Creative cuisine prepared with passion. Classy décor and high-quality service. Expensive, but the 3-course set lunch menu is great value for such a place. Book well in advance.
⚃

Bluebird
◆ H A2
350 King's Road SW3
⊖ Sloane Square
Tel. 020 7559 1000
Open daily lunchtime and evening (call for opening times)
Created by Terence Conran, this restaurant can accommodate up to 240 people. The building, with an art deco façade, also houses a café, a kitchen shop, a florist and a bar. Chef Neil Haydock specializes in updated traditional as well as seafood dishes. Famous for its sorbets. Special reduced-price theater menu (two courses).
⚂

Chutney Mary
◆ H B1
535 King's Rd SW10
⊖ Fulham Broadway
Tel. 020 7351 3113
Open Mon–Fri 6.30–11.30pm; Sat–Sun 12.30–3.30pm, 6.30–10.30pm
Excellent Anglo-Indian cuisine. Reasonably-priced menus on Sundays. Bookings essential.
⚂

La Famiglia
◆ H B1
7 Langton St SW10
⊖ Fulham Broadway
Tel. 020 7351 0761
Open noon–2.30pm, 7–11pm
Friendly, relaxed (very Italian) atmosphere in this restaurant that serves top quality Tuscan cuisine. Very popular so book for dinner. Garden tables in good weather.
⚁

Gordon Ramsay
◆ E D3
68 Royal Hospital Rd SW3
⊖ Sloane Square
Tel. 020 735 4441
Open Mon–Fri noon–2pm and 6.45–11pm. Closed Sat–Sun.
Deservedly won its third Michelin star in 2000. The restaurant is classically French in almost every respect, aside from the name, and is probably the best London has to offer. It is small and elegant – restaurants aiming for triple stardom tend to be. The service has considerable charm, and the food immense elegance. The attention to detail is prodigious, the effects often close to sublime. Altogether a pretty senior experience. Set meals available.
⚃

Do not be deterred by the high prices som luxury restaurants offer. Many also off cheaper set lunches or dinners which mak an extraordinary culinary experience possib for all. Book well in advance thoug

CITY

Sweetings
◆ G A1
39 Queen Victoria St EC4
Mansion House
Tel. 020 7248 3062
Open 11am–3pm. Closed Sat–Sun.
This fish restaurant, established in the 19th century, is a real institution. You can lunch either at the bar or the table (oysters, poached, grilled or fried halibut, shrimp and jam roly-poly). Good selection of wines and beers.

The Place Below
◆ G A1
St-Mary-le-Bow Church
Cheapside EC2
St Paul's
Tel. 020 7329 0789
Open 7.30am–9pm. Closed Sat–Sun.
Creative and high-quality vegetarian cuisine served in the crypt of a church built by Christopher Wren.

COVENT GARDEN

Belgo Centraal
◆ F A2
50 Earlham St WC2
Covent Garden
Tel. 020 7813 2233
Open Mon–Thu noon–11.30pm; Fri–Sat noon–midnight; Sun noon–10.30pm
Belgian restaurant with industrial décor featuring a glassed-in passageway and a huge factory lift. The waiters are dressed as monks and the dining room is candle-lit. Specialties: mussels and fries. Good selection of beers. Prices on the steep side.

Cork and Bottle
◆ F B2
44–46 Cranbourn St WC2
Tel. 020 7734 6592
Leicester Sq
Mon–Sat 11am–11.20pm; Sun noon–9.50pm
A basement wine bar, full of dark private corners, very handy if you want a drink and a bite before or after the movies. Often busy.

Food For Thought
◆ F A2
31 Neal St WC2
Covent Garden
Tel. 020 7836 0239
Open Mon–Fri 9.30am–11.30pm; Sat noon–6.30pm; Sun noon–4pm
Appetizing vegetarian dishes to eat in or take away.

RULES
FUNG SHING

Fung Shing
◆ F A2
15 Lisle St WC2
Leicester Square
Tel. 020 7437 1539
Open noon–11.30pm
A sure bet amongst the many Chinatown restaurants. Traditional Chinese dishes: steamed eels with buns, etc.

Gordon's Wine Bar
◆ F B2
47 Villiers St WC2
Embankment
Tel. 020 7930 1408
Closed Sun.
Extraordinary wine bar with dark vaulted cellars and barrels. Candle-lit tables and musty atmosphere. Wines from all around the world. Packed after work.

Incognico
◆ F A2
117 Shaftesbury Ave WC2
Leicester Square or Tottenham Crt Rd
Tel. 020 7836 8866
The old master, Nico Ladenis, is actually resident in the South of France, but his spirit lives on in Shaftesbury Avenue. The menu, which he supervises, is studded with French classics, produced with the famous attention to depth of flavors, supercharged sauces and all the rest. The staff are smart and friendly and the set price lunch is one of the bargains of the decade.

Joe Allen
◆ F A2
13 Exeter St WC2
Covent Garden
Tel. 020 7836 0651
Open Mon–Fri noon–12.45am; Sat 11.30am–12.45am; Sun 11.30am–11.15pm
Popular restaurant – in a basement with a good atmosphere and live jazz music some evenings. Delicious burgers.

Orso
◆ F A2/3
27 Wellington St WC2
Covent Garden
Tel. 020 7240 5269
Open noon–midnigh
Basement restaurant. Fashionable place to dine either before or after the theater.

Rules
◆ F A2/3
35 Maiden Lane WC2
Covent Garden
Tel. 020 7836 5314
Open noon–11.30pm
It claims to be the oldest restaurant in London, and at first sight Rules seems to be caught in a time warp, all Edwardian illustrations, discrete dining areas, cigar smoke and clubby camraderie. On close inspection it turns out to be a clever disguise for a model, modern watering hole, with serious cooking from David Chambers using best British ingredients (Aberdeen Angus beef, game in season etc). A short, intelligent, well priced wine list (and fixed priced lunch) and crisp service.

Simpson's-in-the Strand
◆ F B2
100 Strand WC2
Charing Cross
Tel. 020 7836 9112
Open Mon–Sat 12.15–2.30pm, 5.30–11pm; Sun noon–2.30pm, 5.30–11pm. Breakfast Mon–Fri 7.15–10am.

▪ < £15 per person for two courses; not including drinks
▪ £15 to £25
▪ £25 to £45
▪ > £45

A British institution. Sumptuous Edwardian décor and traditional English cuisine. Recommended for Sunday lunch of roast beef and Yorkshire pudding. Booking essential.
▪

GREENWICH

Green Village Restaurant
11–13 Greenwich Church St SE10
Greenwich railway station)
Tel. 020 8858 2348
Open 11am–midnight
A pretty restaurant, popular with local residents. Typical English cuisine.
▪

Plume of Feathers
19 Park Vista
Greenwich SE10
Maze Hill railway station)
Tel. 020 8858 1661
Open Mon–Wed noon–3pm; Thu–Fri 7–11pm; Sun 1–4pm
300-year-old pub (there is a plaque in the saloon). Local clientele. Great view over Greenwich Park. Typically English dishes and barbecue.
▪

Spread Eagle
1–2 Stockwell St SE10
Greenwich railway station)
Tel. 020 8853 2333
Open Mon–Sat noon–3pm; 6.30–10.30pm; Sun noon–3.30pm. Closed at Christmas.
The predominantly French menu changes each month. Warm service. Specialties: Scottish grouse and marquise au chocolat.
▪

ANGEL-ISLINGTON CLERKENWELL

The Clerkenwell Dining Room and Bar
◆ C C1
69 St John St EC1
⊖ Barbican
Tel. 020 7253 9000
Open Mon–Fri noon–2.30pm, 6–11.30pm; Sat 6–11.30pm. Closed Sun.
A few steps away from the Barbican center. Tasty Modern European cuisine with an extensive and well-chosen wine list that complements the menu.
▪

Club Gascon
◆ C C1
57 West Smithfield EC1
⊖ Farringdon
Tel. 020 7796 0600
Open Mon–Fri noon–2pm, 7–10.30pm; Sat 7–10.30pm. Closed Sun.
Instant hit with virtually all critics since it opened in 1998. Chef Pascal Aussignac brings flair and an innovative sleight of hand to the grand food of southwest France – foie gras, duck and cassoulet – generally lightening their impact for the modern stomach. Clean, clear décor (though usually cluttered with happy eaters). Service pretty French (read into that what you like).
▪▪

Eagle Pub
◆ C C1
159 Farringdon Rd EC1
⊖ Farringdon
Tel. 020 7837 1353
Open Mon–Fri 12.30–2.30pm, 6.30–10.30pm; Sat–Sun 12.30–3.30pm
The first of the gastro-pubs, and in many ways still the best. Smart but laid-back young professional customers seem to think so because they pack in in big numbers lunchtime and evening. Basic Mediterranean fare, with emphasis on Spain and Portugal. Lots of grills, mountainous salads and the finest steak sandwich in town. A few well-chosen wines and beers.
▪

Moro
◆ C C1
34-36 Exmouth Market, EC1
⊖ Holland Park
Tel. 020 7833 8336
Sam and Sam Clarke (husband and wife) are largely responsible for giving a fashionable lick to the food of North Africa and Spain. Open-plan kitchen, modish, laid-back décor, long bar for tapas, plus formidable range of sherries. The food has a terrific, tastebud-tingling appeal based on superlative basic ingredients and a deft feel for how to combine them to bring the best out of them. Best bread in London.
▪

The Peasant
◆ C C1
240 St John St EC1
⊖ Farringdon
Tel. 020 7336 7726
Open Tue–Fri 12.30–3pm; Tue-Sat 6.30–11pm. Bar food only on Mon. Closed Sun.
With the Eagle, one of the forerunners of the gastropub revolution. Sensational bar with round horseshoe counter and mosaic floors at street level, beautiful restaurant upstairs, with high ceilings and wide windows; the food is Modern European and scrumptious.
▪

Saint-John
◆ C C1
26 St John's St EC1
⊖ Farringdon
Tel. 020 7251 0848
Open noon–3pm, 6–11pm. Closed Sat. lunchtime, Sun.
Chef's favorite, critics favorite, offal lovers' favorite. Fergus Henderson has turned this highly individual, stark, canteen-like space into a place of pilgrimage for anyone seriously interested in contemporary eating. The food is plain but perfect (mostly). The restaurant's motto "Nose to Tail Eating" is slightly exaggerated, but it may be the only place in the country to have squirrel on the menu (albeit occasionally). The point is that it is very good squirrel, very well cooked.
▪

KENSINGTON HOLLAND PARK

The Belvedere
◆ D C3
Holland House, off Abbotsbury Rd W8
⊖ Holland Park or Olympia
Tel. 020 7602 1238
Open Mon–Sat noon–3pm, 6–10.30pm; Sun noon–3.30pm. Closed at Christmas.
Elegant surroundings in the heart of Holland Park. British nouvelle cuisine. Magnificent terrace.
▪

Clarke's
◆ D B4
124 Kensington Church St W8
⊖ Notting Hill Gate
Tel. 020 7221 9225
Open Mon–Fri noon–2.30pm, 7–10pm; Sat 6–10.30pm. Closed Sun.
Small, cozy restaurant that has been going strong for the last 15 years. Clarke's cooking is faultless and imaginative and uses the freshest ingredients. Menus are changed daily but there is only one menu at dinner. Good selection of Californian wines. Sally Carke opened a store next door, selling freshly baked

breads, pastries and other high-quality ingredients used in her restaurant and in others throughout London.

MARYLEBONE

Diwana
◆ B C2
121 Drummond St NW1
Euston Square
Tel. 020 7387 5556
Open noon–11.30pm. Closed at Christmas.
Located northeast of Marylebone and decorated entirely with wood, Diwana's is an address locals would like to keep to themselves. Superb vegetarian Indian cuisine; delicious sweet yoghurt lassis.

The Providores and Tapa Room
◆ B D1
109 Marylebone High St W1
Baker St
Tel. 020 7935 7175
Open Mon–Sat noon–2.45pm, 6–10.45pm; Sun noon–2.45pm, 6–10pm
The Providores opened to rave reviews in fall 2001 and is still going strong. Restaurant on the first floor, and Tapa Room (a mixture of wine-bar, tapas bar and breakfast bar) on the ground floor. Excellent cooking, a fusion of Eastern and Western flavors by New Zealander Peter Gordon (who set up and worked at Sugar Club until 1999) and Anna Hansen.

Villandry
◆ B D2
170 Great Portland St W1 (entrance on Bolsover St in the evening)
Great Portland St or Regent's Park
Tel. 020 7631 3131
Open Mon–Fri 8–11.30am, noon–3pm, 6–10pm; Sat 10am–3pm, 7–10pm; Sun noon–3pm
The restaurant is renowned for the high quality of its ingredients (including organic meats). Next door is the fantastic and pricey deli where you can buy some of these products. Remarkable cheeses and salads. The menu changes daily. Book for dinner.

MAYFAIR

Le Caprice
◆ F B1
Arlington House
Arlington St SW1
Green Park
Tel. 020 7629 2239
Open noon–3pm, 6pm–midnight
Le Caprice has maintained its unrivaled reputation for years thanks to its sensible nouvelle cuisine and impeccable service. Elegant clientele in this luxurious area of St James's. Booking is essential several weeks in advance.

The Cinnamon Club
◆ F C2
The Old Westminster Library
30 Great Smith St W1
St James's Park
Tel. 020 7222 2555
Mon–Fri 7–10am, noon–3pm and 6–11.30pm; Sat 6–11.30pm; Sun noon–4pm
Smooth as a pukka sahib. Set over two floors of the Old Westminster Library it has kept on the old paneling, some of the books and the air of studious calm. New Wave Indian cookery, but all the better for that. Delicate use of spices, controlled exuberance in the sauce department, allied to distinctly Western traditions of plate artistry. A truly civilised experience.

Connaught
◆ E A4
Connaught Hotel
16 Carlos Place W1
Green Park or Bond Street
Tel. 020 7499 7070
Open 12.30–2.30pm and 6.30–10.30pm. Breakfast 7.30–10.30am.
Supremely British décor and fine combination of classic French cuisine with traditional English dishes. The grill is cheaper than the restaurant.

Dorchester Grill Room
◆ E B4
Dorchester Hotel, 54 Park Lane W1
Hyde Park Corner
Tel. 020 7629 8888
Open 12.30–2.30pm, 6–11pm (Sun 7–10pm). Breakfast Mon–Sat 7–11am (10.30am on Sun)
Hotel grill room in the best English tradition. Subtle décor. The menu changes daily and the wine list is superb. Reservations advisable.

Le Gavroche
◆ E A3
43 Upper Brook St W1
Marble Arch
Tel. 020 7408 0881
Open noon–2pm, 7–11pm. Closed Sat–Sun, public hols and one week at Christmas.
The Roux family has been running this place for the past thirty years. Excellent French cuisine, impeccable service and friendly welcome. You should book in advance.

Locanda Locatelli
◆ E A3
Seymour St W1
Marble Arch
Tel. 020 7935 9088
Open noon–3pm and 7–11pm
Giorgio Locatelli was the king of the kitchen when Zafferano was the finest Italian restaurant in London. Now he has his own place, tacked onto the side of the Churchill Hotel. Senior retro-chic design, reassuringly smooth service, classy Italian wine list, and Giorgio's stunning, French-influenced, indubitably Italian food. Flavor in all the right places. Rightly hailed by the critics. No wonder it is one of the most difficult London restaurants to get into.

Greenhouse
◆ E B4
27a Hay's Mews W1
Green Park
Tel. 020 7499 3331
Open Mon–Fri noon–2.30pm, 6.30–11pm; Sat 6.30–11pm; Sun 12.30–3pm, 6–10pm.
Pleasant setting. Modern British cuisine with French and Italian touches. Specialties: veal with bacon, carpaccio, duck paté. Booking essential.

Momo
◆ F B1
27 Heddon St W1
Piccadilly Circus
Tel. 020 7434 4040
Open Mon–Sat noon–2.30pm and 7–11.30pm; Sun. 7–11pm
Open in 1997 by Mourad Mazouz, this Moroccan restaurant has rapidly become one of the most fashionable places in London. The décor is reminiscent of Moorish palaces and the welcome is very warm. The menu has

< £15 per person for two courses; not including drinks
£15 to £25
£25 to £45
> £45

Zaazouk (grilled aubergine salad with coriander, garlic and olive oil), pastilla (pigeon pie with almonds), tagines, chicken with lemon, etc. Book two weeks in advance for dinner.

The Oak Room
◆ F B1
Meridien Piccadilly Hotel
21 Piccadilly W1
Piccadilly Circus
Tel. 020 7734 8000
Mon–Fri 9.30am–9pm;
Sat 10am–9pm;
Sun 10am–1pm
Top-quality cuisine by chef Martin Halls. The lunchtime menu (three courses) enables you to sample the food without putting too much strain on your budget.

NOTTING HILL

Al Waha
◆ D A4
75 Westbourne Grove W2
Notting Hill Gate
Tel. 020 7229 0806
Open daily noon–midnight
Al Waha might not get too many marks for original décor, although it's smart and comfortable, but it will always score highly for the excellence of its food. Classic Lebanese stuff. Modest lunchers can make do with a selection of top grade mezze. More serious eaters may like to explore the more exotic sections of the menu devoted to grills. The service is always ready to help and explain. A glass or two of stylish, hefty Lebanese wines ease any rights of passage.

Geale's
◆ D B3
2 Farmer St W8
Notting Hill Gate
Tel. 020 7727 7528
Open Mon–Sat noon–3pm, 6–11pm; Sun 6–10.30pm.
Closed at Easter and Christmas.
Classic "chippie", all done up with loving care and back to serving hunks of fab fresh fish and chips as they should be, all golden and chunky. Eat in or take away. And a proper wine list as well as heavy-duty tea if you have a mind.

Kensington Place
◆ D B4
205 Kensington Church St W8
Notting Hill Gate
Tel. 020 7727 3184
Open noon–3pm and 6.30–11.45pm
Fashionable place to go to see and to be seen as much as for the inspirational menu direction and cooking of Rowley Leigh – great ingredients and sensible, terrific-tasting European cooking. Good wine list. Very good value set price lunch. Slightly noisy atmosphere.

Leith's
◆ D A3
92 Kensington Park Rd W11
Notting Hill Gate
Tel. 020 4229 4481
Open Tue–Fri 12.15–2.15pm, 7–11.30pm.
Closed Mon and Sat lunchtime and Sun.
This Notting Hill institution is under new management. The two-course menu is the most economical and the most inventive. Excellent wine list and perfect desserts. High-quality vegetarian dishes.

Restaurant 192
◆ D A3
192 Kensington Park Road W11
Ladbroke Grove
Tel. 020 7229 0482
Open 12.30–3pm and 7–11.30pm (11pm Sun)
This wine bar, located near Portobello Road, is always packed. The warm salads are very popular.

The Cow
◆ D A3
89 Westbourne Park Rd W2
Royal Oak or Westbourne Park
Tel. 020 7221 5400
Open Mon–Sat 7–11pm; Sun 12.30–3.30pm, 7.30–10.30pm
Excellent gastropub owned by Tom Conran's, Terence's son. Oysters, seafood and Guinness in the bar and set menus in the more agreeable but posher upstairs dining room. Reasonably-priced two-course menu and a great atmosphere. "Eat Heartily and Give the House a Good Name" is the Cow's slogan and we're happy to do so.

PADDINGTON
BAYSWATER

Bombay Palace
◆ E A2/3
50 Connaught St W2
Marble Arch
Tel. 020 7723 8855
Open noon–3pm and 6–11.30pm
Cuisine from northern India served in an elegant setting with fine views over Hyde Park Square. Attentive service. Booking essential in the evening.

SOHO

Bam-bou
◆ B D2
1 Percy St W1
Tottenham Crt Rd
Tel. 020 7323 9130
Mon–Sat noon–3pm, 6–11.30pm. Closed Sat lunch and Sun.
Delicate French-Vietnamese cuisine in a fantastically elegant townhouse at the bottom of Charlotte Street. Bar on the top floor, restaurant in small rooms on the ground and first. Small terrace in summer. Not cheap but classy.

Gay Hussar
◆ F 2A
2 Greek St W1
Tottenham Crt Rd
Tel. 020 7437 0973
Open 12.30–2.30pm, 5.30–11pm.
Closed Sun.
Hungarian restaurant popular with Soho's literati. Luxurious yet old-fashioned décor and warm atmosphere. Excellent meat dishes from Central Europe. Generous portions.

Lindsay House
◆ F A2
21 Romilly St W1
Piccadilly or Leicester Square
Tel. 020 7439 0450
An 18th-century townhouse in the heart of Soho that retains a distinctively rakish feel. This is largely due to the chef and proprietor Richard Corrigan, who is larger than life in every sense of the word. His cooking has an entirely idiosyncratic brio and style, muscular and robust in flavor, but with the lightest and most delicate of touches. Some of the most distinctive and innovative food in the country.

Pollo
◆ F A2
20 Old Compton St W1

Leicester Square
Tel. 020 7734 5917
Open noon–midnight
Lots of inexpensive delicious pasta dishes. Very popular and often packed.

Rasa Samudra
◆ B D2
1 Charlotte St W1
Tottenham Crt Rd
Tel. 020 7637 0222
Open noon–3pm, 6–11pm. Closed Sun lunchtime.
Remarkable cuisine from southern India (Malabar Coast), based primarily on fish and vegetarian dishes with incredibly delicate flavors.

Saigon
◆ F A2
45 Frith St W1
Leicester Square
Tel. 020 7437 7109
Open noon–11pm. Closed Sun.
Excellent Vietnamese restaurant with a very good choice of dishes. The service is not exactly unfriendly but don't expect many smiles.

The Sugar Club
◆ F A1
21 Warwick St W1
Piccadilly or Oxford Circus
Tel. 020 7437 7776
Open noon–3pm, 6–10.30pm
One of the most innovative restaurants opened in recent years. Peter Gordon has now left to set up The Providores but his influence remains evident in dishes such as spicy kangaroo salad with coriander, grilled scallops with sweet chilli sauce or roast duck with vanilla-scented flageolets. It doesn't come cheap but the experience is worth it.

Yo! Sushi
◆ F A1
52 Poland St W1
Oxford Circus
Tel. 020 7287 0443
Open noon–midnight
Sushis served on a 200-foot-long conveyor belt. Beware, you cannot help taking the dishes as they pass along and the bill can end up being more than you planned. Take-out also available.

SOUTH KENSINGTON

Bibendum
◆ E D2
Michelin Building
81 Fulham Rd SW3
South Kensington
Tel. 020 7581 5817
Open Mon–Fri noon–2.30pm, 7–11.30pm; Sat 12.30–3pm, 7–11.30pm; Sun 12.30–3pm, 7–10.30pm
The favorite and very expensive French bistro of London society. Book ahead. The oyster bar is more reasonable.

Cactus Blue
◆ H A2
86 Fulham Rd SW3
South Kensington
Tel. 020 7823 7858
Open 5.30–11.45pm
Restaurant serving top-quality and authentic Mexican cuisine in a superb décor inspired by desert landscapes.

The Crown
◆ H A2
153 Dovehouse St SW3
South Kensington
Tel. 020 7352 9505
Open noon–2.30pm, 6–11.30pm. Closed Sun.
This gastropub combines a traditional décor with a varied and creative nouvelle cuisine.

BRASSERIE OXO TOWER

BIBENDUM

Fifth Floor
◆ E C3
Top floor of the Harvey Nichols department store, Knightsbridge SW1
Knightsbridge
Tel. 020 7235 5250
Open Mon–Fri noon–3pm, 6–11pm; Sat noon–3.30pm, 6–11pm
Bar and restaurant with superb views of the rooftops of London. Modern English.

Poissonnerie de l'Avenue
◆ E D2/3
78 Sloane Ave SW3
South Kensington
Tel. 020 7589 2457
Mon–Sat noon–2.30pm, 7–11.30pm
1930s décor and large choice of high-quality fish and shellfish. Attractively-priced menus.

Salloos
◆ E C3
62 Kinnerton St SW1
Knightsbridge
Tel. 020 7235 4444
Open noon–3pm, 6–11pm
Pakistani restaurant set up in former mews. Sophisticated setting and tasteful decoration. Do not miss the palak (spicy lamb with spinach).

Wodka
◆ D C4/E C1
12 St Albans Grove W8
High St Kensington or Gloucester Rd
Tel. 020 7937 6513
Open Mon–Fri 12.30–2.30pm, 7–11.15pm. Closed Sat lunchtime and Sun.
Reasonably-priced Polish cuisine and 13 kinds of traditional vodka.

TOWER BRIDGE DOCKLANDS

Café Spice Namaste
◆ G A3
16 Prescot St E1
Tower Hill or Aldgate
Tel. 020 7488 9242
Open Mon.–Fri. noon–3pm and 6.15–10.45pm; Sat. 6.15–10.45pm.

⚀ < £15 per person for two courses; not including drinks
⚁ £15 to £25
⚂ £25 to £45
⚃ > £45

Closed Sun.
A Victorian house near Tower Bridge with bright colors and velvet curtains. Notable Indian cuisine devised by the eminent chef Cyrus Todiwala. Take-out service available.
⚁

WATERLOO LAMBETH

Blue Print Café
G B3
Design Museum SE1
⊖ Tower Hill
Tel. 020 7378 7031
Open noon–3pm and 6–11pm. Closed Sun evening.
Plain and simple décor and a magnificent view over the Thames. The menu has an Asian influence.
⚁

Oxo Tower Restaurant & Bar & Brasserie
◆ F B4
Oxo Tower Warf
Barge House St SE1
⊖ Blackfriars or Waterloo
Tel. 020 7803 3888
Open Mon–Sat noon–2.30pm, 6–11pm; Sun noon–3pm, 6.30–10pm
Chic and expensive restaurant created by Harvey Nichols. If you can't afford dinner, have a drink there and step outside on the terrace. The view from the eighth floor, overlooking St Paul's, is stunning. Refined cuisine. Reservations are recommended for both the restaurant and the brasserie.
⚃ *restaurant*
⚂ *brasserie*

The Fire Station
◆ F C4
150 Waterloo Rd SE1
⊖ Waterloo
Tel. 020 7620 2226
Open Mon–Sat noon–2.45pm, 5.30–11pm; Sun noon–9.30pm
Lively bar-restaurant located in the former barracks of the firemen of Waterloo Station. English nouvelle cuisine.
⚁

Livebait
◆ F C4
43 The Cut SE1
⊖ Waterloo
Tel. 020 7928 7211
Open noon–3pm, 5.30–11.30pm. Closed Sun.
This fish restaurant, used to be a "pie and mash" shop (a type of popular café that serves mainly crusty pies with mashed potatoes). The tiled walls and simple tables and benches recreate its original Victorian charm. First-class fish and shellfish served by young and friendly staff. Reasonable prices. Booking essential. (Other branch at 21 Wellington St, Covent Garden.)
⚁

RSJ
◆ F C4
13a Coin St SE1
⊖ Waterloo
Tel. 020 7928 4554
Open Mon–Fri noon–2pm, 5.30–11pm; Sat 5.30–11pm
Known for its Loire wines and original French cuisine. Attractive theater menu. Book in advance.
⚁

WESTMINSTER BELGRAVIA

Chimes of Pimlico
◆ D D1
26 Churton St SW1
⊖ Pimlico
Tel. 020 7821 7456
Open noon–2.30pm, 6–10.30pm. Closed Sat lunchtime, Sun.
Restaurant located in the heart of Pimlico and serving traditional English specialties: all sorts of pies (mushroom, game, chicken, kidney, etc). Cider list.
⚁

Ken Lo's Memories of China
◆ E D4
67–69 Ebury St SW1
⊖ Victoria
Tel. 020 7730 7734
Open noon–2.15pm, 7–11.15pm. Closed Sun lunchtime.
Prestigious Chinese restaurant with painstakingly prepared dishes that are occasionally over-adapted to Western taste.
⚁

Noura
◆ E C4
16 Hobart Place SW1
⊖ Victoria
Tel. 020 7235 9444
Here's a novelty – a Lebanese brasserie. And it works very well. Big, open space, as sleek and chic as any around. Burly waiters look like enforcers, but are crisp and professional about their business. Some of the best bread in London, hot and puffy from the oven appears regularly throughout a meal. Hot and cold mezze are very reliable and help keep the costs down, but kebabs, fish and other grills are also premier division stuff. Lebanese wines priced higher than elsewhere, but are very drinkable.
⚁

The Seafresh
◆ F D1
80 Wilton Rd SW1
⊖ Victoria
Tel. 020 7828 0747
Open noon–10.30pm. Closed Sun.
Generous portions of seafood are served in this extremely popular restaurant. Take-out dishes also available. Fried or grilled fish, traditional fish and chips and seafood hotpot.
⚀

THE BEST FOOD AT THE BEST HOTELS

Marcus Wareing at **The Savoy Grill**
The Savoy
Strand, WC2
Tel. 020 7592 1600
Daily lunch and dinner
Gordon Ramsay's protégé, also head chef at Pétrus, another gem in London gastronomic landscape.
⚂

Angela Hartnett at **MENU**
The Connaught
Carlos Place W1
Tel. 020 7592 1222
Daily lunch and dinner
Another of Gordon Ramsay's protégée.
⚂

Gordon Ramsay at **Claridge's**
Claridge's Hotel
49 Brook St W1
Tel. 020 7499 0099
Mon–Sat breakfast, lunch and dinner; Sun breakfast and dinner
The man himself, genius chef and restauranteur, who tutored most of the new generation of Michelin-starred chefs.
⚃

David Thompson at **Nahm**
The Halkin
5 Halkin St SW1
Tel. 020 7333 1234
Mon–Fri lunch and dinner; Sat–Sun dinner
Cutting-edge Thai.
⚃

Nobuyuki Matsuhisa at **Nobu**
Metropolitan Hotel
19 Old Park Lane SW1
Tel. 020 7447 4747
Mon–Fri lunch and dinner; Sat–Sun dinner
Michelin-starred food at London's premier Japanese restaurant with South American influences. Book early.
⚃

Eric Chavot at **The Capital Hotel**
22–24 Basil St SW3
Tel. 020 7589 5171
Daily lunch and dinner
French cooking and two Michelin stars for this small, very elegant dining room designed by Nina Campbell.
⚂

PUBS & BARS

CITY

The Blackfriars ◆ F A4
174 Queen Victoria St EC4
Tel. 020 7236 5474
⊖ Blackfriars
Pub with superb Art-Nouveau décor and arts and crafts in marble and wood.

Fox & Anchor ◆ C C1
115 Charterhouse St EC1
Tel. 020 7253 5075
⊖ Barbican
Popular with City workers for its generous breakfast.

Hoop and Grapes Pub ◆ C D4
47 Aldgate High St EC3
Tel. 020 7265 5171
⊖ Aldgate
One of the oldest pubs in London, located in a 17th-century building.

The Old Bell ◆ F A4
95 Fleet St EC4
Tel. 020 7583 0216
⊖ Blackfriars
Typical Fleet Street tavern which has retained its atmosphere. The back door leads to St Brides graveyard.

Prospect of Whitby
57 Wapping Wall E1
⊖ Wapping
Tel. 020 7481 1095
The oldest pub north of the Thames, with a good view over the river. It enjoyed the patronage of such famous people as Samuel Pepys, Turner and Whistler.

Ye Olde Cheshire Cheese ◆ F A4
145 Fleet St EC4
Tel. 020 7353 6170
⊖ Blackfriars
One of the oldest British pubs, once patronised by Dickens. Its décor has not changed much since it was rebuilt after the Great Fire of London in 1666. Low ceiling with exposed beams and floor covered in sawdust.

CHELSEA
SLOANE SQUARE

Bunch of Grapes ◆ E D4
207 Brompton Rd SW2
Tel. 020 7589 4944
⊖ Knightsbridge
This magnificent pub, just a few steps away from Harrods, has retained much of its original Victorian decoration.

The Orange Brewery ◆ E D4
37–39 Pimlico Rd SW1
Tel. 020 7730 5984
⊖ Sloane Square
Still brews its own beer. Cumberland sausages and delicious pies for those small pangs of hunger.

Surprise ◆ E D4
6 Christchurch Terrace SW3
Tel. 020 7349 1821
⊖ Sloane Square
Real pub, with darts and billiards. Perfect for those who want to read their newspaper in peace.

COVENT GARDEN
AND THE STRAND

Dog and Duck ◆ F A1
18 Bateman St W1
Tel. 020 7494 0697
⊖ Tottenham Crt Rd
A small, old-fashioned pub, with Edwardian interior, engraved mirrors and green-and-orange tilework. It's very hard to get to the bar at the end. You can enjoy a drink standing outside or in the "snug", a small den upstairs.

Princess Louise ◆ B D3
208 High Holborn WC1
Tel. 020 7405 8816
⊖ Holborn
Pub dating from 1891, famous for its multicolored tiles and its engraved mirrors.

The Lamb and Flag ◆ F A2
33 Rose St (Garrick St) WC2
Tel. 020 7497 9504
⊖ Covent Garden
Authentic Covent Garden pub located in a small alleyway.

Waxy O'Connors ◆ F A2
14–16 Rupert St W1
Tel. 020 7287 0255
⊖ Piccadilly Circus
A beech tree grows on two stories inside this huge Irish pub! Seafood dishes.

KENSINGTON
KNIGHTSBRIDGE

Grenadier ◆ E C3
Wilton Row SW1
Tel. 020 7235 3074
⊖ Hyde Park Corner
In a tiny mews street behind Hyde Park Corner, former meeting place of the Grenadier Guards. Weapon displays on the walls, wood-burning fireplace and brass counter in the shape of a horseshoe. As cozy as a pair of old slippers.

MARYLEBONE

Barley Mow ◆ A D4
8 Dorset St W1
Tel. 020 7935 7318
⊖ Baker St
The pawnbroker's counter is an unusual feature of this old pub.

The Chapel ◆ E C4
48 Chapel St NW1
Tel. 020 7402 9220
⊖ Edgware Road
Very trendy, with good selection of draft beers and friendly waiters.

Crockers ◆ A C2
24 Aberdeen Place NW8 (continuation of Maida Avenue)
Tel. 020 7286 6608
⊖ Warwick Avenue
Opens very early in the morning (before 7am). Impressive turn-of-the-century Victorian pub. Marble counter, mahogany woodwork, cut glass and engraved mirrors.

NOTTING HILL

Elbow Room ◆ D A4
103 Westbourne Grove W2
Tel. 020 7221 5211
⊖ Notting Hill
Traditional pub, a must for beer and billiards enthusiasts.

Portobello Gold ◆ D A3
95–97 Portobello Road, W11
Tel. 020 7460 4910
⊖ Notting Hill Gate
Lively bar and restaurant in the heart of Portobello market. Real ales, Belgian wheat beer and a good wine list. Also an internet café.

HAMPSTEAD

Spaniards Inn
Spaniards Rd NW3
⊖ Hampstead
Tel. 020 8455 3276
This 400-year-old inn was frequented by romantic poets and by Charles Dickens, who may have been inspired by it for his novel Barnaby Rudge.

SOHO

Akbar ◆ F A2
77 Dean St W1
Tel. 020 7437 2525
⊖ Tottenham Crt Rd
Dark and exotic cocktail bar in the basement of the Red Fort restaurant. Indian-style fixtures and fittings. Excellent but pricey cocktails.

Alphabet ◆ F A1
61–63 Beak St W1
Tel. 020 7439 2190
⊖ Piccadilly Circus
One of the best bars in Soho. No door policy or silly pretentions, yet cool enough to make you want to return time and again. Good beer and excellent cocktails.

Hakkasan ◆ F A2
8 Hanway Place W1
Tel. 020 7927 7000
⊖ Leicester Square
Big list of cocktails at the bar of the sexiest restaurant in London. Brilliant design, fantastic vibe.

Lab ◆ F A2
12 Old Compton St W1
Tel. 020 7437 7820
⊖ Leicester Square
First-class cocktails

served by some of the best bartenders in London.

Two Floors ◆ F A1
3 Kingly St W1
Tel. 020 7439 1007
⊖ Oxford Circus
This establishment has an exterior free of nomenclature, preferring to rely on word of mouth. Good beer and good surroundings.

SOUTH OF THE RIVER

The George Inn
◆ G B1
77 Borough High St SE1
Tel. 020 7407 2056
⊖ London Bridge or Borough
Only coaching house with wooden galleries left in London, again described by Dickens, this time in Little Dorrit. *Serves homebrewed draft beer. Patio open in summer, and wood-burning fireplace in winter.*

NIGHT & JAZZ CLUBS

CAMDEN TOWN

Jazz Café ◆ B A1
5 Parkway NW1
Tel. 020 7344 0044 (tickets)
020 7916 6060 (restaurant)
⊖ Camden Town
Very popular club with excellent programs ranging from jazz to funk.

CITY

Fabric ◆ C C–D1
77A Charterhouse St
Tel. 020 7336 8898
⊖ Farringdon
Clubber's wonderland: frenetic dancefloors and labyrinthine lairs. Live performances every Friday night.

COVENT GARDEN AND STRAND

Bar Rumba ◆ F A2
36 Shaftesbury Avenue W1
Tel. 020 7287 2715
⊖ Piccadilly Circus
Not very large. Eclectic choice of music, according to the day of the week: house, trip-hop, salsa, dub or funk.

The Borderline
◆ F A2
Orange Yard
Manette St W1
Tel. 020 7734 2095
⊖ Tottenham Crt Rd
A favorite with students for britpop or indie. Live music.

Gardening Club
◆ F A2
4 Covent Garden Piazza WC2
Tel. 020 7497 3154
⊖ Covent Garden
Magical in summer with the windows opened onto the piazza. Torrid house music.

Heaven ◆ F B2
Villiers St WC2
Tel. 020 7930 2020
www.heaven-london.com
⊖ Charing Cross
Several bars and dance floors. Very popular with the gay community.

SOHO

100 Club ◆ F A1
100 Oxford St
Tel. 020 7636 0933
⊖ Oxford Circus or Tottenham Crt Rd
One of London's most celebrated jazz and live music venues for the last 50 years. This is the place that saw the birth of punk.

Cafe de Paris ◆ F B2
3 Coventry St, W1
Tel. 020 7734 7700
⊖ Leicester Square or Piccadilly Circus
One of London's best known nightclubs. Dancefloor and restaurant with a jazz band.

Ronnie Scott's
◆ F A2
47 Frith St W1
Tel. 020 7439 0747
www.ronniescott.co.uk
⊖ Leicester Square or Tottenham Crt Rd
From the most obscure to the most famous, every jazz name has played in this club. Absolutely the best. Reserve well in advance – you will have to eat to get a seat at a table. A little expensive though (£15 entry fee).

SOUTH OF THE RIVER

The Arches ◆ G B3
53 Southwark St SE1
Tel. 020 7403 9643
⊖ London Bridge
Huge, fascinating place. Young audience. Packed at the weekend.

Ministry of Sound
◆ G C1
103 Gaunt St SE1
Tel. 020 7378 6528
www.ministryofsound.com
⊖ Elephant & Castle
One of the most famous clubs in London, and, some say, the best nightclub ever. It has recently been refurbished, with the addition of tables and chairs and a cocktail menu. Eclectic clientele and a now legendary sound system. Not for the faint hearted.

The Fridge ◆ I D4
Town Hall Parade, Brixton Hill SW2
⊖ Brixton
Tel. 020 7326 5100
Its "Love and Muscle" evening has become a cult event. Electronic music.

SOUTHEAST

The Venue
2a Clifton Rise New Cross SE14
⊖ New Cross
Tel. 020 8692 4077
Slightly out of the way, but one of the trendiest places for indie music.

SOUTHWEST

606 Club
90 Lots Rd SW10
Tel. 020 7352 5953
⊖ Fulham Broadway or Earl's Court
Small private members' jazz cellar where non-members are welcome as long as they eat – and the food is really worth it. Gigs every night, trios, quartets etc. Great ambience. Recommended.

SHOPPING

Almost every street in central London boasts a store. Head for Kings Road, Bond Street and Regent's Street for designer fashions and department stores; Covent Garden and Notting Hill for fashion boutiques; Jermyn Street for men's tailoring; Hatton Garden for jewelry; Tottenham Court Road for furniture and electronic goods; and Charing Cross Road for new and second-hand books. Most stores open Mon–Sat 10am–6pm (or 7pm). Many stores close late on Thu (8 or 9pm) and open Sun 11am–5pm.

ARCADES

Burlington Arcade
◆ F B1
Piccadilly W1
⊖ Piccadilly Circus
Next door to the Royal Academy of Arts. Indoor arcades selling expensive, luxury goods.

Hay's Galleria
◆ G B2
Tooley Street SE1
⊖ London Bridge
Former warehouses, covered by a high glass roof supported on iron columns, now containing offices, cafés, restaurants and shops. The glass-covered atrium has stalls and street entertainers.

Royal Exchange
◆ C D3
Corner of Threadneedle St and Cornhill St EC3
⊖ Bank
Former center for commerce now converted into a high-class shopping complex.

MARKETS

Borough Market
◆ G B1
Borough High St SE1
⊖ London Bridge
Fri–Sat
Historic fruit and

vegetable market beneath the railway tracks running into London Bridge. Fine foods market (Sat).

Camden Lock Market
◆ B A1
off Chalk Farm Road, NW1
⊖ Camden Town
Sat–Sun
Now the fourth most-visited tourist attraction in London. Enormous range of goods, from new fashions to second-hand clothes, handmade crafts, new and second-hand street fashions, vegetarian fast-food, books, records and antiques.

Petticoat Lane Market
◆ C D4
Middlesex St and Wentworth St E1
⊖ Aldgate or Aldgate East
Mon–Fri, Sun
Probably the most famous of all London's street markets. Huge variety of goods on sale with a bias toward clothing.

Portobello Road Market ◆ D A3
Portobello Rd W11
⊖ Notting Hill Gate
Antiques Sat; general: Mon–Sat; bric-a-brac: Fri–Sat
Really three or four markets rolled into one. At the Notting Hill end there are antiques, jewelry, paintings, silverware and collectables. Further down the hill are fruit and vegetable stalls. Under the Westway are second-hand clothes, jewelry, records and books.

Spitalfields Market
◆ C D3
Commercial St E1
⊖ Shoreditch
General market: Mon–Fri; organic market: Fri, Sun:
Fruit and vegetable market including a number of organic stalls. Crafts, clothes, jewelry.

FOOD

Charbonnel et Walker
One The Royal Arcade
28 Old Bond St W1
www.charbonnel.co.uk
Founded in 1875, and begun as a partnership between Mrs Walker and Mme Charbonnel's chocolate house in Paris. It is the official supplier of the Queen.

Konditor & Cook
◆ F B4
22 Cornwall Rd SE1
www.konditorandcook.com
⊖ Waterloo
The best patisserie in London. Tempting cakes and a good range of breads.

L'Artisan du Chocolat
◆ E D3
89 Lower Sloane St SW1
www.artisanduchocolat.com
⊖ Sloane Square
Tel. 020 7824 8365
London's premier purveyor of bespoke chocolates.

Millroy's of Soho
◆ F A2
3 Greek St W1
⊖ Tottenham Court Road
Irish and Welsh whiskies. All the Scottish pure malts (from the Lowlands to the Orkneys). Tasting bar in the basement.

Neal's Yard Dairy
◆ F A2
19 Short Gardens WC2
⊖ Covent Garden
Sampling and sale of the best of English and Irish cheeses.

Paxton & Whitfield
◆ F B1
93 Jermyn St SW1
www.paxtonandwhitfield.co.uk
⊖ Piccadilly Circus
Traditional British cheeses plus a good selection of the newer on-farm varieties.

Rococo ◆ E D3
321 King's Road SW3
www.rococochocolates.com
⊖ Sloane Square
For chocolate addicts. Funny flavors.

The Tea House
◆ F A2
15a Neal St WC2
⊖ Covent Garden
Huge range of teas from all over the world. Teapots, cookies, etc.

JEWELRY

Lesley Craze Gallery
◆ C C1
33–35a Clerkenwell Green EC1
www.lesleycrazegallery.co.uk
⊖ Farringdon
Contemporary jewelry, metal-smithing and textiles.

London Silver Vaults
◆ B D4
53 Chancery Lane WC2
www.thesilvervaults.com
⊖ Chancery Lane
Thirty different stalls selling jewelry, silver goods and china in vaults that seem as impregnable as the Bank of England. Bargaining expected.

Steinberg & Tolkien
◆ E D3
193 King's Rd SW3
⊖ Sloane Square
Good place for second-hand clothing and jewelry.

Wright and Teague
◆ F B1
1a Grafton St, off Bond St, W1
www.wrightandteague.com
⊖ Green Park
Internationally acclaimed jewellers.

FASHION

Diesel
◆ F A2
43 Earlham St WC2
⊖ Covent Garden
Temple of grunge, fashion famous for its way-out advertising.

Gieves & Hawkes
◆ F A1
1 Savile Row W1
⊖ Piccadilly Circus
The most famous tailors in Savile Row. Luxurious ready-to-wear shirts.

Harvie & Hudson
◆ F B1
77 Jermyn St SW1
⊖ Green Park
World-famous for its made-to-measure shirts. More affordable ready-to-wear section.

Karen Millen
◆ D C4
Unit 4, Barkers Arcade, Kensington High St W8
⊖ High St Kensington
Very elegant clothes for women, with a touch of stylish originality.

Ozwald Boateng
◆ F B1
9 Vigo St W1
⊖ Piccadilly Circus
The best of English eccentricity which never goes out of style. Unequalled comfort.

Paul Smith
◆ F A2
40–44 Floral St WC2
www.paulsmith.co.uk
⊖ Covent Garden
A man who manages to mix eccentricity with classical tailoring.

Red or Dead
◆ F A2
33 Neal St WC2
⊖ Covent Garden
Shoes and evening dress for mad partying.

HATS

Bates the Hatter
◆ F B1
21a Jermyn St SW1
www.bates-hats.co.uk
⊖ Piccadilly Circus
All the great British classics, with the guaranty of quality. Jermyn Street itself, facing the pretty St James's Church, is worth the detour.

Stephen Jones
◆ B D3
36 Great Queen St WC2
www.stephenjonesmillinery.com

⊖ Holborn
Hats for all tastes: from town hats to country hats.

SHOES

Church's
◆ F A1
201 Regent St W1
⊖ Oxford Circus
Famous for high-quality traditional British shoes and boots.

Dr. Marten Department Store
◆ F A2
1–4 King St WC2
⊖ Covent Garden
Toughness is the word at Doc Marten's. Hard-wearing footwear (even for babies) on six floors. You have to be a fan.

John Lobb
◆ F B1
88 Jermyn St SW1
⊖ Green Park
For men. This boutique, worthy of any museum, is reserved for the select few who can afford the shoemaker's made-to-measure footwear. Prices are reasonable though, bearing in mind the quality.

Manolo Blahnik
◆ H A2
49–51 Old Church St SW3
⊖ Sloane Square
Very fashionable and extremely expensive shoes for Sarah Jessica Parker to wear in Sex and the City, and a million other women to dream about.

DEPARTMENT STORES

Fortnum & Mason
◆ F A/B1
181 Piccadilly W1
Tel. 020 7734 8040
Closed Sunday
www.fortnumandmason.com
⊖ Piccadilly Circus
The Queen's department store, worth visiting for its wonderful food section. The motto of this famous store is "prestige and tradition".

Harrods ◆ F B1
87–135 Brompton Rd SW1
Tel. 020 7730 1234
www.harrods.com
⊖ Knightsbridge
You have to go there at least once in your life. The January and July sales are not to be missed.

Harvey Nichols
◆ E C3
109 Knightsbridge SW1
Tel. 020 7235 5000
www.harveynichols.com
⊖ Knightsbridge
Better than Harrods according to fashion lovers. All the great names in fashion design are gathered here. Excellent food store and restaurant (see p. 380).

Liberty
◆ F A1
210–220 Regent St W1
Tel. 020 7734 1234
www.liberty.co.uk
⊖ Oxford Circus
A visit to London would not be complete without dropping into Liberty, famous for its printed fabrics, jewelry, accessories, etc., but also for its charming Victorian décor in the Tudor style. Wonderful women's fashion departments.

Selfridges
◆ E A4
400 Oxford St W1
Tel. 020 7629 1234
www.selfridges.co.uk
⊖ Bond St
Elegant store in a superb Edwardian-style building erected between 1907 and 1928. Renowned cosmetics department.

TOYS

Hamley's
◆ F A1
186 Regent St W1
Tel. 020 7494 2000
www.hamleys.co.uk
⊖ Oxford Circus
The biggest toy store in the world, on seven levels.

BOOKSTORES

Books for Cooks
◆ D A2
4 Blenheim Crescent W11
⊖ Notting Hill
Every cookery book ever published and two tables at the back where you cab lunch on whatever special the owners have decided to cook that day.

Garden Books ◆ D A2
11 Blenheim Crescent W11
⊖ Notting Hill
Every book published on gardening.

Hatchards Bookshop
◆ E C3
187 Piccadilly W1
⊖ Piccadilly Circus
Wonderful bookshop founded in 1797.

Murder One ◆ F A2
71–73 Charing Cross Road
⊖ Leicester Square
Europe's largest crime and mystery bookshop.

FURNITURE

The Conran Shop
◆ E D2
Michelin House
81 Fulham Rd SW3
www.conran.co.uk
⊖ South Kensington
Best of Sir Terence's furniture and furnishings design.

David Black Oriental Carpets
◆ D B2
96 Portland Rd W11
⊖ Holland Park
Finest Oriental rugs and carpets. Beautiful antique kilims.

Designer's Guild
◆ H A2
267–271 & 275–277 King's Rd SW3
www.designersguild.com
⊖ Sloane Square
Beautiful fabrics, wallpapers, bedlinen and China.

Heal's ◆ B D2
196 Tottenham Crt Rd W1
www.heals.co.uk
⊖ Goodge St
Several floors of stylish and expensive furniture and home furnishings. Habitat is next door, and other fine furniture stores, such as Lombok (no. 108), The Pier (no. 200) Purves & Purves (no. 202), Elephant (no. 230) and BO Concept (no. 158), on the same road.

The Holding Company
241–245 Kings Rd SW3
www.theholdingcompany.co.uk
⊖ Sloane Square
Everything for storage. Beautiful furniture for bathroom, bedroom and office. Baskets, shelves, leather chests and boxes, denim organisers... you name it.

Jean Sewell Antiques
◆ D B3
3 Campden St W8
⊖ Notting Hill Gate
Exquisite English porcelain and earthenware.

FLOWERS

Paula Pryke Flowers
◆ B B4
20 Penton Street N1
www.paula-pryke-flowers.com
⊖ Angel
A spacious and elegant flower shop with magical window displays. There's also a concession at Liberty.

Wild at Heart
◆ D A3
49A Ledbury Rd W11
www.wildatheart.com
⊖ Notting Hill Gate or Westbourne Park
This florist supplies bouquets to the fashion industry and the media. The flowers school offers one-day courses.

The Wild Bunch
◆ F A2
17–22 Earlham Street WC2
⊖ Covent Garden or Leicester Square tube
A high-quality, bustling flower stall with a vast choice. Competitive prices.

(THE) ADELPHI 7 Adam Street WC2	*Sumptuous neoclassical building by the Adam Brothers built between 1768 and 1774.*	▲ 267 F B2/3
ADMIRALTY HOUSE Whitehall	*Former official building turned into a hotel south of Trafalgar Square.*	▲ 144 F B2
ALBERT MEMORIAL Hyde Park SW7	*Impressive and well-restored neogothic monument opposite the Royal Albert Hall.*	▲ 236 E C1
ALBERY THEATRE 85 St Martin's Lane WC2 Tel. 020 7369 1700	*Built at the beginning of the 19th century, this West End theater stands back to back with the Wyndham's Theatre in Charing Cross.*	● 55 F B2
ALFIE'S ANTIQUE MARKET 13–25 Church Street NW8 Tel. 020 7723 6066	*Open Tue–Sat 10am–6pm. Closed Sun–Mon. Huge multi-storied indoor market selling antiques and second-hand goods.*	A C/D3
ALL HALLOWS CHURCH Throgmorton St London Wall EC2	*Neoclassical church built by George Dance the Young. Vestiges of the Roman wall in the garden.*	▲ 181 C D3
ALL SAINTS CHURCH, FULHAM ⊖ Fulham Broadway	*Interesting 18th-century tombs inside the church and outside in the churchyard.*	▲ 343
(THE) ANGEL 101 Berdmondsey Wall East SE16 Tel. 020 7237 3608	*Legend has it that Captain Cook came here for a drink before setting out to Australia. Do not miss the trap door used by smugglers.*	▲ 340 G B4
ANTIQUARIUS 131–141 King's Road SW3 Tel. 020 7351 5353	*Antique market with around 120 stores.*	▲ 197 H A2
APSLEY HOUSE (WELLINGTON MUSEUM) 149 Piccadilly, Hyde Park Corner W1 Tel. 020 7499 5676	*Open 11am–5pm. Closed Mon. The Duke of Wellington's address was "Number One, London" and Londoners still refer to it in this way. Gallery on the 2nd floor.*	▲ 247 E B4
ARCHITECTURAL ASSOCIATION 34 Bedford Square WC1 Tel. 020 7636 0974	*Temporary exhibitions and conferences all year round.*	▲ 300 B D3
(THE) ARK Hammersmith W6	*Visible from Hammersmith Flyover, this 1992 building resembles a huge ship.*	● 92 D D1
ASHBURNHAM HOUSE (WESTMINSTER SCHOOL) Dean's Yard SW1 Tel. 020 7963 1000/1079	*Visits by appointment only during school vacation. Well-preserved 17th-century interior decoration and famous square staircase.*	▲ 142 F C2
ATHENAEUM CLUB 107 Pall Mall Tel. 020 7930 4843	*Open to members and their guests only.*	▲ 278 F B2
BANK OF ENGLAND MUSEUM Bartholomew Lane EC2 Tel. 020 7601 5545 *www.bankofengland.co.uk*	*Open Mon–Fri 10am–5pm. Closed Sat, Sun and public hols. Located in the same building as the Bank of England, whose history is presented since its founding in 1694.*	▲ 150 C D2/3
BANQUETING HOUSE Whitehall SW1 Tel. 0870 751 5178	*Open 10am–5pm. Closed Sun, public hols and Dec 24–Jan. The work of Inigo Jones, it is the first classical Renaissance building in London (1622).*	▲ 144 F B2
BARBICAN CENTRE FOR THE ARTS Silk Street EC2 Tel. 020 7638 4141 (box office) 020 7638 8891 (gallery) 020 7582 7000 (cinema) *www.barbican.org.uk*	*Open Mon–Sat 10am–6.45pm (Tue 5.45pm), Sun and public hols noon–6.45pm. Movie theater, theaters, concert halls (London Symphony Orchestra), art galleries, restaurants. Exhibitions of paintings at the Barbican Art Gallery on the 9th floor.*	▲ 181 C C2
BATTERSEA PARK Albert Bridge Road/ Prince of Wales Drive Battersea SW11 *www.batterseapark.org*	*Open every day during daylight hours. Pleasant park south of the Thames, opposite Chelsea. Sports and leisure facilities for children. Entertainment and events throughout the year. Jazz at the Lakeside Café on Tue and Fri eve.*	H B3
BATTERSEA POWER STATION Chelsea Bridge SW8	*Disused red-brick monument dating back to the 1930s. There are plans to develop the building into a multi-purpose center.*	● 90 H B4
BERMONDSEY ANTIQUES MARKET NEW CALEDONIAN MARKET Corner of Bermondsey St, Long Lane and Tower Bridge Rd SE1	*Open to the public Fri 7am–2pm. Open to the trade from 5am. Come early to this popular market for real bargains.*	▲ 340 G C2
BERRY BROTHERS & RUDD 3 St James Street SW1 Tel. 020 7396 9600	*Eight successive generations have run this spirit and wine store (the oldest in Great Britain) opened in 1698.*	▲ 279 F B1
BERWICK STREET MARKET Soho W1	*Open 9am–6pm. Closed Sun. Fruit, vegetables, herbs, spices, cheeses.*	▲ 297 F A1

BETHNAL GREEN MUSEUM OF CHILDHOOD Corner of Cambridge Heath Road and Old Ford Road E2 ⊖ Bethnal Green Tel. 020 8983 5200	*Open daily, except Tue 10am–5.50pm. Annex of the Victoria and Albert Museum. Antique games and toys, dolls houses, puppet theaters and children's clothes. Exhibitions and workshops.*	▲ 313
BISHOP'S PARK Bishop's Park Road, Fulham SW6 ⊖ Putney Bridge	*Open during daylight hours. Thoroughly enjoyable walk along the Thames.*	▲ 343
BOROUGH MARKET Between Borough High Street and Bedale Street, Winchester Walk and Stoney Street SE1	*Open Fri noon–6pm, Sat 9am–4pm.*	G B1
BRAMAH TEA & COFFEE MUSEUM 38 Soutwark Street SE1 Tel. 020 7403 5650	*Open daily 10am–6pm. Two museums in one. History of the tea and coffee trades.*	▲ 340 G B3
BRITISH FILM INSTITUTE IMAX CINEMA 1 Chaplin Walk, South Bank SE1 Tel. 020 7901 1234 *www.bfi.org.uk*	*Open Tue–Sun 11am–5pm (last ticket sales 4.30pm). Group rates (Tel. 020 7902 1220).*	▲ 322 F B3
BRITISH LIBRARY 96 Euston Road W1 Tel. 020 7412 7000 *www.bl.uk*	*Open Mon–Fri 9.30am–6pm (8pm Tue, 5pm Sat), Sun 11am–5pm. Access to books (letter of introduction required) Mon 10am–6pm, Tue–Thur 9.30am–6pm, Fri–Sat 9.30am–4.30pm. Permanent interactive exhibition on the history of illumination. Temporary exhibitions.*	▲ 308 B B3
BRITISH MUSEUM Great Russell Street WC1 Tel. 020 7323 8000 *www.british-museum. ac.uk*	*Open Mon–Sat 10am–5pm, Sun noon–6pm. Free (except for special exhibitions). National archeological collections. The famous Reading Room has been restored and houses bookstores and multimedia stalls.*	▲ 300 B D3
BRIXTON MARKET Brixton SW9	*Open Mon–Sat 8am–6pm (3pm Wed). Huge open-air market famous for its exotic produce in a rapidly developing area.*	1 D4
BROADCASTING HOUSE Portland Place W1 Tel. 0870 010 0222 *www.bbc.co.uk*	*Open Mon 1–4.30pm, Tue–Sun 9.30am–4.30pm. Numerous cultural activities and events. Interactive exhibition "BBC Experience".*	▲ 253 B D2
BROMPTON ORATORY Brompton Road SW7 Tel. 020 7808 0900	*Open 6.30–8pm. Latin mass Sun at 11am. Catholic church in the Italian Baroque style. Organ of great repute.*	▲ 236 E C2
BUCKINGHAM PALACE The Mall SW1 Tel. 020 7373 3333 *www.buckingham-index.co.uk*	*Visit of the State Rooms from Aug 6 until Oct 3 only; daily 9.30am–4.30pm. Queen's Gallery (see separate entry). Royal Mews: Mon–Thur noon–4pm.*	▲ 242 E C4
BURLINGTON ARCADE W1	*Around forty luxury boutiques can be found in this beautiful Regency gallery, set up in 1819.*	▲ 280 F B1
CABINET WAR ROOMS Clive Steps King Charles Street SW1 Tel. 020 7930 6961	*Open daily: Apr–Sep 9.30am–6pm; Oct–Mar 10am–6pm (last admissions 5.15pm). Closed Dec 24–26. Underground bunker that housed the most vital sections of the War Ministry during the Blitz.*	▲ 143 F C2
CAFÉ ROYAL 68 Regent Street W1 Tel. 020 7437 9090	*Prestigious and historical meeting place for late-19th-century artists and writers.*	▲ 282 F B2
CAMDEN LOCK MARKET Chalk Farm Road NW1	*Daily. Picturesque and – touristic – flea market along the canal.*	▲ 259 B A1
CAMDEN PASSAGE off Upper Street N1	*Second-hand goods, silver, books, prints. The stalls vary from day to day.*	▲ 259 B A2
CAMLEY STREET PARK 12 Camley Street NW1 Tel. 020 7833 2311	*Open Mon–Thur 9am–5pm, Sat–Sun 11am–4pm. Behind King's Cross, nature takes over again in this small, but well-preserved space.*	B B3
CANADA HOUSE Trafalgar Square W1	*Canadian showcase in London. Do not miss the elegant staircase and reading room.*	▲ 285 F B2
CANARY WHARF TOWER Canada Square	*The work of Cesar Pelli. The 800-foot (240-m) steel tower is not open to the public.*	▲ 338
CARLYLE'S HOUSE 24 Cheyne Row SW3 Tel. 020 7352 7087 (custodian)	*Open Apr–Oct: Wed–Fri 2–5pm, Sat–Sun 11am–5pm. Museum and residence of the Scottish writer and historian Thomas Carlyle.*	▲ 202 H B2

CARLTON CINEMA Islington N1	*This former movie theater dating back from 1929 with a neo-Egyptian façade of multicolored tiles is now a Bingo club.*	● 85 C A1
CHANGING OF THE GUARDS Buckingham Palace SW1 Tel. 0906 866 3344	*Apr–Jul: daily 11.30am; Aug–Mar: daily 11.30am (canceled if the weather is bad).*	▲ 142 H A4 F C1
CHELSEA ANTIQUES MARKET 245–253 King's Road SW3	*Mon–Sat 10am–6pm. Books, prints and antique maps.*	▲ 197 H A2
CHELSEA OLD CHURCH Old Church Street Cheyne Walk SW3 Tel. 020 7352 5627	*Open Mon–Fri noon–4pm, Sun 8am–7pm. Closed Sat. Also known as All Saints Church. The square tower was rebuilt after the 1941 bombings.*	▲ 202 H B2
CHELSEA PHYSIC GARDEN 66 Royal Hospital Road SW3 Tel. 020 7352 5646	*Open Apr–Oct: Wed 2–5pm, Sun 2–6pm. Closed Nov–Mar. Rare and medicinal plants.*	▲ 200 H A3
CHELSEA OLD TOWN HALL King's Road SW3	*Second-hand goods and jumble sales on Sat. Elegant weddings often held here.*	▲ 197 H A2
CHINA WHARF Mill Street SE1	*Building, erected in 1980, in a mix of post-modern and pseudo-Oriental architectural styles.*	● 93 G B3
CHISWICK HOUSE Burlington Lane, Chiswick W4 Chiswick railway st. (Waterloo) Tel. 020 8995 0508	*Open in summer: daily 10am–4pm; in winter: Thur–Sun 10am–4pm. Closed Jan 1–18. Residence built in 1725 in the Palladian style of country houses and set in French gardens.*	▲ 342
CHRIST CHURCH, SPITALFIELDS Commercial Street E1 Tel. 020 7247 7202	*Open Mon–Fri noon–2.30pm; 4th Sun of month 1–4pm. Church currently undergoing restoration but still open to public.*	▲ 197 C C/D4
CHRISTIE'S 8 King Street, SW1 Tel. 020 7839 9060	*Founded in 1766. Amongst the most prestigious auction rooms in the world.*	F B1
CITY HALL The Queen's Walk SE1 Tel. 020 7983 4000	*New building whose ground floor is open to the public Mon–Fri 8am–8pm and occasional weekends through the year. Call for info.*	▲ 192 F B1
CLARENCE HOUSE Stable Yard SW1 Tel. 020 7766 7303	*Open early Aug–mid Oct: daily 9am–7pm, last admission 6pm. Tickets are timed and must be pre-booked by telephone.*	▲ 241 F B1
CLARIDGE'S HOTEL 53 Brook Street W1 Tel. 020 7629 8860	*The 1930s-style décor by Oswald Milnes was kept during the renovation works.*	▲ 282 E A4
CLEOPATRA'S NEEDLE Victoria Embankment WC2	*Dating back to the 15th century BC, the obelisk erected on the Thames embankment in 1878 is one of London's most ancient monuments.*	▲ 268 F B3
CLINK PRISON MUSEUM 1 Clink Street SE1 Tel. 020 7378 1558	*Open daily 10am–6pm. Built on the site of a former jail, this small museum presents a history of the area.*	G B1
CLOTHWORKERS HALL Dunster Court, Mincing Lane EC3 Tel. 020 7623 7041	*Open to the public only on rare occasions. If closed, visits may be arranged by appointment.*	▲ 156 G A2
COLUMBIA ROAD MARKET E2	*Flower market and garden center: Sun 8am–1pm. Crafts at weekend.*	▲ 312 C B4
COTY FACTORY Great West Road W4	*Superb example of Art-Deco architecture on the industrial Great West Road.*	● 90
COUNTY HALL Riverside Building Westminster Bridge Road SE1 Tel. 020 7967 8000	*Formerly the headquarters of the Greater London Council, this building now houses the London Aquarium, the Dalí Universe, the Saatchi Gallery (see separate entries) and the Football Association Premier League Hall of Fame.*	▲ 320 F C3
COURTAULD INSTITUTE GALLERIES Somerset House, Strand WC2 Tel. 020 7873 2526 *www.somerset-house.org.uk*	*Open Mon–Sat 10am–6pm, Sun 2–6pm. Closed for Christmas and Jan 1. Flemish Primitives, Quattrocento, Italian Baroque, Impressionists and modern paintings.*	▲ 270 F A3
COVENT GARDEN MARKET Southampton Street WC2	*Open daily 9am–7pm. Jewelry and crafts in the main hall (Apple Market).*	▲ 312 F A2
CRAFTS COUNCIL GALLERY 44a Pentonville Road N1 Tel. 020 7278 7700	*Open Tue–Sat 11am–6pm, Sun 2–6pm. Old and contemporary crafts. Reference library, cafeteria and boutique.*	B B4
CUMBERLAND TERRACE Regent's Park NW1	*Impressive row of residences by John Nash, on the Western edge of Regent's Park, between Albany Street and the Outer Circle.*	▲ 256 B B1
CUTTY SARK & GIPSY MOTH IV King William Walk SE10 Tel. 020 7858 3445	*Cutty Sark: open Mon–Sat 10am–6pm (5pm Oct–Mar), Sun noon–5pm. Gypsy Moth IV: (Easter–Oct) Mon–Sat 10am–6pm, Sun noon–6pm.*	▲ 327 G B3

Place	Details	Ref.
DAILY EXPRESS BUILDING 121–128 Fleet Street EC1	*With its chromium and mirrored glass this is a typical example of 1930s futuristic architecture.*	● 92 F A4
DALÍ UNIVERSE County Hall, South Bank SE1 Tel. 020 7620 2720	*Open daily 10am–5.30 last entry. Late opening in summer – telephone for opening times. Gallery devoted to the works of Salvador Dalí.*	
DESIGN MUSEUM Butler's Wharf 28 Shad Thames SE1 Tel. 020 7403 6933 *www.designmuseum.org.uk*	*Open daily 11.30am–6pm. Closed at Christmas and Jan 1. The best of design. Temporary collections or exhibitions.*	▲ 340 G B3
DICKENS'S HOUSE MUSEUM 48 Doughty Street WC1 Tel. 020 7405 2127	*Open Mon–Fri 9.45am–5.30pm, Sat 10am–5pm. Dickens resided here from 1837 to 1839. Photographs, portraits, letters and manuscripts.*	▲ 298 B C4
DOCTOR JOHNSON'S HOUSE 17 Gough Square EC4 Tel. 020 7353 3745	*Open Mon–Sat 11am–5.30pm (5pm in winter). Closed Sun and public hols.*	▲ 161 C D1
DULWICH PICTURE GALLERY College Road, Dulwich SE21 West Dulwich railway st. (Victoria) Bus P4 from Brixton subway st. Tel. 020 8693 5254	*Open Tue–Fri 10am–5pm, Sat 11am–5pm, Sun 1–5pm.*	▲ 364
ELTHAM PALACE off Court Road, SE9 Eltham railway st. (Charing Cross) Tel. 020 8294 2548	*Open Apr–Sep: Wed–Fri, Sun and public hols 10am–6pm; Oct: Wed–Fri, Sun 10am–5pm; Nov–Mar: 10am–4pm.*	
ENGLISH NATIONAL OPERA London Coliseum St Martin's Lane WC2 Tel. 020 7632 8300 *www.eno.org*	*Built in 1906, the London Coliseum has retained its Edwardian charm. The first London theater to be equipped with a revolving stage. The foyer and the tiled bathrooms deserve a glance. Completely refurbished in 2003.*	F B2
ETON COLLEGE Eton, Berkshire Train (Paddington or Waterloo) Tel. 01753 671 177	*Open from mid-Mar until mid-Sep. Call for opening times. The museum on life at Eton and the school chapel are worth a visit.*	▲ 361
FASHION & TEXTILE MUSEUM 83 Bermondsey Street SE1 Tel. 020 7403 0222 *www.ftmlondon.org*	*Open Tue–Sun 11am–5.45pm. Closed Mon. Brainchild of fashion designer Zandra Rhodes, the museum exhibits the works of fashion and textile designers, with emphasis on British design from the 1950s to the present day.*	G B2
FENTON HOUSE Windmill Hill NW3 ⊖ Hampstead Tel. 020 7435 3471	*Open Mar 6–Apr 4: Sat–Sun 2–5pm; Apr 7–Oct 31: Mon–Fri 2–5pm, Sat–Sun and Easter vacation 11am–5pm (last admissions 4.30pm). China, embroidery, musical instruments.*	▲ 262
FIREPOWER! THE ROYAL ARTILLERY MUSEUM Royal Arsenal, Woolwich SE18 Train (Woolwich Arsenal) Tel. 020 8855 7755	*Open daily 10am–5pm. An increasingly popular museum about the history of artillery.*	
FLORENCE NIGHTINGALE MUSEUM St Thomas Hospital 2 Lambeth Palace Road SE1 Tel. 020 7620 0374	*Call for opening days and times.*	▲ 320 F C3
FREUD MUSEUM 20 Maresfield Gardens NW3 ⊖ Finchley Road Tel. 020 7435 2002/7435 5167	*Open Wed–Sun noon–5pm. Library, letters, personal mementos and, of course, the famous consulting couch!*	▲ 264
FROGMORE HOUSE Windsor Great Park, Windsor Train (Paddington or Waterloo) Tel. 020 7766 7305 (bookings) or 020 7766 7324 (enquiries)	*Residence open final weekend in Aug 11am–5pm (last admissions 4pm). Royal mausoleum open on the Wed nearest to May 24 (Queen Victoria's birthday). Call for opening times.*	▲ 363
GEFFRYE MUSEUM Kingsland Road E2 Tel. 020 7739 9893 *www.geffrye-museum.org.uk*	*Open Tue–Sat 10am–5pm, Sun and bank holiday Mon noon–5pm. Closed Mon (unless bank holiday), Easter and Christmas. Museum of the changing style of English homes and gardens from 1600 to the present day.*	
GILBERT COLLECTION OF DECORATIVE ARTS Somerset House, Strand WC2 Tel. 020 7240 4080 *www.somerset-house.org.uk*	*Open Mon–Sat 10am–6pm; Sun, public hols noon–6pm. Last admission 5.15pm. 800 works of art, including European silver, gold snuff boxes and Italian mosaics.*	▲ 269 F A3

GRAY'S INN Gray's Inn Road Holborn WC1	*Open Mon–Fri noon–4.30pm (gardens only). Beautiful gardens designed by Sir Francis Bacon in 1606 and restructured in the 19th century.*	▲ 168 B D4
GRAY'S MEWS & GRAY'S ANTIQUE MARKET 1–7 Davies Mews 58 Davies St W1 Tel. 020 7629 7034	*Open Mon–Fri 10am–6pm. Two large antique markets located in former Victorian factories and workshops.*	E A4
GREEN PARK Piccadilly entrance or Constitution Hill SW1	*Open during daylight hours. Large green space linking St James Park to Hyde Park.*	▲ 245 E B4/F B1
GREENWICH MARKET Greenwich High Road SE10 ⊖ Greenwich or Cutty Sark	*Open Sat–Sun 9am–5pm. Antiques.*	
GREENWICH PARK Greenwich or Maze Hill stations (Charing Cross)	*Alleys and flower banks created by the Versailles' landscape designer Lenôtre.*	▲ 329
GROSVENOR CINEMA Rayner's Lane, Harrow Subway and train (Marylebone)	*Unusual movie theater built in 1936.*	● 90
GUILDHALL Gresham Street EC2 Tel. 020 7606 3030 (St Paul's Visitor Centre)	*Library: open Mon–Sat 9.30am–5pm. Guildhall Clock Museum: open Mon–Fri 9.30am–4.45pm. Century-old headquarters of the Corporation of the City of London. A wealth of documents on London.*	▲ 148 C D2
HAM HOUSE Ham, Richmond, Surrey ⊖ Richmond Tel. 020 8940 1950	*Open Sat–Wed 1–5pm. Superb residence in the Stuart style built c.1610 and altered in the 1670s. The gardens are also worth a visit.*	▲ 349
HAMPTON COURT PALACE East Molesey, Surrey Train (Waterloo) Tel. 0870 752 7777	*Open Apr–Oct: Mon 10.15am–6pm, Tue–Sun 9.30am–6pm; Nov–Mar: Mon 10.15am–4.30pm, Tue–Sun 9.30am–4.30pm.*	▲ 352
HAYMARKET THEATRE ROYAL Haymarket SW1 Tel. 0870 901 3356	*Created in 1720, this theater was rebuilt by John Nash in 1820 and has retained the same façade since then. Well worth seeing.*	▲ 296 F B2
HAYWARD GALLERY Belvedere Road SE1 8XZ Tel. 020 7261 0127	*Open Tue–Wed 10am–noon, Thur–Mon 10am–6pm. In the Southbank Centre. Exhibitions on history and contemporary art.*	▲ 322 F B3
HER MAJESTY'S THEATRE Haymarket SW1 Tel. 0870 890 1106	*Built in 1897, this theater puts on popular musical comedies which can run up to ten years.*	F B2
HERMITAGE ROOMS Somerset House The Strand WC2 Tel. 020 7845 4600 *www.somerset-house.org.uk*	*Open daily 10am–6pm (last admission 5pm). Five furnished rooms with changing exhibitions from the State Hermitage Museum in St Petersburg.*	▲ 269 F A3
HIGHGATE CEMETERY Swains Lane N6 ⊖ Archway Tel. 020 8340 1834	*Open 10am–5pm. Closes at 4pm in winter. Guided tours.*	▲ 264
HISTORIC SHIP COLLECTION St Katharine Docks E1	*Collection of historic ships moored in the eastern docks, including HMS* Discovery *which has been turned into a museum.*	▲ 334 G B3
HMS BELFAST Morgan's Lane/Tooley St SE1 Tel. 020 7940 6300	*Open daily 10am–6pm. A Normandy Landing veteran, this cruiser now resides at the foot of Tower Bridge.*	▲ 192 G B2
HOGARTH HOUSE Hogarth Lane Great West Road W4 Chiswick railway st. (Waterloo) Tel. 020 8994 6757	*Open Apr–Oct: Tue–Sun 1–5pm (6pm Sat–Sun); Nov–Mar: Tue–Sun 1–4pm (5pm Sat–Sun). Closed Mon and Jan. Hogarth's country residence which houses around 200 of his illustrations.*	▲ 343
HOLLAND HOUSE Holland Park W8 Tel. 020 7602 7856 (Holland Park Theater)	*Only vestiges and the orangery (now a restaurant) remain of what was once an elegant residence dating back to the reign of James I. The Holland Park Theatre, situated on the front terrace, puts on plays, ballets and operas during the summer.*	▲ 251 D C3
HOLLAND PARK Abbotsbury Road/ Kensington High Street W8	*Open daily from 7.30am until dusk. The prettiest park in London, with peacocks and chipmunks. Japanese garden and Ice House.*	▲ 251 D B/C3

HOLY TRINITY, CLAPHAM Trinity Road, Clapham SW11 Tel. 020 7627 0941 (parish office)	*Elegant neoclassical church in the south of London.*	● 72 I D2
HOLY TRINITY, SLOANE Sloane Street SW1 Tel. 020 7730 7270	*Typical of the 1900 Gothic style, following in the tradition of the Victorian era.*	● 81 E D3
HOME HOUSE 30 Portman Square W1	*Quintessential Robert Adam art in this townhouse.*	▲ 256 E A3
HOOVER BUILDING Western Avenue, Greenford rail and subway (Paddington)	*Built in the 1930s when architects turned factories into palaces. Now a supermarket.*	● 91
HORSE GUARDS Whitehall SW1	*Changing of the Guards: Mon–Sat 11am, Sun 10am. Daily review 4pm. Trooping the Colours: on the 2nd Sun in June.* *The Changing of the Guards takes place on the Horse Guards' Parade esplanade, opposite St James's Park.*	▲ 142 F B2 F D1
HORTICULTURAL HALLS Vincent Square SW1	*Monthly fair in Chelsea: traditional wooden cooking utensils, antique teapots, lampshades.*	F D1
HUNTERIAN MUSEUM Royal College of Surgeons 35–43 Lincoln's Inn Fields WC2 Tel. 020 7973 2190	*Closed for refurbishment. Will reopen in 2005.*	▲ 168 F A3
HYDE PARK AND KENSINGTON GARDENS W2 and W8 Tel. 020 7298 2100	*Both Hyde Park (closes at midnight) and Kensington Gardens (closes at dusk) are linked to form the largest public park in London.*	▲ 245 ▲ 247 E A/B1-3
IMPERIAL COLLEGE OF SCIENCE, TECHNOLOGY AND MEDICINE Exhibition Road SW7 Tel. 020 7589 5111	*The only 19th-century element that remained after the building was pulled down in 1953 is the central tower in a neo-Renaissance Victorian style.*	▲ 229 E C1/2
IMPERIAL WAR MUSEUM Lambeth Road SE1 Tel. 020 7416 5000 or 0900 160 0140 (recorded info)	*Open daily 10am–6pm, free after 4.30pm. Historical aircraft, painters from the two world wars, recreation of World War I trenches, temporary exhibitions.*	▲ 320
INNER TEMPLE Crown Office Row EC4 Tel. 020 7797 8250	*Open 10am–4pm. Closed Sat, Sun and public hols. Church open Mon–Fri 10am–4pm, Sun 12.30–3pm.*	▲ 163 F A4
INSTITUTE OF CONTEMPORARY ARTS (ICA) Nash House, The Mall W1 Tel. 020 930 3647 (box office) or 020 7930 0493 (24 hr ans. svce)	*Gallery open daily noon–7.30pm; bookstore open noon–9pm; café open 12.30–10.30pm. Very up-to-date, with theater and movie theater (daily performances and showings). New talent and media.*	F B2
ISLAND GARDENS East Ferry Road E14 Isle of Dogs ⊖ Island Gardens	*Small park by the Thames south of the Isle of Dogs, with a great view of the Royal Naval Hospital in Greenwich.*	▲ 339
IVORY HOUSE St Katharine's Docks E1	*This enormous brick building dating from 1858 was restored and converted into apartments.*	▲ 334 G A3
THE JEWEL TOWER Abingdon Street SW1 Tel. 020 7222 2219	*Open Apr–Sep: daily 10am–6pm; Oct–Mar: daily 10am–4pm. Closed Dec 24–26 and Jan 1. Relics from the Palace of Westminster and an exhibition on "Parliament Past and Present".*	
JEWISH MUSEUM Raymond Burton House 129–131 Albert Street NW1 Tel. 020 7284 1997	*Open Sun–Thur 10am–4pm; groups by appointment. Closed Fri–Sat, public hols and Jewish hols.* *Cultural center; collection of religious artifacts.*	▲ 262 B B1
JUBILEE GARDEN South Bank SE1	*Small park inaugurated in 1977 for Queen Elizabeth II's Silver Jubilee.*	▲ 321 F B3
JUBILEE MARKET Southampton Street WC2	*Open 9am–6pm.* *Just south of Covent Garden Piazza. Antiques, jewelry, crafts, clothes, food.*	▲ 273 F A2/3
KEATS' HOUSE MUSEUM Wentworth Place Keats Grove NW3 ⊖ Hampstead Tel. 020 7435 2062	*Open Apr–Oct: Mon–Sat 10am–1pm, 2–6pm (Sat 5pm), Sun 2–5pm; Nov–Mar: Mon–Fri 1–5pm, Sat 10am–1pm, 2–5pm, Sun 2–5pm. This double pavilion was the residence of John Keats between 1818 and 1820.*	▲ 261
KENSINGTON PALACE Kensington Gardens W8 Tel. 0870 751 5180 *www.royal.gov.uk*	*Open 10am–5pm.* *Queen Victoria's residence until the age of 18, then later Princess Diana's. Visit the state apartments and costume collection.*	▲ 250 D B4

KENWOOD HOUSE Hampstead Lane NW3 Tel. 020 8348 1286 or 020 7973 3427 (concerts) ⊖ Hampstead	*Open 10am–6pm (4pm Oct–Mar).* *If you do not fancy the long walk from Hampstead subway station, take bus n° 210 from Archway or Golden Green stations.* *The manor house and the gallery of paintings are open to the public. Boutique, café and restaurant. Open-air concerts with firework displays Jul 5–Aug 30 (Tel. 020 7973 3427).*	▲ 263
KEW PALACE – ROYAL BOTANICAL GARDENS Kew Road, Richmond, Surrey TW9 ⊖ Kew Gardens Tel. 020 8332 5655	*Gardens open Nov–Jan 9.30am–4.15pm; Feb–Mar 9.30am–5.30pm; Mar–Aug Mon–Fri 9.30am–6.30pm; Sat–Sun 9.30am–7.30pm; Sep–Oct 9.30am–6pm (exhibitions and greenhouses close 30 minutes before). Restaurant available. Kew Palace currently closed for restoration work. Queen Charlotte's Cottage opens May Day bank holiday only.*	▲ 344
KING'S COLLEGE The Strand WC2 Tel. 020 7836 5454	*Founded in 1828 by the Duke of Wellington, King's College is situated in the eastern wing of Somerset House.*	▲ 269 F A3
LAMBETH PALACE Lambeth Palace Road SE1 Tel. 020 7928 8282	*Group visits by appointment only.* *By the Thames, one of the last feudal palaces, property of the archbishops of Canterbury.*	▲ 319 F D3
LAUDERDALE HOUSE Waterlow Park, Highgate N19 ⊖ Highgate Tel. 020 7348 8716	*Open Tue–Sun 11am–4pm.*	▲ 264
LEADENHALL MARKET Whittington Avenue EC3	*Open daily 9am–5pm.* *Indoor market built in 1881; a superb example of metal architecture (flowers and food).*	▲ 154 C D3
LEIGHTON HOUSE 12 Holland Park Road W1 Tel. 020 7602 3316	*Open Mon–Sat 11am–5pm (6pm when temporary exhibitions are on). Works by Leighton and friends on permanent display.*	▲ 226 D C3
LINCOLN'S INN Chancery Lane WC2 Tel. 020 7405 1393	*Open Mon–Fri 9am–6pm.* *Old hall: visit by appointment only.* *Chapel: open noon–2.30pm. Closed Sat–Sun.*	▲ 165 F A3
LINDSEY HOUSE 95–100 Cheyne Walk SW3	*Whistler, the painter, once lived in this elegant double house built in 1674.*	▲ 165 H B2
LLOYD'S BUILDING 1 Lime Street EC3	*This stunning building completed in 1986 is the work of the architect Richard Rogers. It is not open to the public.*	▲ 153 C D3
LLOYD'S REGISTER OF SHIPPING 71 Fenchurch Street EC3 Tel. 020 7709 9166	*All shipping documents and acts are kept in this Art-Nouveau building.*	▲ 153 C D3
LONDON AQUARIUM County Hall, Riverside Building Westminster Bridge Road SE1 Tel: 020 7967 8000 *www.londonaquarium.co.uk*	*Open daily 10am–6pm, last admission 5pm.* *One of Europe's largest and most spectacular displays of aquatic life.*	▲ 320 F C3
LONDON CENTRAL MEAT MARKET Smithfield EC1	*Typical Victorian central food market.*	▲ 177 C C/D1
LONDON DUNGEON 34 Tooley Street SE1 Tel. 020 7403 7221 (info)	*Open Oct–Mar: 10am–5.30pm; Apr–Sep: 10am–6.30pm.* *Small horror museum located under the arches of London Bridge Station.*	G B2
(BRITISH AIRWAYS) LONDON EYE Jubilee Gardens South Bank SE1 Tel. 0870 500 0600	*Open Nov–Mar: 10am–6pm, Apr–Oct: 9am–late evening.* *Tickets available on-site on first-come-first-served basis or by telephone booking.*	▲ 321 F C3
LONDON PALLADIUM Argyll St W1 Tel. 0870 890 1108	*This sumptuous theater is used for official events, such as the Royal Variety Performance.*	F A1
LONDON PLANETARIUM Marylebone Road NW1 Tel. 0870 400 3000	*Open Apr–Sep 10.40am–5.40pm (5pm Sat–Sun); Oct–Mar 10.20am–5pm. Shows every 40 min.*	▲ 256 A C/D4
LONDON TRANSPORT MUSEUM The Piazza, Covent Garden WC2 Tel. 020 7379 6344	*Open 10am–6pm.* *The history of London public transport throughout the ages.*	▲ 273 F A3
LONDON ZOO Regent's Park NW1 Tel. 020 7722 3333	*Open in summer 10am–5pm; out of season 10am–4pm (last admissions 4pm or 3pm).* *One of the largest zoos in the world.* *Organized activities in summer.*	▲ 258 A B4

LORD'S CRICKET GROUND St John's Wood NW8 Tel. 020 7289 1611	*This is where the greatest cricket trophies are fought over. The futuristic stands reserved for the press are a recent addition. Also home to the MCC Cricket Museum (see separate entry).*	A C3
LOTS ROAD GALLERIES 71 Lots Road SW10 Tel. 020 7351 7771	*Sales every Mon. Exhibition on Thur 5–7pm, Sat 10am–4pm and Sun 11am–5pm.*	▲ 273 H B1
MADAME TUSSAUD'S Marylebone Road (corner of Allsop Place) NW1 Tel. 0870 400 3000	*Open Mon–Fri 10am–5.30pm, Sat–Sun 9.30am–5.30pm. Closed Christmas. World-famous wax museum. Reduced rates with a combined ticket to Planetarium.*	▲ 256 A D4
MANSION HOUSE Walbrook EC4N 8BH	*Open by appointment only for visits by organized groups (min. 15 people, max. 40). Applications should be made in writing.*	▲ 149 C D2
MARBLE ARCH At the end of Park Lane W1	*Triumphal arch first erected in 1828 and transfered to its current site north-east of Hyde Park in 1851.*	▲ 252 E A3
MARBLE HILL HOUSE Richmond Rd, Twickenham TW1 ⊖ Richmond Tel. 020 8892 5115	*Open Apr–Sep: Wed–Sun, public hols 10am–6pm; Oct: Wed–Sun 10am–5pm. Closed Nov–Mar. Anglo-Palladian house. Collection of 18th-century furniture and paintings.*	▲ 349
MARLBOROUGH HOUSE Marlborough Road Pall Mall SW1	*Open to the public one day in Sep. Built by Christopher Wren. Now headquarters of the Commonwealth Conference Institute.*	▲ 229
MARYLEBONE NEW CHURCH Marylebone Road NW1 Tel. 020 7935 7315	*Visits Mon–Fri 9am–5.30pm; Sun 10am–5pm. Services Sun 8am, 11am, 6.30pm and Wed 1.10pm.*	▲ 253 B C/D1
(THE) MAYFLOWER 117 Rotherwhite Street SE16 ⊖ Rotherhithe	*Only recently has this very old pub (1550) been named for the famous ship that sailed for the New World from a nearby dock.*	▲ 339
MCC CRICKET MUSEUM Lord's Cricket Ground St John's Wood Road NW8, entrance through the Grace Gate Tel. 020 7432 1033	*Museum open daily 10am–5pm. 90-minute guided tours of the ground Oct–Mar: daily noon, 2pm; Apr–Sep: daily 10am, noon, 2pm. There are no tours on important match days or preparation days – telephone for availability.*	A C3
MIDDLE TEMPLE Middle Temple Lane EC4 Tel. 020 7427 4800	*Open 10–11.30am and 3–6pm. Closed Sat–Sun.*	▲ 162 F A3/4
(THE) MONUMENT Monument Street EC3 Tel. 020 7626 2717	*Open daily 10am–5.50pm. Stunning view from the top of the 311 steps of the column built by Christopher Wren.*	▲ 156 G A2
MUDCHUTE FARM Pier Street E14 ⊖ Mudchute Tel. 020 7515 5901	*One of many farms in the East End, with a horse-riding center.*	▲ 338
MUSEUM OF LONDON 150 London Wall EC2 Tel. 020 7600 3699	*Open Tue–Sat 10am–5.50pm, Sun noon–5.50pm. Closed Mon and Christmas. History of London and its people.*	▲ 178 C D2
NATIONAL ARMY MUSEUM Royal Hospital Road SW3 Tel. 020 7730 0717	*Open 10am–5.30pm. Closed public hols. History of the British Army since the 16th century.*	▲ 199 H A3
NATIONAL FILM THEATRE (NFT) South Bank SE1 Tel. 020 7633 0274 (info) 020 7928 3232 (reserv.) *www.bfi.org.uk*	*Different programs every day, showing both old and recent movies of excellent quality.*	▲ 338 F B3
(THE) NATIONAL GALLERY Trafalgar Square WC2 Tel. 020 7747 2885 (recorded info) *www.nationalgallery.org.uk*	*Open Mon, Tue,Thur, Sun 10am–6pm, Wed 10am–9pm. Closed public hols. Fabulous collection of 18th-, 19th- and 20th-century paintings. Free, except for special exhibitions.*	▲ 288 F B2
NATIONAL MARITIME MUSEUM Park Row, Greenwich SE10 ⊖ Greenwich or Cutty Sark or Maze Hill railway st. Tel. 020 8858 4422 *www.nmm.ac.uk*	*Open 10am–5pm. Interactive exhibitions on all aspects of navigation, past and present.*	▲ 328
NATIONAL PORTRAIT GALLERY 2 St Martin's Place WC2 Tel. 020 7306 0055 020 7312 2463 (recorded info) *www.npg.org.uk*	*Open 10am–6pm (Sun noon–6pm). Closed public hols. Very popular with national visitors. Portraits of famous British men and women, from the Tudors until today.*	▲ 294 F B2

NATURAL HISTORY MUSEUM Cromwell Road South Kensington SW7 Tel. 020 7942 5000 *www.nhm.ac.uk*	*Open Mon–Sat 10am–5.50pm, Sun 11am–5.50pm. Closed Christmas. Dinosaurs, insects, minerals... Exhibitions on evolution and ecology. Simulation of volcanic eruptions and earthquakes.*	▲ 234 E C1/2
NEW SQUARE Lincoln's Inn (entrance on Carey Street)	*Row of typical 17th-century four-storied houses set around a central lawn. Do not miss the Palladian-style Stones Buildings in Carey Street.*	▲ 168 F A3
OLD OPERATING THEATRE MUSEUM AND HERB GARRET 9a St. Thomas's St SE1 Tel. 020 7955 4791	*Open daily 10.30am–5pm. Closed 15th Dec–5th Jan). Oldest surviving operating theatre in England. Exhibits tell the story of surgery and herbal medicine.*	
OLD ROYAL OBSERVATORY Greenwich Park SE10 ⊖ Greenwich or Maze Hill railway st. Tel. 020 8858 4422 *www.nmm.ac.uk*	*Open 10am–5pm. Located in Flamstead House. Here you will find the longest telescope in the country, as well as astronomical instruments and early watches.*	▲ 327
OLD VIC THEATRE Waterloo Road SE1 Tel. 020 7928 7616	*One of the oldest theaters in London, founded by Lilian Baylis at the turn of the 19th century.*	F C4
OPEN AIR THEATRE Regent's Park Tel. 020 7486 2431	*Open-air performances during the summer months.*	▲ 257 A C4
OSTERLEY PARK HOUSE Osterley, Isleworth, Middlesex ⊖ Osterley Tel. 01494 755 566 (answering service)	*House open Apr–Oct: Wed–Sun 12.30–3.30pm. Closed Mon–Tue. Park and playing fields open daily during daylight hours.*	▲ 348
OXFORD AND CAMBRIDGE UNIVERSITY CLUB 71 Pall Mall SW1 Tel. 020 7930 5151	*Club founded by Lord Palmerston in 1830. The same architect also built the British Museum.*	▲ 279 F B1
PALACE THEATRE Shaftesbury Avenue W1 Tel. 020 7434 0909	*Built in 1891 to house the Royal English Opera company, this monumental theater is today a temple of musical comedy in the West End.*	● 54 F A2
PETTICOAT LANE AND BRICK LANE MARKETS Middlesex St, Cheshire St	*Sun 8am–2pm. Popular flea markets. Second-hand clothes, bric-à-brac, food. Petticoat Lane is more touristic. Indian products in Brick Lane.*	▲ 312 C D3/4 C C/D4
PORTOBELLO ROAD Notting Hill Gate W10–W11	*General market (second-hand clothes, jewelry, house accessories, etc.) on weekdays. Second-hand goods Sat 8am–6pm. Bars, restaurants and galleries.*	D A3
PUPPET THEATRE BARGE 78 Middleton Road E8 Tel. 020 7249 6876	*Barge moored on the canal in Little Venice. Puppet shows Sat and Sun afternoon.*	A D2
QUEEN'S CHAPEL St James Palace SW1	*Open only for Sun mass. Built in the first classical style by Inigo Jones.*	▲ 240 F B1
QUEEN'S GALLERY Buckingham Palace The Mall SW1 Tel. 020 7766 7301	*Open daily 10am–5.30pm (last admission 4.30pm). Entry is by timed ticket. One of the most valuable royal collection of objets d'art in the world.*	▲ 244 F C1
RANGERS HOUSE (WERNHER COLLECTION) Chesterfield Walk, Blackheath SE10 Train Blackheath (Charing Cross) Tel. 020 8853 0035	*Open Apr 31–Sep 30: daily 10am–6pm; Oct: daily 10am–5pm; Nov–Mar: Wed–Sun 10am–4pm.*	
RANELAGH GARDENS Entrances on Royal Hospital Road and Chelsea Embankment SW3	*Open Mon–Sat 10am–1pm and Sun from 2pm until dusk. Closed Christmas. Mozart gave a concert here at the age of 8.*	▲ 199 H A4
REGENT'S PARK NW1	*Open from 3pm until dusk. Built by John Nash in 1817 and 1828. Lively in the summer. Open-air theater (see Open Air Theatre).*	▲ 257 A B/C3/4 B B/C1
RICHMOND PARK Richmond, Surrey ⊖ Richmond	*Open every day during daylight hours. The Richmond district is one of the most popular walking areas amongst Londoners.*	▲ 351
ROCK CIRCUS The London Pavilion 1 Piccadilly Circus W1 Tel. 020 7437 5752	*Open Mon, Wed–Thur and Sun 11am–9pm, Tue noon–9pm, Fri–Sat 11am–10pm. Popular wax museum dedicated to rock stars.*	F B1/2

ROYAL ACADEMY OF ARTS Burlington House, Piccadilly W1 Tel. 020 7300 8000 020 7300 5760 (recorded info) *www.royalacademy.org.uk*	*Open 10am–6pm (8.30pm on Fri). Houses the most important traveling exhibitions.*	▲ 280 F B1
ROYAL ACADEMY OF MUSIC Marylebone Road NW1 Tel. 020 7873 7373 *www.ram.ac.uk*	*Founded in 1822, the Royal Academy is a hive of young composers and interpreters. Offers a lot of free concerts.*	▲ 256 B C1
ROYAL ALBERT HALL Kensington Gore SW7 Tel. 020 7589 8212 *www.royalalberthall.com*	*Tickets available daily 9am–9pm. Temple of music built in 1871. Very popular thanks to the famous "Proms" (Promenade-concerts).*	▲ 236 E C1/2
ROYAL ARCADE Old Bond Street W1	*Shopping arcade with exclusive boutiques. Links the Browns Hotel to Old Bond Street.*	● 84 F B1
ROYAL AUTOMOBILE CLUB 89 Pall Mall W1 Tel. 020 7930 2345	*Opposite St James Square, this beautiful Edwardian building is well worth a visit for its sumptuous Louis XVI interior decoration. Marble swimming pool (members only).*	▲ 279 F B1
ROYAL COURTS OF JUSTICE Aldwych WC2 Tel. 020 7947 6000	*Open Mon–Fri 10.30am–4.30pm. Closed Aug–Sep. Galleries and the Central Hall are open to the public.*	▲ 158 F A3
ROYAL COURT THEATRE Sloane Square SW1 Tel. 020 7565 5000	*Reservations 10am–6pm. Closed Sun. Contemporary repertoire. Restaurant.*	▲ 197 E D3
ROYAL EXCHANGE Corner of Threadneedle Street and Cornhill Street EC3	*The 1844 building, formerly home to the London International Financial Futures Exchange (LIFFE), is now a high-class shopping center.*	▲ 151 C D3
ROYAL FESTIVAL HALL Southbank SE1 Tel. 020 7960 4242 *www.rfh.org.uk*	*Apart from the RFH, this center also includes the Queen Elizabeth Hall and the Purcell Room. Daily concerts, some of them free at lunchtime and in the late afternoon.*	▲ 322 F B3
ROYAL GEOGRAPHICAL SOCIETY 1 Kensington Gore SW7 Tel. 020 7591 3000	*Open 11am–5pm. Closed Sat–Sun. The Map Room contains some 900,000 geographical maps.*	▲ 236 E C1/2
ROYAL HOSPITAL CHELSEA Royal Hospital Road SW3 Tel. 020 7730 0161	*Open 10am–noon and 2–4pm. Closed Sun morning and Christmas. Superb gardens near the Thames (Chelsea Flower Show in May). Small museum that presents the history of this building designed by Christopher Wren to house the Chelsea Pensioners.*	▲ 197 H A3
ROYAL NATIONAL THEATRE South Bank SE1 Tel. 020 7452 3400 (info.) 020 7452 3000 (reserv.) *www.nt-online.org*	*This theatrical complex has three rooms: Olivier, Lyttleton and Cottesloe. Large repertoire.*	▲ 322 F B3
ROYAL NAVAL COLLEGE King William Walk SE10 ⊖ Cutty Sark Tel. 0800 389 3341	*Open 2.30–4.45pm. Former naval hospital designed by Christopher Wren. Do not miss the Painted Hall and the chapel in which concerts are sometimes given.*	▲ 327
ROYAL OPERA HOUSE (COVENT GARDEN) Bow Street WC2 Tel. 020 7304 4000 *www.royalopera.org*	*This harmonious neoclassical building was renovated in 1999 and offers three daily performances in the main hall, as well as concerts, workshops in the Studio Theatre and the Upstairs Studio.*	▲ 274 F A2
RUSSELL HOTEL Russell Square WC1 Tel. 020 7837 6470	*A must for afternoon tea in neogothic surroundings of red brick and marble.*	▲ 298 B D3
SAATCHI GALLERY County Hall, Southbank SE1 Tel. 020 7823 2363 (info) 020 7928 8195 (bookings)	*Open Thur–Sun 10am–8pm, Fri–Sat 10am–10pm (last admissions 45 mins before closing). The Saatchi brothers' collection covers mostly British art.*	A A/B1
ST ALFEGE Greenwich Church St SE10 ⊖ Cutty Sark or Greenwich Tel. 020 8853 2703	*Open Tue–Fri 11am–3pm, Sat–Sun 2–4pm. Closed Mon. Church built in 1714 by Nicholas Hawksmoor.*	▲ 326
ST ANDREW UNDERSHAFT St Mary Axe EC3	*Open by arrangement: telephone Great St Helen's EC3 (020 7283 2231).*	▲ 154 C D3
ST ANNE LIMEHOUSE Commercial Road E14 ⊖ Limehouse	*Open Mon–Fri 2–4pm, Sat–Sun 2.30–5.30pm. Buit by Thomas Hawksmoor between 1714 and 1730.*	▲ 336

ST BARNABAS Pimlico Road SW1	*This small church, designed by Thomas Cundy, is typical of the mid-19th-century Gothic style.*	▲ 206 E D4
ST BARTHOLOMEW HOSPITAL & ST BARTHOLOMEW THE LESS West Smithfield EC1 Tel. 020 7377 7000 (Hospital)	*The work of George Dance the Young and completed in 1789, this neoclassical church with its octogonal dome stands in a 500-year-old hospital complex.*	▲ 176 C D1
ST BARTHOLOMEW THE GREAT West Smithfield EC1 Tel. 020 7606 5171	*Open Jan–mid-Nov 8.30am–5pm; mid-Nov–Dec 8.30am–4.30pm.* *One of the City's oldest churches (built 1123).*	▲ 176 C C/D1/2
ST BOTOLPH'S ALDERSGATE Aldersgate Street EC1 Tel. 020 7283 1670	*Do not miss the murals by Victorian artist G.F. Watts in Postman's Park (former graveyard) praising the courage of ordinary Londoners.*	▲ 181 C D3/4
ST BRIDE'S Bride Lane, Fleet Street EC4 Tel. 020 7427 0133	*The 223-foot (68-m) spire is the highest of all erected by Christopher Wren.*	● 70 C D1
ST CLEMENT DANES The Strand WC2 Tel. 020 7242 8282	*Open 9.30am–3.30pm. Closed Sat–Sun.* *The belltower of this church, built by Wren in 1680, was a later addition by Gibbs in 1720.*	▲ 160 F A3
ST DUNSTAN AND ALL SAINTS Stepney High Street E2 Tel. 020 7702 0685	*The oldest parts of the church date from the 13th century.*	▲ 316 C D4
ST DUNSTAN IN-THE-WEST 184 Fleet Street EC4 Tel. 020 7242 6027	*Open 9am–4.30pm.* *Closed Sat–Sun.*	▲ 164 C D1
ST GEORGE'S BLOOMSBURY Bloomsbury Way WC1 Tel. 020 7405 3044	*Normally open Sun–Thur 9.30am–5.30pm (call to confirm). Unusual 18th-century church with curious belltower.*	▲ 300 B D3
ST GEORGE IN THE EAST Cannon Street Road E1 Tel. 020 7481 1345	*Open 8am–5pm. Closed Mon.* *Built between 1714 and 1726 by Thomas Hawksmoor.*	▲ 335 G A4
ST GILES CRIPPLEGATE Fore Street EC2 Tel. 020 7638 1997	*Open Mon–Fri 9.30am–5.15pm, Sat 9am–1pm and Sun 8am–noon.*	▲ 181 C D2
ST JAMES'S CHURCH PICCADILLY 197 Piccadilly W1 Tel. 020 7734 4511	*Open daily Apr–Sep 9am–6pm; out of season 9am–6pm.* *Regular concerts at lunchtime and in the evening. Café and indoor craft market.*	▲ 276 F B1
ST JAMES'S PALACE St James'Street/The Mall SW1	*This Tudor-style palace is not open to the public.*	▲ 240 F B1
ST JAMES'S PARK The Mall SW1	*Open daily during daylight hours.* *Its lake is a sanctury for ducks, swans and geese. Beautiful trees and flower displays.*	▲ 238 F C1/2
ST JAMES THE LESS 13 Churton Place SW1 Tel. 020 7630 6282	*This church located in Pimlico has a surprising décor of brick and metal, both on the inside and outside.*	● 81 F D1
ST JOHN'S HAMPSTEAD Church Row NW3 ⊖ Hampstead Tel. 020 7794 5808	*Open 8am–5pm.* *14th-century church rebuilt in the 18th and 19th centuries. Constable's grave in graveyard.*	▲ 261
ST JOHN'S SMITH SQUARE Smith Square SW1 Tel. 020 7222 1061	*This Baroque church, rebuilt by Thomas Archer in 1728, has been turned into a concert hall (at lunchtime and in the evening).*	F D2
ST KATHARINE'S DOCKS St Katharine's Way E1 Tel. 020 7481 8350	*Open 6–8.30pm.* *Popular marina. Created for both business and leisure, with restaurants, bars and boutiques.*	▲ 334 G B3
ST LAURENCE JEWRY Gresham Street EC2 Tel. 020 7600 9478	*Open 7.30am–6pm. Closed Sat–Sun.* *Official church of the Corporation of London.*	▲ 149 C D2
ST MARGARET'S CHURCH Parliament Square Westminster SW1	*Open Mon–Fri 9.30am–5.30pm, Sat 9am–2pm, Sun 1–5.30pm.* *15th-century parochial church.*	▲ 137 F C2
ST MARTIN-IN-THE-FIELDS Trafalgar Square WC2 Tel. 020 7839 8362 (concerts) 020 7839 4342 (café)	*Open 8am–6.30pm. Café in the crypt (Mon–Sat 10am–8pm, Sun noon–6pm).* *Lunchtime concerts Mon, Tue and Fri; evening concerts Thur, Fri and Sat (res. 020 7839 4342).*	▲ 286 F B2
ST MARY ABCHURCH Cannon Street EC4 Tel. 020 7626 0306	*Open 10am–2pm (noon Fri).* *The original decoration has been preserved. The painted cupola is particularly notable.*	▲ 157 G A2
ST MARY'S ALDERMARY Watling Street EC4 Tel. 020 8979 2297	*Open Thur 11am–3pm, Fri 11am–2pm.* *Interesting example of perpendicular Gothic by Christopher Wren.*	▲ 157 C D2

ST MARY'S HAMPSTEAD 4 Holly Place NW3 ⊖ Hampstead Tel. 020 7435 6678	*White-painted Catholic church. The two chapels are decorated with mosaics.*	▲ 261
ST MARY, HARMONDSWORTH Southwestern suburbs, near Twickenham	*Built in the 13th century and at the beginning of the 15th century, this church has a red brick square tower in the Tudor style.*	● 73 A C4
ST MARY'S CHURCH, ISLINGTON Upper Street N1 Tel. 020 7354 3427	*The belltower is all that remains from the original building. The porch was added in 1903.*	● 72 C A1
ST MARY-LE-BOW Cheapside EC2 Tel. 020 7248 5139	*Open Mon–Fri 6.30am–6pm (4.15pm Fri). Superb church designed by Christopher Wren between 1670 and 1680.*	▲ 157 C D2
ST MARY-LE-STRAND 171 Strand WC2 Tel. 020 7836 3126	*Open Mon–Fri 11am–4pm, Sun 10am–2pm. Church built in 1724 by James Gibbs. Concerts Wed at 1.15pm and in the evening.*	▲ 267 F A3
ST MARY'S, ROTHERHITHE SE16 Rotherhithe or ⊖ Canada Water	*Open 7.30am–5.15pm. Closed Sat–Sun. Christopher Jones, captain of the* Mayflower, *was buried here.*	▲ 339
ST MARY'S, STOKE NEWINGTON Church Street, Stoke Newington railway st (Liverpool St.) Tel. 020 7254 6072	*Tudor-style church with a wooden spire added in 1829.*	● 73
ST MARY THE VIRGIN, PERIVALE Oldfield Road ⊖ Perivale	*Medieval stone church with a wooden belltower dating from the 16th century.*	● 73
ST MARY THE VIRGIN, WANSTEAD High Street ⊖ Wanstead Tel. 020 8989 9240 (curator)	*Charming interior. Palm leaf carvings in the pillars of the pulpit.*	● 72
ST MARY WOOLNOTH Lombard Street EC3 Tel. 020 7626 9701	*Can only be seen during services. Built by Nicholas Hawksmoor, it is the most original church in the City.*	● 72 C D2/3
ST MATHIAS CHURCH Poplar High Street E14 ⊖ Poplar Tel. 020 7987 0459	*Open Mon–Fri 8.30am–5.30pm, Sun 10.30am–1.30pm, Sat by appointment.*	▲ 336
ST MICHAEL'S CHURCH South Grove, Highgate N6 ⊖ Archway Tel. 020 8340 7279	*Neogothic church famous mainly for its graveyard (see Highgate Cemetery).*	▲ 264
ST MICHAEL-IN-CORNHILL EC3 Tel. 020 7626 8841	*The tower was rebuilt at the beginning of the 18th century by Nicholas Hawksmoor.*	▲ 155 C D3
ST PANCRAS (STATION AND HOTEL) Euston Road NW1	*The finest examples of Victorian monumental Gothic completed in 1874 by Sir George Gilbert Scott. Recently renovated.*	● 80 B B3
ST PAUL'S CATHEDRAL Ludgate Hill EC4 Tel. 020 7236 4128	*Open 8.30am–4pm. Visits to the crypt and the galleries: Mon–Sat 10am–4pm. Guided tours 11am, 11.30am,1.30pm and 2pm.*	▲ 171 C D1
ST PAUL'S CHURCH Covent Garden Piazza WC2	*Also known as the Actor's Church, it is the work of Inigo Jones and is the oldest building on the square today.*	▲ 274 F A2
ST PETER-UPON-CORNHILL Cornhill EC3 Tel. 020 7220 7571	*Visits Mon–Fri 9am–5pm but not during services. Information and keys available from St Helen's Church (Great St Helen's EC3).*	▲ 155 C D3
ST SAVIOUR'S CHURCH, PIMLICO George Square SW1 Tel. 020 7592 9733	*Designed by Thomas Cundy the Young and built in 1864.*	▲ 206 I A1/2
ST SAVIOUR'S CHURCH ELTHAM Eltham SE9	*Austere building of modern brick design south of the river dating from the 1930s.*	● 91
ST STEPHEN WALBROOK Walbrook EC4 Tel. 020 7283 4444	*Open Mon–Thur 10am–4pm (3pm Fri). Closed Sat–Sun. Church built by Wren. The modern altar is the work of Henry Moore.*	▲ 149 C D2
(THE) SAVOY The Strand WC2 Tel. 020 7836 4343	*The marble lobby and the 1920s décor of this prestigious hotel next to the theater bearing the same name are well worth seeing.*	▲ 268 F B3
SCIENCE MUSEUM Exhibition Road SW7 Tel. 020 7942 4000 *www.sciencemuseum.org.uk*	*Open daily. 10am–6pm. History of science and industry on five different levels. Old train engines and spaceships. Many exciting activities for children.*	▲ 234 E C2

Place	Description	Ref.
SERPENTINE GALLERY Kensington Gardens W2 Tel. 020 7402 6075	*Open 10am–6pm. Contemporary art exhibitions.*	▲ 246 E B2
SHAKESPEARE GLOBE THEATRE New Globe Walk, Bankside SE1 Tel. 020 7401 9919 *www.shakespeares-globe.org*	*Open 10am–5pm. Closed public hols. Built on the site of the 16th-century theater.*	▲ 322 G A1
SHELL-MEX HOUSE The Strand, WC2	*1931 art deco building whose clock was designed to surpass that of Big Ben in size. Recently renovated.*	▲ 269 F B3
SHEPHERD'S MARKET Entrance on Curzon Street and Half Moon Street W1	*Antique dealers, restaurants and food stores in narrow little streets and courtyards where the former "May Fair" used to take place and which gave its name to the elegant Mayfair area.*	▲ 281 E B4
SHERLOCK HOLMES MUSEUM 221b Baker Street NW1 Tel. 020 7935 3130 *www.sherlock-holmes.co.uk*	*The home of one of the most famous detectives has been recreated on four different levels. The true address of Sherlock Holmes, according to Conan Doyle, was n° 221b, but this number does not correspond to any existing house.*	A D4
SIR JOHN SOANE'S MUSEUM 13 Lincoln's Inn Fields WC2 Tel. 020 7405 2107 *www.soane.org*	*Open 10am–5pm. Late-night opening 6–9pm every first Tue of the month. Closed on Sun, Mon and public hols. Former house of John Soane, architect of the Bank of England. Amongst its treasures are paintings by Canaletto, Hogarth and Turner.*	▲ 166 F A3
SKIN FLOOR Highway Buildings, Wapping Lane, Tobacco Docks	*One of the few remaining examples of what the former docks looked like before the area was redeveloped.*	▲ 335 G A4
SOMERSET HOUSE *www.somerset-house.org.uk*	*Houses King's College, the Courtauld Institute Galleries, the Gilbert Collection of Decorative Arts and the Hermitage Rooms (see individual entries). Ice rink in Dec–Jan.*	▲ 269 F A3
SOTHEBY'S 34 New Bond Street Tel. 020 7293 5000	*Amongst the most prestigious of auction rooms, together with Christie's.*	E A4
SOUTH BANK CENTRE *www.sbc.org.uk*	*Complex built south of the Thames, by Waterloo Bridge. It includes the Royal National Theatre, the National Film Theatre, the Hayward Gallery, the Royal Festival Hall and the NFI IMAX Cinema.*	▲ 322 F B3
SOUTHWARK CATHEDRAL Montague Close London Bridge SE1 Tel. 020 7367 6700	*Open Mon–Fri 8am–6pm, Sat 9am–6pm, Sun 8.45am–6pm. First Gothic style, restored in the 19th century. The most beautiful building south of the river.*	▲ 323 G B2
STAPLE INN Holborn WC2 Tel. 020 7242 2435	*Open (courtyard only) Mon–Fri 8am–8pm. This Elizabethan building is unique.*	▲ 164 B D4
STOCK EXCHANGE Old Broad Street EC2 Tel. 020 7588 2355	*The current building dates from 1969.*	▲ 151 C D3
STORMWATER PUMPING STATION Isle of Dogs E14 ⊖ South Quay	*Astonishing modern building with brilliant colors and a façade decorated in the Egyptian style favored in the 19th century.*	● 93
STRAWBERRY HILL Waldegrave Road, Twickenham Surrey By train (from Waterloo) Tel. 020 8892 0051	*Visits by appointment only. This miniature castle, built in the mid-18th century for Sir Horace Walpole and used today as a college, is one of the best examples from the English Gothic Revival period.*	▲ 349
SURREY DOCK FARM Rotherwhite Street SE16 ⊖ Canada Water Tel. 020 7231 1010	*Open Tue–Thur 10am–5pm, Fri, Sat–Sun 10am–1pm and 2–5pm. Closed school vacation. Eggs, honey and pure wax candles sold in the store.*	▲ 339
SYON HOUSE Brentford, Middlesex ⊖ Kew Bridge Tel. 020 8560 0882	*Open Mar 15–Oct 31 Wed–Thur, Sun and public hols 11am–5pm. Closed in winter. Gardens open daily all year around 10am–6pm. 16th-century residence.*	▲ 343
TATE BRITAIN Millbank SW1 Tel. 20 7887 8000 or 020 7887 8008 (recorded info) *www.tate.org.uk*	*Open daily 10am–5.50pm. Superb collection of British works from the 16th to the 20th century, as well as regular special exhibitions. The adjoining Clore Gallery houses the works of J.M.W. Turner.*	▲ 206 F D2

TATE MODERN 25 Sumner Street, Bankside SE1 Tel. 20 7887 8000 or 020 7887 8008 (recorded info) *www.tate.org.uk*	*Open Mon–Thur, Sun 10am–6pm, last entry 5pm; Fri–Sat 10am–10pm.* *Collection of modern and contemporary international art from 1900 to the present, in magnificent, renovated pump station.*	▲ 206 G A1
TEMPLE BAR MEMORIAL Fleet Street EC1	*The bronze griffin, erected in 1880, marks the official entrance to the City.*	▲ 160 F A4
TEMPLE CHURCH Inner Temple EC4 Tel. 020 7353 3470	*Open 10am–4pm. Closed Tue.* *Sole vestige from the Templars' era.*	▲ 161 F A4
THAMES BARRIER VISITOR'S CENTRE 1 Unity Way, Woolwich SE18 North Woolwich railway st. Tel. 020 8305 4188	*Open 10am–5pm (Sat–Sun 10.30am–5.30pm). Closed Christmas.* *Exhibitions on the barrier built in order to protect London from floods.*	
THEATRE MUSEUM Russell Street WC2 Tel. 020 7943 4700	*Open 11am–7pm. Closed Mon.* *Located in what was formerly the Covent Garden flower market. Collections related to the theater and to opera.*	▲ 273 F A2
THEATRE ROYAL DRURY LANE Catherine Street WC2 Tel. 0870 890 1109	*Nell Gwyn started her stage career here in 1665.* *The theater is now used for musical comedies.*	▲ 274 F A3
TOWER BRIDGE Southwark SE1 Tel. 020 7403 3761 Bridge Lift Information (for bridge opening hours): 020 7378 7000 *www.towerbridge.org.uk*	*Open winter 9.30am–6pm, summer 10am–6pm.* *Superb view. In the two towers are the Engine Room Museum and the steam engines which used to operate the bascule bridge.*	▲ 188 G B3
TOWER HILL PAGEANT 1 Tower Hill Terrace EC3 Tel. 020 7709 0081	*Open 9.30am–5.30pm (4.30pm Nov–Mar). Closed Christmas.* *Small automatic cars carry visitors along a historical route from Roman times until now.*	G A3
TOWER HOUSE 29 Melbury Road W14	*This curious neo-medieval tower was built in 1880 by the architect William Burgess who used it as his residence.*	▲ 226 D C3
TOWER OF LONDON Tower Hill EC3 Tel. 0870 756 6060 (recorded info)	*Open Mar–Oct: Mon–Sat 9am–5pm, Sun 10am–5pm; Nov–Feb: Tue–Sat 9am–4pm, Sun–Mon 10am–4pm.* *Former royal residence, prison and place of execution. The Jewel House still attracts scores of visitors.*	▲ 182 G A3
TROCADERO 1 Piccadilly Circus W1 Tel. 0906 888 1100	*Open 10am–midnight.* *Boutiques, video games, discotheque, movie theaters.*	F B1
TWICKENHAM Rugby Road, Twickenham By train (from Waterloo) Tel. 020 8892 2000	*The temple of rugby, host of the Six Nations Tournament. Museum open Tue–Sat 10am–5pm, Sun 2–5pm. Closed school vacations, Christmas and Good Friday.*	
UNICORN AT THE PLEASANCE THEATRE North Road/Caledonian Road N7 ⊖ Caledonian Road Tel. 020 7700 0702	*Performances Sat (matinees and evenings) and Sun (matinees).* *Theater for children. The former Unicorn Theatre for Children has been transferred from the West End to the New Pleasance Theatre.*	
UNIVERSITY COLLEGE Gower Street W1 Tel. 020 7679 2000	*The Slade School of Art is located in the north wing of this college, which was founded in 1826 and built by William Wilkins.*	▲ 298 B C2
VICTORIA & ALBERT MUSEUM Cromwell Road South Kensington SW7 Tel. 020 7942 2000 *www.vam.ac.uk*	*Open Mon noon–5.45pm, Tue–Sun 10am–5.45pm. Late-night opening Wed 6.30–9pm. Closed Christmas and Jan 1.* *The most eclectic of all the great museums not only for its architecture but also for the variety of its collections. It houses the National Art Library. The British Gallery is being renovated and is due to reopen in 2002.*	▲ 229 E C2
VINOPOLIS CITY OF WINE 1 Bank End SE1 Tel. 0870 444 4777 *www.vinopolis.co.uk*	*Open Mon, Fri–Sat noon–9pm; Tue–Thur, Sun noon–6pm. Last entry to the tour is two hours before closing.* *Multimedia exhibition on the history of wine from around the world. Admission price includes wine tasting.*	G B1

WALLACE COLLECTION Hertford House Manchester Square W1 Tel. 020 7563 9500 *www.the-wallace-collection.org.uk*	*Open 10am–5pm. Closed Chrismas and Jan 1. The largest collection of 18th-century French paintings, as well as miniatures, furniture, fine china and weapons in recently renovated surroundings.*	▲ 254 A D4
WELLINGTON ARCH Hyde Park Corner SW1 Tel. 020 7930 2726	*Open Apr–Sep: Wed–Sun 10am–6pm; Oct: Wed–Sun 10am–5pm, Nov–Mar: Wed–Sun 10am–4pm.*	▲ 245 E B4
WESLEY'S CHAPEL 49 City Road EC1 Tel. 020 7253 2262	*Open Mon–Sat 10am–4pm, Sun noon–2pm. Visit the house, museums and the chapel.*	▲ 181 C B1
WESTMINSTER CATHEDRAL Parliament Square SW1 Tel. 020 7222 5152 *www.westminster-abbey.org/* Guided tours 020 7222 7110	*Abbey and royal chapels: open Mon–Fri 9.15am– 4.45pm (last admissions 3.45pm), Sat 9.15am–2.45pm (last admissions 1.45pm). Late-night opening Wed 6–8pm (cheaper and only time when photos are permitted). Closed Sun except for services (free admission). Supplement payable for the visit of the Chapter room and the museum. Guided tours 10am–3pm (12.30pm Sat).*	▲ 137 F C2
WESTMINSTER CATHEDRAL Ashley Place SW1 Tel. 020 7798 9055	*Open Mon–Sat 7am–7pm (Sun 8pm). Lift to the bell-tower: Apr–Oct: daily 9am–5pm; out of season: Thur–Sun 9am–5pm.*	▲ 316
WESTMINSTER PALACE (HOUSES OF PARLIAMENT) Parliament Square SW1 House of Lords Tel. 020 7219 3000 House of Commons Tel. 020 7219 3000 *www.parliament.uk/TOURS*	*The Strangers Gallery of the two houses are open to the public during work sessions: Oct 15–beg. of Jul, generally Mon–Wed 2.30pm, Thur 3pm and Fri 11am. Come to St Stephens' Entrance 30 min. before. To visit Westminster Hall and Jewel Tower (groups not exceeding 16 persons, Fri only), a special pass must be requested from the Parliamentary Educational Unit (Tel. 020 7219 2105).*	▲ 135 F C2
WHITECHAPEL AND MILE END WASTE MARKET ⊖ Whitechapel	*Animated market, opposite the London Hospital.*	▲ 316
WHITECHAPEL ART GALLERY 80 Whitechapel Road E1 Tel. 020 7522 7878 *www.whitechapel.org*	*Open 11am–5pm (8pm Wed). Closed Mon and Christmas. Art-nouveau gallery, temporary modern art exhibitions and very friendly café.*	▲ 316 C D4
WHITECHAPEL BELL FOUNDRY 34 Whitechapel Road E1 Tel. 020 7247 2599	*Open Mon–Fri 9am–5pm.*	▲ 316 C D4
WHITE CUBE ART GALLERY Hoxton Square N1 Tel. 020 7930 5373 *www.whitecube.com*	*Open Tue–Sat 10am–6pm.*	C B3
WHITE LODGE	*See under Richmond Park.*	
WIGMORE HALL 36 Wigmore Street Tel. 020 7935 2141 *www.wigmore-hall.org.uk*	*Built in 1901 for the piano maker Friedrich Bechstein, this lovely concert offers concerts at lunchtime and in the evening.*	B D1
WINDSOR CASTLE Castle Hill Windsor railway st. (Waterloo) Tel. 020 7766 7304	*Open Nov–Feb 9.45am–3pm (4pm in summer). Visit of the royal palace, collection of paintings. Info. available from the Windsor Tourist Office (Tel. 01753 743 900).*	
WINDSOR GREAT PARK Long Walk, Windsor	*Beautiful park with a wonderful view over Windsor Castle. Since 1996 it has been home to Legoland Windsor (Tel. 0990 040 404).*	▲ 356

ESSENTIAL READING

◆ ACKROYD (P.): *Dickens' London*, Headline Books, 1989.
◆ BARKER (F.): *London: Two Thousand Years of a City and its People* , Macmillan, 1984.
◆ BURKHARDT (W.): *A Guide to the Architecture of London*, Weidenfeld & Nicolson, 1983.
◆ HALSEY (A.H.): *Trends in British Society Since 1900*, London, 1972.
◆ HIBBERT (C.): *London, The Biography of a City*, Longman, 1969.
◆ KITCHEN (P.): *Poets' London*, Longman, 1980.
◆ LAWSON (A.): *Discover Unexpected London*, Phaidon, 1979.
◆ LEBRECHT (N.): *Music in London: a History and Handbook*, Aurum Press, 1991.
◆ LLOYD (T.O.): *Empire to Welfare State, 1906–76*, 2nd ed., Oxford University Press, 1979.
◆ MITCHELL (R.J.): *A History of London Life*, Penguin, 1969.
◆ PALIS (L.M.): *The Blue Plaques of London*, Equation, Wellingborough, 1989.
◆ PEVSNER (N.): *London*, Penguin, 1973.
◆ PIPER (D.): *Artists' London*, Weidenfeld & Nicolson, 1982.
◆ WEINREB (B.) and HIBBERT (C.): *The London Encyclopaedia*, Dictionary of London Ltd, Macmillan, 1983.
◆ WILSON (A.N.) ed.: *The Faber Book of London*, Faber and Faber, 1993

GENERAL

◆ ALFRY (S.): *London Life*, Wayland, Hove, 1978.
◆ BETJEMAN (J.): *Victorian and Edwardian London from Old Photographs*, Batsford, 1969.
◆ BUSH (G.), DIXEN (H.) BOOL (A.) and BOOL (J.): *Old London*, Academy Editions, 1975.
◆ CAMERON (R.): *Above London*, Bodley Head, 1980.
◆ CLAYTON (R.): *Portrait of London*, Robert Hale (Portrait Books), 1980.
◆ *A Cockney Camera* (Compiled by G. Winter), Penguin, 1975.
◆ CRACKNELL (B.): *Portrait of London's River*, 2nd edn, Hale, 1980.
◆ FITZGIBBON (T.): *A Taste of London*, Pan Books, 1976.
◆ FRIEDMAN (J.), photographer: Aprahamian (P.): *Inside London: Discovering London's Period Interiors*, Phaidon, 1988.
◆ GENTLEMAN (D.): *London*, Weidenfeld & Nicolson, 1986.
◆ GIROUARD (M.): *Victorian Pubs*, Studio VIsta and Yale University Press, 1975.
◆ GREEN (Benny.): *London*, Oxford University Press, 1984.
◆ JACOBS (M.): *Art in London*, Jarrold, Norwich 1980.
◆ LEJEUNE (A.): *The Gentlemen's Clubs of London*, Macdonald & Jane's, 1979.
◆ NELSON (W.H.): *The Londoners*, Hutchinson, 1975.
◆ NORRIE (I.): *A Celebration of London*, André Deutsch, 1984.
◆ PEARLMUTTER (K.): *London Street Markets*, Wildwood, 1983.
◆ UNDERWOOD (P.): *Haunted London*, Fontana, 1975.
◆ WITCHOUSE (R.): *A London Album: Early Photographs Recording the History of the City and its People from 1840 to 1915*, Secker & Warburg, 1980.
◆ WITTICH (J.): *London Villages*, Shire Publications, Aylesbury, reprinted 1992.

URBAN DEVELOPMENT

◆ BETJEMAN (J.): *London's Historic Railway Stations*, John Murray, 1978.
◆ BIGNELL (J.): *Chelsea Seen from its Earliest Days*, 2nd ed., Robert Hale, 1987.
◆ DAY (J.R.): *The Story of London's Underground*, London Transport Executive, 1974.
◆ DROGHEDA (C.G.P.M.): *The Covent Garden Album: 250 Years of Theatre, Opera and Ballet*, Routledge & Kegan Paul, 1981.
◆ DYOS (H.J.) and WOLFF (M.): *The Victorian City: Images and Realities*, 2 vols., Routledge & Kegan Paul, 1973.
◆ HARRISON (M.): *The London that was Rome. The Imperial City Recreated by the New Archeology: the Remapping of Londinium Augusta, Capital of Maxima Caesariensis, Chief of the Four Provinces of Britain*, Allen & Unwin, 1971.
◆ LOBEL (M.D.): *The City of London from Prehistoric Times to c. 1520*, Oxford University Press, 1989.
◆ *London 1500–1700: The Making of the Metropolis*, (ed. A.L. Barir, R. Finlay), Longman, 1986.
◆ *London Docklands: Past, Present and Future*, (edited by S.K. al Naib), Thames & Hudson, 1990.
◆ *The Making of Modern London*, 4 vols.: *1815–1914* by G. Weightman and S. Humphries; *1914–39*; by G. Weightman and S. Humphries; *1939–45*; by G. Weightman and J. Taylor; *1945–85*, by J. Mack and S. Humphries, Sidgwick and Jackson, *1984–6*
◆ MARSDEN (P.): *Roman London*, Thames & Hudson, 1986.
◆ MEARS (K.J.): *The Tower of London: Nine Hundred Years of English History*, Phaidon, 1988.
◆ OLSEN (D.J.): *Town Planning in London: the 18th and 19th Centuries*, Yale University Press, 1964;
The Growth of Victorian London, Batsford, 1976.
◆ ROSE (M.): *The East End of London*, C. Chivers, 1973.
◆ STAMP (G.): *The Changing Metropolis: Earliest Photographs of London, 1839–79*, Viking, 1984.
◆ THOMPSON (F.M.L.): *The Rise of Suburbia*, Leicester University Press, 1982.
◆ TRENT (C.): *Greater London: its Growth and Development through Two Thousand Years*, Phoenix House, 1965.
◆ YOUNG (K.) and GARSIDE (P.L.): *Metropolitan London: Politics and Urban Change, 1837–1981*, Edward Arnold, 1982.

HISTORY

◆ BARKER (F.) and JACKSON (P.): *The History of London in Maps*, Barrie & Jenkins, 1990.
◆ BARKER (T.C.) and ROBBINS (M.): *A History of London Transport*, 2 vols., Allen & Unwin, 1974.
◆ BARTLETT (C.J.): *A History of Post-war Britain, 1945–74*, London, 1977.
◆ BOLTON (J.L.): *The Medieval English Economy 1150–1500*, London, 1980.
◆ BUSHELL (P.): *London's Secret History*, Constable, 1983.
◆ *The Cambridge Historical Encyclopaedia of Great Britain and Northern Ireland*, (Edited by C. Haigh), Cambridge University Press, 1985.
◆ CAMPBELL (J.): *The Anglo-Saxons*, Penguin, 1991.
◆ CHURCHILL (Winston.): *A History of the English-speaking Peoples*, first publ. 1951–6, Cassell, 1991.
◆ COWARD (B.): *The Stuart Age*, Longman, 1980.
◆ DAVIS (J.): *Reforming London: the London Government Problem 1855–1900*, Clarendon Press, 1990.
◆ *The English Parliament in the Middle Ages* (edited by R.G. Davies and J.H. Denton, Manchester, 1981.
◆ MARGRETSON (S.): *Regency London*, Cassell, 1971.
◆ MERRIFIELD (R.): *London: City of the Romans*, Batsford, 1983.
◆ MOSLEY (L.): *London under Fire: 1939–45*, Pan Books, 1971.
◆ OWEN (J.B.): *The Eighteenth Century, 1714–1815*, London, 1974.
◆ *The Oxford Illustrated History of Britain* (edited by K.O. Morgan), Oxford University Press, 1984.
◆ ROSEN (A.): *Rise Up Women*, London, 1974.
◆ RUDÉ (G.): *Hanoverian London 1714–80*, Secker and Warburg, 1971.
◆ RUSSEL (C.): *The Crisis of Parliaments 1509–1660*, Oxford, 1971.
◆ STRONG (R.): *The Cult of Elizabeth: Elizabethan Portraiture and Pageantry*, Thames & Hudson, 1977.
◆ THOMPSON (E.P.): *The Making of the English Working Class*, London, 1963.
◆ TRENCH (R.): *London under London*, John Murray, 1984.
◆ WHITE (H.P.): *London Railways History*, David & Charles, 1971.
◆ WILLIAMS (G.A.): *Medieval London: from*

Commune to Capital, London, 1963

GEOGRAPHY

◆ *Atlas of London and the Region* (edited by E. Jones and D.J. Sinclair), Pergamon Press, 1969.
◆ DYOS (H.J.): *Collins's Illustrated Atlas of London*, Leicester University Press, 1973.
◆ *The Geography of Greater London* (edited by R. Clayton), G. Philip & Son, 1964.,
◆ HOWGEGO (J.): *Printed Maps of London circa 1553–1850*, Dawson & Son, Folkestone, 1978.
◆ RAYNS (A.W.): *The London Region*, G. Bell, 1971.

NATURE

◆ CROWE (A.): *The Parks and Woodlands of London*, Fourth Estate, 1987.
◆ FITTER (R.S.R.): *London's Natural History*, Collins, 1945; reprinted Bloomsbury, 1990.
◆ MCLEOD (D.): *The Gardener's London: Four Centuries of Gardening, Gardeners and Garden Usage*, Duckworth, 1972.

TRADITIONS

◆ COLLOWAY (S.): *The House of Liberty: Masters of Style and Decoration*, Thames & Hudson, 1992.
◆ *The Criers and Hawkers of London* (edited by S. Shesgreen, with engravings and drawings by M. Laroon), Stanford University Press, 1990.
◆ FRANKLIN (J.): *The Cockney. A survey of London Life and Language*, André Deutsch, 1953.

SOCIETY

◆ ALDERMAN (G.): *London Jewry and London Politics: 1889–1986*, Routledge, 1989.
◆ ALEXANDER (S.): *Women's Work in Nineteenth Century London*, Journeyman, 1983.
◆ ANDREW (D.T.): *Philanthropy and Police: London Charity in the 18th Century*, Princeton University Press, 1989.
◆ ARCHER (I.W.): *The Pursuit of Stability: Social Relations in Elizabethan London*, Cambridge University Press, 1991.
◆ AUBREY (J.): *Brief Lives*, Penguin, 1962.
◆ BISHOP (J.): *Social History of the First World War*, Angus & Robertson, 1982.
◆ BLAIR (T.): *New Britain*, Fourth Estate, 1998.
◆ BRANDT (B.): *London in the Thirties*, Gordon Fraser, 1983.
◆ BRIGGS (A.): *The Age of Improvement*, London, 1959.
◆ CATHCART (B.): *Were You Still Up For Portillo?*, Penguin, 1997.
◆ CRUICKSHANK (D.): *Life in the Georgian City*, Viking, 1990.
◆ DEKREY (G.S.): *A Fractured Society: the Politics of London in the First Age of Party 1688–1715*, Clarendon Press, 1985.
◆ *Development of English Society* (edited by D. Marshall), 4 vols., Charles Scribner's 1973–9.
◆ DU BOULAY (F.R.H.): *An Age of Ambition*, London, 1970.
◆ FOSTER (J.): *The Class Struggle in the Industrial Revolution*, London, 1974.
◆ GEORGE (M.D.): *London Life in the Eighteenth Century*, London, 1925.
◆ HARRIS (T.): *London Crowds in the Reign of Charles II: Propaganda and Politics from the Restoration until the Exclusion*, Cambridge University Press, 1987.
◆ *The History of British Society 1832–1939*, 7 vols. (edited by E.J. Hobsbawn), Weidenfeld & Nicolson, 1971
◆ HOOK (J.): *The Baroque Age in England*, Thames & Hudson, 1976.
◆ HUTTON (W.): *The State We're In*, Vintage, 1996.
◆ JONES (G.S.): *Outcast London*, Penguin, 1976.
◆ JORDAN (W.K.): *The Charities of London 1480–1660. The Aspirations and the Achievements of the Urban Society*, Allen & Unwin, 1960.
◆ LANDES (D.): *The Unbound Prometheus: Technological Change 1750 to the Present*, Cambridge, 1969.
◆ LASLETT (P.): *The World we Have Lost*, London, 1971.
◆ LEES LYNN (H.): *Exiles of Erin, Irish Migrants in Victorian London*, Manchester University Press, 1979.
◆ MALCOMSON (R.W.): *Life and Labour in England, 1700–80*, Hutchinson, 1981.
◆ MARWICK (A.): *The Explosion of British Society, 1914–70*, Macmillan, 1971.
◆ MORTON (A.): *Diana, Her True Story, In Her Own Words*, Michael O'Mara Books Ltd., 1997.
◆ MOWAT (C.L.): *Britain Between the Wars*, London, 1955.
◆ NEEDHAM (L.W.): *Fifty Years of Fleet Street*, Michael Joseph, 1973.
◆ PALLISER (D.M.): *The Age of Elizabeth*, London, 1983.
◆ PELLING (H.): *A History of British Trade Unionism*, 2nd ed., London 1971.
◆ PERKIN (H.): *The Origins of Modern English Society, 1780–1880*, Routledge & Kegan Paul, 1969; *The Rise of Professional Society. England since 1880.* Routledge & Kegan Paul, 1989.
◆ PORTER (R.): *English Society in the Eighteenth Century*, Penguin, 1984.
◆ SEAMAN (L.C.B.): *Life in Victorian London*, Batsford, 1973.
◆ SHEPHERD (J.): *A Social Atlas of London*, Clarendon Press, 1974.
◆ SMITH (C.M.): *Curiosity of London Life or Phases, Physiological and Social, of the Great Metropolis*, F. Cass, 1972.
◆ *Society and Industry in the 19th Century: a Documentary Approach*, 6 vols. (edited by K. Dawson and P. Wall), Oxford University Press, 1968–70.
◆ STEDMAN (J.): *Outcast London: a Study in Relationship between Classes in Victorian Society*, Oxford University Press, 1971.
◆ STENTON (D.M.): *English Society in the Early Middle Ages 1066–1307*, 2nd ed., Penguin, 1952.
◆ STONE (L.): *The Crisis of the Aristocracy*, Oxford University Press, 1965; *The Family, Sex and Marriage, 1500–1800*, Weidenfeld & Nicolson, 1977.
◆ THATCHER (M.): *The Downing Street Years*, Harper Collins Publisher, 1993.
◆ THOMPSON (F.M.L.): *The Cambridge Social History of Britain*, Cambridge University Press, 1990
◆ *The Victorian City* (edited by H.J. Dyos and M. Wolff), 2 vols., London 1973.
◆ WALKOWITZ (J.R.): *City of Dreadful Delight: Narrative of Sexual Danger in Late Victorian London*, Virago, 1992.
◆ WHITE (J.): *The Worst Street in North London, Campbell Bunk, Islington between the Wars*, Routledge & Kegan Paul, 1986.
◆ WILKES (J.): *The London Police in the 19th Century*, Cambridge University Press, 1977.
◆ WRIGHTSON (K.): *English Society 1580–1680*, Hutchinson, 1983.
◆ YOUNG (G.M.): *Victorian England: the Portrait of an Age*, Oxford, 1936.
◆ YOUNG (M.) and WILLMOTT (P.): *Family and Kinship in East London*, Routledge, 1957; *Family and Clan in a London Suburb*, Routledge, 1960.

RELIGION

◆ BARLOW (F.): *The English Church 1066–1154*, Longman, 1979
◆ BEDE: *Ecclesiastical History of the English People*, trans. L. Sherley-Price, rev. ed., Penguin, 1968.
◆ BOOTH (C.): *Life and Labour of the People in London. Third Series: Religious Influence*, 7 vols., Macmillan, 1902–1904: Ams Press, New York 1970.
◆ CHADWICK (O.): *The Victorian Church*, 2 vols., 3rd ed., London, 1973
◆ COBB (G.): *London City Churches*, Batsford, 1977.
◆ GAY (J.D.): *The Geography of Religion in Britain*, Duckworth, 1971.
◆ HARVEY (B.): *Westminster Abbey and its Estate in the Middle Ages*, Oxford University Press, 1977.
◆ HIBBERT (C.): *London's Churches*, Queen Anne Press, 1988.
◆ KENYON (J.P.): *The Popish Plot*, London, 1972.
◆ LAMONT (W.N.): *Godly Rules: Politics and Religion 1603–60*, Macmillan, 1969.

◆ Liu (T.): *Puritan London: a Study of Religion and Society in the City Parishes*, University of Delaware Press, Associated Uni Corp., 1986.
◆ McGrath (P.): *Papists and Puritans under Elizabeth I*, London, 1967.
◆ Pettigrew (A.): *Foreign Protestant Communities in 16th-Century London*, Clarendon Press, 1986.
◆ Reardon (B.M.G.): *From Coleridge to Gore. A Century of Religious Thought in Britain*, Longman, 1971.
◆ Thomas (K.): *Religion and the Decline of Magic*, London, 1971.
◆ Young (E.): *Old London Churches*, Faber & Faber, 1956.

ARCHITECTURE AND SCULPTURE

◆ Astaire (L.), photographer Boys (M.): *Living in London*, Thames and Hudson, 1990.
◆ Baker (M.): *London Statues and Monuments*, Shire Publications, reprinted 1992.
◆ Byron (A.): *London Statues: a Guide to London's Outdoor Statues and Sculptures*, Constable, 1981.
◆ Campbell (K.): *Home Sweet Home: Housing Designed by the London County Council and Greater London Council Architects: 1888–1975*, Academy Editions, 1976.
◆ Crook (J.M.): *The British Museum: a Case Study in Architectural Politics*, Penguin, 1972.
◆ Cruickshank (D.): *London: the Art of Georgian Building*, Architectural Press, 1975.
◆ Downes (K.): *Hawksmoor*, rev. ed., Thames & Hudson, 1987.
◆ Hardingham (S.): *London: A Guide to Recent Architecture*, Könemann, 1996. *Eat London: Architecture Eating and Drinking*, Ellipsis London Ltd., 1998.
◆ Heal (A.): *The London Furniture Makers from the Restoration to the Victorian Era: 1660–1840*, Dover, 1972.
◆ *A History of English Architecture* (edited by P. Kidson, P. Murray and P. Thompson), London 1979.
◆ Mordaunt Cook (J.): *Victorian Architecture: a Visual Anthology*, Johnson Reprint Corp., New York, 1971.
◆ Murray (P.) and Stevens (M.A.): *New Urban Environments, British Architecture and its European Context,* Prestel Munich–New York, 1998.
◆ Nellist (J.B.): *British Architecture and its Background*, Macmillan, London, St Martin's Press, New York, 1967.
◆ Olsen (D.J.): *The City as a Work of Art: London, Paris, Vienna*, Yale University Press, 1986.
◆ Pearce (D.): *London's Mansions: the Palatial Houses of the Nobility*, Batsford, 1986
◆ Pevsner (N) and Cherry (B.): *The Buildings of England: London*, vol. 1: *The Cities of London and Westminster*, vol. 2: *South*, vol. 3: *North West*, Penguin, 1973, 1983, 1991.
◆ Port (M.H.): *The Houses of Parliament*, Yale University Press, 1976.
◆ Roseneau (H.): *Social Purpose in Architecture. Paris and London 1760–1800*, Studio Vista, 1970.
◆ Saunders (A.): *The Art and Architecture of London: an Illustrated Guide*, Phaidon, 1984.
◆ Schofield (J.): *The Building of London from the Conquest to the Great Fire*, British Museum Publications, 1984.
◆ Service (A.): *The Architects of London and their Buildings: from 1066 to the Present Day*, Architectural Press, 1979. *London: 1900*, Granada, 1979.
◆ Summerson (J.N.): *The London Building World of the Eighteen-sixties*, Thames & Hudson, 1974; *The Architecture of Victorian London*, University Press of Virginia, 1976;
Architecture in Britain: 1530 to 1830, Penguin, 1977;
Georgian London, rev. ed., Penguin, 1978.
The Life and Works of John Nash, Architect, Allen & Unwin, 1981.
◆ Thackrah (J.R.): *The Royal Albert Hall*, T. Dalton, 1983.
◆ *Victorian London*, Victorian Society/ London Transport Executive, 1975.
◆ Whinney (M.): *Wren*, Thames & Hudson, 1985.

LITERATURE

◆ Ackroyd (P.): *Hawksmoor*, Abacus Books, 1986
◆ Conan Doyle (A.): *The Penguin Complete Adventures of Sherlock Holmes*, Penguin, 1984.
◆ *A Personal Record*, J.M. Dent & Sons, 1975.
◆ Conrad (J.): *The Secret Agent* (edited by R. Tennant), Oxford University Press, 1983.
◆ Dickens (C.): *Oliver Twist*, (edited by K. Tillotson), Oxford University Press, 1982; *A Tale of Two Cities* (edited by G. Woodcock), Penguin, 1970;
The Old Curiosity Shop (edited by A. Basson), Penguin, 1972.
◆ Fielding (H.): *Bridget Jones's Diary,* Picador, 1996.
◆ Forster (E.M): *Howard's End*, Penguin, 1989.
◆ James (H.): *Washington Square*, Penguin, 1984.
◆ James (P.D.): *A Mind to Murder*, Penguin, 1963.
◆ Kerouac (J.): *The Lonesome Traveler*, Paladin, 1990.
◆ *London in Verse* (edited by C Logue), Secker & Warburg, 1982.
◆ Rutherford (E.): *London the Novel,* Arrow Books Ltd., 1998.
◆ Stevenson (R.L.): *Dr Jekyll and Mr Hyde*, Dover Publications, 1991.
◆ Updike (J.): *Bech: a Book*, Penguin, 1972.
◆ Wilde (O.): *The Picture of Dorian Gray*, Oxford University Press, 1981.

FIRST-HAND ACCOUNTS

◆ Hanff (H.): *84 Charing Cross Road*, Futura Publications, 1979.
◆ *The Illustrated Pepys* (edited by R.C. Latham), London, 1978.
◆ Orwell (G.): *Down and Out in Paris and London* (edited by D. Murphy), Penguin, 1989.
◆ Welsh (I.): *Trainspotting*, 1993.
◆ Trench (S.): *Bury Me in my Boots*, Hodder & Stoughton, 1983.
◆ Woolf (V.): *The London Scene*, Hogarth Press, 1982.

CRITICAL WORKS

◆ Baer (M.): *Theatre and Disorder in Late Georgian London*, Clarendon Press, 1992.
◆ Bradbrook (M.C.): *The Living Monument: Shakespeare and the Theatre of his Time,*, Cambridge University Press, 1977.
◆ Byrd (M.): *London Transformed: Images of the City in the 18th Century*, Yale University Press, 1978.
◆ Chalfant (F.C.): *Ben Jonson's London*, University of Georgia Press, 1978.
◆ Collins (P.): *Trollope's London*, University of Leicester, 1982.
◆ Gardner (J.): *Yeats and the Rhymer's Club: a Nineties' Perspective*, P. Lang, 1989.
◆ Gross (J.): *Rise and Fall of the English Man of Letters*, London, 1969.
◆ Harrison (M.): *The London of Sherlock Holmes*, David & Charles, 1972.
◆ Hewison (R.): *Under Siege: Literary Life in London 1939–45*, Weidenfeld & Nicolson, 1977.
◆ Hodges (W.C.): *Shakespeare's Second Globe: the Missing Monument*, Oxford University Press, 1973.
◆ Kimmey (J.L.): *Henry James and London: the City in his Fiction*, P. Lang, 1991.
◆ *Literature and the Social Order in Eighteenth-Century England* (edited by S. Copley), Croom Helm, 1984.
◆ Lucas (V.): *Tolstoy in London*, Evans Bros., 1979.
◆ *The Pelican Guide to English Literature* (Edited by B. Ford), Penguin, 1973.
◆ Schwarzbach (F.S.): *Dickens and the City*, Athlone Press, 1979.
◆ Weintraub (S.): *The London Yankees*, W.H. Allen, 1979.

MUSIC

◆ Hogwood (C.): *Handel*, Thames & Hudson, 1988.
◆ Mackerness (E.D.): *A Social History of English*

Music, Routledge & Kegan Paul, 1964.
◆ MILLIGAN (T.B.): *The Concerto and London's Musical Culture in the Late Eighteenth Century*, UMI Research Press, 1983.
◆ ORGA (A.): *The Proms*, David & Charles, 1974.
◆ POHL (C.F.): *Mozart and Haydn in London*, Da Capo Press, 1970.
◆ WEBER (W.): *Music and the Middle class: the Social Structure of Concert Life in London, Paris and Vienna,* 1975.
◆ YOUNG (P.): *A History of British Music*, London, 1967.

PAINTING AND DECORATIVE ARTS

◆ ANSCOMBE (I.): *Omega and After: Bloomsbury and the Decorative Arts*, Thames & Hudson, 1985.
◆ ARCHER (M.): *Indian Painting for the British: 1770–1880*, Oxford University Press., 1955.
◆ BINDMAN (D.): *Hogarth*, Thames & Hudson, 1981.
◆ BLAYNEY BROWN (D.): *The Art of J.M.W. Turner*, Headline, 1990.
◆ *British Art and the Modern Movement, 1930–40*, exh. cat. Arts Council, 1962.
◆ COOPER (J.): *Victorian and Edwardian Furniture and Interiors: from the Gothic Revival to Art Nouveau*, Thames & Hudson, 1987.
◆ DE MARÉ (E.): *The London Doré Saw: a Victorian Evocation*, Saint Martin's Press, 1973.
Farr (D.): *English Art 1870–1940*, Oxford, 1978.
◆ GAUNT (W.): *English Painting: a Concise History*, Thames & Hudson, 1985.
◆ HARRIS (J.): *The Artist and the Country House*, 1979.
◆ HILTON (T.): *The Pre-Raphaelites*, Thames & Hudson, 1970.
◆ HUTCHISON (H.C.): *The History of the Royal Academy, 1768–1968*, 1968.
◆ MURDOCH (J.), MURRELL (J.), NOON (P.) and STRONG (R.): *The English Miniature*, 1981.
◆ PIPER (D.): *The English Face*, 1957;
The Genius of British Painting, Weidenfeld & Nicolson, 1975.
◆ PRESTON (H.): *London and the Thames: Paintings of Three Centuries*, exh. cat., National Maritime Museum, undated.
◆ ROSENTHAL (M.): *British Landscape Painting*, 1982;
Constable, Thames & Hudson, 1987.
◆ SHONE (R.): *Bloomsbury Portraits: Vanessa Bell, Duncan Grant and their Circle*, Phaidon, 1976
◆ SUNDERLAND (J.):*Painting in Britain: 1525–1975*, Phaidon, 1976.
◆ *The Thames & Hudson Encyclopaedia of British Art* (edited by D. Bindman), Thames & Hudson, 1985.
◆ TREVHERZ (J.): *Victorian Painting*, Thames & Hudson, 1993.
◆ WALPOLE (H.): *Anecdotes of Painting in England, 1762–80, Penguin, 1954.*
◆ WATERHOUSE (E.): *Painting in Britain 1530 to 1790*, Penguin, 1954.
◆ *William Morris: Selected Writings and Designs,* (edited by A. Briggs), London, 1962.

GUIDES

◆ ADBURGHAM (A.): *Shopping in Style*, Thames & Hudson, 1979.
◆ BAILEY (C.): *Harrap's Guide to Famous London Graves*, Harraps, 1975.
◆ BANKS (F.R.): *The Penguin Guide to London*, 7th ed., Penguin, 1977.
◆ BARKER (F.) and SILVESTER CARR (D.): *The Black Plague Guide to London*, Constable, 1987.
◆ BLACKWOOD (A.): *London: a Times Bartholomew Guide*, Times Books, 1987.
◆ BORER (M.C.): *London Walks and Legends*, Granada, 1981.
◆ BUSHELL (P.): *London's Secret History*, Constable, 1983.
◆ CLARKE (J.): *In our Grandmothers' Footsteps*, Virago, 1984.
◆ DAVIES (A.) and HAZELTON (F.): *Walk in London: Forty Selected Walks in Central London,* John Bartholomew & Son (A Bartholomew Map and Guide), Edinburgh, 1988.
◆ DOWNIE (R.A.): *Murder in London: a Topological Guide to Famous Crimes*, A. Barker, 1973.
◆ DUNCAN (F.), GLASS (L.) AND SHARPE (C.): *London up Close*, Passport Books, Lincolnwood (Chicago), 1992.
◆ FAIRFAX (B.): *Walking London's Waterways,* David & Charles, 1985.
◆ *Fodor's London*, Hodder & Stoughton, 1979.
◆ GIBSON (P.): *The Capital Companion: a Street-by-street Guide to London and its Inhabitants*, Webb & Bower, 1985.
◆ GREEN (M.): *A Guide to London's Best Pubs*, Virgin, 1982.
◆ KAY (F.G.): *London,* rev. ed., Collins, 1984.
◆ LANE (E.): *A Guide to Literary London*, Hippocrene Books, undated.
◆ *London,* Michelin Guide, 1990.
◆ *London,* Blue Guide, 1990.
◆ PEARSON (M.M.): *Discovering London for Children*, 6th ed., Shire Publications, Aylesbury, 1983.
◆ PEPLOW (M.): *London for Free*, Panther, 1984.
◆ SAUNDERS (N.): *Alternative London*, 5th ed., WIldwood House, 1977.
◆ TWORT (D.): *London (Guide in Jeans)*, Octopus, 1980.
◆ WILLIAMS (G.): *Guide to Literary London*, Batsford, 1973.
◆ WITTICH (J.): *Discovering London Street Names*, Shire Publications, Aylesbury, reprinted 1990.

MUSEUMS

◆ DANTO (E.): *Undiscovered Museums of London*, Surrey Books, Chicago, 1991.
◆ FARR (D.) and NEWMAN (J.): *Guide to the Courtauld Institute Galleries at Somerset House*, Courtauld Institute of Art, 1990.
◆ GRAVES (A.): *Treasures of the Royal Academy*, 1963.
◆ *Guide to London Museums and Galleries*, Her Majesty's Stationery Office, 1974.
◆ INGAMELLS (J.): *The Wallace Collection*, Scala, 1990.
◆ *The National Gallery*, *London* (intro. by M. Wilson), Letts, 1978.
◆ *The National Maritime Museum* (edited by B. Greenhill), Philip Wilson, 1982.
◆ NICOLSON (B.): *The Treasures of the Foundling Hospital*, 1972.
◆ *The Tate Gallery: an Illustrated Companion to the National Collections of British and Foreign Modern Art*, Tate Gallery Publications, 1979.
◆ *The Victoria and Albert Museum*, Scala, 1991.

ACKNOWLEDGEMENTS

We would like to thank the following publishers or copyright-holders for permission to reproduce the quotations on pages 105–20.

◆ HARCOURT BRACE & COMPANY and FABER AND FABER LTD: Excerpt from "The Waste Land" in *Collected Poems 1909–1962* by T.S. Eliot, copyright © 1963, 1964 by T.S. Eliot. Rights outside the U.S. administered by Faber and Faber Ltd., London. Reprinted by permission of the publishers.
◆ HARCOURT BRACE & COMPANY and A.M. HEATH & COMPANY LTD: Excerpt from *Down and Out in Paris and London* by George Orwell, copyright © 1933 by George Orwell, copyright renewed 1961 by Sonia Pitt-Rivers. Rights outisde the U.S. administered by A.M. Heath & Company Ltd, London on behalf of the Estate of the late Sonia Brownell Orwell and Martin Secker & Warburg Ltd. Reprinted by permission of the publishers.

◆ VIKING PENGUIN and PETERS FRASER & DUNLOP: Excerpt from *Money* by Martin Amis, copyright © 1984 by Martin Amis. Rights outside the U.S. administered by Peters Fraser & Dunlop Group Ltd. Reprinted by permission of Viking Penguin, a division of Penguin Books U.S.A. Inc., and the Peters Fraser & Dunlop Group Ltd.

Front cover (US): Tower Bridge. Coll. Peter Jackson. Poster for the Southern Railway. Reproduced with the kind permission of the National Railway Museum, York. Phone box, photo S. Bosman. Endsleigh Street, photo idem. Dickens' House, Doughty Street. Sparrow, drawing by Jean Chevallier.
Spine (US): Entrance to the Gallipoli Bathhouse. Coldstream Guard.
Back cover (US): Thames barge, 1805. Coll. Peter Jackson. Map by Jean-Yves Duhoo. Street sign, photo S. Bosman. Royal Albert Hall. *Mr Hughes' Ball*, drawing by Richard Doughty. Coll. Peter Jackson. Pub sign, Kennington, photo Geoff Howard/Collections.
Front endpaper Westminster, photo Anthony Kersting. St Paul's Cathedral, photo British Tourist Authority. Tower of London, photo The Corporation of London. The Meat Hall, Harrods, photo Harrods. The Picture Gallery, Buckingham Palace © H.M. the Queen. Deckchairs in Hyde Park, photo British Tourist Agency. Shakespeare's Globe Theatre, photo Richard Kalina.
10/11 Urchins bathing in the docks, photo c. 1910. Coll. Peter Jackson. The Thames at Billingsgate with Tower Bridge in the background, photo Museum in Docklands Project, London.
11/12 Barges at Greenwich, photo Museum in Docklands Project, London. The *Mauritania* in 1939. Idem.
14 Hatter, photo c. 1910. Coll. Peter Jackson. Nature section. Photographs copyright:
16 © A.F. Kersting © London Ecology Unit (LEU)
17 © Skyscan balloon photography
19 © LEU
20 © LEU
21 © Jacana
22 © David Bevan, Natural History Society
23 © LEU
26/27 © LEU
28 © LEU
30/31 © LEU
33 *Lord Mayor's Barge*, David Roberts, watercolor, 1830. Guildhall Art Library, Corporation of London, photo Bridgeman Art Library.
34 Coin from the late 3rd century depicting Emperor Constantine, electrotype. Museum of London. Roman mosaic discovered in a basement in the City. Charles d'Orléans in the Tower of London, manuscript c. 1500. British Library.
35 *Henry VI and St Edmund*, painting/wood, c. 1500. St Catherine's Church, Ludham, Norfolk, photo Angelo Hornak Library. Effigy of Richard II, Westminster Abbey, with the kind permission of the Dean and Chapter of Westminster Abbey, photo Angelo Hornak Library. *Old London Bridge before 1760*, by Samuel Scott, oil/canvas. Guildhall Art Gallery, Corporation of London, photo Bridgeman Art Library.
36 *Elisabeth I*, oil/panel, 1585, attributed to William Segar. Reproduced with the permission of the Earl of Salisbury, Hatfield House. *Southwark Cathedral*, engraving by W. Hollar, 1647. Coll. Peter Jackson. *The Fire of London*, Flemish school, oil/canvas, 1666. Museum of London.
37 *George IV's Coronation Procession*, 1821, W. Heath, colored aquatint. Coll. Peter Jackson. *The Prince Regent*, hand-colored engraving, 1815. Coll. Peter Jackson. *The Opening of Tower Bridge*, 1894, William Lionel Wyllie, oil/canvas, 1894–5. Guildhall Art Gallery, Corporation of London, photo Bridgeman Art Library.
38 *Queen Victoria's Coronation*, anonymous artist, oil/canvas, 1838. Bradford Art Galleries and Museums, photo Bridgeman Art Library. *Crystal Palace in 1851*, lithograph. Coll. Peter Jackson. *St Pancras Station* after 1869, hand-colored lithograph. Idem. Harrods, old postcard. Idem.
39 Fleet Street, photo c. 1930, Hulton Picture Company. Churchill in the rubble of the Blitz, photo Popperfoto. The Lloyd's building, photo S. Bosman.
40/41 *The Fire of London*, 1666, anonymous artist, oil/canvas. Worshipful Company of Goldsmiths. *The Fire of London*, Griffier the Elder, oil/canvas. Museum of London. *The Fire of London*, by Waggoner, oil/canvas. Guildhall Art Gallery, Corporation of London, photo Bridgeman Art Library.
42 St Paul's Cathedral during the Blitz, photo Popperfoto. Firemen in the ruins, photo Hulton Picture Company.
43 Firemen, photo Popperfoto. Ludgate Hill in May 1941, photo Hulton Picture Company. Street scene, photo idem.
44 *Bill-Stickers near Charing Cross*, hand-colored engraving. Coll. Peter Jackson. Women talking in the street, photo idem.
45 Urchins playing cards, photo idem.
46 *Personnages londoniens* (*People in London*), engraving by Gustave Doré, in Louis Enault, *Londres*, 1876.
47 Shopfront, photo c. 1910. Coll. Peter Jackson.
48 The orb, made for Charles II's coronation, Crown Copyright, photo A.C. Cooper. Procession in Westminster Abbey, before Queen Elizabeth II's coronation, photo in *The Queen Elizabeth Coronation Souvenir*, 1953. Queen Elizabeth in her carriage, photo Hulton Picture Company.
48/49 *King George V and Queen Mary at a Thanksgiving Service in Westminster Abbey*, 1935, Frank Salisbury, oil/canvas, 1935–6. Guildhall Art Gallery, Corporation of London, photo Bridgeman Art Library.
49 Queen Elizabeth and her family on the balcony of Buckingham Palace after the coronation, photo Hulton Picture Company. Queen Victoria and her Indian servant Abdul Karim, photo Hill & Saunders, 1893. National Portrait Gallery, London. Henry II at Prayer before the tomb of Thomas Becket, stained glass window, Canterbury Cathedral, photo Angelo Hornak Library. The scepter holding the Cullinan Diamond. Crown Copyright, photo A.C. Cooper.
50 Recruitment poster for the Welsh Guards, 1915. Guards Museum, London. *The Battle of Alma* (detail), oil/canvas, 1854. Reproduced with kind permission of the Regimental Lieutenant Colonel, Scots Guards. Blues and Royals (1), Life Guards (2), Grenadier Guard (3), drawings by Jonathan Shock.
51 Standard of the Welsh Guards. Reproduced with kind permission of the Welsh Guards. Standard of the Life Guards, Household Cavalry Museum, Windsor. Coldstream Guard (4), Welsh Guard (6) and Scots Guard, drawings by Jonathan Shock. Irish Guard (5). Reproduced with kind permission of the Irish Guards.
52 Trumpeter at the Lord Mayor's election, photo Brian Shuel/Collections. Beating the bounds, photo idem. Pearly Queen, photo idem.
52/53 Trooping the Colour, photo Headquarters London District Public Information.
53 Lord Mayor's Barge, David Roberts, watercolor, 1830. Guildhall Art Library, Corporation of London, photo Bridgeman Art Library. The Lord Mayor's

Peter Jackson.
132 The bell, Big Ben. Controller of Her Majesty's Stationery Office (Crown Copyright). *Sketch for the Clock Tower*, Charles Barry, watercolor, c. 1840–5. British Architectural Library, RIBA, London. *George Thomas, First Viscount Tonypandy, Speaker 1976–83*, George J.D. Bruce, oil/canvas. Controller of Her Majesty's Stationery Office (Crown Copyright).
131 *Procession of Queen Victoria Returning from the House of Lords after the Opening of Parliament*, Joseph Nash, watercolor. © H.M. the Queen.
133 *William Pitt the Younger Speaking in the House of Commons*, Carl Anton Hickel, oil/canvas, 1793. National Portrait Gallery. *Gladstone Presenting the Irish Land Bill to the House of Commons in 1881*, F. Sargent, oil/canvas, 1882. Controller of Her Majesty's Stationery Office (Crown Copyright). *Queen Anne at the House of Lords*, Peter Tillemans, oil/canvas, c. 1710. Controller of Her Majesty's Stationery Office (Crown Copyright). *St Stephen's Hall*, engraving, 1859. Controller of Her Majesty's Stationery Office (Crown Copyright).
136 *The Old House of Commons*, B. Cole, hand-colored engraving. Coll. Peter Jackson.
136/137 Houses of Parliament, old postcard. Idem.
137 Westminster seen from the South Bank, photo Antony Kersting. *Big Ben*, colored engraving in the *Illustrated London News*, 1859. Coll. Peter Jackson. Central Lobby, Houses of Parliament, photo Geoff Howard/ Collections.
138 Invitation card to George IV's coronation at Westminster Abbey. Coll. Peter Jackson. *Westminster Abbey*, J. Bowles, hand-colored engraving. Idem. *Procession of the Knights of the Order of the Bath*, Canaletto, oil/canvas, after 1749. Dean and Chapter of Westminster Abbey, photo Bridgeman Art Library.
139 North transept of Westminster Abbey, photo Antony Kersting. *Henry VII's Chapel in Westminster Abbey*, C. Wild, colored aquatint, 1828. Coll. Peter Jackson. Choirboys in Westminster Abbey, photo Geoff Howard/Collections.
140 Recumbent effigy of William of Valence. Westminster Abbey, photo Antony Kersting. *Coronation of William IV*, hand-colored engraving. Coll. Peter Jackson. The nave in Westminster Abbey, photo Antony Kersting.
141 Poets' Corner, south transept, photo idem. Tomb of Edward the Confessor, photo idem. Tomb of Queen Elizabeth I, photo idem.
142 10 Downing Street and 11 Downing Street, photo Hulton Picture Company.
142/143 *Horseguards Parade,* John Chapman, oil/canvas, c. 1750. Private coll ., photo Bridgeman Art Library.
143 Horseguards, Whitehall, photo Antony Kersting. *Horse Guards*, hand-colored lithograph. Coll. Peter Jackson. Officer in the Life Guards, Whitehall, photo Geoff Howard/Collections.
144 *Ceiling of the Banqueting House*, Rubens, photo Antony Kersting. Admiralty Arch, old postcard. Coll. Peter Jackson. The Mall, photo S. Bosman.
145 Westminster Cathedral, photo Antony Kersting. Poster for the Southern Railway. Reproduced with the kind permission of the National Railway Museum, York. Westminster Cathedral at night, photo S. Bosman.
146 *Queen Victoria on her Way to Guildhall on November 9, 1837*, James Henry Dix, oil/canvas, 1838. Guildhall Art Library, Corporation of London, photo Bridgeman Art Library.
147 Lord Mayor's carriage, photo Brian Shuel/Collections. *The Ninth November: The Procession of Mayor James Whitehead*, William Logsdail, oil/canvas, 1888. Guildhall Art Gallery, Corporation of London, photo Bridgeman Art Library.
148 *Lord Mayor's Banquet*, Guildhall, colored aquatint, 1830. Coll. Peter Jackson. Guildhall, photo Antony Kersting. *St Lawrence Jewry and Guildhall*, Thomas Malton, oil/canvas, 1783. Guildhall Art Gallery, Corporation of London.
148/149 *London Bridge and the City Seen from Somerset House*, Francis Smith, oil/canvas, late 18th-century. Guildhall Art Gallery, Corporation of London, photo Bridgeman Art Library.
149 St Mary Woolnoth, photo S. Bosman. Mansion House Street and the Royal Exchange, photo c. 1900. Coll. Peter Jackson. *The Interior of St Stephen Walbrook*, Thomas Rowlandson, colored aquatint, 1809. Idem.
150 The vaults of the Bank of England. Bank of England Museum, with the permission of the Governor and Company of the Bank of England. *A Shop near the Royal Exchange, Cornhill,* C.J. Richardson, watercolor, 1871. Coll. Peter Jackson. Mansion House, photo c. 1900. Idem.
150/151 *Bank of England*, Sir John Soane, watercolor, 1807. Reproduced with the kind permission of the Sir John Soane Museum.
151 *Dividend Day at the Bank of England*, G.E. Hicks, oil/canvas, 1859. Bank of England Museum, with the permission of the Governor and Company of the Bank of England.
152 The tower of the National Westminster Bank, photo Geoff Howard/Collections. The tower of the National Westminster Bank, photo Charles Lane. *The City of London*, watercolor, in David Gentleman, London, 1986. © David Gentleman.
153 Signs in the City, photo S. Bosman. The Lloyd's building, photo Antony Kersting. Plaque, photo S. Bosman.
154 Leadenhall Market, photo S. Bosman. *Leadenhall Market*, watercolor, in David Gentleman, London, 1986. © David Gentleman. Porter at Billingsgate market, photo c. 1920. Coll. Peter Jackson.
155 Cheapside, old postcard. Coll. Peter Jackson. *Alexander Pope*, William Hoare, pastel. National Portrait Gallery. Cheapside, photo c. 1900. Coll. Peter Jackson.
156 *157–9 Fenchurch Street*, architect Leo Sylvester Sullivan, drawing by L. D. Coombs, 1911. *Billingsgate Market*, Thomas Rowlandson, colored aquatint. Coll. Peter Jackson. *The Monument and Fish Street Hill*, Canaletto, oil/canvas, c. 1750. Guildhall Art Gallery, Corporation of London, photo Bridgeman Art Library.
157 *Old London Bridge in the Seventeenth Century*, Claude de Jongh, oil/canvas. Iveagh Bequest, Kenwood House, photo Bridgeman Art Library. St Mary le Bow, photo Clémence Jacquinet.
158 *The Mouth of Fleet River*, Samuel Scott, oil/canvas, c. 1750. Guildhall Art Gallery, Corporation of London, photo Bridgeman Art Library.
159 Fleet Street, photo 1921, Hulton Picture Company.
160 St Clement Danes church, interior of St Clement Danes, photo S. Bosman. *Mail Guard Passing through Temple Bar*, J.L. Agasse, colored aquatint, 1825. Coll. Peter Jackson. Temple

Coll. Peter Jackson. *Physic Garden*, engraving 1751. Idem. Brick motif, Chelsea Embankment, Chelsea Old Church, photo S. Bosman.
201 Cheyne Walk, photo S. Bosman. *Carlyle Square*, watercolor, in David Gentleman, *London*, 1986. © David Gentleman.
202 Paultons Square, Cheyne Walk, photo S. Bosman. *Cheyne Walk*, Henry Greaves and Walter Greaves, oil/canvas, 1857. Private coll., photo Bridgeman Art Library.
203 Cheyne Walk, photo c. 1910. The Thames at Chelsea Embankment, statue of Thomas Carlyle, photo S. Bosman.
204/205 *Millbank Penitentiary*, engravings, 19th century. Coll. Peter Jackson.
206 *Vauxhall Gardens*, Canaletto, oil/canvas, 1751. Lord Trevor. *Sir Henry Tate*, oil/canvas. Coll. Tate and Lyle.
207 Tate Gallery, old postcard. Coll. Peter Jackson. Clore Gallery by James Stirling, photo S. Bosman.
208 *Pompeii*, Hans Hofmann, oil/canvas, 1959. Tate Gallery. *Self-portrait*, Joseph Mallord William Turner, oil/canvas, c. 1797. Idem.
209 *Faa Iheihe*, Paul Gauguin, oil/canvas, 1898. Idem.
210 *The Forge*, Joseph Wright of Derby, oil/canvas, 1772. Idem. *The Painter and his Dog*, Paul Hogarth, oil/canvas, 1745. Idem.
211 *Captain Thomas Lee*, Marcus Gheeraerts, oil/canvas, 1594. Idem. *The Saltonstall Family*, David des Granges, oil/canvas, c. 1636–7. Idem.
212 *The Three Daughters of Sir William Montgomery as "The Graces Adorning a Term of Hymen"*, Joshua Reynolds, oil/canvas, 1773. Idem.
213 *The Reapers*, George Stubbs, oil/wood, 1785. Idem. *Giovanna Baccelli*, Thomas Gainsborough, oil/canvas, 1782. Idem.
214 *Beatrice on the Car*, William Blake, watercolor and ink on paper, c. 1824–7. Idem. *Blind Violinist*, David Wilkie, oil/wood, 1806. Idem. *The Opening of Waterloo Bridge*, John Constable, oil/canvas, 1832. Idem.
215 *The Bridge of Sighs, the Ducal Palace and the Customs-house*, Joseph Mallord William Turner, oil/canvas, 1833. Idem. *The Dogano, San Giorgio, Citella, Seen from the Steps of the Europa*, Joseph Mallord William Turner, oil/canvas, 1842. Idem. *Petworth: Sunset in the Park*, Joseph Mallord William Turner, watercolor, c. 1830. Idem.
216/217 *Snowstorm: Steamboat off a Harbour Mouth*, Joseph Mallord William Turner, oil/canvas, 1842. Idem.
218 *Beata Beatrix*, Dante Gabriel Rossetti, oil/canvas, 1860–70. Idem. *Ophelia*, John Everett Millais, oil/canvas, 1851. Idem.
219 *The Awakening Conscience*, William Holman Hunt, oil/canvas, 1852. Idem. *The Golden Stairs*, Edward Burne-Jones, oil/canvas, 1880. Idem.
220 *Three Studies of Figures at the Foot of a Crucifixion*, Francis Bacon, oil/board, c. 1944. Idem. *Mr and Mrs Clark and Percy*, David Hockney, acrylic/canvas, 1970–1. Idem. *Red and Black*, Mark Rothko, oil/canvas, 1957. Idem. *Whaam!*, Roy Lichtenstein, acrylic/canvas, 1963. Idem.
221 *Woman in Tears*, Pablo Picasso, oil/canvas, 1937. Idem.
222 *Figure, Nanjizal*, Barbara Hepworth, carved yew wood, 1958. Idem. *The Matador*, Joan Miró, engraving and collage, 1969. Idem.
223 *Early One Morning*, Antony Caro, colored sculpture, 1962. Idem. *The End of the Twentieth Century*, Joseph Beuys, sculpture, 1983–5. Idem.
222/223 *Woman Reclining*, Henry Moore, sculpture, 1951. Idem.
224 *Terraces*, watercolor, in David Gentleman, London, 1986. © David Gentleman.
225 The Meat Hall, Harrods, photo Harrods
226/227 Views of Kensington, photo S. Bosman.
228 View of the Albert Memorial and the Albert Hall from the air, photo Skyscan Balloon Photo-graphy Copyright. *Prince Albert*, Franz Xavier Winterhalter, oil/canvas, 1867. National Portrait Gallery.
229 Watercolor, in David Gentleman, *London*, 1986. © David Gentleman. Victoria and Albert Museum, photo S. Bosman.
230 *Handing Over the Keys*, sketch by Raphael. © H.M. the Queen, (Victoria and Albert Museum). *Flatford Mill from a Lock on the Stour*, John Constable, oil, c. 1811. Victoria and Albert Museum. *Miniature of a Courtesan*, Nicholas Hilliard, on vellum, 16th century. Idem.
231 *St Paul Preaching in Athens*, sketch by Raphael. © H.M. the Queen (Victoria and Albert Museum). River goddess Yamuna, sculpture, Central India, c. 900. Victoria and Albert Museum. *Prince on Horseback*, Moghul miniature, gouache on paper, c. 1720. Idem. Tipoo's Tiger, painted wood carving, c. 1700. Idem.
232 Evening dress, Callot sisters, 1922. Idem. sculpture gallery, Victoria and Albert Museum, photo S. Bosman. The plaster cast room. Victoria and Albert Museum.
233 Snuff box, P.F. Drais, 1775–7. Idem. *The Alarm, or the Loyal Governess*, Jean François de Troy, oil/canvas, 1785. Idem. Sèvres vase Idem. Cabinet, 1867. Idem.
234 *View of the Dinosaur Gallery*, Alfred Waterhouse, ink/paper, 1870–1. British Architectural Library, RIBA, London. Exterior of the Natural History Museum, photo Emily Lane.
234/235 *Natural History Museum*, Alfred Waterhouse, watercolor, c. 1870. Victoria and Albert Museum, photo Bridgeman Art Library.
235 Natural History Museum, old postcard. Coll. Peter Jackson.
236 The auditorium of the Albert Hall, photo c. 1900. Coll. Peter Jackson. Albert Memorial, photo Antony Kersting. *Brompton Oratory*, Herbert A. Gribble, watercolor, c. 1870. Fathers of the London Oratory, photo Bridgeman Art Library.
237 *People in Hyde Park*, Charles James Conder, oil/canvas. Private coll., photo Bridgeman Art Library.
238 Deck chairs, St James' Park, photo S. Bosman. *St James's Park*, Benjamin Read, colored aquatint, c. 1838. Guildhall Library, Corporation of London, photo Bridgeman Art Library.
239 *St James's Park*, Chatelain, hand-colored engraving, 18th century. Coll. Peter Jackson.
240 *German Chapel, St James's*, hand-colored engraving in W.H. Pyne, *Royal Residences*, 1819. Coll. Peter Jackson. Interior of St James' Palace. Idem. Exterior of St James' Palace. Idem.
241 *St James's Palace*, Christopher Clark, poster. Reproduced with the kind permission of the National Railway Museum, York. Buckingham Palace seen from St James' Park, old postcard. Coll. Peter Jackson.
242 The Picture Gallery, Buckingham Palace. © H.M. the Queen. The Green

Archive.
359 Windsor, Ball Room. Hand-colored engraving in W.H. Pyne *Royal Residences*, 1819. Windsor, King's Drawing Room, idem. Views of Windsor, photos S. Bosman.
360 View of Windsor, idem.
361 *Cricket on the Green at Eton*, William Evans, oil on canvas, c.1843. Eton College, E.T. Archive. Illustration in J. Ryman *A Few Recollections of Eton*, 1840, E.T. Archive.
362-3 *Frogmore*, handcolored engraving in W.H. Pyne *Royal Residences*, 1819.
362 Eton College Chapel, photo S. Bosman. Cloisters Chapel, idem. Illustration in J. Ryman *A Few Recollections of Eton*, 1840, E.T. Archive.
363 The Library of Eton College, photo S. Bosman.
364 *St John the Baptist*, Guido Reni, oil/canvas, 1640–2. Dulwich Picture Gallery. Exterior of Dulwich Picture Gallery, photo Antony Kersting. *The Triumph of David*, Nicolas Poussin, oil/canvas, 1628–31. Dulwich Picture Gallery.
367 British Tourist Authority.
368 British Tourist Authority.
370 Tower of London, photo The Corporation of London, British Tourist Authority.
376 *Rules*. *Fung Shing*, photo Seymourina Cruse.
380 *Bibendum, Brasserie Oxo Tower*, photo Chris Gascoigne.
422-439 *Street maps* © Touring Editora/Nouveaux Loisirs, Édigraphie edition.
Back endpaper Map. Gallimard Nouveaux Loisirs/ Édigraphie

Illustrators:
16/17 Gilbert Houbre, Jean Chevallier, François Desbordes, William Donohoe, Claire Felloni, Pascal Robin.
18/19 François Desbordes, Jean Chevallier, Claire Felloni, Pascal Robin.
20/21 Jean Chevallier, François Desbordes, Claire Felloni, Catherine Lachaux, Guy Michel.
22/23 Jean Chevallier, Claire Felloni, Catherine Lachaux, Guy Michel.
24/25 Jean Chevallier, Claire Felloni, Catherine Lachaux.
26/27 Jean Chevallier, Richard Coombes, Claire Felloni.
28/29 Jean Chevallier, François Desbordes, Claire Felloni, Guy Michel, John Wilkinson.
30/31 Jean Chevallier, François Desbordes, Claire Felloni, Guy Michel, François Crozat.
32 Jean Chevallier, François Desbordes, Claire Felloni, Guy Michel, John Wilkinson.
Illustrators for the practical information section and list of adresses: Maurice Pommier and Raymond Stottel.
Computer graphics: Paul Coulbois and Danièle Guitton.

We have not been able to trace the heirs or publishers of certain documents. An account is being held open for them at our offices.

A

B

C

D

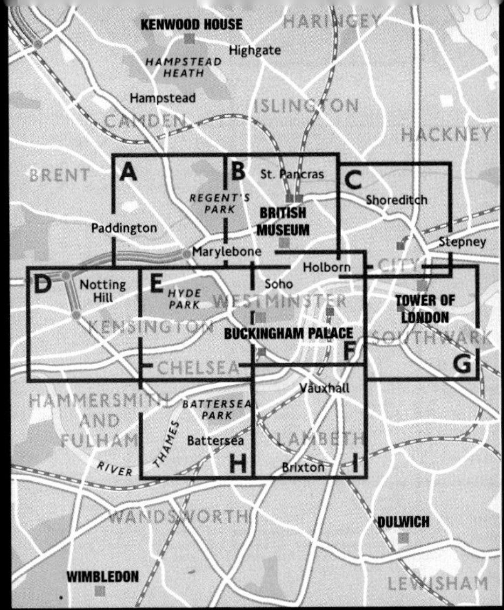

Map Section

Key

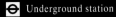

M4 Motorway	Airport
A2 Main road	Underground station
Railroad	Hospital
Monument	

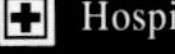

◆ The London Underground

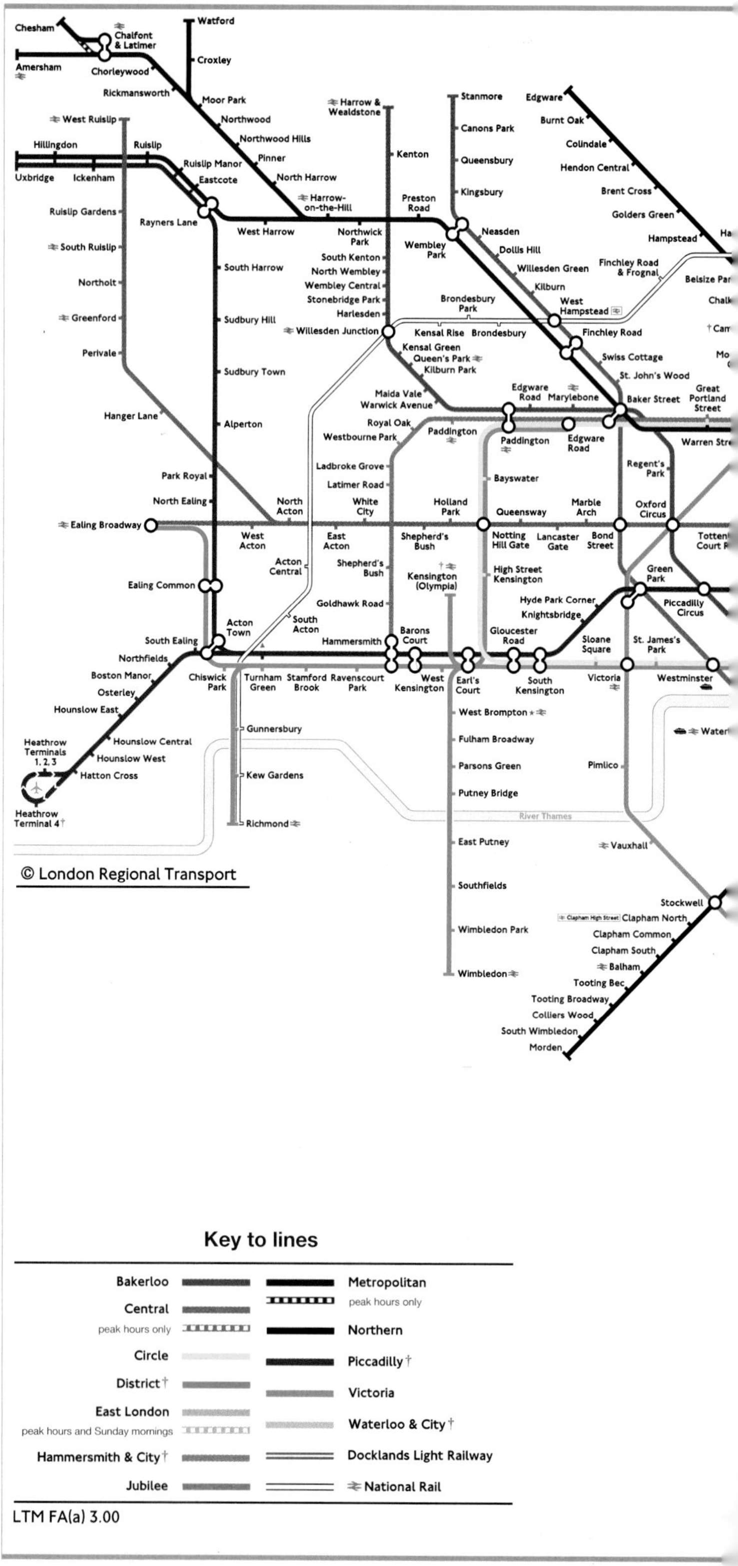

Chesham
Chalfont & Latimer
Watford
Amersham
Chorleywood
Croxley
Rickmansworth
Moor Park
Northwood
Northwood Hills
Pinner
North Harrow
Harrow-on-the-Hill
West Ruislip
Hillingdon
Ruislip
Uxbridge
Ickenham
Ruislip Manor
Eastcote
Ruislip Gardens
Rayners Lane
South Ruislip
Northolt
Greenford
Perivale
Hanger Lane
West Harrow
South Harrow
Sudbury Hill
Sudbury Town
Alperton
Park Royal
North Ealing
Ealing Broadway
West Acton
North Acton
Ealing Common
Acton Town
South Ealing
Northfields
Boston Manor
Osterley
Hounslow East
Hounslow Central
Hounslow West
Hatton Cross
Heathrow Terminals 1, 2, 3
Heathrow Terminal 4 †
Harrow & Wealdstone
Kenton
Preston Road
Northwick Park
South Kenton
North Wembley
Wembley Central
Stonebridge Park
Harlesden
Willesden Junction
Wembley Park
Stanmore
Canons Park
Queensbury
Kingsbury
Neasden
Dollis Hill
Willesden Green
Kilburn
Brondesbury Park
Kensal Rise
Brondesbury
West Hampstead
Finchley Road & Frognal
Finchley Road
Swiss Cottage
St. John's Wood
Edgware
Burnt Oak
Colindale
Hendon Central
Brent Cross
Golders Green
Hampstead
Belsize Park
Kensal Green
Queen's Park
Kilburn Park
Maida Vale
Warwick Avenue
Royal Oak
Westbourne Park
Paddington
Edgware Road
Marylebone
Baker Street
Great Portland Street
Warren Street
Regent's Park
Ladbroke Grove
Latimer Road
White City
East Acton
Acton Central
Holland Park
Shepherd's Bush
Queensway
Bayswater
Lancaster Gate
Marble Arch
Bond Street
Oxford Circus
Notting Hill Gate
Kensington (Olympia) †
High Street Kensington
Green Park
Piccadilly Circus
Hyde Park Corner
Knightsbridge
Goldhawk Road
South Acton
Hammersmith
Barons Court
Gloucester Road
Sloane Square
St. James's Park
Chiswick Park
Turnham Green
Stamford Brook
Ravenscourt Park
West Kensington
Earl's Court
South Kensington
Victoria
Westminster
Gunnersbury
Kew Gardens
Richmond
West Brompton
Fulham Broadway
Parsons Green
Putney Bridge
East Putney
Southfields
Wimbledon Park
Wimbledon
Pimlico
River Thames
Vauxhall
Stockwell
Clapham High Street
Clapham North
Clapham Common
Clapham South
Balham
Tooting Bec
Tooting Broadway
Colliers Wood
South Wimbledon
Morden

Key to lines

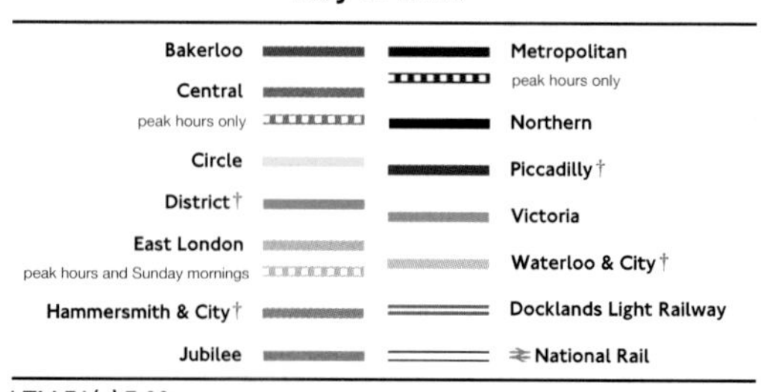

LTM FA(a) 3.00

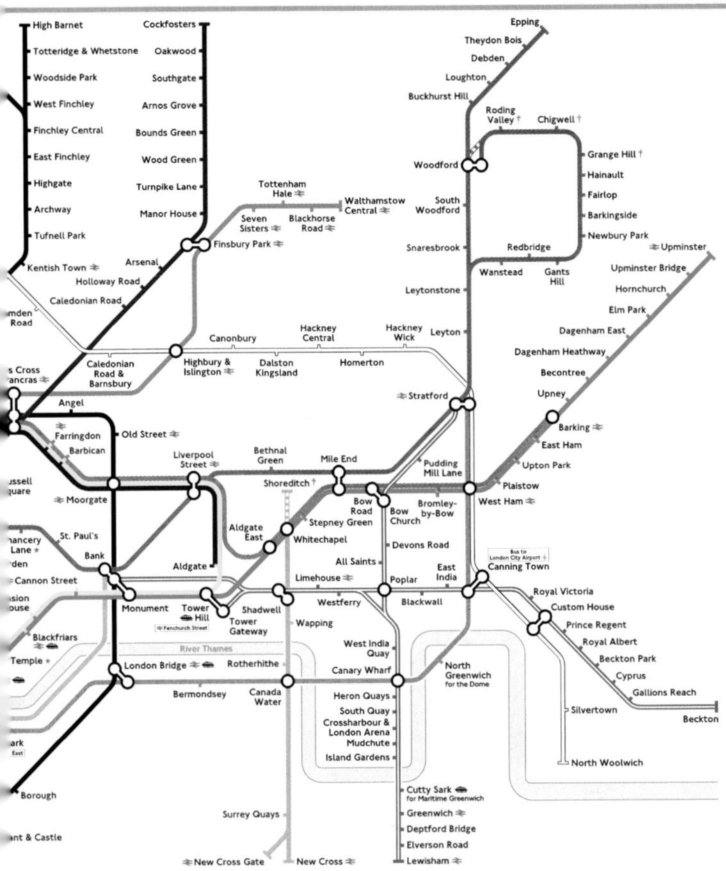

High Barnet
Totteridge & Whetstone
Woodside Park
West Finchley
Finchley Central
East Finchley
Highgate
Archway
Tufnell Park
Kentish Town
Cockfosters
Oakwood
Southgate
Arnos Grove
Bounds Green
Wood Green
Turnpike Lane
Manor House
Arsenal
Holloway Road
Caledonian Road
Finsbury Park
Tottenham Hale
Seven Sisters
Blackhorse Road
Walthamstow Central
Epping
Theydon Bois
Debden
Loughton
Buckhurst Hill
Roding Valley †
Chigwell †
Grange Hill †
Hainault
Fairlop
Barkingside
Newbury Park
Woodford
South Woodford
Snaresbrook
Redbridge
Wanstead
Gants Hill
Leytonstone
Leyton
Upminster
Upminster Bridge
Hornchurch
Elm Park
Dagenham East
Dagenham Heathway
Becontree
Upney
Barking
East Ham
Upton Park
Plaistow
West Ham
mden Road
Caledonian Road & Barnsbury
Canonbury
Highbury & Islington
Dalston Kingsland
Hackney Central
Homerton
Hackney Wick
Stratford
s Cross ancras
Angel
Farringdon
Barbican
Old Street
Liverpool Street
Bethnal Green
Mile End
Pudding Mill Lane
ussell uare
Moorgate
Shoreditch †
Bow Road
Bow Church
Bromley-by-Bow
Stepney Green
Whitechapel
Aldgate East
Aldgate
ancery Lane
St. Paul's
rden
Bank
Cannon Street
Devons Road
All Saints
Limehouse
Poplar
East India
Bus to London City Airport
Canning Town
sion ouse
Monument
Tower Hill
Fenchurch Street
Tower Gateway
Shadwell
Westferry
Blackwall
Royal Victoria
Custom House
Prince Regent
Royal Albert
Beckton Park
Cyprus
Gallions Reach
Beckton
Blackfriars
Temple
Wapping
River Thames
West India Quay
Canary Wharf
North Greenwich for the Dome
London Bridge
Rotherhithe
Bermondsey
Canada Water
Heron Quays
South Quay
Crossharbour & London Arena
Mudchute
Island Gardens
Silvertown
North Woolwich
ark
East
Borough
Cutty Sark for Maritime Greenwich
Greenwich
Deptford Bridge
Elverson Road
Lewisham
Surrey Quays
ant & Castle
New Cross Gate
New Cross

London Travel Information
020 7222 1234
24 hours

Minicom
020 7918 3015

- Interchange stations
- Connections with National Rail
- Connections with National Rail within walking distance
- Connections with riverboat services
- Airport interchange
- ★ Closed Sundays
- ▲ Served by Piccadilly line trains early morning and late evening
- † For opening times see poster journey planners. Certains stations are closed on public holidays.

Reg. user No. 00/3325

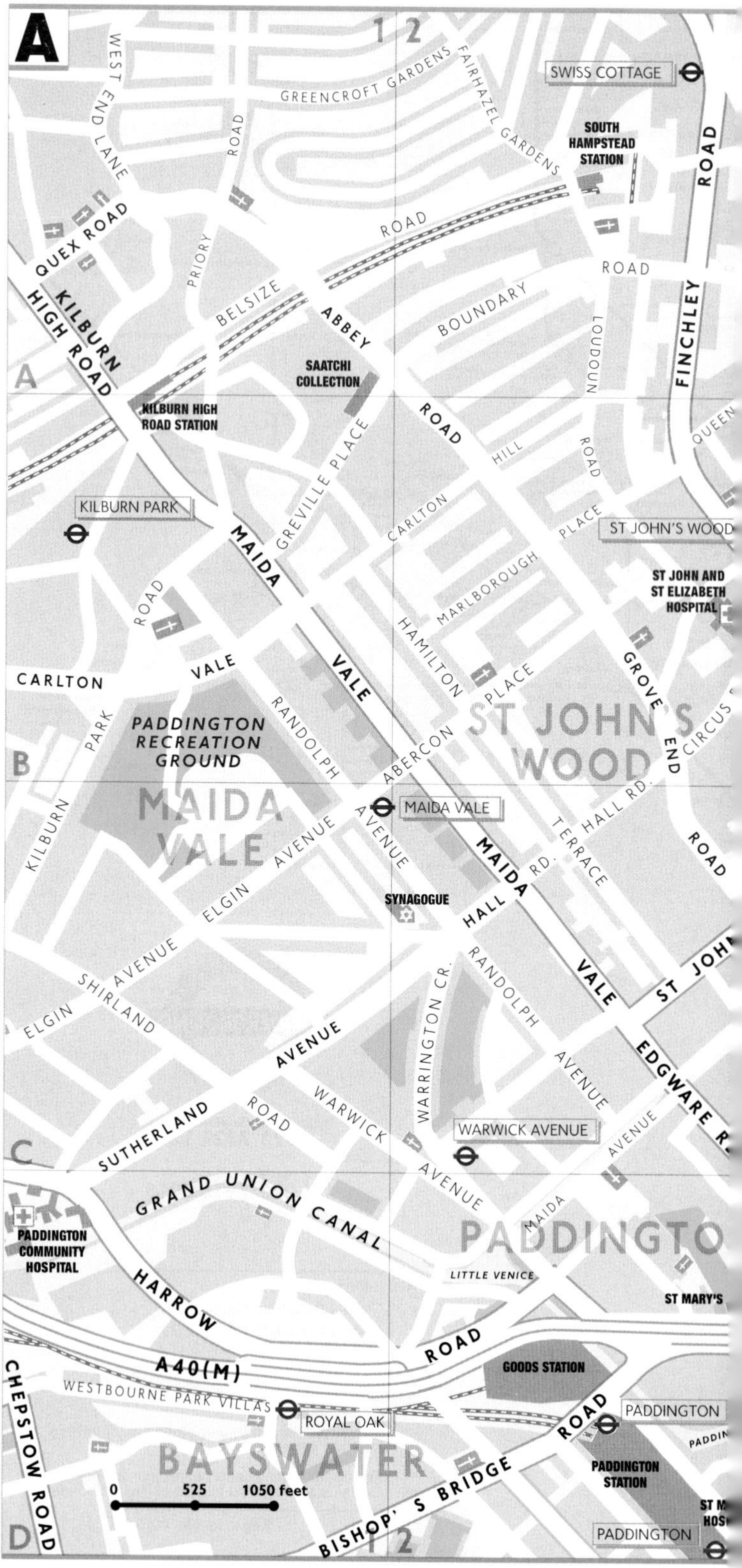
A
1 2
SWISS COTTAGE
SOUTH HAMPSTEAD STATION
WEST END LANE
GREENCROFT GARDENS
FAIRHAZEL GARDENS
PRIORY ROAD
QUEX ROAD
BELSIZE ROAD
KILBURN HIGH ROAD
ABBEY ROAD
BOUNDARY ROAD
LOUDOUN ROAD
FINCHLEY ROAD
SAATCHI COLLECTION
KILBURN HIGH ROAD STATION
KILBURN PARK
GREVILLE PLACE
HILL ROAD
CARLTON HILL
QUEEN'S
ST JOHN'S WOOD
PLACE
MAIDA VALE
MARLBOROUGH PLACE
ST JOHN AND ST ELIZABETH HOSPITAL
CARLTON VALE
HAMILTON TERRACE
GROVE END ROAD
PADDINGTON RECREATION GROUND
RANDOLPH AVENUE
ST JOHN'S WOOD
KILBURN PARK ROAD
ABERCORN PLACE
CIRCUS ROAD
MAIDA VALE
HALL RD.
ELGIN AVENUE
SYNAGOGUE
HALL ROAD
SHIRLAND ROAD
ELGIN AVENUE
ST JOHN'S
SUTHERLAND AVENUE
WARRINGTON CR.
RANDOLPH AVENUE
EDGWARE ROAD
WARWICK AVENUE
WARWICK AVENUE
MAIDA AVENUE
GRAND UNION CANAL
PADDINGTON COMMUNITY HOSPITAL
PADDINGTON
LITTLE VENICE
HARROW ROAD
ST MARY'S
A40(M)
GOODS STATION
WESTBOURNE PARK VILLAS
ROYAL OAK
PADDINGTON
CHEPSTOW ROAD
BAYSWATER
PADDINGTON STATION
0 525 1050 feet
BISHOP'S BRIDGE ROAD
PADDINGTON
B
C
D

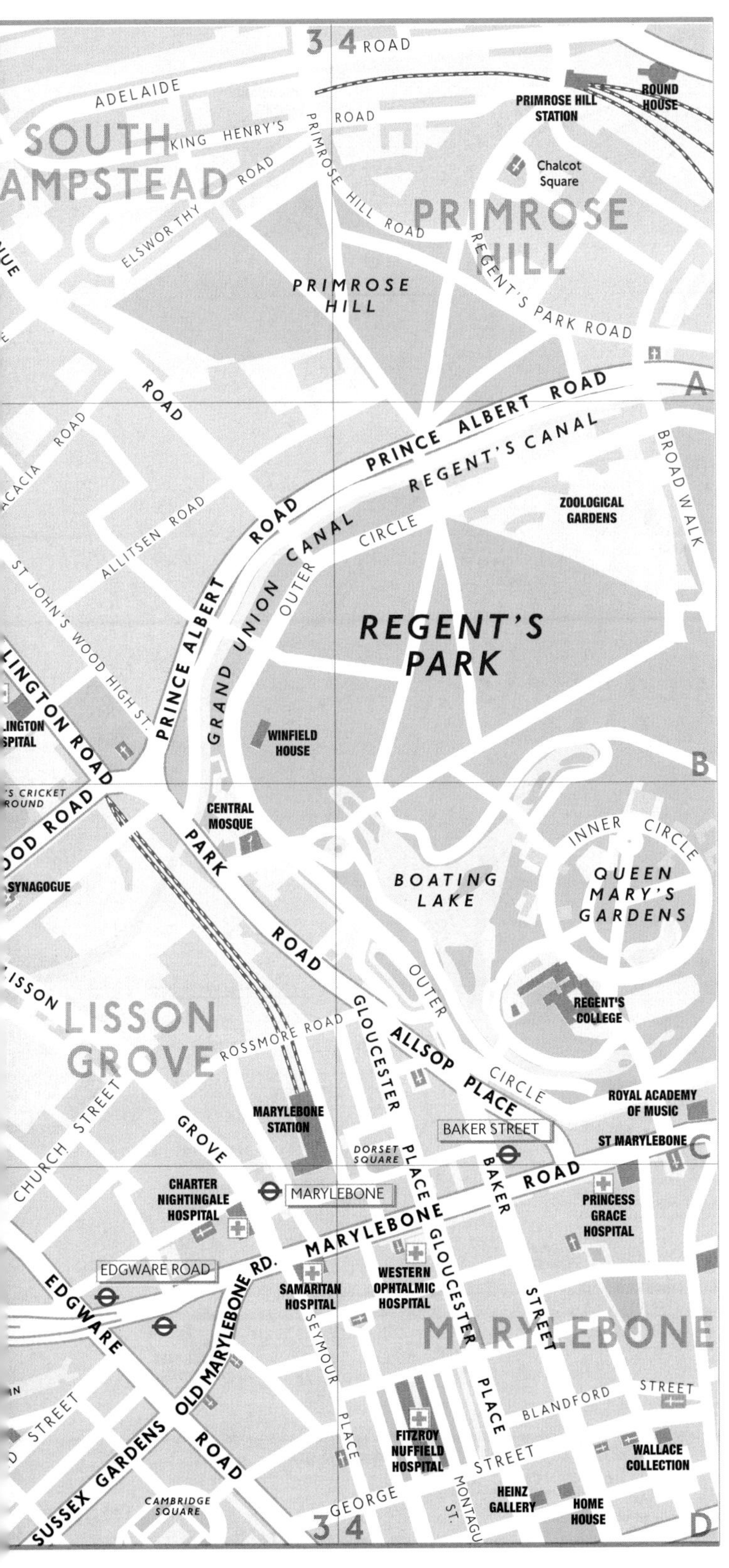

3 4
ROAD
ADELAIDE
SOUTH HAMPSTEAD
KING HENRY'S
ROAD
PRIMROSE HILL ROAD
ROAD
ELSWORTHY
PRIMROSE HILL STATION
ROUND HOUSE
Chalcot Square
PRIMROSE HILL
REGENT'S PARK ROAD
PRIMROSE HILL
A
ROAD
ACACIA ROAD
PRINCE ALBERT ROAD
REGENT'S CANAL
BROAD WALK
ZOOLOGICAL GARDENS
ALLITSEN ROAD
GRAND UNION CANAL
OUTER CIRCLE
ST JOHN'S WOOD HIGH ST.
REGENT'S PARK
PRINCE ALBERT ROAD
WINFIELD HOUSE
B
CENTRAL MOSQUE
PARK ROAD
INNER CIRCLE
SYNAGOGUE
BOATING LAKE
QUEEN MARY'S GARDENS
OUTER CIRCLE
REGENT'S COLLEGE
LISSON GROVE
ROSSMORE ROAD
GLOUCESTER
ALLSOP PLACE
MARYLEBONE STATION
ROYAL ACADEMY OF MUSIC
BAKER STREET
ST MARYLEBONE
C
CHURCH STREET
GROVE
DORSET SQUARE
PLACE
BAKER
ROAD
CHARTER NIGHTINGALE HOSPITAL
MARYLEBONE
PRINCESS GRACE HOSPITAL
EDGWARE ROAD
MARYLEBONE RD.
WESTERN OPHTALMIC HOSPITAL
SAMARITAN HOSPITAL
EDGWARE
GLOUCESTER
STREET
OLD MARYLEBONE
SEYMOUR
MARYLEBONE
BLANDFORD STREET
PLACE
SUSSEX GARDENS
ROAD
FITZROY NUFFIELD HOSPITAL
STREET
WALLACE COLLECTION
CAMBRIDGE SQUARE
GEORGE
MONTAGU ST.
HEINZ GALLERY
HOME HOUSE
3 4
D

B
ROUND HOUSE
CHALK FARM ROAD
CAMDEN ROAD STATION
KENTISH TOWN
ROAD
SAINT
AGAR
PANCRAS WAY
PRIMROSE HILL
CAMDEN TOWN
ROYAL COLLEGE STREET
CAMDEN
CAMDEN STREET
OVAL ROAD
REGENT'S PARK ROAD
PRINCE ALBERT RD.
PARKWAY
CAMDEN HIGH STREET
DELANCEY ST.
OUTER CIRCLE
PARK VILLAGE EAST
CROWNDALE ROAD
MORNINGTON CRESCENT
Harrington Square
Lidlington place
ZOOLOGICAL GARDENS
ST JOHN
ALBANY STREET
BROAD WALK
CHALTON
EVERSHOLT STREET
REGENT'S PARK
STANHOPE STREET
HAMPSTEAD ROAD
EUSTON STATION
EUSTON
ROBERT STREET
QUEEN MARY'S GARDENS
Munster Square
EUSTON SQUARE
Euston
EUSTON
HOLY TRINITY
WARREN ST.
PARK SQUARE GARDENS
GOWER
UNIV. COLL. HOSPITAL
GREAT PORTLAND ST.
ROYAL ACADEMY OF MUSIC
REGENT'S PARK
ST LUXE'S HOSPITAL
TOTTENHAM
MARYLEBONE ROAD
PARK CRESCENT
Fitzroy Square
ST MARYLEBONE
PORTLAND HOSP.
ROYAL NAT. ORTH. HOSPITAL
LONDON FOOT HOSPITAL
CLEVELAND STREET
LONDON TELECOM TOWER
TOTTENHAM COURT
ROYAL EAR HOSPITAL
KING EDWARD VII HOSPITAL
TOY MUSEUM
GOODGE
DEVONSHIRE HOSPITAL
MARYLEBONE
GREAT PORTLAND PLACE
WIMPOLE STREET
MARYLEBONE HIGH ST.
STREET
CHARLOTTE ST.
NEW CAVENDISH
TITCHFIELD STREET
CHANDOS HOUSE
B.B.C.
ALL SOULS CHURCH
MIDDLESEX HOSPITAL
NEWMAN ST.
PERCY ST.
GEORGE ST.
Langham Place
UNIVERSITY OF WESTMINSTER
0
525
1050 feet
Cavendish Square
WIGMORE ST.
OXFORD STREET
ST PATRICK
A
B
C
D
1
2

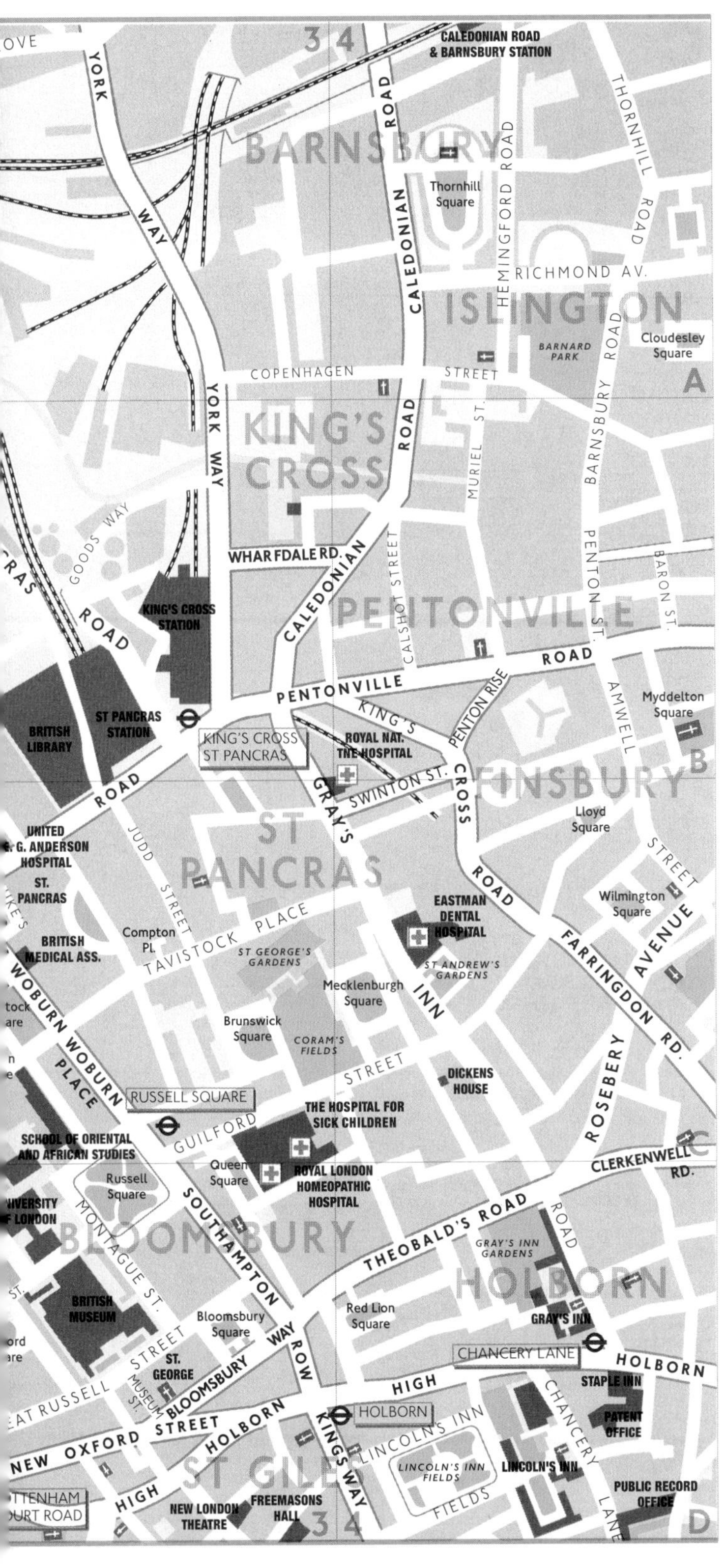

3 4
CALEDONIAN ROAD & BARNSBURY STATION
YORK WAY
CALEDONIAN ROAD
BARNSBURY
Thornhill Square
HEMINGFORD ROAD
THORNHILL ROAD
RICHMOND AV.
ISLINGTON
BARNARD PARK
BARNSBURY ROAD
Cloudesley Square
COPENHAGEN STREET
A
KING'S CROSS
MURIEL ST.
GOODS WAY
WHARFDALE RD.
CALSHOT STREET
PENTON ST.
BARON ST.
KING'S CROSS STATION
PENTONVILLE
ROAD
PENTONVILLE ROAD
BRITISH LIBRARY
ST PANCRAS STATION
KING'S CROSS ST PANCRAS
ROYAL NAT. TNE HOSPITAL
KING'S CROSS ROAD
PENTON RISE
AMWELL
Myddelton Square
B
FINSBURY
SWINTON ST.
GRAY'S INN ROAD
Lloyd Square
UNITED G. ANDERSON HOSPITAL
ST. PANCRAS
JUDD STREET
ST PANCRAS
Wilmington Square
STREET
EASTMAN DENTAL HOSPITAL
BRITISH MEDICAL ASS.
Compton Pl.
TAVISTOCK PLACE
ST GEORGE'S GARDENS
ST ANDREW'S GARDENS
FARRINGDON RD.
AVENUE
WOBURN
Mecklenburgh Square
Brunswick Square
CORAM'S FIELDS
WOBURN PLACE
STREET
DICKENS HOUSE
RUSSELL SQUARE
THE HOSPITAL FOR SICK CHILDREN
ROSEBERY
GUILFORD
SCHOOL OF ORIENTAL AND AFRICAN STUDIES
Queen Square
ROYAL LONDON HOMEOPATHIC HOSPITAL
CLERKENWELL RD.
C
Russell Square
SOUTHAMPTON ROW
THEOBALD'S ROAD
MONTAGUE ST.
BLOOMSBURY
GRAY'S INN GARDENS
HOLBORN
BRITISH MUSEUM
Bloomsbury Square
Red Lion Square
GRAY'S INN
CHANCERY LANE
HOLBORN
STREET
ST. GEORGE
BLOOMSBURY WAY
MUSEUM ST.
HIGH
STAPLE INN
PATENT OFFICE
HOLBORN
KINGSWAY
LINCOLN'S INN
CHANCERY LANE
NEW OXFORD STREET
HIGH HOLBORN
LINCOLN'S INN FIELDS
LINCOLN'S INN
ST GILES
FIELDS
PUBLIC RECORD OFFICE
NEW LONDON THEATRE
FREEMASONS HALL
D

C

Milner Square
Lonsdale Square
ALMEIDA THEATRE
ESSEX ROAD
NEW NORTH ROAD
ISLINGTON
BASIRE ST.
SHEPPERTON
Wilton Square
Cloudesley Square
PACKINGTON ST.
BUSINESS DESIGN CENTRE
UPPER STREET
ESSEX ROAD
Arlington Square
LIVERPOOL ROAD
ST PETER'S STREET
GRAND UNION
EAGLE WHARF RD.
CROPLEY STREET
CHAPEL MARKET
ANGEL
DUNCAN TERRACE ROW
NOEL ROAD
BARON ST.
WHITE LION ST.
CITY ROAD BASIN
WHARF ROAD
WENLOCK BASIN
SHEPHERDESS WALK
MURRAY GRO
PROVOST ST.
Myddelton Square
ST. JOHN STREET
GOSWELL ROAD
CITY ROAD
SADLER'S WELLS THEATRE
AVENUE
CITY UNIVERSITY
CENTRAL STREET
BATH STREET
MOORFIELDS EYE HOSPITAL
ROSEBERY
FINSBURY
LEVER STREET
PERCIVAL ST.
ST JOHN STREET
GOSWELL ROAD
BUNHILL ROW
OLD STREET
WHITECROSS ST.
FARRINGDON ROAD
CLERKENWELL
ST LUKE'S
GOLDEN LANE
ST JOHN
CLERKENWELL ROAD
CHARTERHOUSE
Charterhouse Square
ALDERSGATE STREET
CHISWELL ST.
BEECH STREET
BARBICAN CENTRE
SILK ST.
FARRINGDON
BARBICAN
THE BARBICAN
MOORGATE
GREVILLE ST.
CHARTERHOUSE ST.
LONG LANE
CENTRAL MARKETS
HOLBORN
ST BARTHOLOMEW THE GREAT
ST GILES CRIPPLEGATE
ELY CHAPEL
SMITHFIELD ST.
West Smithfield
MUSEUM OF LONDON
LONDON WALL
Holborn Circus
PATENT OFFICE
HOLBORN VIADUCT
ST ANDREW
CITY TEMPLE
ST BARTHOLOMEW'S HOSPITAL
ST ANNE
GUILDHALL MUSEUM
SHOE LANE
FARRINGDON ST.
GEN. POST OFFICE
G.P.O.
PUBLIC RECORD OFFICE
NEWGATE ST
GRESHAM STREET
GUILDHALL
ST PAUL'S STATION
CENTRAL CRIMINAL COURT
ST PAUL'S
ST MARGARET LOTHBURY
ST DUNSTAN IN THE WEST
CITY
ST VEDAST
KING ST.
BANK OF ENGLAND
CHEAPSIDE
POULTRY
MIDLAND BANK
STRAND
FLEET ST.
Ludgate Circus
LUDGATE HILL
ST PAUL'S CATHEDRAL
ST MARY LE BOW
TEMPLE CHURCH
ST BRIDE
N. BRIDGE ST.
ST. PAUL'S CH. YARD
ST MARY ALD.
THE TEMPLE
ST ANDREW'S BY THE W.
FARADAY BUILDING
COLLEGE OF ARMS
TEMPLE OF MITHRAS
BLACKFRIARS
QUEEN VICTORIA ST.
MANSION HOUSE

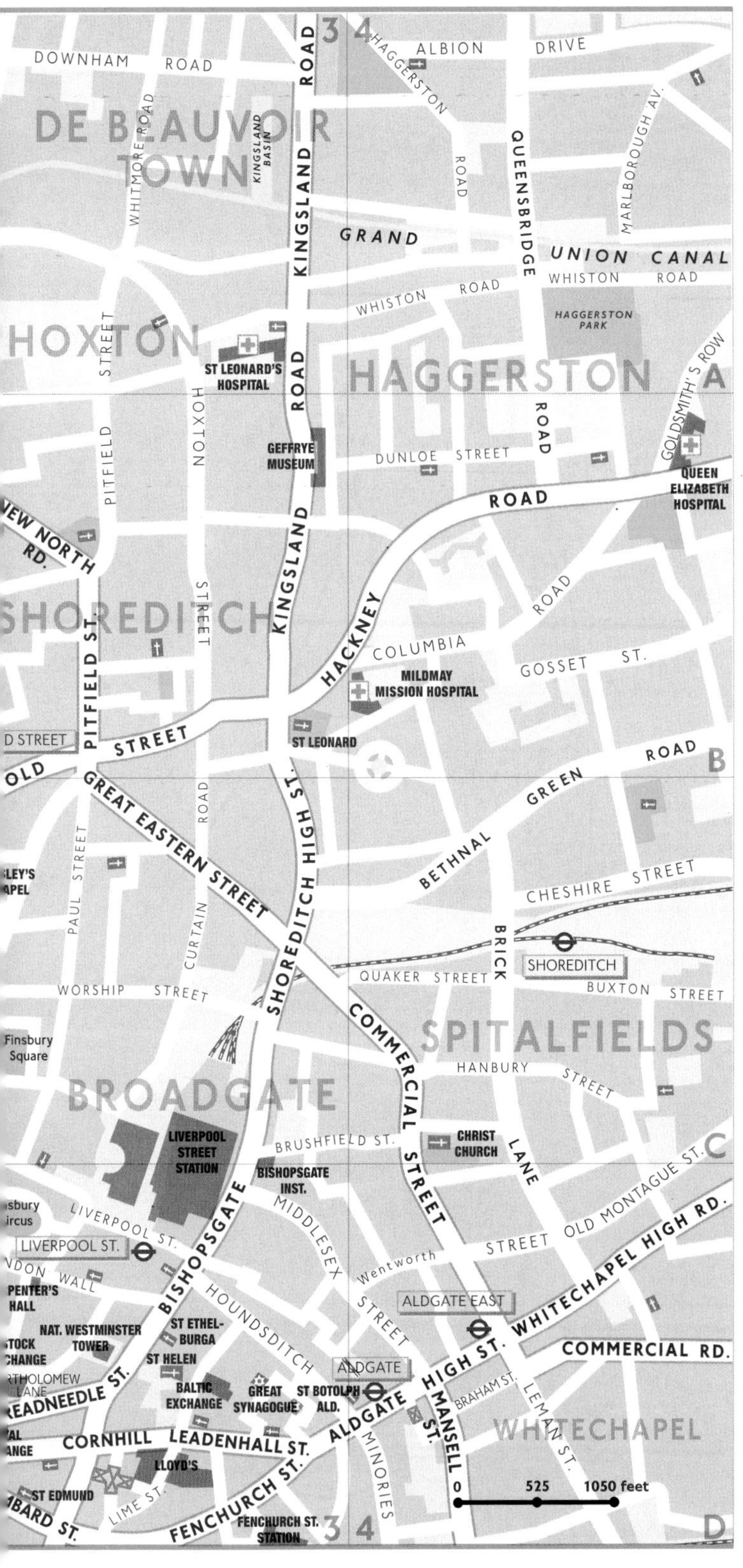

DE BEAUVOIR TOWN
HOXTON
HAGGERSTON
SHOREDITCH
SPITALFIELDS
BROADGATE
WHITECHAPEL
DOWNHAM ROAD
ALBION DRIVE
HAGGERSTON ROAD
QUEENSBRIDGE ROAD
MARLBOROUGH AV.
WHITMORE ROAD
KINGSLAND BASIN
KINGSLAND ROAD
GRAND UNION CANAL
WHISTON ROAD
HAGGERSTON PARK
GOLDSMITH'S ROW
ST LEONARD'S HOSPITAL
HOXTON STREET
PITFIELD STREET
GEFFRYE MUSEUM
DUNLOE STREET
HACKNEY ROAD
QUEEN ELIZABETH HOSPITAL
NEW NORTH RD.
COLUMBIA ROAD
GOSSET ST.
MILDMAY MISSION HOSPITAL
ST LEONARD
OLD STREET
PITFIELD ST.
GREAT EASTERN STREET
SHOREDITCH HIGH ST.
BETHNAL GREEN ROAD
CURTAIN ROAD
PAUL STREET
CHESHIRE STREET
BRICK LANE
SHOREDITCH
QUAKER STREET
BUXTON STREET
WORSHIP STREET
COMMERCIAL STREET
Finsbury Square
HANBURY STREET
LIVERPOOL STREET STATION
BRUSHFIELD ST.
CHRIST CHURCH
BISHOPSGATE INST.
OLD MONTAGUE ST.
LIVERPOOL ST.
MIDDLESEX STREET
Wentworth STREET
WHITECHAPEL HIGH RD.
BISHOPSGATE
HOUNDSDITCH
ALDGATE EAST
NAT. WESTMINSTER TOWER
ST ETHELBURGA
COMMERCIAL RD.
ST HELEN
ALDGATE
BALTIC EXCHANGE
GREAT SYNAGOGUE
ST BOTOLPH ALD.
HIGH ST.
BRAHAM ST.
LEMAN ST.
MANSELL ST.
ALDGATE
MINORIES
CORNHILL
LEADENHALL ST.
LLOYD'S
ST EDMUND
LIME ST.
FENCHURCH ST.
FENCHURCH ST. STATION
0 525 1050 feet
3 4
A B C D

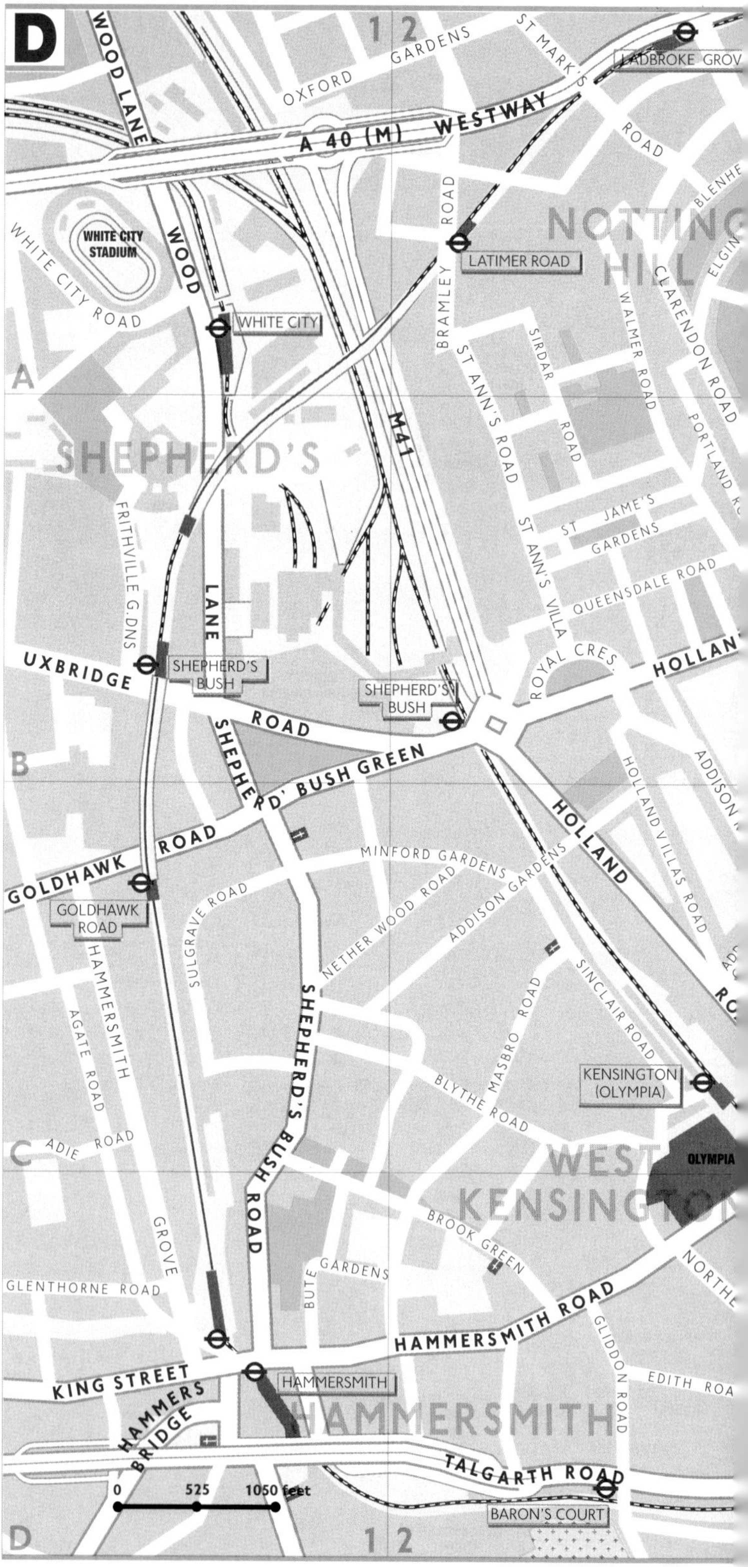
D
1 2
A
B
C
D
WOOD LANE
OXFORD GARDENS
ST MARK'S ROAD
LADBROKE GROV
A 40 (M) WESTWAY
WHITE CITY STADIUM
WHITE CITY ROAD
WOOD LANE
WHITE CITY
BRAMLEY ROAD
LATIMER ROAD
NOTTING HILL
BLENHE
ELGIN
CLARENDON ROAD
WALMER ROAD
SIRDAR ROAD
ST ANN'S ROAD
PORTLAND R
SHEPHERD'S
M41
FRITHVILLE G.DNS
ST JAMES'S GARDENS
ST ANN'S VILLA
QUEENSDALE ROAD
ROYAL CRES.
HOLLAN
UXBRIDGE ROAD
SHEPHERD'S BUSH
SHEPHERD'S BUSH
SHEPHERD'S BUSH GREEN
HOLLAND ROAD
HOLLAND VILLAS ROAD
ADDISON
GOLDHAWK ROAD
GOLDHAWK ROAD
MINFORD GARDENS
SULGRAVE ROAD
NETHER WOOD ROAD
ADDISON GARDENS
HAMMERSMITH GROVE
AGATE ROAD
SHEPHERD'S BUSH ROAD
MASBRO ROAD
SINCLAIR ROAD
BLYTHE ROAD
KENSINGTON (OLYMPIA)
OLYMPIA
ADIE ROAD
WEST KENSINGTON
BROOK GREEN
BUTE GARDENS
GLENTHORNE ROAD
NORTHE
HAMMERSMITH ROAD
GLIDDON ROAD
EDITH ROA
KING STREET
HAMMERSMITH
HAMMERSMITH
HAMMERS BRIDGE
TALGARTH ROAD
0
525
1050 feet
BARON'S COURT

BAYSWATER
KENSINGTON
EARL'S COURT
HOLLAND PARK
WESTBOURNE GROVE
BISHOP'S BRIDGE
CHEPSTOW RD.
PEMBRIDGE VILLAS
PEMBRIDGE RD.
NOTTING HILL GATE
BAYSWATER ROAD
KENSINGTON CHURCH STREET
KENSINGTON PALACE GARDENS
THE BROAD WALK
QUEENSWAY
INVERNESS TERRACE
MOSCOW ROAD
NEWTON RD.
Prince's Square
DAWSON PL.
Pembridge Square
PEMBRIDGE G.DNS
TALBOT ROAD
LEDBURY ROAD
ARTESIAN ROAD
COLVILLE TERR.
LONSDALE ROAD
WESTBOURNE PARK RD.
PORTOBELLO ROAD
KENSINGTON PARK ROAD
CHEPSTOW VILLAS
LADBROKE PARK G.DNS
LADBROKE SQ.
LADBROKE ROAD
GROVE
HOLLAND PARK
KENSINGTON PL.
AUBREY WALK
PALACE GARDENS TERRACE
ORANGERIE
KENSINGTON PALACE
CAMPDEN HILL
CAMPDEN HILL ROAD
QUEEN ELIZABETH COLLEGE
HORNTON STREET
HOLLAND HOUSE
HOLLAND WALK
CRICKET GROUND
PLACE ROAD
COMMONWEALTH INSTITUTE
HIGH STREET KENSINGTON
KENSINGTON HIGH STREET
EARL'S
ABINGDON VILLAS
ABINGDON RD.
MARLOES RD.
CORNWALL GARDENS
Edwardes Square
WARWICK G.DNS
WARWICK
PEMBROKE ROAD
LEXHAM GARDENS
CROMWELL ROAD
CROMWELL CRES
COURTFIELD
COLLINGHAM ROAD
COLLINGHAM GARDENS
WEST CROMWELL ROAD
NEVERN PLACE
Nevern Square
EARL'S COURT
COURT ROAD
EARL'S COURT ROAD
PHILBEACH GARDENS
TREBOVIR RD.
Earl's Court Square
BOLTON GARDENS
OLD BROMPTON ROAD
EARL'S COURT EXHIBITION BUILDING
WEST KENSINGTON
NOTTIN GHILL GATE
3
4
A
B
C
D

◆ HYDE PARK, MAYFAIR, SOUTH KENSINGTON

E

PADDINGTON STATION
GLOUCESTER
WESTBOURNE
EASTBOURNE TERR
CHILWORTH ST
PRAED ST.
NORFOLK SQUARE
SUSSEX GARDENS
Cambridge Square
Oxford Square
Cleveland Square
TERRACE
PADDINGTON
INVERNESS TERRACE
LEINSTER GARDENS
DEVONSHIRE TERRACE
PORCHESTER GARD.
QUEEN'S GARDENS
CRAVEN HILL G.DNS
CRAVEN HILL
TERRACE
LANCASTER TERR.
SUSSEX
GLOUCESTER SQUARE
CONNAU
Sussex Square
STANHOPE TERRACE
BAYSWATER ROAD
THE RING
BAYSWATER
QUEENSWAY
LANCASTER GATE
LANCASTER GATE
BAYSWATER ROAD
A
QUEENSWAY
KENSINGTON GARDENS
THE LONG WATER
THE RING
NURSERY
PHYSICAL ENERGY STATUE
ROUND POND
THE SERPENTIN
SERPENTINE GALLERY
KENSINGTON PALACE
B
ALBERT MEMORIAL
KENSINGTON ROAD
KENSINGTON GORE
KENSINGTON
ROAD
ROYAL ALBERT HALL
KNIGHTSBRIDGE
VICTORIA ROAD
PALACE GATE
QUEEN'S GATE
PRINCE CONSORT RD
EXHIBITION ROAD
IMPERIAL COLLEGE OF SCIENCE AND TECHNOLOGY
ELVASTON PLACE
GLOUCESTER ROAD
SCIENCE MUSEUM
BROMPTON ORATORY
VICTORIA AND ALBERT MUSEUM
CORNWALL GARDENS
BRITISH MUSEUM OF NATURAL HISTORY
BROMPTON
C
CROMWELL ROAD
Cromwell Pl.
ISMAIL CENTRE
Thurloe Square
SOUTH KENSINGTON
GLOUCESTER ROAD
SOUTH TERR.
WAL
SOUTH KENSINGTON
PELHAM ST.
DRAYC
SLO
COLLINGHAM ROAD
HARRINGTON GARDENS
GLOUCESTER ROAD
ROAD
SUMNER PLACE
Onslow Square
WETHERBY GARDENS
BINA GARDENS
BROMPTON
ROAD
POND PLACE
IXWORTH PL.
SYDNEY STREET
CALE STREET
ROLAND GARDENS
CRANLEY GARDENS
DRAYTON GARDENS
THE BOLTONS
FULHAM
Chelsea Square
BRITTEN STRE
D
1
2

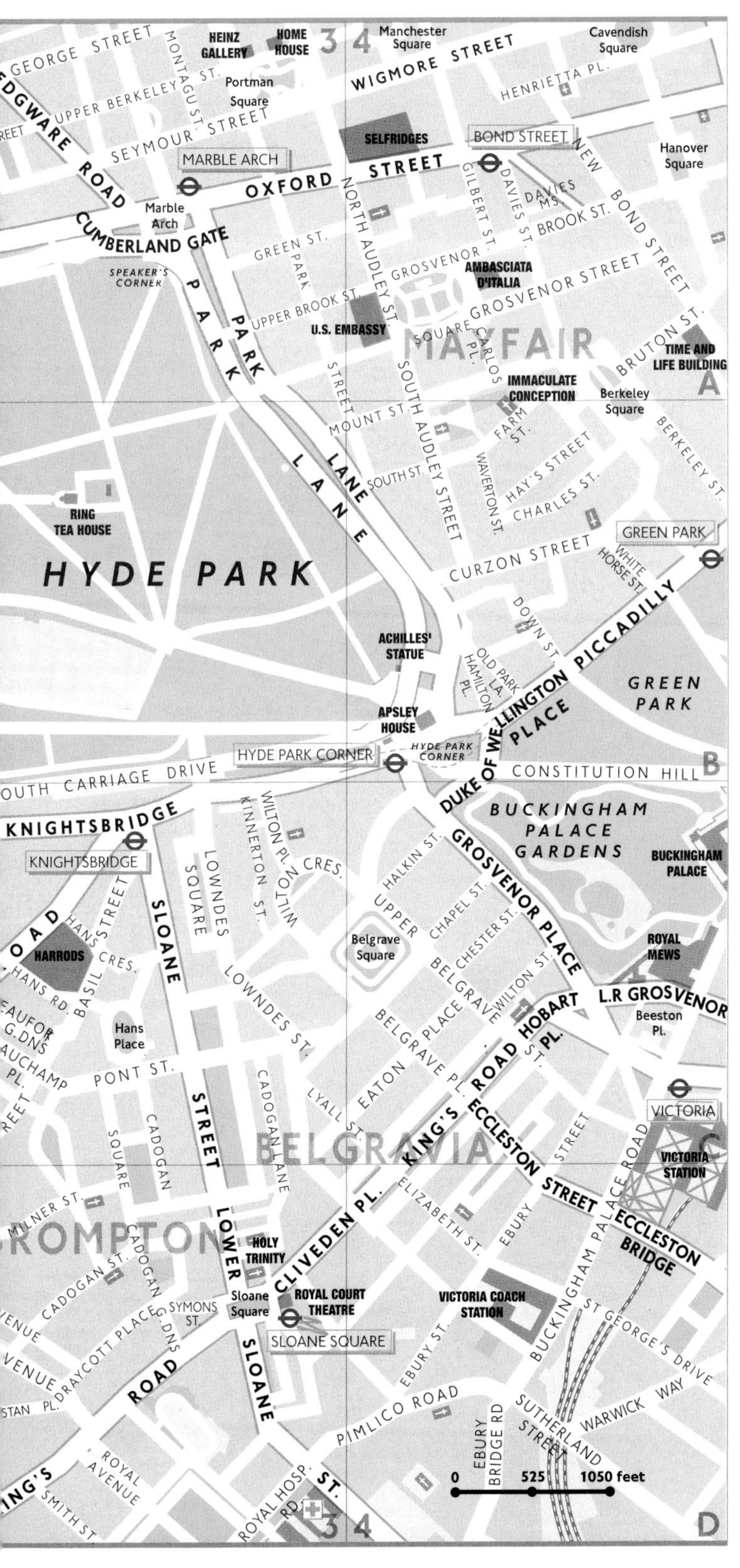

GEORGE STREET
MONTAGU ST.
HEINZ GALLERY
HOME HOUSE
Manchester Square
Cavendish Square
WIGMORE STREET
HENRIETTA PL.
EDGWARE ROAD
UPPER BERKELEY ST.
Portman Square
SEYMOUR STREET
SELFRIDGES
BOND STREET
Hanover Square
MARBLE ARCH
OXFORD STREET
NEW BOND STREET
Marble Arch
NORTH AUDLEY ST.
GILBERT ST.
DAVIES ST.
DAVIES MS.
BROOK ST.
CUMBERLAND GATE
GREEN ST.
PARK
GROSVENOR
AMBASCIATA D'ITALIA
GROSVENOR STREET
SPEAKER'S CORNER
UPPER BROOK ST.
U.S. EMBASSY
SQUARE
CARLOS PL.
MAYFAIR
BRUTON ST.
TIME AND LIFE BUILDING
PARK
STREET
SOUTH AUDLEY STREET
IMMACULATE CONCEPTION
Berkeley Square
MOUNT ST.
FARM ST.
BERKELEY ST.
PARK LANE
SOUTH ST.
WAVERTON ST.
HAY'S STREET
CHARLES ST.
RING TEA HOUSE
GREEN PARK
HYDE PARK
CURZON STREET
WHITE HORSE ST.
DOWN ST.
PICCADILLY
ACHILLES' STATUE
OLD PARK LA.
HAMILTON PL.
GREEN PARK
APSLEY HOUSE
DUKE OF WELLINGTON PLACE
HYDE PARK CORNER
HYDE PARK CORNER
SOUTH CARRIAGE DRIVE
CONSTITUTION HILL
KNIGHTSBRIDGE
KINNERTON ST.
WILTON PL.
BUCKINGHAM PALACE GARDENS
KNIGHTSBRIDGE
LOWNDES SQUARE
WILTON CRES.
HALKIN ST.
GROSVENOR PLACE
BUCKINGHAM PALACE
ROAD
HANS STREET
SLOANE
UPPER
CHAPEL ST.
HARRODS
HANS CRES.
Belgrave Square
CHESTER ST.
ROYAL MEWS
HANS RD.
BASIL
LOWNDES ST.
BELGRAVE
WILTON ST.
HOBART PL.
L.R GROSVENOR
BEAUFORT G.DNS
Hans Place
BELGRAVE PLACE
Beeston Pl.
BEAUCHAMP PL.
PONT ST.
EATON
ROAD
ST.
LYALL ST.
BELGRAVE PL.
CADOGAN
STREET
CADOGAN LANE
VICTORIA
SQUARE
CADOGAN
BELGRAVIA
KING'S
ECCLESTON
STREET
VICTORIA STATION
MILNER ST.
STREET
ELIZABETH ST.
ROAD
BROMPTON
LOWER
CLIVEDEN PL.
HOLY TRINITY
EBURY
ECCLESTON BRIDGE
CADOGAN ST.
CADOGAN G.DNS
Sloane Square
ROYAL COURT THEATRE
VICTORIA COACH STATION
BUCKINGHAM PALACE
AVENUE
SYMONS ST.
DRAYCOTT PLACE
SLOANE SQUARE
ST GEORGE'S DRIVE
AVENUE
ROAD
SLOANE
EBURY ST.
STAN PL.
PIMLICO ROAD
WARWICK WAY
EBURY BRIDGE RD
SUTHERLAND STREET
KING'S
ROYAL AVENUE
ROYAL HOSP. RD
ST.
SMITH ST.
0
525
1050 feet
3
4
A
B
C
D

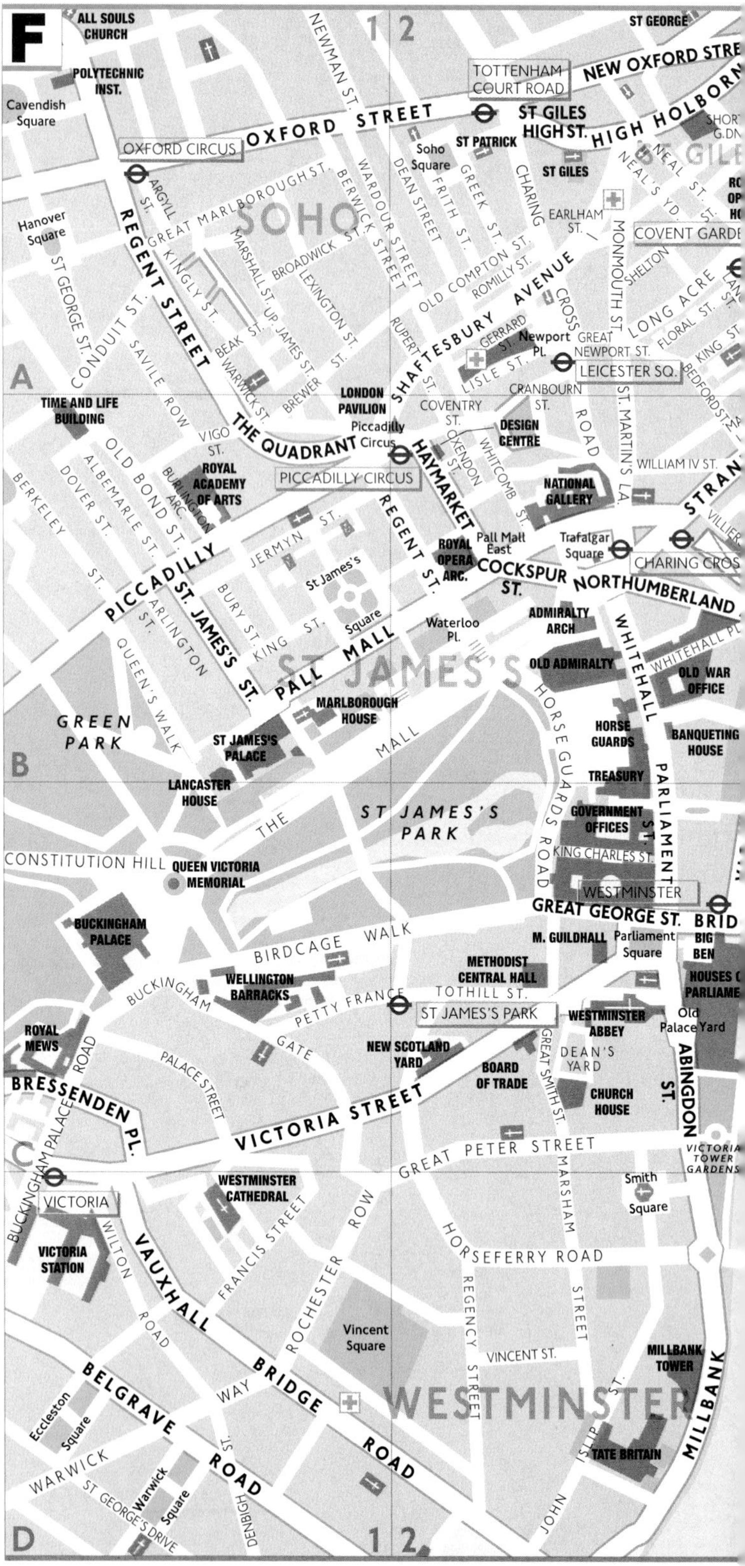

◆ Soho, Covent Garden, Westminster

F

ALL SOULS CHURCH
POLYTECHNIC INST.
Cavendish Square
OXFORD CIRCUS
OXFORD STREET
NEWMAN ST.
TOTTENHAM COURT ROAD
NEW OXFORD STREET
ST GEORGE
ST GILES HIGH ST.
HIGH HOLBORN
ST GILES
ST PATRICK
Soho Square
SOHO
Hanover Square
REGENT STREET
ARGYLL ST.
GREAT MARLBOROUGH ST.
BERWICK STREET
WARDOUR STREET
DEAN STREET
FRITH ST.
GREEK ST.
CHARING CROSS ROAD
EARLHAM ST.
MONMOUTH ST.
NEAL'S YD.
NEAL ST.
COVENT GARDEN
SHELTON
KINGLY ST.
MARSHALL ST.
BROADWICK ST.
LEXINGTON ST.
UP. JAMES ST.
OLD COMPTON ST.
ROMILLY ST.
SHAFTESBURY AVENUE
ST GEORGE ST.
CONDUIT ST.
SAVILE ROW
BEAK ST.
WARWICK ST.
BREWER ST.
RUPERT ST.
GERRARD ST.
LISLE ST.
Newport Pl.
GREAT NEWPORT ST.
LONG ACRE
FLORAL ST.
KING ST.
BEDFORD ST.
LEICESTER SQ.
A
TIME AND LIFE BUILDING
LONDON PAVILION
COVENTRY ST.
CRANBOURN ST.
THE QUADRANT
Piccadilly Circus
VIGO ST.
OXENDON ST.
WHITCOMB ST.
DESIGN CENTRE
ST. MARTIN'S LA.
WILLIAM IV ST.
STRAND
HAYMARKET
PICCADILLY CIRCUS
ROYAL ACADEMY OF ARTS
BURLINGTON ARC.
OLD BOND ST.
ALBEMARLE ST.
DOVER ST.
BERKELEY ST.
NATIONAL GALLERY
VILLIERS
JERMYN ST.
REGENT ST.
ROYAL OPERA ARC.
Pall Mall East
Trafalgar Square
CHARING CROSS
St James's Square
BURY ST.
COCKSPUR ST.
NORTHUMBERLAND
PICCADILLY
ST. JAMES'S ST.
ARLINGTON ST.
KING ST.
PALL MALL
Waterloo Pl.
ADMIRALTY ARCH
WHITEHALL
WHITEHALL PL.
ST JAMES'S
OLD ADMIRALTY
OLD WAR OFFICE
QUEEN'S WALK
GREEN PARK
MARLBOROUGH HOUSE
HORSE GUARDS ROAD
HORSE GUARDS
BANQUETING HOUSE
ST JAMES'S PALACE
THE MALL
B
LANCASTER HOUSE
TREASURY
PARLIAMENT ST.
ST JAMES'S PARK
GOVERNMENT OFFICES
THE
CONSTITUTION HILL
QUEEN VICTORIA MEMORIAL
KING CHARLES ST.
WESTMINSTER
GREAT GEORGE ST.
BRID
BUCKINGHAM PALACE
BIRDCAGE WALK
M. GUILDHALL
Parliament Square
BIG BEN
METHODIST CENTRAL HALL
HOUSES OF PARLIAME
WELLINGTON BARRACKS
BUCKINGHAM GATE
TOTHILL ST.
PETTY FRANCE
ST JAMES'S PARK
WESTMINSTER ABBEY
Old Palace Yard
ROYAL MEWS
NEW SCOTLAND YARD
GREAT SMITH ST.
DEAN'S YARD
PALACE STREET
BOARD OF TRADE
ABINGDON ST.
BRESSENDEN PL.
BUCKINGHAM PALACE ROAD
CHURCH HOUSE
VICTORIA STREET
GREAT PETER STREET
VICTORIA TOWER GARDENS
C
VICTORIA
WESTMINSTER CATHEDRAL
MARSHAM STREET
Smith Square
VICTORIA STATION
WILTON ROAD
FRANCIS STREET
ROCHESTER ROW
HORSEFERRY ROAD
VAUXHALL BRIDGE ROAD
Vincent Square
REGENCY STREET
VINCENT ST.
MILLBANK TOWER
BELGRAVE ROAD
WAY
WESTMINSTER
MILLBANK
Eccleston Square
ST.
ISLIP ST.
TATE BRITAIN
WARWICK WAY
Warwick Square
ST GEORGE'S DRIVE
DENBIGH ST.
JOHN ISLIP
D
1 2

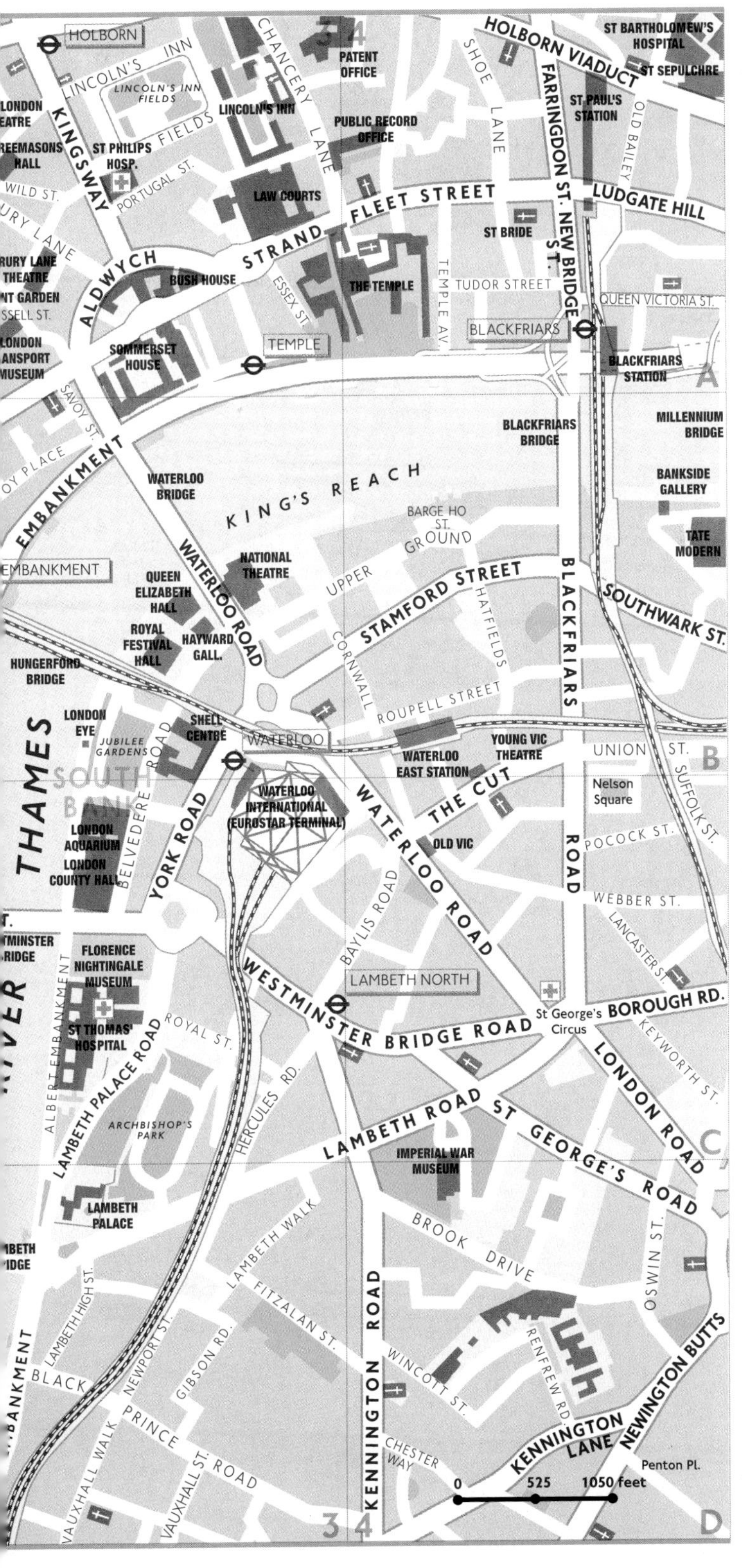
HOLBORN
LINCOLN'S INN FIELDS
LINCOLN'S INN
CHANCERY LANE
PATENT OFFICE
PUBLIC RECORD OFFICE
HOLBORN VIADUCT
ST BARTHOLOMEW'S HOSPITAL
ST SEPULCHRE
FARRINGDON ST.
ST PAUL'S STATION
OLD BAILEY
SHOE LANE
KINGSWAY
ST PHILIPS HOSP.
PORTUGAL ST.
WILD ST.
LAW COURTS
FLEET STREET
LUDGATE HILL
NEW BRIDGE ST.
ST BRIDE
STRAND
ALDWYCH
BUSH HOUSE
ESSEX ST.
THE TEMPLE
TEMPLE AV.
TUDOR STREET
QUEEN VICTORIA ST.
BLACKFRIARS
TEMPLE
SOMMERSET HOUSE
BLACKFRIARS STATION
SAVOY ST.
BLACKFRIARS BRIDGE
MILLENNIUM BRIDGE
BANKSIDE GALLERY
TATE MODERN
EMBANKMENT
WATERLOO BRIDGE
KING'S REACH
BARGE HO ST.
UPPER GROUND
NATIONAL THEATRE
QUEEN ELIZABETH HALL
ROYAL FESTIVAL HALL
HAYWARD GALL.
WATERLOO ROAD
STAMFORD STREET
HATFIELDS
CORNWALL
BLACKFRIARS ROAD
SOUTHWARK ST.
HUNGERFORD BRIDGE
LONDON EYE
JUBILEE GARDENS
SHELL CENTRE
WATERLOO
ROUPELL STREET
WATERLOO EAST STATION
YOUNG VIC THEATRE
UNION ST.
SUFFOLK ST.
Nelson Square
THAMES
SOUTH BANK
LONDON AQUARIUM
LONDON COUNTY HALL
BELVEDERE ROAD
YORK ROAD
WATERLOO INTERNATIONAL (EUROSTAR TERMINAL)
THE CUT
OLD VIC
POCOCK ST.
WEBBER ST.
LANCASTER ST.
BAYLIS ROAD
FLORENCE NIGHTINGALE MUSEUM
ST THOMAS' HOSPITAL
ALBERT EMBANKMENT
WESTMINSTER BRIDGE ROAD
LAMBETH NORTH
St George's Circus
BOROUGH RD.
KEYWORTH ST.
LONDON ROAD
ROYAL ST.
LAMBETH PALACE ROAD
ARCHBISHOP'S PARK
HERCULES RD.
LAMBETH ROAD
ST GEORGE'S ROAD
IMPERIAL WAR MUSEUM
LAMBETH PALACE
LAMBETH WALK
BROOK DRIVE
OSWIN ST.
LAMBETH HIGH ST.
FITZALAN ST.
KENNINGTON ROAD
RENFREW RD.
WINCOTT ST.
NEWINGTON BUTTS
KENNINGTON LANE
BLACK PRINCE ROAD
NEWPORT ST.
GIBSON RD.
VAUXHALL WALK
VAUXHALL ST.
CHESTER WAY
Penton Pl.
0
525
1050 feet
A
B
C
D
3
4

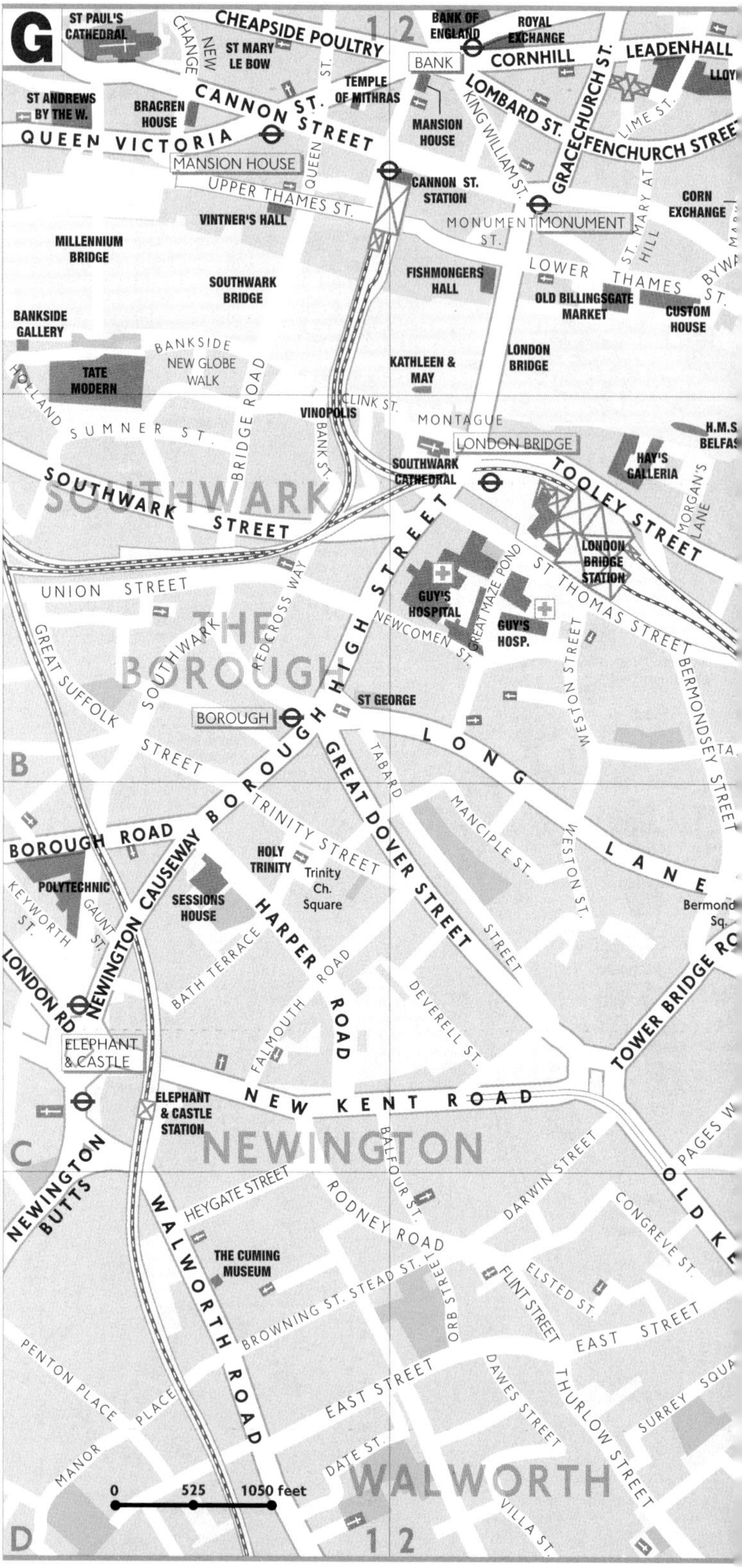

◆ SOUTHWARK, TOWER BRIDGE

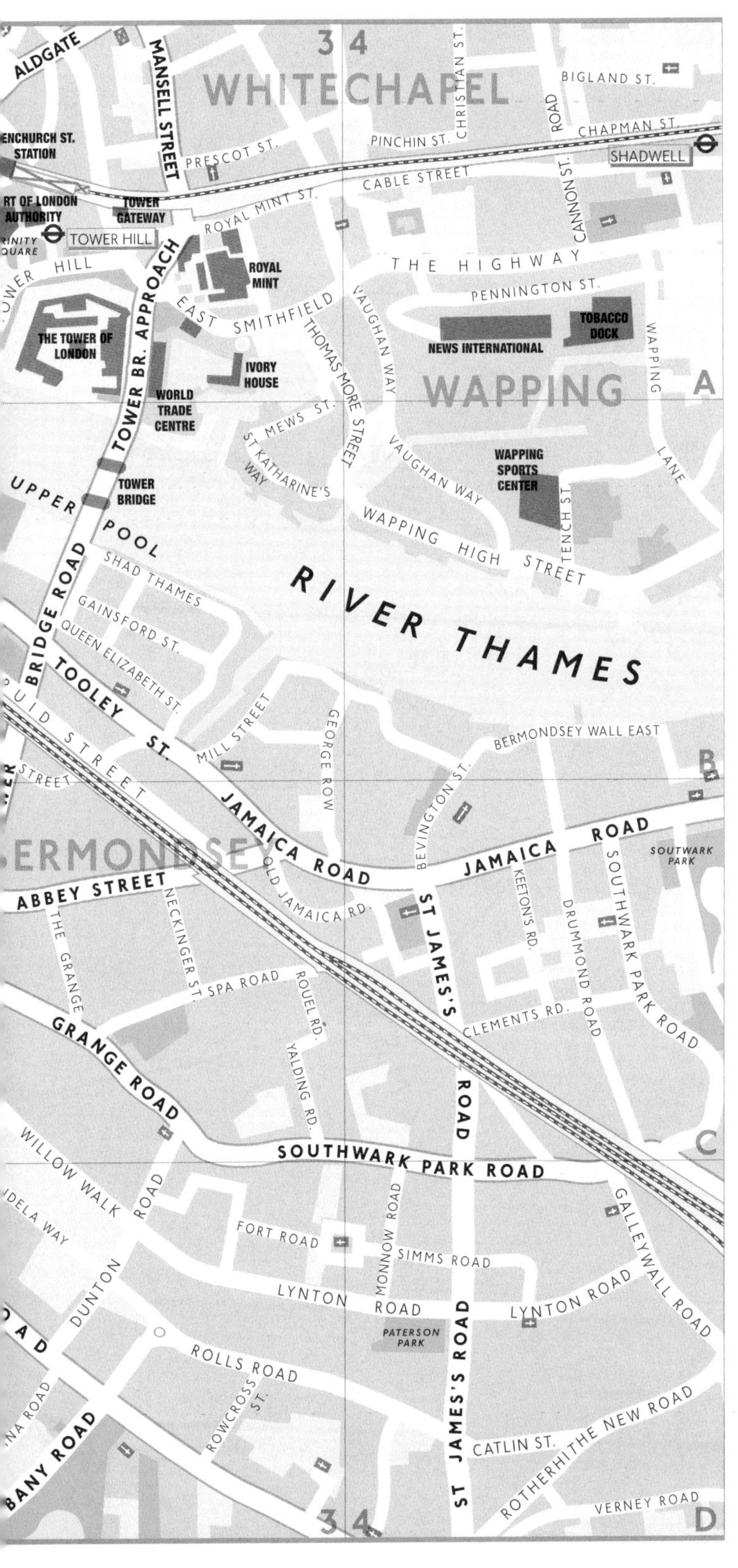

34
WHITECHAPEL
ALDGATE
MANSELL STREET
CHRISTIAN ST.
BIGLAND ST.
ROAD
CHAPMAN ST.
PINCHIN ST.
SHADWELL
ENCHURCH ST. STATION
PRESCOT ST.
CABLE STREET
CANNON ST.
RT OF LONDON AUTHORITY
TOWER GATEWAY
ROYAL MINT ST.
TOWER HILL
RINITY QUARE
ROYAL MINT
THE HIGHWAY
OWER HILL
TOWER BR. APPROACH
EAST SMITHFIELD
PENNINGTON ST.
TOBACCO DOCK
THE TOWER OF LONDON
THOMAS MORE STREET
VAUGHAN WAY
NEWS INTERNATIONAL
WAPPING
IVORY HOUSE
WAPPING
A
WORLD TRADE CENTRE
MEWS ST.
ST KATHARINE'S WAY
VAUGHAN WAY
WAPPING SPORTS CENTER
LANE
TOWER BRIDGE
UPPER POOL
TENCH ST.
WAPPING HIGH STREET
BRIDGE ROAD
SHAD THAMES
RIVER THAMES
GAINSFORD ST.
QUEEN ELIZABETH ST.
TOOLEY ST.
DRUID STREET
MILL STREET
GEORGE ROW
BERMONDSEY WALL EAST
B
STREET
BEVINGTON ST.
JAMAICA ROAD
JAMAICA ROAD
SOUTWARK PARK
BERMONDSEY
KEETON'S RD.
ABBEY STREET
OLD JAMAICA RD.
ST JAMES'S ROAD
DRUMMOND ROAD
SOUTHWARK PARK ROAD
THE GRANGE
NECKINGER ST.
SPA ROAD
ROUEL RD.
CLEMENTS RD.
GRANGE ROAD
YALDING RD.
C
SOUTHWARK PARK ROAD
WILLOW WALK
ROAD
GALLEYWALL ROAD
DELA WAY
FORT ROAD
MONNOW ROAD
SIMMS ROAD
DUNTON
LYNTON ROAD
LYNTON ROAD
PATERSON PARK
ROLLS ROAD
ROWCROSS ST.
ROTHERHITHE NEW ROAD
CATLIN ST.
BANY ROAD
ST JAMES'S ROAD
VERNEY ROAD
D
34

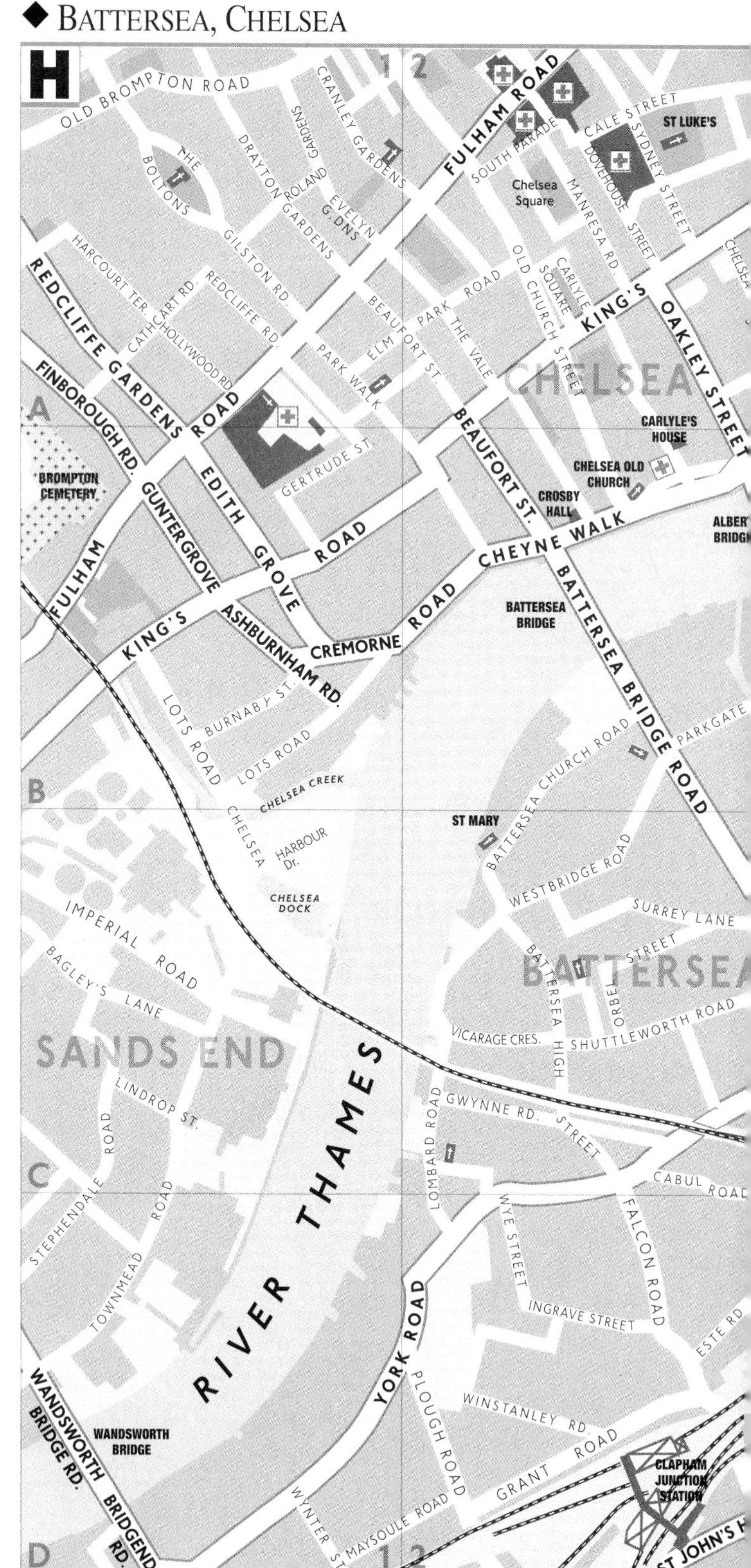
H
OLD BROMPTON ROAD
THE BOLTONS
CRANLEY GARDENS
DRAYTON GARDENS
ROLAND GARDENS
EVELYN G.DNS
FULHAM ROAD
SOUTH PARADE
CALE STREET
ST LUKE'S
SYDNEY STREET
DOVEHOUSE STREET
Chelsea Square
MANRESA RD.
HARCOURT TER.
GILSTON RD.
REDCLIFFE GARDENS
CATHCART RD.
REDCLIFFE RD.
HOLLYWOOD RD.
PARK ROAD
ELM PARK ROAD
BEAUFORT ST.
THE VALE
OLD CHURCH STREET
CARLYLE SQUARE
KING'S
OAKLEY STREET
CHELSEA
FINBOROUGH RD.
PARK WALK
ROAD
CARLYLE'S HOUSE
BROMPTON CEMETERY
GERTRUDE ST.
EDITH GROVE
CHELSEA OLD CHURCH
CROSBY HALL
CHEYNE WALK
ALBERT BRIDGE
GUNTER GROVE
FULHAM
ROAD
BATTERSEA BRIDGE
KING'S
ASHBURNHAM RD.
CREMORNE ROAD
BATTERSEA BRIDGE ROAD
LOTS ROAD
BURNABY ST.
LOTS ROAD
BATTERSEA CHURCH ROAD
PARKGATE
CHELSEA CREEK
CHELSEA HARBOUR Dr.
ST MARY
WESTBRIDGE ROAD
CHELSEA DOCK
SURREY LANE
IMPERIAL ROAD
BATTERSEA HIGH STREET
ORBEL STREET
BATTERSEA
BAGLEY'S LANE
VICARAGE CRES.
SHUTTLEWORTH ROAD
SANDS END
LINDROP ST.
LOMBARD ROAD
GWYNNE RD.
RIVER THAMES
ROAD
CABUL ROAD
STEPHENDALE ROAD
WYE STREET
FALCON ROAD
TOWNMEAD ROAD
INGRAVE STREET
ESTE RD
YORK ROAD
PLOUGH ROAD
WINSTANLEY RD.
WANDSWORTH BRIDGE RD.
WANDSWORTH BRIDGE
GRANT ROAD
CLAPHAM JUNCTION STATION
BRIDGEND RD.
WYNTER ST
MAYSOULE ROAD
ST JOHN'S H
A
B
C
D
1
2

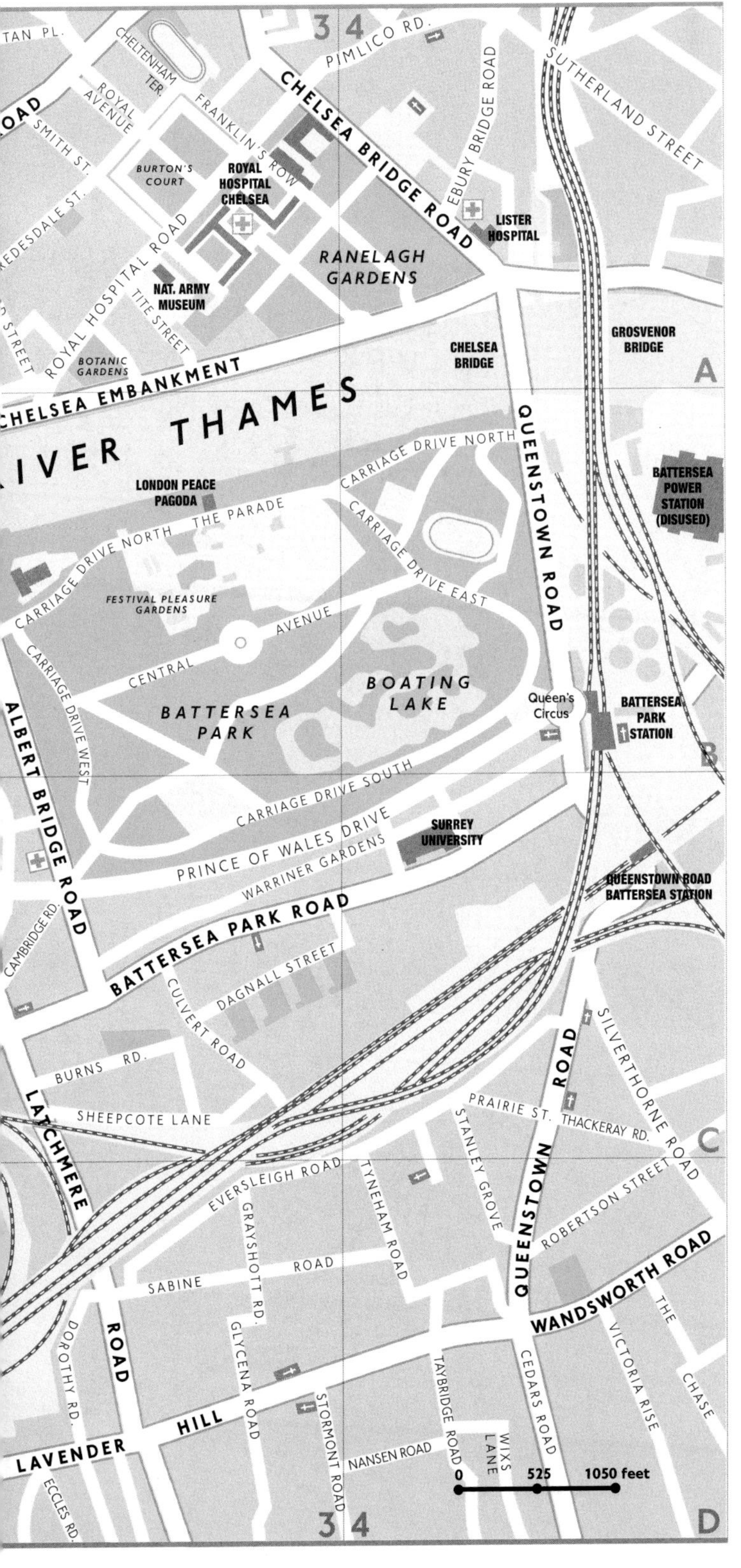

CHELSEA BRIDGE ROAD
PIMLICO RD.
SUTHERLAND STREET
EBURY BRIDGE ROAD
ROYAL HOSPITAL CHELSEA
LISTER HOSPITAL
BURTON'S COURT
FRANKLIN'S ROW
ROYAL AVENUE
CHELTENHAM TER.
SMITH ST.
ROYAL HOSPITAL ROAD
TITE STREET
NAT. ARMY MUSEUM
RANELAGH GARDENS
BOTANIC GARDENS
CHELSEA EMBANKMENT
CHELSEA BRIDGE
GROSVENOR BRIDGE
RIVER THAMES
QUEENSTOWN ROAD
CARRIAGE DRIVE NORTH
LONDON PEACE PAGODA
THE PARADE
BATTERSEA POWER STATION (DISUSED)
CARRIAGE DRIVE EAST
FESTIVAL PLEASURE GARDENS
AVENUE
CENTRAL
BOATING LAKE
BATTERSEA PARK
Queen's Circus
BATTERSEA PARK STATION
CARRIAGE DRIVE WEST
ALBERT BRIDGE ROAD
CARRIAGE DRIVE SOUTH
SURREY UNIVERSITY
PRINCE OF WALES DRIVE
WARRINER GARDENS
QUEENSTOWN ROAD BATTERSEA STATION
BATTERSEA PARK ROAD
CAMBRIDGE RD.
CULVERT ROAD
DAGNALL STREET
SILVERTHORNE ROAD
BURNS RD.
LATCHMERE
SHEEPCOTE LANE
PRAIRIE ST.
THACKERAY RD.
STANLEY GROVE
EVERSLEIGH ROAD
TYNEHAM ROAD
ROBERTSON STREET
GRAYSHOTT RD.
SABINE ROAD
WANDSWORTH ROAD
THE CHASE
VICTORIA RISE
CEDARS ROAD
DOROTHY RD.
ROAD
GLYCENA ROAD
STORMONT ROAD
TAYBRIDGE ROAD
WIXS LANE
HILL
LAVENDER
NANSEN ROAD
ECCLES RD.
0 525 1050 feet
A
B
C
D
3 4

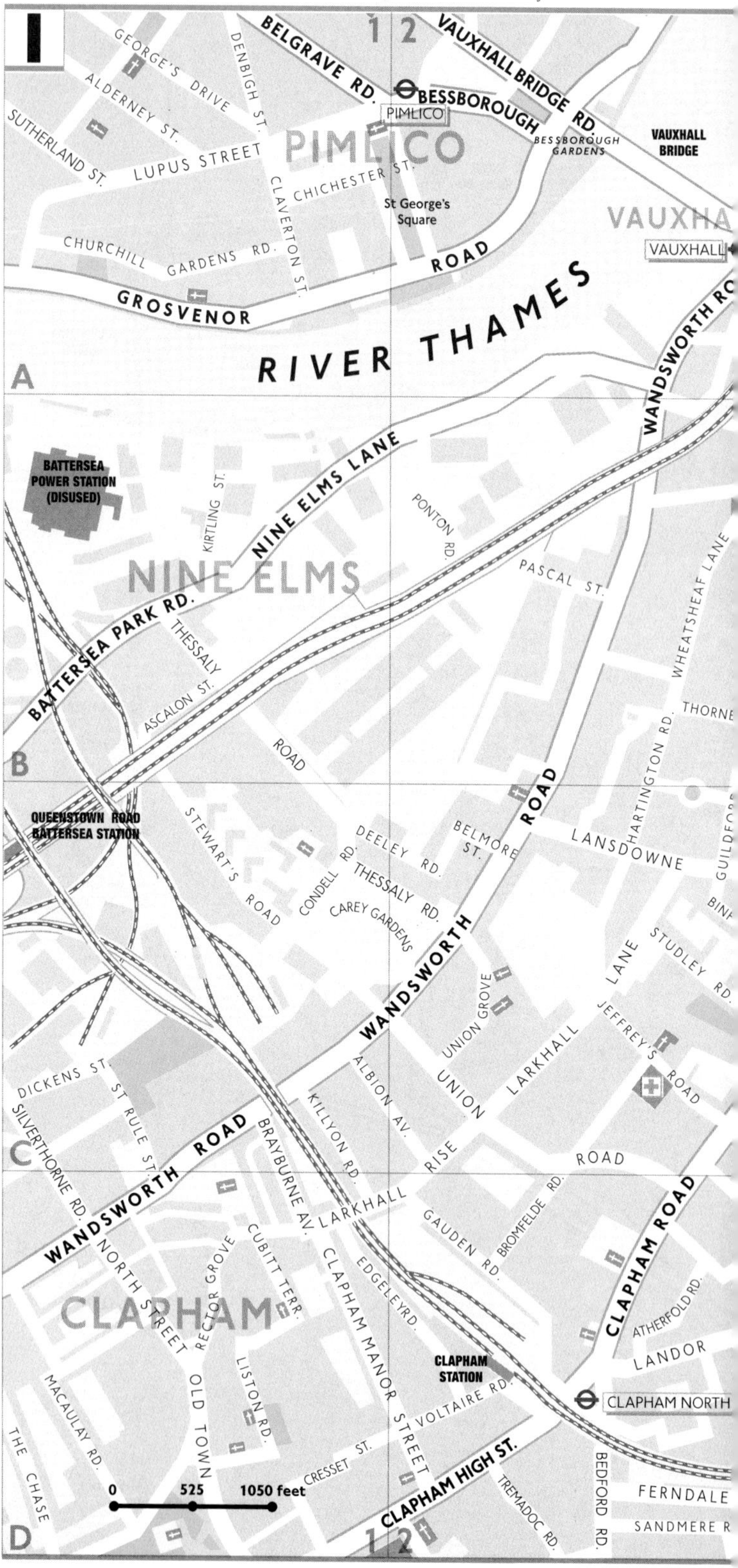

1
1 2
BELGRAVE RD.
VAUXHALL BRIDGE RD.
BESSBOROUGH
PIMLICO
BESSBOROUGH GARDENS
VAUXHALL BRIDGE
GEORGE'S DRIVE
DENBIGH ST.
ALDERNEY ST.
SUTHERLAND ST.
LUPUS STREET
PIMLICO
CHICHESTER ST.
CLAVERTON ST.
St George's Square
VAUXHA
VAUXHALL
CHURCHILL GARDENS RD.
ROAD
GROSVENOR
RIVER THAMES
WANDSWORTH RO
A
BATTERSEA POWER STATION (DISUSED)
KIRTLING ST.
NINE ELMS LANE
PONTON RD.
NINE ELMS
PASCAL ST.
WHEATSHEAF LANE
BATTERSEA PARK RD.
THESSALY
ASCALON ST.
ROAD
THORNE
HARTINGTON RD.
B
QUEENSTOWN ROAD BATTERSEA STATION
STEWART'S ROAD
DEELEY RD.
CONDELL RD.
THESSALY RD.
CAREY GARDENS
BELMORE ST.
ROAD
LANSDOWNE
GUILDFORD
BINF
STUDLEY RD.
WANDSWORTH
UNION GROVE
LANE
JEFFREY'S ROAD
LARKHALL
UNION
ALBION AV.
KILLYON RD.
DICKENS ST.
ST RULE ST.
SILVERTHORNE RD.
C
ROAD
BRAYBURNE AV.
RISE
ROAD
WANDSWORTH ROAD
LARKHALL
GAUDEN RD.
BROMFELDE RD.
CLAPHAM ROAD
NORTH STREET
RECTOR GROVE
CUBITT TERR.
CLAPHAM MANOR STREET
EDGELEY RD.
ATHERFOLD RD.
CLAPHAM
LANDOR
CLAPHAM STATION
CLAPHAM NORTH
MACAULAY RD.
OLD TOWN
LISTON RD.
VOLTAIRE RD.
THE CHASE
CRESSET ST.
CLAPHAM HIGH ST.
TREMADOC RD.
BEDFORD RD.
FERNDALE
SANDMERE R
0 525 1050 feet
D
1 2

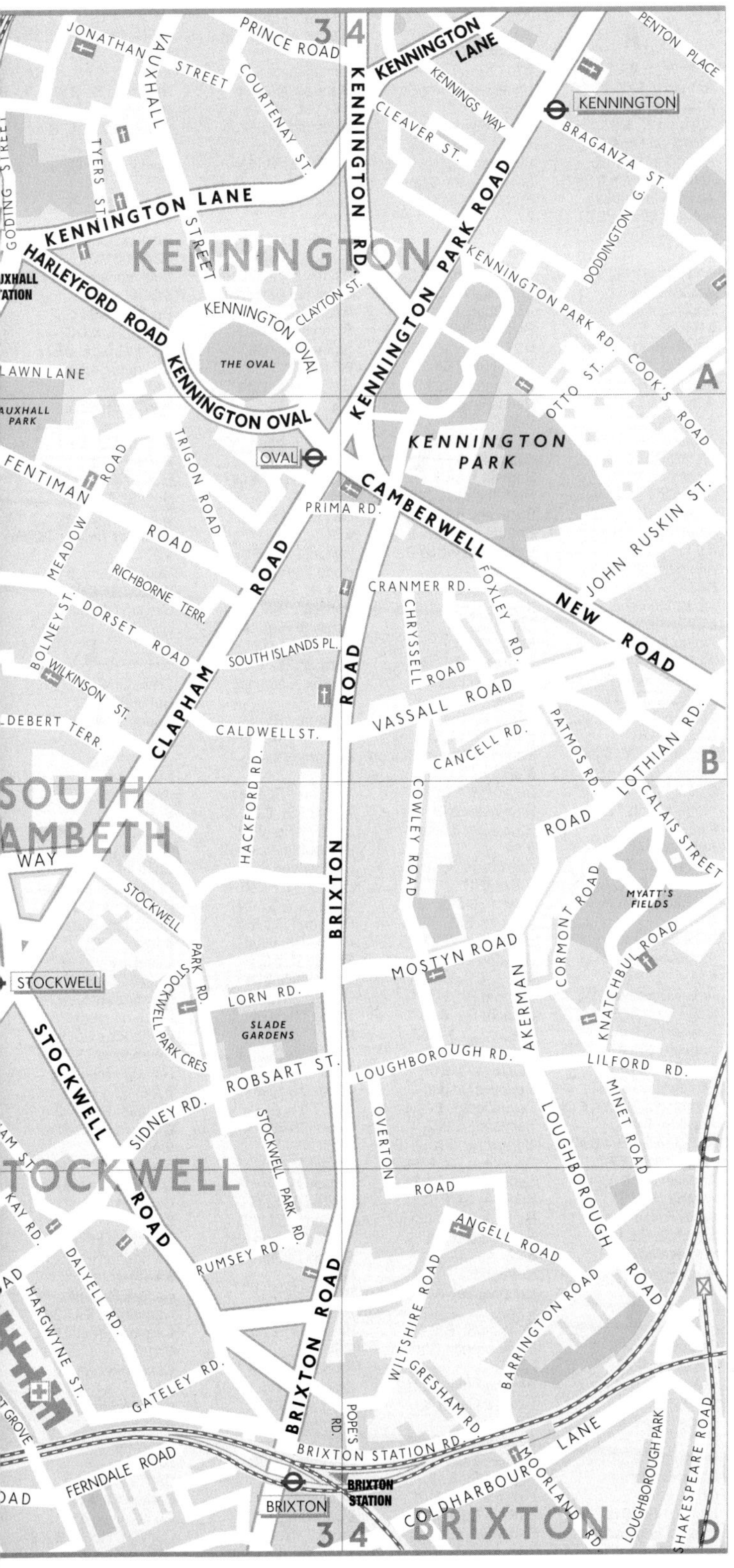
3
4
KENNINGTON
SOUTH LAMBETH
STOCKWELL
BRIXTON
KENNINGTON PARK
THE OVAL
SLADE GARDENS
MYATT'S FIELDS
KENNINGTON
OVAL
STOCKWELL
BRIXTON
BRIXTON STATION
KENNINGTON LANE
KENNINGTON RD.
KENNINGTON PARK ROAD
KENNINGTON ROAD
KENNINGTON OVAL
HARLEYFORD ROAD
CLAPHAM ROAD
BRIXTON ROAD
CAMBERWELL NEW ROAD
STOCKWELL ROAD
LOUGHBOROUGH ROAD
COLDHARBOUR LANE
JONATHAN STREET
VAUXHALL STREET
PRINCE ROAD
COURTENAY ST.
TYERS ST.
KENNINGS WAY
CLEAVER ST.
PENTON PLACE
BRAGANZA ST.
DODDINGTON G.
KENNINGTON PARK RD.
COOK'S ROAD
OTTO ST.
CLAYTON ST.
LAWN LANE
FENTIMAN ROAD
MEADOW ROAD
TRIGON ROAD
RICHBORNE TERR.
DORSET ROAD
BOLNEY ST.
WILKINSON ST.
DEBERT TERR.
PRIMA RD.
CRANMER RD.
CHRYSSELL ROAD
FOXLEY RD.
JOHN RUSKIN ST.
SOUTH ISLANDS PL.
VASSALL ROAD
CALDWELL ST.
CANCELL RD.
PATMOS RD.
LOTHIAN RD.
CALAIS STREET
HACKFORD RD.
COWLEY ROAD
WAY
STOCKWELL PARK RD.
STOCKWELL PARK CRES
CORMONT ROAD
KNATCHBULL ROAD
MOSTYN ROAD
AKERMAN ROAD
LORN RD.
ROBSART ST.
LOUGHBOROUGH RD.
LILFORD RD.
MINET ROAD
SIDNEY RD.
STOCKWELL PARK RD.
OVERTON ROAD
ANGELL ROAD
KAY RD.
DALYELL RD.
RUMSEY RD.
HARGWYNE ST.
WILTSHIRE ROAD
BARRINGTON ROAD
GRESHAM RD.
GATELEY RD.
POPE'S RD.
BRIXTON STATION RD.
FERNDALE ROAD
MOORLAND RD.
LOUGHBOROUGH PARK
SHAKESPEARE ROAD
A
B
C
D

A

B

C

D

E

F

G

H

I

J

K

L

M

N

U

V

W